ENCYCLOPEDIA OF AMERICAN CIVIL RIGHTS AND LIBERTIES

ENCYCLOPEDIA OF AMERICAN CIVIL RIGHTS AND LIBERTIES

Volume 2: H-R

Edited by
Otis H. Stephens, Jr.
John M. Scheb II
Kara E. Stooksbury

GREENWOOD PRESS
Westport, Connecticut • London

Library of Congress Cataloging-in-Publication Data

Encyclopedia of American civil rights and liberties / edited by Otis H. Stephens, Jr., John M. Scheb II, Kara E. Stooksbury.

   p. cm.

  Includes bibliographical references and index.

  ISBN 0-313-32758-0 (set : alk. paper) — ISBN 0-313-32759-9 (v. 1 : alk. paper) — ISBN 0-313-32760-2 (v. 2 : alk. paper) — ISBN 0-313-32761-0 (v. 3 : alk. paper)

  1. Civil rights—United States—Cases. 2. Civil rights—United States—Encyclopedias. I. Stephens, Otis H., 1936– II. Scheb, John M., 1955– III. Stooksbury, Kara Elizabeth, 1969–
KF4748.E53 2006
342.7308'5—dc22   2006012037

British Library Cataloguing in Publication Data is available.

This book is included in the African American Experience database from Greenwood Electronic Media. For more Information, visit: www.africanamericanexperience.com.

Library of Congress Catalog Card Number: 2006012037
ISBN: 0–313–32758–0 (set)
     0–313–32759–9 (vol. 1)
     0–313–32760–2 (vol. 2)
     0–313–32761–0 (vol. 3)
First published in 2006

Greenwood Press, 88 Post Road West, Westport, CT 06881
An imprint of Greenwood Publishing Group, Inc.
www.greenwood.com

Printed in the United States of America

The paper used in this book complies with the Permanent Paper Standard issued by the National Information Standards Organization (Z39.48–1984).

10 9 8 7 6 5 4 3 2 1

Dedicated, with love, to our parents:

Otis H., Sr, and Margaret F. Stephens

John M., I, and Mary B. Scheb

Kyle and Betty Stooksbury

CONTENTS

LIST OF ENTRIES

GUIDE TO RELATED TOPICS

Civil Rights

Constitutional Provisions

Court Decisions

Dworkin, Andrea

Dworkin, Ronald

Evers, Medgar

Fortas, Abe

Frank, Leo

Frankfurter, Felix

Ginsburg, Ruth Bader

Goldberg, Arthur

Hand, Learned

Harlan, John Marshall

Harlan, John Marshall, II

Hart, H.L.A.

Hobbes, Thomas

Holmes, Oliver Wendell, Jr.

Jackson, Jesse

Jackson, Robert H.

Jefferson, Thomas

Kennedy, Anthony

Kennedy, Robert F.

King, Martin Luther, Jr.

King, Rodney

Kuntsler, William

Lincoln, Abraham

Locke, John

Machiavelli, Niccolò

Madison, James

Malcolm X

Marshall, John

Marshall, Thurgood

McCarthy, Joseph R.

McReynolds, James Clark

Meese, Edwin, III

Meredith, James

O'Connor, Sandra Day

Paine, Thomas

Parks, Rosa

Plato

Powell, Lewis F., Jr.

Rawls, John

Reed, Stanley F.

Rehnquist, William H.

Reno, Janet

Roosevelt, Eleanor

Roosevelt, Franklin D.

Rousseau, Jean-Jacques

Scalia, Antonin

Sharpton, Alfred Charles

Socrates

Souter, David H.

Stanton, Elizabeth Cady

Stevens, John Paul

Stewart, Potter

Stone, Harlan Fiske

Story, Joseph

Taft, William Howard

Taney, Roger B.

Thomas, Clarence

Thoreau, Henry David

Truth, Sojourner

Vinson, Fred M.

Waite, Morrison Remick

Warren, Earl

Washington, Booker T.

White, Byron R.

Zenger, John Peter

Key Concepts

Contempt, Power of

Fundamental Rights

Harmless Error, Doctrine of

Interpretivism

Judicial Activism

Judicial Restraint

Living Constitution

Original Intent, Doctrine of

Rational Basis Test

State Action Doctrine

Strict Scrutiny

Unconstitutional as Applied

Warren Court

Citizenship

Civil Disobedience

Conservatism

Democracy, Constitutional

Democracy, Representative

Diversity

Equity

Hate Crimes

In Loco Parentis

American Nazi Party

Americans United for Separation of Church and State

Anti-Defamation League

Center for Individual Rights

Church of Jesus Christ of Latter-day Saints

Communist Party USA

Concerned Women of America

Congress of Racial Equality

Congressional Women's Caucus

Human Rights Watch

Jehovah's Witnesses

John Birch Society

Ku Klux Klan

Motion Picture Association of America

National Association for the Advancement of Colored People

Nation of Islam

National Abortion Rights Action League

National Organization for Women

National Right to Life Committee

Native American Church

Operation Rescue

People for Ethical Treatment of Animals

People for the American Way

Planned Parenthood

Quakers

Reporters Committee for Freedom of the Press

Seventh-Day Adventists

Southern Baptist Convention

Southern Christian Leadership Conference

Southern Poverty Law Center

Student Nonviolent Coordinating Committee

Student Press Law Center

Students for a Democratic Society

Unitarian Universalism

Privacy, Reproductive and Family Rights

Abortion, Public Funding of

Abortion, Right to

Adoption

Die, Right to

Drugs, Private Use of

Griswold v. Connecticut

Lawrence v. Texas

Living Will

Loving v. Virginia

Medical Treatment, Right to Refuse

Meyer v. Nebraska

Parental Rights

Pierce v. Society of Sisters

Poe v. Ullman

Privacy, Constitutional Right of

Privacy, Informational

Privacy, Invasion of

Pro-choice Position

Pro-life Movement

Pro-life Position

Reproductive Freedom

Roe v. Wade

Seat Belt Laws

Sterilization, Compulsory

Substituted Judgment, Doctrine of

Suicide, Doctor-Assisted

Surrogate Motherhood

Religious Freedom

Abington School District v. Schempp

Americans United for Separation of Church and State

Bob Jones University v. United States

Cantwell v. Connecticut

Church of Jesus Christ of Latter-Day Saints

Conscience, Freedom of

Employment Division, Department of Human Resources of Oregon v. Smith

Establishment Clause

Everson v. Board of Education

Evolution/Creationism Controversy

First Amendment

Free Exercise Clause

Freedom from Religion Foundation

Jehovah's Witnesses

Lemon v. Kurtzman

"Memorial and Remonstrance"

Moment of Silence Laws

Nation of Islam

Religion, Freedom of

LIST OF PRIMARY DOCUMENTS

"Against the Writs of Assistance" (James Otis, 1761)

Alien and Sedition Acts (1798)

Assize of Clarendon (1166)

Bank of the United States Recharter: President Jackson's Veto Message (1832)

Bill of Rights (English, 1689)

"Civil Disobedience" (Henry David Thoreau, 1849)

Constitution of the United States of America (1787)

Declaration of Abolitionist Sentiments (1833)

Declaration of Independence (1776)

Declaration of the Rights of Man (1789)

Emancipation Proclamation (Abraham Lincoln, 1863)

Executive Order 9066 (Franklin D. Roosevelt, 1942)

Federalist Papers (Alexander Hamilton and James Madison, 1787 and 1788)

"Fireside Chat" (Franklin D. Roosevelt, 1937)

First Inaugural Address (Abraham Lincoln, 1861)

First Inaugural Address (Thomas Jefferson, 1801)

"The Four Freedoms" (Franklin D. Roosevelt, 1941)

Fundamental Orders of Connecticut (1639)

Georgia Resolution of Secession from the Union (1861)

Gettysburg Address (Abraham Lincoln, 1863)

Habeas Corpus Act (1679)

"I Have a Dream" (Martin Luther King, Jr., 1963)

Judiciary Act of 1789

Kentucky and Virginia Resolutions (Thomas Jefferson and James Madison, 1798)

"Letter from a Birmingham Jail" (Martin Luther King, Jr., 1963)

"Letter to the Danbury Baptist Association" (Thomas Jefferson, 1802)

Magna Carta (1215)

Mayflower Compact (1620)

"Memorial and Remonstrance" (James Madison, 1785)

Northwest Ordinance (1787)

"On Liberty" (John Winthrop, 1645)

Petition of Right (1628)

"A Plea for Religious Liberty" (Roger Williams, 1644)

Ratification of the Constitution by the State of New York (1788)

"Second Treatise of Government" (John Locke, 1690)

Seneca Falls Declaration (Elizabeth Cady Stanton, 1848)

Universal Declaration of Human Rights (1948)

Virginia Statute for Religious Freedom (1786)

PREFACE

The *Encyclopedia of American Civil Rights and Liberties* is designed as a reference tool for students, teachers, scholars, and citizens interested in the broad subject of civil rights and liberties. Covering topics ranging from abortion to zoning, the *Encyclopedia* provides current, comprehensive, and sophisticated coverage of *both* civil rights and liberties in the United States. No other volume currently available covers both these topics in such a detailed yet readable manner. The term "civil rights" refers to the issues that arise from the democratic commitment to equality. In the United States, civil rights protections stem both from constitutional guarantees of equal protection of the laws and antidiscrimination legislation enacted by Congress, state legislatures, and local governments. "Civil liberties," on the other hand, denotes the numerous disputes pitting claims of individual freedom against assertions of governmental power. In large part, these claims are based on provisions of the United States Constitution and the state constitutions. Most noteworthy among these provisions are the Bill of Rights of the United States Constitution and similar enumerations of rights found in state constitutions. This encyclopedia encompasses both the civil rights and civil liberties dimensions. Although these are distinctive fields of law and policy, they are closely interrelated and equally important in reflecting the core values of a democratic society.

The *Encyclopedia*'s 627 alphabetically arranged entries include articles on major historical developments and social movements, such as the feminist and civil rights movements, and important legislation, such as the USA PATRIOT Act of 2001; the Espionage Act of 1917; and the seven Civil Rights Acts, ranging from the first such statute passed in 1866 to the last enacted in 1988. Other entries cover landmark Supreme Court decisions, such as *Plessy v. Feguson* (1896), *Wisconsin v. Yoder* (1972), and *Hustler Magazine v. Falwell* (1988); influential individuals, such as Rosa Parks and John Peter Zenger; groundbreaking justices of the U.S. Supreme Court, such as Benjamin Cardozo and Louis D. Brandeis; key constitutional provisions, such as the cruel and unusual punishments clause and the establishment clause; relevant groups and organizations, such as the National Right to Life Committee and the Nation of Islam; important government departments and agencies, such as the Department of Homeland Security and the Equal Employment Opportunity Commission; controversial issues, such as school prayer, smoking bans, and flag burning; and crucial legal and philosophical concepts and doctrines, such as judicial immunity and the fruit of the poisonous tree doctrine. In addition, the *Encyclopedia* contains the text of a set of original documents that have figured prominently in the development of civil rights and liberties in the Anglo-American legal and political traditions. These documents include the Mayflower Compact, Abraham Lincoln's first inaugural address, Martin Luther King's "Letter from a Birmingham Jail," the English Petition of Right of 1628, and the Universal Declaration of Human Rights of 1948.

Contributors to the *Encyclopedia* include scholars from diverse fields of study, including law, history, philosophy, political science, sociology, and related disciplines in the social sciences and humanities, as well as judges and practitioners of the law. Although the entries reflect the diversity of our contributors, as editors we have endeavored to make each article accessible to an educated lay audience by minimizing legal and academic jargon. And because issues of rights and liberties are matters over which reasonable and conscientious people can and will disagree, we have insisted that contributors avoid polemics and provide fair and balanced coverage of their respective topics.

With few exceptions, the entries conclude with a bibliography listing books, articles, or Web sites that were used in the preparation of the entry or where additional useful information can be found. Each entry also contains a "see also" line listing cross-references to related entries elsewhere in the *Encyclopedia*. To assist readers in navigating through the entries, we have included a guide to related topics, which breaks the entries down into broad categories and will allow readers to quickly and easily trace all relevant entries relating to Supreme Court justices, civil rights, or religious issues. Finally, the *Encyclopedia* contains a general bibliography listing numerous works that have contributed significantly to scholarship in the civil rights and liberties fields, as well as a comprehensive table of cases listing all the judicial decisions cited throughout the *Encyclopedia*.

Otis H. Stephens, Jr., John M. Scheb II, and Kara E. Stooksbury

ACKNOWLEDGMENTS

During the preparation of this compendium, we have received strong encouragement and helpful suggestions from our colleagues in the College of Law and the Department of Political Science at the University of Tennessee. Summer grants provided by the College of Law in 2004 and 2005 greatly facilitated completion of the project.

We have also been assisted by a great number of people, including all our contributors, many of whom reviewed the contributions of others. Special thanks are due to Judge John M. Scheb for his extraordinary effort in conducting research, reviewing numerous articles, and authoring many more entries than he was originally assigned. Others whose efforts surpassed the call of duty include Aaron Belville, Martin Carcieri, Mary Walker Michael R. Fitzgerald, David Folz, Lori Maxwell, Linda C. Noe, Charles Patrick, Rachel Pearsall, Chapman Rackaway, Adam Ruf, Mary Walker, and Caitlin Shockey. We also wish to thank Steven Vetrano, our editor at Greenwood Press, and John Wagner, the development editor on this project, for their patience and flexibility. Finally, we would like to thank our families and friends for putting up with our preoccupation with this project for the last three years.

We assume responsibility for all errors of commission or omission and invite readers to contact us to point out any such errors.

H

HABEAS CORPUS

Grounded in English common law, the writ of habeas corpus is designed to effectuate the right of the individual not to be held in unlawful custody. A Latin phrase meaning, "You have the body," habeas corpus enables a court of law to order the release of an individual who is being held in custody illegally. In his celebrated *Commentaries on the Laws of England* (1765–1769), Sir William Blackstone characterized habeas corpus as "the great and efficacious writ, in all manner of illegal confinement."

The writ of habeas corpus is directed to a party, usually an executive official, alleged to be holding a person in unlawful custody. The custodian is required to appear in court to provide a legal justification for the custody. Failure to respond to the writ is punishable as a contempt of court. Typically, the court issuing the writ will hold a hearing to allow opposing counsel to make arguments and present evidence as to the legality of the custody at issue. Habeas corpus has many applications, including child custody disputes, but the most common is one in which an individual confined to a jail or prison challenges the legality of an arrest, denial of bail, or criminal conviction. Today, habeas corpus often serves as a mechanism for postconviction relief where a prisoner has exhausted other avenues of appeal.

What the United States Constitution refers to as "the privilege of the Writ of Habeas Corpus" is the right to seek a writ of habeas corpus from a court of appropriate jurisdiction, either to challenge one's own custody or the custody of another person. In *Ex parte Yerger* (1868), Chief Justice Salmon P. Chase called habeas corpus "the most important human right in the Constitution" and "the best and only sufficient defense of personal freedom." More recently, Justice Abe Fortas, speaking for the Supreme Court in *Harris v. Nelson* (1969), observed that "habeas corpus is the fundamental instrument for safeguarding individual freedom against arbitrary and lawless state action."

Origin and Development of the Writ

The writ of habeas corpus first appeared in the English common law in the early fourteenth century, although some commentators link it historically with the Magna Carta (1215). Certainly the function of the writ is consistent with the provision in Magna Carta that states, "No freeman shall be taken or imprisoned or disseised or exiled or in any way destroyed, nor will we go upon him nor send upon him, except by the lawful judgment of his peers or by the law of the land." Common law courts developed the writ of habeas corpus as a legal mechanism to bring a defendant to court for arraignment and trial and to ensure that subjects of the Crown would not be subjected to arbitrary arrest or confinement. The frequent refusals of sheriffs and other public officials promptly to obey writs of habeas corpus led the English Parliament to pass the Habeas Corpus Act of 1679, which levied fines on officials who refused to obey the writ.

Because England's colonial courts followed the common law, the writ of habeas corpus came to be firmly established in the American colonies. Prior to the American Revolution, some colonial courts refused to issue writs of habeas corpus when colonists suspected of fomenting insurrection were taken into custody by British military authorities. This refusal to honor the common-law rights of Englishmen contributed to the spread of revolutionary fervor in the colonies.

Because the English common law was adopted by the new American states after independence was declared, state courts in this country have always exercised the power to issue writs of habeas corpus. The writ was widely recognized in state constitutional provisions and state statutes enacted during the founding era. However, neither Congress nor the federal courts adopted the English common law. Therefore, as Chief Justice John Marshall recognized in *Ex parte Bollman* (1807), federal courts derive their power to issue writs of habeas corpus from statutes enacted by Congress. Section 14 of the Judiciary Act of 1789 granted authority to federal courts to issue writs of habeas corpus, but also provided that such writs "shall in no case extend to prisoners in gaol, unless where they are in custody, under or by colour of the authority of the United States, or are committed for trial before some court of the same, or are necessary to be brought into court to testify." Thus, state prisoners were unable to obtain habeas corpus relief from the federal courts, but only from state courts.

Federal Habeas Corpus Jurisdiction Over State Prisoners

In 1867, Congress significantly expanded federal jurisdiction in this field by authorizing federal courts to issue writs of habeas corpus in cases where state authorities held persons in custody "in violation of the Constitution or laws or treaties of the United States." Ostensibly designed to protect the rights of the newly freed former slaves, federal

habeas corpus jurisdiction would evolve into a means by which federal courts could review state criminal convictions and conditions of confinement in state prisons. In *Frank v. Mangum* (1915), the Supreme Court broadened federal habeas corpus review to ensure that states supplied some "corrective process" whereby criminal defendants could seek to vindicate their federal constitutional rights.

Under Chief Justice Earl Warren, the Supreme Court broadened the scope of federal habeas corpus review by permitting state prisoners to raise issues in federal court that they did not raise in their state appeals. In *Fay v. Noia* (1963) the Supreme Court held that a state prisoner did not have to take a direct appeal to the state supreme court to seek federal habeas corpus review. Nor was the prisoner barred from raising constitutional issues in federal court merely because the issues had not been raised on direct appeal in state courts.

A number of the Supreme Court's most important rulings in the area of criminal procedure originated as federal habeas corpus petitions brought by state prisoners. Probably the most famous and consequential of these is *Gideon v. Wainwright* (1963), where the Court held that states denied due process of law by failing to provide counsel at public expense to indigent defendants accused of felonies.

Under Chief Justices Warren E. Burger and William H. Rehnquist, a more conservative Court significantly restricted state prisoners' access to federal habeas corpus. For example, in *Stone v. Powell* (1976), the Burger Court held that state prisoners could not use federal habeas corpus hearings to challenge searches and seizures as long they had been provided an opportunity for full and fair litigation of their Fourth Amendment claims in the state courts. In *Brecht v. Abrahamson* (1993), the Rehnquist Court ruled that federal courts may not overturn a state criminal conviction unless the petitioner can show that he or she suffered "actual prejudice" from errors committed by the trial court. Prior to this ruling, the state carried the burden of proving beyond a reasonable doubt that any constitutional error committed during or before trial was "harmless"—that is, not prejudicial to the defendant. *Brecht v. Abrahamson* had the effect of shifting the burden of proof from the state to the petitioner in a federal habeas corpus hearing, thus making it harder for state prisoners to prevail in challenging their convictions in federal court.

Despite these and other similar rulings, a continuing controversy over federal habeas corpus review of state criminal convictions prompted Congress to place further restrictions on the availability of the writ. The Antiterrorism and Effective Death Penalty Act of 1996 curtailed habeas corpus petitions by state prisoners who have already filed such petitions in federal court.

Of course, because Congress initially provided this jurisdiction to the federal courts by statute, Congress may modify or abolish this jurisdiction if it so desires. It is unlikely, though, that Congress would eliminate federal habeas review of state criminal cases altogether.

Suspension of Habeas Corpus

Article I, Section 9, of the Constitution states that "the privilege of the Writ of Habeas Corpus shall not be suspended, unless when in Cases of Invasion or Rebellion the public Safety may require it." In adopting the habeas corpus provision of Article I, Section 9, the framers wanted not only to recognize the right but also to limit its suspension to emergency situations.

The Constitution is somewhat ambiguous as to which branch of government has the authority to suspend the writ of habeas corpus during emergencies. In the early days of the Civil War, President Abraham Lincoln authorized Union military commanders to suspend the writ of habeas corpus in areas occupied by the Union army. In April of 1861, the Union army occupied Baltimore, Maryland, and arrested several Confederate sympathizers, including one John Merryman, who was charged with treason and held incommunicado at Fort McHenry. In *Ex parte Merryman* (1861), Chief Justice Roger B. Taney, acting in his capacity as circuit judge, issued a writ of habeas corpus to the commanding general at Fort McHenry, directing him to bring Merry-

man before the court. After the military authorities refused to honor the writ, Taney filed an opinion holding that the military had no right to arrest and detain a civilian and that President Lincoln was not authorized to suspend the writ of habeas corpus. Taney's opinion sounded an alarm bell, but it was drowned out in the cacophony of war: "I can only say that if the authority which the constitution has confided to the judiciary department and judicial officers, may thus, upon any pretext or under any circumstances, be usurped by the military power, at its discretion, the people of the United States are no longer living under a government of laws." Although Lincoln never replied directly to Taney's opinion, he did ask Congress for legislation suspending habeas corpus, and in 1863, Congress complied with this request. Eventually, Merryman was turned over to civilian authorities.

In the year following the cessation of the Civil War, the Supreme Court ruled that, although Congress could suspend the "privilege" of seeking the writ of habeas corpus, it could not prohibit federal courts from issuing the writ. In *Ex parte Milligan* (1866), a case involving a Southern sympathizer arrested and tried by the Union army in Indiana, the Court said: "The suspension of the privilege of the writ of habeas corpus does not suspend the writ itself. The writ issues as a matter of course, and, on the return made to it, the court decides whether the party applying is denied the right of proceeding any further with it." In *Milligan,* the Court also condemned President Lincoln's order establishing military jurisdiction over civilians outside of the immediate war area. It strongly affirmed the fundamental right of a civilian to be tried in a regular court of law, with all the procedural safeguards that characterize due process of law.

Immediately following the Japanese attack on Pearl Harbor on December 7, 1941, the governor of Hawaii issued an order declaring martial law in the territory and suspending the privilege of the writ of habeas corpus. The Hawaiian Organic Act, adopted by Congress in 1900, explicitly authorized the territorial governor to order these measures "in case of rebellion or invasion, or imminent danger thereof, when the public safety requires it." After assuming power under martial law, the commanding general issued an order closing the civilian courts and establishing military tribunals to act in their place. As the American war in the Pacific progressed, tensions eased in Hawaii and the civilian courts were reopened. Yet military tribunals continued to try and sentence civilians. In 1944, the federal district court in Honolulu issued writs of habeas corpus in two cases where civilians had been arrested and tried by military authorities for ordinary criminal offenses having nothing to do with national security or the war effort. In *Duncan v. Kahanamoku* (1946), the Supreme Court ruled that the martial law authorized by Congress under the Hawaii Organic Act, "while intended to authorize the military to act vigorously for the maintenance of an orderly civil government and for the defense of the island against actual or threatened rebellion or invasion, was not intended to authorize the supplanting of courts by military tribunals." The Court did not speak directly to the suspension of habeas corpus, but the implication of the Court's opinion was that the district court in Honolulu acted properly in issuing the writ.

Who Is Eligible to Seek a Writ of Habeas Corpus?

Federal law authorizes federal district courts to issue writs of habeas corpus in "all cases where any person may be restrained of his or her liberty in violation of the constitution, or of any treaty or law of the United States." Yet in *Johnson v. Eisentrager* (1950), the Supreme Court ruled that "enemy aliens" captured and held outside of American territory at the end of World War II did not have the right to seek habeas corpus relief in the federal courts. On the other hand, in *Braden v. 30th Judicial Circuit Court of Kentucky* (1973), the Court held that a prisoner's presence within the territorial jurisdiction of a district court is not "an invariable prerequisite" to the exercise of that court's habeas corpus jurisdiction. As long as an executive officer with legal responsibility for the custody can "be reached by service of process," the district court can issue the writ.

After September 11, 2001, the United States embarked upon a "war on terrorism" that included an invasion of Afghanistan, the government of which was harboring terrorists responsible for the September 11 attacks. In early 2002, the military transferred hundreds of suspected terrorists captured in Afghanistan and elsewhere to a detention center at the American naval base at Guantanamo, Cuba. Relatives of some of these detainees sought writs of habeas corpus to challenge the legality of their detention. The government claimed that because the base at Guantanamo is not territory over which the United States has sovereignty, federal courts have no jurisdiction to issue writs of habeas corpus with respect to enemy aliens held there. In *Rasul v. Bush* (2004), the Supreme Court rejected the government's position and held that the district court did have jurisdiction to hear these cases. Writing for the Court, Justice John P. Stevens noted that the government conceded that "the habeas statute would create federal-court jurisdiction over the claims of an American citizen held at the base." Stevens reasoned that because the federal habeas corpus statute does not distinguish between Americans and aliens, "there is little reason to think that Congress intended the geographical coverage of the statute to vary depending on the detainee's citizenship."

See also Blackstone, William; Burger Court; Common-Law Background of American Civil Rights and Liberties; Due Process Clauses; Fortas, Abe; *Gideon v. Wainwright* (1963); Habeas Corpus, Federal; Lincoln, Abraham; Magna Carta; *Milligan, Ex parte* (1866); Rehnquist Court; Stevens, John Paul; Terrorism, War on; Warren Court

Bibliography

Duker, William F. 1980. *A Constitutional History of Habeas Corpus.* Westport, CT: Greenwood Press.

Freedman, Eric N. 2003. *Habeas Corpus: Rethinking the Great Writ of Liberty.* New York: New York University Press.

Meador, Daniel J. 1966. *Habeas Corpus and Magna Carta: Dualism of Power and Liberty.* Charlottesville: University of Virginia Press.

     John M. Scheb II and Otis H. Stephens, Jr.

HABEAS CORPUS, FEDERAL

No writ is more celebrated in the annals of Anglo-American jurisprudence than the "Great Writ" of habeas corpus, whose ancient origins arguably trace to Magna Carta (1215). From William Blackstone to Zechariah Chafee, jurists and judicial scholars have long praised it as a formidable device to confront governmental oppression or caprice. Habeas corpus is a collateral civil remedy, informed by equitable principles and available within a state or federal jurisdiction and, as noted below, between them. While the writ features five variations, its most basic and familiar form is *habeas corpus ad subjiciendum*. Under its terms, a judge may investigate the cause of personal detention and, if the detention is found illegal, afford appropriate relief, including in rare instances the actual release of a confined or imprisoned person.

Despite its historic prominence as a guarantor of freedom, the writ of habeas corpus, in its primary American usage as a postconviction remedy, has also become a power distributor, stirring latent tensions between federal and state courts and their judges. The post-Civil War Habeas Corpus Act of 1867, an important historical catalyst for this intersystem friction, first extended federal review to state prisoners through a *writ of error* to the U.S. Supreme Court. In response, some state judiciaries asserted in unprecedented fashion the reciprocal prerogative of discharging persons in federal custody. Without hesitation, the Court quickly and decisively circumscribed state power on predictable grounds of federal supremacy (see *Tarble's Case,* 1872).

Because this entry focuses on *federal* habeas corpus, it is important to comment on the modern administrative and political considerations that have framed this friction point of judicial federalism. Over the course of the twentieth century, federal and state judges alike, for differing reasons, objected to the consequences of the jurisdictional overlap between court systems. On the one hand, thousands of habeas petitions from state prisoners imposed rather routine caseload congestion on federal district courts. Evidence showed that less than one percent of these docketed petitions raised legitimate claims that merited review, much less judicial relief. Yet all petitions, including frivolous ones, were dutifully evaluated by federal judges, straining already heavy workloads in most districts. On the other hand, state judges bristled at the politically motivated suggestion that incompetent and inferior state criminal proceedings caused the deluge of applications for federal habeas relief. The unique exception to the time-honored doctrine of *res judicata*—namely, that it did not apply in habeas proceedings—further undermined the finality of state judgments and exacerbated interjudicial tension.

The issue of the limits of federal relief engaged both the Congress and the U.S. Supreme Court from the 1940s forward. In response to lobbying efforts by jurists, such as John J. Parker and Kimbrough Stone, to minimize the opportunity for federal relief, national lawmakers in 1948 revised the federal Code and included (in Title 28, chapter 153, §§ 2241–2255) renewed deference to the principle of exhaustion of state remedies in matters of habeas corpus. Thereafter, the Supreme Court took the scope of habeas relief into its own interpretive hands, first expanding coverage of the writ and then contracting it. Expansion came through relaxed exhaustion rules and newly identified grounds for substantive relief. *Brown v. Allen* (1953), for example, held that federal judges may redetermine the merits of constitutional claims previously adjudicated by state courts. That conclusion alarmed Justice Robert Jackson, who lamented that the Court majority had " sanctioned progressive trivialization of the writ until floods of stale, frivolous petitions inundate the docket of the lower courts and swell our own." A decade later, however, the Warren Court in a 1963 trilogy of rulings (*Sanders v. United States, Townsend v. Sain,* and *Fay v. Noia*) expanded the writ's coverage still further. In the latter case, the court announced that an adequate and independent state ground for decision did not foreclose federal jurisdiction on collateral review. Furthermore, the now familiar and systematic nationalization of federally protected rights by the Warren Court opened new grounds of substantive relief for state inmates. Taken together, these sets of rulings contributed to increased writ-writing and, in turn, prompted further judicial and legislative actions.

A decade or so later, the ruling in *Stone v. Powell* (1976) restored a modicum of comity to federal-state judicial relations by setting new boundaries for federal habeas relief. The Court held that once state courts had provided a full and fair *opportunity* for a litigant to present a claim (not whether the petitioner actually did so), then federal judges would not revisit the Fourteenth Amendment claim. Subsequent rulings, by the Rehnquist Court, in particular, have also contracted available remedies, and three deserve mention here. *Teague v. Lane* (1989), for example, revised the retroactivity doctrine to narrow available habeas relief. With limited exception, the Court held that state prisoners could no longer litigate new interpretive rules announced after their convictions and sentences had been finalized. Four years later in *Herrera v. Collins* (1993), the Court ruled that, in the absence of a context of other constitutional violations, an inmate's claim of innocence (even based on newly found and arguably exculpatory evidence) was insufficient to merit further review by federal courts. In other words, and importantly, state prisoners no longer enjoyed entitlement nor even the presumption of innocence. It should be noted that this narrowed view of the function of federal habeas corpus now has special meaning for the emerging issue of postconviction DNA testing, so much so that some two dozen states, in response to *Herrera*, have instituted their own mechanisms to insure prisoner access to that testing. As a final note, the Rehnquist Court in *Felker v. Turpin* (1996) renewed its longstanding displeasure with the practice of filing so-called "successive" or "abusive" habeas petitions in district courts.

Of significance in the discussion of contemporary federal habeas corpus is the recent passage of the Antiterrorism and Effective Death Penalty Act (AEDPA) of 1996. Portions of this statute have modified (some observers say significantly) the use of habeas corpus as a postconviction remedy for state prisoners, and will no doubt continue to invite litigation in the years ahead. While the law appears for the most part to restate current habeas concepts and processes, some variations are noteworthy. Under AEDPA, for example, a state petitioner must now seek permission from a federal court of appeals before filing a second or successive petition in a district court. How federal courts, especially the Supreme Court, construe the meaning of this statute may impact the vitality of habeas corpus as a symbolic and substantive guardian of individual liberty.

See also Accused, Rights of the; Antiterrorism and Effective Death Penalty Act; Common Law Background of American Civil Rights and Liberties; Due Process Clauses; Habeas Corpus; Lincoln, Abraham; Leo Frank Case; Magna Carta; *Milligan, Ex parte* (1866); Rehnquist Court; Stevens, John Paul; Terrorism, War on; Warren Court

Bibliography

Bator, Paul. 1963. "Finality in Criminal Law and Federal Habeas Corpus for State Prisoners." *Harvard Law Review* 76: 441.

Meador, Daniel J. 1966. *Habeas Corpus and Magna Carta: Dualism of Power and Liberty*. Charlottesville: University of Virginia Press.

Winkle, John W., III. 1985. "Judges as Lobbyists: Habeas Corpus Reform in the 1940s." *Judicature* 68: 263.

John W. Winkle III

HABITUAL OFFENDER LAWS

Habitual offender laws impose enhanced penalties on chronic offenders. All states define some form of repeated criminal activity that is eligible for enhanced penalties. Many states define a specific number of repeat offenses as habitual conduct under state criminal codes. The definition of "habitual offender" varies from state to state, and habitual offender status is typically imposed for a third conviction within a specific time period. Habitual offender statutes most commonly apply to repeat felony offenses (offenses for which the penalty is incarceration for a minimum of one year).

Many states incorporate repeated violent conduct into state habitual offender laws. States also include habitual offender provisions in state vehicle codes, to revoke driving privileges for offenders previously convicted of serious driving offenses. In some states, habitual offender statutes are triggered by conduct that qualifies as a misdemeanor offense when taken alone, but that becomes a felony by virtue of the offender's previous conduct. The most notable habitual offender statutes are known as "three strikes, you're out" laws, because the penalty for the third offense incapacitates the offender for a significant period of time.

Penalty enhancements have been in existence for decades; however, the "three strikes" approach has diffused rapidly across the states since the early 1990s. In 1994, California adopted the most onerous of these laws amid a public backlash over the murder of a young girl, Polly Klaas, by a man on parole. Today, the federal government and approximately half of the states have enacted some form of "three strikes" legislation.

California cases account for the vast majority of the prosecutions in the states. California sentencing enhancements under the "three strikes" law impose a 25-year-to-life term for third-time felons and double the nominal sentence for second-time offenders. A consequence of California's law is that a potential misdemeanor offense can result in a life sentence as a third offense.

The significant minimum sentences imposed on habitual offenders may present a punishment that is excessive under the Eighth Amendment to the United States Constitution, which prohibits punishments that are cruel and unusual. A significant minimum sentence may also violate state constitutional provisions that provide similar protections. Of particular concern are cases in which an enhanced sentence is imposed for a relatively minor, nonviolent third offense such as shoplifting or petty theft.

For decades, the United States Supreme Court has declined to find that sentencing enhancements for habitual offenders amount to constitutional infringements of the protections against double jeopardy, ex post facto laws, cruel and unusual punishment, due process, and equal protection under the law. In *Rummel v. Estelle* (1980), the Supreme Court upheld a life sentence imposed under a Texas habitual offender statute for three nonviolent theft offenses which totaled $229.11. Although the Eighth Amendment prohibits imposition of a sentence that is grossly disproportionate to the severity of the crime, for the moment the Court appears to reserve the application of this proposition to cases involving the death penalty.

The California Supreme Court has struck down some indeterminate sentences as excessive and in violation of the California constitutional protection against cruel and unusual punishment but has not rendered such an opinion with respect to "three strikes" penalties. Federal courts have been more inclined to find that constitutional provisions have been violated by these sentencing statutes. The Ninth Circuit Court of Appeals has overturned several California "three strikes" sentences as grossly disproportionate punishments in violation of the Eighth Amendment.

The United States Supreme Court, however, has overturned those opinions and upheld the California law in its 2003 decisions in the cases of Leandro Andrade and Gary Ewing. Andrade was sentenced to two consecutive terms of 25 years to life for a third offense of stealing videos from a K-Mart store. Ewing was convicted of attempting to steal three golf clubs valued at $1,200 and sentenced to 25 years to life. In five-to-four decisions in both cases, the Supreme Court determined that the California law did not violate the constitutional ban on cruel and unusual punishment. Dissenting justices argued that both defendants would receive drastically lower sentences in other states and in the federal system (see *Lockyer v. Andrade; Ewing v. California*).

The argument behind sentencing enhancements for habitual offenders is that offenders commit numerous crimes before actually being caught, and that early identification and incapacitation for longer periods of time will reduce the revolving door of recidivism. The identification of habitual offenders and the potential benefits of stringent sentencing provisions are based on the work of the National Resource Council, Peter Greenwood, and the RAND Corporation (1982). Habitual offender statutes are credited by some with reducing the crime rate in California and with removing violent and career criminals from society. However, the research on this point is not resolved. Critics of this policy strategy argue that any effect of habitual offender statutes on crime is marginal at best, and that "three strikes" laws actually increase prison populations by imposing long prison sentences on offenders convicted of nonviolent, relatively petty crimes (Jones 2003; Zimring, Hawkins and Kamin 2001).

See also Cruel and Unusual Punishments Clause; Eighth Amendment; Retribution; "Three Strikes" Laws

Bibliography

Jones, Nolan E. 2003. "Three Strikes and You're Out: A Symbolic Crime Policy?" In *Crime Control and Social Justice: The Delicate Balance,* eds. Darnell E. Hawkins, Samuel L. Myers, Jr., and Randolph N. Stone, 53–66. Westport, CT: Greenwood Press.

Zeigler, Frank A., and Del Carmen, Rolando V. 1996. "Constitutional Issues Arising from 'Three Strikes and You're Out' Legislation." In *Three Strikes and You're Out: Vengeance as Public Policy,* eds. David Shichor and Dale K. Secrest. Thousand Oaks, CA: Sage.

Zimring, Franklin E., Gordon Hawkins, and Sam Kamin. 2001. *Punishment and Democracy: Three Strikes and You're Out in California.* New York: Oxford University Press.

Kathleen Hale

HAMILTON V. REGENTS OF THE UNIVERSITY OF CALIFORNIA (1934)

The significance of *Hamilton v. Regents of the University of California* (1934) rests in its conclusion that the duty of the government to ensure military readiness outweighs the rights of individuals to refuse military training. The Court considered national security to be more important than the rights of individuals to assume the status of conscientious objectors.

Hamilton and his co-litigants had been students at the University of California. The statute that created that institution specified that "all able-bodied male students of the University … shall receive instruction and discipline in military tactics." The state constitution also required that the university include military tactics in its curriculum. In turn the Regents ordered that all able-bodied students who were younger than 24 years old and not at least juniors were required to take six units of military science and tactics. Hamilton and the others belonged to a church that had clearly stated its opposition to war. In accordance with their religious beliefs, they had refused to take the military courses, and the university, as a result, suspended them. This case ensued.

First, the students claimed that their suspension violated the Privileges or Immunities Clause of the Fourteenth Amendment, which reads "no State shall make or enforce any law which shall abridge the privileges or immunities of citizens of the United States." In response, Justice Pierce Butler cited in his opinion for the Court a series of earlier cases in which the Court had held that the privileges and immunities protected by the Amendment are based on the Constitution itself or on federal laws (see, especially, the Slaughterhouse Cases). Butler went on to state that the privilege of attending the university was bestowed by the state, and so was not covered by the clause. In addition, the immunity at issue, freedom from the military training requirement, was part of the liberty interest protected by the Due Process Clause of the same amendment and was to be considered along with that part of the case. This switch from privileges and immunities to the Due Process or Equal Protection Clauses of the Fourteenth Amendment is in line with the modern development of privilege and immunity law. In fact, that portion of the Fourteenth Amendment is virtually a dead letter.

The argument founded upon the Due Process Clause was the plaintiffs' strongest. They argued, with some plausibility, that they had been deprived of liberty (which the Court viewed as the freedom to remain as students without taking military science courses) without due process of law. The Court rebutted that contention by asserting three arguments. The first was that in return for the state's maintenance of peace and order and enforcement of the law each citizen was bound "to support and defend government against all enemies." The Court apparently meant that there was no freedom from military obligations. The Court's second argument was that citizens are relieved of military obligations not by the Constitution but by statutes such as the ones that recognize conscientious objection. The third argument was that the "war powers," the basis of which is not specified, being "well-nigh limitless," include the right to compel military service. The common theme in these arguments is that military necessity trumps whatever constitutional rights the litigants had.

The would-be students' third argument was that the university's requirement was repugnant to the Kellogg-Briand Peace Pact. The constitutional underpinning of that argument is found in the Supremacy Clause (Article VI, clause 2), which specifies that the Constitution, federal laws made in pursuance of it, and treaties "shall be the supreme Law of the Land." Not surprisingly, the law on the supremacy of treaties is more complicated than the relevant general statement in the Constitution suggests. For example, questions have arisen regarding the force of treaties that are not self-executing but require action by Congress to go into effect—the relation between treaties and conflicting laws and the effect of the presumption against preemption of laws by treaties complicate the interpretation of the Supremacy Clause. However, the Court avoided the tangles of this law by tersely pointing out that there was no conflict between the pact, which condemned war, and the University of California's military science requirement.

Based on the facts of the case, it is reasonable to conclude that the main argument would be that the liberty interest that is protected by the Due Process Clause and that might have been abridged by the university is the First Amendment guarantee of freedom of religion. After all, the would-be students argued that their religious beliefs led them to resist military training. The majority opinion does mention an assertion to that effect, but it immediately holds that the only liberty right at issue is the freedom to attend the university without taking military science courses. As we have seen, the opinion quickly disposes of that argument. However, Justice Benjamin N. Cardozo's concurring opinion, which two other justices joined, does seriously consider the argument about religious freedom. Nevertheless, Cardozo was not persuaded by the students' arguments.

The difficulty with *Hamilton* is that the Court, due to the military context in which the case arose, brushed aside arguments having to do with rights that were based on religious beliefs. *Hamilton* is not the only case in which religious beliefs were ignored in favor of military exigencies. Proponents of civil rights will probably continue to struggle with this decision in the future.

See also Bill of Rights, Incorporation of; Cardozo, Benjamin N.; Conscience, Freedom of; Conscientious Objection to Military Service; Due Process Clauses; Equal Protection Clause; First Amendment; Fourteenth Amendment (1868); Free Exercise Clause; Liberty; Privileges or Immunities Clause; Slaughterhouse Cases

Jack Stark

HAND, LEARNED (1872–1961)

Sometimes called the "Tenth Justice" because he never served on the United States Supreme Court but was as respected and influential as if he had, Learned Hand served as a district and circuit court judge for over a half century. Although he suspected that his controversial wartime free speech decision in *Masses Publishing Co. v. Patten* (1917) may have prevented his later appointment to the Supreme Court, legal scholars believe the general politics of judicial appointments as well as the timing of vacancies on the Court during Hand's career were the more likely reasons. Regardless, Hand's courageous defense of the freedom of speech during World War

I remains perhaps his most enduring legacy. Nearly a century after *Masses,* Professor Geoffrey Stone characterized Hand's opinion as "quite brilliant," and as having had an "enormous impact on our understanding of the First Amendment." (Stone 2003, 335)

Born Billings Learned Hand in Albany, New York, on January 27, 1872, Learned Hand was the son of Samuel Hand, a lawyer and judge, and Lydia Coit Hand, a homemaker. Both Samuel and Lydia Hand's families had long histories of legal and judicial service. This family legacy, coupled with his father's death when Learned was just 14, heavily influenced Learned Hand's pursuit of a career in law.

Learned Hand graduated *summa* cum laude from Harvard University in 1893, receiving both a bachelor's and master's degree in philosophy, having studied under such giants in the field as George Santayana and William James. Hand graduated with honors from Harvard Law School in 1896, and worked in private practice in Albany and New York City from 1897 to 1909, but never achieved significant success as a lawyer. Despite its lower pay, a judgeship was more fitting to his introspective, philosophical temperament ("the modern Hamlet" as Justice Felix Frankfurter described him). He was appointed to the Federal District Court for the Southern District of New York by President William Howard Taft in 1909. In 1924 President Calvin Coolidge appointed Hand to the United States Court of Appeals for the Second Circuit, where he spent the rest of his career.

Hand was known for both the quantity and the quality of the opinions he wrote. In over 50 years on the bench, he authored some 4,000 opinions in an eloquent literary style that is still celebrated as among the best in American legal history. He was a popular speaker at commencements and professional functions. He was one of the founders of the American Law Institute and contributed to the drafting of several ALI "Restatements of the Law." He was similarly instrumental in launching *The New Republic* magazine in 1914. Also a voluminous letter-writer, Hand left behind correspondence with his wife, Frances Fincke Hand, and his friends and colleagues, such as Justice Oliver Wendell Holmes, that has provided biographers and scholars with a treasure trove of insights into both his personal and professional lives.

In addition, Hand published several law review articles, beginning in 1908 with "Due Process of Law and the Eight-Hour Day," in which he harshly criticized the Supreme Court's *Lochner v. New York* (1905) decision as an abuse of judicial power. Throughout his career Hand eschewed judicial activism, committed to the belief that judges should retain their independence and objectivity and, regardless of their own political or personal preferences, apply the laws that are properly created only by the legislative branch. And he practiced the judicial restraint he preached: only twice in his long career did he declare a statute unconstitutional. "[T]his power," he stated in *The Bill of Rights,* "should be confined to occasions when the statute or order was outside the grant of power to the grantee, and should not include a review of how the power has been exercised." (Hand 1958, 66)

Among Hand's memorable opinions was *United States v. Carroll Towing* (1947), still well-known to law students as the source of the algebraic "Hand Test" for determining the standard of care for the tort of negligence. Hand is also known for influential opinions in patent/trademark and antitrust cases (e.g., *U.S. v. Aluminum Co. of America* [1945]). He presaged the modern obscenity law of "community standards" in *United States v. Kennerley* (1913), writing that obscenity statutes "do not embalm the precise morals of an age or place," but rather should be "left to the gradual development of general notions about what is decent."

But it is Hand's courageous defense of the First Amendment in *Masses Publishing Co. v. Patten* (1917), an opinion overturned only months later by the appellate court and cited only a handful of times by any court since 1919, that remains perhaps his most influential work, his ideas still debated by constitutional scholars today. Professor Vincent Blasi has said:

The opinion's most important contribution lies … in the structure of reasoning Judge Hand employed to justify his direct-advocacy-of-crime test. Hand was the first judge to place heavy reliance on democratic theory in seeking to understand the meaning of the first amendment, the first judge to hold that speech integral to the democratic process must be protected even when it may cause substantial harm. The premises Hand invoked and the reasoning process he employed to draw out implications from those premises have become the basic, though often unacknowledged, features of modern first amendment analysis. (Blasi 1990, 4-5)

The case involved the effect of the Espionage Act of 1917 on the distribution of a self-described "revolutionary" magazine, *The Masses.* The Postmaster General of the United States refused to allow mailing of the August 1917 issue of *The Masses,* citing four antiwar cartoons and other content praising jailed antidraft activists Emma Goldman and Alexander Berkman as violations of provisions of the Espionage Act prohibiting any person from willfully causing or attempting to cause "insubordination, disloyalty, mutiny, or refusal of duty in the military or naval forces" or to "obstruct the recruiting or enlistment service of the United States." The magazine's publisher sought an injunction to permit mailing of the issue. Despite knowing it would be politically unpopular to do so during wartime, but faithful to his philosophy of judicial restraint, Hand granted the injunction, proposing a "direct incitement to violence" test. Hand notes in his opinion that, "Words are not only the keys of persuasion, but the triggers of action, and those which have no purport but to counsel the violation of law cannot by any latitude of interpretation be a part of that public opinion which is the final source of government in a democratic state." He goes on to say:

Yet to assimilate agitation, legitimate as such, with direct incitement to violent resistance, is to disregard the tolerance of all methods of political agitation which in normal times is a safeguard of free government. The distinction is not a scholastic subterfuge, but a hard-bought acquisition in the fight for freedom, and the purpose to disregard it must be evident when the power exists. If one stops short of urging upon others that it is their duty or their interest to resist the law, it seems to me one should not be held to have attempted to cause its violation. If that be not the test, I can see no escape from the conclusion that under

this section every political agitation which can be shown to be apt to create a seditious temper is illegal. I am confident that by such language Congress had no such revolutionary purpose in view. It seems to me, however, quite plain that none of the language and none of the cartoons in this paper can be thought directly to counsel or advise insubordination or mutiny.

The Circuit Court of Appeals overturned Hand's opinion just four months later, and the Supreme Court adopted the more restrictive "clear and present danger" test beginning with *Schenck v. U.S.,* another Espionage Act case, in 1919. Ironically, it was Hand's friend and judicial idol Oliver Wendell Holmes who wrote the opinion for the unanimous Court in *Schenck,* including the famous example of shouting "Fire!" in a crowded theater. However, as Professor Blasi notes:

The great Holmes and Brandeis opinions that turned the clear-and-present-danger test into a meaningful constraint on the power to punish dissent … employed a logic very similar to, and almost surely derived from, that introduced by Judge Hand in his *Masses* opinion. In this respect, the impact of Hand's approach to first amendment interpretation has been far more pervasive, and far more profound, than even his admirers have recognized. (Blasi 1990, 5)

Learned Hand officially retired from the Second Circuit Court in 1951 but remained active in the law until his death on August 18, 1961.

See also Brandeis, Louis D.; Clear and Present Danger Doctrine; Clear and Probable Danger Doctrine; Due Process Clauses; Espionage Act of 1917; First Amendment; Holmes, Oliver Wendell, Jr.; Judicial Activism; Judicial Restraint; *Lochner v. New York* (1905); Obscenity and Pornography; Speech, Freedom of; Taft, William Howard; United States Courts of Appeals

Bibliography

Blasi, Vincent. 1990. "Learned Hand and the Self-Government Theory of the First Amendment: *Masses Publishing Co. v. Patten.*" *University of Colorado Law Review* 61: 1.

Gunther, Gerald. 1994. *Learned Hand: The Man and the Judge.* New York: Knopf.

Hand, Learned. 1908. "Due Process of Law and the Eight-Hour Day." *Harvard Law Review* 21: 495.

Hand, Learned. 1958. *The Bill of Rights.* Cambridge, MA: Harvard University Press.

Stone, Geoffrey R. 2003. "Judge Learned Hand and the Espionage Act of 1917: A Mystery Unraveled." *University of Chicago Law Review* 70: 335.

Julie A. Thomas

HARLAN, JOHN MARSHALL (1833–1911)

John Marshall Harlan was born in Harlan's Station in Boyle County, Kentucky on June 1, 1833, into a prominent, slave-owning family. He was the sixth of nine children born to James and Eliza Harlan. James Harlan was a lawyer and two-term Congressman. He also held several positions in Kentucky government. Thus, John Marshall Harlan grew up steeped in both politics and the law. He graduated from Centre College in Kentucky in 1850 and studied law at Transylvania University for two years, read law in his father's law office for one year, and was admitted to the bar in 1853. Harlan held several offices in Kentucky including service as a county judge and attorney general. Harlan's political platform was consistently proslavery. Perhaps surprisingly, he was an officer in the Union army during the Civil War.

After having been affiliated with several political parties, Harlan supported Republican Rutherford B. Hayes in the disputed presidential election of 1876. When a vacancy opened on the Court in 1877, Hayes nominated Harlan to fill the vacant seat. According to Henry Abraham, it would be "wrong to attribute Harlan's nomination solely to political considerations—indeed at the time of his selection Harlan could have been looked on as both nonpartisan and bipartisan, a characterization not at all inconsistent with his complex and eclectic political history" (Abraham 1999, 100). Harlan was confirmed by the Senate on November 29, 1877. During Harlan's 34-year tenure on the Court, he wrote dissents in several landmark cases, earning the title of the Great Dissenter.

Although his family had owned slaves and Harlan himself had initially been opposed to the Civil War Amendments, by the time Harlan reached the Supreme Court he had changed his position on slavery and legal equality for former slaves. Scholars have offered a number of reasons for this shift including political expediency, in that by joining the Republican Party, which opposed slavery, he would have an easier path to higher political office. Another reason was his family's view on the institution of slavery, which tended toward the paternalistic. According to family lore, James Harlan had once admonished a slave driver on the streets of Frankfort, Kentucky, as a "damned scoundrel." Moreover, Harlan's wife Malvina was reportedly opposed to the practice. Further explanation of this shift concerned his half-brother Robert, who was a slave. Harlan was acutely aware of the racism Robert endured (Thompson 1996). Harlan prosecuted members of the Ku Klux Klan during his four-year tenure (1863–1867) as Attorney General of Kentucky. He also became an advocate of the Civil War Amendments before he reached the High Court.

Evidence of Harlan's views on the Civil War Amendments can be found in his dissenting opinion in the Civil Rights Cases (1883), a consolidation of five cases each presenting the question of whether the Civil Rights Act of 1875 could be enforced against private entities. Justice Joseph Bradley's majority opinion offered a narrow interpretation of the Fourteenth Amendment. According to Bradley, the Fourteenth Amendment only applied to discrimination by the state and thus the Civil Rights Act was unconstitutional as applied to private entities. Harlan dissented, claiming that the Civil Rights Act declared "that since the nation has established universal freedom in this country for all time, there shall be no discrimination, based merely upon race or color, in respect of the legal rights in the accommodations and advantages of public conveyances, inns, and places of public amusement." He argued that such discrimination constituted "a badge of servitude" forbidden by the Thirteenth Amendment and was within the purview of Congress to forbid. Harlan also argued for a broad interpretation of the Fourteenth Amendment, asserting that Section 5 of the Fourteenth Amendment was a sufficient basis for the legislation as it protected rights guaranteed by the amendment.

Harlan wrote: "Citizenship in this country necessarily imports equality of civil rights among citizens of every race in the same state. It is fundamental in American citizenship that, in respect of such rights, there shall be no discrimination by the state, or its officers, or by individuals, or corporations exercising public functions or authority, against any citizen because of his race or previous condition of servitude." According to his wife's memoirs, Harlan had difficulty writing this opinion as he was the youngest member of the Court and because "he felt that, on a question of such far-reaching importance, he must speak, not only forcibly but wisely" (quoted in Przybyszewski 2003, 67).

Harlan's commitment to equal treatment under the law is perhaps best exemplified in his lone dissent in *Plessy v. Ferguson* (1896). In *Plessy*, the Court considered the constitutionality of a Louisiana law mandating racially segregated railroad passenger cars against claims that the law violated the Thirteenth Amendment and the Equal Protection Clause. The Court upheld the law claiming that there was no constitutional violation and ushered in the "separate but equal" doctrine as the authoritative interpretation of the Equal Protection Clause. Harlan's dissent argued that in "the eye of the law there is in this country no superior, dominant, ruling class of citizens. There is no caste here. Our Constitution is color-blind and neither knows nor tolerates classes among citizens." Harlan also noted that the Court's opinion would incite racial hatred and promote the view of the legal inferiority of African Americans. This view was not vindicated until the Supreme Court's ruling more than 50 years later in *Brown v. Board of Education* (1954).

Despite Harlan's commitment to equal treatment under the law for whites and African Americans, his family's experience with slavery continued to influence his views on race. Harlan subscribed to the racial identity theory, under which whites were considered socially superior to blacks (Przybyszewski 2003, 68). Just prior to his oft-quoted statement in the *Plessy* dissent that the Constitution is color-blind, Harlan wrote that, "The white race deems itself to be the dominant race in this country.

And so it is, in prestige, in achievements, in education, in wealth, and in power. So, I doubt not, it will continue to be for all time, if it remains true to its great heritage and holds fast to the principles of constitutional liberty." This view could explain his votes in several post-*Plessy* cases regarding race. For instance, he did not believe that the Fourteenth Amendment granted citizenship to Chinese-Americans (see, e.g., *United States v. Wong Kim Ark*, 1898). He also voted with the majority in *Pace v. Alabama* (1882) in which the Court upheld a law punishing interracial adultery more harshly than same-race adultery. Moreover, he deferred to state authorities in upholding racially segregated public schools in his majority opinion in *Cummings v. Richmond Board of Education* (1899) (Przybyszewski 2003, 68).

When the Supreme Court interpreted the Fourteenth Amendment as protecting the right to freedom of contract, Harlan again found himself in dissent, although this time he was not alone. In *Lochner v. New York* (1905), the Court ruled that a New York law limiting working hours for bakery employees was unconstitutional because it denied the employer and the employee their right of liberty of contract protected by the Due Process Clause of the Fourteenth Amendment. Harlan dissented because he believed that the majority expanded the Fourteenth Amendment beyond its original purpose. He also believed the law was a legitimate exercise of state police power to protect the health of bakery employees who often worked more than 100 hours per week in less than sanitary conditions.

Harlan strongly believed that the Fourteenth Amendment guaranteed state citizens the protections afforded by the Bill of Rights because that was the intent of the framers of the Fourteenth Amendment, particularly with regard to the Privileges or Immunities Clause. He became the initial proponent of the doctrine of incorporation in *Chicago, Burlington, and Quincy Railroad Co. v. Chicago* (1897). In this case, the Court held that the Due Process Clause required the states to provide just compensation when it took private property for public use. This case is significant in applying protections of the Bill of Rights to the states. It is also significant in the context of protecting the property rights of individuals against encroachment by corporations.

John Marshall Harlan's reputation as the lone dissenter was initially due to his many votes involving economic liberties in which he voted to protect the individual over the corporation. It was not until public opinion towards race relations changed significantly that Harlan was commended for his early efforts on behalf of civil rights. Harlan's views on both civil rights and incorporation provided the framework for many of the landmark rulings of the Warren Court era. Ironically, his own grandson, Associate Justice John Marshall Harlan II, who served during the Warren Court, disavowed any interpretation of the Constitution that advocated incorporation of the Bill of Rights to the states; yet he was an advocate of civil rights. The elder Harlan died on October 14, 1911, and is routinely mentioned among the greatest justices to have ever served on the United States Supreme Court (Pederson and Provizer 2003).

See also Bill of Rights, Incorporation of; *Brown v. Board of Education* (1954; 1955); Civil Rights Act of 1875; The Civil Rights Cases (1883); Due Process Clause; Due Process, Substantive; Economic Freedom; Equal Protection Clause; Fourteenth Amendment (1868); Harlan, John Marshall, II; Ku Klux Klan; *Lochner v. New York* (1905); *Plessy v. Ferguson* (1896); Police Power; Privileges or Immunities Clause; Fourteenth Amendment, Section 5 of the; Segregation in Public Education; Slavery; Thirteenth Amendment; Warren Court

Bibliography

Abraham, Henry. 1999. *Justices, Presidents, and Senators.* Lanham, MD: Rowman & Littlefield.

Pederson, William D., and Norman W. Provizer, eds. 2003. *Leaders of the Pack: Polls and Case Studies of Great Supreme Court Justices.* New York: Peter Lane.

Przybyszewski, Linda. 2003. "John Marshall Harlan the Elder: Color-Blind Justice." In *Leaders of the Pack: Polls and Case Studies of Great Supreme Court Justices,* eds. William D. Pederson and Norman W. Provizer. New York: Peter Lane.

Thompson, Charles. 1996. *Harlan's Great Dissent.* Available at: http://library.louisville.edu/law/harlan/harlthom.html. Accessed 17 October 2005.

Kara E. Stooksbury

HARLAN, JOHN MARSHALL, II (1899–1971)

John Marshall Harlan was born in Chicago, Illinois, on May 20, 1899. Harlan was the namesake of his grandfather John Marshall Harlan, an Associate Justice on the High Court from 1877 to 1911. Born into a distinguished, upper-class family, Harlan earned an undergraduate degree from Princeton University in 1920 and attended Oxford University on a Rhodes Scholarship. In 1925, he earned a law degree from New York Law School.

Harlan obtained a position at one of New York's most prestigious Wall Street firms. During his employment, however, he also took leaves of absence to hold various positions in public service and to serve in the Air Force in World War II. "By the early 1950's, he was considered one of the nation's foremost litigators in anti-trust and related suits" (Yarbrough 2000, 48). Harlan was a long-time supporter of the Republican Party, yet "he had always kept a low political profile and was widely regarded to be nonpartisan" (Abraham 1999, 197). He was appointed by President Eisenhower to the U.S. Court of Appeals for the Second Circuit in 1954. After the death of Justice Robert Jackson in October 1954, Eisenhower nominated Harlan to the U.S. Supreme Court on November 8, 1954. Harlan was confirmed on March 16, 1955, after delays by senators who believed that "he was 'ultra-liberal,' hostile to the South, [and] dedicated to reforming the Constitution by 'judicial fiat'" (Abraham 1999, 197). Harlan's detractors could not have been more wrong. Indeed, his record on the Court evinced a jurist strongly committed to the principle of judicial restraint.

His restrained posture can be explained in terms of his view of the role of a judge within our constitutional arrangement of separation of powers. Harlan, much like his colleague Felix Frankfurter, believed that the Court should not disturb the system of federalism crafted by the Constitution's framers. This view put him at odds with the liberal majority of the Warren Court on reapportionment cases. For instance, in *Reynolds v. Sims* (1964) Harlan was the lone dissenter from the majority's holding that state legislatures must adhere to the "one person, one vote" doctrine when redrawing electoral district lines. He wrote that the Court's ruling would "have the effect of placing basic aspects of state political systems under the pervasive overlordship of the federal judiciary" and was thus contrary to the Constitution.

Harlan also dissented in a number of criminal justice cases decided by the Warren Court. In *Miranda v. Arizona* (1966), he disagreed with the holding that police were required to apprise suspects of their Fifth Amendment right against self-incrimination. According to Harlan, the majority's decision was not compelled by the Fifth Amendment and thus represented "poor constitutional law." In the same vein, he rejected the Court's holding in *Mapp v. Ohio* (1961) extending the exclusionary rule to the states because he rejected the doctrine of incorporation, a concept ironically espoused by his late grandfather.

"Harlan's regard for the passive virtues of judicial self-restraint did not mean, of course, that he invariably rejected civil liberties claims" (Yarbrough 2000, 51). In fact, he authored majority opinions in several of the most significant free speech cases decided during the Warren Court era (Mendelson 1991, 196). His majority opinion in *NAACP v. Alabama* (1958), for instance, upheld the right to freedom of association as protected by the First Amendment, despite the lack of wording in the amendment guaranteeing such a right. His advocacy of free speech continued into the Burger Court era in opinions such as *Cohen v. California* (1971), in which he limited the power of the state to prosecute individuals for engaging in political speech that it found to be vulgar.

Harlan was also committed to limiting government in the realm of individual privacy. In *Poe v. Ullman* (1961), he dissented when a majority of the Court dismissed a case involving a Connecticut anti–birth control law. Harlan wrote that the law presented an "intolerable and unjustifiable invasion of privacy" in violation of the Fourteenth Amendment, a forerunner of the right to privacy the Court would recognize four years later in *Griswold v. Connecticut* (1965). Harlan, however, wrote a concurring opinion in *Griswold* because he believed the right to privacy was implicit in the concept of ordered liberty and thus protected by the Due Process Clause. He therefore rejected Justice William O. Douglas's rationale that the right to privacy was contained in the Bill of Rights and incorporated in the Due Process Clause.

Harlan's views on the Fourteenth Amendment as applied to racial discrimination centered on the concept of state action. In other words, he believed that the amendment only limited actions undertaken by state government, not private citizens. He voted with a unanimous Court in the *Brown II* (1955) school desegregation opinion requiring integration with "all deliberate speed." He also voted with the majority in *Swann v. Charlotte-Mecklenburg County Board of Education* (1971), which set forth guidelines eliminating *de jure* segregation of public schools.

Overall, John Marshall Harlan's jurisprudence was guided by the belief that judicial restraint was a prudent course of action so that "sweeping rulings [would not have] broad future impact as binding precedent" (Yarbrough 2000, 54). Harlan retired from the Court in 1971 after serving for 16 years. He died on December 29, 1971.

See also Association, Freedom of; Bill of Rights, Incorporation of; Burger Court; *Cohen v. California* (1971); Douglas, William O.; Due Process Clauses; Due Process, Substantive; Federalism and Civil Rights and Liberties; Fifth Amendment; First Amendment; Fourteenth Amendment (1868); Frankfurter, Felix; *Griswold v. Connecticut* (1965); Harlan, John Marshall; Jackson, Robert H.; Judicial Restraint; *Mapp v. Ohio* (1961); *Miranda v. Arizona* (1966); *Poe v. Ullman* (1961); Privacy, Constitutional Right of; *Reynolds v. Sims* (1964); Segregation, De Jure and De Facto; Segregation in Public Education; Speech, Freedom of; State Action Doctrine; Warren Court

Bibliography

Abraham, Henry. 1999. *Justices, Presidents, and Senators*. Lanham, MD: Rowman & Littlefield.

Mendelson, Wallace. 1991. "Justice John Marshall Harlan: *Non sub Homine …*" in *The Burger Court: Political and Judicial Profiles*, eds. Charles M. Lamb and Stephen C. Halpern. Chicago: University of Illinois Press.

Yarbrough, Tinsley. 2000. *The Burger Court: Justices, Rulings, and Legacy*. Santa Barbara, CA: ABC-CLIO, Inc.

Kara E. Stooksbury

HARMLESS ERROR, DOCTRINE OF

One of the principal functions of appellate courts is to correct errors made by trial courts. However, not all errors necessitate reversal of a lower tribunal's order, judgment, or sentence. The doctrine of harmless error holds that appellate courts should reverse trial court judgments only when errors committed by the trial court prejudiced the complaining party in the outcome of a case. The doctrine is sometimes memorialized by statute; in other instances it is part of the decisional law. The burden is on the party bringing the appeal to persuade the appellate court that the outcome of the hearing or trial would have been different in the absence of the alleged error. Although specific standards vary across jurisdictions, all appellate courts operate on the principle that reversal is required only when substantial, as distinct from merely technical, errors are committed by trial courts. Of course, appellate courts do not consider each error at trial in isolation. Rather, they will consider the cumulative effect of a series of errors. Thus, an appellant might secure reversal of a criminal conviction where the trial judge committed a series of errors, even though each particular error might be considered harmless in and of itself.

In *Chapman v. California* (1967), the United States Supreme Court held that even violations of defendants' constitutional rights are subject to harmless error analysis. Writing for the Court, Justice Hugo Black observed that "there may be some constitutional errors which in the setting of a particular case are so unimportant and insignificant that they may, consistent with the Federal Constitution, be deemed harmless, not requiring the automatic reversal of the conviction." However, the Court held that appellate courts must find beyond a reasonable doubt that constitutional errors were harmless to affirm the decision of a trial court on the basis of the harmless error doctrine.

The harmless error doctrine has been applied to a number of serious constitutional errors, including the denial of the defendant's right to be present at trial (see *United States v. Hasting,* 1983); the trial judge's failure to allow defense counsel to cross-examine a prosecution witness to prove bias (see *Rushen v. Spain,* 1983); the admission of evidence against the defendant that should have been suppressed because it was obtained in violation of the Fourth Amendment (see *Chambers v. Maroney,* 1970); and the use of a confession obtained in violation of the defendant's right to counsel (see *Milton v. Wainwright,* 1972).

In *Chapman v. California* the Court also indicated that violations of rights essential to a fair trial are not subject to harmless error analysis. As Justice Hugo Black noted in his majority opinion, "some constitutional rights are so basic to a fair trial that their infraction can never be treated as harmless error." It is axiomatic that such violations require reversal on appeal. Similarly, in *Rose v. Clark* (1986), the Supreme Court observed that "some errors necessarily render a trial fundamentally unfair." The Court in *Rose* went on to identify the right to counsel and the right to trial before an impartial judge and jury as "basic protections" that, if violated, necessarily require reversal of a trial court's judgment.

See also Accused, Rights of the; Appeal, Right to; Black, Hugo L.; Counsel, Right to; Due Process, Procedural; Interrogation and Confessions; Reasonable Doubt Standard

Bibliography

Childs, William G. 1999. "The Intersection of Peremptory Challenges, Challenges for Cause, and Harmless Error." *American Journal of Criminal Law* 27: 49.

Pizzi, William T., and Morris B. Hoffman. 2001. "Jury Selection Errors on Appeal." *American Criminal Law Review* 38: 1391.

John M. Scheb II and Otis H. Stephens, Jr.

HART, H.L.A. (1907–1992)

Herbert Lionel Adolphus Hart, who became widely known as H. L. A. Hart, was a noted English legal philosopher of the twentieth century. He was educated at New College, University of Oxford, admitted to the bar, and practiced as a barrister from 1932 to 1940. He became a tutor at Oxford in 1945, and in 1952 Oxford named him the Professor of Jurisprudence, a chair he held until his resignation in 1969.

Professor Hart was essentially a legal positivist. Legal positivists advocate that law is a social fact enforced by a sovereign authority; that law consists of statutes and codes that separate the law from the concept of natural law and morality. Hart agreed that law is a social fact and that law and morality are conceptually separate. But Hart took a normative approach to legal positivism, arguing that the positivist approach was derived too greatly from coercive rules. Rather, he posited that law is composed of both primary and secondary rules.

In *The Concept of Law* (1961), Hart expounded on his philosophy of law and legal systems. In it he criticized the approach of John Austin (1790–1859), the earlier English legal philosopher who advocated that law was a sovereign command backed by sanction. Hart found the Austinian approach relied too much on a criminal pattern, failed to provide for a continuity of legislative authority, and lacked the "idea of a rule" that would make people feel bound by the law. He explained that primary rules prescribe what people should or should not do, for example, laws that define crimes. They are basic to even primitive societies. But, he argued, primary rules alone are static and lack arbiters who are essential to maintain the primary rules. A modern legal system, he posited, must also have secondary rules. These are rules that allocate basic political power and identify the lawmakers who can introduce change and eliminate old rules. Secondary rules include those regulating legislative and judicial procedures and must provide a basis for adjudication of disputes, the latter being essential to empower individuals to authoritatively determine when a primary rule is violated. Hart opined that it is this union of primary and secondary rules that form the core of a modern legal system.

Professor Hart took issue with many legal philosophers of the twentieth century, but perhaps his most famous challenge was to Patrick Devlin (1906–1992), who later became Lord Chief Justice of England. Devlin was a legal moralist who advocated that it was necessary for the state to legislate morality, particularly with respect to sexual conduct. In *Law, Liberty, and Morality*, Oxford published Hart's series of lectures at Stanford University in 1962. In contrast to Devlin's views, Hart argued that deviation from accepted standards of sexual morality was no threat to society. In one of his lectures at Stanford he sharply contrasted crimes that are harmful to others with immoral sexual practices conducted in private (even when made unlawful) between consenting adults. These contrasting views have a special relevance in contemporary society in the United States where debate continues to rage on issues of abortion, prostitution, homosexuality, and same-sex marriage.

Hart strongly supported personal liberties, particularly in addressing the enforcement of morality by the criminal law. He once cautioned that "even when popular morality is supported by an overwhelming majority or marked by widespread intolerance, indignation, and disgust" that loyalty to democratic principles does not justify its imposition on a minority.

Hart was succeeded at Oxford by Ronald Dworkin (1931–). Dworkin supported Hart's analytical approach to law but departed from Hart's philosophy by holding that rights are premised on moral principles that are not necessarily separable from law. Until his demise in 1992 Professor Hart continued to lecture and write.

See also Abortion, Right to; Dworkin, Ronald; Same-Sex Marriage

Bibliography

Hart, H. L. A. 1972. *Law, Liberty and Morality*. Palo Alto, CA: Stanford University Press.

Hart, H. L. A. 1994. *The Concept of Law*. 2nd ed. New York: Oxford University Press.

Lacey, Niccola. 2004. *A Life of H. L. A. Hart: The Nightmare and the Noble Dream*. New York: Oxford University Press.

Hon. John M. Scheb

HATCH ACT (1939)

The Hatch Act became federal law in August 1939. It was designed to prevent various types of political activity by federal employees as well as the inappropriate use of federal employees by candidates in political campaigns. The law was passed in the wake of several scandals that involved the misuse of federal civil servants in various New Deal agencies during the administration of Franklin D. Roosevelt. Amidst widespread allegations that the Works Progress Administration (WPA) funds had been misused by staff members and local Democratic politicians during the congressional elections of 1938, many Republican office holders at the time believed that the WPA had gone even further by intimidating staff members, pressuring clients, and using public funds for political purposes. This concern explains the Hatch Act's most restrictive original provision—that persons below the policy making level in the executive branch of the federal government must not only refrain from political practices that would be illegal for any citizen but must abstain from "any active part" in political campaigns. A 1940 amendment to the law extended coverage to state and local employees whose salaries included any federal funds.

The original Hatch Act prohibited the use of public funds designated for relief or public works for any electoral purposes and forbade government employees from raising funds for candidates, giving partisan public speeches, or volunteering for any candidate or party. It also forbade federal employees to promise jobs, promotion, finan-

cial assistance, contracts, or any other benefit to secure campaign contributions or political support for candidates. The Hatch Act's ban on federal workers' involvement in political campaigns was appealed to the U.S. Supreme Court in 1947 and 1973 but was upheld both times. (See *United Public Workers v. Mitchell* [1947]; *United States Civil Service Comm'n v. National Ass'n of Letter Carriers, AFL-CIO* [1973].) In both cases, the Supreme Court upheld the Hatch Act provisions that forbade federal employees from taking an active part in political management or political campaigns. In 1987, a proposed amendment to the Hatch Act to permit federal workers to participate in political campaigns passed the House but not the Senate. In 1990, a similar bill passed both houses but was vetoed by President George Bush.

In 1993, however, Congress eliminated many of the restrictions that had previously cabined the political activities of federal employees. The amendments to the Hatch Act signed into law by President Clinton permitted most federal employees to take part in political management or in political campaigns. The allowable political activities by federal employees are found in the Hatch Act regulations in 5 U.S.C. § 7321 and a number of advisory opinions issued by the Hatch Act Unit of the U.S. Office of Special Counsel. For example, most federal employees may contribute money to political campaigns, give partisan public speeches, and volunteer for any candidate or party, so long as these activities are done outside the workplace and government employees do not exploit their positions for political purposes. Federal employees also now may run for public office in nonpartisan elections, assist in voter registration drives, express opinions about candidates and issues, solicit contributions for their own race in a nonpartisan election, campaign for or against candidates in partisan elections, and hold office in political clubs or parties.

However, some federal agencies and categories of employees remain "hatched" and continue to be prohibited from engaging in partisan political activities. For example, employees in the Customs Service, the Office of Investigative Programs and the career

Senior Executive Service (SES) are still prohibited from engaging in partisan political activity, and their political activities remain circumscribed by the provisions of the original Hatch Act. However, the 1993 amendment specifically allows employees of the Executive Office of the President to engage in "political activity." The law defined political activity to include anything campaign-related—organizing events, planning party strategy—except fundraising, which it completely prohibited. These same limits now apply to cabinet secretaries and all other presidential appointees approved by the Senate. A president's campaign or party must reimburse the government for the use of its offices and resources for permitted political activities.

In the wake of the 1993 amendments, some political activities remain generally impermissible for all federal employees (see, e.g., § 2(a), 107 Stat. 1002) regardless of whether they are on or off duty. Chief among these are prohibitions on federal employees soliciting, accepting, or receiving political contributions. A federal employee, for example, cannot host a political fundraiser at his or her home or solicit funds at any other fundraiser for a partisan candidate. They cannot, for instance, directly or indirectly pressure or coerce other employees to contribute to any partisan political campaign that includes activities such as selling tickets to a political fundraising event. All federal employees are prohibited from becoming a candidate in a partisan election where any of the candidates are running as a representative of any party. They also may not orchestrate any type of write-in candidacy for themselves or others during a partisan election. Federal employees also are barred from using their official authority or influence in political campaigns. For example, they cannot circulate a letter among coworkers asking for campaign volunteers and use the title of their position for identity in the letter. They also cannot solicit others to volunteer to work for any partisan political campaign or have their name appear on any invitation to a partisan fundraiser as a sponsor or point of contact.

All federal employees remain barred from either soliciting or discouraging the political activity of anyone with whom the agency specifically does

business. For example, an employee of a federal agency may address a large diverse group (outside the workplace), give a keynote address, and urge attendees to support a partisan political candidate. However, if that group has any official business with the agency, such a solicitation is prohibited. In any event, a federal employee is prohibited from soliciting monetary contributions from anyone at such a partisan political affair. Moreover, all federal employees are prohibited from engaging in any political activity while on duty, in a government office, while wearing an official uniform, or while using a government vehicle. An employee for example, cannot display a political poster, bumper sticker, or campaign button either in a government office or in any common areas of federal buildings. Yet, an employee is allowed to display a bumper sticker on a vehicle that the employee parks in a private lot or garage for which the employee receives a parking fee subsidy from his or her agency.

The provisions of the Hatch Act apply not only to federal workers, but they also restrict the political activities of individuals principally employed by state, county, or municipal executive agencies who have duties in connection with an activity financed in whole or in part by federal loans or grants. The notable exceptions to the law's application to non-federal employees include those individuals who have no duties in connection with federally funded activities and those individuals employed by publicly financed educational or research institutions, including state university systems and local public school systems. Also, the Hatch Act only applies to the employees of private nonprofit organizations if the statute through which the organization derives its federal funding contains a provision that deems the recipient organizations to be state or local government agencies for purposes of the Hatch Act. The conduct of state and local government employees is subject to various "Little Hatch Acts" that have been enacted at the state and local levels, but nothing in those state and local laws affect the political activities proscribed by the federal Hatch Act.

The U.S. Office of Special Counsel (OSC) is authorized to enforce the Hatch Act's provisions on permissible and impermissible political activities by government employees. The OSC is the agency authorized to prosecute violations of the act that are adjudicated by the Merit Systems Protection Board (MSPB). The Special Counsel may ask the MSPB to impose any penalty ranging from a 30-day suspension without pay to removal from the federal service.

The Hatch Act's original prohibitions on political activities by civil servants reflect, in many ways, the historic application of the doctrine of privilege to civil servants. This doctrine asserted that public employees enjoy no right to government employment; they choose their jobs voluntarily. Accordingly, public employees can claim few constitutional rights that the state, in its capacity as employer, cannot abridge. The 1993 amendments to the Hatch Act reflect the gradual erosion of the doctrine of privilege that has occurred in the course of several U.S. Supreme Court rulings since the 1950s. While no grand doctrine has emerged to replace the privilege doctrine, the unmistakable trend during the last 50 years has been to afford public employees greater constitutional protections within the context of their employment. Hence, the 1993 amendments to the Hatch Act embrace many of the legal victories won by public employees to greater freedom of speech and association without recrimination by their employer, especially during off-duty hours. In accord with the aspirations of government reformers to assure a politically neutral civil service, many of the limits on partisan political activities remain firmly entrenched in law. However, the amendments to the Hatch Act now make it clear that a politically neutral civil service can now be more narrowly construed as one that is neutral only in terms of partisanship.

See also Merit Systems Protection Board; The New Deal; Public Employees, Constitutional Rights of; Roosevelt, Franklin D.; Speech, Freedom of

David H. Folz

HATE CRIMES

The modern, accepted definition of hate crimes includes "crimes that manifest evidence of prejudice based on race, religion, sexual orientation, or ethnicity, including where appropriate the crimes of murder and non-negligent manslaughter; forcible rape; aggravated assault, simple assault, intimidation; arson; and destruction, damage or vandalism of property" as well as crimes committed against those with disabilities, both physical and mental (Hate Crimes Statistics Act of 1990 and Violent Crime Control and Law Enforcement Act of 1994). Some of the most widely condemned hate crimes are cross or church burnings, vandalism involving symbols or terms associated with hate (such as swastikas), and physical attacks (such as lynchings). As a result, hate crime laws have evolved from antilynching, anti-Klan, and group libel laws (Levin 2002). Currently, scholars of hate crimes have shifted their focus from defining those crimes to issues concerning the enforcement of hate crime penalties.

In recent decades, the Supreme Court has retreated from the decisions of the liberal Warren Court of the 1960s to develop a more conservative and narrowly focused jurisprudence for hate crime laws under the Burger and Rehnquist Courts. The foundations of Supreme Court hate crime law are found in *United States v. Guest* (1966) and *United States v. Price* (1966), which dealt with the denial of services and rights based upon the race of the victims. In these cases, the Court prohibited interference with government services or federally funded services on the basis of race, color, religion, or national origin. To reach this result, the Court upheld the federal statutes making it a crime for public or private actors to deprive people of their civil rights. (See 18 U.S.C. §§ 241 and 242.) The 1968 Federally Protected Rights law later codified this premise.

In *Barclay v. Florida* (1983) the Court upheld the use of the death penalty for a murder committed as a hate crime. However, in *Dawson v. Delaware* (1992), the Rehnquist Court reversed the trend of broadening the application of hate crimes laws and narrowed the definition of what constitutes a hate crime by ruling that a defendant's affiliation with hate groups could not be introduced into evidence unless it had some relevance to the crime committed. The Court further restricted the definition of hate crimes in *R.A.V. v. City of St. Paul* (1992), with its ruling that a municipal "hate crime" ordinance, which was used to prosecute a skinhead who burned a cross in the yard of a black family, was unconstitutional under the First Amendment.

The Rehnquist Court, however, has allowed prosecutors and judges to use some hate-related evidence. In the 1993 case of *Wisconsin* v. *Mitchell* the Court upheld a penalty enhancement for a defendant who selected his victim on the basis of race. In a unanimous opinion authored by the Chief Justice, the Court carefully distinguished between the protections that the Constitution affords even hate speech, and the entirely unprotected nature of racist violence. The Court also emphasized the constitutional permissibility of considering a defendant's motives during the penalty phase of trial.

A New Jersey "hate crime" statute provided for an enhanced prison sentence of 10 to 20 years if the trial judge found, by a preponderance of the evidence, that the accused had committed a crime with the intent to intimidate an individual or group on the basis of designated characteristics including race. Charles C. Apprendi had fired several shots into the home of an African-American family that had previously moved into an all-white neighborhood. Following a guilty plea, an evidentiary hearing was conducted to determine Apprendi's "purpose" for the shooting. The trial judge concluded that the preponderance of the evidence supported a finding "that the crime was motivated by racial bias." Accordingly, the trial judge applied the penalty enhancement provision by adding 2 years to the maximum sentence of 10 years on one count of the indictment. In reversing Apprendi's conviction, the Supreme Court, in a five-to-four decision, held that the Due Process Clause of the Fourteenth Amendment requires that any fact that increases the penalty for a state crime beyond the statutory maximum—other than the fact of a prior conviction—must be submitted to a jury and proved beyond a reasonable doubt. (*Apprendi v. New Jersey*, 2000)

During the Clinton Administration, Congress followed the Supreme Court's lead by passing legislation focused on penalty enhancements. The Hate Crime Sentencing Enhancement Act (1994), increased sentences for federal offenders by 30 percent when the prosecution established beyond a reasonable doubt that the victim was selected because of race, color, religion, national origin, ethnicity, gender, disability, or sexual orientation. In 1996, the Church Arson Prevention Act further increased the coverage and penalties for hate crimes.

As a result of these Court rulings and Congressional initiatives, federal hate crimes law currently works through penalty enhancements for criminals who target their victims based upon their race, religion, color, disability, sexual orientation, national origin, or ancestry. More recent attempts to strengthen hate crime legislation by providing support and guidance to law enforcement for the prosecutions of hate crimes through a "Hate Crime Prevention Act" have failed.

See also Burger Court; Due Process Clauses; First Amendment; Fourteenth Amendment (1868); Ku Klux Klan; Reasonable Doubt Standard; Rehnquist Court; Speech, Freedom of; Warren Court

Bibliography

Glenn, Richard A., and Otis H. Stephens. 1997. "Campus Hate Speech and Equal Protection: Competing Constitutional Values." *Widener Journal of Public Law* 6: 349.

Levin, Brian. 2002. "The Vindication of Hate Violence Victims Via Criminal and Civil Adjudications." *Journal of Hate Studies* 1: 133.

Jennifer R. Woodward

HATE SPEECH

Hate speech laws are highly controversial because the diverse nature of our country often produces sharp division between different groups, sometimes resulting in highly offensive and hateful speech. The two sides of the debate about what constitutes hate speech view the Constitution in very different ways. Proponents of these laws argue that the Fourteenth Amendment guarantees every citizen equal citizenship. They argue that minority groups cannot become truly equal citizens unless they are protected from purely bias-motivated hate. Opponents counter that the First Amendment was designed to protect speech even when it is highly offensive to most listeners; if bias-motivated speech is prohibited, soon other forms of offensive speech will come under fire. The Court must weigh the right of citizens to speak, even when their words are hateful, against the right of other citizens to live their lives unharassed by such speech.

The first Supreme Court case to address a hate speech law was *Beauharnais v. Illinois* (1952). Beauharnais was arrested under an Illinois law prohibiting the distribution of materials portraying "depravity, criminality, unchastity, or lack of virtue of a class of citizens, of any race, color, creed, or religion." As the president of the White Circle League, he had handed out racist leaflets. In this case, the Supreme Court said that libel against groups (group libel) was little different than libel against individuals and upheld Beauharnais' conviction. Although *Beauharnais* has not been explicitly overturned, later decisions have brought its validity into question. Now, criminal libel consists only of false statements of fact against nonpublic persons, not against groups and public figures, such as elected officials.

More recently, the Court addressed hate speech in *R.A.V. v. City of St. Paul* (1992). In this case, the Supreme Court addressed the St. Paul, Minnesota Bias-Motivated Crime Ordinance, which banned the use of swastikas, burning crosses, and similar symbols to arouse fear or anger on the basis of race, color, creed, religion, or gender. A group of white teenagers had burned a cross on the lawn of a black neighbor and were arrested under this ordinance. The city of St. Paul argued that the law did no more than prohibit "fighting words," a category of speech unprotected by the First Amendment. However, the Supreme Court disagreed, ruling that the ordinance represented "viewpoint discrimination," that is, it allowed fighting words for the tolerant, but did not

allow them for the intolerant. The Court emphasized that the First Amendment is intended to protect speech even if the ideas it contains are offensive to most listeners. The ordinance also banned offensive symbols such as swastikas and burning crosses only when used by the proponents of racial and religious hatred. A protester could, for example, display a swastika as part of a protest against Nazism. The ordinance was unconstitutional because the symbols and offensive speech that were banned were based on the viewpoint of the speaker; therefore the law violated a longstanding First Amendment speech principle—that the government cannot limit speech based on its content.

Furthermore, the ordinance was considered content-based because it did not prohibit speech biased in regard to characteristics other than race, color, creed, religion, or gender. For example, symbols meant to arouse fear on the basis of sexual orientation would not be prohibited.

Though the Court decision was unanimous, a concurring opinion signed by four justices cited very different reasons for invalidating the St. Paul antibias law. Justices in the concurrence emphasized that the law was too broad. It did not specify that for fighting words to be unconstitutional they must communicate ideas in a threatening rather than simply in an obnoxious manner. It banned all use of the symbols when used in a bias-motivated manner, even if the particular situation was not specifically threatening. Therefore, officials could have used the ordinance to restrict speech that would otherwise be protected.

The Court again dealt with cross burning in *Virginia v. Black* (2003). Here, the Court allowed laws banning cross burning only when the action is carried out with an intent to intimidate. The ruling was consistent with *R.A.V. v. St. Paul* because it ruled specifically on cross burning, noting that this particular act has a long history in the United States and that in certain circumstances burning a cross becomes a truly threatening action rather than being simply speech. When used in situations of intimidation, where the perpetrator is using the symbol to cause fear, the state may regulate it because it is a "true threat," a threat in which the speaker is communicating a serious expression of intent to commit an act of unlawful violence to a particular individual or group of individuals. Because the Ku Klux Klan often used the burning of crosses to relay this message, it still holds the same threat today, and is therefore not protected when used to intimidate in this manner. The burning cross's place in our history as a particularly dangerous form of intimidation makes it legal for the state to single it out for prohibition.

The Court has also permitted states to punish crimes motivated by racial hatred more harshly. In *Wisconsin v. Mitchell* (1993), the Court considered a Wisconsin hate-crime act that allowed for stricter punishments if a crime was motivated by bias. Many of the same problems of St. Paul's ordinance remained: Wisconsin opted to punish racially motivated crimes while not punishing, for example, crimes motivated by bias against the poor. The Court ruled that the law was constitutional, because it was aimed at conduct rather than speech. Just as employers may be punished for discriminatory hiring practices, when a crime is similarly motivated by bias, it has ceased to be simple speech and therefore loses First Amendment protection.

Many other nations, including Canada and Germany, do permit laws against speech that is biased against racial, ethnic, and religious groups, even if no specific intimidation is demonstrated. Unlike the United States, they allow laws that are invoked simply based on the content of the speech. Free speech principles in the United States require far more neutral standards in their application. They do not allow government to limit speech based solely on content. They can, however, limit speech intended to intimidate.

See also American Nazi Party; *Brandenburg v. Ohio* (1969); Clear and Present Danger Doctrine; Fighting Words Doctrine; First Amendment; Fourteenth Amendment (1868); Hate Crimes; Ku Klux Klan; Speech, Freedom of; Speech/Conduct Distinction; Symbolic Speech

Bibliography

Bollinger, Lee C., and Geoffrey R. Stone. "Dialogue." In *Eternally Vigilant: Free Speech in the Modern Era*, eds. Lee C. Bollinger and Geoffrey R. Stone, 1–31. Chicago: University of Chicago Press, 2002.

Delgado, Richard, and Kean Stefancic. *Must We Defend the Nazis?: Hate Speech, Pornography, and the First Amendment*. New York: New York University Press, 1996.

Greenawalt, Kent. *Fighting Words: Individuals, Communities, and the Liberties of Speech*. Princeton, NJ: Princeton University Press, 1995.

Ronald Kahn

HEALTH INSURANCE PORTABILITY AND ACCOUNTABILITY ACT OF 1996. *See* Privacy, Informational

HEARING, ELEMENTS OF A

The right to a hearing, that is, the right to present one's side in a criminal prosecution, a civil suit, an administrative proceeding, or a dispute or disciplinary action, is a fundamental right, embodied in the United States Constitution in the Fifth and Fourteenth Amendment rights to due process of law. But what constitutes a hearing? When is it required? What are the fundamental elements of a hearing?

Black's Law Dictionary defines a hearing as "A proceeding of relative formality, generally public, with definite issues of fact or of law to be tried, in which parties proceeded against have right to be heard, and is much the same as a trial and may terminate in final order." Further, hearings generally include the possibility of depriving someone or some business entity or government agency of life, liberty, or property. By far, the greatest numbers of hearings concern property.

All trial or trial-like proceedings include, in varying degrees, the same general elements or requirements. The most formal, stringent, and detailed requirements for a hearing are found in a criminal proceeding. Closely following in complexity is a civil suit for money damages, declaratory relief, or injunction. The least formal actions, though not necessarily the least important, are administrative proceedings.

Once it is determined that a hearing is required, what are the fundamental elements and procedures? First, the formality of hearings can vary substantially. A hearing might mean nothing more than a relatively informal meeting, with an opportunity to explain your position to the deciding official if you feel the adverse action against you is not justified. At the opposite end of the spectrum of hearings is a formal trial, in which each side appears in a courtroom before a judge, with the proceedings transcribed by a court reporter, with or without a jury and representation by attorneys. The parties may make opening and closing statements; may call witnesses who testify under oath; may offer documentary or forensic evidence, including scientific studies and expert testimony; may cross-examine witnesses; and may challenge the legal authenticity of documentary or forensic evidence offered by the opposing side. In a criminal trial, charges must be proven beyond a reasonable doubt. For civil trials, most claims should be proven by a preponderance (more than 50%) of the evidence. There also is a formal right to appeal a final order or judgment to a higher court.

Many of the circumstances requiring a hearing arise in the field of employment. A hearing is required when a public office, agency, or division terminates or otherwise deprives an employee of some tangible benefit, such as a grade of rank or a level on the pay scale. Other possible losses of benefits might be claimed for employment changes such as a transfer to the night shift for punitive reasons, though that is more questionable. Outside of the realm of employment, a hearing requirement may arise when a governmental agency takes some action that deprives an individual or a business entity subject to its regulation of a tangible benefit or right, or bestows on an individual or business entity a tangible benefit.

Examples of the first would include the restriction of the right to manufacture and sell certain chemical products, or pharmaceutical products, or the right to discharge pollutants into waters subject to Environmental Protection Agency regulations and permits. Examples of the second include

decisions to grant or deny such things as a license to practice optometry or to sell alcoholic beverages.

The Administrative Procedure Act, which is the federal law that regulates how public agencies must conduct themselves, provides a guide to what a formal hearing on the record must include in Sections 554, 556, and 557. Most states have their own state administrative procedure acts, which are modeled on the federal act. These hearings are sometimes called quasi-judicial. The distinguishing characteristics are: (1) notice to all parties of the time and place of the hearing, (2) an impartial hearing officer, often an administrative law judge, (3) that both parties have the right to make a statement, (4) that both sides may present documentary evidence or the testimony of witnesses, (5) that the evidentiary burden is on the proponent of a rule or order (6) that different evidentiary standards may apply, from substantial evidence to a preponderance, to clear and convincing evidence, (7) that formal rules of evidence may be relaxed, for example, hearsay testimony may be allowed and documents may be admitted without authentication, (8) that there is a right to cross-examine witnesses in some instances, and (9) that the hearing officer must make written findings of fact and conclusions of law.

As mentioned previously, these standards may be relaxed and certain elements may be omitted, depending on the nature of the hearing. The United States Supreme Court has even held that in certain circumstances, a post-termination hearing may be sufficient. That means an employee can be fired first and then have a hearing after the fact.

While administrative hearings are by far the most numerous form of claims review, some limits are placed on their availability. First, unless there is a written, contractual obligation, or a customary or institutionalized obligation to provide for a hearing, no private or nonpublic employer or organization is required to provide a hearing before taking lawful adverse, disciplinary, or termination actions against an employee or a third party.

Under the laws of most states, a private employer does not even have to give employees a reason for terminating their employment if they are employees at will, that is, without a written contract of employment. In fact, employers are best advised not to provide a reason for termination, so as to reduce the risk of a constitutional challenge to the dismissal on equal protection grounds such as racial or sexual discrimination.

See also Due Process Clauses; Due Process, Procedural; Equal Employment Opportunity Commission (EEOC); Equal Protection Clause; Fundamental Rights; Public Employees, Constitutional Rights of

Bibliography

Cann, Steven J. 2001. *Administrative Law*. 3rd ed. Thousand Oaks, CA: Sage Publications.

Rosenbloom, David. 2003. *Administrative Law for Public Managers*. Boulder, CO: Westview Press.

James V. Cornehls

HEARING, RIGHT TO. *See* Due Process, Procedural

HEART OF ATLANTA MOTEL V. UNITED STATES (1964)

In the Civil Rights Cases (1883), the Supreme Court held that Congress did not have the power under Section 5 of the Fourteenth Amendment to prohibit racial discrimination by hotels, theaters and other privately owned places of public accommodation. Because state and local governments were disinclined to prohibit such discrimination, places of public accommodation in the South and many other areas of the country remained free to refuse service to African Americans altogether. As late as the early 1960s, black people traveling in the South could not count on staying in a hotel or eating a meal in a restaurant. Often they were reduced to sleeping in their cars and eating sandwiches by the side of the road.

When Congress finally moved to address this problem by passing the Civil Rights Act of 1964, it relied not only on its powers under the Fourteenth Amendment but its power to regulate interstate commerce conferred by Article I, Section 8 of the Constitution. As early as *Gibbons v. Ogden* (1824),

the Supreme Court had recognized the power of Congress to facilitate interstate travel.

Title II of the Civil Rights Act provided: "All persons shall be entitled to the full and equal enjoyment of the goods, services, facilities, privileges, advantages, and accommodations of any place of public accommodation, as defined in this section, without discrimination or segregation on the ground of race, color, religion, or national origin." Title II also provided that any "establishment which serves the public is a place of public accommodation within the meaning of this title if its operations affect commerce."

In addition to restaurants, movie theaters, and sports arenas, Title II applied to "any inn, hotel, motel, or other establishment which provides lodging to transient guests, other than an establishment located within a building which contains not more than five rooms for rent or hire and which is actually occupied by the proprietor of such establishment as his residence."

The owner of the Heart of Atlanta Motel filed suit in federal district court seeking an injunction against the enforcement of Title II against his business. He claimed, among other things, that in enacting Title II, Congress had exceeded its powers under the Commerce Clause. That clause permits Congress to regulate "commerce among the States." The owner claimed that his hotel business was a local activity beyond the reach of federal power over interstate commerce.

The motel at issue was located in downtown Atlanta not far from the intersection of two interstate highways—one running east-to-west, the other running north-to-south. Three-fourths of the hotel's guests were interstate travelers. A three-judge panel of the federal district court rejected the challenge to the statute and, on counterclaim of the government, permanently enjoined the motel owner from refusing to accommodate African American patrons.

On appeal, the Supreme Court affirmed the district court by a unanimous vote. Writing for the Court, Justice Tom Clark stressed the broad powers of Congress over the field of interstate commerce. Citing Chief Justice John Marshall's opinion in *Gibbons v. Ogden* (1824), Clark noted that interstate travel had long been considered an aspect of interstate commerce subject to congressional regulation. He also emphasized the "overwhelming evidence that discrimination by hotels and motels impedes interstate travel." In Clark's view, this impediment "empowered Congress to enact appropriate legislation, and, given this basis for the exercise of its power, Congress was not restricted by the fact that the particular obstruction to interstate commerce with which it was dealing was also deemed a moral and social wrong."

In *Katzenbach v. McClung,* decided the same day as *Heart of Atlanta Motel,* the Court upheld the validity of Title II as applied to a Birmingham restaurant that catered to a primarily local clientele. Together, these decisions provided substantial legitimacy for the Civil Rights Act of 1964 and went a long way toward ending the legal and political battles over segregation by places of public accommodation in this country.

See also Civil Rights Act of 1875; Civil Rights Act of 1964; The Civil Rights Cases; Civil Rights Movement; Discrimination; *Katzenbach v. McClung* (1964); Public Accommodation, Places of; Segregation, De Facto and De Jure.

Bibliography

Cortner, Richard C. 2001. *Civil Rights and Public Accommodations: The Heart of Atlanta Motel and McClung Cases.* Lawrence: University Press of Kansas.

John M. Scheb II and Otis H. Stephens, Jr.

HIGHLANDER FOLK SCHOOL. *See* Civil Rights Movement; Parks, Rosa

HOBBES, THOMAS (1588–1679)

The English philosopher Thomas Hobbes is considered to be one of the forerunners of modern political theory because he was both the first to focus on the role of the individual and the first to espouse the idea of the social contract. Hobbes's profound conservatism, and in particular his espousal in the *Leviathan* of an all-powerful government, inspired John Locke to produce his own

works of political theory in opposition to Hobbes. Together Hobbes and Locke helped frame the conservative and liberal dialectic within American political thought.

Hobbes can rightly be said to be to the first philosopher to focus on the role of the individual vis-à-vis the state. Ancient philosophers typically focused on the role of the state or polis, the church, royalty, or the rule of law. Hobbes' unit of analysis, though, is the individual citizen. This is often used as the demarcation point between ancient and modern political philosophy. Whereas ancient political thinkers viewed governments as divinely ordained or, in the Greek tradition, the ultimate good that people must serve, Hobbes defined government as existing to serve the people. Hobbes believed that the existence of government rested on the social contract: the tacit consent among the people to trade the freedom of the "state of nature" for the security ensured by government.

Although the social contract is widely seen as the theoretical underpinning of democracy, as in our own government "of the people, by the people, and for the people," Hobbes never envisioned a democracy. Rather, he called for an "authoritarian monarchy" (Ebenstein and Ebenstein 2000, 361) to control the very people the government sought to protect. Because Hobbes believed man to be inherently evil, he believed that in the absence of a powerful government, society would degenerate into "war of every one against every one."

This is where Hobbesian conservatism really began to show. Hobbes believed that rational men would sacrifice liberty in order to secure the protection that a strong government would afford, and his views later found favor with the conservative Founding Fathers, especially the Hamiltonians. Conversely, Locke believed that government could be limited to that which is necessary to secure life, liberty, and property. Locke would later add to the social contract a key component: the right of the people to resist the government—its ultimate exposition being the right to revolution. This would ensure that the people were always stronger than the government, and it was based upon a notion of the inherent goodness of man. The Jeffersonians embraced this more liberal ideological approach. The early conservatives became the Federalists, the forerunners of today's Republican Party; something that, had he been alive, would surely have made Hobbes proud.

Yet, Hobbes could surprise the reader. In fact, his conservatism was based on an underlying egalitarianism that was rare for his time period. He believed that the strong government was necessitated by the inherent equality of all men, as seen in the following passage:

> From this equality of ability, ariseth equality of hope in the attaining of our ends. And therefore if any two men desire the same thing, which nevertheless they cannot both enjoy, they become enemies. (reprinted in Cohen and Fermon 1996, 207)

Just how strong the government was to be is made clear by the title of Hobbes' seminal work, *Leviathan*. A leviathan is literally a biblical sea monster of mythical proportions. Of course, Hobbes' leviathan was the government. In other words, it is better that one suffer under an authoritarian monster than be subject to the terrible freedom of being left to fend for oneself. Nevertheless, despite the overwhelming strength of the leviathan, there was one thing it could not require of a citizen. It could not unjustly require of a man his life, because this would be a violation of self-preservation and would be placing the individual essentially right back into the feared, chaotic state of nature. Just causes, though, such as military service and a trial and sentencing were allowed because they served the betterment of the leviathan. This, then, would help the self-preservation of many others.

Subsequent critics have challenged various aspects of Hobbesian thought. Of course, scholars now know that the American Indians, to whom he referred as his primary example of the chaotic state of nature, actually lived orderly, peaceful lives until their way of life was largely destroyed by westward expansion. Other scholars have challenged his definition of the social contract. David Gauthier, for instance, argues that individuals who are wholly focused on self-preservation would not give up their rights to a completely sovereign king who might require them to die in combat. He proposes the notion of an "alienation social contract" where there is either limited sovereignty or the "citizens merely loan their rights to the sovereign" but can take them back (Gauthier 1969, 70). This allows for the right to revolution if self-preservation is being violated but still allows for an authoritarian government if the citizens remain motivated, as in Hobbes, by fear of the state of nature, where life will be "nasty, brutish, and short."

In conclusion, Thomas Hobbes had the honor of accomplishing many firsts in political philosophy. He was one of the first authors to focus on the role of the individual, thus making him one of the very first authors of modern political theory. He was the first author to create and define the notion of a social contract—something that we take for granted today. He was far ahead of his time in thinking that all men were inherently equal. And yet from these egalitarian beginnings, he is now known as one of the fathers of conservatism because Hobbes believed that men were inherently evil and that they must be controlled by an authoritarian government. He documents this necessity in his most famous work, the *Leviathan*. Because Hobbes was so very conservative, John Locke was soon inspired to write in opposition to him, and together they helped form an ideological framework debated by the Founding Fathers and alive still somewhat today in our political party system.

See also Conservatism; Individualism; Liberalism; Locke, John

Bibliography

Cohen, Mitchell, and Nicole Fermon, eds. 1996. *Princeton Readings in Political Thought*. Princeton, NJ: Princeton University Press.

Ebenstein, William, and Alan Ebenstein. 2000. *Great Political Thinkers from Plato to the Present*. 6th ed. Fort Worth, TX: Harcourt.

Gauthier, David P. 1969. *The Logic of Leviathan: The Moral and Political Theory of Thomas Hobbes*. Oxford: Clarendon Press.

Morris, Christopher W., ed. 1999. *The Social Contract Theorists*. Lanham, MD: Rowan and Littlefield.

Lori Maxwell

HOLMES, OLIVER WENDELL, JR. (1841–1935)

Oliver Wendell Holmes, Jr., was the celebrated lawyer, scholar, and Supreme Court Justice whose influential work in the late nineteenth and early twentieth centuries helped modernize constitutional thinking about the development of the law, the role of judges, and the expanse of free speech. Holmes propounded the then-controversial but now entirely mainstream view that law was not a fixed and pre-ordained set of logical principles, but rather a constantly shifting accumulation of political, social, and economic arrangements among society's dominant interests. Believing that in a democracy, and under our constitutional system, policy outcomes were meant to be worked out primarily in the competitive setting of the legislature, Holmes authored some of the most famous opinions advocating judicial restraint and supporting the broad discretion of Congress and state legislatures to enact economic and social measures. In the area of free speech, however, Holmes believed that the First Amendment's prohibition against making laws imposed major limitations on legislative power in order to create a free market place of ideas. Holmes often expressed these now classic constitutional propositions in dissenting Supreme Court opinions, earning the famous title of "Great Dissenter" among many legal observers.

The eldest of three children, Holmes was born into one of Boston's great intellectual patrician families. His father was Dr. Oliver Wendell Holmes, Sr., the eminent physician, Harvard professor, essayist, and poet. His mother was Amelia Lee Jackson Holmes, the daughter of a justice of the Supreme Judicial Court of Massachusetts. Raised in a privileged family environment, Holmes acquired from his youth an unrelenting ambition to do his duty and to achieve greatness.

A passionate abolitionist upon graduation from Harvard in 1861, Holmes enlisted in the Union Army. He suffered three serious wounds,

two of them nearly fatal. The horrors of the Civil War prompted him to develop a distanced and skeptical worldview, suspicious of dogma, in which he saw conflict and the victory of the strong as great formative social forces. This outlook led him to embrace the popular Social Darwinism of his day, an attitude that later significantly influenced his judicial thinking.

Obtaining his law degree from Harvard Law School in 1866, Holmes entered the practice of law in Boston, where for the next 16 years he devoted his full energies to achieving both professional distinction and scholarly recognition. He married Fanny Bowditch Dixwell in 1872. The couple had no children. During his private Boston years, Holmes became a prominent commercial attorney and an accomplished legal thinker. He produced a new edition of James Kent's *Commentaries on American Law,* contributed a steady stream of articles to *The American Law Review,* which he edited for three years, and in 1881 authored the pivotal book, *The Common Law,* an adaptation of lectures he had delivered at the Lowell Institute. Holmes propounded a provocative thesis in *The Common Law:*

The life of the law has not been logic: it has been experience. The felt necessities of the time, the prevalent moral and political theories, intuitions of public policy, avowed or unconscious, even the prejudices which judges share with their fellow men, have had a good deal more to do than the syllogism in determining the rules by which men should be governed.

Those words, emphasizing the sociopolitical rather than the logical roots of the law, attracted immediate scholarly interest. They secured for him a professorship at Harvard Law School and established him as a pioneer of what would eventually become known as legal realism.

In 1882 Holmes was named to the Supreme Judicial Court of Massachusetts, a post he held for 20 years, the last three as Chief Justice. He was disappointed to find that the court's docket consisted mostly of ordinary cases. Two dissents, in *Vegelahn v. Guntner* (1896) and *Plant v. Woods*

(1900), raised his judicial profile, however, and provided a glimpse of his developing judicial philosophy. Holmes backed the right of workers to engage in organized union activities, such as strikes and boycotts, in both cases. He did so, not because he supported the cause of labor, but because he felt political and economic reality made it impossible to distinguish between the actions of employees and those of employers to combine and compete.

The dissents in the state cases were a preview. In 1902 President Theodore Roosevelt appointed Holmes, then 61, to the U.S. Supreme Court, where for the next 29 years Holmes used his position to refine and advance his particular notions of judicial restraint. They embodied a jurisprudence of abstention laced with detachment, skepticism, and cynicism. Holmes believed that legislative majorities, representing the dominant desires of the people, deserved to get their way—for good or for ill—unless the objectives sought were specifically forbidden by the U.S. Constitution. An elitist to the core, Holmes maintained that the strong were entitled to their victories, regardless of whether he personally approved of the results (which he often did not). "[I]f my fellow citizens want to go to Hell," he once wrote, "I will help them. It's my job."

Holmes' tenure on the high bench coincided with the rise of American Progressivism, a movement dedicated to improving the conditions of the masses, in part by enacting laws facilitating unionization, restricting child labor, and imposing maximum work hours and minimum wages. It also coincided with the presence of a conservative majority on the high court ideologically opposed to such legislation and intent on using a variety of judicially crafted legal doctrines, including the due process "liberty of contract" doctrine, to strike down the statutes. Holmes' unswerving commitment to judicial restraint in the face of the conservative activism of his colleagues won him wide acclaim among Progressives and turned him into a national symbol of judicial reasonableness.

Many of the Holmes dissents advocating judicial abstention have become classics. In *Lochner v. New York* (1905), for example, Holmes wrote:

The Fourteenth Amendment does not enact Mr. Herbert Spencer's Social Statics.... [A] constitution is not intended to embody a particular economic theory.... It is made for people of fundamentally differing views, and the accident of our finding certain opinions natural and familiar or novel and even shocking ought not to conclude our judgment.... I think that the word liberty in the Fourteenth Amendment is perverted when it is held to prevent the natural outcome of a dominant opinion, unless it can be said that a rational and fair man necessarily would admit that the statute proposed would infringe fundamental principles as they have been understood by the traditions of our people and our law.

Holmes' position of approving reasonable economic and social welfare legislation not specifically forbidden by the Constitution was a stance he would assert again and again, in dissent, in a long list of cases including *Adair v. United States* (1908), *Coppage v. Kansas* (1915), *Hammer v. Dagenhart* (1918), *Truax v. Corrigan* (1921), *Adkins v. Children's Hospital* (1923), and *Tyson & Brother v. Banton* (1927). Eventually, after his death, Holmes' view became the majority position of the Court and the constitutional norm of the land.

Holmes' deference to the legislative will, however, could sometimes be overly generous and lead him down some dangerous paths. In the notorious decision of *Buck v. Bell* (1927), for example, Holmes upheld Virginia's statutory scheme for sterilizing "mental defectives." His opinion for the Court coldly reasoned that "the public welfare may call upon the best citizens for their lives. It would be strange if it could not call upon those who already sap the strength of the State for these lesser sacrifices."

Holmes' opinions on the First Amendment freedom of speech are the ones that have most contributed to his reputation as a great civil libertarian. Those pronouncements sought to develop a standard for protecting a broad zone of liberty against an onslaught of legislation criminalizing antigovernment speech during the World War I period. The result of Holmes' efforts was the "clear and present danger" test, which he first introduced for a unanimous Court in *Schenck v. United States*

(1919), and which he subsequently elaborated and strengthened in dissenting opinions in cases such as *Abrams v. United States* (1919), *Gitlow v. New York* (1925), and *United States v. Schwimmer* (1929). With increasing firmness, Holmes argued that the government could limit speech only if the statement "immediately" threatened the constitutional order. Holmes also sought to develop an overall guiding rationale for free speech, and in his *Abrams* dissent he introduced the concept of a "marketplace of ideas." The concept is now the accepted theoretical framework around which modern free speech jurisprudence has been built, and the clear and present danger test is the progenitor of the "imminent lawless action" test set forth in *Brandenburg v. Ohio* (1969).

Holmes developed a close relationship on the bench with Justice Louis Brandeis, a Progressive lawyer and social reformer who joined the Court in 1916. Many observers speculate that Holmes' evolution on free speech was influenced in part by Brandeis' strong civil libertarianism. Holmes deeply respected Brandeis' intellectual brilliance and his understanding of the political dimensions of the law. Brandeis believed in actively pursuing social experimentation through law. Holmes, on the other hand, believed in simply tolerating social experimentation under law. Both men often dissented together, and Holmes admitted that on several occasions it was Brandeis who had convinced him to write "another dissent on burning themes."

Near the end of his tenure on the Court, Holmes began to deteriorate noticeably. On the advice of his colleagues, gently conveyed to him by the Chief Justice, Holmes resigned on January 12, 1932. He died on March 6, 1935, two days short of his 94th birthday.

See also Bad Tendency Test; Brandeis, Louis D.; *Brandenburg v. Ohio* (1969); Clear and Present Danger Doctrine; Common Law Background of American Civil Rights and Liberties; Due Process Clauses; Due Process, Substantive; First Amendment; Fourteenth Amendment (1868); Free Marketplace of Ideas; *Gitlow v. New York* (1925); Judicial Activism; Judicial Restraint; *Lochner v. New York* (1905); *Schenck v. United States* (1919); Speech, Freedom of

Bibliography

Aichele, Gary J. 1989. *Oliver Wendell Holmes, Jr.: Soldier, Scholar, Judge.* Boston: Twayne Publishers.

Alschuler, Albert W. 2000. *Law Without Values: The Life, Work, and Legacy of Justice Holmes.* Chicago: University of Chicago Press.

Baker, Liva. 1991. *The Justice from Beacon Hill: The Life and Times of Oliver Wendell Holmes.* New York: HarperCollins Publishers.

Howe, Mark DeWolfe. 1957. *Justice Oliver Wendell Holmes: The Shaping Years, 1841–1870.* Cambridge, MA: Harvard University Press.

Howe, Mark DeWolfe. 1963. *Justice Oliver Wendell Holmes: The Proving Years, 1870–1882.* Cambridge, MA: Harvard University Press.

Novick, Sheldon M. 1989. *Honorable Justice: The Life of Oliver Wendell Holmes.* Boston: Little, Brown.

White, G. Edward. 1993. *Justice Oliver Wendell Holmes: Law and the Inner Self.* New York: Oxford University Press.

Alain L. Sanders

HOMELAND SECURITY, DEPARTMENT OF (DHS)

The mission of the U.S. Department of Homeland Security (DHS) is to prevent terrorist attacks in the United States, to protect the rights of Americans affected by natural disasters, and to improve immigration services. It does this by grouping functions previously assigned to the departments of Justice, Treasury, Agriculture, GSA, Transportation, Commerce, Defense, and Energy, among other government agencies. DHS also brings together many different government agencies with the purpose of securing the nation's homeland.

After the terrorist attacks of September 11, 2001, the United States Government was looking for a better way to organize the prevention of emergency situations and response to them, particularly to possible terrorist actions. President Bush proposed the establishment of a new department whose primary responsibility was homeland security. Prior to this proposal, homeland security functions were allocated to more than one hundred different public agencies. The proposal resulted in the enactment of the Homeland Security Act, which was the legal framework for the creation of the Department of Homeland Security.

Due to its multiple objectives, DHS is divided into five major divisions or directorates: (1) Border and Transportation Security; (2) Emergency Preparedness and Response; (3) Science and Technology; (4) Information Analysis and Infrastructure Protection; and (5) Management. Border and Transportation Security (BTS) has the responsibility of securing the borders and transportation systems within the United States. It also enforces immigration laws aimed at preventing illegal entry of terrorists and terrorism-related materials or equipment.

The Emergency Preparedness and Response (EP&R) directorate is committed to continuing the efforts of the Federal Emergency Management Agency (FEMA) in reducing loss of life and property. It also aims to protect the nation's institutions from all types of hazard through a comprehensive, risk-based emergency management program of preparedness, prevention, response, and recovery. Working in collaboration with FEMA, EP&R is directing its efforts at changing the nation's view of disasters from one of reaction to emergency situations to that of preparation and development of plans to reduce the impact of any potential disaster.

The Science and Technology division focuses on organizing and coordinating research efforts to prevent and mitigate potential terrorist attacks. To meet these objectives, it makes use of current scientific and technological developments and provides financial and coordinating support for new research in areas related to potential vulnerabilities, such as vaccines and antidotes against biological or chemical warfare.

The Information Analysis and Infrastructure Protection (IA&IP) directorate has the advantage of combining such functions as gathering intelligence, assessing vulnerabilities, and protecting infrastructures. One of its main objectives is to gather and analyze information about terrorists and potential terrorist actions. In addition, this directorate is the coordinating federal agency for securing the nation's critical infrastructure.

Finally, the Management Directorate "is responsible for budget, appropriations, expenditure of funds, accounting and finance; procurement; human resources and personnel; information technology systems; facilities, property, equipment, and other material resources; and identification and tracking of performance measurements relating to the responsibilities of the Department" (DHS, 2003).

In addition to the five directorates, there is a Homeland Security Advisory Council composed of a chair, a vice-chair, and 16 members representing state and local governments, first responder communities, the private sector, and academia. The main objective of the council is to give advice and make recommendations to the secretary about issues related to homeland security.

In order to preserve American civil liberties and personal privacy, the position of Chief Privacy Officer was created. This office is tasked with the responsibility of compliance with the Privacy Act and for evaluating legislative and regulatory proposals involving the collection, use, and disclosure of personal information by the federal government (DHS, 2003). The office also guarantees privacy compliance across DHS in gathering, managing, analyzing, and sharing information.

Finally, the Coast Guard, the Secret Service, and the Bureau of Citizenship and Immigration Services (former Immigration and Naturalization Service) are also part of DHS. These not only perform their original duties, but now they also can coordinate with each other and take advantage of information and analysis performed by IA&IP.

Bibliography

Department of Homeland Security. (2003). *U.S. Department of Homeland Security.* Available at: www. dhs.gov. Accessed 25 August 2003.

J. Ramon Gil-Garcia

HOMOSEXUALITY. *See* Gay Rights Movement; *Lawrence v. Texas* (2003); Sexual Orientation, Discrimination Based on; Same-Sex Marriage and Civil Unions

HOOVER, J. EDGAR. *See* Federal Bureau of Investigation (FBI)

HOT PURSUIT, DOCTRINE OF

Also known as "fresh pursuit," hot pursuit is the doctrine developed at common law under which a law enforcement officer may cross a jurisdictional line in order to arrest a fleeing suspect. Nearly every state has adopted the Uniform Law on Fresh Pursuit, which authorizes hot pursuit across state lines in pursuit of fleeing felons. Tennessee's version of the statute, codified at T. C. A. sec. 40-7-203, provides:

Any member of a duly organized state, county or municipal peace unit of another state, who enters this state in fresh pursuit, and continues within this state in such fresh pursuit, of a person in order to arrest the person on grounds that the person is believed to have committed a felony in such other state, shall have the same authority to arrest and hold such person in custody as has any member of any duly organized state, county or municipal peace unit of this state to arrest and hold in custody a person on the ground that the person is believed to have committed a felony in this state.

In addition to this uniform act most states have laws permitting officers to make arrests for misdemeanors in fresh pursuit, but some states restrict misdemeanor arrests to the officer's jurisdiction, for example, within the county.

In Fourth Amendment jurisprudence, the doctrine of hot pursuit allows police to pursue a fleeing suspect into a protected place, such as a home, without having to abandon their pursuit until a warrant can be obtained. The hot pursuit doctrine requires four elements: (1) probable cause to make the arrest; (2) an attempted arrest in a public location; (3) flight from that location to a home or other private place; and (4) pursuit by a police officer (Stephens and Glenn 2006, 120).

In *Warden v. Hayden* (1967), the Supreme Court upheld a warrantless entry into a home to arrest

a fleeing armed robbery suspect. Writing for the Court, Justice William Brennan, Jr., opined, "Under the circumstances of this case, 'the exigencies of the situation made that course imperative.'" Similarly, in *United States v. Santana* (1976), the Court upheld a warrantless entry into a home to arrest a suspected drug dealer. Noting that police had probable cause to make an arrest, the Court held that the suspect's retreat into the vestibule of her home did not immunize her from warrantless arrest. In his majority opinion, Justice William H. Rehnquist characterized the police entry into the vestibule as "hot pursuit":

This case, involving a true "hot pursuit," is clearly governed by *Warden* [*v. Hayden*]; the need to act quickly here is even greater than in that case while the intrusion is much less. The District Court was correct in concluding that "hot pursuit" means some sort of a chase, but it need not be an extended hue and cry "in and about [the] public streets." The fact that the pursuit here ended almost as soon as it began did not render it any the less a "hot pursuit" sufficient to justify the warrantless entry into Santana's house.

In *Welsh v. Wisconsin* (1984), the Court placed a limit on the hot pursuit doctrine, holding that it allows a warrantless entry into the home only when there is "immediate or continuous pursuit of the petitioner from the scene of a crime."

See also Brennan, William J., Jr.; Fourth Amendment; Probable Cause; Rehnquist, William H.; Warrantless Searches

Bibliography

Scheb, John M., and John M. Scheb II. 2006. *Criminal Procedure.* Belmont, CA: Thomson/Wadsworth.

Stephens, Otis H., Jr., and Richard A. Glenn. 2006. *Unreasonable Searches and Seizures: Rights and Liberties under the Law.* Santa Barbara, CA: ABC-Clio.

John M. Scheb II and Otis H. Stephens, Jr.

HOUSE ARREST

With increasing jail and prison populations, alternatives to physical incarceration have become an economic necessity in recent years. House arrest or home detention, as used in the American criminal justice system, is a form of intermediate sanction that is stricter than probation, but not as severe as a prison sentence. House arrest allows a sentenced individual to serve his or her sentence at home rather than in a correctional facility. It has been recognized as a form of sanction in the United States since 1971, when it was first used to detain juvenile offenders in St. Louis, Missouri. The use of house arrest gained momentum in the 1980s as a more suitable detention alternative for "special needs" offenders, for example, pregnant women. Today, its use is widespread in the American correctional system because it is inexpensive and relieves prison overcrowding.

There are basically two types of court orders that can impose house arrest: the probation order and the conditional sentence type order. A probation order is typically imposed on juvenile offenders, whereas the conditional type is reserved for adults. Both types allow a judge to determine the conditions and duration of the detention, usually in terms of months. The consequences for violating a conditional sentence order is a jail sentence, while a violation of the probation order causes the offender to be subject to the entire criminal justice process. House arrest programs gained widespread public attention due to Martha Stewart's widely publicized home detention in 2005.

Intermediate sanctions, such as house arrest, are used for nonviolent offenders and promote the offender's integration back into society as a rehabilitated productive citizen. House arrest programs, currently monitored by private companies and organizations, cite numerous benefits to this form of sanction.

In a house arrest situation, the individual is monitored by a variety of methods depending upon which one is available or assigned to the offender. These methods include, but are not limited to, ankle bracelets, global positioning satellites (GPS), breath alcohol testers, and interactive voice response systems via telephone. The offender typically bears the expense of utilizing one of these devices. The ankle bracelet, worn continuously, uses an electronic sensor that is linked to

telephone lines to a centrally located computer that tracks the signal. If there is any interruption in the signal, the violator could be subject to arrest. Individuals placed on house arrest are sometimes allowed to leave their residence with permission to attend work and other approved functions. The GPS systems are used in additional to conventional house arrest in that they can track and record an offender's movements on a daily basis. This monitoring system is especially helpful in tracking sex offenders, stalkers, and more high-risk violent offenders. The breath alcohol testers are administered by calling an offender at random and requesting that he blow into the tester device, which sends the results to the monitoring station insuring the offender is at his residence and is sober. The interactive voice response system utilizes the offender's telephone by placing random calls to his home during curfew hours. The calls are monitored; any missed calls made to the offender are reported to the supervising officer. Another form of house arrest, from a global aspect, is the detaining of an individual, usually a political dissident, in his or her residence by government authorities.

Despite the benefits to house arrest to the offender and taxpayer, critics of electronic monitoring claim violent offenders placed on house arrest find ways to defeat the system. Other critics cite possible violations of constitutional guarantees of privacy as well as the expensive price tag for offenders who are already economically disadvantaged.

See also Accused, Rights of the; Juvenile Justice; Privacy, Constitutional Right of; Probation and Parole; Sentencing, Eighth Amendment and; Sex Offenders, Rights of

Bibliography

Carlson, Nelson, Karen M. Hess, and Christine M. H. Orthmann. 1999. *Corrections in the 21st Century. Alternatives to Incarceration: Probation and Other Sanctions.* Belmont, CA: Wadsworth.

McCarthy, Bernard J. 1992. "Community Residential Centers: An Intermediate Sanction for the 1990s." In *Corrections: Dilemmas and Directions,* eds. Peter

J. Benekos and Alida V. Merio, 173–192. Cincinnati: Anderson Publishing. Co.

Schmalleger, John Ortiz Smykla. 2005. *Corrections in the 21st Century: Intermediate Sanctions,* 2nd ed. New York: McGraw-Hill.

Cassie Adams-Walls

HOUSE UN-AMERICAN ACTIVITIES COMMITTEE (HUAC)

During the 1950s, at the height of the Cold War, the House Committee on Un-American Activities was at the center of an intense ideological controversy between competing claims on behalf of national security and First Amendment freedoms. Defenders of the committee praised its efforts to combat disloyalty and subversion largely through highly publicized hearings designed to ferret out leaders of the Communist Party. The committee's disregard of procedural safeguards in questioning targeted witnesses aroused little criticism among many of those who regarded "Communist subversion" as a genuine menace to American national security. Critics of the House Un-American Activities Committee, on the other hand, saw HUAC as the embodiment of a governmental betrayal of principles announced by the Framers of the Constitution and one of the most insidious intrusions upon freedom of thought and association in our history. Created in 1938 to investigate disloyalty and subversion, the committee languished in relative obscurity for decades. As concern about the Soviet Union and the spread of communism grew in the postwar era, the House Committee on Un-American Activities assumed a prominence matched only by the red-baiting Senator from Wisconsin, Joseph McCarthy.

HUAC investigated a wide range of areas. Unions and academia, perceived by many to be saturated with communists, presented inviting targets for the committee. Another high-profile area of investigation by HUAC involved the executive branch. This inquiry produced one of the most controversial and highly covered episodes, as Whitaker Chambers, a former communist and writer for *Time* magazine, testified against State Department official Alger Hiss and accused him of spying for the Soviet

Union. Hiss would later be convicted of perjury for the testimony he gave to the committee. One of the most intensely pursued targets of investigation for HUAC was the film industry. Members of the committee feared that a Hollywood community inundated with communists would brainwash unsuspecting Americans in movie theaters across the nation. The film industry was also an inviting target given the publicity that this investigation would produce for ambitious politicians.

The committee's modus operandi was to subpoena individuals it believed to have communist links. These witnesses would be sworn and asked whether they were now, or ever had been, members of the Communist Party. A refusal to respond would be met with a citation for contempt of Congress. A negative response would likely render the witness guilty of perjury. Finally, an affirmative response would result in even more intense grilling from the committee and a demand to name the names of other communists, which would provide HUAC with more witnesses and continue the cycle. Frequently the culmination of an appearance before the House Un-American Activities Committee would be the loss of a job or the end of a career in a nation gripped by paranoia and hysteria.

One of the most intriguing questions about the committee's reign of inquisition was the lack of intervention by the political institution designed to protect against governmental abuse of power and violation of individual liberties: the Supreme Court. Where was the Court during this period? In the 1957 decision of *Watkins v. United States* the Supreme Court provided a flash of judicial vigilance when it overturned the conviction of an individual who refused to answer questions from the committee. Chief Justice Earl Warren, writing for the majority, asserted that "Abuses of the investigative process may imperceptibly lead to abridgement of protected freedoms. The mere summoning of a witness and compelling him to testify, against his will, about his beliefs, expressions or associations is a measure of governmental interference. And when those forced revelations concern matters that are unorthodox, unpopular, or even hateful to the general public, the reaction in the life of the witnesses may be disastrous." Clearly this was a Supreme Court that understood the dangers associated with HUAC's investigation.

This promise of vigorous protection of the lone individual facing the investigative power of the government proved to be an empty one. Two years later, possibly responding to intense congressional criticism of the Watkins decision, the Supreme Court took a much different approach in *Barenblatt v. United States*. A former teaching fellow at the University of Michigan refused to answer the question of whether he had ever been a member of the Communist Party. Barenblatt's objection was that the committee was infringing upon his rights under the First Amendment. The Supreme Court, dividing five to four, rejected his position. Writing for the majority, Justice John M. Harlan (the younger) conceded that "the First Amendment in some circumstances protects an individual from being compelled to disclose associational relationships." However, Harlan went on to state "Where First Amendment rights are asserted to bar governmental interrogation, resolution of the issue always involves a balancing by the courts of the competing private and public interests at stake in the particular circumstances shown." The specter of communism led the majority to "conclude that the balance between the individual and governmental interests here at stake must be struck in favor of the latter, and that therefore the provisions of the First Amendment have not been offended."

Justice Hugo Black wrote passionately in dissenting from the Court's decision in *Barenblatt*: "Ultimately all the questions in this case really boil down to one—whether we as a people will try fearfully and futilely to preserve democracy by adopting totalitarian methods, or whether in accordance with our traditions and our Constitution we will have the confidence and courage to be free." Those who appreciate Black's perspective will likely view HUAC as a dark stain on our constitutional democracy. Those who reject Black's position as naïve are likely to see the House Committee on Un-American Activities as an essential development during one of the most dangerous periods in our history.

See also Black, Hugo L.; Communist Party USA; Due Process, Procedural; Federal Bureau of Investigation; First Amendment; Harlan, John Marshall, II; Legislative Investigations; McCarthy, Joseph R.; Warren, Earl; *Watkins v. United States* (1957)

Bibliography

Bentley, Eric, ed. 2002. *Thirty Years of Treason: Excerpts from Hearings Before the House Committee on Un-American Activities, 1938–1968.* New York: Thunder's Mouth Press.

Goodman, Walter. 1968. *The Committee: The Extraordinary Career of the House Committee on Un-American Activities.* New York: Farrar, Straus & Giroux.

Simmons, Jerrold. 1986. *Operation Abolition: The Campaign to Abolish the House Un-American Activities Committee 1938–1975.* New York: Taylor & Francis.

Anthony Simones

HOUSING, DISCRIMINATION IN

Historically, racial discrimination in the United States permeated every aspect of American society extending even to discrimination in housing. While the Supreme Court held in The Civil Rights Cases (1883) that Congress lacked the authority to prohibit discrimination in places of public accommodation, such as hotels and restaurants, it also acknowledged that Congress had the power under the Civil Rights Act of 1866 "to secure to all citizens of every race and color, without regard to previous servitude, those fundamental rights which are the essence of civil freedom" including the right to "inherit, purchase, lease, sell and convey property." Despite the legal protection afforded by this legislation, the property rights of African Americans were subject to Jim Crow laws segregating residences; this pattern continued well into the modern era.

Due to pre-Civil War housing patterns, neighborhoods in many Southern cities remained integrated after the war. However, as rural blacks began to move to the cities in search of economic opportunities, whites began to push for residential segregation through the enactment of city ordinances (Klarman 2004, 79). In 1917, the U.S. Supreme Court struck down such an ordinance in *Buchanan v. Warley* (1917). This case centered on a Louisville, Kentucky ordinance stipulating that houses sold on majority-white blocks could be occupied only by whites; similarly, houses sold on majority-black blocks could only be occupied by blacks. Several cities had adopted similar ordinances since Baltimore had enacted the first in 1910 (Klarman 2004). Despite the argument by the city that the ordinance prevented violence and "ill-feeling" between whites and blacks, the Court unanimously held that such ordinances violated the Due Process Clause of the Fourteenth Amendment. This case ended official governmental residential segregation.

In order to circumvent the Court's ruling, private racially restrictive covenants replaced official policies of residential segregation. These agreements required white residents to sell or lease their homes to whites only. In *Corrigan v. Buckley* (1926), the Supreme Court dismissed a challenge to a restrictive covenant finding that the Constitution only prohibited government-sponsored discrimination. Restrictive covenants were ultimately outlawed by the Court 22 years later in *Shelley v. Kraemer* (1948). In this case, the Court held that restrictive covenants were private agreements and did not violate the Constitution; however, the judicial enforcement of such agreements constituted state action and thus the enforcement of the covenants was unconstitutional.

The impact of this case was evident in two subsequent cases involving housing discrimination. In *Barrows v. Jackson* (1953), the Court held that state courts could not require an individual who had signed a restrictive covenant to pay damages to the other parties for breaking the covenant. The action by the courts, like that in *Shelley,* was deemed unconstitutional under the Equal Protection Clause of the Fourteenth Amendment.

The issue of state action was also central in *Reitman v. Mulkey* (1967), a case involving a 1964 California constitutional amendment barring the state from interfering with the individual's right to sell or refuse to sell property to anyone for any reason. The U.S. Supreme Court upheld the decision of the California Supreme Court that the amendment violated the Equal Protection Clause because the state had implicitly sanctioned racial discrimination. The Court applied the same logic to a charter amendment to an Akron fair housing ordinance that required a referendum on any ordinance concerning race and housing. In *Hunter v. Erickson* (1969), the Court held that such a policy violated the Equal Protection Clause because it contained "an explicitly racial classification treating racial housing matters differently from other racial and housing matters and place[d] special burdens on racial and religious minorities within the governmental process by making it more difficult for them to secure legislation on their behalf." The only instance in which the Court upheld a referendum with regard to fair housing was in *James v. Valtierra* (1971). In this case, the Court held that an amendment to the California constitution requiring voter approval for the construction of low-income housing was constitutional because it did not single out race, but rather low-rent housing projects—a racially neutral category.

A year after the Court's ruling in *Reitman,* Congress enacted the Fair Housing Act of 1968 to combat discrimination in housing shortly after the assassination of Martin Luther King, Jr. It banned discrimination in the sale and rental of approximately 80 percent of the nation's housing (Barker et al. 1999, 559). The Department of Housing and Urban Development (HUD) was charged with the responsibility of seeking voluntary compliance with the law's nondiscrimination requirements. Because there was still widespread discrimination in housing, a bill was introduced during the late 1970s to increase the authority of HUD. The bill died, however, during a Senate filibuster (Barker et al. 1999, 559). The issue of strengthening the Fair Housing Act was not taken up again until 1988 when the Fair Housing Amendments Act of 1988 was enacted. This legislation allowed HUD to initiate stronger penalties for noncompliance with the law. It also allowed administrative law judges to impose fines on those who violated the act. According to the HUD web site, the law currently "prohibits discrimination in the sale, rental, and financing of dwellings, and in other housing-related transactions, based on race, color, national origin, religion, sex, familial status (including children under the age of 18 living with parents of legal custodians, pregnant women, and people securing custody of children under the age of 18), and handicap (disability)."

Not long after the Fair Housing Act went into effect in 1968, the Supreme Court offered an alternative means of eliminating housing discrimination. In *Jones v. Alfred Mayer Co.* (1968), the Court dealt with a claim by Jones that the defendants refused to sell a home to him because he was black. He brought a claim under Title 42, section 1982 of the U.S. Code (legislation previously known as the Civil Rights Act of 1866), which forbids racial discrimination in the sale of property. The key question was whether this legislation included private conduct. The Court held that section 1982 "bars all racial discrimination, private as well as public, in the sale or rental of property, and that the statute, thus construed, is a valid exercise of the power of Congress to enforce the Thirteenth Amendment." Justice Potter Stewart distinguished section 1982 from the Fair Housing Act by noting that section 1982 was more limited because the Fair Housing Act applied to a number of discriminatory actions. Thus, private discrimination could be prohibited due to Congressional enforcement power under the Thirteenth Amendment.

During the 1970s, many issues of housing discrimination involved zoning ordinances and discrimination based on factors other than race. For instance in *Village of Belle Terre v. Boraas* (1974), the Court upheld a New York village's zoning ordinance against a Fourteenth Amendment challenge. The ordinance prohibited more than two unrelated people from cohabitating in a single family home, while no restrictions were placed on the number of related people (i.e. related by blood, adoption, or marriage) sharing a house. The owners of a house in the village who had rented it to six unrelated college students were cited for violating the ordinance. The Court upheld the law

by reasoning that the ordinance was not discriminatory and that the objective of maintaining an atmosphere conducive to family needs was legitimate.

In *Village of Arlington Heights v. Metropolitan Housing Development Corporation* (1977) the Court upheld a village's refusal to rezone property from that of single-family dwelling to multiple-family dwelling in order to prevent construction of low to moderate income housing. Justice Lewis Powell's majority opinion found that there was no intent to discriminate on the basis of race; therefore, there was no violation of the Equal Protection Clause.

Thus, while the Court dealt with housing discrimination in a plethora of cases, it has only considered appropriate remedies for such discrimination in one case, *Hills v. Gautreaux* (1976) (Savage 2004, 291–292). In this case, the Court upheld a metropolitan area-wide remedy imposed by a federal judge who found that the Chicago Housing Authority (CHA) "had deliberately selected family public housing sites in Chicago to 'avoid the placement of Negro families in white neighborhoods' in violation of federal statutes and the Fourteenth Amendment, and that HUD had assisted in that policy by providing financial assistance and other support for CHA's discriminatory housing projects." HUD had asked the Court to limit the remedy to the Chicago city limits. Justice Stewart, however, stated that given HUD's history of discrimination a metropolitan area-wide remedy was acceptable. Moreover, according to Stewart, the appropriate area for the development of fair housing was not the Chicago city limits, but the Chicago housing market, which extended beyond those limits. The Court, thus, distinguished this case from its holding in *Millikin v. Bradley* (1974), which had held that a multidistrict remedy was inappropriate for busing because only a few of the districts had policies of segregation.

Currently there are several federal laws in addition to the Fair Housing Act that prohibit discrimination in housing. These include Title VI of the Civil Rights Act of 1964, which prohibits racial discrimination in activities receiving federal funding, Title IX of the Education Amendments Act of 1972, which prohibits gender-based discrimination by federally funded programs, and Section 504 of the Rehabilitation Act of 1973, which prohibits discrimination based on disability in activities that rely on federal funds. HUD's website, located at www.hud.gov, offers substantial information about these and other laws and about various federal programs to promote access to housing.

Finally, it should be noted that while federal law currently does not prohibit housing discrimination on the basis of sexual orientation, a number of states and municipalities have prohibited discrimination in housing on this basis.

See also Busing Controversy; Civil Rights Cases, The; Due Process Clauses; Equal Protection Clause; Fair Housing Act (1968); Fourteenth Amendment (1868); King, Martin Luther, Jr.; Powell, Lewis F. Jr.; Restrictive Covenants; Segregation, De Facto and De Jure; Sexual Orientation, Discrimination Based on; *Shelley v. Kraemer* (1948); Stewart, Potter; Thirteenth Amendment; Zoning

Bibliography

Barker, Lucius, et al. 1999. *Civil Liberties and the Constitution: Cases and Commentaries.* 8th ed. Prentice Hall: Upper Saddle River, New Jersey.

Klarman, Michael J. 2004. *From Jim Crow to Civil Rights: The Supreme Court and the Struggle for Racial Equality.* New York: Oxford University Press.

Savage, David. 2004. *The Supreme Court and Individual Rights.* 4th ed. Washington, DC: CQ Press.

Kara E. Stooksbury

HRW. *See* Human Rights Watch (HRW)

HUAC. *See* House Un-American Activities Committee (HUAC)

HUMAN LIFE AMENDMENT. *See* Pro-Life Movement

HUMAN RIGHTS WATCH (HRW)

The largest U.S.-based international human rights organization, Human Rights Watch (HRW) is a nongovernmental organization (NGO) with the express mission of "protecting human rights of people around the world" through "even-handed and accurate" reporting of rights violations. The organization began in 1978 as Helsinki Watch, a group formed to monitor Soviet bloc compliance with the Helsinki Accords of 1975. Over the next 10 years, similar groups were created to investigate human rights abuses in other parts of the world: Asia Watch, Americas Watch, and so forth. In 1988, those groups were united into one organization, Human Rights Watch.

HRW operates without accepting government funds, directly or indirectly, with funding coming mainly through private donations from individuals and corporate entities. Only in "egregious" cases does HRW resort to litigation to achieve its goals. Rather, HRW's preferred method of operation is to "investigate and expose human rights violations and hold abusers accountable." To do this, HRW sends fact-finders into the area of interest to interview victims and witnesses of alleged abusive practices by both governments and nonstate actors. Reports are then published, giving rise to extensive media coverage and, HRW hopes, worldwide attention that will shame human rights violators and lead to diplomatic and economic pressures to end the abuse from governments and institutions, including the United Nations.

HRW publishes dozens of such reports each year. It also publishes an *Annual Report* and, also annually, *World Report,* a compilation of HRW reports reflecting the scope of the organization's investigative work during that year. Many reports are available from HRW's Web page (http://www.hrw.org/), which offers content in 7 main languages, and 13 additional languages, including Swahili and Persian.

To further disseminate its message, HRW sponsors an International Film Festival featuring fiction, documentary and animated films, and videos with human rights themes. It also awards Hellman-Hammett Grants, funded from the estates of writers Lillian Hellman and Dashiell Hammett, to international authors struggling with political persecution and financial need. Since the grants were first awarded in 1990, over 400 writers have received monetary support from HRW.

Since 1993, HRW, under current executive director Kenneth Roth, has extensively broadened its geographic scope and has added economic, social, and cultural rights to its interventionist agenda, formerly limited to civil and political rights. Special projects have been launched to defend the rights of specific groups, including child soldiers (Coalition to Stop the Use of Child Soldiers), women, gays, academics, HIV/AIDS patients, and refugees. As a member of the International Campaign to Ban Landmines, HRW shared the 1997 Nobel Peace Prize. The group is also a member of the International Freedom of Expression Exchange. Its focus is not just on distant Third World countries—among regular targets of its reports is the United States, for issues such as continuing use of the death penalty, incidents of police brutality, discriminatory treatment of African Americans in the criminal justice system, and opposition to a permanent International Criminal Court.

In addition to its contributions to achieving bans against land mines and child soldiers, HRW numbers among its other successes early identification of the need for an international war crimes tribunal for the former Yugoslavia, expert testimony supporting convictions in the Rwandan genocide, and aiding in the legal action against former Chilean dictator Augusto Pinochet, which led to the establishment of the "Pinochet precedent," whereby dictators can no longer escape international prosecution by blocking prosecution in their own country.

Some critics of HRW denounce its assumption that the ideology, values, and standards of the United States, such as freedom of association and freedom of speech, are universally applicable. Others insist that HRW is procommunist and ignores human rights violations of leftist governments, and claim that it is prone to exaggeration in its reporting.

Currently, HRW has nearly 200 staff members, headquartered in New York, but with over a dozen worldwide offices located from Toronto to Tashkent. Operating expenses for 2002/2003 exceeded $21 million.

See also Accused, Rights of the; Association, Freedom of; Death Penalty; Human Rights; International Law; Speech, Freedom of; Universal Declaration of Human Rights

Bibliography

Blitt, Robert Charles, 2004. "Who Will Watch the Watchdogs? Human Rights Nongovernmental Organizations and the Case for Regulation." *Buffalo Human Rights Law Review* 10: 261.

Mosse, Gail M. L. 1997. "U.S. Constitutional Freedom of Association: Its Potential for Human Rights NGOs at Home and Abroad." *Human Rights Quarterly* 19: 738.

Welch, Claude E., Jr., ed. 2001. *NGOs and Human Rights: Promise and Performance*. Philadelphia: University of Pennsylvania Press.

Wiegandt, Manfred. 1996. "The Pitfalls of International Human Rights Monitoring: Some Critical Remarks on the 1995 Human Rights Watch/Helsinki Report on Xenophobia in Germany." *Human Rights Quarterly* 18: 833.

Julie A. Thomas

HUNG JURY

The term *hung jury*, also called a *deadlocked jury*, refers to a jury in a civil or criminal trial that is unable to reach a verdict. In jurisdictions that follow the traditional common rule that verdicts must be unanimous, a hung jury is not a rare phenomenon. If the jury cannot reach a verdict, the court has no choice but to declare a mistrial. A mistrial is often frustrating and costly to lawyers and litigants, and judges generally prefer not to have to declare one. From one perspective, a mistrial represents a failure of the system—the inability to resolve a controversy.

When a jury first reports that it is deadlocked, the trial judge will often exhort the jury to continue to deliberate. Sometimes the judge will give a supplemental instruction known as an *Allen* charge, so called because the Supreme Court approved its use in *Allen v. United States* (1896). The *Allen* charge encourages the jury to reach a unanimous verdict so as to avoid a mistrial. Some appellate courts have criticized the use of the *Allen* charge as an attempt to pressure the dissenting members of the jury to change their views. In some states, such as Montana, the courts have prohibited the use of the *Allen* charge. Other jurisdictions have developed alternative jury instructions to be followed when the court faces the prospect of a deadlocked jury. These model instructions generally urge the jurors holding majority and minority views to carefully consider each other's positions and attempt to arrive at a unanimous verdict.

See also Jury, Trial by

Bibliography

Scheb, John M., and John M. Scheb II. 2006. *Criminal Procedure.* Belmont, CA: Thomson/Wadsworth.

John M. Scheb II and Otis H. Stephens, Jr.

HUSTLER MAGAZINE V. FALWELL (1988)

In its November 1983 issue, *Hustler* magazine ran a fictional advertisement entitled "Jerry Falwell talks about his first time." The ad, which was a spoof on a popular ad campaign for Campari liqueur, portrayed Rev. Falwell as a hypocritical drunkard whose "first time" involved sex with his mother in an outhouse. At the bottom of the page, in fine print, was the disclaimer "Ad parody—not to be taken seriously."

Despite the disclaimer, Falwell brought suit in federal court charging *Hustler* with invasion of privacy, libel, and infliction of emotional distress. After the trial, the court granted *Hustler*'s motion for a directed verdict on the invasion of privacy claim, but allowed the jury to consider the remaining charges. The jury returned a verdict for the defendant on the libel claim, finding that *Hustler*'s parody could not "reasonably be understood as describing actual facts about [Falwell] or actual events in which [Falwell] participated." However, on the claim of infliction of emotional distress, the court found for Rev. Falwell, awarding him $100,000 in compensatory damages and another $100,000 in punitive damages.

The U.S. Court of Appeals for the Fourth Circuit affirmed the judgment, rejecting *Hustler*'s contention that because the plaintiff was a well-known public figure, his claim for emotional distress was governed by the "actual malice" standard articulated in *New York Times Co. v. Sullivan* (1964) and *Curtis Publishing Co. v. Butts* (1967). In *Sullivan,* the Supreme Court held that a public official is barred from recovering damages for libel unless the defendant acted with actual malice. In *Butts,* the Court extended this holding to public figures. In the *Hustler* case, the appellate court recognized that Rev. Falwell was a public figure, but held that the actual malice standard was not applicable to claims of infliction of emotional distress.

The United States Supreme Court reversed, holding that Falwell, as a public figure, could not recover damages without showing that *Hustler* had published a false statement of fact with actual malice. Writing for a unanimous bench, Chief Justice William H. Rehnquist concluded that extending the actual malice standard to the tort of infliction of emotional distress was "necessary to give adequate 'breathing space' to the freedoms protected by the First Amendment." "Were we to hold otherwise," Rehnquist observed, "there can be little doubt that political cartoonists and satirists would be subjected to damages awards without any showing that their work falsely defamed its subject."

In his opinion concurring in the judgment only, Justice Byron White questioned the relevance of *New York Times Co. v. Sullivan,* inasmuch as "the jury found that the ad contained no assertion of fact." But he concluded nevertheless that in these circumstances, a judgment for infliction of emotional distress "cannot be squared with the First Amendment."

See also Defamation; First Amendment; Free Marketplace of Ideas; *New York Times v. Sullivan* (1964); Press, Freedom of the; Privacy, Invasion of; Rehnquist, William H.; Speech, Freedom of; White, Byron R.

Bibliography

Smolla, Rodney A. 1988. *Jerry Falwell v. Larry Flynt: The First Amendment on Trial.* New York: St. Martin's Press.

John M. Scheb II and Otis H. Stephens, Jr.

HYDE AMENDMENT. *See* Abortion, Public Funding of

I

IDENTIFICATION, POLICE REQUEST FOR. *See* Stop and Frisk

IMMIGRATION AND NATIONALITY ACT. *See* Asylum, Right to; Immigrants and Aliens, Rights of

IMMIGRATION APPEALS, BOARD OF. *See* Asylum, Right to

IMMIGRANTS AND ALIENS, RIGHTS OF

In the United States, all noncitizens are by law considered to be aliens. Within the broad category of aliens are included immigrant noncitizens and nonimmigrant noncitizens (immigrant citizens are not considered to be aliens because a citizen, by definition, cannot be an alien). Immigrant noncitizens, as well as nonimmigrant noncitizens, have a status of being either documented (legal) or undocumented (illegal). The main distinction between immigrant noncitizens and nonimmigrant noncitizens is that immigrant noncitizens are persons who have migrated to the United States to become permanent residents and perhaps ultimately citizens. In order for an alien to fall under immigrant status they must declare their intent to permanently reside in the United States and apply for "lawful permanent residency" (LPR) status. Only after achieving this status can an immigrant noncitizen apply for citizenship. The process by which immigrant noncitizens achieve citizenship is called naturalization (Dinnerstein

and Reimers 1982). Nonimmigrant noncitizens, on the other hand, are persons who have entered the country for the purposes of visiting, furthering their education, conducting research, or working, and who plan to stay for an indefinite period of time (nonresident aliens). Immigrant noncitizens and nonimmigrant noncitizens are not, however, afforded the same level of protections under the laws as U.S. citizens. Rather, they hold a special status under immigration laws established by the federal government.

The United States Congress establishes rules for immigration and naturalization of noncitizens. Constitutional authority to regulate immigration, although not expressly stated in the United States Constitution, is implicitly vested in Congress via a number of important Constitutional clauses (Jasper 1996). The Commerce Clause (Article I, Section 8, Clause 3) empowers Congress to regulate commerce with foreign nations. The Naturalization Clause (Article I, Section 8, Clause 4) gives Congress the power to establish uniform rule of naturalization. The Migration and Importation Clause (Article I, Section 9, Clause 1), which mainly considers slavery, limits Congress from prohibiting the admission of "such persons as the States ... shall think proper to admit prior to 1808."

Early in the history of American politics, there was debate over who had the legal authority to regulate the rights of immigrants. In addition, there were questions about whether immigrants were afforded any rights under the U.S. Constitution. In the landmark case of *Henderson v. Mayor of New York* (1876), the Court answered the first of these questions. In *Henderson,* the Court declared that the regulation of immigration was the exclusive right of Congress, and "whenever the statute of a State invades the domain of legislation which belongs exclusively to the Congress of the United States, it is void, no matter under what class of powers it may fall." (See also *Smith v. Turner* [*The Passenger Cases*], 1849). Over time, the Supreme Court continued to recognize Congress as having plenary power in dealing with aliens as well as establishing rules of immigration and naturalization. In effect, the Court recognized Congress had full discretion to promulgate statutory rules regulating the expulsion or inclusion of aliens (Dinnerstein and Reimers 1982).

Subsequent to the *Henderson* case, Congress began to pass various laws restricting immigration in response to the fears of the states over competition for jobs by new immigrants. One of the first laws of this nature was the Chinese Exclusion Act of 1882. Upon review of the act, the Court held that congressional annulment of reentry certificates for Chinese laborers was a constitutional exercise of power (*Chae Chan Ping v. United States* [1889]). This case, along with a series of other cases, became known as the *Chinese Exclusion Cases.* In a second important case, *Fong Yue Ting v. United States* (1893), the Court recognized that aliens are "subject to the power of Congress to expel them, or to order them to be removed and deported from the country whenever in its judgment their removal is necessary or expedient for the public interest." This case upheld Congress' power to require Chinese laborers already in the United States to obtain a certificate of residence or face expulsion from the country. As a consequence of the Court's decision in these and more recent cases, the states have typically been barred from setting conditions on noncitizens that would put them at any legal disadvantage not proscribed by the Congress (Dinnerstein and Reimers 1982).

The Court has typically struck down state challenges to congressional authority in the realm of regulating immigration and naturalization. In *Truax v. Reich* (1915), the Court held that "the assertion of an authority to deny to aliens the opportunity of earning a livelihood when lawfully admitted to the state would be tantamount to the assertion of the right to deny them entrance and abode for in ordinary cases, they cannot live where they cannot work." As a result, an Arizona statue requiring 80 percent of all workers in any company to be qualified electors or native-born citizens was held to be an unconstitutional exercise of power by the state. Over time, the Court, with few exceptions, did not waver in its stance with regards to striking down state laws aimed at circumscribing the rights of immigrants (see also *Clarke v. Deckebach* [1927] and *Plyer v. Doe* [1982]). In fact, the Court began to recognize the need for stronger protections of immigrants against state actions that discriminated based on alienage. Accordingly, in *Graham v. Richardson* (1971), the Court held that classifications based on alienage, like those based on nationality or race, are inherently subject to close judicial scrutiny (Dinnerstein and Reimers 1982).

The Supreme Court first recognized the application of Constitutional protections to noncitizens in the landmark decision in *Yick Wo v. Hopkins* (1885). In this case, the Court established the principle that the Fourteenth Amendment to the Constitution requires states to grant equal protection of the laws to all persons without regard of nationality. The case dealt with a challenge to San Francisco's denial of a special license to a resident alien, Yick Wo, to operate a laundry in the city. The Court recognized that the Equal Protection and Due Process Clauses applied not only to citizens, but "persons" as well. Likewise, in the case of *Wong Wing v. U.S.* (1896), the Supreme Court said that Chinese immigrants should be afforded the right to a fair trial in accordance with Fourteenth Amendment due process protections. Two years later, in the landmark case of *U.S. v. Wong Kim Ark* (1898), the Court took on the question as to whether an individual born on U.S. soil, but to parents who were not American citizens, was in fact a citizen of the United States. Basing its ruling on the language of the Fourteenth Amendment, which reads, "all persons born or naturalized in the United States, and subject to the jurisdiction thereof, are citizens of the United States and of the State wherein they reside," the Court held that Wong Kim Ark, who as a child was born in the United States to parents of Chinese citizenship, was indeed a citizen of the United States (for more discussion on the expansion of the civil rights of noncitizens, see also *Wong Yang Sung v. McGrath* [1950] and *U.S. v. Brignoni-Ponce* [1975]).

Congressional regulation of immigration has been provided for through two main avenues: statutes and treaties. There have been many immigration acts passed by Congress since the first federal exclusionary immigration law, the Alien and Sedition Act of 1798 (Jasper 1996, Bau 1985). The Chinese Exclusionary Act of 1882, often recognized as the nation's first general federal immigration law, banned Chinese (as well as other classes of persons) from entering the country and levied a head tax of 50 cents on each immigrant. This law was not repealed until 1943. Likewise, the Alien Contract Labor laws of 1885 and 1887 prohibited certain laborers from immigrating to the United States (Smith 1998). These statutes spurred the need for and creation of a federal enforcement agency. The Immigration Act of 1891 created the office of the Superior of Immigration, located within the Treasury Department, to oversee the inspection and processing of all immigrants seeking admission into the United States.

In 1906, Congress passed the Basic Naturalization Act, which mandated national standards for naturalization forms and expanded the Bureau of Immigration into the Bureau of Immigration and Naturalization. The 1906 act created the framework for rules of naturalization that are used today (Smith 1998). With regards to immigration, the Immigration and Nationality Act (INA), passed in 1952, became the basic immigration law of the United States. The most prominent change to the INA, made in 1965, did away with natural origin provisions and established a new quota system. This legislation created a cap of 20,000 immigrants per annum from all countries in the western hemisphere. While most countries in Latin America and the Caribbean benefited greatly, Mexico did not. In response to the high volumes of undocumented workers entering the United States from the country's porous southern border, Congress passed the Immigration Reform and Control Act of 1986, which made it illegal to knowingly hire an undocumented worker. Most recently, the Immigration and Naturalization Service (INS) became the Bureau of Citizenship and Immigration Services (BCIS) in a newly created Department of Homeland Security. This change took place on March 31, 2003.

The executive branch plays a secondary role in the development of the rights of immigrants through statutes and treaties. The bulk of presidential power in this area, however, lies within the scope of individuals who fall under refugee status. One of the major sources of presidential statutory power over the rights of immigrants emanates from the Alien Enemies Act of 1798. This act gave the executive branch the right to stop the entry of aliens and to apprehend, restrain, secure, and remove alien enemies from the United States in instances where Congress has declared war (Jasper 1996). With regards to treaties, immigrants retain a limited number of rights emanating from specific agreements that have been made between the United States and foreign nations. For example, U.S. immigration laws provide nonimmigrant visa status for a citizen of a country with which the United States has a treaty of commerce and navigation. Referred to as an "E Treaty Visa," these apply only to a national of a foreign treaty country who comes to the United States to carry on substantial trade. In addition, numerous human rights treaties (e.g., the Geneva Convention) mandate specific performance by the executive branch with regards to humane treatment of aliens in foreign territories.

Immigrant noncitizens, other types of aliens, and even naturalized citizens do not enjoy complete coterminous rights with natural-born American citizens. Of these groups, naturalized citizens retain the most rights under the U.S. Constitution. However, naturalized citizens, as mandated by the Constitution, cannot become president or vice president of the country. Aliens, on the other hand, do not receive the same degree of rights as naturalized citizens. Even though guaranteed Fourteenth Amendment due process protections, aliens face more stringent repercussions for their actions while in the United States. For example, noncitizens can be deported from the country for reasons ranging from entering the United States without an inspection or a valid visa, to questionable political activity, violating the terms of their visa, firearms and weapons offenses, committing crimes, espionage, or sabotage, or having a serious communicable disease. Even legal permanent resident aliens, as the result of a 1996 law passed by Congress, can be deported upon their conviction of one or more various types of crimes. In addition, the Supreme Court has ruled that deportation is a civil proceeding; therefore, it doesn't involve the same level of due process as criminal proceedings (*Harisiades v. Shaughnessy* [1952]).

U.S. immigration law provides for the issuance of immigrant visas in four general categories: immediate relatives, family based, employment based, and Diversity Immigrant Visa Program (referred to as the "green card" lottery). Noncitizens can sometimes also fall into the category of refugee/asylee. Refugee status is applied for from abroad while those already in the United States or at a port of entry can request asylum. Refugee/asylum status may lead to temporary protective status—which is available only to those individuals whose home countries have been deemed by the U.S. Attorney General to be too dangerous to return to. In addition, the president has the power to specify the conditions under which an individual can be defined as an asylee or refugee. Typically, refugee/asylum status is a temporary condition; however, this status can lead to legal permanent resident status.

See also Asylum, Right to; Bureau of Citizenship and Immigration Services; Homeland Security, Department of (DHA); International Law; *Yick Wo v. Hopkins* (1886)

Bibliography

Bau, Ignatius. 1985. *This Ground is Holy: Church Sanctuary and Central American Refugees.* Mahwah, NJ. Paulist Press.

Dinnerstein, Leonard, and David M. Reimers. 1982. *Ethnic Americans.* New York: Harper and Row.

Jasper, Margaret. 1996. *The Law of Immigration.* Dobbs Ferry, NY: Oceana Publications.

Reimers, David M. 1985. *Still The Golden Door.* New York: Columbia University Press.

Schuck, Peter H. 1984. "The Transformation of Immigration Law." *Columbia Law Review* 84: 1.

Schuck, Peter H. 1983. "Developments in the Law—Immigration Policy and the Rights of Aliens." *Harvard Law Review* 96: 1286.

Smith, Marian L. 1998. "History INS Overview." In *A Historical Guide to the U.S. Government,* ed. George T. Kurian. 350. New York: Oxford University Press.

Richard T. Middleton, IV

IMMINENT LAWLESS ACTION. *See Brandenburg v. Ohio;* Clear and Present Danger Doctrine

IMMUNITY, JUDICIAL

The doctrine of judicial immunity, the concept that judges cannot be sued for actions taken while acting in their official judicial capacity, dates from seventeenth-century English common law. Judicial immunity was created by judges to protect themselves from lawsuits. It has been criticized and challenged on numerous occasions. But, at least in the United States, it has become even stronger in modern times, sometimes protecting judges from suit even when their actions are clearly biased and violate the civil rights of individuals.

The strongest argument in favor of judicial immunity is that judges could not be objective or impartial in rendering their decisions if they were constantly under the threat of facing lawsuits challenging their rulings. Moreover, since inevitable mistakes are made in every case that goes to trial, judges would be exposed to suits for negligence for the most trivial errors. According to the proponents of judicial immunity, this would render a judge's duties impossible to perform.

While many public officials enjoy varying degrees of qualified immunity, judges and prosecutors are cloaked with absolute immunity. That means that there are no exceptions to their immunity so long as they are acting in an official capacity.

Arguments for prosecutorial immunity are essentially the same as those for judicial immunity. If every prosecutor could be sued by every person s/he convicted, prosecutors would be reluctant to prosecute certain cases, especially cases against wealthy individuals with the financial means and sophistication to sue them.

The argument against judicial immunity is that there are corrupt judges, just as there are corrupt individuals in every profession. Judges can be bought, they can hold grudges, and they can be biased against certain groups or individuals. Why should judges, of all people, sworn to uphold the law, get a free pass?

In the United States, state judges did not enjoy immunity from suits for civil rights violations brought against them under the Civil Rights Act of 1871, until courts themselves determined that they were immune. The doctrine was established by the U.S. Supreme Court in *Pierson v. Ray* (1967). Critics argue that Congress never intended to give judges immunity from claims made pursuant to the Civil Rights Act of 1871.

Opponents of judicial immunity argue that the doctrine conflicts directly with constitutional guarantees, most notably the Due Process Clauses of the Fifth and Fourteenth Amendments. Due process mandates that an individual who has been wronged, charged with a crime, or otherwise deprived of a fundamental right is entitled to a fair hearing. This would include the right to sue. Opponents of judicial immunity point out that absolutely immunizing judges from civil suit effectively deprives victims of judicial error or misconduct of their right to due process of law.

Courts have been equivocal on this issue in an effort to carve out meaningful standards for judicial immunity. These standards include tests to determine whether the action in question was a judicial act or simply an official act of an administrator.

In the latter instance judicial immunity would not apply.

Possibly the most definitive statement of judicial immunity was made by the U.S. Supreme Court in 1978. The case involved a slightly retarded 15-year-old girl. The trial judge, without a hearing, approved the involuntary sterilization of the girl during an appendectomy because her mother told the judge the girl was promiscuous. Subsequently, when the girl married and discovered she was sterile she sued the judge. In *Stump v. Sparkman* (1978), the Supreme Court found that the doctrine of judicial immunity barred suit against the judge. The absolute nature of judicial immunity could hardly be better illustrated than by the harsh result in this case.

See also Civil Rights Act of 1871; Common Law Background of American Civil Rights and Liberties; Due Process Clauses; Due Process, Procedural; Fifth Amendment; Fourteenth Amendment (1868); Fundamental Rights

Bibliography

Murphey, Martha. 1983. *Judicial Immunity and Indemnification of State Officers and Employees*. Williamsburg, VA: National Center for State Courts.

Olowofoveku, Abimbola A. 1993. *Suing Judges: A Study of Judicial Immunity*. Oxford: Oxford University Press.

James V. Cornehls

IMMUNITY FROM CRIMINAL PROSECUTION

It is well established that courts of law, grand juries, legislative committees and government agencies have the power to compel witnesses to appear before them and give testimony. Concurring in *Murphy v. Waterfront Commission* (1964), Justice Byron White observed, "Among the necessary and most important of the powers of the States as well as the Federal Government to assure the effective functioning of government in an ordered society is the broad power to compel residents to testify in court or before grand juries or agencies."

One who refuses to comply with a subpoena issued by a governmental entity may be prosecuted for contempt. On the other hand, the Fifth Amendment to the United States Constitution, as well as similar provisions of the 50 state constitutions, protects witnesses from being compelled to incriminate themselves. A conflict seems to have arisen between these two doctrines. Granting immunity to witnesses addresses this problem. The federal government and all 50 states have laws under which witnesses can be granted immunity from criminal prosecution in order to secure their testimony. As the U.S. Supreme Court recognized in *United States v. Kastigar* (1972), the concept of immunity represents "a rational accommodation between the imperatives of the privilege and the legitimate demands of government to compel citizens to testify."

There are essentially two types of immunity: use immunity and transactional immunity. Strictly speaking, use immunity applies only to the immunized testimony itself. In most instances, however, the grant of use immunity also applies to derivative evidence. When a witness is granted use and derivative use immunity, the government cannot use the immunized testimony, or any evidence obtained solely as the result of this testimony, in a criminal prosecution of this witness. The government may, however, prosecute the witness for a crime to which he or she admitted under the grant of immunity, as long as the government bases its case entirely on evidence that is independent of the immunized testimony. As the Supreme Court explained in *Hoffman* v. *United States* (1951), "The privilege afforded not only extends to answers that would in themselves support a conviction under a federal criminal statute but likewise embraces those which would furnish a link in the chain of evidence needed to prosecute the claimant for a federal crime."

Transactional immunity is broader than use immunity, and is sometimes referred to as full immunity. A grant of transactional immunity bars the government from prosecuting the witness for the crime that was the subject of his or her testimony. In effect, transactional immunity is a pardon in advance of conviction.

Prosecutors often arrange for immunity in order to induce persons involved in criminal activity to testify against others, especially those who occupy higher positions in organized crime syndicates. Congress has also made extensive use of immunity in order to facilitate its own investigations of organized crime, corporate wrongdoing, and political scandals.

Frequently, the prosecution and witness will negotiate an immunity agreement as part of a plea bargain. The witness may agree to "turn state's evidence" in exchange for the prosecutor dropping or reducing some of the charges as well as granting use immunity with respect to the testimony sought or transactional immunity with respect to crimes that may be revealed in this investigation.

See also Accused, Rights of the; Clemency, Executive; Fifth Amendment; Grand Jury; Immunity, Judicial; Legislative Investigations; Plea Bargaining; Self-Incrimination Clause; White, Byron H.

John M. Scheb II and Otis H. Stephens, Jr.

IMMUNITY, LEGISLATIVE. *See* Legislative Investigations

IMMUNITY, OFFICIAL. *See* Section 1983 Actions

IMMUNITY, PROSECUTORIAL. *See* Immunity, Judicial

IMMUNITY, TRANSACTIONAL. *See* Immunity from Criminal Prosecution

IMMUNITY, USE. *See* Immunity from Criminal Prosecution

IMPEACHMENT OF WITNESSES

Facts are presented at trial through the sworn testimony of witnesses and the presentation of exhibits, which may include physical items, documents, and photographs. When facts are established through a witness's testimony, the witness's truthfulness becomes very important. Before being allowed to testify, a witness must take an oath declaring that he or she will "testify truthfully."

The familiar oath, still used in many jurisdictions, requires the witness to "tell the truth, the whole truth, and nothing but the truth."

Because a testifying witness has taken an oath to tell the truth in front of the fact finder, be it judge or jury, if the witness is shown to be testifying falsely or to be untruthful, the impact on the fact finder may be significant. This process by which the truthfulness of a witness is challenged is known as impeachment.

A more formal definition of impeachment is offered by *Black's Law Dictionary*. To impeach a witness is "to call in question the veracity of a witness, by means of evidence adduced for such purpose, or the adducing of proof that a witness is unworthy of belief." Thus, a witness may be impeached by a variety of methods, all of which are aimed at discrediting the witness or the witness' testimony.

A witness is called to testify by one side or the other in a lawsuit. After the party calling the witness has questioned the witness, by a process known as *direct examination,* the opposing party has the right to *cross-examine* the witness. Cross-examination is accomplished through leading questions, which narrowly limit a witness' response, generally to an affirmation or denial of a statement made by opposing counsel. It is usually during cross-examination that the witness is impeached, although modern evidence rules allow either party, even the one calling the witness, to impeach the witness.

During cross-examination, a witness may be forced into contradictions or inconsistencies that suggest untruthfulness. Sometimes, a witness will have made prior statements that differ from the witness's testimony at trial. These statements, known as prior inconsistent statements, may be used to impeach the witness. When a witness has admitted contradictions or has made prior inconsistent statements, the fact finder may doubt not only the trustworthiness of the trial testimony, but the general trustworthiness of the witness.

Another method of impeachment is by the proof of contradictory facts. If a witness's statement is contradicted by physical facts that make the statement unlikely or unbelievable, the witness, too, may seem unreliable or unbelievable. Similarly, if a witness is shown to have some bias, motive, interest in the outcome or prejudice for or against a party that affects the testimony, the testimony may seem less reliable and trustworthy.

The law also recognizes that the character of a witness may affect the witness's credibility and, thus, the reliability of the witness's testimony. When, for example, a witness has a reputation for being untruthful, or when the witness has been convicted of certain serious crimes or crimes involving dishonesty, the fact finder is entitled to consider the witness's conduct in weighing the testimony that the witness gives.

In the final analysis, whether a witness has been impeached based on prior inconsistent statements, bias, contradictory facts, or character evidence is up to the judge or jury who is determining the facts in the case. The fact finder may ignore the impeachment evidence and believe the witness's testimony; may rely on some, but not all, of the witness' testimony; or may disregard the witness' testimony altogether. The fact finders' reaction will depend not only on how they are affected by the impeachment evidence, but also on how they view the witness's demeanor on the witness stand and how well the witness is able to narrate or explain his or her testimony.

A witness whose credibility has been questioned by some method of impeachment may be rehabilitated by the introduction of evidence tending to support the witness' credibility. The nature of the rehabilitation evidence will also affect, in the final analysis, whether the fact finder believes the witness's testimony.

See also Accused, Rights of the; Bench Trial; Confrontation, Right of; Counsel, Right to; Jury, Trial by

Bibliography

Aron, Roberto, Kevin Thomas Duffy, and Jonathan L. Rosner. 1990. *Impeachment of Witnesses.* New York: Shepards/McGraw-Hill.

Givens, Richard A. 1985. *Advocacy: The Art of Pleading a Cause.* 2nd ed. New York: Shepards/McGraw-Hill.

Timony, James P. 2000. "Demeanor Credibility." *Catholic University Law Review* 49: 903.

Penny White

IMPLIED CONSENT STATUTES

To facilitate testing of motorists suspected of driving under the influence of alcohol or drugs, all states have enacted implied consent statutes requiring motorists to submit to chemical testing for drugs and blood, breath, or urine testing to determine blood-alcohol content. The refusal to submit to such testing results in an immediate administrative suspension of the driver's license. Statutory provisions vary but usually require that a driver be informed of the consequences of a refusal to take such tests.

In *Mackey v. Montrym* (1979), the U.S. Supreme Court upheld the validity of a Massachusetts law providing for suspension of the driver's license of a person who refused to take a breathalyzer test. Writing for a five-to-four majority, Chief Justice Warren E. Burger observed:

The Commonwealth's interest in public safety is substantially served in several ways by the summary suspension of those who refuse to take a breath-analysis test upon arrest. First, the very existence of the summary sanction of the statute serves as a deterrent to drunken driving. Second, it provides strong inducement to take the breath-analysis test and thus effectuates the Commonwealth's interest in obtaining reliable and relevant evidence for use in subsequent criminal proceedings. Third, in promptly removing such drivers from the road, the summary sanction of the statute contributes to the safety of public highways.

Critics charge that implied consent statutes permit police to violate motorists' Fourth Amendment right to be free from unreasonable searches and seizures as well as their Fifth Amendment protection against compulsory self-incrimination. State courts have generally rejected challenges based on Fourth Amendment grounds but have divided on whether a driver's refusal to submit to blood, breath, or urine testing can be admitted into evidence at trial. However, in 1983 in *South Dakota v. Neville,* the Supreme Court held that admission into evidence of an individual's refusal to submit to a blood-alcohol test does not violate the Fifth Amendment to the U.S. Constitution.

Civil libertarians continue to object to the automatic suspension of a driver's license under implied consent laws, contending such suspensions violate federal and state constitutional protections of due process of law. Given the magnitude of the public safety interest at stake, and the fact that courts consider driving is a privilege and not a constitutional right, they have been reluctant to accept these arguments.

See also Accused, Rights of the; Burger, Warren E.; Due Process Clauses; Due Process, Procedural; Fifth Amendment; Fourth Amendment; Self-Incrimination Clause

John M. Scheb II

INCHOATE OFFENSES

Inchoate offenses are actions taken in furtherance of a substantive criminal act that has either not yet occurred or has failed. Often referred to as anticipatory or incomplete offenses, inchoate crimes include the crimes of attempt, solicitation, and conspiracy. While definitions vary, all states and the Model Penal Code criminalize attempt, solicitation, and conspiracy in some form.

The purpose behind separating substantive offenses from inchoate (incomplete) crimes is to allow the state to prosecute those who have taken steps towards the commission of a crime but have yet to commit the criminal act. The difficulty for the states is in defining what constitutes an attempt. Mere preparation for a crime is not sufficient. Under common law, the proximity approach, which asks whether the person has taken the *last step* in furtherance of the criminal act, was the test to determine attempt. However, most states (and the Model Penal Code) have now opted for the stricter "substantial step" test, only requiring significant activity undertaken in furtherance of the criminal goal. Many jurisdictions have defined "substantial step" as an overt act towards the commission of the crime.

Defenses to a charge of criminal attempt include abandonment and impossibility, though not all jurisdictions accept both. Abandonment requires that the defendant voluntarily renounce the steps he or she took toward the completion of the crime. Waiting for a better opportunity or a better victim does not constitute abandonment. The second and less popular defense to attempt is impossibility. Attempting to kill an already dead person would be a factual impossibility. A legal impossibility would be when there is no law against the crime one is charged with.

A conspiracy exists when two or more persons agree to commit or take steps in furtherance of a criminal act. Most states and the federal government categorize conspiracy as a felony. A conspiracy charge also requires culpable intent on the part of the defendants. Conspiracies generally take two forms: a wheel conspiracy and a chain conspiracy. A wheel conspiracy exists when the conspirators do not interact with each other but only with the one ringleader, or hub. The ringleader is the only person who communicates with all members of the conspiratorial community. Chain conspiracies are usually found in the illegal drug trade, where there exists a succession of individuals, each playing a crucial part in the illegal activity.

Conspiracy is a powerful prosecutorial tool because it is, in the words of Judge Learned Hand, fundamentally "formless" (see *Harrison v. United States,* 1925). The elements of a conspiracy charge are easy to prove and hard to defend against. Therefore, defenses to conspiracy usually take one of two forms: denying that one is a party to the conspiracy or alleging that one withdrew from it. Conspiracies are a favorite target of criticism for lawyers since only *mens rea* (guilty mind) is present, but not *actus reus* (criminal act). For this crime, the *actus reus* is the collection of guilty minds working towards one separate and distinct criminal act.

The last inchoate crime is that of criminal solicitation, which occurs when someone requests, encourages, counsels, or induces another person to commit a crime. In most states, the crime consists of asking someone to commit the crime (or requesting a person to find someone else to commit the crime) and is not dependent on whether the person agrees

to do so. The intent is of the person asking, not the person who was asked. Generally, criminal solicitation requires that the request for criminal activity be made to (a) specific person(s), not to some larger group.

Due to accomplice and complicity law, a solicitation charge is only brought if the crime sought was not attempted or was not successful. For example, if Joe solicits Betty to kill Rachel and Betty is successful, both Joe and Betty will be charged with murder. Likewise, if Betty attempts to kill Rachel but is unsuccessful, both Joe and Betty will both be charged with attempted murder. It is also possible that if Betty agrees to Joe's request, a prosecutor would bring conspiracy charges against both Joe and Betty rather than just solicitation charges against Joe.

Though solicitation, conspiracy, and attempt are all inchoate crimes, conspiracy is different from the other two in one major respect. While both solicitation and attempt merge into a separate offense if the inchoate crime becomes complete, a conspiracy charge can be added on to the completed crime. For example, if Joe and Betty are successful in killing Rachel they can be charged with both murder and the lesser charge, conspiracy to commit murder. The only way Joe and Betty can be charged with either solicitation or attempt is if they failed to complete the crime.

The rationale for punishing inchoate offenses has always posed difficulties. It does not appear to be deterrence since the threat of punishment for an attempt will not dissuade those who are willing to take the risk of being punished for the completed crime. The need to allay social harm is also not a forceful argument since determining the harm of an attempt is not abundantly clear. Many have argued that the lack of any apparent rationale for criminalizing inchoate offenses leaves us to conclude that the end result is the criminalizing of mere evil thoughts, a clear prohibition of criminal law. At the very least, attempt, solicitation, and conspiracy are criminalized because society is not willing to sanction, through inaction, significant steps taken by individuals in furtherance of criminal action.

See also Accused, Rights of the; Common Law Background of American Civil Rights and Liberties; Conspiracy; Drugs, War on; Hand, Learned

Bibliography

Scheb, John M., and John M. Scheb II. 2005. *Criminal Law and Procedure.* Belmont, CA: Thomson/ Wadsworth.

Kyle Kreider

"INCORPORATION PLUS." *See* Bill of Rights, Incorporation of

INDEFINITE AND INDETERMINATE SENTENCING

For a considerable part of United States history, most criminal sentencing was definite; that is, those convicted were sentenced to a fixed period of incarceration with no parole. Indeterminate sentences were initially applied in New York in 1924 (Inciardi 2002). Indeterminate sentences are defined as "a range of time between minimum date of parole eligibility and a maximum discharge date" (Rush 2003, 314). In its purest or most ideal form, an indeterminate sentence is a completely indefinite period of incarceration, that is, a minimum of one day with the possibility of life incarceration. No state has ever applied an ideal or pure indeterminate sentencing structure for all offenses, so it is probably more correct to refer to these flexible and unpredictable sentencing provisions as indefinite and not indeterminate. Still, the terms are often used interchangeably.

Whether indefinite or indeterminate, these sentencing systems rest on the primacy of rehabilitation in criminal punishment and the need for flexibility with respect to sentence length. Although virtually all states relied on indefinite or indeterminate sentencing laws between 1924 and the 1970s, there has been and still is considerable variation. Some state statutes simply sentenced convicted felons to the custody of the pertinent correctional or prison authority; others required that a particular portion of the minimum term had to be served before parole consideration, and

still others set upper limits on the maximum that could be served (Branham 2002).

Although there have been sweeping changes in sentencing laws over the past 30 years, many states still retain indefinite or indeterminate sentencing structures. As recently as 2001, Reitz concluded that "a majority of U.S. jurisdictions continue to plow ahead with the high-discretion model of indeterminate sentencing for the bulk of their punishment decisions" (Reitz 2001, 231). Still, it is important to recognize that virtually every state and the federal government have adopted mandatory minimum or definite or determinate sentences of one kind or another, even those jurisdictions that established sentencing guidelines.

Indefinite or indeterminate sentences have been subject to considerable criticism for more than 30 years. Perhaps the first and most searing criticism came in 1973 from Marvin Frankel, a federal judge, who argued that such sentencing provisions resulted in disparate and discriminatory punishment that could never be justified. Other critics charged that lack of predictability about sentences and the vagaries of parole authorities intensified prison tension and exacerbated the difficulty of administration.

Indefinite and indeterminate sentencing laws are defended, implicitly or explicitly, by the fact that there is some residual support for rehabilitation, that judges have fought to retain sentencing discretion, and/or that legislatures are unable to undertake comprehensive sentencing changes or unwilling to delegate that authority to an administrative agency. Interestingly, the underlying feature of a state's sentencing system does not invariably correlate with escalating rates of incarceration. Texas, which has one of the highest rates of incarceration at 711 per 100,000 for 2001, and North Dakota, which features one of the lowest at 161, both have sentencing systems that are fundamentally indefinite or indeterminate (Cole and Smith 2004, 433).

See also Accused, Rights of the; Plea Bargaining; Presentence Investigation Reports (PSIR);

Sentencing Hearing; Sentencing, Definite and Determinate; Sentencing, Eighth Amendment and; Sentencing Guidelines; Sentencing, Proportionality in; Sixth Amendment

Bibliography

Branham, Lynn S. 2002. *The Law of Sentencing, Corrections, and Prisoners' Rights.* St. Paul, MN: West.

Cole, George F., and Christopher E. Smith. 2004. *The American System of Criminal Justice.* Belmont, CA: Wadsworth/Thomson.

Frankel, Marvin E. 1973. *Criminal Sentences: Law without Order.* New York: Hill and Wang.

Inciardi, James A. 2002. *Criminal Justice.* New York: Oxford University Press.

Reitz, Kevin R. 2001. "The Disassembly and Reassembly of U.S. Sentencing Practices." In *Sentencing and Sanctions in Western Countries,* eds. Michael Tonry and Richard S. Frase, 222–58. New York: Oxford University Press.

Rush, George E. 2003. *The Dictionary of Criminal Justice.* New York: Dushkin/McGraw-Hill.

Susette M. Talarico

INDEPENDENT SOURCE DOCTRINE. *See* Fruit of the Poisonous Tree Doctrine

INDIAN CIVIL RIGHTS ACT OF 1968. *See* Native Americans, Civil Rights of

INDICTMENT

Deeply rooted in the English common law, an indictment is a formal document handed down by a grand jury accusing one or more persons of a crime or crimes. The Fifth Amendment to the United States Constitution states that "[n]o person shall be held to answer for a capital, or otherwise infamous crime, unless on a presentment or indictment of a grand jury …" These provisions require federal prosecutors to obtain an indictment or "true bill" from a grand jury to formally charge a person with an offense. Once indicted, the accused is arraigned, that is, brought to court to enter a plea. Petty offenses for which no sentence of imprisonment will be imposed may be tried by indictment, or by less formal means, for example, a citation or violation notice.

In *Hurtado v. California* (1884), the U.S. Supreme Court held that the Due Process Clause of the Fourteenth Amendment does not require states to abide by the grand jury requirement imposed on the federal courts by the Fifth Amendment. Nevertheless, about half the states have constitutions that require grand jury indictments for prosecution of felonies, with some allowing misdemeanors to be prosecuted on basis of an information, an accusatory document filed under oath by a prosecutor.

In other states, prosecutors charge persons with crimes through an information. Some, however, require an indictment to charge a capital crime. Where a felony crime is charged by an information, a court will hold a preliminary hearing, an adversary hearing presided over by a magistrate or judge. Its purpose is to determine whether there is probable cause to allow a criminal prosecution to go forward. Because the preliminary hearing is held in open court, whereas only the government presents a case to a grand jury, most commentators believe the information is preferable to the indictment as a charging mechanism.

See also Accused, Rights of the; Common Law Background of American Civil Rights and Liberties; Due Process Clauses; Due Process, Procedural; Fifth Amendment; Fourteenth Amendment; Grand Jury; Preliminary Hearing

Bibliography

Scheb, John M., and John M. Scheb II. 2005. *Criminal Law and Procedure.* 5th ed. Belmont, CA: Thomson/Wadsworth.

John M. Scheb II and Otis H. Stephens, Jr.

INDIVIDUALISM

The term *individualism* has several levels of meaning, all of which are relevant to civil rights and liberties. At the most basic level, the term refers to a conception of society as a collection of individuals, as distinct from a holistic or organic conception of society. It was this conception of society that led the philosophers of the Enlightenment to reject monarchy and other forms of top-down political control and embrace instead liberal and democratic ideas of governance. The idea that human beings are born with certain inalienable rights, including the right to pursue happiness on their own terms, is predicated on an individualistic conception of society. In this sense, John Locke, Thomas Jefferson, and other architects of liberal democracy were most certainly individualists.

Economic Individualism

Economically, individualism is the idea that each person is responsible for his or her own welfare. He or she must make his or her own economic choices and must live with the consequences. While individuals are entitled to the unrestricted acquisition and use of property and the unlimited enjoyment of the fruits of their labor, they should not look to government or society to rescue them from misfortune. In its most extreme form, economic individualism is synonymous with social Darwinism, the nineteenth-century idea that social progress is promoted through unrelenting competition and the "survival of the fittest." It is also closely linked to the theory of laissez-faire capitalism, an economic model based on private property, free enterprise, and minimal government involvement in the marketplace. Economic individualism is thus incompatible with socialism, communism, or other forms of collectivism.

Economic individualism is deeply rooted in American culture, which explains why capitalism has been successful in this country and why socialism and communism have never generated mass appeal. However, in the modern era, individualism has been tempered by a general agreement that government must assume some responsibility for assuring a modicum of social welfare and promoting interests, such as environmental protection, that are not strongly promoted by the free market.

Historically, some of the most contentious questions facing the courts boiled down to whether the United States Constitution is wedded to economic individualism or permits governmental control of the economy to foster the general welfare. Certainly this can be seen in the Supreme Court's tenacious defense of laissez-faire capitalism in the late nineteenth and early twentieth centuries, culminating in a showdown with President Franklin D. Roosevelt over the constitutionality of the New Deal. In a well-known dissent in *Lochner v. New York* (1905), Justice Oliver Wendell Holmes, Jr., insisted that the Constitution "is made for people of fundamentally differing views" and that the "14th Amendment does not enact Mr. Herbert Spencer's *Social Statics*" (a book propounding Spencer's individualistic philosophy). Reflecting the ultimate victory of the Holmesian perspective, the Supreme Court declared in *Ferguson v. Skrupa* (1963), "Whether the legislature takes for its textbook Adam Smith, Herbert Spencer, Lord Keynes, or some other is no concern of ours." Today, only libertarians (and some conservatives) maintain strict fidelity to the theory of economic individualism.

Ethical Individualism

At the ethical level, individualism is the theory that individuals can or should set their own moral compass without the control or guidance of others. It rejects the idea of universal moral truth and thus is incompatible with traditional theological notions of God as the supreme lawgiver of the universe and the church as the authoritative interpreter of divine law. Philosophically, ethical individualism is related to existentialism, hedonism, and utilitarianism. In the Anglo-American tradition, its best known exponents are John Stuart Mill and Henry David Thoreau. Culturally, ethical individualism has become much more prevalent in the modern era, most notably since the social upheavals of the 1960s. As ethical individualism has taken hold, the influence of traditional values and institutions has declined. Politically, the rise of ethical individualism is manifested in increased demands for government to remove itself from the business of fostering and regulating morality. Legally, the rise of ethical individualism is linked to the increased assertion and judicial recognition of constitutional rights of privacy and personal autonomy.

Some of the most divisive contemporary controversies in the realm of civil rights and liberties, most notably abortion, euthanasia, and gay rights, are at bottom cultural conflicts over the issue of ethical individualism. Just as liberals and socialists condemned the unbridled economic individualism of an earlier era, conservatives and communitarians reject the ethical individualism that characterizes postmodern American society.

See also Abortion, Right to; Right to Die; Economic Freedom; Gay Rights Movement; Holmes, Oliver Wendell, Jr.; Jefferson, Thomas; Liberalism; Libertarianism; *Lochner v. New York* (1905); Locke, John; The New Deal; Privacy, Constitutional right of; Roosevelt, Franklin D.; Thoreau, Henry David

Bibliography

Franck, Thomas M. 2001. The *Empowered Self: Law and Society in an Age of Individualism.* New York: Oxford University Press.

Madsen, Richard, et al., eds. 1996. *Habits of the Heart: Individualism and Commitment in American Life.* Berkeley, CA: University of California Press.

Shain, Barry Alan. 1996. *The Myth of American Individualism.* Princeton, NJ: Princeton University Press.

John M. Scheb II

INDIVIDUAL RIGHTS

Individual rights lie at the heart of the American system of government. When Thomas Jefferson drafted the Declaration of Independence in 1776, he drew upon the thinking of John Locke, an English philosopher. Locke had postulated that before governments existed, human beings lived in what he called a "state of nature," where they enjoyed complete liberty but where they were in danger of others seeking to take it from them. They came together and created government to protect that liberty, giving to the government only those powers that were necessary and retaining all others for themselves.

Jefferson's version was that all human beings were created by God as equals—not in wealth or intelligence or other such attributes, but in their possession of human rights. "The God who gave us life," he wrote, "gave us liberty at the same time."

Those liberties, or "inalienable rights," could be ceded by them to government, but government had no intrinsic power; that is, government could not take away the liberties of the governed without their consent. Rebutting the idea that kings ruled by divine right, Jefferson argued that while God created people, God did not create governments. People created governments to provide them with physical safety and whatever other benefits they considered necessary.

When the drafters of the Constitution came together in Philadelphia in the summer of 1787, they were so certain that governments could exercise only the powers specifically given to them by the people that, paradoxically, they made almost no mention of individual rights. Their assumption, a secularized version of the inalienable rights theory, was that since the document gave only limited powers to the new federal government, all unmentioned powers and individual liberties remained in the hands of the people. That, however, was not good enough for people in many of the states, who worried about what they believed was the propensity of governments to seek ever-increasing power at the expense of individual rights. Their threat to withhold ratification of the Constitution elicited the promise that the first Congress would enact a Bill of Rights. It did so, and the first 10 amendments to the Constitution were ratified by the states and came into force in 1791.

As listed in the Bill of Rights, individual rights were a prohibition on action by the federal government. The First Amendment, for example, states that Congress cannot interfere with the people's rights of religion, speech, press, and assembly; the Fourth Amendment prohibits the federal government from carrying out unreasonable searches and seizures; the Fifth, from holding people in double jeopardy; the Sixth, from punishing an accused person without a fair and public trial. Taken together, the 10 amendments seek to protect each person's physical liberty and his or her right to function both in private and as a member of society: to worship alone or with others, to communicate with others, and to take an active role in political life. Recognizing that such a list might be read as giving government permission to interfere with any rights not explicitly mentioned, the Ninth and Tenth Amendments proclaim that "The enumeration in the Constitution, of certain rights, shall not be construed to deny or disparage others retained by the people," and that "The powers not delegated to the United States by the Constitution, nor prohibited by it to the states, are reserved to the states respectively, or to the people." The Bill of Rights is therefore a dynamic rather than a static entity and was written so that it could be interpreted to include individual rights that were not listed.

That kind of interpretation has occurred most dramatically in the enunciation by the U.S. Supreme Court of the right to privacy. Looking at enumerated rights such as the right to be private in one's speech (First Amendment) and in one's home (Fourth Amendment), the Court has held (*Griswold v. Connecticut,* 1965) that there is a constitutional right to privacy. That right was subsequently interpreted to mean, for example, that the government could not wiretap without a warrant (*Katz v. United States,* 1967), forbid most abortions (*Roe v. Wade,* 1973), prevent decisions by terminally ill people or their legal guardians to end their lives (*Cruzan v. Director, Missouri Department of Health,* 1990), or interfere with the private sexual behavior of gays and lesbians (*Lawrence v. Texas,* 2003).

Other parts of the Bill of Rights have also been interpreted in accordance with the changing needs of society. When the Constitution was written, the telephone or the Internet could not be imagined. The Supreme Court has nonetheless held that the First Amendment's guarantee of free speech applies to messages sent across the Internet (*Reno v. American Civil Liberties Union,* 1997). Similarly, the Congress that forbade "unreasonable searches and seizures" in the Fourth Amendment could not have envisioned electronic eavesdropping or thermal-imaging devices, but the Supreme Court has held that the physical intrusion required to plant an eavesdropping device constituted an illegal search, as did a thermal-imaging device used without a warrant in an attempt to ascertain whether marijuana

was being grown inside a house (*Berger v. New York,* 1967; *Kyllo v. United States,* 2001).

For more than a century, the Bill of Rights applied only to the federal government. The First Amendment says that "Congress shall make no law ...," reflecting the view of its authors that the citizens of each state could decide what individual rights were to be protected from their state and local governments. That, in democratic fashion, left it to the majority in a state to define rights for themselves and include whatever protections they chose in their state laws and constitutions. It thereby left state majorities free to conclude either, for example, that slavery violated individual rights and was not to be countenanced or that some people, being considered less than people, could be held as slaves. The Thirteenth, Fourteenth and Fifteenth Amendments, enacted after the Civil War, prohibited slavery throughout the nation and forbade the states from taking anyone's "life, liberty or property, without due process of law." It also required the states to give all people the "equal protection of the laws." The right to equal treatment by the government was thereby defined as an individual right, and the Supreme Court gradually interpreted that right to mean that individuals cannot be discriminated against on the basis of their race (*Brown v. Board of Education,* 1954) or gender (*Reed v. Reed,* 1971).

The states also came to be limited by the Bill of Rights. In 1925, the Supreme Court ruled that the First Amendment guarantees of speech and press are so basic to a democratic governmental system that the Fourteenth Amendment's injunction against taking "liberty" without due process of law must necessarily include those guarantees (*Gitlow v. New York,* 1925). In the years thereafter, the other parts of the Bill of Rights were held to be binding on the states, so that the Bill of Rights' recognition of individual rights now applies equally to the federal government and the states.

One of the seeming paradoxes of individual rights is that they are crucial to a democratic society and yet they constitute a limitation on the majority. If democracy is defined only as rule by the majority, then individual rights would seem to play no role. Logically, if the majority rules absolutely, then it should, for example, have the power to prohibit speech that it considers dangerous or obnoxious (or, as discussed above, to legitimize slavery). If, however, people are not free to try out unpopular ideas and see whether, in Justice Oliver Wendell Holmes' phrase, they can make their way in "the marketplace of ideas," free speech means little and the society may lose important thinking. Acknowledging that, the Supreme Court has held that the government elected by the majority cannot punish unpopular speech unless it presents an imminent danger of illegal action (*Brandenburg v. Ohio*, 1969).

The concept of individual rights has changed from the late eighteenth century. In an era when the phrase "human rights" has become a force around the world, individual rights may be viewed as the gift of God, or the more secularized birthright of all human beings, or as necessary to human fulfillment. What has not changed since Jefferson's time is the recognition that individual rights are crucial to a democratic political system. Democracy does mean rule by the people, but the Founding Fathers assumed that the people who participate in the democratic process would be informed. Members of a democratic society must have access to all ideas, so they can decide for themselves which ones are valid, and they must be able to hear and express ideas without fear of being subjected to punishment by the government. What Jefferson and the writers of the Constitution understood is that the real definition of democracy is rule by the majority with full protection for the rights of the individual.

See also Accused, Rights of the; Assembly, Freedom of; Bill of Rights (American) (1789); Bill of Rights, Incorporation of; *Brandenburg v. Ohio* (1969); *Brown v. Board of Education* (1954; 1955); Declaration of Independence (1776); Democracy, Constitutional; Democracy, Representative; Equal Protection Clause; Electronic Surveillance; Equality; Federalism and Civil Rights and Liberties; Fifteenth Amendment; Fifth Amendment; Fourteenth Amendment; Fourth Amendment; Gender-Based Discrimination; *Gitlow v. New York* (1925); Holmes, Oliver Wendell, Jr.; Human Rights; Individualism; Internet, Free Speech on; Jefferson, Thomas; *Katz v. United States* (1967); *Lawrence v. Texas* (2003); Liberty; Locke, John; Natural Law and Natural Rights; Ninth Amendment; Press, Freedom of the; Religion, Freedom of; *Reno v. American Civil Liberties Union* (1997); *Roe v. Wade* (1973); Sixth Amendment; Speech, Freedom of; Tenth Amendment; Thirteenth Amendment;

Bibliography

Wermiel, Stephen J. 1992. "Rights in the Modern Era: Applying the Bill of Rights to the States." *William & Mary Bill of Rights Journal* 1: 121.

Philippa Strum

INEVITABLE DISCOVERY EXCEPTION. *See* Fruit of the Poisonous Tree Doctrine

INFORMANTS, ANONYMOUS AND CONFIDENTIAL

In the course of their investigations, police often rely on tips from informants. Essentially there are two types. An anonymous informant is usually a citizen who may not desire or be in a position to reveal his or her identity. Yet these anonymous informants often provide the police with valuable information about criminal activity. On the other hand, a confidential informant, commonly called a CI, is a person who is known to the police, who provides information, and who typically is seeking some reward or favorable consideration with respect to his or her own offenses. Tips from anonymous and confidential informants are often the basis for an investigation that may ultimately lead to probable cause to conduct a search or make an arrest. Today police frequently find it necessary to rely on information supplied from informants in enforcement of drug laws.

Anonymous Informants

By itself, an anonymous tip about criminal activity does not constitute probable cause to make an arrest; indeed, without corroboration, it is unlikely to even provide "reasonable suspicion" to allow police to conduct an investigatory detention. Anonymous tips often cause the police a dilemma. Should they act on unverified information that may be inaccurate, realizing their actions may run afoul of Fourth Amendment rights? The U.S. Supreme Court has provided guidance, but some questions remain.

In *Alabama v. White* (1990), police received an anonymous tip that a certain female was carrying cocaine and indicated that she would leave a certain apartment at a specified time, get into a car matching a particular description, and drive to a particular motel. The police conducted surveillance of the woman, which verified elements of the tip. Only then did they move in to stop her car, detain her, and seize the cocaine. Characterizing the case as a "close" one, the Court upheld the action by the police, but noted that the tip alone would not have justified the stop and frisk. Here, however, the Court pointed out that the informant's basis of knowledge was established because the tip described not only existing conditions but also unpredictable future activity.

A decade later in *Florida v. J.L.* (2000), the Court ruled that an anonymous tip lacking in reliability that a person is carrying a gun is not sufficient justification for the police to detain and search that individual. Although it declined to speculate about the circumstances under which the danger alleged in an anonymous tip might be so great as to justify a search even without a showing of reliability, the Court commented:

We do not say, for example, that a report of a person carrying a bomb need bear the indicia of reliability we demand for a report of a person carrying a firearm before the police can constitutionally conduct a frisk. Nor do we hold that public safety officials in quarters where the reasonable expectation of Fourth Amendment privacy is diminished, such as airports and schools, cannot conduct protective searches on the basis of information insufficient to justify searches elsewhere

Considering the current threat of terrorism, the Court's expression assumes great significance. It has caused a split among lower federal and state courts as to what type of threats might merit a less stringent standard in evaluating anonymous tips.

Some have interpreted the Court's language in *J.L.* to hold that the focus of inquiry should be on the level of danger alleged while other courts continue to place their emphasis on the reliability and corroboration of the anonymous tip.

Confidential Informants

Unlike the typical public-spirited citizen who furnishes the police an anonymous tip, a confidential informant is usually looking to be compensated by the police or rewarded by mitigating the informant's own situation. A tip from a confidential informant is stronger from an evidentiary point of view than an anonymous tip, especially if the informant is well known to the police to be credible and has a proven track record of providing reliable information about criminal activity.

Prior to 1983, the Supreme Court required magistrates to follow a rigorous two-pronged test in reviewing police applications for search warrants based on tips from informants. This test was derived from two decisions of the Court under Chief Justice Earl Warren: *Aguilar v. Texas* (1964) and *Spinelli v. United States* (1969). The *Aguilar–Spinelli* test required that the officer's affidavit satisfy two criteria: (1) it had to demonstrate that the informant was both credible and reliable, and (2) it had to reveal the informant's basis of knowledge. This test made it very difficult for police to rely on anonymous tips and often resulted in courts invalidating search warrants and suppressing contraband and other fruits of searches.

In *Illinois v. Gates* (1983) the Supreme Court under Chief Justice Warren E. Burger rejected the two-pronged *Aguilar–Spinelli* test in favor of a "totality of circumstances" approach that "traditionally has informed probable cause determinations." This relaxed test permits magistrates to consider the totality of circumstances when evaluating applications based on hearsay evidence and makes it easier for police to obtain warrants based on tips from informants. The following year, in *Massachusetts v. Upton* (1984), the Court held that the standard for determining probable cause announced in the *Gates* decision was to be given a broad interpretation by lower courts.

Despite the Supreme Court's relaxed standard for determining probable cause based on tips from informants, courts in several states have chosen to follow the stricter standards formerly imposed by the *Aguilar* and *Spinelli* decisions. This, of course, is their prerogative under our system of federalism.

Defendants often demand to know the identity of the informant who provided the police with information on which they based their investigation or which formed the basis for their affidavit for a search warrant. In some instances defense counsel may insist that a CI appear at a trial. When this arises courts face a delicate problem. Once a CI's identity is disclosed that person's value to law enforcement has been severely compromised. Indeed, the CI's personal safety may be jeopardized.

In *Roviaro v. United States* (1957), the Supreme Court held that in "furtherance and protection of the public interest in effective law enforcement" the government has a limited privilege to withhold the identity of a confidential informant from disclosure. In determining whether to require disclosure, a court must balance the interest of the public in preserving the anonymity of the informant against the defendant's need to have this information to prepare a defense. "Where the disclosure of an informer's identity, or of the contents of his communication, is relevant and helpful to the defense of an accused, or is essential to a fair determination of a cause," the Court observed, "the privilege must give way." Here again, state courts may adopt their own rules relative to disclosure of the identity of an informant as long as they do not contravene federal constitutional rights as interpreted by the U.S. Supreme Court.

See also Accused, Rights of the; Arrest, Constitutional Limits on; Automobile Stops and Searches; Burger Court; Burger, Warren E.; Fourth Amendment; Probable Cause; Search Warrants; Stop and Frisk; Warren Court; Warren, Earl

Bibliography

Bryk, Jason Kyle. 2003. "Anonymous Tips to Law Enforcement and the Fourth Amendment: Arguments for Adopting an Imminent Danger Exception and Retaining the Totality of the Circumstances Test." *George Mason University Civil Rights Law Journal* 13: 277.

Dunn, Tiffany A. 1999. "Constitutional Law—Fourth Amendment—Using an Informant as the Basis of a Search or Seizure." *Tennessee Law Review* 66: 531.

Mauet, Thomas A. 1995. "Informant Disclosure and Production: A Second Look at Paid Informants." *Arizona Law Review* 37: 563.

Scheb, John M., and John M. Scheb II. 2006. *Criminal Procedure*. Belmont, CA: Thomson/Wadsworth.

Hon. John M. Scheb and John M. Scheb II

INFORMATIONAL PRIVACY. *See* Privacy, Informational

INITIAL APPEARANCE IN CRIMINAL CASES

People charged with felonies and major misdemeanors are typically arrested prior to making an appearance in court. Rule 5(a) of the Federal Rules of Criminal Procedure provides that a person arrested for a federal offense shall be taken "without unnecessary delay" for a first appearance before a federal magistrate judge, or before a state or local judicial officer. Rule 5(f) now allows video teleconferencing for an initial appearance if the accused consents.

State courts have their own rules in this regard, but most require that a person arrested must be brought before a judge or magistrate within 24 hours (or 48 hours if the arrest is made on a weekend). Like the federal rule, some states now allow an initial appearance through video. In *County of Riverside v. McLaughlin* (1991), the U.S. Supreme Court held that suspects may be detained for as long as 48 hours before their first appearance in court. The purpose of these rules is to make sure an accused is fully advised of his or her constitutional rights by a judicial officer—not an enforcement officer—before making incriminating statements. In some instances courts have invalidated an accused's confession where the initial appearance was not promptly conducted.

In the first appearance, the charges are read to the accused; the accused is informed of relevant constitutional rights, including the right to remain silent and the right to counsel. The judicial officer also determines whether the accused should be released pending trial, and, if so, the conditions of release, or remanded to custody to await the disposition of the case. The first appearance is sometimes incorrectly termed an "arraignment," which refers to a defendant's entry of a plea before a trial court. After the first appearance, the case will go either before a grand jury (federal cases) or a grand jury or preliminary hearing (state cases) to determine whether the defendant should be bound over for trial.

See also Accused, Rights of the; Arraignment; Bail, Right to; Critical Pretrial Stages; Due Process, Procedural; Grand Jury; Pleas in Criminal Cases; Preliminary Hearing; Pretrial Detention

Bibliography

Scheb, John M., and John M. Scheb II. 2006. *Criminal Procedure*. Belmont, CA: Thomson/Wadsworth.

John M. Scheb II and Otis H. Stephens, Jr.

IN LOCO PARENTIS

Literally meaning "in the place of the parents," *in loco parentis* is the common-law doctrine under which a party having custody of a minor can exercise authority over that minor and make decisions on his or her behalf.

An adult who acts *in loco parentis* voluntarily assumes the duties that a parent normally provides to his or her child. Although a stepparent or grandparent does not necessarily stand *in loco parentis,* some voluntarily adopt that role. Where this occurs the rights and liabilities arising out of that relation are substantially the same as between a parent and child, and the adult must act in the same manner as an actual parent.

Historically courts often considered the doctrine of *in loco parentis* when called on to determine whether a child should be treated as a child of an in loco parent for purposes of an entitlement to certain benefits provided by law, for example, workers compensation benefits of an injured or deceased in loco parent. In recent years, however, the doctrine has been more frequently applied in divorce cases where courts sometimes consider whether the in loco parent should be awarded custodial or visitation rights.

Teachers, coaches, day care providers, and camp counselors act *in loco parentis* when they have temporary custody of other people's children. Of course, with the authority to make decisions on a minor's behalf comes the responsibility for the safekeeping and welfare of that minor. Persons acting *in loco parentis* have a duty to act reasonably to protect minors in their care from foreseeable harm. The failure to perform this duty exposes the custodian to civil and in some instances criminal liability.

Writing for the U.S. Supreme Court in *Vernonia School District 47J v. Acton* (1995), Justice Antonin Scalia quoted Sir William Blackstone in stating the *in loco parentis* doctrine in the context of the private school:

When parents place minor children in private schools for their education, the teachers and administrators of those schools stand in loco parentis over the children entrusted to them. In fact, the tutor or schoolmaster is the very prototype of that status. As Blackstone describes it, a parent "may ... delegate part of his parental authority, during his life, to the tutor or schoolmaster of his child; who is then in loco parentis, and has such a portion of the power of the parent committed to his charge, viz. that of restraint and correction, as may be necessary to answer the purposes for which he is employed." 1 W. Blackstone, Commentaries on the Laws of England 441 (1769).

Historically, many courts took the view that public schools also stand *in loco parentis* and, therefore, public school students may not assert constitutional rights vis-à-vis their teachers and principals. This began to change in the late 1960s. In *Tinker v. Des Moines Independent Community School District* (1969), the Supreme Court held that students in public schools do not "shed their constitutional rights to freedom of speech or expression at the schoolhouse gate." In *Goss v. Lopez* (1975), the

Supreme Court held that public school students subjected to disciplinary actions are entitled to due process of law. And in *New Jersey v. T.L.O.* (1985), the Court held that the Fourth Amendment's protection against unreasonable searches and seizures is applicable, albeit in an attenuated form, to the public school environment. Writing for the Court in *T.L.O.*, Justice Byron White observed, "If school authorities are state actors for purposes of the constitutional guarantees of freedom of expression and due process, it is difficult to understand why they should be deemed to be exercising parental rather than public authority when conducting searches of their students."

While not returning to the traditional view that public school officials stand *in loco parentis,* in recent years a more conservative Supreme Court has tempered the application of constitutional rights to the public school environment. In the *Vernonia School District v. Acton* (1995), the Court upheld a drug-testing requirement for public high school students who chose to participate in athletics. Recognizing that a suspicionless, mandatory drug testing program would not be constitutionally permissible in another context, Justice Scalia's majority opinion reflected on the application of constitutional rights to the public school environment:

In *T.L.O.* we rejected the notion that public schools, like private schools, exercise only parental power over their students, which of course is not subject to constitutional constraints.... Such a view of things, we said, "is not entirely 'consonant with compulsory education laws'" ... and is inconsistent with our prior decisions treating school officials as state actors for purposes of the Due Process and Free Speech Clauses.... But while denying that the State's power over schoolchildren is formally no more than the delegated power of their parents, *T.L.O.* did not deny, but indeed emphasized, that the nature of that power is custodial and tutelary, permitting a degree of supervision and control that could not be exercised over free adults.... Thus, while children assuredly do not "shed their constitutional rights ... at the schoolhouse gate," ... the nature of those rights is what is appropriate for children in school.

See also Blackstone, William; Common Law Background of American Civil Rights and Liberties; Drug Testing; Due Process Clauses; Due Process, Procedural; First Amendment; Fourth Amendment; Public Schools, Searches and Seizures in; Scalia, Antonin; Speech, Freedom of; *Tinker v. Des Moines Independent Community School District* (1969); White, Byron

Hon. John M. Scheb, John M. Scheb II, and Otis H. Stephens, Jr.

INSANITY DEFENSE

From a legal standpoint insanity refers to a mental condition that prevents a person from having the capacity to formulate intent to commit a crime. In the United States, courts generally followed the English common-law development of the defense of insanity. Congress has now defined the criteria for establishing the defense in federal courts; however, insanity remains defined by decisional law in some states, by statute in others, and in a few states the legislature has eliminated it as a defense. Juries infrequently find a defendant not guilty by reason of insanity, and when they do the defendant is usually committed to a mental institution or otherwise exposed to medical treatment. Insanity has sometimes been referred to as "a rich man's defense" because defendants who invoke it often expend considerable resources in presenting psychiatric testimony.

A public outcry occurred when a federal court jury found John Hinckley not guilty by reason of insanity in the 1981 shooting of President Ronald Reagan, his press secretary, and two law officers. Congress responded by enacting the Insanity Defense Reform Act of 1984 to establish standards for federal prosecutions. States also began to reassess their standards for the insanity defense.

A brief history assists in understanding how the law has developed in this area. Common-law crimes included a mental element (*mens rea*), yet the English courts were slow to develop any standard that would excuse a person from criminal responsibility. In 1843, Daniel M'Naghten shot and killed Edward Drummond, believing Drummond to be Sir Robert Peel, the British Home Secretary. M'Naghten's barristers won an acquittal by convincing the jury that M'Naghten was insane at the time of the killing. In response to Queen Victoria's indignation over the verdict, the House of Lords announced in *M'Naghten's Case* that in order to establish insanity as a defense to a crime it must be shown that "at the time of committing the act, the party accused was labouring under such a defect of reason, from disease of the mind, as not to know the nature and quality of the act he was doing; or, if he did know it, that he did not know what he was doing was wrong."

This standard, known as the M'Naghten Rule (or the "right from wrong" test) is essentially a cognitive test and was soon imported to the United States and followed by federal and state courts. As new theories of mental capacity emerged, courts developed new tests to determine whether a defendant was insane when he or she committed an offense. During the early twentieth century a number of state courts added to the M'Naghten Rule by incorporating the irresistible impulse test that stressed volition, that is, self-control, and authorized a court to find a defendant insane even though he or she knew an act was wrong, but committed a criminal act under an uncontrollable desire. Either by statute or judicial decision most states have now rejected the irresistible impulse test, often observing that it cannot be applied with precision. But in *Vann v. Commonwealth* (2001), a Virginia appellate court observed, "Virginia law recognizes ... the M'Naghten Rule and the irresistible impulse doctrine" and noted "[t]he irresistible impulse defense is available when the accused's mind has become so impaired by disease that he is totally deprived of the mental power to control or restrain his act."

In *Durham v. United States* (1954), the U.S. Court of Appeals for the D.C. Circuit opined that a person was not criminally responsible if that person's unlawful act was "the product of mental disease or defect." This "Durham test" did not gain wide acceptance and was eventually discarded in favor of a new test recommended by the American Law Institute.

In 1962 the American Law Institute (ALI), developed the "ALI or substantial capacity" test, which proposed: "A person is not responsible for criminal conduct if at the time of such conduct, as a result of mental disease or defect, a person lacks substantial capacity either to appreciate the wrongfulness of his conduct or to conform his conduct to the requirement of the law." Most federal courts adopted this as the standard for the defense of insanity. Including "appreciate the wrongfulness of his conduct" added flexibility to former tests for insanity. It was this test that the court and jury applied in the John Hinckley case.

The verdict in the Hinckley case motivated Congress to enact the Insanity Defense Reform Act of 1984, codified at 18 U.S.C. sec. 17(a), which provides that in federal courts:

It is an affirmative defense to a prosecution under a federal statute that, at the time of the commission of the acts constituting the offense, the defendant, as a result of severe mental disease or defect, was unable to appreciate the nature and quality or the wrongfulness of his acts.

The new federal standard effectively eliminated the volitional prong of the ALI test. The new statute stipulates that [t]he defendant has the burden of proving the defense of insanity by clear and convincing evidence" (see 18 U.S.C. § 17[b]). A "not guilty by reason of insanity" verdict can authorize federal civil commitment proceedings under 18 U.S.C. sec. 4242(b).

Most criminal prosecutions occur in state courts where courts generally follow either the M'Naghten (right from wrong) test or the ALI (substantial capacity) test. In some states insanity is an affirmative defense. For example, Tenn. Code Ann. sec. 39–11–501, enacted in 1997, provides that insanity is an affirmative defense and the defendant bears the burden of establishing the defense by clear and convincing evidence (see *State v. Flake*, 2002). In other states, Florida for example, once a defendant introduces evidence that raises a reasonable doubt relative to the defendant's sanity the presumption of sanity disappears and the State must prove beyond a reasonable doubt that the defendant was sane at the time of commission of the crime (see *Yohn v. State*, 1985).

Where the evidence is not sufficient to warrant a finding of insanity, some states have recently resorted to verdicts of "guilty but mentally ill" to require that a defendant be treated in addition to being incarcerated. First adopted in Michigan in 1975, Mich. Comp. Laws sec. 768.36, several states have followed this approach.

A few state legislatures have simply abolished the defense of insanity. Idaho, for example, now provides that a "mental condition shall not be a defense to any charge of criminal conduct" (see Idaho Code § 18–207[1]). The statute allows admission of expert evidence on any issue regarding a defendant's state of mind that is an element of the crime, but a defendant's mental condition cannot provide a complete defense to a crime where the defendant has the ability to form intent and to control his or her actions (see *State v. Card*, 1991).

See also Common-Law Background; Death Penalty and Mental Incompetence

Bibliography

Bonnie, Richard C., Peter W. Low, and John C. Jeffries, Jr. 2000. *The Trial of John W. Hinckley, Jr.: A Case Study in the Insanity Defense.* New York: Foundation.

Robison, Daniel N. 1998. *Wild Beasts and Idle Humours: The Insanity Defense from Antiquity to the Present.* Cambridge, MA: Harvard University Press.

Hon. John M. Scheb

INTEREST GROUPS

Interest groups (or "organized interests" as I will call them in this précis) are ubiquitous in the United States. Recent estimates indicate that in Washington, D.C., alone there are well over 15,000 active organized interests. Outside of Washington, in states and cities across the United States, there may be as many as 200,000 more (Hrebenar 1997, 17). Organized interests are active across a wide range of issues. Not surprisingly, they are (and have always been) active in the politics surrounding civil rights and liberties. In this entry, I will briefly examine the role of organized interests in the politics of civil rights and liberties in the United States. I will start with a brief survey of the types of organized interests active on civil rights and liberties issues. From here, I will outline how organized interests seek to influence government decisions concerning civil rights and liberties. Finally, I will conclude with three brief case studies that point up a number of fundamental facts about organized interests and civil rights and liberties.

Organized Interests: What They Are and Why They Lobby Government

An organized interest is defined as *an organization that lobbies government* (Nownes 2001, 8). Here, I use the term *lobby* to denote *any attempt to influence what government does.* Among people who study them, the term *organized interest* has largely taken the place of the term *interest group*. Traditionally, the term *interest group* has been used to describe a membership organization with political goals, and thus conjures up thoughts of groups like the National Rifle Association (NRA), the National Organization for Women (NOW), and the Sierra Club. While groups like these are indeed active in American politics, they represent only a fraction of the lobbying organizations in the United States. Thus, the term *organized interest* has been adopted to account for the myriad lobbying organizations active in the United States today.

The universe of organized interests comprises several types of organizations. Among the most numerous are *citizen groups* (membership groups open to any citizen, such as the NRA or NOW), *corporations, political action committees* (organizations that exist to collect and donate money to candidates' campaigns), *professional associations* (groups of professionals, such as the American Medical Association and American Bar Association), and *trade associations* (organized groups of businesses, such as the National Association of Manufacturers and the U.S. Chamber of Commerce). Other less plentiful but no less active types of organized interests include *coalitions* (temporary groupings of individuals and organized interests that form around specific issues), *foreign countries, governmental entities* (such as counties, cities, states, and individual government agencies), *labor unions, public interest law firms,* and *think tanks* (research organizations that produce policy papers and manuscripts).

Not all organizations lobby government, and thus not all organizations are organized interests. Many organizations including fan clubs, book clubs, hobby clubs, fraternities and sororities, and some corporations choose not to lobby government. This begs the following question: Why do so many organizations choose to lobby? The answer is simple. Organizations lobby government because what the government does affects them. Many corporations, for example, lobby the federal government because its tax policies profoundly affect their financial status. Similarly, citizen groups such as the American Association of Retired Persons (AARP), the NRA, and the Sierra Club lobby the federal government as well as local or state governments because what the government does affects the well-being of the elderly, gun enthusiasts, and the environment, respectively.

It is safe to say that at some point organizations within each of these categories of organized interests have been active in the politics of civil rights and liberties in the United States. Nonetheless, some types of organized interests are more active on civil rights and liberties issues than others. Specifically, citizen groups are often at the forefront of civil rights and liberties advocacy. Among the most influential and well-known citizen groups active in these areas are the American Civil Liberties Union (ACLU), the Congress of Racial Equality (CORE), the National Abortion Rights Action League (NARAL), the NRA, the National Right to Life Committee (NRTLC), the National Association for the Advancement of Colored People (NAACP), the National Gay and Lesbian Task Force, Planned Parenthood, and the Southern Christian Leadership Conference (SCLC). This is by no means an exhaustive list! There are perhaps as many as 2,500 citizen groups in Washington alone, and many of

these groups are active on civil rights and liberties issues (Nownes 2001, 29).

The high level of citizen group activity notwithstanding, other types of organized interests are also quite active on civil rights and liberties issues. For example, think tanks such as the Heritage Foundation, the Cato Institute, and the American Enterprise Institute count among their issue interests affirmative action, civil rights, privacy rights, property rights, and homosexual rights. Similarly, a number of political action committees, including EMILY's List (a PAC that provides money to prochoice female Democratic candidates for public office) are active in elections. In addition, it is not unusual for foreign countries (Mexico, for example), governmental entities (such as cities and towns), labor unions, professional associations, and trade associations to actively lobby on civil rights and liberties issues.

Lobbying: How Organized Interests Seek to Influence Policy

Organized interests lobby in an attempt to influence what the government does. For many people, the term *lobbying* conjures up images of shady backroom deals. The real world of lobbying is far more mundane than this image. The most common lobbying techniques used by organized interests are helping to draft legislation, meeting face-to-face with legislators or their aides, and testifying at legislative hearings. Other less common but still widespread techniques are attempting to influence appointment to public office (e.g., the Supreme Court), campaigning for candidates for public office, contributing money to political campaigns, engaging in informal contacts (e.g., "wining and dining") with government officials, filing lawsuits, helping to draft regulations, meeting with bureaucrats, meeting with chief executives or their aides, mounting grassroots campaigns, running advertisements in media, serving on advisory boards and commissions, and submitting amicus curiae briefs (Nownes and Freeman 1998, 92; Schlozman and Tierney 1983, 357).

Studies of lobbying consistently show that neither organized interests nor lobbyists tend to specialize in one or a few lobbying techniques (Baumgartner and Leech 1998, 154). In other words, many organized interests seek to influence policy across the branches of government. The ACLU, for example, lobbies Congress, executive branch officials, and the federal judiciary (through filing lawsuits and submitting amicus briefs). Similarly, many organized interests are active across *levels* of government. Many corporations, for example, dispatch lobbyists to state capitals and cities as well as Washington, D.C. (Rosenthal 2001). In the same vein, several of the largest and most powerful citizen groups in the United States including the AARP, the NRA, and the Sierra Club have state or local chapters or affiliates that actively lobby subnational governments.

In sum, the United States is home to tens of thousands of organized interests—organizations that seek to influence what the government does. Organized interests are active at all levels of American government, and the typical organized interest lobbies policy makers across the branches of government. With so many organized interests attempting to influence government, it is no surprise that organized interests and their lobbyists are active in the politics surrounding civil rights and liberties. Citizen groups are particularly active, but other types of organized interests are active as well.

Three Case Studies: Organized Interests and Civil Rights and Liberties

I have already listed several organized interests that are active participants in the politics of civil liberties and civil rights. There are literally tens of thousands more. Among the civil rights and liberties issues that continue to attract considerable attention from organized interests are abortion rights, affirmative action, environmental racism, free speech rights, gay and lesbian rights, religious freedoms, and women's rights. Among the more specific civil rights and liberties issues that have motivated substantial organized interest activity in recent years are flag burning, gay marriage, the PATRIOT Act, the posting of the Ten Commandments in public buildings, racial profiling, sodomy

laws, and university admissions quotas. Unfortunately, there are so many organized interests engaging in so much activity *vis-à-vis* policies related to civil rights and liberties, that a full rendering of such activity is impossible. Instead of a full rendering, I will conclude with three brief case studies designed to point out the role of organized interests in the politics of civil liberties and civil rights.

The NRA: Citizen Group Behemoth

The NRA was founded in the aftermath of the Civil War to improve the marksmanship of American soldiers. For approximately the first 100 years of its existence, the NRA was a reasonably quiescent organization focused on serving its members (Spitzer 1995, 99–115). In the 20 years or so after Congress acted to restrict gun ownership in the wake of the Martin Luther King Jr. and Robert Kennedy assassinations, the NRA grew into a political force. It designed new benefits to attract members and began to forge its now well-known uncompromising position against virtually all policies aimed at restricting gun ownership (Patterson and Singer 2002, 55–78). Today, the NRA's membership stands at over four million, and the group continues to be a force in national and state politics. More important for our purposes, the case of the NRA shows how organized interests exert influence over policies concerning civil liberties.

The NRA uses a wide variety of lobbying techniques. First, it has a stable of lobbyists who regularly attempt to influence judicial and executive branch appointments, engage in informal contacts with government officials, help to draft legislation and regulations, meet with bureaucrats, meet with chief executives or their aides, and testify at legislative hearings. In the past couple of years, for example, in the aftermath of city government initiated lawsuits against gun manufacturers and distributors, NRA lobbyists have lobbied state legislatures across the country to pass laws that would restrict the ability of cities and individuals to sue gun manufacturers and distributors for negligence.

Second, the NRA has a large PAC that contributes money to pro-gun candidates for office. Between

1978 and 2000, the NRA's Political Victory Fund donated over $25 million to candidates for federal office, and the group and its affiliates provided millions more to candidates for subnational offices (Patterson and Singer 2002, 68). Fourth and perhaps most important, the NRA uses a wide range of grassroots lobbying techniques. For example, virtually every time a gun control bill (or conversely, a bill to loosen controls on gun ownership or possession) is introduced in Congress or a state legislature, the NRA contacts its members and urges them to write letters, send electronic mail, or telephone policy makers to register their opposition to (or support of) the proposed policy. For example, in 1993, President Clinton began to push for legislation that required a five-day waiting period for the purchase of handguns. Soon, the NRA sprang into action. As Congress considered the bill, the NRA sent several million letters to its members urging them to contact members of Congress and express their opposition to the Brady Bill. Eventually, the Brady Bill passed, primarily because it had overwhelming public support. Nonetheless, the NRA's campaign was by all accounts nearly successful, as NRA members responded to the group's call for action and flooded Congress with communiqués (Stone 1993, 1334–38). In recent years the NRA has also used other grassroots techniques including advertising on radio and television and running infomercials (featuring Charlton Heston) on television.

Not surprisingly, the NRA has a number of enemies. In fact, the group itself recently received a torrent of media attention over an "enemies list" on its website (www.nraila.org). The NRA's primary nemeses are anti-gun groups such as the Brady Campaign (formerly Handgun Control Inc.) and the Coalition to Stop Gun Violence, two citizen groups that use many of the same lobbying techniques as the NRA. However, the NRA also counts among its opponents professional associations including the American Medical Association and the American Academy of Family Physicians, both of which in 1996 actively opposed the NRA-supported dismantling of a Centers for Disease Control (CDC) unit that conducted research on gun violence. In addition, the NRA has battled labor unions including

the AFL-CIO, the International Garment Workers Union, and the National Education Association, as well as individual cities including Chicago, New Orleans, and Miami, which filed lawsuits against gun manufacturers. In short, the NRA almost always faces strong opposition. And though it occasionally loses political battles (in 2004, for example, Congress failed to pass a federal law that would ban lawsuits against the gun industry), it continues to wield considerable influence in American politics.

How much influence has the NRA had on gun control policy in this country? It is impossible to answer this question definitively. Each specific policy outcome is a function of several factors (e.g., public opinion, the opinions of public officials), and determining the true impact of any single factor (such as organized interest lobbying) is virtually impossible. Nonetheless, there is a good deal of evidence that the NRA has played a large role in shaping gun control policy in the United States. For example, the NRA spent millions of dollars in support of George W. Bush's 2000 presidential election campaign, and the Bush administration has been consistently hostile to the kinds of gun controls that the Clinton administration favored. Similarly, the NRA's Political Victory Fund spent millions on Senate and House races across the country in the 1990s, and it is no coincidence that the Republican Party took control of Congress during this period (Patterson and Singer 2002, 68–72). Finally, every year in this country, legislators in Washington, D.C., and elsewhere propose tighter restrictions on gun ownership and sales, and yet most of these measures fail. In short, though it is impossible to prove, it is safe to conclude that the NRA, through its wide variety of lobbying activities, its deep pockets, and its passionate membership, has profoundly shaped Second Amendment interpretation and how guns are regulated.

Brown vs. Board of Education: An Interest Group Success Story

In the aftermath of the Civil War, Congress and the states added the Fourteenth Amendment to the Constitution, which ostensibly guaranteed "equal protection of the laws" to African Americans. The constitutional guarantee of equal protection notwithstanding, from 1868 (when the amendment was added) until at least the mid-1960s, many state and local governments adopted discriminatory "separate but equal" policies designed to keep blacks from achieving true equality. By now the story is a familiar one: black Americans were required to attend separate schools and colleges, could not marry whites, and were subject to all sorts of discrimination in voting, hiring, housing, and public facilities (Kluger 1975). From its inception in 1909, the NAACP fought for equal rights and against separate but equal policies. Throughout the 1910s, 1920s, and 1930s, for example, the NAACP lobbied policy makers directly, and filed lawsuits on behalf of individuals who felt they had been discriminated against. The NAACP hit pay dirt in the early 1950s when it filed a series of class action lawsuits against school systems that discriminated against black students.

In one of the most famous cases in all of American law, the NAACP sponsored litigation challenging the "separate but equal" doctrine. Specifically, the NAACP assisted a Topeka, Kansas girl named Linda Brown in her federal lawsuit against the Topeka Board of Education. Brown lived less than a block from a white public school but was forced to attend a black school much farther away. The NAACP's lawsuit, spearheaded by future Supreme Court justice Thurgood Marshall, sought an injunction against the Board of Education of Topeka, Kansas, that would prohibit it from segregating public schools. The NAACP's lawsuit forcefully argued but that requiring Ms. Brown to attend a segregated school far from her home was an unconstitutional violation of Brown's Fourteenth Amendment right to equal protection of the law. Not only did being forced to attend a segregated school inconvenience Ms. Brown and other black students, the NAACP argued, but it also sent a message to black children that they were second-class citizens who did not deserve the same treatment as white children. The NAACP was assisting plaintiffs (by providing legal help) in a number of other cases involving school segregation during the same period and the group's

ultimate goal was to have the segregation of public schools declared unconstitutional.

The *Brown* case reached the Supreme Court in 1951, and the Court reached a decision in 1954. The Court's decision declared segregated public schools unconstitutional and thus sounded the death knell for the entire separate but equal system—a system that had been in existence since the immediate aftermath of the Civil War. The Supreme Court's decision in *Brown* was one of the most far-reaching and important in American history. It also provided a textbook example of how organized interests could use the courts to influence public policy. Turning to the courts is not always the best option for organized interests. The main reason that the NAACP chose to "lobby the courts" is that it had consistently received lukewarm receptions from elected policy makers in the legislative and executive branches (Lowery and Brasher 2004, 243). Nonetheless, on the heels of the NAACP's landmark success in court, a plethora of other organizations have turned to the courts to effect policy change (Lowery and Brasher 2004, 234–236).

Abortion Since *Roe v. Wade*

At least since the landmark Supreme Court decision *Roe v. Wade,* which effectively legalized abortion in this country, organized interests of all stripes have done battle over abortion policy in the United States. Almost immediately after the decision (which was rendered in 1973), antiabortion groups (whose term for themselves is *pro-life*) sprang into action to reverse it and lessen its impact. Among the most prominent anti-abortion groups were (and still are) the American Life League, the Christian Coalition, the National Right to Life Committee, and the U.S. Catholic Conference (Woliver 1998, 328). On the "pro-choice" side, prominent groups including the ACLU, the National Abortion and Reproductive Rights Action League (now known as NARAL Pro-Choice America), NOW, and Planned Parenthood tried just as hard (and are still trying) to protect abortion rights. As is often the case with civil rights and liberties politics, the main organized interest actors in abortion politics have consistently been citizen groups.

Pro-life groups have used a variety of techniques to mitigate the effects of the far-reaching *Roe v. Wade* decision, and have sought to overturn it as well. On the federal level, pro-life organizations have lobbied Congress and the executive branch (especially during Republican administrations) relentlessly by engaging in informal contacts with government officials, meeting with executive branch personnel, meeting with legislators and their aides, and testifying at congressional hearings. In addition, pro-life groups have contributed money to congressional and presidential candidates, filed amicus briefs in abortion cases, mounted grassroots campaigns, and run advertisements in the media (Blanchard 1994). Throughout the 1980s and 1990s, a number of grassroots citizen groups such as Operation Rescue took pro-life advocacy in a radical direction and engaged in "direct action" by mounting large public protests at abortion clinics, and in some cases illegally blocking entry to such clinics (Woliver 1998, 329). Finally, since the *Roe* decision, pro-life groups have expended considerable effort in states across the country by attempting to influence appointments to executive and judicial positions, contributing money and personnel to election campaigns, engaging in grassroots lobbying campaigns, lobbying executive branch personnel, lobbying legislators and their aides, and running advertisements in the media. In short, at both the federal and state levels of government, pro-life groups have used virtually the entire array of lobbying techniques.

What do these pro-life groups want? At the state level, pro-life groups have pushed for (and in some cases gotten) policies that restrict access to abortion such as parental consent, mandatory counseling, and waiting periods. At the state and federal levels pro-life groups have consistently pushed for the appointment of pro-life judges to judgeships. Finally, pro-life groups have sought to make abortion less accessible and more unpleasant. By this, I mean that through protest tactics (it is not unusual for abortion protesters to wield large placards displaying gruesome photographs of aborted fetuses) and media campaigns, pro-life groups have tried hard to make women who would have abortions think twice and consider other options.

Of course, pro-life groups do not operate unopposed. As I mention above, an array of pro-choice groups including the ACLU, NARAL Pro-Choice America, NOW, and Planned Parenthood, oppose pro-life groups at every turn. These groups (and other pro-choice citizen groups like them) utilize the same array of tactics as their pro-life counterparts, and like these groups, also operate at the state level as well as the federal level. Just like pro-life groups, pro-choice groups utilize conventional lobbying strategies such as attempting to influence appointment to judicial and executive branch positions, contributing money and help to electoral campaigns, and meeting with policy makers, as well as less traditional tactics such as conducting grassroots e-mail, telephone, and regular mail campaigns, and engaging in public protests.

Abortion politics is a battleground for organized interests. In fact, few issues attract as much and as frenzied organized interest attention as abortion. There is no question that organized interests have profoundly affected abortion policy in this country. Who's "winning" the "abortion wars"? There is no straightforward answer to this question. On the one hand, a number of legislative and judicial decisions since *Roe* have narrowed the scope of abortion rights in this country. In *Webster vs. Reproductive Health Services* (1989), for example, the Supreme Court upheld parts of a statute that restricted access to abortion. In addition, pro-life groups have successfully lobbied for a federal ban on late-term abortions, as well as a ban on federal funding for abortion. On the other hand, *Roe v. Wade* is still the law of the land, and abortion remains legal in the United States.

Summary: The Cases and What They Tell Us

It would be impossible in such a limited space fully to describe the role of organized interests in the politics of civil rights and liberties. Nonetheless, the three brief case studies I present above allow us to reach several conclusions about organized interests and their impact on policies concerning civil rights and liberties in the United States. Specifically, the case studies point up the following essential facts:

1. *Organized interests are active on a wide range of issues related to civil rights and liberties.* Organized interests are present virtually everywhere that policies concerning civil rights or liberties are made.
2. *Organized interests that lobby on policies related to civil rights and liberties are active at the state and local levels of government as well as the federal level.* While the media tend to focus on Washington politics to the exclusion of state and local politics, organized interests realize that policies concerning civil rights and liberties are made at the state and local levels of government as well as the federal level. Thus, they are active across levels of government.
3. *Several types of organized interests are active on civil rights and liberties issues, but citizen groups tend to be the most active.* While a number of issues related to civil rights and liberties attract the attention of professional groups, think tanks, labor unions, and other types of noncitizen groups, citizen groups tend to be the primary players in the politics of controversial civil rights and liberties issues.
4. *Organized interests that attempt to affect civil rights and liberties policies use a large variety of techniques.* The groups that attempt to influence government policies on abortion, civil rights, gun control, and other civil liberties and rights issues use traditional lobbying techniques such as meeting with public officials face-to-face, but also rely upon less traditional techniques such as engaging in grassroots campaigns, filing lawsuits or amicus briefs, and protesting.
5. *Organized interests historically have exerted and continue to exert profound influence over civil rights and liberties policies in the United States.* It would be difficult to overestimate how influential organized interests have been in shaping civil rights and liberties policies in the United States. Some of the biggest

and most important policy decisions in American history—including the Supreme Court's *Roe v. Wade* and *Brown v. Board of Education* decisions—have featured organized interests prominently.

Conclusion

Organized interests are everywhere in America—they and their lobbyists operate in Washington, D.C., as well as in state capitals and city halls across the country. As numerous entries in these volumes attest, the nature of civil liberties and civil rights in America is ever-changing. Laws and regulations are adopted and abandoned, court cases are decided, and civil rights and liberties are clarified, narrowed, or broadened. The primary lesson of this entry is this: when policy makers—be they legislative, executive, or judicial branch officials—make policies concerning civil rights and liberties, organized interests are there and they are often influential.

See also Abortion, Right to; Affirmative Action; American Civil Liberties Union; Arms, Right to Keep and Bear; *Brown v. Board of Education* (1954); Civil Rights Movement; Congress of Racial Equality (CORE); Conservatism; Federalism and Civil Rights and Liberties; Feminist Movement; Flag Burning; Gay Rights Movement; Gender-Based Discrimination; Jim Crow Laws; Liberalism; Marshall, Thurgood; National Abortion Rights Action League; National Association for the Advancement of Colored People; National Organization for Women; National Right to Life Committee (NRLC); Operation Rescue; People for the American Way; Planned Parenthood; Racial Profiling; *Roe v. Wade;* Same-Sex Marriage and Civil Unions; Southern Christian Leadership Conference; Ten Commandments, Public Display of the; USA PATRIOT Act (2001)

Bibliography

Baumgartner, Frank R., and Beth L. Leech. 1998. *Basic Interests: The Importance of Groups in Politics and Political Science.* Princeton, NJ: Princeton University Press.

Blanchard, Dallas A. 1994. *The Anti-Abortion Movement and the Rise of the Religious Right.* New York: Twayne.

Hrebenar, Ronald J. 1997. *Interest Group Politics in America.* 3rd ed. Armonk, NY: M.E. Sharpe.

Kluger, Richard. 1975. *Simple Justice: The History of Brown v. Board of Education and Black America's Struggle for Equality.* New York: Vintage Books.

Lowery, David, and Holly Brasher. 2004. *Organized Interests and American Government.* New York: McGraw-Hill.

Nownes, Anthony J. 2001. *Pressure and Power: Organized Interests in American Politics.* Boston: Houghton Mifflin.

Nownes, Anthony J., and Patricia K. Freeman. 1998. "Interest Group Activity in the States." *Journal of Politics* 60: 92.

Patterson, Kelly D., and Matthew M. Singer. 2002. "The National Rifle Association in the Face of the Clinton Challenge." In *Interest Group Politics,* eds. Allan J. Cigler and Burdett A. Loomis. 6th ed. Washington, DC: CQ Press (55).

Rosenthal, Alan. 2001. *The Third House: Lobbyists and Lobbying in the States.* 2nd ed. Washington, DC: CQ Press.

Schlozman, Kay Lehman, and John T. Tierney. 1983. "More of the Same: Washington Pressure Group Activity in a Decade of Change." *Journal of Politics* 45: 357.

Spitzer, Robert. 1995. *The Politics of Gun Control.* Chatham, NJ: Chatham House.

Stone, Peter H. 1993. "Under the Gun." *The National Journal* (5 June): 1334–38.

Woliver, Laura. 1998. "Abortion Interests: From the Usual Suspects to Expanded Coalitions." In *Interest Group Politics,* eds. Allan J. Cigler and Burdett A. Loomis (327). 5th ed. Washington, DC: CQ Press.

Anthony J. Nownes

INTERMEDIATE SCRUTINY. *See* Levels of Judicial Scrutiny

INTERNAL REVENUE SERVICE (IRS)

Located within the U.S. Department of the Treasury, the Internal Revenue Service (IRS) is responsible for the implementation and enforcement of federal tax laws other than those relating to alcohol, tobacco, and firearms. Prior to 1953, the agency

was known as the Bureau of Internal Revenue. The bureau was created with the passage of the Internal Revenue Act of 1862, a response to the growing cost of the Civil War. The previously limited federal government had been stretched beyond its original, available sources of revenue.

A decade later, Congress repealed the act, although debate over its constitutionality continued until 1881, when the Supreme Court decided in *Springer v. United States* that the income tax was an indirect tax not subject to the apportionment requirement of the Constitution. Until the ratification of the Sixteenth Amendment in 1913, the United States Constitution did not explicitly authorize Congress to enact an income tax. Article I, Section 9 of the U.S. Constitution requires that "direct taxes shall be apportioned among the several States ... according to their respective numbers." Many commentators believed that this language precluded the Congress from establishing an income tax unless the tax burden is apportioned among the states according to population.

In 1894 Congress again faced a revenue shortfall and established several new taxes and tariffs, one of which imposed a 2 percent tax on incomes of more than $4,000 a year. The Supreme Court, however, had grown more conservative since the *Springer* decision, and declared the tax unconstitutional in *Pollock v. Farmer's Loan and Trust Company* (1895). Splitting five-to-four, the Court held that the new income tax was a direct tax insofar as it was based on incomes derived from land and, as such, had to be apportioned among the states. Since the law did not provide for apportionment, it was deemed unconstitutional.

In the early twentieth century, progressive reformers favored the enactment of an income tax in order to fund the expansion of federal regulatory and service functions. In 1913, the states ratified the Sixteenth Amendment, which provides that "Congress shall have power to lay and collect taxes on incomes, from whatever source derived, without apportionment among the several States, and without regard to any census or enumeration." That same year, Congress imposed a one percent tax on incomes over $3,000 and a 6 percent surtax on incomes of more than $500,000. During World War I, federal income tax rates increased dramatically in order to fund America's role in the conflict. The rates were lowered during the Roaring Twenties, but rose again during the Great Depression. During the Second World War, Congress enacted legislation allowing the IRS to implement payroll withholding and quarterly tax payments.

The modern Internal Revenue Service (IRS) is responsible for administering and enforcing all internal (domestic) revenue laws except those relating to alcohol, tobacco, firearms, and explosives. The major sources of revenue, in descending order, are: the individual income tax, employment taxes (for example, Social Security and Medicare), the corporate income tax, excise taxes, and estate and gift taxes. In Fiscal Year 2004 the IRS collected over $1.7 trillion in net revenues (gross revenue less deductions). The more than 130 million individual income tax returns alone netted in excess of $762 billion. The agency has approximately 100,000 employees and a budget of $10 billion.

In 1997 Congress held hearings that investigated alleged abuses by the IRS, at which an array of witnesses related often grizzly stories of mistreatment from the agency. The hearings resulted in the Internal Revenue Service Restructuring and Reform Act of 1998, a rather historic overhaul of the IRS. The IRS's new mission statement was to: "Provide America's taxpayers top-quality service by helping them understand and meet their tax responsibilities and by applying the tax law with integrity and fairness to all." The legislation granted new rights and protections to taxpayers when dealing with the agency, revised the schedule of penalties and interest charges, and opened up the IRS to legal actions by taxpayers alleging disregard of the tax code. The law transformed the administrative structure of the agency, and established an oversight board on which six of the nine members would be drawn from the private sector. These changes and others mandate that the IRS work to simplify the tax code and in so doing help taxpayers meet their obligations. The ultimate goal of these reforms is to achieve fuller and more user-friendly compliance with the law.

Bibliography

Chommie, John C. 1970. *The Internal Revenue Service.* Belmont, CA: Thomson.

Rossotti, Charles O. 2005. *Many Unhappy Returns: One Man's Quest to Turn Around the Most Unpopular Organization in America.* Cambridge, MA: Harvard Business School Press.

Yancey, Richard. 2004. *Confessions of a Tax Collector: One Man's Tour of Duty Inside the IRS.* New York: Harper Collins.

Gerard S. Gryski

INTERNATIONAL LAW

Human rights law focuses on the conduct of states toward their own people, unlike the rest of international law, which is concerned with the behavior of states toward other states. States endorsed the radical notion of human rights in horrified response to the atrocities of World War II. For the first time in history, states conceded that their own people had rights beyond the rights established under their own domestic law, rights that even the states themselves could not legally abrogate.

The United States was eager to declare its support for international human rights after the war, and quickly recognized the need for other states to guarantee them, but it was reluctant to expose itself to international scrutiny and criticism. In 1948, the United States signed the Universal Declaration of Human Rights, which, like the United States Declaration of Independence, was aspirational. Thus, the United States was able to express its rhetorical support for human rights without assuming any legally binding obligations.

It was not until the 1960s, and the emergence of former colonies as newly independent states, that the Universal Declaration was divided into two legally binding instruments: the International Covenant on Civil and Political Rights (the Civil Covenant) and the International Covenant on Economic, Social, and Cultural Rights (the Economic Covenant). The Civil Covenant addresses negative rights, such as freedoms of religion and expression and freedom from arbitrary arrest or detention. These rights are familiar to Americans because they are guaranteed by the Bill of Rights of the United States Constitution.

The rights set out in the Economic Covenant, in contrast, have historically been marginalized in this country. The Economic Covenant addresses positive rights. By ratifying the Economic Covenant, a government "commits itself to its best efforts to secure for its citizens the basic standards of material existence." Although some trace the Economic Covenant to President Roosevelt's "freedom from want," the United States is the only major industrialized democracy that has not ratified it. Together with the Universal Declaration, the two covenants comprise the International Bill of Rights, globally recognized as the definitive law of international human rights.

The Civil Rights Movement

The United States did not ratify the Civil Covenant until the end of the Cold War in 1992. Human rights norms, especially the norm against discrimination set out in both covenants as well as the Universal Declaration, nevertheless had a profound impact on the American Civil Rights Movement. The Soviets broadcasted over 1,400 photographs of the American civil rights struggle to an appalled world. The photos had a profound impact, especially on people in underdeveloped countries. As Mary Dudziak (1988: 62–63) has explained:

[T]he international focus on U.S. racial problems meant that the image of American democracy was tarnished.... U.S. government officials realized that their ability to sell democracy to the Third World was seriously hampered by continuing racial injustice at home. Accordingly, efforts to promote civil rights in the United States were consistent with, and important to, the more central U.S. mission of fighting world communism.

As the Justice Department made clear in the amicus brief it submitted in the groundbreaking case of *Brown v. Board of Education,* desegregation had become a Cold War imperative.

Since the End of the Cold War

In addition to ratifying the Civil Covenant, the United States has ratified the International Convention on the Elimination of All Forms of Racial Discrimination ("CERD"), the Convention Against Torture, the Convention on the Prevention and Punishment of Genocide, and the two Optional Protocols to the Convention on the Rights of the Child (CRC). But the United States has taken the position that human rights treaties are not self-executing; that is, that such treaties require implementing legislation before they may be relied upon in U.S. courts. Such legislation has only been enacted in connection with the Torture Convention and the Genocide Convention, so the other conventions cannot be relied upon as binding law in U.S. courts. In addition, the United States has taken reservations, or exceptions, to many provisions of the treaties it has ratified, further limiting their domestic application.

Despite these restrictions, the norms of international human rights law shape U.S. jurisprudence at the highest levels. In *Grutter v. Bollinger* (2003), for example, the U.S. Supreme Court cited both the CERD and the Convention on the Elimination of All Forms of Discrimination Against Women (CEDAW) to show international support for the Court's understanding of affirmative action as a temporary measure to level the playing field. In *Lawrence v. Texas* (2003), similarly, the Court cited the European Court of Human Rights to show that its rejection of *Bowers v. Hardwick* (1986), upholding a state's criminalization of homosexual conduct, reflected "values we share with a wider civilization."

In *Roper v. Simmons* (2005), the Court finally joined the rest of the world in rejecting the juvenile death penalty. While expressly noting that "The overwhelming weight of international opinion against the juvenile death penalty is not controlling here," Justice Kennedy stressed that such opinion

provides respected and significant confirmation for the Court's determination that the penalty is disproportionate punishment for offenders under 18. The United States is the only country in the world that continues to give official sanction to the juvenile penalty. It does not lessen fidelity to the Constitution or pride in its origins to acknowledge that the express affirmation of certain fundamental rights by other nations and peoples underscores the centrality of those same rights within our own heritage of freedom.

Other U.S. courts, on the federal as well as the state level, are increasingly receptive to claims grounded in or supported by human rights law. The Torture Convention, for example, along with its implementing legislation, has been relied upon in immigration decisions by the federal courts. In *Ogbudimkpa v. Ashcroft* (2003), the Third Circuit held that an alien could bring a Torture Convention claim on habeas corpus. In *Zubeda v. Ashcroft* (2003), the same court held that rape could amount to "torture" under the Convention.

In addition, holocaust restitution cases, the slavery reparation cases inspired by them, and claims by foreign torture victims under the Alien Tort Claims Act show the ongoing internationalization of civil rights and liberties in the United States. Developments subsequent to September 11, 2001, including challenges to the interrogation and detention of War on Terrorism detainees, while not explicitly relying on international law, demonstrate an encouraging respect for its norms, particularly respect for the rule of law. In *Rasul v. Bush* (2004), the Court held that U.S. District Courts have jurisdiction to hear challenges to legality of detention of foreign nationals captured abroad and incarcerated at Guantanamo Bay, Cuba. In *Hamdi v. Rumsfeld* (2004), in a decision delivered by Justice O'Connor, the Court held that a citizen detained by the United States as an "enemy combatant" had to be given a meaningful opportunity to challenge that detention before a neutral decision maker, even if the detention was authorized by Congress.

There is evidence of a countertrend, however. The Supreme Court decision in *Sosa v. Alvarez-Machain* (2004), for example, reversed the Ninth U.S. Circuit's decision that the extraterritorial arrest and detention of Alvarez gave rise to a cause of action under the ATCA, holding that the act enabled federal courts to hear claims in "a very limited category" of cases. In May 2005, the Court dismissed its own writ of certiorari in the *Medellin*

case. This involved the effect of the International Court of Justice's decision in *Avena,* holding that U.S. courts must reconsider cases where foreign criminal defendants had not been advised of their rights under the Consular Convention. The failure to comply with the convention in several cases in which foreign defendants received the death penalty outraged U.S. treaty partners.

As of this writing, the Court is at a crossroads. While international human rights norms are increasingly relied upon in domestic civil rights and civil liberties litigation, there is at the same time a distinct backlash, a resistance to foreign influence, buttressed by growing concerns about national security.

See also Affirmative Action; *Brown v. Board of Education* (1954; 1955); Civil Rights Movement; Death Penalty and the Supreme Court; Death Penalty for Juveniles; Declaration of Independence (1776); Habeas Corpus; Human Rights Watch (HRW); Kennedy, Anthony; *Lawrence v. Texas* (2003); Natural Law and Natural Rights; O'Connor, Sandra Day; Reparations for Slavery; Roosevelt, Eleanor; Roosevelt, Franklin D.; Terrorism, War on; United States Constitution; Universal Declaration of Human Rights (UDHR)

Bibliography

Dudziak, Mary. 1988. "Desegregation as a Cold War Imperative." *Stanford Law Review* 41: 61.

Barbara Stark

INTERNET, ACCESS TO

In 2001, more than half-a-dozen separate bills containing provisions for increasing the Internet access rates of schoolchildren were introduced in the U.S. House of Representatives. These bills, notably including the No Child Left Behind Act, were based on the belief that the Internet is necessary for full participation in contemporary American society. Essentially, Congress recognized the importance of Internet access for all Americans during 2001 and declared that Internet literacy was becoming a necessary skill. Since then, bills have also been introduced in Congress to alleviate taxes on Internet access, to provide increased access for the poor, and to undermine attempts by other nations to censor the Internet. There is even litigation under way seeking to declare Internet Service Providers and commercial Web sites "public accommodations" for the purpose of enhancing online access for the visually impaired under the Americans with Disabilities Act.

While Internet skills and access were becoming crucial, Internet crime was also growing at a tremendous pace. Currently experts estimate that up to 90 percent of all e-mail is unsolicited commercial e-mail (Spam), a substantial proportion of which involves various sorts of fraudulent schemes. Intentional dissemination of computer viruses, hacking, blackmail, harassment and intimidation, and "phishing" (fraudulently obtaining private information) have all become regular topics in current news reports about the Internet.

In recent years, bills have been introduced into Congress to reverse this trend. As a result, the loss of Internet privileges has become a realistic possibility. Currently, the privilege of accessing the Internet is in a state of limbo. It is neither a guaranteed right nor purely a privilege. Court cases rather than legislation at this time define the scope of the right of Internet access. In most instances, Internet access is curtailed as a condition of probation or supervised release from prison.

Sex offenses involving children are considered grounds for suspension or curtailment of Internet access rights (see *United States v. Zinn*, 2003; *United States v. Paul*, 2001; *United States v. Walser*, 2001). These restrictions are considered appropriate because the Internet is the distribution method of choice for many child pornographers and because child molesters often use the Internet to "troll" for victims. But Internet restrictions have been imposed for a range of offenses and are not limited to pedophilia cases. Defendants convicted of hacking, phishing, online harassment, and disseminating viruses have had their access to the Internet curtailed by courts as conditions of probation or supervised release.

In *United States v. Crandon* (1999), the U.S. Court of Appeals for the Third Circuit upheld a total ban on Internet access in certain circumstances, and in *United States v. Sines* (2002) the Seventh Circuit also approved of this measure. However, these courts distinguished between crimes dependent on the Internet and crimes committed independent of the Internet. Penalties relating to restrictions on Internet access are appropriate only for crimes involving the Internet.

In *United States v. Scott* (2003), the Seventh Circuit held that total Internet access bans can only be applied when there is no "less severe" alternative and only when the defendant has had the opportunity to propose alternatives. This ruling attempts to reconcile the criminal's need to use the Internet in everyday life and the public's special vulnerability to criminal conduct perpetrated through this medium.

These standards for imposing complete Internet access bans have been reaffirmed by the Third U.S. Circuit Court of Appeals (*United States v. Freeman*, 2003). The Ninth U.S. Circuit Court of Appeals has held that restricted access to the Internet can be included in release terms (*United States v. Mitnick*, 1998), while the Eighth Circuit has upheld restrictions on Internet access by offenders (*United States v. Ristine*, 2003).

The Internet has proved to be a useful tool, for good and for ill, to prisoners serving time. Death row inmates have been able to post their writings on the Internet using friends and relatives as intermediaries. Inmates with access through a prison library can use courts' information systems and online legal services to research their cases and prepare lawsuits against prison administrators.

The exact form of access to the Internet as a right has not been settled. There are some limitations, both legislative and judicial in nature. But legislatures and the judiciary have both acted to broaden Internet rights. The right to use the Internet is a new right, and lawmakers in all jurisdictions will need more time to settle the questions it raises.

See also First Amendment; Internet, Free Speech on; Prisoners' Rights; Probation and Parole; Public Accommodation, Places of; Speech, Freedom of

Bibliography

Brinson, J. Diane, and Mark F. Radcliffe. 2000. *Internet Law and Business Handbook: A Practical Overview.* Chicago: Independent Publishers Group.

Ferraro, Monique, and Eoghan Casey. 2004. *Investigating Child Exploitation and Pornography: The Internet, Law and Forensic Science.* Burlington, MA: Academic Press.

Hiller, Janine, and Ronnie Cohen. 2002. *Internet Law and Policy.* Upper Saddle River, NJ: Prentice Hall.

David B. Conklin

INTERNET, FREE SPEECH ON

The Internet has presented new challenges to the Supreme Court in deciding First Amendment cases. Although past decisions remain important as precedent, the Internet often produces situations that are fundamentally different and require new solutions to properly balance speech rights and valid concerns of the state. Because the Internet makes it possible to spread materials more quickly and to a wider audience than ever before, some argue that it requires special regulation.

Congress has on various occasions attempted to protect minors through laws regulating speech on the Internet. In 1996, Congress passed the Communications Decency Act (CDA) in an attempt to prevent minors from accessing inappropriate materials online. In *Reno v. ACLU* (1997), the Supreme Court struck down two provisions of this law. One prohibited the knowing transfer of any "obscene" material to a minor. The other prohibited posting any "patently offensive" materials in a location that would be available to any minor.

The Court found both provisions to be too ambiguous because they extended to material that would otherwise enjoy First Amendment protection. Also, speakers would be unclear on whether what they were saying was illegal. Additionally, the Court found that the act was not the "least restrictive means" to accomplish the goal of protecting minors.

In 1996, Congress passed the Child Pornography Prevention Act (CPPA), which criminalized virtual child pornography, that is, "sexually explicit depictions that appear to be minors [or that] 'convey the impression' that they contain … depictions of minors." The statute was primarily aimed at computer-generated or altered works that were advertised as and virtually indistinguishable from actual child pornography. The CPPA banned virtual child pornography largely because of secondary effects, such as its use to "seduce … other children into sexual activity."

However, in *Free Speech Coalition v. Reno* (1999), the U.S. Court of Appeals for the Ninth Circuit found that the act was overbroad and overly vague. As with the CDA, the CPPA banned materials that would otherwise be protected by the First Amendment. For example, even if a director used actors over the age of 18, the director could be prosecuted if the film "conveyed the impression" that the actors were minors.

The Internet also provides new avenues in which individuals may be harmed by speech. In *United States v. Alkhabaz* (6th Cir. 1997), the Sixth Circuit Court of Appeals addressed the conviction of a man who posted stories on the Internet that graphically described sexual violence toward women. He was charged with the interstate transmission of a threat, based on a series of e-mails between Baker, Jake Abraham Alkabaz's alias, and another man who seemed to be planning to act out one of the stories. Baker claimed that the e-mails were merely an extension of the stories—that they too were only fantasy. Baker's conviction was overturned because the e-mails did not constitute "true threats"—that is, they were not "conveyed to effect some change or achieve some goal through intimidation."

Similarly, the quick and widespread dissemination of information can be dangerous. *Planned Parenthood v. American Coalition of Life Activists* (2002) centered on a Web site that listed personal contact information for abortion doctors. Although the Web site did not contain explicit threats, the names of murdered doctors were crossed out, as if it were a hit list. The doctors interpreted the site as a serious threat; some even wore bulletproof vests to work after learning their names were listed. Moreover, the wide audience that the Internet provided made the information available to anyone who was considering committing crimes against abortion providers. In a closely split decision, a six-judge majority of the Ninth Circuit (sitting *en banc*) ruled that the coalition could be held civilly liable because here the Web site constituted a threat. The five dissenting judges disagreed, citing the U.S. Supreme Court's landmark decision in *Brandenburg v. Ohio* (1969), and arguing that the Web site would have been unprotected only if the harm it caused was both likely and imminent.

Another current debate regarding the Internet and free speech rights concerns copyright law. The Constitution allows Congress to limit First Amendment freedom of speech by providing for limited licenses—copyrights. The purpose of this limitation is to encourage artists to create new work. Without copyrights, there would be less financial incentive to continue doing so. When Congress attempted to increase the length of copyrights by several years, the law was challenged in Court as essentially providing artists with an unlimited copyright, and unfairly limiting which materials would be placed in the public domain. (The public domain consists of all materials not covered by copyright; all individuals are free to reprint these works as they wish, whether or not they are the creator themselves.) With the Internet, plaintiffs argued, materials not readily available to the public could be made available; however, if lengthy copyrights remained in place, this process would be seriously hampered. Nevertheless, the Court determined that the Constitution did not set a maximum length for copyrights; Congress may determine the duration of copyright protection as it sees fit.

See also *Brandenburg v. Ohio;* First Amendment; Overbreadth, Doctrine of; Press, Freedom of the; *Reno v. American Civil Liberties Union* (1997); Speech, Freedom of; Vagueness Doctrine

Bibliography

Alexander, Mark C. 2001. "The First Amendment and Problems of Political Viability: The Case of Internet Pornography." *Harvard Journal of Law and Public Policy* 25 (Fall): 977–1030.

Lessig, Lawrence. 1999. *Code and Other Laws of Cyberspace.* New York: Basic Books.

Lessig, Lawrence. 2002. "Copyrights' First Amendment." *University of California Law Review* 48 (June): 1057–73.

Schachter, Madeline. 2002. *Law of Internet Speech, Second Edition.* Durham, North Carolina: Carolina Academic Press.

Ronald Kahn

INTERPOSITION, DOCTRINE OF. *See* States' Rights, Doctrine of

INTERPRETIVISM

The term *interpretivism* has two distinct usages, one in philosophy of law, the other in jurisprudence. In philosophy of law, interpretivism (also known as constructive interpretivism, constructivism, law as integrity, and the third theory) is a theory of law and adjudication that owes its foundation to Ronald Dworkin. The theory is grounded in the general claim that the law includes not only statutory norms and norms promulgated by judges but also the moral principles that show these norms in the best moral light. Interpretivism in this sense has three distinct dimensions: conceptual, normative, and empirical.

The conceptual dimension is concerned with the conditions that a norm must satisfy to be properly characterized as a law. According to Dworkin, it is part of the nature of law (or implicit in the concept of law) that its function is to provide a moral justification for the use of the state's coercive enforcement mechanisms. As he explained:

I suggest, that the most abstract and fundamental point of legal practice is to guide and constrain the power of government in the following way. Law insists that force not be used or withheld, no matter how useful that would be to ends in view, no matter how beneficial or noble these ends, except as licensed or required by individual rights and responsibilities flowing from past political decisions about when collective force is justified. (Dworkin 1986, 93)

What is essential (or necessary) to law, on this view, is that it is a system of norms that constrain and justify state coercion. In every society that is properly characterized as having a legal system, the law necessarily includes not only those norms that have been formally promulgated by legislatures and courts, but also the moral principles that best justify those norms at any given point in time.

While the conceptual claim is a claim about law as such, the normative and empirical claims are specific to judicial decision-making and are properly characterized as comprising a theory of adjudication—and not as comprising a general theory of law. According to Dworkin's normative theory of adjudication:

[J]udges *should* decide hard cases by interpreting the political structure of their community in the following special way: by trying to find the best justification they can find, in principles of political morality, for the structure as a whole, from the most profound constitutional rules and arrangements to the details of, for example, the private law of tort or contract. (Dworkin 1982, 165)

Dworkin's normative theory of adjudication distinguishes the complementary dimensions of fit and justification. First, since an interpretation is successful insofar as it justifies the preexisting legal materials (i.e., statutory and judicial decisions), the interpretation must minimally *fit* (or cohere) with those materials; this, after all, is what makes the process one of law-*interpretation* rather than law-creation. Second, since an interpretation should provide a *moral justification* for those preexisting materials, it should present them in the best possible moral light by interpreting them as incorporating those moral principles most likely to legitimate those materials. Thus, an interpretation is successful, on Dworkin's view, if and only if (1) the interpretation coheres to some threshold level with existing legal materials; and (2) the interpretation is the most morally attractive standard that satisfies (1). The correct interpretation, then, is the one that makes the law the moral best it can be.

Dworkin also views his theory as empirically descriptive, arguing that judges generally base their decisions on moral arguments:

[U]noriginal judicial decisions that merely enforce the clear terms of some plainly valid statute are always

justified on arguments of principle, even if the statute itself was generated by policy.... But if the case at hand is a hard case, when no settled rule dictates a decision either way, then it might seem that a proper decision could be generated by either policy or principle.... I propose, nevertheless, the thesis that judicial decisions in civil cases, even in hard cases ... *characteristically are* ... generated by principle not policy. (Dworkin 1978, 83–84; emphasis added)

These remarks are empirical claims about what most judges do when interpreting the law—and not conceptual or normative claims. Dworkin believes that most judges attempt to decide cases in a way that shows the entire legal system in its best moral light and justifies the use of the state's police power in enforcing the court's decision.

Both the conceptual and normative claims are controversial. While Dworkin believes that law and morality are different concepts, he nonetheless believes that the criteria of legality (i.e., the criteria that determine which norms count as law and which norms do not) necessarily contain a moral criterion—the criterion that the law includes those moral principles that show formally promulgated legal norms in their best moral light. This stands Dworkin's view in opposition to two influential conceptual theories of law: classical natural law theory and legal positivism. The former holds that there are necessary moral constraints on the content of law that even formally promulgated norms must satisfy to count as law, while the latter holds that there are no necessary moral constraints at all on what counts as law.

Dworkin's normative claims about how judges should interpret the law are disputed by a variety of theories of interpretation. Originalists, like Robert Bork, believe that judges should interpret the terms of statutes and constitutional provisions in accordance with the common understandings of those terms at the time the relevant provisions were promulgated. Strict constructionists believe that the terms of such laws should be interpreted according to their "plain meanings." Evolutionist theories believe that all legal norms should be interpreted to conform to evolving *conventional* (as opposed to objectively correct) standards of morality.

Within the field of American constitutional jurisprudence, the term *interpretivism* takes on a very different meaning. In his seminal book *Democracy and Distrust* (1980), John Hart Ely juxtaposes interpretivism and noninterpretivism, the former "indicating that judges deciding constitutional issues should confine themselves to enforcing norms that are stated or clearly implicit in the written Constitution." Noninterpretivism, on the other hand, advances the view that "courts should go beyond that set of references and enforce norms that cannot be discovered within the four corners of the document" (Ely 1980, 1). Ely was quick to point out that one should not "suppose that there is any necessary correlation between an interpretivist approach to constitutional adjudication and political conservatism or even what is commonly called judicial self-restraint." Ely elaborated on his definition of interpretivism by explaining that interpretivism is distinguished from noninterpretivism by "its insistence that the work of the political branches is to be invalidated only in accord with an inference whose starting point, whose underlying premise, is fairly discoverable in the Constitution" (p. 2).

While Justice Hugo Black could not accurately be described as an historical literalist, he is recognized by Ely and others as "the quintessential interpretivist." The most prominent example of Black's interpretivism is his dissent in *Griswold v. Connecticut* (1965) in which he denied the existence of a constitutional right of privacy. While he found the anti–birth control law at issue in that case personally offensive, Black was not persuaded by "talk [in the majority opinion of Justice Douglas] about a constitutional 'right of privacy' as an emanation from one or more constitutional provisions." In memorable language he added: "I like my privacy as well as the next one, but I am nevertheless compelled to admit that government has a right to invade it unless prohibited by some specific constitutional provision." In analyzing Black's position, Ely noted that when Black's "constitutional philosophy (interpretivism) and his political philosophy (liberalism) diverged, as they did in *Griswold,* 'the Judge' went with his constitutional philosophy."

Rightly or wrongly, interpretivism as a philosophical perspective in American constitutional law has often been identified with "originalism" or "original intent." Of course many judges and legal scholars reject this perspective as impractical and undesirable in light of the demands placed on contemporary judicial decision making. These noninterpretivists view the Constitution as a living document, "the meaning of which evolves according to what Justice Oliver Wendell Holmes called the 'felt necessities' of the times" (Stephens and Scheb 2003, 43). Noninterpretivist views range from recommendations that judges attempt to reflect societal consensus to suggestions that "the [Supreme] Court adopt an explicit position of moral leadership, striving to elevate and enlighten society rather than merely reflect prevailing norms" (Stephens and Scheb 2003, 43).

Ely explained the basic difference between interpretivism and noninterpretivism by pointing out that: "The noninterpretivist would have politically unaccountable judges select and define the values to be placed beyond majority control, but the interpretivist takes his values from the Constitution, which means, since the Constitution itself was submitted for and received popular ratification, that they ultimately come from the people" (Ely 1980, 8).

See also Black, Hugo L.; Bork, Robert; Dworkin, Ronald; *Griswold v. Connecticut* (1965); Holmes, Oliver Wendell, Jr.; Judicial Activism; Judicial Restraint; Liberty; Living Constitution; Original Intent, Doctrine of

Bibliography

Dworkin, Ronald. 1982. "'Natural' Law Revisited." *University of Florida Law Review* 35: 165.

Dworkin, Ronald. 1986. *Law's Empire.* Cambridge, MA: Harvard University Press.

Dworkin, Ronald. 1978. *Taking Rights Seriously.* Cambridge, MA.: Harvard University Press.

Ely, John Hart, 1980. *Democracy and Distrust: A Theory of Judicial Review.* Cambridge, MA: Harvard University Press.

Stephens, Otis H., Jr. and Scheb, John M., II, 2003. *American Constitutional Law.* 3rd ed. Belmont, CA: Wadsworth/Thomson Learning.
    Kenneth Einar Himma and Otis H. Stephens, Jr.

INTERRACIAL MARRIAGE

Laws prohibiting interracial marriage in the United States were initially enacted during the colonial era in the 1660s and were originally applied to marital or sexual relationships between whites, African slaves, and former slaves. After the Civil War, laws prohibiting interracial marriage were popularly known as *antimiscegenation* laws. The term *miscegenation* was coined by David Croly in an 1863 pamphlet as part of an elaborate political hoax cleverly designed to defeat the Republicans during upcoming elections by portraying them as proponents of racial mixing (Kaplan 1949). As the concept was originally used in the 1860s, the word *miscegenation* was not used in a neutral, scientific context, but rather it was used in ways to convey white supremacy and racism. Religious arguments were also used to justify laws prohibiting racial intermarriage, and Charles Darwin's theories of racial inferiority were cited as scientific authority justifying the enactment of antimiscegenation statutes. States relied on the Tenth Amendment to justify laws prohibiting interracial marriage on the grounds that states had the authority to regulate marriage.

The antimiscegenation laws were unique in several important respects when compared to other forms of statutory discrimination under the regime of Jim Crow. For example, these laws restricted the liberty of desired relationships by both parties on account of race. The antimiscegenation laws contained more specific racial categories compared to other Jim Crow statutes in that they were extended to American Indians, Chinese, Japanese, Koreans, Filipinos, and Hindus. The geographic landscape of laws prohibiting racial intermarriage went beyond the Jim Crow South to the West Coast, Midwest, and East Coast regions of the country. The antimiscegenation laws have the distinction of being among the last of the Jim Crow laws struck down by the Supreme Court.

In 1948 the California Supreme Court became the first tribunal to declare an antimiscegenation statute unconstitutional (see *Perez v. Sharp*). In this case, the county clerk of Los Angeles County refused to issue a marriage license to Andrea Perez, a white woman, and Sylvester Davis, an African American male, on account of race. Sections 60 and 69 of the California Civil Code prohibited the issuance of marriage licenses to a white person and a Negro, mulatto, Mongolian, or member of the Malay race. The state justified the statute on the grounds that the Caucasian race would be contaminated by races whose members were physically and morally inferior to Caucasians. Justice Traynor, writing for the majority, rejected the state's argument on the grounds that no scientific proof established that one race is superior to another. Justice Traynor was not persuaded by the state's reliance on *Pace v. Alabama* (1883) as he distinguished the two cases. The California Supreme Court also invalidated the codes on the grounds that they were too vague because they made no provisions for applying the statute to persons of mixed ancestry. The California Supreme Court concluded that Sections 60 and 69 also violated the Equal Protection Clause by impairing the right of individuals to marry on the basis of race alone and by arbitrarily and unreasonably discriminating against certain racial groups.

The U.S. Supreme Court avoided the question of the constitutionality of laws prohibiting mixed marriages in *Naim v. Naim* (1955), but 12 years later it squarely confronted the issue in the landmark case of *Loving v. Virginia* (1967). In June 1958, Mildred Jeter, a black woman, and Richard Loving, a white man, were married in Washington, D.C. Shortly after they married, the Lovings returned to Virginia and established residence in Caroline County where they were arrested and indicted for violating Virginia's antimiscegenation statutes. Virginia was one of 15 states at the time that had a law forbidding racial intermarriage. The Lovings pleaded guilty and were sentenced to one year in jail. The trial judge suspended the sentence for a period of 25 years on the condition that the

Lovings leave the state and not return together. After residing in the District of Columbia, the Lovings challenged their convictions on the grounds that the Virginia statute violated the Equal Protection Clause of the Fourteenth Amendment.

In *Loving,* Virginia argued that because its antimiscegenation statutes punished equally both blacks and whites in an interracial marriage, there was no discrimination based on race. In a unanimous opinion, the Supreme Court rejected Virginia's argument on two grounds. Chief Justice Earl Warren rejected the equal application theory on the grounds that the fact of equal application does not immunize the statute from the heavy burden of justification which the Fourteenth Amendment has traditionally required of state statutes drawn according to race. The Court also rejected Virginia's reliance on *Pace v. Alabama* (1883) where an Alabama statute provided for a more severe punishment for whites and blacks found guilty of adultery or fornication than for persons of the same race. The Court reasoned that the Equal Protection Clause required the consideration of whether the classification drawn by any statute constitutes an arbitrary and invidious discrimination. This requirement is important because the purpose of the Fourteenth Amendment was to eliminate all official state sources of invidious racial discrimination. Chief Justice Warren found no legitimate overriding purpose for invidious racial discrimination, which justified the prohibition on interracial marriage; therefore, restricting the freedom to marry based solely on race violated the central meaning of the Equal Protection Clause.

The *Loving* case is also significant because the Court ruled that the right to marry is a fundamental right under the strict scrutiny standard of equal protection analysis. Chief Justice Warren reasoned that the right to marry has long been recognized as one of the vital personal rights essential to the orderly pursuit of happiness. The Fourteenth Amendment requires that the freedom to marry a person of another race rests with the individual and may not be restricted by invidious racial discrimination. *Loving* established that because marriage is essential to the pursuit of happiness, it is not purely a domestic matter but is within the purview of the federal courts.

See also *Brown v. Board of Education* (1954; 1955); Equal Protection Clause; Fourteenth Amendment; Jim Crow Laws; *Loving v. Virginia* (1967); Marriage, Rights Pertaining to; *Plessy v. Ferguson* (1896); Race, Discrimination Based on; Same-Sex Marriage; Tenth Amendment; Warren, Earl

Bibliography

Kaplan, Sidney. 1949 "The Miscegenation Issue in the Election of 1864." *The Journal of Negro History* 34 (July): 274–343.

Pascoe, Peggy. 1996. "Miscegenation Law, Court Cases, and Ideologies of 'Race' in Twentieth-Century America." *The Journal of American History* 83 (June): 44–69.

Barbara L. Graham

INTERROGATION AND CONFESSIONS

The Fifth Amendment to the U.S. Constitution protects persons against compulsory self-incrimination. In the 1897 case of *Bram v. United States,* the Supreme Court held that a coerced confession violated the Self-Incrimination Clause. In *Bram* the Court stated that to be admissible in court, a confession must be "free and voluntary: that is, [it] must not be extracted by any sort of threats or violence, nor obtained by any direct or implied promises, however slight, nor by the exertion of any improper influence." Because the Self-Incrimination Clause was not applied to the states until the mid-1960s, the Court's ruling in *Bram* applied only to federal law enforcement agencies. Meanwhile, state and local police remained free to use any means they deemed necessary to extract confessions from suspects. Often, these means were highly coercive, and sometimes they were downright brutal.

In 1931, the National Commission on Law Observance and Enforcement (better known as the Wickersham Commission) released a report concluding that "[t]he third degree—that is, the use of physical brutality, or other forms of cruelty, to obtain involuntary confessions or admissions—is widespread" (National Commission on Law Observance and Enforcement 1931, 4). Police tactics documented by the Wickersham Commission included protracted questioning, intimidation, brutality, and refusal to allow suspects to meet with their lawyers. The commission's report stirred widespread outrage and was, perhaps, a motivating factor behind the Supreme Court's unanimous 1936 decision in *Brown v. Mississippi*, which held that a coerced confession deprives a state criminal defendant of the due process of law guaranteed by the Fourteenth Amendment.

Until the mid-1960s, the traditional test used by the courts in determining the admissibility of confessions obtained by state and local law enforcement officers was whether it could reasonably be deemed to have been voluntary. This was a difficult test to apply and, consequently, the judicial decisions as to the admissibility of confessions were often unclear and inconsistent. For example, in *Ashcraft v. Tennessee* (1944), the Supreme Court overturned a murder conviction on grounds that the defendant's confession was coerced because it had been preceded by a 36-hour period of continuous police interrogation. A month later, in *Lyons v. Oklahoma* (1944), the Court upheld a confession repeated some 12 hours after the suspect had been made to hold a pan containing the charred bones of his alleged murder victims. In a sharp dissent, Justice Frank Murphy characterized the police tactics at issue as a "flagrant abuse by a state of the rights of an American citizen."

In 1961, the Civil Rights Commission issued a report stating that "some policemen still resort to physical force to obtain confessions" (U.S. Commission on Civil Rights 1961, Book 5, 17). The report documented one particularly egregious incident in which police in Kings County, New York, subjected a man under interrogation to beating, kicking, and burning with lighted cigarettes. By the early1960s, many commentators believed that another approach to the law governing police interrogation was necessary.

The McNabb-Mallory Rule

Although the Supreme Court did not overrule the *Bram* decision, it did not rely on it in federal police interrogation cases for many decades. Rather, the justices based their most important decisions in this area on an extra-constitutional source of authority; namely the Supreme Court's supervisory power over the administration of criminal justice in federal courts. In *McNabb v. United States* (1943) and *Mallory v. United States* (1957) the Court fashioned a "prompt arraignment" standard requiring that criminal suspects, prior to interrogation, be brought before a committing magistrate without "unnecessary delay." The *McNabb-Mallory* Rule drew sharp criticism from vocal minorities in both houses of Congress, especially during the period of Court-bashing in the aftermath of the school desegregation and pro-free speech cases of the middle and late 1950s.

The Warren Court's Landmark Decisions

The Supreme Court's decision in *Malloy v. Hogan* (1964) to apply the Self-Incrimination Clause to the states via the Fourteenth Amendment set the stage for a stricter attitude toward police interrogation. Writing for the Court in *Malloy*, Justice William J. Brennan observed, "Governments, state and federal, are ... constitutionally compelled to establish guilt by evidence independently and freely secured, and may not by coercion prove a charge against an accused out of his own mouth."

A sharp break with the voluntariness approach came in 1964 when the Supreme Court decided *Escobedo v. Illinois*. There the Court held that once a police interrogation "has begun to focus on a particular suspect, the suspect has been taken into custody, the police carry out a process of interrogations that lends itself to incriminating statements, the suspect has requested and been denied an opportunity to consult with his lawyer, and the police have not effectively warned him of his absolute constitutional right to remain silent ... no statement elicited by the police during the interrogation may be used against him during the criminal trial."

Two years later, in *Miranda v. Arizona,* the Court developed the well-known *Miranda* warnings. Unless police inform suspects of their rights to remain silent and have an attorney present during questioning and unless police obtain voluntary waivers of these rights, suspects' confessions and other statements are inadmissible at trial. In addition to *Miranda v. Arizona* itself, this landmark decision actually covered three state cases and one federal case, all decided on the same day, June 13, 1966. Each of these four cases involved the admissibility of statements obtained from suspects during periods of private interrogation characterized either by failure to advise them of their constitutional rights or by the absence of "knowing and intelligent" waiver of those rights (Stephens 1973, 127). By thus reviewing state and federal cases in a single decision, the Court "officially erased" the substantial differences that, up until the *Miranda* decision, had existed between interrogation requirements at state and federal levels of law enforcement (Stephens 1973, 129).

Chief Justice Earl Warren's majority opinion in *Miranda* insisted that the decision was "not intended to hamper the traditional function of police officers in investigating crime." In dissent, Justice White disagreed, suggesting that the ruling would "measurably weaken" the ability of law enforcement to ferret out crime. White speculated that "[i]n some unknown number of cases the Court's rule will return a killer, a rapist or other criminal to the streets and to the environment which produced him, to repeat his crime whenever it pleases him."

The *Miranda* decision was widely criticized for "coddling criminals" and "hamstringing the police." As it turned out, however, most suspects readily waived their Miranda rights and submitted to private interrogation. Accordingly, the practice of "Mirandizing" suspects soon became standard operating procedure in law enforcement. Today, most police and prosecutors support the *Miranda* decision as a means of professionalizing law enforcement practices and, perhaps more importantly, protecting legitimate confessions from later challenges. Moreover, the *Miranda* decision is firmly established in the Supreme Court's jurisprudence, as evidenced by the Court's reaffirmation in *United States v. Dickerson* (2000). Writing for the Court in *Dickerson,* Chief Justice William H. Rehnquist, one of *Miranda*'s strongest early critics, observed that "*Miranda* has become embedded in routine police practice to the point where the warnings have become part of our national culture."

Post-*Miranda* Confessions Jurisprudence

Although the Supreme Court has reaffirmed the *Miranda* decision, it has also reduced its impact by delimiting its applicability and by recognizing exceptions. For example, in *Harris v. New York* (1971), the Court ruled that confessions excluded from trial under *Miranda* could nevertheless be used to impeach the credibility of a defendant who takes the stand to testify in his or her own behalf. In *New York v. Quarles* (1984), the Supreme Court created a "public safety exception" that allows police to engage in limited questioning of suspects before giving the Miranda warnings in order to address imminent threats to public safety. And in *Nix v. Williams* (1984), the Court created an "inevitable discovery exception" to the rule that excludes from trial other evidence discovered as the result of inadmissible statements made to police.

The Supreme Court has also refused to expand the scope of custodial interrogation beyond an actual arrest or significant "deprivation of freedom." In *Oregon v. Mathiason* (1977), the Court allowed the use of a confession obtained by police by questioning a suspect who was not then under arrest. In the *Mathiason* case a police officer obtained a confession after falsely informing the suspect that his fingerprints had been found at the scene of the crime. However, because Mathiason was not under formal arrest at the time and had even come to the station house unescorted to talk to police, the Court held that *Miranda* did not apply.

In one of the most significant decisions in this area, *Arizona v. Fulminante* (1991), the Supreme Court held that an illegally obtained confession is subject to harmless error analysis. Prior to *Fulminante,* a defendant was automatically entitled to reversal of a conviction if an unlawfully obtained confession had been introduced into evidence at trial. Under *Fulminante,* an appellate court may affirm a conviction if it determines that the defendant would have been convicted on the basis of other evidence.

See also Accused, Rights of the; Arraignment; Bill of Rights, Incorporation of; Brennan, William J., Jr.; Counsel, Right to; Critical Pretrial Stages; Due Process Clauses; Exclusionary Rule; Fifth Amendment; Fourteenth Amendment; Fruit of the Poisonous Tree Doctrine; Harmless Error, Doctrine of; *Miranda v. Arizona* (1966); *Miranda,* Exceptions to; Rehnquist, William H.; Self-Incrimination Clause; Warren Court; Warren, Earl; White, Byron

Bibliography

National Commission on Law Observance and Enforcement. 1931. *Report on Lawlessness in Law Enforcement.* Washington, DC: U.S. Government Printing Office.
Stephens, Otis H., Jr. 1973. *The Supreme Court and Confessions of Guilt.* Knoxville: University of Tennessee Press.
U.S. Commission on Civil Rights. 1961. *Report.* Washington, DC: U.S. Government Printing Office.

Otis H. Stephens, Jr. and John M. Scheb II

INVENTORY SEARCHES

Law enforcement officers frequently impound motor vehicles that are parked illegally, abandoned, or left because the driver has been arrested and there is no passenger able to lawfully operate the vehicle. Once impounded, a vehicle typically will be searched, valuables removed, and its contents inventoried. These inventory searches are justified by the need for protection of the owner's property while the vehicle remains in police custody, protection of the police from claims of lost property, and protection of the police from potential dangers that might be lurking inside closed automobiles.

Often inventory searches will produce contraband or other evidence of crime. In *South Dakota v. Opperman* (1976), the Supreme Court upheld the use in evidence of contraband found by police in a glove compartment during a routine inventory search of an impounded vehicle. Chief Justice Warren Burger's opinion for the Court stressed the reduced privacy expectations associated with automobiles, the need to protect personal property and public safety, and the fact that inventory searches had long been upheld by state and federal appellate courts.

In *Colorado v. Bertine* (1987), the Supreme Court upheld the use in evidence of controlled substances found in a closed backpack in an automobile that had been impounded by police. In a pretrial hearing on the defendant's motion to suppress the evidence, the trial court noted that the inventory was conducted in a "slipshod" fashion, but concluded that "the search of the backpack was done for the purpose of protecting the owner's property, protection of the police from subsequent claims of loss or stolen property, and the protection of the police from dangerous instrumentalities." Writing for the Supreme Court, Chief Justice William H. Rehnquist observed that "reasonable police regulations relating to inventory procedures administered in good faith satisfy the Fourth Amendment." Addressing the argument that police should not have opened the closed backpack, Rehnquist quoted from the Court's decision in *United States v. Ross* (1982): "When a legitimate search is underway, and when its purpose and its limits have been precisely defined, nice distinctions between closets, drawers, and containers, in the case of a home, or between glove compartments, upholstered seats, trunks, and wrapped packages, in the case of a vehicle, must give way to the interest in the prompt and efficient completion of the task at hand." Dissenting, Justice Thurgood Marshall accused the majority of ignoring the defendant's reasonable expectation in the privacy of his backpack: "Whatever his expectation of privacy in his automobile generally, our prior decisions clearly establish that he retained a reasonable expectation of privacy in the backpack and its contents."

In *Opperman,* Chief Justice Burger observed that the disputed inventory search was "standard procedure" and was not conducted as "a pretext concealing an investigatory police motive." Similarly, in *Bertine,* Chief Justice Rehnquist noted that the challenged inventory search was not performed "for the sole purpose of investigation." As these comments imply, police are not permitted to use an inventory search as a pretext for a criminal investigation. Nevertheless, once the police have legitimately taken a vehicle into custody, they are not required to overlook contraband articles discovered during a valid inventory search, and such items may be used as evidence. Lower federal and state courts have emphasized that an inventory search must be in accordance with established inventory procedures.

When a person is taken into custody and confined in a jail or detention facility, police will inventory his or her personal belongings. In *Illinois v. Lafayette* (1983), the Supreme Court held that "it is not 'unreasonable' for police, as part of the routine procedure incident to incarcerating an arrested person, to search any container or article in his possession, in accordance with established inventory procedures." Concurring in the judgment, Justice Marshall agreed that "the practical necessities of securing persons and property in a jailhouse setting justify an inventory search as part of the standard procedure incident to incarceration."

Although state courts are free to interpret their respective state constitutions to provide greater protection against searches and seizures, the state courts have by and large accepted the concept of the warrantless inventory search of a lawfully impounded vehicle. A common thread running through the state court decisions is that police must not use the inventory searches as pretexts to conduct otherwise impermissible searches of motor vehicles. A number of state court decisions have also held that impoundment of vehicles by the police is lawful only as a last resort and that any inventory search of an illegally impounded vehicle is likewise invalid.

See also Automobile Stops and Searches; Burger, Warren E.; Fourth Amendment; Marshall, Thurgood; Privacy, Reasonable Expectations of; Rehnquist, William H.; Warrantless Searches

Bibliography

Johnson, Octavia. 1992. "How Far Can We Go? The Inventory Search Exception to the Warrant Requirement." *Thurgood Marshall Law Review* 18: 181.

LaFave, Wayne R. 1996. *Search and Seizure: A Treatise on the Fourth Amendment.* 3rd ed. St. Paul, MN: West Publishing Co.

Scheb, John M., and John M. Scheb II. 2006. *Criminal Procedure.* Belmont, CA: Thomson/Wadsworth.

John M. Scheb II and Otis H. Stephens, Jr.

IRS. *See* Internal Revenue Service

J

JACKSON, JESSE (1941–)

Jesse Louis Jackson was born on October 8, 1941, in Greenville, South Carolina. He attended the University of Illinois on a football scholarship, but transferred to North Carolina A&T after his freshman year due to racial discrimination that he encountered. He graduated with a bachelor's degree in Sociology in 1964. During his college years, Jackson became committed to the cause of civil rights and was a leader in the student sit-in movement designed to draw attention to segregated public facilities. After graduation, Jackson attended the Chicago Theological Seminary for two years (he would later earn a Master's of Divinity in 2000), during which time he was appointed national director of Operation Breadbasket, the economic arm of the Southern Christian Leadership Conference, by Dr. Martin Luther King, Jr. (Hatch and Watkins 1987). Jackson became a close associate of Dr. King's and was with him when King was assassinated in Memphis, Tennessee on April 4, 1968.

Jackson, along with other civil rights leaders, established PUSH (People United to Serve Humanity) in Chicago on December 25, 1971, an organization dedicated to increasing economic opportunities for racial minorities. Under the auspices of PUSH's Economic Justice Campaign, Jackson negotiated multimillion dollar agreements with several large corporations to increase economic opportunities for minorities and women. According to Hatch and Watkins (1987), PUSH is also dedicated to the cause of furthering international human rights. PUSH even initiated voter registration drives and was involved in grassroots politics.

Jackson ran for the Democratic nomination for the presidency in 1984, which "marked the first full-scale effort by an African American to capture the nation's highest office" (Hatch and Watkins 1987, xiii). Jackson's campaign was associated with the multiracial National Rainbow Coalition, an organization attempting to provide a voice to disempowered groups in the American political system. After a strong showing in the primaries, Jackson bowed out to former Vice President Walter Mondale. In 1988, Jackson again launched a failed bid for the presidency, but his impressive support made him an important voice in the Democratic Party. In 1996, PUSH and the Rainbow Coalition merged into one organization, Rainbow/PUSH, dedicated to social, racial, and economic justice.

President Bill Clinton appointed Jackson as a special envoy to Africa in 1997. In 2000, Clinton also awarded Jackson the Presidential Medal of Freedom, the nation's highest civilian honor. Jackson has continued his dedication to fairness in the political process, educational and economic opportunities for minorities and women, the labor movement, and international human rights through his work with Rainbow/PUSH.

See also Civil Disobedience; Civil Rights Movement; Discrimination; Interest Groups; King, Martin Luther, Jr.; Sit-Ins; Southern Christian Leadership Conference

Bibliography

Hatch, Roger D., and Frank Watkins, eds.1987. *Straight From the Heart.* Philadelphia: Fortress Press.
Rainbow/PUSH. "Founder." Available at http://www.rainbowpush.org.

Kara E. Stooksbury

JACKSON, ROBERT H. (1892–1954)

Robert Houghwout Jackson was born on February 13, 1892. Jackson's paternal ancestors helped settle Pennsylvania, and his maternal ancestors arrived before the British purchased Manhattan. His parents imparted to their son the values of industry, self-reliance, respect, and restraint common in pioneer stock, although it is clear that Jackson also learned about ambition somewhere along the line.

Early in his life, the Jackson family relocated to upstate New York, and it was here that Jackson began his rise to prominence while holding to the values and lessons learned living in a country setting. An avid and active Democrat in a Republican bastion, Jackson's partisanship foretold his approach to political and judicial life. Independent of mind and spirit, Jackson read law and earned a law degree from Albany College in 1912. He went on to build a successful and lucrative law practice in his home community. Owing success to one or two large clients, Jackson believed, would taint the ability of a lawyer to serve his clients. Thus, Jackson built a practice that included large and small clients, and served all to the best of his ability. He did not specialize in any area of law, but succeeded in most. Though meant derogatorily, Jackson relished his title of "country lawyer" and never lost touch with the pragmatic approach to the law developed in his years in Jamestown.

His ability and personality enabled Jackson to rise to local prominence quickly. His reputation as an advocate earned him an early appointment as Corporation Counsel for the City of Jamestown in 1918, only five years after he entered private practice. This is one of many political appointments that would elevate Jackson to the national stage. As his success grew, so did his reputation, leading to an appointment in 1931 to the Commission to Investigate the Administration of Justice in New York State. This appointment was the first of many Jackson received from future President, then Governor, Franklin D. Roosevelt.

In 1934, after turning down positions with both the state and federal government, Jackson was lured from his hometown and his private practice to become General Counsel for the Bureau of Internal Revenue. Loathe to leave a lucrative private practice, Jackson accepted the appointment hoping to continue to practicing law part-time. This arrangement did not last long, as President Roosevelt called on Jackson as an advisor as early as 1935. That same year, Jackson transferred to the Department of Justice, became an Assistant Attorney General in the Tax Division, and was Special Counsel for the Securities and Exchange Commission. By 1937, Jackson was head of the Anti-Trust Division at Justice.

In 1938, President Roosevelt appointed him to the post of Solicitor General—an appointment that Jackson relished. In retrospect, this position may be where Jackson was most happy and successful. He was an extremely able Solicitor General, winning almost every case he argued. In 1940, the President called upon Jackson to head the Department of Justice. Jackson's tenure at Justice occurred as the war in Europe escalated. Jackson served as a critical advisor to the president as Roosevelt walked the tightrope of supporting allies, and maintaining neutrality. Still, Jackson had traveled to Europe for the administration in 1935, and it was during this trip that he began to form a philosophy regarding aggressors and international law.

Soon after his appointment to the cabinet, Jackson was considered for the position of Chief Justice of the United States due to the retirement of Charles Evans Hughes. However, given the increasing likelihood of war and the need for unity, Roosevelt elevated Associate Justice Harlan Fiske

Stone, a Republican, to Chief Justice instead, and appointed Jackson as an Associate Justice. Though Jackson was willing to serve as the president requested, it was clear that Jackson had his sights set on the chief's spot. Jackson's personality was generally winning, but he clashed with some of his brethren. The battles between Jackson and Black are notorious, and generally credited with keeping Jackson from becoming chief justice.

The work of a judge, however, is not the work of an advocate; fundamentally, Jackson was an advocate. He had the knack of getting to the kernel of an argument, but also could do so with literary aplomb. The work of the Court provided an outlet for his judicial acumen and his pen, but the chance to take up the role as advocate led Jackson to interrupt his work as a justice. In 1945, Jackson suspended his service on the Court to serve as chief prosecutor at the Nuremberg trials. Jackson was steadfast in his belief that not all wars are legal ones, and that the aggressors should be held accountable. The undertaking was large and uncertain, but Jackson's skill and industriousness brought the first war crimes tribunal to a successful close, and ushered in a new era of international law. While some criticized Jackson's absence from the Court, including some of the brethren, Jackson believed his service at Nuremberg to be "the most satisfying and gratifying experience" and one of greater significance than his service as Associate Justice.

After returning to the states, Jackson settled into his position as Associate Justice. The public feuding between Black and Jackson after the sudden death of Chief Justice Stone closed off any future ambition for the center seat. Jackson would serve on the Court as an Associate Justice until his death on October 9, 1954.

Jackson's opinions remain a favorite for students of the Court; his style is direct and forthright, and he had a knack for turning a memorable phrase. Jackson's civil liberties jurisprudence is not unlike the man himself. Jackson believed in respect, tolerance, and individualism. Government should neither coerce nor compel any person to adopt any idea, be it religious, partisan, or patriotic.

Perhaps his best-known work comes from his critique of Justice Frankfurter's opinion in *Minersville v. Gobitas* (1940), when Jackson wrote for the majority to overturn the three-year-old precedent in *West Virginia v. Barnette* (1943), which upheld the right of Jehovah's Witnesses to refrain from saluting the flag and reciting the Pledge of Allegiance. According to Jackson:

If there is any fixed star in our constitutional constellation, it is that no official, high or petty, can prescribe what shall be orthodox in politics, national, religion, or other matters of opinion, or force citizens to confess by word or act their faith therein.

This same theme permeated Jackson's other work, and became a cornerstone of First Amendment jurisprudence. Jackson returned to this idea in a string of Establishment Clause cases: *Everson v. Board of Education* (1947), *McCollum v. Board of Education* (1948), and *Zorach v. Clauson* (1952). In each instance, he held that state support of religious teaching either through reimbursement for transportation, daily instruction, or release time involved some coercion by the state on individual beliefs. His jurisprudence was consistent, and restrained as evinced by his dissent in *U.S. v. Ballard* (1944) where he deviated from the Court because he did not agree that "religious fraud" could be prosecuted without trampling on the free exercise of religion or governmental coercion. These opinions set the stage for later religious freedom cases such as *Wisconsin v. Yoder* (1972).

Tolerance and individualism are at the heart of his judicial philosophy, but tolerance did not require an absolutist interpretation of the rights of speech and free exercise of religion. Certainly this position, which placed him as the conservative among liberals, was further sustained when he dissented in *Terminiello v. Chicago* (1949), a case involving a priest who was arrested for disorderly conduct for addressing a sympathetic audience in an auditorium while a hostile crowd gathered outside. However, his opinion is not out of character. Jackson, ever the lawyer-judge, relied on the facts of the situation, and the precedent of *Chaplinsky v. NH* (1942) to guide his opinion.

Typical of the pragmatist, Jackson concluded that "[the] choice is not between order and liberty. It is between liberty with order and anarchy without either." This type of temperance or relativism when applying the clear and present danger test would soon become precedent for the Court in *Dennis v. U.S.* (1951).

In terms of civil liberties, Jackson's legacy is built upon concurring and dissenting opinions that often presented a clear and judicious opinion for lower courts and future judges to follow. Jackson's words from *Barnette,* in particular, have echoed in landmark First Amendment decisions, consolidating two divergent and important doctrines. One doctrine that emanates from *Barnette* prohibits government from discriminating based upon the content of the speech or excising particular types of speech from the "marketplace of ideas," and so local governments, as in *NSPA v. Skokie* (1977), cannot pass ordinances to prevent a hate group from marching in their regalia, nor can cities criminalize racist, misogynist, or anti-Semitic speech as St. Paul, Minnesota did in *R.A.V. v. St. Paul* (1992). Additionally, the Court has held in *U.S. v. Eichman* (1990) and *Texas v. Johnson* (1989) that neither the federal nor the state government can set the flag apart as a symbol of particular meaning and deserving of greater respect by prohibiting the desecration of the flag.

The second doctrine is as important as the first. From *Barnette* and Jackson, the Court has established that government cannot compel or enforce one view over another. The continued application of this important principle is evident in *Hurley v. Irish-American Gay Group of Boston* (1995) where the Court again refused to force speech upon one group even when balanced against the right to speak of another group.

Barnette is not the only example of Jackson standing against the tide of rampant patriotism to the detriment of civil liberties. Jackson stood against the majority and against the racist hysteria that led to the Court's much maligned ruling in *Korematsu v. U.S.* (1944). Despite his relationship with the president, Jackson would not support a policy that branded people without due process

of law. According to Jackson's dissent, "[i]f any fundamental assumption underlies our system, it is that guilt is personal and not inheritable." His position has been vindicated by history, and stands as a testament to his consistent and fervent beliefs in individual rights.

Justice Jackson appeared before the bench during the great battles of the New Deal era and sat on the bench during some of the most important, foundational civil liberties cases. He provided a critical vote in *Brown v. Board of Education* (1954), and though he was quite ill he appeared in Court for the reading of the opinion. Jackson believed that the opinion needed unanimity in writing and announcement. His contributions to American jurisprudence and international law are hard to underestimate, and his 13 years on the bench were productive as he wrote over 300 opinions. His career included such auspicious posts as solicitor general, attorney general, and chief prosecutor at Nuremburg. Robert Jackson's legacy, though formidable in civil liberties, extends equally to areas of commerce, federalism, and international law.

See also Black, Hugo; *Brown v. Board of Education* (1954; 1955); Establishment Clause; Fighting Words Doctrine; Flag Burning; Flag Salute Controversy; Free Exercise Clause; Free Marketplace of Ideas; Hate Speech; Jehovah's Witnesses; *Korematsu v. United States* (1944); Religion, Freedom of; Roosevelt, Franklin; Speech, Freedom of; Symbolic Speech; *West Virginia Board of Education v. Barnette* (1943); *Wisconsin v. Yoder* (1972)

Bibliography

Gerhart, Eugene C. 1958. *America's Advocate: Robert H. Jackson.* New York: Bobbs-Merrill.

Irons, Peter. 1999. *A People's History of the Supreme Court.* New York: Penguin Books.

Jackson, Robert H. 2003. *That Man: An Insider's Portrait of Franklin D. Roosevelt.* Ed. John Q. Barrett. New York: Oxford.

Schubert, Glendon. 1969. *Dispassionate Justice: A Synthesis of the Judicial Opinions of Robert H. Jackson.* New York: Bobbs-Merrill.

Schwartz, Bernard. 1993. *A History of the Supreme Court*. New York: Oxford University Press.

Rorie Spill Solberg

JAPANESE AMERICANS, RELOCATION OF

World War II placed ethnic Japanese in America at the center of a domestic crisis during wartime where democratic ideals and civil liberties gave way to national security concerns. Weeks after the Japanese attack on Pearl Harbor on December 7, 1941, intense anti-Japanese sentiment arose on the West Coast, fueled in part by decades of vilification against the "Yellow Peril," wartime hysteria, and prejudice against a people whose ethnicity linked them to the enemy. Issues of military security were assigned to Lieutenant General John L. DeWitt. As commanding general responsible for West Coast security, DeWitt's beliefs about the Japanese, that they were disloyal and were an enemy race, played a major role in their eventual internment (Report of the Commission on Wartime Relocation and Internment of Civilians 1997, 86–92).

On February 19, 1942, President Franklin Roosevelt signed Executive Order 9066, which authorized the secretary of war and military commanders to exclude "any or all persons" from designated areas to protect against espionage and against sabotage to national defense materials, premises, and utilities. The order was used to exclude persons of Japanese ancestry, both citizens and resident aliens. According to General DeWitt's report to the secretary of war, shore-to-ship signaling to enemy submarines and the discovery of arms and contraband were the significant indicators of military danger. Although the Department of Justice offered no evidence for widespread ethnic Japanese disloyalty; it took the position widely reported on the West Coast that Japanese disloyalty was likely to occur. General DeWitt first ordered voluntary resettlement of the ethnic Japanese away from the restricted military zones on the West Coast. This policy was abandoned because of its impracticality and later the government ordered mandatory mass evacuations of persons of Japanese ancestry. Ethnic Japanese were initially sent to temporary assembly centers and later to "relocation centers" in the interior of the United States.

The U.S. Congress' role in the exclusion and evacuation of the ethnic Japanese took the form of legislation that imposed criminal penalties for violations of the curfew and evacuation orders. As one form of protest against the exclusion policy, ethnic Japanese brought lawsuits challenging the constitutionality of the curfew and evacuation orders. Gordon Hirabayashi, an American citizen of Japanese ancestry, violated a curfew order mandating that ethnic Japanese remain in their places of residence between the hours of 8:00 P.M. and 6:00 A.M. Hirabayashi argued that the curfew order was an unconstitutional delegation of Congressional power. In *Hirabayashi v. United States* (1943), the U.S. Supreme Court ruled unanimously that Congress and the Executive acting together had the constitutional authority to impose the curfew as an emergency war measure.

Fred Korematsu, an American-born citizen of Japanese ancestry, refused to leave his home in California after the evacuation order was issued. He was convicted of violating the order and was sentenced to five years in prison. Korematsu challenged his conviction on the grounds that Civilian Exclusion Order #34, which was based on Executive Order #9066, was beyond the war power of Congress and the Executive. In a six-to-three ruling, the Supreme Court, in the landmark case of *Korematsu v. United States* (1944), found that the exclusion order was a valid expression of the power of the government to take steps necessary to prevent espionage and sabotage in areas threatened by Japanese attack. The Court established for the first time that classifications based on race are suspect and therefore will be subjected to strict scrutiny. Only "pressing public necessity" may justify classifications, which curtail the civil rights of a racial group. On the one hand, Justice Black's majority opinion acknowledged the hardships of war and how compulsory exclusion of large groups of citizens from their homes is inconsistent with American democracy; yet he concluded that, "when under conditions of modern warfare our shores are threatened by hostile forces; the power to protect must be commensurate with the threatened danger." The dissenters, Justices Roberts, Murphy, and Jackson, sharply criticized the majority for ignoring the lack of evidence of disloyalty against the ethnic Japanese and recognized the need for limits to military discretion, especially where martial law had not yet been declared. The dissenters also argued that the exclusion order deprived persons of Japanese ancestry of their constitutional rights and thus amounted to the legalization of racism against ethnic Japanese.

The implementation of Exclusion Order #9066 resulted in the notorious deprivation of civil liberties, extreme personal hardships, and devastating financial losses for persons of Japanese ancestry interned at the camps. The internment camps were located on federal lands in several western states, often situated in harsh climates and desert areas. The relocation centers were barbed-wire camps with guards where freedom of movement was restricted. More than 100,000 ethnic Japanese interned at the camps lived under wretched living conditions, had inadequate medical care, few opportunities for work, and minimal education for their children.

The exclusion order was rescinded on December 17, 1944. The ethnic Japanese faced considerable uncertainty, hostility, and discrimination, and lacked economic resources to rebuild their lives. In 1981, the Japanese American redress movement persuaded Congress to establish a commission to review the exclusion program and to propose remedies for legal wrongs (Irons 1988, p. 47). The Commission on Wartime Relocation and Internment of Civilians held 20 days of hearings, heard testimony from more than 750 witnesses, and examined a range of sources of information. One important finding by the commission was that there was no credible evidence of military necessity that justified the exclusion of the ethnic Japanese from the West Coast. Among other things, the commission recommended that Congress pass a joint resolution offering a national apology for the exclusion and a compensatory payment of $20,000 to each of the surviving excluded members. In 1988, Congress passed the Civil Liberties Act of 1988, apologizing

on behalf of the nation and awarding $20,000 to each of the surviving internees.

See also Black, Hugo L.; Constitutional Democracy; Jackson, Robert H.; *Korematsu v. United States* (1944); Roosevelt, Franklin D.; Strict Scrutiny; Civil Rights and Liberties During Wartime

Bibliography

Irons, Peter. 1988. *The Courage of their Convictions.* New York: Penguin Books.

Report of the Commission on Wartime Relocation and Internment of Civilians. 1997. *Personal Justice Denied.* Seattle: University of Washington Press.

Barbara L. Graham

JEFFERSON, THOMAS (1743–1826)

Few figures in American history are more controversial than Thomas Jefferson. Unquestionably respected as the author of the Declaration of Independence and as a proponent of the unique brand of American liberty, Jefferson is criticized and often reviled for failing to embody the very standards that he himself proffered. Jefferson, best known for authoring the Declaration of Independence, relied primarily on the writings of John Locke and Lord Kames to justify his belief in limiting the power of the central government. To the extent to which the federal government must exercise power, its authorization should come from the legislative branch. Jefferson's skepticism regarding the concentration of power in the hands of the executive reflects the antimonarchical spirit of the American Revolution. Although his philosophy evolved over time, Jefferson never entirely abandoned the ideas most closely associated with the Declaration.

In the 1780s, as others of the revolutionary generation came to see the need for a stronger centralized authority, Jefferson remained reluctant to endorse such a move. According to Jefferson, the concentration of power can never be achieved without running the grave risk of tyranny. This was the reason for Jefferson's less than enthusiastic attitude regarding ratification of the Constitution. While others found solace in the assurance that the office of chief executive would be held by George

Washington, Jefferson was less sanguine, believing that eventually even the best of men succumb to corruption, and the law will never succeed in constraining the most egocentric among us. Aristocracy and ultimately tyranny are never far from the surface of human political interaction. In order for the law to serve as an effective deterrent to dictatorship, an egalitarian culture must necessarily be cultivated.

It was this belief that the culture itself must be transformed if the law was to serve as an effective barrier to the abuse of power that separated the thought of Thomas Jefferson from many of his contemporaries. Jefferson, who was serving as American minister in Paris, was a witness to the French Revolution and its messages of social as well as political revolution. Thus, Jefferson's penchant for dressing in informal attire and shunning most vestiges of executive ceremony, practices embraced by his two predecessors, was more than just a personal preference. It was, in fact, part of his legal and political philosophy. For the law to function properly, Jefferson believed that there must be an egalitarian culture serving the negative function of restraining aristocratic pretension. Jefferson chafed at what he considered the monarchical practices of his two predecessors, Washington and Adams.

As Secretary of State under Washington, he helped to form the nation's first political party. The Jeffersonian Democrats were committed to reigning in the power of the central government, empowering states, and limiting the power of the financial interests of the industrial northeast. Jefferson opposed the expansion of the military and urged the use of militias instead. This Lockean fear of Leviathan remained a central element of Jefferson's thought throughout his tenure in Washington's cabinet and gained expression in his opposition to the active role that Jefferson's nemesis Alexander Hamilton envisioned for the federal government. An agrarian society, decentralized, and relying for governance on the legislature instead of a strong executive were the bedrock principles of Jefferson's new party.

Late in the 1790s, while serving as Vice-President, Jefferson became increasingly alarmed by what he regarded as the sinister misuse of the law. With Alexander Hamilton at the head of the nation's military, and President Adams enforcing legislative provisions that censored speech and restricted citizenship, Jefferson came to regard the young republic as teetering on the brink of dictatorship. Accordingly, he and his partner James Madison, who had been allied with Hamilton just a decade earlier, took up their pens and argued in favor of states' rights in the face of unjust federal abuses of power. The dispute over the Alien and Sedition Acts fueled a broader debate between Jefferson's followers and the Federalist defenders of the Adams Administration regarding the nature of federalism, free speech, and the rights of the citizen vis-à-vis the federal government. These arguments culminated in the election of 1800 when Jefferson defeated Adams' bid for a second term.

As President, Jefferson appeared less committed to his bedrock principles. Through the Louisiana Purchase, he effectively doubled the size of the United States without the expressed constitutional power to do so. He dramatically expanded the power of the federal government as he attempted to enforce his ill-fated "non-intercourse" policy, which effectively ended trade with both England and France and severely crippled the nation's economy.

Later in his life, after leaving the presidency, Jefferson searched for ways to ensure citizen participation in the affairs of governance. His most famous proposal was for the counties of Virginia to be divided into wards. Modeled on the New England town meeting, Jefferson hoped to see the lawmaking process delegated to local communities. In keeping with his older Lockean ideas, his newly minted republicanism was designed to provide structural impediments to the centralization of power. While Jefferson's legal and political philosophy displayed unmistakable signs of evolution, his commitment to limiting state power and increasing the empowerment of individual citizens was a consistent theme throughout his career.

See also Alien and Sedition Acts; Bill of Rights (American) (1789); Citizenship; Declaration of Independence; Constitutional Democracy;

Representative Democracy; Equality; Federalism and Civil Rights and Liberties; Hobbes, Thomas; Kentucky and Virginia Resolutions; Liberalism; Libertarianism; Liberty; Locke, John; Religion, Freedom of; Separation of Church and State; Speech, Freedom of; States' Rights, Doctrine of

Bibliography

Becker, Carl. 1960. *The Declaration of Independence: A Study in the History of Political Ideas.* New York: Alfred A. Knopf.

Fliegelman, Jay. 1993. *Declaring Independence: Jefferson, Natural Language, and the Culture of Performance.* Palo Alto, CA: Stanford University Press.

Mayer, David M. 1995. *The Constitutional Thought of Thomas Jefferson.* Charlottesville: University of Virginia Press, 1995

John Wilson Wells

JEHOVAH'S WITNESSES

The Jehovah's Witnesses is a religious denomination of more than six million members worldwide. Founded in the 1870s by Charles Taze Russell, the Jehovah's Witnesses describe themselves as a Christian organization; however, they do not subscribe to traditional Christian theology, nor do they acknowledge the divinity of Christ. The creed of the Jehovah's Witnesses prohibits blood transfusions, celebration of holidays, participation in sports, and saluting the flag. The unconventional beliefs and practices of the Jehovah's Witnesses, along with their active proselytizing, have generated considerable antipathy toward the organization. Jehovah's Witnesses are often regarded as nuisances, especially when they go door-to-door to solicit and distribute their literature. Thus it is not surprising that members of this sect have been involved in many of the most important Supreme Court decisions in the area of free exercise of religion.

The right to proselytize and solicit is protected by the Free Exercise Clause of the First Amendment. Although assembly and expression in the public forum are subject to reasonable time, place, and manner restrictions, religious speech is afforded a high degree of constitutional protection. In a long series of decisions, the Supreme Court has made it very clear that laws aimed at restricting the religious freedom of certain groups are unacceptable. Yet during the 1930s and 1940s, a number of states and communities enacted measures specifically to counter the activities of the Jehovah's Witnesses.

Solicitation

In *Cantwell v. Connecticut* (1940), in a case involving a Connecticut statute aimed at preventing the Jehovah's Witnesses from proselytizing, the Supreme Court ruled that states cannot prohibit solicitation based on religion and that the mere act of proselytizing by itself is not a disturbance of the peace. With this decision, the Court established an important principle—that people cannot be prevented from promoting their religious beliefs in public. Significantly, in also ruling that the Free Exercise Clause applied to the states, the Court paved the way for other challenges to state laws.

In 1942, in *City of Opelika v. Alabama,* the Supreme Court upheld ordinances adopted by several cities requiring itinerant sellers of books and magazines to obtain licenses. The ordinances had been passed specifically to restrict door-to-door solicitation by the Jehovah's Witnesses. The following term, the Court overturned the *Opelika* decision by striking down a similar Pennsylvania tax on solicitation. Writing for the Supreme Court in *Murdock v. Pennsylvania* (1943), Justice William O. Douglas observed that "a person cannot be compelled to purchase … a privilege freely granted by the Constitution." *Murdock* effectively allowed the Jehovah's Witnesses (as well as other religious groups) to avoid paying licensing fees to distribute their literature door-to-door.

In a more recent case, the Supreme Court struck down a local ordinance requiring both a permit and an identification badge to be carried by door-to-door proselytizers. In *Watchtower Bible v. Stratton* (2002), the Court stated that "it is offensive, not only to the values protected by the First Amendment, but to the very notion of a free society, that in the context of everyday public discourse a citizen must first inform the government of her desire to speak to her neighbors and then obtain a permit to do so."

Access to the Public Forum

In *Cox v. New Hampshire* (1941), the Supreme Court upheld the convictions of five Jehovah's Witnesses who had been arrested for engaging in a public parade without first obtaining a permit. Writing for a unanimous bench, Chief Justice Charles Evans Hughes characterized the ordinance on which the convictions were based as a conventional time, place, and manner restriction. However, in *Niemotko v. Maryland* (1951) the Supreme Court ruled that permits cannot be used to prevent an unpopular group, to wit, the Jehovah's Witnesses, from gaining access to the public forum. In *Niemotko* the Court reversed the disorderly conduct convictions of two Jehovah's Witnesses who held a religious meeting in a public park after having been denied a permit to hold the meeting. In a unanimous decision, the Supreme Court noted that "the use of the park was denied because of the City Council's dislike for or disagreement with the Witnesses or their views." The Court observed that the regulation of the exercise of First Amendment rights must have "a firmer foundation than the whims or personal opinions of a local governing body."

The Flag Salute Controversy

Jehovah's Witnesses believe that to participate in a flag salute exercise is to violate Scripture, specifically the passages from Exodus (20:3–5) that enjoin the making of "any graven image" and "bow[ing] down thyself to them…" When the Minersville, Pennsylvania school board expelled two children who were Jehovah's Witnesses because they refused to salute the American flag and recite the Pledge of Allegiance, the Supreme Court was asked to consider for the first time whether freedom of religion includes the right to refuse to participate in patriotic rituals. In *Minersville School District v. Gobitis* (1940), the Court ruled that the governmental interest in creating national unity was compelling and that requiring the recitation of the Pledge of Allegiance was a reasonable means of

accomplishing that goal. But only three years later, in another case involving the Jehovah's Witnesses, the Court reversed itself and ruled that school children cannot be forced to salute the flag. In *West Virginia State Board of Education v. Barnette* (1943), the Court said that "no official, high or petty, can prescribe what shall be orthodox in politics, nationalism, religion, or other matters of opinion or force citizens to confess by word or act their faith therein." Thus, the Jehovah's Witnesses prevailed in their opposition to the compulsory flag salute.

Refusal of Blood Transfusions

Jehovah's Witnesses accept most medical treatments, but most members do not accept blood transfusions. Some even carry cards that read: "No Blood Transfusion! As a God-fearing Christian and a believer in Jehovah God's word, the Bible; I hereby demand that blood, in any way, shape or form, is NOT to be fed into my body…." It is now well established in the law that a competent adult is legally entitled to refuse unwanted medical treatments, even those necessary to save his or her life. This right is based not only on the Free Exercise of Religion Clause of the First Amendment, but also on the common-law doctrine of informed consent. Moreover, in *Cruzan v. Director, Missouri Dept. of Health*, the Supreme Court recognized under the Due Process Clause of the Fourteenth Amendment a significant liberty interest in refusing medical treatment. Thus, Jehovah's Witnesses are on solid legal ground in refusing blood transfusions for themselves. Refusing life-saving transfusions for their children is another matter. Courts have uniformly held that parents may not refuse to allow medical professionals to administer blood when it is necessary to save the life of their child.

The State's Role in Protecting the Welfare of Children

The issue of blood transfusions is but one aspect of a legal problem posed by the unusual beliefs and practices of the Jehovah's Witnesses. It has long been established that parents have a fundamental right to determine the upbringing of their children, certainly with regard to religious instruction and training, but it is also axiomatic that the state has the right to intervene into the family in order to protect children from harm. Thus, in *Prince v. Massachusetts* (1944), the Supreme Court rejected a challenge to a law that prohibited boys under twelve and girls under eighteen from selling newspapers on the streets. The challenge came from a member of the Jehovah's Witnesses whose children normally assisted her in the sale and distribution of religious literature. Writing for the Court, Justice Wiley Rutledge outlined the state's authority in protecting the welfare of children, even against the religious views of their parents.

Acting to guard the general interest in youth's well being, the state as *parens patriae* may restrict the parent's control by requiring school attendance, regulating or prohibiting the child's labor, and in many other ways. Its authority is not nullified merely because the parent grounds his claim to control the child's course of conduct on religion or conscience. Thus, he cannot claim freedom from compulsory vaccination for the child more than for himself on religious grounds. The right to practice religion freely does not include liberty to expose the community or the child to communicable disease or the latter to ill health or death.

An individual waving a Bible and urging passersby to "Repent!" is a sight common to most urban areas. However, the right to engage in this behavior was not affirmed until around the middle of the twentieth century. Street preachers of today are direct beneficiaries of a number of Supreme Court cases involving Jehovah's Witnesses. Though they are a fairly small group when contrasted with many other religious groups in the United States, the Jehovah's Witnesses have clearly had an impact on religious freedom that far surpasses their size.

See also *Cantwell v. Connecticut* (1940); Conscience, Freedom of; Douglas, William O.; First Amendment; Flag Salute Controversy; Free Exercise Clause; Medical Treatment, Right to Refuse; Parens Patriae, Doctrine of; Religion, Freedom of; Religious Speech; *West Virginia State Board of Education v. Barnette* (1943)

Bibliography

Peters, Shawn Francis. 2002. *Judging Jehovah's Witnesses: Religious Persecution and the Dawn of the Rights Revolution.* Reprint ed. Lawrence, KS: University Press of Kansas.

Gay Henry Lyons

JENCKS ACT (1957)

The *Jencks* Act is a federal statute pertaining to pretrial discovery in federal criminal cases. Under this statute, which is codified at 18 U.S.C.A. sec. 3500, a federal criminal defendant is not entitled to inspect a statement or report prepared by a government witness "until said witness has testified on direct examination in the trial of the case." After a witness testifies, if the defense so requests, the government must produce "any statement of the witness in the possession of the United States which relates to the subject matter as to which the witness has testified." Such statements may include those verbatim transcripts of the witness's oral statements that are written, signed, or otherwise approved by the witness, including the witness's testimony before a grand jury.

The defense's purpose in making such a request is to determine whether there are inconsistencies between the witness' testimony and a prior statement in possession of the government. Such inconsistencies can be used to impeach the credibility of the witness and possibly expose the witness to prosecution for perjury. If the government fails to disclose the requested statement, the court must either strike the testimony of the government's witness or declare a mistrial.

The statute is commonly referred to as the *Jencks* Act because it was adopted shortly after and in response to the Supreme Court's decision in *Jencks v. United States* (1957). In that case, Jencks, the president of a labor union, was convicted of violating a provision of the National Labor Relations Act by submitting a false affidavit claiming that he was affiliated with the Communist Party. Crucial testimony for the prosecution came from two paid F.B.I. informants who admitted on cross-examination that they had made a series of written reports to the

F.B.I. on matters relating to their testimony. Defense counsel moved then that these reports be produced in court. The prosecution objected, arguing that the defense had not established sufficient foundation for the production of the reports. The trial judge agreed and denied the motion. The appeals court affirmed. Speaking through Justice William J. Brennan, the Supreme Court reversed, holding that the defense "was not required to lay a preliminary foundation of inconsistency, because a sufficient foundation was established by the testimony...."

The decision in *Jencks* was not based on constitutional law, although one could make an argument that the holding was required by the Confrontation Clause of the Sixth Amendment. Rather, the Court based its decision on its broad power to supervise the administration of justice in the federal courts. The Court's decision in *Jencks* was greeted with a barrage of criticism from the Congress. A number of members expressed concern that a broad reading of *Jencks* might lead lower federal courts to compel disclosure of material that would adversely affect criminal investigations and even national security. Writing for the Supreme Court in *Palermo v. United States* (1959), Justice Felix Frankfurter observed: "Not only was it strongly feared that disclosure of memoranda containing the investigative agent's interpretations and impressions might reveal the inner workings of the investigative process and thereby injure the national interest, but it was felt to be grossly unfair to allow the defense to use statements to impeach a witness which could not fairly be said to be the witness' own rather than the product of the investigator's selections, interpretations and interpolations." Such concerns led Congress to enact the *Jencks* Act, which became law in September 1957, barely three months after the Supreme Court's decision in *Jencks v. United States*. The purpose of the legislation was to limit compelled disclosure of witnesses' statements to the narrow categories delineated above. Today, the *Jencks* Act is a staple of federal criminal procedure, and federal courts continue to wrestle with the application of its provisions.

See also Brennan, William J., Jr.; Confrontation, Right of; Pretrial Discovery; Sixth Amendment

John M. Scheb II

JIM CROW LAWS

Named for a character in a minstrel show, the Jim Crow laws were enacted by Southern states beginning, for the most part, in the 1880s as a reaction against the national government's imposition of Reconstruction measures in the states of the former Confederacy. These laws required racial segregation in every aspect of public life. To students of American history, the most familiar of the Jim Crow laws were those requiring segregated trains, trolleys, buses, and public schools. But the Jim Crow laws went much further. They also prohibited white nurses from attending black patients and vice versa. They forbade whites and blacks to play sports together or even use the same recreational facilities. They prohibited blacks and whites from being buried in the same cemeteries. They forbade interracial marriage or cohabitation. They required segregation in parks, at beaches, in hospitals, in theaters and other places of public accommodation, and even in courtrooms. The Jim Crow laws required separate public restrooms, drinking fountains, and even telephone booths for blacks and whites. Perhaps the most ludicrous law was that which required white and black witnesses in court to take their oaths on separate Bibles!

Mississippi went so far as to criminalize the advocacy of racial equality, threatening to punish anyone for "printing, publishing or circulating printed, typewritten or written matter urging or presenting for public acceptance or general information, arguments or suggestions in favor of social equality or of intermarriage between whites and Negroes." Clearly, the Jim Crow laws established a regime of racial apartheid in the American South, despite the fact that the Fourteenth Amendment to the U.S. Constitution prohibited states from denying persons equal protection of the laws.

In *Plessy v. Ferguson* (1896), the Supreme Court upheld one of the Jim Crow laws that was challenged under the Equal Protection Clause, but its decision provided a rationale for the entire regime of segregation. At issue in *Plessy* was an 1890 Louisiana law requiring passenger trains operating within the state to provide "equal but separate" accommodations for the "white and colored races." Dividing seven to one (Justice David Brewer not participating), the Court sustained the Louisiana statute. Writing for the majority, Justice Henry Billings Brown asserted that "in the nature of things, [the Fourteenth Amendment] could not have been intended to abolish distinctions based upon color, or to enforce social, as distinguished from political, equality, or a commingling of the two races upon terms unsatisfactory to either." In the Court's view, racial separation did not necessarily imply racial inequality. Hence, the Court's decision in *Plessy* gave rise to the "separate but equal" doctrine that would be used for more than half a century to insulate Jim Crow laws from constitutional scrutiny.

Justice John M. Harlan (the elder) dissented vehemently in *Plessy*. For Justice Harlan, who was, ironically, a former Kentucky slave owner, the "arbitrary separation of citizens on the basis of race" was tantamount to imposing a "badge of servitude" on the black race. In one of the most widely quoted statements in American constitutional history, Harlan asserted that "our Constitution is color-blind, and neither knows nor tolerates classes among citizens."

The separate-but-equal doctrine approved in *Plessy* remained the authoritative interpretation of the Equal Protection Clause for 58 years. Ultimately, of course, it was repudiated by the Supreme Court under Chief Justice Earl Warren in a series of cases beginning with *Brown v. Board of Education of Topeka* (1954) and ending with *Loving v. Virginia* (1967). The Warren Court made clear in these decisions that compulsory segregation is inherently unequal. By 1967, the Jim Crow laws had been abolished. The Supreme Court's equal protection decisions together with the far-reaching Civil Rights Act of 1964 provided a strong impetus for racial integration, especially in the field of public accommodations and, at least through the 1970s,

in public education. Nevertheless, de facto racial segregation persists, most notably in residential patterns that clearly define the racial composition of local communities throughout the United States.

See also *Brown v. Board of Education* (1954;1955); Civil Rights Act of 1964; Equality; Equal Protection Clause; Equal Protection Jurisprudence; Federalism and Civil Rights and Liberties; Fourteenth Amendment; Interracial Marriage; *Loving v. Virginia* (1967); *Plessy v. Ferguson* (1896); Public Accommodation, Places of; Reconstruction; Segregation in Public Education; Segregation, De Facto and De Jure

Bibliography

Klarman, Michael J. 2004. *From Jim Crow to Civil Rights*. New York: Oxford University Press.

Stephens, Otis H., Jr., and John M. Scheb II. 2003. *American Constitutional Law*. 3rd ed. Belmont, CA: Wadsworth.

Woodward, C. Vann. 1968. *The Strange Career of Jim Crow*. New York: Oxford University Press.

Wormser, Richard. 2003. *The Rise and Fall of Jim Crow*. New York: St. Martin's Press.

Otis H. Stephens, Jr. and John M. Scheb II

JOHN BIRCH SOCIETY

The John Birch Society is an ultraconservative group that opposes ideas and trends that the organization deems to be contradictory to the U.S. Constitution. The Society was initially founded to fight the Communist conspiracy that was perceived to be a threat during the 1950s. The organization sought to educate citizens in the United States regarding the dangers of communism and expose communists everywhere. During its membership peak in the mid-1960s, hundreds of chapters of the John Birch Society were established across the country with over 100,000 members. Today, the headquarters of the John Birch Society are located in Appleton, Wisconsin, and local chapters exist in all 50 states.

The philosophical foundations of the John Birch Society are attributed to Robert Henry Winborne Welch, Jr., a retired candy maker from Massachusetts. Welch was born on December 1, 1899, in

Chowan County, North Carolina. At age 12, he became the youngest student to be admitted to The University of North Carolina at Chapel. A year after graduating from the University in June 1916, Welch entered the U.S. Naval Academy. He resigned two years later and returned to Stockton, North Carolina to write commentaries for four newspapers. Following a brief period of study at Harvard Law School, Welch started his own candy making company, worked for Brach and Sons, and became vice-president in charge of sales and advertising for the James O. Welch Company owned by his brother. As he achieved success in the business and financial world, Welch began to pursue his profound interests in scholarship, travel, and politics. He served as vice chairman of the Massachusetts Republican Finance Committee during the 1948 election and campaigned as a candidate for lieutenant governor of Massachusetts in the 1950 Republican primary.

The John Birch Society was formed in December 1958 in an Indianapolis, Indiana hotel. Welch delivered a two-day-long speech to 11 other businessmen in which he identified the "Communist conspiracy" in the United States as an immediate threat to individual freedom in this country. This speech was published as *The Blue Book of the John Birch Society*. In his speech, Welch summarized the purpose of the organization as "to promote less government, more responsibility, and a better world" (Welch 1961). He felt the society should be named for John Birch, a U.S. Army captain from Macon, Georgia, who was killed by communist Chinese soldiers in August 1945 after the end of World War II. Birch was a fundamentalist Baptist preacher and missionary who had joined General Chennault's 14th Air Force six months after the war was declared between the United States and Japan. Welch and many others theorized that Birch was murdered because of the influence he could have inspired against communism in postwar China.

Membership in the John Birch Society experienced a decline in the latter part of the twentieth century as the Cold War came to an end and the threat of nuclear war decreased significantly. The Society continued to exist, however, as the members' collective focus shifted to more immediate political issues facing the nation. During the 1970s and 1980s, the organization delivered over 11 million signatures to Congress petitioning the United States to withdraw from membership in the United Nations. In the late 1990s, the society launched an "Impeach Clinton Now" campaign before congressional hearings regarding the President were even proposed. The organization experienced some growth in membership and chapter numbers as the society has focused on its core mission to help American citizens understand the proper role of government in a free society. Since its inception, the John Birch Society has published over one hundred books including *Financial Terrorism* and *Shadows of Power*. In addition, the *New American* magazine is printed biweekly, and a monthly *Bulletin* is distributed describing the Society's agenda and current legislation which is of concern to its members. Information for the Tax Reform Immediately Movement (TRIM) is also published and distributed three times each year. This report provides the voting records of members of the House of Representatives regarding eight big spending issues. Other outlets utilized to distribute information on issues of concern to the John Birch Society include videocassettes, youth camps, and New American Clubs on college campuses.

See also Communist Party USA; Conservatism; Liberalism

Bibliography

Epstein, Benjamin R., and Arnold Forster. 1966. *The Radical Right: Report on the John Birch Society and Its Allies.* New York: Random House.

Griffin, G. Edward. 1975. *The Life and Words of Robert Welch.* Thousand Oaks, CA: American Media.

Schomp, Gerald. 1970. *Birchism Was My Business.* London: The MacMillian Company.

Stewart, Charles J. 2002. "The Master Conspiracy of the John Birch Society: From Communism to the New World Order." *Western Journal of Communication* 66(4): 424–48.

Welch, Robert. 1959. *The Blue Book of The John Birch Society.* Belmont, MA: Western Islands Publishers.

P. Edward French

JOHNSON V. EISENTRAGER (1950)

After the U.S. military action in Afghanistan, more than 600 people were taken captive and held at the U.S. Naval base in Guantanamo Bay, Cuba. These people were held without access to attorneys or to the U.S. court system. In defending its position, the Bush Administration asserted that these people were neither prisoners of war (and thus subject to the Third Geneva Convention), nor lawful combatants (and thus entitled to access the U.S. court system). The first conclusion rested on the assertion that the Taliban soldiers had not distinguished themselves sufficiently from Afghan civilians, nor had they followed the laws of war. The second conclusion rested on two U.S. Supreme Court decisions, *Ex Parte Quirin* (1942) and *Johnson v. Eisentrager* (1950). The first dealt with unlawful combatants; the second with enemy nonresident aliens.

The *Eisentrager* case began at the end of World War II, between the unconditional surrender of Germany and that of Japan. Following the German surrender in early May 1945, Lothar Eisentrager and 26 other German citizens continued their war against the United States by aiding the Japanese, primarily through espionage. Captured on Chinese soil, the U.S. military commission tried them and found 21 of them guilty of espionage and violations of the laws of war–of being unlawful combatants. The trial, although conducted on Chinese soil, was a purely American affair, since the Chinese were not involved. Upon review by the military reviewing authority, the commission was deemed to have been properly constructed, the trial was properly conducted, and the sentences appropriate for the crimes committed.

After sentencing, the convicted Germans were returned to West Germany to serve out their sentences on a U.S. Army base. While in Germany, the prisoners petitioned for a writ of habeas corpus; they wanted to be tried by the U.S. civilian court system. The District Court for the District of Columbia, as the court of original jurisdiction, heard their case. The burden of proof in a habeas corpus case is upon the government to show that the petitioners are not entitled to relief. The District Court held that the U.S. government did not sufficiently show that they were not entitled to a civil hearing and accordingly the petition was granted. Much of this decision was based on *Ex Parte Milligan* (1866), in which the Court determined that civilian prisoners were allowed access to civilian courts as long as the courts were open and operating.

The government appealed, basing its argument on two distinguishing facts. First, Eisentrager and the others, unlike Milligan, were not American citizens. As noncitizens, they were not given the same level of rights and access to the U.S. court system. Second, the 21 were never residents of America. In fact, they never set foot upon American soil.

The Court handed down a split decision (six-to-three) in favor of denying the petition. Delivering the opinion, Justice Robert Jackson focused on the fact that the 21 were nonresident enemy aliens. Jackson found the dispute over their actual status, vis-à-vis military or civilian, as immaterial to the decision.

While the U.S. Constitution does not specifically state that the Bill of Rights (including the Fifth and Sixth Amendments) applies only to citizens, it is long-held that citizens receive a higher level of rights than do noncitizens. Jackson continued this gradation of guaranteed rights. Even resident aliens are granted access to civil courts (see *Yick Wo v. Hopkins,* 1886). However, there is a considerable difference between aliens of friendly countries and aliens of enemy countries. Nonresident enemy aliens have no right of access to our courts in times of war. William Blackstone, the eminent English jurist, would have agreed. Jackson quotes him in the opinion to the effect that "alien enemies have no rights, no privileges, unless by the king's special favour, during the time of war."

The dissenting opinion, penned by Hugo L. Black, pointed out that previous court decisions, specifically, *Ex parte Quirin* and *In re Yamashita* (1946), allow for enemy aliens to contest conviction through habeas corpus proceedings. Thus, since the opinion explicitly asserted that it did not contradict either of these two findings, the relevant point of fact must be the defendants' capture, conviction, and incarceration outside American territory. Black regarded this as a dangerous precedent, because American occupation of foreign lands would then fall outside Court oversight.

As a result, the decision meant that Eisentrager and the other 20 prisoners had to serve out their sentences. It also meant that nonresident enemy aliens could be tried and convicted without civilian oversight *as long as* they never set foot upon American soil. Did this mean actual American soil, or did it also include American-controlled territory?

The concerns of Justice Hugo Black find new relevance today. Two recent cases underline the importance of the *Eisentrager* decision: *Rasul v. Bush* and *al Odah v. United States,* both decided in 2004. Because of the *Eisentrager* precedent, the Court had to determine whether Guantanamo Bay, Cuba was de facto part of the United States. In both cases, by six-to-three decisions, the Court answered yes. But the question remains: Who deserves the protections of the U.S. civil court system?

See also Bill of Rights (American) (1789); Black, Hugo L.; Blackstone, William; Fifth Amendment; Habeas Corpus; Jackson, Robert H.; *Milligan, Ex parte; Quirin, Ex parte* (1942); Sixth Amendment; Terrorism, War on; *Yick Wo v. Hopkins*

Ole J. Forsberg

JUDEO-CHRISTIAN MORALITY. *See* Natural Law and Natural Rights

JUDICIAL ACTIVISM

The term *judicial activism* figures prominently in both scholarly and popular commentary on the courts, although the term is often employed to mean different things and is difficult to define with precision. Sometimes the term denotes a proclivity to strike down statutes and other actions of government, whereas judicial self-restraint counsels deference to policies made by the other branches. But is it judicial activism for a court to declare invalid a statute that clearly violates the Constitution, or is it merely the proper exercise of judicial review? Dissenting in *Massachusetts v. Laird* (1970), Justice

William O. Douglas remarked, "It is far more important to be respectful to the Constitution than to a coordinate branch of government." Of course, there are different theories as to how the Constitution should be understood and interpreted, and seldom does the U.S. Supreme Court review a statute where good arguments cannot be made for and against its constitutionality.

Today, the term judicial activism is used more commonly to mean "legislating from the bench," that is, merely using a statute or the Constitution as a means of advancing a judge's personal policy goal. The recognition of new rights by the courts, such as the constitutional right of privacy established in *Griswold v. Connecticut* (1965), is widely regarded as a clear example of judicial activism. *Roe v. Wade* (1973), in which the Supreme Court effectively legalized abortion on the basis of a broad reading of the Due Process Clause of the Fourteenth Amendment, is often singled out as another prominent example of judicial activism. But those who believe that *Roe* was wrongly decided and ought to be overturned are also accused of condoning judicial activism. For example, sharply divided decisions of the Rehnquist Court striking down congressional measures abolishing state sovereign immunity in the areas of age and disability discrimination were assailed as blatant instances of conservative judicial activism (see *Kimel v. Board of Regents,* 2000; *Board of Trustees v. Garrett,* 2001).

Activism is used to refer to a judge's willingness to overturn precedent, whereas judicial restraint entails respect for *stare decisis.* But what if the precedent under consideration is not well established and is based on erroneous reasoning? Is correcting such an error activism?

Court decisions that manifest all three of the foregoing characteristics (striking down legislation; overturning precedent; recognizing new rights) are most likely to be dubbed activist decisions. For example, in *Lawrence v. Texas* (2003), the Supreme Court overturned precedent (*Bowers v. Hardwick,* 1986) and declared unconstitutional a Texas law criminalizing private, consensual homosexual activity. Because the text of the Constitution does not address such issues, the decision was based on a broad interpretation of the term "liberty" found within the Fourteenth Amendment. In dissent, Justice Antonin Scalia asserted that the decision was really "the product of a Court, which is the product of a law-profession culture, that has largely signed on to the so-called homosexual agenda, by which I mean the agenda promoted by some homosexual activists directed at eliminating the moral opprobrium that has traditionally attached to homosexual conduct."

It should be emphasized that judicial power can be used for liberal or conservative policy goals. For example, in the Dred Scott Case (1857), a conservative Supreme Court actively defended the institution of slavery on dubious constitutional grounds. Similarly, in *Lochner v. New York* (1905), a conservative Court used its power to frustrate the implementation of progressive economic legislation. Accordingly, the terms judicial activism and judicial self-restraint are not correctly identified with either liberal or conservative political ideologies.

Much of American constitutional law can be seen as an ongoing debate between judicial activism and judicial restraint. In a system committed both to representative democracy and avoiding the tyranny of the majority, it is inevitable that the courts will wrestle with the problem of defining the proper judicial role. This dynamic tension is most visible in the Supreme Court's exercise of the power of judicial review.

See also Conservatism; Douglas, William O.; Dred Scott Case; Due Process Clauses; Fourteenth Amendment; *Griswold v. Connecticut* (1965); Judicial Restraint; *Lawrence v. Texas* (2003); Liberalism; *Lochner v. New York* (1905); Privacy, Constitutional Right of; *Roe v. Wade* (1973); Scalia, Antonin; Tyranny of the Majority

Bibliography

Halpern, Stephen C., and Charles M. Lamb, eds. 1982. *Supreme Court Activism and Restraint.* Lexington, MA: Lexington Books.

Powers, Stephen P., and Stanley Rothman. 2002. *The Least Dangerous Branch?: Consequences of Judicial Activism.* Westport, CT: Praeger.

Schwartz, Herman. 2002. *The Rehnquist Court: Judicial Activism on the Right.* New York: Hill and Wang.

Wolfe, Christopher. 1997. *Judicial Activism.* Lanham, MD: Rowman and Littlefield.

Otis H. Stephens, Jr. and John M. Scheb II

JUDICIAL IMMUNITY. *See* Immunity, Judicial

JUDICIAL RESTRAINT

Judicial restraint is a philosophy of judicial review that counsels courts to exercise their powers cautiously and to avoid conflicts with other branches of government. Advocates of judicial restraint do not regard courts as the primary custodians of the general welfare; in their view, that role belongs to Congress and the state legislatures. Judicial restraintists believe that courts should by and large defer to the policy choices of the people's elected representatives. Typically, advocates of judicial restraint do not favor aggressive enforcement of civil rights and liberties by the courts.

Judicial restraint requires judges to give substantial deference to the intentions of the legislature that enacted a particular statute, rather than to apply their own understanding of the underlying issue and political solution to the problem addressed by that legislation. This reflects the concept that democratic elections most accurately reflect the popular will through authority transmitted from voters to representatives who act on their behalf. Thus, judges appointed to lifetime terms without direct public involvement are seen as too far removed from the citizenry to serve as their delegates. Instead, their role is to arbitrate disputes through the application of a law to a specific situation, not to assess or challenge the wisdom of the law-making body's particular response to a social issue. Implicit in this view is that judges should not be swayed by popular sentiment or political pressure on the system to reach their decision on critical issues of the day.

With respect to constitutional matters, advocates of judicial restraint believe that constitutional questions should be avoided if at all possible. Thus, if a case can be decided on statutory grounds rather than constitutional grounds, courts should opt for the former. If, however, a constitutional question cannot be avoided, courts should operate with a presumption that a challenged law is constitutional. That is, the burden falls on the party bringing the challenge to demonstrate that the statute violates constitutional principles. In exercising judicial review of legislation, courts should strive to find a way to validate the policy choices of the people's representatives. If a statute can be interpreted in a way so as to preserve its constitutionality, courts should opt for this "saving construction." Judicial restraintists also believe that courts should interpret constitutional provisions carefully, maintaining fidelity to text, intentions of the framers, history, and precedent, lest judges use constitutional interpretation as a guise for the enactment of their own policy preferences.

Supreme Court Justice Felix Frankfurter often is cited as a prime example of this approach. His dissenting opinion in *West Virginia State Board of Education v. Barnette* (1943) contains a classic statement of the philosophy of judicial self-restraint:

As a member of this Court I am not justified in writing my private notions of policy into the Constitution, no matter how deeply I may cherish them or how mischievous I may deem their disregard. The duty of a judge who must decide which of two claims before the Court shall prevail…is not that of the ordinary person. It can never be emphasized too much that one's own opinion about the wisdom or evil of a law should be excluded altogether when one is doing one's duty on the bench.

Frankfurter goes on to insist that "[j]udicial self-restraint is equally necessary whenever an exercise of political or legislative power is challenged."

Justice Oliver Wendell Holmes, Jr.'s dissenting opinion in *Lochner v. New York* (1905) also contains a classic statement of judicial restraint. Objecting to the Court's employment of the Fourteenth Amendment to strike down a state law limiting the hours of work in bakeries, Holmes wrote: "I think that the word 'liberty,' in the 14th Amendment, is perverted when it is held to prevent the natural outcome of a dominant opinion, unless it can be said that a rational and fair man necessarily would admit

that the statute proposed would infringe fundamental principles as they have been understood by the traditions of our people and our law." In *Griswold v. Connecticut* (1965), where the Supreme Court first recognized a constitutional right of privacy in striking down a state law banning contraceptives, Justice Potter Stewart's dissenting opinion sounded a similar theme:

It is the essence of judicial duty to subordinate our own personal views, our own ideas of what legislation is wise and what is not. If, as I should surely hope, the law before us does not reflect the standards of the people of Connecticut, the people of Connecticut can freely exercise their true Ninth and Tenth Amendment rights to persuade their elected representative to repeal it. That is the constitutional way to take this law off the books.

Among contemporary constitutional commentators, Robert Bork is the best-known exponent of judicial restraint. For Bork, the abandonment of judicial restraint by the modern courts in cases like *Griswold v. Connecticut* has meant that the country is "increasingly governed not by law or elected representatives but by an unelected, unrepresentative, unaccountable committee of lawyers applying no will but their own" (Bork 130). Bork's vocal criticism of modern constitutional law, regarded as reactionary in some quarters, cost him a seat on the United States Supreme Court. During his ill-fated Senate confirmation hearing in 1987, anti-Bork protesters gathered in the streets chanting, among other things, "Hey hey, ho ho, judicial restraint has got to go."

See also Bork, Robert H.; Due Process, Substantive; Fourteenth Amendment (1868); Frankfurter, Felix; Holmes, Oliver Wendell, Jr.; *Griswold v. Connecticut* (1965); Interpretivism; Judicial Activism; *Lochner v. New York* (1905); Original Intent, Doctrine of; Privacy, Rights of; Stewart, Potter; *West Virginia Board of Education v. Barnette* (1943)

Bibliography

Bork, Robert H. 1990. *The Tempting of America: The Political Seduction of the Law.* New York: The Free Press.

Lamb, Charles. 1982. "Judicial Restraint on the Supreme Court." In *Supreme Court Activism and Restraint*, eds. Stephen C. Halperin and Charles M. Lamb. Lexington, MA: Lexington Books.

James Gilchrist

JURY, TRIAL BY

The origins of the American jury system are rooted in English history and common law. The concept and practice of jury trials evolved over a long period beginning with the early trials by battle and ordeal and leading to the creation of presenting (grand) juries that decided whether there was enough evidence to bring a suspected criminal to trial. Trial (petit) juries judging between guilt and innocence emerged after 1215 a.d. in the wake of two important events. One was a directive from Rome that priests were to abandon their long-held positions as arbiters of guilt at trials by ordeal (Dwyer 2002, 34). In the absence of divine judgments, royal judges turned to members of local communities to decide disputes. At the same time, King John was forced by his barons to agree to a list of stipulations, later known as the Magna Carta, designed to protect them from the King's arbitrary rule. Not least among the demands of the Magna Carta was that, "no free man shall be seized or imprisoned … or outlawed or exiled … except by the lawful judgment of his equals or by the law of the land." Together, these events represented an important step away from religious and arbitrary resolution of disputes towards more secular and predictable means of dispute resolution.

Over the next several hundred years, the character and power of juries developed. The first juries operated in an environment lacking systematic rules and procedures for dispute resolution; indeed, there were few lawyers and the judges were strangers to the community. Thus, juries consisted of locals who had first-hand knowledge of the crime or litigants. Personal observations and impressions were critical to the determination of guilt or innocence. As populations grew, communities became more complex, and the state apparatus developed, dispute resolution became more organized and formal. Jurors were less connected to the facts and the disputants. Instead, they based their judgments on evidence presented by both sides of the conflict, and were required to make unanimous verdicts through their evaluation of the information heard at trial.

Throughout this time, juries exercised great power insofar as they were largely independent of the other court actors, making decisions based on their own judgments of the information presented. Even in the latter period, when they were less personally connected to the cases they heard, jurors were expected to use their common sense and consciences in understanding and application of the law (Green 1985, 26–27). Not infrequently, and particularly in capital cases, juries tempered the stringency of British law by acquitting guilty defendants or lessening penalties. The function and power of the English jury demonstrates the political as well as legal role of the institution, and had significant implications for the development of American juries.

The earliest American political documents illustrate the significance of the political consequences of jury trials. The Declaration of Independence (1776) made a specific complaint to King George about the deprivation of trials by jury to the colonies; according to the Declaration's author, Thomas Jefferson, juries were a means of protecting individuals against despotism, a safeguard of liberties essential to a free government. The most meaningful statements of the political importance of juries were made in the Constitution (1789) and the Bill of Rights (1791). While the Federalists and Anti-Federalists struggled over the relative authority of the federal and state governments to administer jury trials, there was no disagreement about the value of juries. As Alexis de Tocqueville (1835) noted, the jury was like the suffrage, "an eminently republican element in the government … [placing] the real direction of society in the hands of the governed, or of a portion of the governed, and not in that of the government." (Tocqueville 1981, 166)

Thus, jury trial was one method, in addition to others built into the new Constitution, of holding the new government accountable to the people. True, the early jury selection processes, like then existing qualifications for voting, excluded many citizens. The concept of peers was still vital, however, insofar as it guaranteed that lay people would have an independent and powerful role in politics. Article III, Section 2 of the Constitution insists that:

The trial of all crimes, except in cases of impeachment, shall be by jury; and such trial shall be held in the state where the said crimes shall have been committed; but when not committed within any state, the trial shall be at such place or places as the Congress may by law have directed.

Additionally, the Sixth Amendment requires that "In all criminal prosecutions, the accused shall enjoy the right to a speedy and public trial, by an impartial jury of the state and district wherein the crime shall have been committed…" and the Seventh Amendment reads in part: "In suits at common law, where the value in controversy shall exceed twenty dollars, the right of trial by jury shall be preserved …."

Of course, it is one thing to include protections of this kind in the Constitution; it is a different and more difficult task fully to understand and administer them. There are many ambiguities in the text of these constitutional guarantees. First of all, to whom do the guarantees apply? Because these rights to trial by jury were made in the federal Constitution, they were applicable originally only to defendants or other litigants tried in federal courts. While many states had similar protections in their laws and constitutions, the right to trial by jury protected by the Constitution was not applicable to the states. This changed, however, when the United States Supreme Court issued its ruling in *Duncan v. Louisiana* (1968), a case involving a misdemeanor conviction. According to the Louisiana Constitution, defendants charged with misdemeanors did not have the right to a jury trial. Duncan, whose case was tried before a judge, appealed his conviction for misdemeanor battery. He argued that trial by jury is a fundamental right protected by the U.S. Constitution. The Supreme Court agreed:

Because we believe that trial by jury in criminal cases is fundamental to the American scheme of justice, we hold that the Fourteenth Amendment guarantees a right of jury trial in all criminal cases which—were they to be tried in a federal court—would come within the Sixth Amendment's guarantee.

In so arguing, the Court incorporated the jury trial provision of the Sixth Amendment into the Fourteenth Amendment, making it applicable to the states. By contrast, the Seventh Amendment has never been incorporated, thus the right to trial by jury does not apply to civil cases brought in state courts. Some states do guarantee jury trials to civil litigants, but there is no federal mandate requiring them to do so.

Another ambiguity in the constitutional text concerns the question of just what constitutes a jury. For example, how many jurors should sit on a jury? In the context of criminal trials, the early interpretations by the Court were based on English common law that established 12-person juries (see, for example, *Thompson v. Utah*, 1898). But in the last several decades, the Supreme Court has turned from common law explanations to the framers of the Constitution for guidance, and has found no requirement of a 12-person jury. Thus, in *Williams v. Florida* (1970), the Court ruled that a Florida law requiring a 12-member jury *only* in capital cases did not violate the Sixth Amendment as applied to the states through the Fourteenth Amendment. In the Court's words, the rule of 12 was an "historical accident" with no confirmation in the Constitution. Recognizing that there was little empirical evidence available on the reliability of juries of different sizes, the Court still concluded that the Sixth Amendment required only that there be enough jurors to encourage deliberation, to prevent intimidation, and to represent the community. Smaller juries, such as the six-person jury empanelled for Williams, fulfilled this condition (as they did for civil juries also; see *Colgrove v. Battin*, 1973). In his dissent, Justice Harlan wondered, "… if 12 jurors are not essential, why are six?" In other words, at what point is a jury too small to meet constitutional requirements?

Eight years later, and with the benefit of empirical research on the effects of jury size, the Court presented an answer. In *Ballew v. Georgia* (1978), the Court acknowledged the evidence that juries of six were significantly more likely than juries of 12 to reach incorrect verdicts, less likely to deliberate effectively, and more likely to be missing minority representation. Nevertheless, the Court maintained the precedent established in *Williams* and drew the constitutional line at six jurors when it agreed with the defendant that a five-person jury was unconstitutional. According to the Court, the Sixth Amendment requires that a jury consist of at least six jurors to provide the requisite protection of the defendant and representation of the community. Although the majority of states empanel 12 jurors in felony cases, most states allow fewer than 12 jurors in misdemeanor criminal cases and in civil cases.

The issue of representation highlighted in *Ballew* is another critical aspect of trial by jury, one that is not specified in the Constitution. *Who* should be jurors? The answer relies on two related concepts: peers and impartiality. Historically, peers were simply lay people, members of the community in which a crime or dispute occurred; their most essential characteristic was that they were not officials of government or members of the nobility. In other words, they were in a position to protect defendants and other litigants from the power of the state by being more like the defendant than they were like the government. A point of debate for some time has been how similar to the defendant jurors should be. Generally, legislators and judges have determined that, as a group, jurors should reflect the diversity in a community. However, this does not mean that every juror, or even the majority of jurors, should look, act, or think like the defendant in order to be considered his or her peer. In 1968, Congress passed the Jury Selection Act, confirming this conception by requiring federal juries to be chosen by a "fair cross section" of the community. To meet this requirement, potential jurors are identified by Department of Motor Vehicles or voter registration records, and then are randomly assigned to a *venire,* or panel, from which jurors for particular cases will be chosen.

Several years later, the Supreme Court made the provisions of the Jury Selection Act applicable to state jury selection in *Taylor v. Louisiana* (1975). Taylor, a male, was convicted by a jury that included no women because Louisiana had constitutional and statutory requirements that women not be selected for jury duty unless they declared in writing their wish to serve. The defendant argued that his right to trial by jury had been violated by the absence of women, which diminished the representative nature and function of his jury. Relying on precedent as well as the Jury Selection Act, the Court agreed that Taylor's Sixth Amendment right to trial by jury had been violated.

The idea of a fair cross section of the community reflects the concern for the impartiality of juries; importantly, the number of jurors also implicates impartiality. Note that the emphasis here is not on impartial jur*ors,* but rather impartial jur*ies.* In other words, the expectation of individual jurors is that they will be biased in potentially important ways. To combat the problems associated with individual biases, jury selection processes are designed to have a minimum number of jurors seated but also to choose jurors who have different prejudices and who are then obliged to deliberate and work through them towards the most just outcome for the defendant and the community. Through *voir dire* (which means "to speak the truth"), potential jurors are questioned by judges and lawyers to determine the amount and type of knowledge and views that they bring to the decision-making process. As part of the adversarial nature of trials, but also as a method of selecting an impartial jury, jurors can be eliminated through two types of challenges: for cause, which requires that lawyers provide a specific reason for eliminating a juror; and, peremptory challenges, which require no explanation and are often based on lawyers' intuition about which jurors will be most likely to find for their client.

The Supreme Court has been asked to step in many times to clarify the appropriate criteria for choosing jurors, and in so doing, has clarified the purpose of juries in the justice system and in American politics more generally. In part, the Court addressed impartiality when it recognized in *Ballew* that individual jurors would bring their biases to their judgments; requiring a minimum number of jurors was a method of balancing these biases to create just outcomes. But the Court's attention to impartiality has been more complicated than *Ballew* suggests because the process of jury selection is beset with attempts to exclude, often systematically, particular people from jury service in an attempt to obtain desired outcomes.

As long ago as 1879, the Court addressed the issue of discriminating against certain types of jurors. In *Strauder v. West Virginia* (1879), the Court ruled that prohibiting blacks from being members of the venire because of their race was a violation of the Equal Protection Clause of the Fourteenth Amendment; citizens may not be denied participation in the administration of justice based on their race. More recently, the Court has addressed the constitutionality of race- and gender-based peremptory challenges in cases such as *Swain v. Alabama* (1965), *Batson v. Kentucky* (1986), *J.E.B. v. Alabama* (1994), *Miller-El v. Cockrell* (2003), and *Miller-El v. Dretke* (2005).

Closely related to these discussions about the constitutional requirements and purpose of trial juries is the ongoing debate about the efficacy of the jury. The debate has at least two related elements. One is jury nullification, the authority of the jury to use its unique political responsibility in the justice system to circumvent what it believes to be an illegitimate law to achieve a just outcome. Importantly, this is not a right that juries have; indeed, juries are often unaware of this authority, and judges make a practice of not informing juries about nullification and often instruct them not to nullify. Instead, nullification is a power that dates to English common law juries, and both English and American history are replete with examples of nullifying juries.

The debate about the merits of jury nullification is as old as the power itself. In many instances, this is a battle about the independence of juries and control over outcomes; the contemporary discussion about nullification is largely about dissatisfaction with jury verdicts that appear to circumvent the established legal process. It is also about jury deliberation, because the ability of jurors to discuss their consciences and debate the merits of laws may be an important part of reaching a verdict (Abramson 1994, 93).

Moreover, the conflict is also about competing principles of American democracy. In *United States v. Battiste* (1835), Justice Joseph Story made a controversial, yet compelling, ruling that juries should not determine the law. While the value of republicanism is fundamental to American democracy, and jurors fulfill an important republican purpose when they decide issues of fact, the value of equal protection of the laws is just as significant to the proper functioning of democracy. According to Story, if jurors were allowed to decided issues of law, then litigants would face a legal system absent the uniform and predictable application of laws (Abramson 1994, 79). Laws would be applied differently depending on the jury drawn in any particular case. Only judges, regular participants in the justice system, trained and experienced in the law, could be trusted with the responsibility of ensuring the equal protection requirements of the Constitution.

The second significant element of the discussion about the efficacy of the jury is the requirement of unanimity. Also a significant part of English common law, the idea of a unanimous verdict has been integral to the American conception of criminal trials by jury. Or it was until 1972, when the Supreme Court ruled in *Johnson v. Louisiana* (1972) and *Apodaca v. Oregon* (1972) that the Constitution did not require states to have unanimous juries (federal law requires that federal juries reach unanimous verdicts). In reasoning similar to rulings about the size of juries, the Court argued that allowing juries to split either 10–2 (as in *Apodaca*) or 9–3 (as in *Johnson*) would not diminish their reliability or representativeness (significantly, the Court has ruled that 5–1 verdicts are unconstitutional because they essentially amount to a verdict by 5-person juries; see *Burch v. Louisiana* [1979]). In so finding, the Court diminished as arbitrary the historical common-law basis of unanimity, just as it did for the 12-person jury.

The debate about whether juries should reach unanimous verdicts focuses, like nullification, on outcomes and deliberation. There are many who are concerned with the incidence of hung juries and the difficulty of obtaining guilty verdicts. They promote majority verdicts as a solution to both of these problems. There are others who stress the significance of unanimity to deliberation and the representativeness of juries. The requirement of unanimity means that jurors must convince each other of the validity of their interpretations of facts. In the absence of unanimity, majority views win at the expense of minority views, lessening the influence of representation on juries.

This essay suggests that the development of the American trial jury reflects the constitutional, political, and legal debates that characterize American politics more generally. As the debate about the role and structure of the jury continues, it is valuable to remember that the jury is both a legal and a political institution. With recommendations for change should come careful consideration of the potential consequences of significant alterations to a fundamentally political institution designed to increase popular control over the power of the state. This is not to argue that institutions should not be adapted to the changing needs and desires of the community, but to recognize that doing so may come with costs to fundamental rights and, more broadly, to democracy itself.

See also Accused, Rights of the; Bill of Rights (American) (1789); Bill of Rights, Incorporation of; Challenges for Cause; Common Law Background of American Civil Rights and Liberties; Death-Qualified Juries; Declaration of Independence; Fourteenth Amendment (1868); Fundamental Rights; Grand Jury; Jefferson, Thomas; Magna Carta; Peremptory Challenges to Prospective Jurors; Seventh Amendment; Sixth Amendment

Bibliography

Abramson, Jeffrey. 1994. *We, the Jury: The Jury System and the Ideal of Democracy.* New York: Basic Books.

Dwyer, William L. 2002. *In the Hands of the People: The Trial Jury's Origins, Triumphs, Troubles, and Future in American Democracy.* New York: St. Martin's Press.

Green, Thomas Andrew. 1985. *Verdict According to Conscience.* Chicago: University of Chicago Press.

Tocqueville, Alexis de. 1981. *Democracy in America.* Abridged with Introduction by Thomas Bender. New York: Random House.

Jennifer Segal Diascro

JUST COMPENSATION CLAUSE

The Takings Clause of the Fifth Amendment to the Constitution states "nor shall private property be taken for public use, without just compensation." This language tacitly recognizes the federal government's inherent power of eminent domain; as the United States Supreme Court said in *Boom Co. v. Patterson* (1879), this power "appertains to every independent government. It requires no constitutional recognition; it is an attribute of sovereignty."

Prior to the adoption of the Fourteenth Amendment, the power of eminent domain of state governments was unrestrained by any federal authority. In *Barron v. Baltimore* (1833), the Supreme Court held that the just compensation provision of the Fifth Amendment did not apply to the States. In *Chicago, Burlington, & Quincy Railroad Co. v. Chicago* (1897), however, the Court embraced the argument that the Due Process Clause of the Fourteenth Amendment afforded property owners the same measure of protection against the states as the Fifth Amendment did against the federal government. It ruled that, although a state "legislature may prescribe a form of procedure to be observed in the taking of private property for public use, ... it is not due process of law if provision be not made for compensation.... The mere form of the proceeding instituted against the owner ... cannot convert the process used into due process of law, if the necessary result be to deprive him of his property without compensation." While the federal and state guarantees of just compensation flow from different sources, the standards used by the Court in dealing with the issues appear to be identical, whether they arise in federal or state cases.

The purpose of requiring just compensation is, according to the Court in *Armstrong v. United States* (1960), "to bar Government from forcing some people alone to bear public burdens which, in all fairness and justice, should be borne by the public as a whole." What just compensation means was defined by the Court in *Monongahela Navigation Co. v. United States* (1893) as "a full and perfect equivalent for the property taken." This has come to mean the market value of the property, that is, what a willing buyer would pay a willing seller. Since property is ordinarily taken under a condemnation suit upon the payment of the money award by the condemner, no interest accrues. However, if the property is taken before payment is made, the courts have held that just compensation requires the payment of interest.

At its simplest, just compensation requires that, if real property is condemned, the market value of that property must be paid to the owner. Things, however, are seldom that simple, as there are many kinds of property and many uses of property, which cause problems in computing just compensation. For example, if only a portion of a tract of land is taken, the owner's compensation is to include any element of value arising out of the relation of the part taken to the entire tract, unless the taking has in fact benefited the owner, in which case the benefit may be set off against the value of the land condemned (even then, however, any benefit that the owner receives in common with the rest of the public may not be set off). Moreover, interests in intangible as well as tangible property are protected, and compensation must be paid for the taking of contract rights, patent rights, and even trade secrets.

The courts have long held that legislatures are free to decide on the nature and character of the tribunals that determine compensation; as a consequence, they may be regular courts, special legislative courts, commissions, or administrative bodies. Proceedings to condemn land for the benefit of the United States are brought in the federal district court for the district in which the land is located.

When a government itself initiates a condemnation proceeding against someone's property, the question of whether that property has been "taken," with the consequent requirement of just compensation, does not arise. However, questions of whether there has been a taking do arise when physical damage results to property because of government action, or when regulatory action limits activity on the property or otherwise deprives it of value.

In *Pumpelly v. Green Bay Co.* (1872), the Court determined that land can be "taken" in the constitutional sense by physical invasion or occupation by the government, as occurs when government floods land. More recently, it held in *Griggs v. Allegheny County* (1962) that operators of airports are required to compensate the owners of adjacent land when the noise, glare, and fear of injury occasioned by low-altitude over-flights during takeoffs and landings made the land unfit for the use to which the owners had applied it. Cases such as these, where the government has not instituted formal condemnation proceedings but instead property owners have sued for just compensation claiming that governmental action or regulation has "taken" their property, are described as "inverse condemnation."

Regulation may deprive owners of most or all beneficial use of their property or may destroy the values of the property for the purposes to which it is suited. Does such regulation also constitute a taking? Initially, the Court flatly denied the possibility of compensation for this diminution of property values; however, in *Pennsylvania Coal Co. v. Mahon* (1922), it established as a general principle that "if regulation goes too far it will be recognized as a taking." But, how far is "too far"?

While the Court confessed in *Penn Central Transportation Co. v. City of New York* (1978) that it had failed to develop a "set formula to determine where regulation ends and taking begins," it has responded to increasing governmental regulation of property over the years in terms of zoning and land-use controls, environmental regulations, and so forth, by formulating general principles for determining whether a regulatory taking has occurred. One guideline was spelled out in *Penn Central:* Courts must consider the "economic impact of the regulation on the claimant and, particularly, the extent to which the regulation has interfered with reasonable investment-backed expectations." A second, announced in *Loretto v. Teleprompter Manhattan CATV Corp.* (1982), involves physical invasions: when government permanently occupies or authorizes someone else to occupy property, the action constitutes a taking and compensation must be paid regardless of the public interests served by the occupation or the extent of damage to the parcel as a whole.

A third guideline was spelled out by the Court in *Agins v. City of Tiburon* (1980): A land use regulation must "substantially advance legitimate governmental interests." Applying that guideline in *Nollan v. California Coastal Commission* (1987), the Court held that extraction of a public access easement across a strip of beach as a condition for a permit to enlarge a beachfront home did not "substantially advance" the state's legitimate interest in preserving the public's view of the beach from the street in front of the lot. A fourth guideline was also announced in *Agins:* The regulation cannot deny a property owner "economically viable use of his land." The Court elaborated on this guideline in *Lucas v. South Carolina Coastal Council* (1992), a case in which a landowner was deprived of all "economically viable use" of his $1 million property when the state enacted a coastal zone act, designed to prevent beach erosion, that prevented him from building a beachfront home on his property: "When the owner of real property has been called upon to sacrifice all economically beneficial uses in the name of the common good, that is, to leave his property economically idle, he has suffered a taking."

Finally, a fifth guideline was provided by the Court in *Tahoe-Sierra Preservation Council* v. *Tahoe Regional Planning Agency* (2002). In it, the Court held that no compensation is due to property owners who are temporarily deprived of all economically viable use of their land through, as in this case, the imposition of moratoria on development imposed by governmental agencies during the process of drafting a comprehensive land-use plan.

See also *Barron v. Baltimore* (1833); Bill of Rights (American) (1789); *Chicago, Burlington, & Quincy Railroad Co. v. Chicago* (1897); Due Process, Procedural; Due Process, Substantive; Fifth Amendment; Fourteenth Amendment (1868); Property Rights; Public Use Clause

Bibliography

Epstein, Richard. 1989. *Takings: Private Property and the Power of Eminent Domain.* Cambridge, MA: Harvard University Press.

Mercuro, Nicholas, ed. 1992. *Taking Property and Just Compensation: Law and Economics Perspectives of the Takings Issue.* Dordrecht, Netherlands: Kluwer Academic Publishers.

Ralph A. Rossum

JUVENILE DEATH PENALTY. *See* Death Penalty for Juveniles

JUVENILE JUSTICE

The juvenile justice system includes law enforcement agencies, social services agencies, specialized courts, and corrections facilities designed to address problems of juvenile delinquency as well as child neglect and abuse, the latter often being handled apart from juvenile court proceedings. *Delinquency* refers to conduct that would be criminal if committed by an adult. In addition to being charged with delinquency, young people may be subjected to the jurisdiction of a juvenile court for engaging in conduct that is prohibited only for minors, for example, purchasing alcoholic beverages or violating curfews. They may also be taken into custody for such prohibited behavior as truancy (chronic absence from school) and incorrigibility, which are often referred to as *status offenses* because they are peculiar to the status of children.

Of the roughly two million juveniles taken into custody every year, more than half are dealt with by specialized juvenile courts. Of course, some juveniles are charged with very serious crimes, such as murder, rape, aggravated assault, and armed robbery. These grave offenses, especially when committed by older juveniles, are sometimes adjudicated by the regular criminal courts. Indeed, as juvenile crime escalated in the 1980s and 1990s, many states enacted laws making it easier to prosecute and punish juvenile offenders, age 14 or older, as adults. In recent years, rates of juvenile crime have declined, but there is no consensus as to whether the decline is related to the increased tendency to treat juvenile offenders as adults.

The Common-Law Background

Although the English common law did not recognize specific protections for juveniles, it created an irrebuttable presumption that children under the age of 7 were incapable of *mens rea* (criminal intent), and therefore immune from criminal responsibility. Children between the ages of 7 and 14 were also presumed not to be responsible for criminal acts, but the presumption was rebuttable. The common law treated all persons above the age of 14 as adults.

Because the American legal system was based on English common law, American courts followed the common-law rules for the treatment of juveniles. Young teenagers were treated essentially as adults for the purposes of criminal justice. In 1646, Massachusetts enacted a Stubborn Child Law, an early introduction to status offenses. During the colonial period of American history families often imposed corporal punishment; however, it was not uncommon for teenagers to be hanged, flogged, or placed in the public pillory as punishment for serious crimes. Later, as state penitentiaries were established, it was not unusual for 20 percent of prison populations to be juveniles.

Establishment of the Juvenile Justice System

In the late nineteenth century, public outcry against treating juveniles like adults led to the establishment of a separate justice system for juveniles. The first state to act was Illinois, which in 1899 passed "An Act to Regulate the Treatment and Control of Dependent, Neglected, and Delinquent Children." By the 1920s, many states had followed suit, and by 1945 juvenile court legislation had been enacted by Congress and all state legislatures.

The new juvenile courts were created to deal with young offenders not as hardened criminals, but as misguided youth in need of special care. This special treatment was justified legally by the concept of *parens patriae,* which is the power of the state to act as a sort of super-parent to protect the welfare of children and others who are unable to protect themselves.

The newly created juvenile courts were usually separate from the regular tribunals; often the judges or referees presiding over these courts had no formal legal training. Generally unconcerned with procedural regularity or strict rules of evidence, juvenile judges often assumed the role of benign patriarch. Juvenile delinquency proceedings were generally nonadversarial, and there was little in the way of consistent procedure or even the opportunity for the juvenile offender to confront his or her accusers. In fact, juvenile delinquency proceedings were conceived as civil, as opposed to criminal, proceedings. Dispositions of cases were usually nonpunitive in character; therefore, accused juvenile offenders were not afforded most of the rights of criminal defendants. Typically, juveniles were not represented by counsel. They often had little opportunity to prepare a defense, obtain favorable witnesses, or even confront adverse witnesses. Because juvenile courts usually were not courts of record, rarely were delinquency proceedings transcribed. Appeals to higher courts were rare.

Because the juvenile justice system emphasized rehabilitation (rather than retribution, incapacitation, or deterrence), juveniles who were found delinquent were often placed in reformatories for indeterminate periods, sometimes until they reached the age of majority. Juvenile courts were often under-funded, suffered from judges who had no formal legal training, and lacked trained staffs and adequate facilities. By the 1960s, a period of significant legal reforms in the United States, a system conceived by reformers to rehabilitate juvenile offenders—indeed the concept of *parens patriae* itself—were under attack by a new generation of reformers.

The *Gault* Decision and Subsequent Developments

The abuses that came to be associated with juvenile courts were addressed by the U.S. Supreme Court in the landmark case of *In re Gault* (1967). In *Gault,* the Court recognized that juvenile delinquency hearings threatened the loss of liberty and required juvenile courts to adhere to standards of due process, applying most of the basic procedural safeguards enjoyed by adults accused of crimes. Specifically, the Court held that juveniles charged with delinquency must be provided fair notice of the charges and an opportunity to prepare a defense; the right to be represented by counsel; the right to subpoena favorable witnesses and cross-examine hostile ones; and the right to be free from compulsory self-incrimination.

In *In re Winship* (1970), the Supreme Court continued down the path it had blazed in *Gault* by holding that the reasonable doubt standard characteristic of adult criminal trials is a constitutional requisite in juvenile delinquency proceedings. In the wake of *Gault* and *Winship,* a number of states revised their juvenile codes to reflect the requirements of those decisions and, moreover, to increase the qualifications of persons serving as juvenile judges and to transform juvenile courts into courts of record.

In *McKeiver v. Pennsylvania* (1971), the Court refused to extend the right to trial by jury to juvenile proceedings. Writing for a plurality, Justice Harry Blackmun concluded that juries are not indispensable to fair and equitable juvenile proceedings. But in *Breed v. Jones* (1975), the Court extended the Fifth Amendment protection against double jeopardy to juvenile delinquency proceedings. In justifying this holding, Chief Justice Burger's opinion for the Court noted that "in terms of potential consequences, there is little to distinguish an adjudicatory hearing such as was held in this case from a traditional criminal prosecution." Despite

what many observers consider a fiction, courts continue to distinguish a juvenile adjudication from a trial and deny juveniles charged with serious offenses the right to a trial by jury.

Thirteen years later, in *Schall v. Martin* (1984), the Court upheld a pretrial detention program for juveniles that might well have been found violative of due process had it applied to adults. Writing for the Court, Justice William H. Rehnquist stressed that "the Constitution does not mandate elimination of all differences in the treatment of juveniles." While it is likely that the Supreme Court will maintain the requirements imposed in *Gault* and subsequent cases, at this time further expansion of juvenile due process seems unlikely.

Adjudication of Juvenile Delinquency Cases

Despite *In re Gault* and efforts to make the juvenile courts conform to due process requirements, juvenile delinquency proceedings are still, strictly speaking, civil matters, although they now possess many of the accoutrements of criminal cases. The delinquency petition is the juvenile justice counterpart to a grand jury indictment or an information filed by a prosecutor. It is a formal document charging that one or more delinquent acts have been committed by a particular juvenile and requesting that he or she be subjected to the court's disciplinary authority. Petitions are usually filed by law enforcement or social welfare agencies. Where the juvenile is not in custody, the petition is often accompanied by a request for an order to take the juvenile into custody.

Once a petition for delinquency has been filed, it must be determined whether the juvenile is to be detained pending a disposition of the case. This is usually accomplished through a formal detention hearing. The juvenile has the right to be represented by counsel at such hearings, and most states require juvenile judges to appoint counsel to represent indigent juveniles in these circumstances. However, parents or guardians who are financially able to retain counsel but refuse to do so may be ordered to reimburse the state for the costs of providing counsel.

In some instances the decision to detain may be based on whether a parent or guardian is willing and able to guarantee that the juvenile will appear in court when required to do so. In other instances a juvenile may be detained for his or her own protection or, particularly in the case of serious charges, to prevent the juvenile from committing additional offenses pending an adjudicatory hearing. In *Schall v. Martin* the U.S. Supreme Court upheld a state statute that permitted detention of a juvenile found to pose a serious threat to the community. Indicating a more conservative trend in its approach to juvenile cases, the Court observed that any attempt to structure juvenile rights "must be qualified by the recognition that juveniles, unlike adults, are always in some form of custody." A juvenile can attack an excessive or unreasonable detention decision by petitioning for a writ of habeas corpus.

Because there is no formal arraignment per se, the first stage of a juvenile delinquency hearing is the juvenile's answer to the delinquency petition. The juvenile has two options; he or she may admit to or deny the charges. These terms, which are functionally equivalent to pleas of "guilty" and "not guilty," are used to distinguish the juvenile justice system from the adult criminal process. A juvenile who "stands mute" (i.e., refuses to answer) is assumed to have denied the charges. If the juvenile admits to the charges, the juvenile court judge must determine that such admission is voluntary, that there is a factual basis for the offense or other conduct charged, and that the juvenile understands the charges before being adjudged delinquent; the only question remaining is that of appropriate treatment or punishment. If, on the other hand, the juvenile denies the charges, then a hearing must be held to determine their validity. As the Supreme Court held in the *Winship* case, prosecutors must prove their case beyond a reasonable doubt, and, as noted, the hearing proceeds with the juvenile afforded most of the procedural due process rights accorded to an adult charged with a criminal offense.

As noted earlier, the Supreme Court has held that the Sixth Amendment right of trial by jury does not extend to juvenile delinquency proceedings.

However, under the federal system, states are free to provide greater protections to citizens than those mandated by the federal Constitution. Some states permit juveniles to demand a jury trial if they are accused of offenses that would be triable by a jury if committed by an adult.

The courts have also ruled that juvenile court proceedings are not subject to the constitutional "public trial" requirement. The Federal Juvenile Delinquency Act gives federal judges discretion on the issue of whether to close proceedings involving a child and whether to grant public access to the records of the proceedings. State laws vary, often allowing the presiding judge to exercise discretion in these matters.

The typical statute governing disposition of juvenile delinquency cases provides the following dispositional alternatives: dismissal of the petition; suspended judgment; probation; placement in a treatment program; and, finally, commitment to a juvenile correctional institution. Once a juvenile is found to be delinquent the judge conducts a dispositional hearing usually involving all interested persons—prosecutor, defense counsel, parents, the child, and probation officer—in a rather informal meeting to determine what disposition is in the best interest of the child and the community. As a general rule, dispositions in juvenile cases tend to be more lenient and place more emphasis on rehabilitation than do sentences imposed on adults convicted of crimes. Increasingly, states are providing for community-based alternatives to incarceration, for example, commitment to a training school, probation, community service, restitution, and the like. In *United States v. R.L.C.* (1992), the Supreme Court held that a juvenile offender may not be incarcerated for a term exceeding that which would be imposed on an adult convicted of the same offense.

The U.S. Supreme Court has not decided whether a juvenile who is confined for an offense has a constitutional right to rehabilitative treatment. However, some courts and numerous commentators have suggested as much. Of course, like adult prisoners, juveniles in custody have the right to be assured of a reasonably safe and sanitary environment, as well as adequate health care. Future cases will undoubtedly bring to the forefront the question of whether a confined juvenile must be afforded rehabilitative treatment.

In the *Gault* case, the Supreme Court stopped short of holding that juveniles have a constitutional right to appeal, or that due process required that juveniles be afforded the same appellate remedies available to adults convicted of crimes. Some states do provide a right of appeal in juvenile delinquency cases, either by statute, court rule, or judicial decision. Others permit a *de novo* hearing (a new hearing) in a higher trial court. All states make available the writ of habeas corpus, or some equivalent postconviction procedure, by which a juvenile who believes that he or she is being wrongfully held in custody may challenge the custody in court. Availability of these remedies permits juveniles adjudicated delinquent an opportunity to have their cases reviewed by higher courts.

Trying Juveniles as Adults

Whether a juvenile is to be tried as an adult is subject to considerable variation among jurisdictions. In some states, a prosecutor can elect to try an older juvenile as an adult for certain major offenses. Moreover, in many states a juvenile charged with a nonfelony traffic violation is routinely tried in adult court. Although older juveniles accused of serious offenses are increasingly being tried as adults, this usually entails a waiver of the jurisdiction of the juvenile court. In *Kent v. United States* (1966), the Supreme Court held that a juvenile court must conduct a hearing before it can waive its jurisdiction and transfer a juvenile to the criminal court. As a consequence of this decision, waiver hearings are now commonly held throughout the United States. Although this hearing may be informal, the juvenile must be represented by counsel, and the records of social services agencies that have dealt with the juvenile must be made available to counsel, and in many jurisdictions a judge who grants a waiver must generally make detailed findings of fact to justify waiver of jurisdiction. Those who favor trying

certain juveniles as adults stress the need for incapacitation and deterrence of, as well as retribution against, dangerous offenders. Some have noted that overall rates of juvenile crime have dropped as the frequency of trying juveniles as adults has increased, but not everyone is convinced there is a causal relationship. There is also evidence to indicate that juvenile offenders who are punished as adults are more likely to commit future crimes than offenders who are dealt with by the juvenile justice system. Rehabilitation is extremely difficult to accomplish in the environment of the adult prison; the juvenile justice system affords greater opportunities for successful intervention.

Execution of Juveniles Convicted of Capital Crimes

In *Roper v. Simmons*, decided on March 1, 2005, the U.S. Supreme Court overturned precedent and declared unconstitutional the execution of juvenile offenders. In *Stanford v. Kentucky* (1989), the Court had held that the death penalty could be imposed on juveniles who were above the age of 15 when they committed their offenses. In *Trop v. Dulles* (1958), Chief Justice Earl Warren had expressed the view that the Eighth Amendment provision against cruel and unusual punishments "must draw its meaning from the evolving standards of decency that mark the progress of a maturing society." Some years before the *Roper* decision, this formulation was extended to death penalty issues and was in fact invoked in the 1989 decision upholding the juvenile death penalty. Noting that a number of states had abolished the juvenile death penalty in recent years, the *Roper* majority overruled *Stanford v. Kentucky*. Writing for a sharply divided Court, Justice Anthony Kennedy concluded that: "The Eighth and Fourteenth Amendments forbid imposition of the death penalty on offenders who were under the age of 18 when their crimes were committed."

Conclusion

The juvenile justice system is not without critics. The due process model of juvenile justice is now a given; yet juvenile courts share their functions with social agencies, and there are considerable variations in the adjudication and disposition of juvenile offenders. Some critics contend that dispositions are too lenient. Others fault the system for being too punitive. Yet, most thoughtful observers recognize a greater need for more effective parental supervision, more emphasis on schooling of juveniles, and the need for more community involvement by adults. Most also agree with the need for community-based sanctions for juvenile offenders with institutionalization to be reserved for the most serious offenders.

See also Accused, Rights of the; Adversary System of Justice; Appeal, Right of; Arraignment; Self-Incrimination Clause; Counsel, Right to; Cruel and Unusual Punishments Clause; Death Penalty for Juvenile Offenders; Double Jeopardy, Prohibition of; Due Process Clauses; Due Process, Procedural; Fortas, Abe; *Gault, In re* (1967); Habeas Corpus; Kennedy, Anthony; *Parens Patriae,* Doctrine of; Parental Rights; Pretrial Detention; Public Trial, Right to a; Reasonable Doubt Standard; Jury, Trial by; Warren, Earl

Bibliography

Coalition for Juvenile Justice. 1998. *A Celebration or a Wake? The Juvenile Court After 100 Years.* Washington, DC: Coalition for Juvenile Justice.

Platt, A.M. 1977 (Revised from 1969). *The Child Savers: The Invention of Delinquency.* 2nd ed. Chicago: University of Chicago Press.

Hon. John M. Scheb

K

KATZENBACH V. MCCLUNG (1964)

In adopting Title II of the Civil Rights Act of 1964, Congress prohibited places of public accommodation from discriminating against patrons on the ground of race, color, religion, or national origin. The prohibition was based on Congress's broad powers under the Commerce Clause of Article I, Section 8 of the United States Constitution. In *United States v. Wrightwood Dairy Co.* (1942), the Supreme Court observed that congressional power under the Commerce Clause "extends to those activities intrastate which so affect interstate commerce, or the exertion of the power of Congress over it, as to make regulation of them appropriate means to the attainment of a legitimate end, the effective execution of the granted power to regulate interstate commerce."

Opponents of the Civil Rights Act objected to the extension of federal power to matters long within the jurisdiction of state and local governments. Of course, throughout the South and in many other parts of the country, state and local governments permitted restaurants, hotels, and other places of public accommodation to segregate patrons by race or even to refuse service altogether to minorities.

In *Heart of Atlanta Motel v. United States,* decided the same day as *Katzenbach v. McClung,* the Supreme Court upheld the constitutionality of Title II as applied to an inner-city hotel that catered primarily to interstate travelers. The Court's decision in the *Heart of Atlanta Motel* case left open the question of whether Title II could be constitutionally applied to a place of public accommodation that serves a primarily local clientele. That question was addressed in *Katzenbach v. McClung.*

Since it opened in 1927, Ollie's Barbecue, a family-owned restaurant in Birmingham, Alabama, had refused sit-down service to blacks, although it did offer them carryout service. Although the great majority of customers were local residents, as distinct from interstate travelers, a substantial portion of the food served by Ollie's Barbecue was procured from out-of-state sources. Ollie McClung, the owner of the restaurant, brought suit in the federal district court in Birmingham, seeking to enjoin the enforcement of Title II against his business. He argued, among other things, that because Ollie's Barbecue was a local commercial activity with minimal impact on interstate commerce, it was beyond the reach of federal regulatory authority. McClung claimed that his restaurant business would be devastated if he were forced to allow black patrons to eat there.

The federal district court sided with McClung and declared Title II unconstitutional as applied to Ollie's Barbecue and similar establishments. The court found that there was not "a close and substantial relation between local activities and interstate commerce" to justify congressional regulation in this context. The court enjoined the attorney general, Nicholas Katzenbach, from enforcing Title II against McClung's business. Supreme Court Justice Hugo Black, however, stayed the injunction.

On appeal, the Supreme Court reversed the district court by a unanimous vote. The High Court found sufficient connection with interstate commerce in the restaurant's purchase of food and equipment from sources outside Alabama. The Court brushed aside McClung's argument that his restaurant's racial practices in no way impeded the free flow of foodstuffs across state lines. Justice Tom Clark's opinion for the Court asserted that "[t]he absence of direct evidence connecting discriminatory restaurant service with the flow of interstate food, a factor on which the appellees place much reliance, is not, given the evidence as to the effect of such practices on other aspects of commerce, a crucial matter." Clark stressed that Congress had "ample basis for the conclusion that established restaurants in such areas sold less interstate goods because of the discrimination, that interstate travel was obstructed directly by it, that business in general suffered and that many new businesses refrained from establishing there as a result of it." He concluded that Title II was "plainly appropriate in the resolution of what the Congress found to be a national commercial problem of the first magnitude."

The Supreme Court's emphatic decision in *Katzenbach v. McClung* effectively muted the legal controversy over the constitutionality of Title II and its applicability to places of public accommodation throughout the country. Today, businesses do not challenge the applicability of the Civil Rights Act, because racial segregation by places of public accommodation has become socially, as well as legally, unacceptable.

See also Civil Rights Act of 1875; Civil Rights Act of 1964; Civil Rights Cases, The; Civil Rights Movement; Clark, Tom C.; Discrimination; *Heart of Atlanta Motel v. United States* (1964); Public Accommodation, Places of; Segregation, De Facto and De Jure

Bibliography

Cortner, Richard C. 2001. *Civil Rights and Public Accommodations: The Heart of Atlanta Motel and McClung Cases.* Lawrence: University Press of Kansas.

John M. Scheb II and Otis H. Stephens, Jr.

KATZ V. UNITED STATES (1967)

The Fourth Amendment prohibits government agents from conducting unreasonable searches and seizures. In *Olmstead v. United States* (1928), the U.S. Supreme Court held that this prohibition was limited to unlawful searches of a person or "actual physical invasion of his house 'or curtilage' for the purpose of making a seizure." Thus, surveillance without physical contact with the suspect or the suspect's property, such as wiretapping, was deemed to fall outside the scope of the Fourth Amendment. In *Katz v. United States* (1967), the Supreme Court overturned *Olmstead v. United States* and significantly expanded the scope of Fourth Amendment protection.

In *Katz*, the Court reversed a conviction in which government agents, acting without a warrant, attached a "bug," or listening device, to the outside of a public telephone booth from which a suspected bookie often placed calls. Noting that "the Fourth Amendment protects people—not places," Justice Potter Stewart's majority opinion concluded that "[t]he Government's activities in electronically listening to and recording the petitioner's words violated the privacy upon which he justifiably relied while using the telephone booth and thus constituted a 'search and seizure' within the meaning of the Fourth Amendment."

According to Justice John M. Harlan's concurrence, which has come to be regarded as the most important opinion in *Katz,* the Fourth Amendment extends to any place or thing in which an individual "exhibited an actual (subjective) expectation of privacy ... that society is prepared to recognize as 'reasonable.'" In numerous later decisions (see, for example, *Kyllo v. United States,* 2001), the Supreme Court has adopted the "reasonable expectation of privacy" test in determining whether the Fourth Amendment applies in a particular context.

See also Exclusionary Rule; Fourth Amendment; Harlan, John Marshall, II; Privacy, Reasonable Expectations of; Search Warrants; Stewart, Potter;

Bibliography

Landynski, Jacob W. 1966. *Search and Seizure and the Supreme Court: A Study in Constitutional Interpretation*. Baltimore, MD: Johns Hopkins Press.

McWhirter, Darien A. 1994. *Search, Seizure, and Privacy*. Westport, CT: Oryx Press.

John M. Scheb II and Otis H. Stephens, Jr.

KELO V. CITY OF NEW LONDON (2005)

The Fifth Amendment to the U.S. Constitution states that "private property [shall not] be taken for public use, without just compensation." Referred to as the Takings Clause of the Fifth Amendment, this restriction on the federal government is also made applicable to the states through the Fourteenth Amendment (see *Chicago, B&Q RR v. Chicago,* 1897). From a strict constructionist view, the Takings Clause identifies property as a fundamental right unequivocally guaranteed the same protections as life and liberty, thereby providing a consequential limitation on the government's use of eminent domain—the power of the government to take away private property without the owner's consent. However, in the recent case of *Kelo v. City of New London* (2005), the Supreme Court's deferential treatment and broad interpretation of the "public use" component of the Takings Clause effectively weakened the constitutional protections afforded to citizens with respect to the fundamental right of property ownership.

In the latter part of the 1990s, the City of New London, Connecticut was facing challenges common to many municipalities throughout the United States, namely decades of economic decline, a dwindling population, and high unemployment. In an effort to revitalize a distressed economy, the city and its common council reactivated the New London Development Corporation (NLDC) and formally adopted an integrated redevelopment plan with the approval of the state. The development plan encompassed seven parcels of property constituting 90 acres, which included 115 privately owned properties, for purposes of revitalizing the city's downtown and waterfront areas and with projections of creating over 1,000 jobs and increasing tax and other revenues for the city. In addition, ownership of a portion of the earmarked property would be turned over to Pfizer Inc. to build a $300 million research facility adjacent to the targeted redevelopment area. The majority of the privately-owned property was purchased from willing sellers. However, 15 of the properties were owned by nine individuals unwilling to relinquish their property rights. In response, the city implemented its power of eminent domain and initiated condemnation proceedings against those unwilling to sell, which led to a lawsuit filed by the property owners against the City of New London. In its ruling, the trial court upheld some of the property takings, but granted a restraining order to prohibit the taking of other properties. On appeal, the Connecticut Supreme Court affirmed the lower court decision in part and reversed in part, thereby upholding all of the proposed takings although there was no allegation that the petitioners' properties were blighted or in poor condition.

Upon review by the Supreme Court, the question under consideration was whether the city's proposed disposition of the property to Pfizer, Inc. qualified as a "public use" within the meaning of the Fifth Amendment. In short, the Court ruled to affirm the judgment of the Supreme Court of Connecticut, effectively upholding all of the property takings as satisfying the public use requirement. With a broad interpretation of the public use requirement and an unmasked preference for deference with respect to the Takings Clause, the Court in its ruling essentially redefined the term *public use* to that which serves a "public purpose."

In the majority opinion, Justice John Paul Stevens explained that although there was no need to remove blight in the area targeted for redevelopment, the city's determination that the area was sufficiently distressed to justify a program of economic revitalization was entitled to the court's deference. Stevens argued that the Court's "public use jurisprudence has wisely eschewed rigid formulas and intrusive scrutiny in favor of affording legislatures broad latitude in determining what public needs justify the use of the takings power." He noted that the City of New London carefully formulated a redevelopment plan with expectations of appreciable benefits accruing to the community, including new jobs and increased tax revenue. Stevens conceded that the government's pursuit of a public purpose will often benefit individual private parties, and that "public ownership is [not] the sole method of promoting the public purposes of community redevelopment projects," but concluded that "[t]he public end may be as well or better served through an agency of private enterprise than through a department of government."

Invoking the Court's 1954 decision in *Berman v. Parker,* Stevens concluded that community redevelopment programs need not be considered for public use on a piecemeal basis—lot by lot, building by building—because an area must be planned as a whole for the plan to be successful. Therefore, given the city's intentions, the Court made the determination that the development plan unquestionably served a public purpose, thereby satisfying the public use requirement of the Fifth Amendment.

In her dissenting opinion, Justice Sandra Day O'Connor distinguished New London's use of eminent domain from takings the Court had approved in its earlier decisions, in particular *Hawaii Housing Authority v. Midkiff* (1984), where O'Connor had authored the majority opinion. She predicted that the beneficiaries of New London's decision "are likely to be those citizens with disproportionate influence and power in the political process, including large corporations and development firms." She bemoaned the fact that "government now has license to transfer property from those with fewer resources to those with more" and insisted that the framers of the Constitution "cannot have intended this perverse result."

Also dissenting, Justice Clarence Thomas characterized the *Kelo* decision as "simply the latest in a string of our cases construing the Public Use Clause to be a virtual nullity, without the slightest nod to its original meaning."

While the *Kelo* decision gives elected officials broad latitude with respect to eminent domain, courts can still invalidate particular takings if it can be shown that a private party that will benefit from the condemnation exercised undue influence over the decision.

See also Bill of Rights, Incorporation of; Eminent Domain; Fifth Amendment; Fundamental Rights; Judicial Restraint; Just Compensation Clause; O'Connor, Sandra Day; Property Rights; Public Use Clause; Stevens, John Paul; Thomas, Clarence

Deborah A. Carroll

KENNEDY, ANTHONY (1936–)

Anthony Kennedy was born on July 23, 1936, in Sacramento, California. Kennedy was a model child who served as an altar boy in his Catholic church. Kennedy would often joke with his friends that his father "had offered to pay him $100 if just once he would do something requiring his parents to come pick him up at the local police station" (Abraham 1999, 299); the young Kennedy never obliged. He was an honor roll student in high school and completed his undergraduate studies at Stanford University in three years. Kennedy studied for a year at the London School of Economics before returning to graduate Phi Beta Kappa from Stanford in 1958. He then attended law school at Harvard University, graduating with honors in 1961. After graduation, Kennedy returned to his native California to practice law. Due to the unexpected death of his father in 1963, Kennedy returned to Sacramento to take over his father's practice. He became involved in Republican politics and worked as both an attorney and a lobbyist; he also found time to teach law at McGeorge School of Law of the University of the Pacific. Kennedy was instrumental in drafting California Governor Ronald Reagan's tax limitation initiative, which impressed Reagan so much that he recommended Kennedy to President Gerald Ford for a federal judgeship. Ford appointed Kennedy to the Ninth U.S. Circuit Court of Appeals in 1975 where he served until 1988.

When Justice Lewis Powell retired in 1987, President Reagan initially nominated Robert Bork to fill the vacancy; however, Bork's controversial nomination was rejected by the Senate. Reagan's second choice to fill Powell's seat, Douglas Ginsburg, was forced to withdraw his nomination after revelations of past marijuana use. Kennedy was ultimately nominated due to his conservative record on the Ninth Circuit and his respect for judicial restraint. He was unanimously confirmed by the Senate on February 3, 1988.

In his early years on the Court, Kennedy, unlike Powell, tended to vote more with the conservative justices (Abraham 1999, 300). Over time, however, Kennedy has assumed a more centrist position while leaning to the right in certain areas, particularly those concerning federalism. Due to his moderate stance, Kennedy has often provided crucial votes in a number of cases dealing with civil liberties and civil rights.

Throughout his tenure on the Court, Kennedy has consistently voted to narrow the use of affirmative action programs. In 2003, for instance, Kennedy dissented in *Grutter v. Bollinger* (2003), an affirmative action case in which a majority of the Court upheld the use of race as a factor in law school admissions decisions. Kennedy admonished the majority for abandoning Justice Powell's condition set forth in the *Bakke* (1978) decision that strict scrutiny must be applied to educational institutions using race as a factor in admissions. While Kennedy believed that "appropriate consideration" should be given to race, he believed that the Court had been too deferential to the law school in this particular case.

Kennedy authored the majority opinion in *Freeman v. Pitts* (1992), another case involving race and education, which was one in a series of cases in which the Supreme Court began to limit the power of federal district courts to implement remedies in instances of public school segregation. This ruling allowed district courts to cease supervision of areas where desegregation had been achieved, even if full compliance with requirements established in prior desegregation cases had not.

Kennedy has written several significant majority opinions involving religious freedom. In *Lee v. Weisman* (1992), the Court, speaking through Justice Kennedy, held that school prayers at graduation ceremonies were in violation of the Establishment Clause of the First Amendment. He based his opinion on the involvement of state officials with the prayer and the potential for indirect coercion on minors; activities forbidden by precedent. In another Establishment Clause case, *Rosenberger v. University of Virginia* (1995), Kennedy wrote for a five-member majority in holding that the university's guideline barring payment of a subsidy to a student organization for its religious activity constituted viewpoint discrimination in violation of the organization's free speech rights. This violation was not excused by the necessity of complying with the Establishment Clause. He has also authored opinions concerning the Free Exercise of religion. In *Church of the Lukumi Babalu Aye, Inc. v. Hialeah* (1993), Kennedy invalidated a city ordinance prohibiting animal sacrifice because the ordinance was not generally applicable as the city had asserted but rather was targeted to prevent church members from practicing rituals associated with their religious beliefs.

In *City of Boerne v. Flores* (1997), the key issue was over the extent of congressional power in enforcing the Fourteenth Amendment, but the implications for religious freedom were apparent. In this case, Kennedy wrote for the majority, asserting that Congress lacked the power to pass the Religious Freedom Restoration Act on the basis of Section 5 of the Fourteenth Amendment. The RFRA was enacted as a result of the Court's ruling in *Employment Division v. Smith* (1990) in which the Court held that Native Americans who ingested peyote during religious worship were not exempt from criminal laws regarding drug use. Congress asserted that the RFRA was an attempt to prevent a generally applicable law from burdening religious freedom; Kennedy countered that it was the responsibility of the judicial branch, not the Congress, to determine the permissibility of such policies. Moreover, the requirements imposed on the states by this legislation violated the separation of powers instituted by the Constitution's framers.

Kennedy's most controversial opinions have dealt with issues concerning the right to privacy and gay rights. Kennedy was among the plurality in *Planned Parenthood v. Casey* (1992) that reaffirmed the central holding of *Roe v. Wade* (1973). However in *Stenberg v. Carhart* (2000) he dissented from the majority's ruling that a ban on late-term abortions imposed an "undue burden" on a woman's right to choose.

In the area of gay rights, Kennedy authored the opinion in *Romer v. Evans* (1996) invalidating an amendment to Colorado's constitution on the basis of the Equal Protection Clause. Amendment 2, enacted through a referendum, precluded executive, legislative, or judicial action undertaken to protect the status of gays, lesbians, and bisexuals. Kennedy, quoting Justice John Marshall Harlan's dissent in *Plessy v. Ferguson* (1896), stated "that the Constitution 'neither knows nor tolerates classes among citizens.'" Because Amendment 2 denied homosexuals the equal protection of the law, it was unconstitutional. In *Lawrence v. Texas* (2003), Kennedy invalidated a Texas homosexual anti-sodomy law on due process grounds, overturning *Bowers v. Hardwick* (1986), which had held that there was no constitutionally protected right to engage in sodomy. He wrote that, "The liberty protected by the Constitution allows homosexual persons the right to choose to enter upon relationships in the confines of their homes and their own private lives and still retain their dignity as free persons." Kennedy's opinion was criticized by Justice Antonin Scalia's dissent, which argued that the majority opinion opened the door for legalizing gay marriages.

Kennedy was also criticized by Scalia for his majority opinion in *Roper v. Simmons* (2005) in which the Court held that the Eighth Amendment's Cruel and Unusual Punishments Clause prohibited the execution of minors convicted of capital offenses. Shortly after Kennedy arrived on the Court, he voted with the majority in *Stanford v. Kentucky* (1989), which held that executing individuals who

were 16 or 17 at the time of a capital crime was constitutional. His opinion in *Roper* emphasized that more states now had statutory prohibitions on executing minors than at the time of *Stanford*. These statutes provided evidence of society's evolving standards of decency. Kennedy also noted that international opinion against the death penalty, especially as applied to minors, was persuasive.

Justices Kennedy and O'Connor occupied pivotal positions as centrists on the Rehnquist Court. Chief Justice Rehnquist died in the summer of 2005, and Justice O'Connor's previously announced retirement became effective early in 2006 upon the confirmation of her successor, Justice Samuel Alito. If, as many observers have predicted, Alito joins the conservative wing of the Court, and if the new Chief Justice, John Roberts, does not depart sharply from the views of his predecessor, Justice Kennedy's centrist role could become even more critical.

See also Abortion, Right to; Affirmative Action; Bork, Robert; Cruel and Unusual Punishments Clause; Death Penalty for Juvenile Offenders; Eighth Amendment; *Employment Division v. Smith;* Establishment Clause; First Amendment; Free Exercise Clause; Gay Rights Movement; Harlan, John Marshall; Judicial Restraint; *Lawrence v. Texas* (2003); O'Connor, Sandra Day; *Plessy v. Ferguson* (1896); Powell, Lewis F., Jr.; Privacy, Constitutional Right of; Rehnquist Court; Religion, Freedom of; Religious Freedom Restoration Act; *Roe v. Wade* (1973); *Romer v. Evans (1996);* Same-Sex Marriage and Civil Unions; Scalia, Antonin; School Prayer Decisions; Segregation in Public Education; Separation of Church and State; Sexual Orientation, Discrimination on the Basis of

Bibliography

Abraham, Henry. 1999. *Justices, Presidents, and Senators.* Lanham, MD: Rowman and Littlefield.

Belsky, Martin H., ed. 2002. *The Rehnquist Court: A Retrospective.* New York: Oxford University Press.

Mauro, Tony. 2005. "A Lost Chance to Be the Chief." *Legal Times* (7 March): 1.

Schwartz, Herman, ed. 2002. *The Rehnquist Court: Judicial Activism on the Right*. New York: Hill and Wang.

Tushnet, Mark. 2005. *A Court Divided: The Rehnquist Court and the Future of Constitutional Law*. New York: W.W. Norton.

Yarbrough, Tinsley E. 2000. *The Rehnquist Court and the Constitution*. New York: Oxford University Press.

Kara E. Stooksbury

KENNEDY, ROBERT F. (1925–1968)

Robert Francis Kennedy (RFK), the younger brother of President John Fitzgerald Kennedy (JFK), was born in Brookline, Massachusetts, on November 20, 1925. Robert was the seventh of nine children, and eight years younger than JFK. He studied at Harvard University until World War II, at which point he joined the U.S. Navy. Upon completion of his service, he returned to Harvard to finish his baccalaureate degree in 1948. In 1951, he received an LL.B. from the University of Virginia Law School. While attending law school, Robert met Ethel Skakel, and they married in 1950. In 1951, he became an attorney for the U.S. Department of Justice, but left this job after one year to manage his brother John's campaign for the U.S. Senate. When the campaign ended, Robert used family connections to work as counsel for several Senate committees, including Senator Joseph McCarthy's Committee on Government Operations. Robert first gained national prominence as the chief counsel of the Senate Permanent Investigations Committee from 1955 to 1957 during the investigation of corruption by Teamster Union executives David Beck and James Hoffa.

In 1960, Robert served as campaign manager for John's presidential race. After John's victory, he selected Robert to become United States Attorney General. In this position, Robert Kennedy was a strong supporter of civil rights. It was Robert who ordered U.S. Marshals to provide protection for James Meredith, the first African-American student admitted to the University of Mississippi.

Robert's most pivotal role in his brother's presidential administration was as an advisor on Cuba.

The failure of the Bay of Pigs invasion in April 1961 was a disaster for the Kennedy administration. Many believed Cuba would continue to be a problem unless the leader of Cuba, Fidel Castro, could be removed from power. President Kennedy believed that his previous advisors had betrayed him in the Bay of Pigs invasion. Thus, he turned to his brother to handle the matter of Cuba. Robert thought the best way to overthrow Castro was to instigate sabotage and chaos in Cuba through covert operations using Castro's own people and the CIA.

The Kennedy Administration received bipartisan pressure to resolve the Castro situation. Hence, Robert began a secret project, code named "Operation Mongoose," consisting of small, covert operations designed to instigate a counterinsurgency. The operation cost more than $100 million in manpower and equipment. Many believe that Operation Mongoose included a plot to assassinate Castro. Although previous attempts on Castro's life had been made by the U.S. government, records indicate that Operation Mongoose was not one of these attempts. Moreover, there are no records tying either of the Kennedy brothers to an assassination plot. The operation was a failure and tension between Cuba and the United States climaxed during the Cold War.

On October 15, 1962, an American U-2 spy plane photographed Soviet ballistic missiles in Cuba. Later, declassified documents and photographs would reveal that there were 134 Soviet warheads in Cuba. In response to what soon became known as the Cuban Missile Crisis, President Kennedy formed the Executive Committee of the National Security Council (ExComm), consisting of both current and former cabinet members, including his bother Robert. Eventually, the Kennedy brothers determined that negotiations would be the best way to resolve the situation. The president informed Soviet Premier Nikita Khrushchev that he and his brother would be conducting negotiations.

Negotiations began on October 23, 1962, when Robert contacted Soviet ambassador Anatoly Dobrynin. During these negotiations, tensions were heightened by a U.S. naval blockade of Cuba and the Soviets' shooting down of an American U-2. Although on the brink of war, the situation was finally resolved on October 28, when Khrushchev publicly agreed to remove the missiles in Cuba if the United States would not invade Cuba. Furthermore, in private, the president promised to remove American missiles from Turkey. Neither side consulted Fidel Castro during the negotiations; Castro later declared that Khrushchev lacked *"cojones"* in the negotiations. The Cuban Missile Crisis was the greatest test the Kennedy brothers faced, and both received global recognition for their handling of the crisis.

After President Kennedy's assassination in 1963, Robert resigned his position as Attorney General, and was elected U.S. Senator from New York in 1964. His greatest concerns were socioeconomic issues, including poverty and urban ghettos. Robert often sponsored legislation that sought to improve the situation of the poverty-stricken. He also advocated these same reforms in Eastern Europe, Latin America, and South Africa. During this time, Robert became the personification of modern liberalism.

In 1968, Robert Kennedy sought the Democratic Party's presidential nomination, calling for an end to the Vietnam War and the expansion of civil rights at home. In April of 1968, Martin Luther King, Jr. was assassinated, and African Americans across the nation rioted in the streets. Robert informed his audience in Indianapolis of his rage at the situation, but called for restraint. As a result, Indianapolis was one of the few cities that did not experience riots.

By June of 1968, Robert Kennedy had won presidential primaries in Indiana, Nebraska, and California, and many observers believed that he would follow in his brother's footsteps and become the next president. However, at a victory party in a Los Angeles hotel following the California primary, Robert was shot by a Jordanian named Sirhan Bishara Sirhan. He died the next day on June 6, 1968. Robert Kennedy was only 42-years-old at the time of his assassination. He was survived by his wife and 11 children, one of whom was born

after his death. He is buried in Arlington National Cemetery next to his brother John.

See also Civil Rights Movement; Freedom Rides; King, Martin Luther, Jr.; Liberalism; Meredith, James

Bibliography

Schlesinger, Arthur M., Jr. 1980. *Robert Kennedy and His Times.* Boston: Houghton-Mifflin.

Thomas, Evan. 1992. *Robert Kennedy: His Life.* New York: Simon & Schuster

Ann M. Bennett

KENTUCKY AND VIRGINIA RESOLUTIONS (1798)

In a clash over the limits of federal authority, the legislatures of the Commonwealths of Kentucky and Virginia passed separate resolutions expressing strong opposition to four federal laws known collectively as the Alien and Sedition Acts. Passed in late 1798, these resolutions were both principled defenses of civil liberties and statements of political philosophy that supported Thomas Jefferson's presidential campaign against the Federalists. They enunciated a theory that the Constitution was a "compact" between states. Introducing the ideas of "interposition" and "nullification," the resolutions advanced a position that states were ultimately sovereign over domestic policy. Just such a construction of states' rights, asserted in a more strident form, would later become the South's rationale for seceding from the Union and forming the Confederacy.

At a time when adversarial political parties were beginning to define national politics (Federalists vs. Democratic-Republicans), a Federalist-dominated U.S. Congress, fearing war with Napoleon's France, enacted the far-reaching Alien and Sedition Acts in the early summer of 1798. These acts were intended to prevent wartime domestic subversion by, among other considerations: lengthening the time required for aliens to become citizens (Naturalization Law); giving President Adams the power for two years (June 25, 1800), in peace or war, to judge and deport "dangerous" aliens (Alien Friends Law); giving the presidency, during any time of war and without expiration, the power to set the conditions of control, arrest, and deportation of aliens (Alien Enemies Law); and, finally, giving unprecedented power until March 3, 1801 to the Federalists to prosecute critics of the government in any court of jurisdiction. Guilty verdicts imposed fines and imprisonment.

Democratic-Republicans, led by Adams' vice-president, Thomas Jefferson, opposed the acts. Politically, they were seen as attacks on the future membership of Jefferson's party. Legally, the Kentucky and Virginia Resolutions presented the Alien Acts as multiple violations of the Constitution (allocating judicial powers to the president; usurping states' authority; violating due process and the right to trial by jury) and the Sedition Act as a blatant violation of the First Amendment's guarantee of free speech. Jefferson composed the Kentucky Resolutions and arranged for his close friend, James Madison, to write the Virginia Resolution. To avoid political attack, however, both men concealed this for many years.

The Kentucky Resolutions were nine resolves: the first declared the "compact" theory of the Constitution; resolves two through seven enumerated the offenses contained in the Alien and Sedition Acts and branded them "unconstitutional" and "void and of no force"; resolve number eight committed Kentucky's representatives in the federal Congress to the repeal of these acts; and resolve number nine declared that Kentucky would not submit tamely to unlimited federal power and encouraged declarations in kind from her co-states.

Madison's Virginia Resolution, a more moderate and reasoned statement, also asserted that the Alien and Sedition Acts were unconstitutional and, like Kentucky, sought the concurrence of the other states in this judgment. While maintaining that a state had a duty to "interpose" itself when the national government exercised dangerous and unfounded power, the Virginia Resolution eschewed a tone of belligerent defiance.

All states rejected the Kentucky and Virginia invitation to declare in kind. Ten states—Maryland,

Delaware, Pennsylvania, New Jersey, New York, Connecticut, Rhode Island, Massachusetts, New Hampshire, and Vermont—passed resolutions of condemnation, while the remaining states stayed silent. As far as we know, only New York and New Hampshire specifically referenced Kentucky in their response.

In the face of such unfavorable reactions, Jefferson and Madison were determined to renew the Kentucky and Virginia Resolutions. The federal compact theory was a cardinal principle in the struggle against centralized federal power and an important tenet in Jeffersonian Republicanism. Not to forcefully defend it would leave the party looking weak. In a private letter, Jefferson even contemplated separation "from that union we so much value," so strongly did he perceive a federal threat to a state's right to self-government. He directed both states to reaffirm their resolves.

Kentucky, renewing its resolution in 1799 with a shorter restatement, introduced for the first time in print the controversial and prophetic term *nullification* (South Carolina would revive the term 30 years later) as a state's rightful remedy to unconstitutional assumptions of power. The resolution, however, did not then seek to nullify the Alien and Sedition Acts, but described itself as a "solemn protest" only.

The Madison Report, Virginia's resolution restatement, argued with subtlety and force against the concept of nullification. It declared that a state's right to interpose was limited to an act of last resort and solely to check federal usurpation. States, meaning the sovereign people within a boundary and not the governmental apparatus within that boundary, had submitted—through the Constitutional compact—to the binding judgment of federal courts in all Constitutional matters. A state, therefore, did not have the legal power to overturn or "nullify" a federal law. Any single state delivering a resolution was, in fact, delivering an "opinion" without force or legal finality.

Jefferson's election in 1800, the expiration of the Alien Friends Act and the Sedition Act, the rewriting of the Naturalization Act, and the dormancy of the Alien Enemies Act (written for a war that never materialized) closed the controversy.

See also Alien and Sedition Acts; First Amendment; Jefferson, Thomas; Madison, James; Speech, Freedom of; States' Rights, Doctrine of

Bibliography

Anderson, Frank M. 1899. "Contemporary Opinion of the Virginia and Kentucky Resolutions, I & II." *American Historical Review* 5: 1.

Harrison, Lowell H. 1969. *John Breckenridge*. Louisville, Kentucky: Filson Club.

Koch, Adrienne, and Harry Ammon. 1948. "The Virginia and Kentucky Resolutions." *William and Mary Quarterly* 5: 145.

Loring, Caleb W. 1893. *Nullification, Secession Webster's Argument*. New York and London: G.P Putnam's Sons.

Warfield, Ethelbert D. 1894. *The Kentucky Resolutions of 1798*. New York and London: G. P. Putnam's Sons.

Kevin Collins

KEVORKIAN, JACK. *See* Right to Die

KING, MARTIN LUTHER, JR. (1929–1968)

Martin Luther King, Jr., was a complex and controversial figure during his brief life. In death, he is in danger of being reduced to either icon or target. During his adult life, Martin Luther King, Jr., was an eloquent voice and effective organizer for the rights of people of color. He also was subjected to virulent racial hatred and FBI wiretaps. Since his assassination on April 4, 1968, King has been domesticated and demonized. On the one hand, a national holiday has been created to commemorate King's birth, and numerous public facilities, events, and streets have been named after him, lauding a legendary public figure while taming the power of King's methods, the forcefulness of his critique, and the breadth of his vision of "The Beloved Community." On the other hand, King has been pilloried as a philanderer and a plagiarist.

Martin Luther King, Jr. was born Michael Luther King, to Martin Luther King, Sr. (Daddy King) and schoolteacher Alberta Williams King,

on January 15, 1929 (Michael was renamed Martin when he was six). Martin's father succeeded his father-in-law, the Rev. A. D. Williams—who was a founder of the Atlanta Chapter of the National Association for the Advancement of Colored People (NAACP)—as pastor of the Ebenezer Baptist Church in Atlanta, Georgia. Thus, the young Martin was steeped in the African American Baptist Church and the civil rights struggle. This heritage would provide the twin sources of his influence throughout his life's work, in which religion and liberation were thoroughly intertwined.

King was educated at Morehouse College, Crozer Theological Seminary, and Boston University. After he completed his doctoral coursework at Boston University, he was appointed pastor of the Dexter Avenue Baptist Church in Montgomery, Alabama in September, 1954—three and a half months after the Supreme Court had handed down *Brown v. Board of Education*. Shortly after King's arrival, Montgomery became embroiled in a conflict over Jim Crow laws and segregation that became a defining chapter in the Civil Rights Movement. Rosa Parks, former secretary of the local NAACP chapter, was arrested on December 1, 1955 for refusing to surrender her seat on a city bus to a white passenger and move to the rear. Parks' arrest galvanized local blacks, who had been confronting segregation as early as Claudette Colvin's similar act of resistance on March 2, 1955. A Montgomery resident, JoAnn Robinson of the Women's Political Committee, called for a one-day protest.

Fortuitously, King was in the right place at the right time. He joined with other religious, student, and community leaders, to form the Montgomery Improvement Association (MIA). The MIA organized a successful boycott, supported by a highly effective car-pooling arrangement called "private taxis." The boycott, together with a federal district court decision applying *Brown* to hold segregated Montgomery buses in violation of the Fourteenth Amendment, ended Jim Crow public transportation (see *Browder v. Gayle*, 1956; affirmed per curiam in *Gayle v. Browder*, 1956). Amidst the heat of the Montgomery struggle, on January 30, 1956, the King family home was dynamited.

King's Montgomery experience provided the template for the remainder of his career. Using black churches as his organizing base—as a "black preacher in the black church," as he put it—he eventually became a preacher in a larger social venue, advocating community solidarity and nonviolent tactics in the cause of black liberation. Death threats, assassination attempts, and arrests continued to dog him. The Southern Christian Leadership Conference, King's primary organizational vehicle, also emerged out of the Montgomery struggle.

A representative example of King's rhetorical brilliance, as well as the substance of his message, is his April 16, 1963 "Letter from a Birmingham Jail." Written while he was incarcerated for participating in protests against discriminatory hiring practices and segregated department store facilities in a city known as "Bombingham" for its history of violence against blacks, King's missive ostensibly is his reply to unsolicited advice tendered by eight Alabama Jewish and Christian clergy that blacks stop protesting and patiently await social justice—advice criticizing King's activities as "unwise and untimely." King's moving use of language renders his letter compelling. His essential message is that the time has come to act:

> For years now I have heard the words [sic] 'Wait!' It rings in the ear of every Negro with a piercing familiarity. This 'Wait' has almost always meant 'Never.' ... [W]e find it difficult to wait. There comes a time when the cup of endurance runs over, and men are no longer willing to be plunged into an abyss of despair.... We must come to see that human progress never rolls in on wheels of inevitability. It comes through the tireless efforts and persistent work of men willing to be co-workers with God, and without this hard work time itself becomes an ally of the forces of social stagnation.... Now is the time to lift our national policy from the quicksand of racial injustice to the solid rock of human dignity.

For sheer emotional power, King's letter surpasses his more famous "I Have a Dream" speech delivered on August 28, 1963, at the March on Washington for Jobs and Freedom.

King did not survive to see his dream realized. He was shot and killed on April 4, 1968, in Memphis, Tennessee where he was supporting striking sanitation workers. Prior to his murder, King revised his critique of American society and his vision of social justice to be more fundamental: "[O]ne day we must ask the question of whether an edifice which produces beggars must not be restructured and refurbished." In this regard, King's work resonated with that of Malcolm X, whom he met only once in Washington, D.C., on March 26, 1964.

See also Boycotts; *Brown v. Board of Education* (1954;1955); Civil Disobedience; Civil Rights; Civil Rights Movement; Federal Bureau of Investigation; Jim Crow laws; Malcolm X; National Association for the Advancement of Colored People (NAACP); Parks, Rosa

Bibliography

Baldwin, Lewis V. 2002. *Between Cross and Crescent: Christian and Muslim Perspectives on Malcolm and Martin.* Gainesville: University Press of Florida.

Cone, James H. 1992. *Malcolm & Martin & America: A Dream or A Nightmare.* Maryknoll, New York: Orbis Books.

Frady, Marshall. 2002. *Martin Luther King, Jr.* New York: Penguin.

Garrow, David J. 1986. *Bearing the Cross: Martin Luther King, Jr. and the Southern Christian Leadership Conference.* New York: W. Morrow.

Stetson, Jeff. 1990. *The Meeting: A One-Act Play.* New York: Dramatists Play Service.

James C. Foster

KING, RODNEY. *See* Rodney King Incident (1991)

KNOCK AND ANNOUNCE. *See* Castle Doctrine

KOREMATSU V. UNITED STATES (1944)

In the aftermath of the Japanese attack on Pearl Harbor on December 7, 1941, and the United States' subsequent entry into World War II, President Franklin Roosevelt issued a series of executive orders severely limiting the civil liberties of individuals of Japanese descent residing on the West Coast. Due to an active role by the press in reassuring the American public, individuals of Japanese ancestry were not initially subject to discrimination. Public opinion suddenly changed in early January 1942, however, when both the press and prominent public officials demanded that Japanese-Americans be removed. Responding to this pressure, President Roosevelt signed Executive Order 9066, which allowed the secretary of war to designate military zones from which individuals could be excluded. Pursuant to this order, General John DeWitt, the West Coast army commander, issued exclusion orders which required Japanese-Americans living on the West Coast to leave their homes and report to relocation centers. Refusal to report to the center was punishable by a fine of up to $5,000 and one year's imprisonment. Ultimately, more than 110,000 Japanese-Americans, most of whom were U.S. citizens, would be forced to leave their homes for these camps without any justification on the part of the government that any of them individually posed a threat to national security.

Fred Korematsu, an American citizen of Japanese ancestry, was charged with violating the exclusion order because he remained at his home in San Leandro, California, which had been designated a military zone. The question before the Supreme Court in *Korematsu v. United States* was whether the exclusion order was constitutional. In a six-to-three ruling, the Court held that it was. Writing for the majority, Justice Hugo Black stated that laws which treated people differently on the basis of race are subject to the highest level of scrutiny. He added that while "pressing public necessity may sometimes justify the existence of such restrictions; racial antagonism never can." Black deferred to the judgment and expertise of the military and Congress in assessing the threat posed by Japanese-Americans. Because of the impracticability of determining individualized guilt and because of the presumed threat posed by Japanese-Americans, Black declared that the exclusion order was constitutionally valid. He noted that ordinarily removing people from their homes was "inconsistent with

our basic governmental institutions"; however during a time of war, the government must be allowed to protect its citizens. Ultimately Black concluded that: "Korematsu was not excluded from the Military Area because of hostility to him or his race. He was excluded because we are at war with the Japanese Empire."

Justice Owen Roberts dissented from what he perceived to be a "clear violation of Constitutional rights." Justice Frank Murphy, also in dissent, argued that there was no evidence of an "immediate, imminent, and impending" public threat posed by Japanese-Americans. He asserted that the government's decision was based on the "erroneous assumption of racial guilt." He cited General DeWitt's report in which the general referred to "all individuals of Japanese descent as 'subversive,' as belonging to 'an enemy race' whose 'racial strains are undiluted,' and as constituting over '112,000 potential enemies.'" In Murphy's view, the government failed to justify why it had not held hearings to determine individual guilt and characterized the majority opinion as "legalized racism."

Similarly, Justice Robert Jackson emphasized that under the Constitution "guilt is personal and not inheritable." He pointed out that Korematsu was both a U.S. citizen and a citizen of California who was being singled out because of his parents' heritage, not because there was any evidence that he was disloyal to the United States. Jackson also criticized the majority opinion for its deference to a military order of questionable credibility. The only thing worse than blind adherence to a military order, in Jackson's view, was the principle the Court established by upholding it. He asserted that the principle upheld here "lies about like a loaded weapon ready for the hand of any authority that can bring forward a plausible claim of an urgent need."

The *Korematsu* decision is widely considered to be one of the Supreme Court's biggest mistakes, exceeded only by the Dred Scott ruling. Fred Korematsu's conviction was eventually overturned by a federal district court in 1983. Five years later, Congress issued an official apology to all those of Japanese ancestry that were confined to internment camps. This legislation also provided $20,000 to each of the approximately 60,000 Japanese-Americans who were interned and still alive. Fred Korematsu received the nation's highest civilian honor in January 1998 when he was awarded the Medal of Freedom by President Bill Clinton. In 2004, as the question of the constitutionality of detaining U.S. citizens as enemy combatants reached the U.S. Supreme Court, Korematsu filed an amicus curiae brief in *Hamdi v. Rumsfeld* (2004) and *Rasul v. Bush* (2004), urging the Court to remember the injustices he suffered when civil rights and liberties took a back seat to war. He died on March 30, 2005, at the age of 86.

See also Black, Hugo; Dred Scott Case; Jackson, Robert H.; Japanese Americans, Relocation of; Roosevelt, Franklin D.; Strict Scrutiny; Terrorism, War on; Civil Rights and Liberties During Wartime

Bibliography

Irons, Peter. 1983. *Justice at War*. New York: Oxford University Press.

Kara E. Stooksbury

KU KLUX KLAN (KKK)

The organization known as the Ku Klux Klan (the Klan, KKK) has existed in three distinct forms in three different eras. The Klan first appeared in the South during Reconstruction following the Civil War. It disappeared and then reappeared with an expanded agenda in 1915. It disappeared again in 1945 and made its final appearance in the 1960s. Its modern remnants serve as icons of hatred and intolerance.

1865–1871

The KKK originated in Pulaski, Tennessee, in 1865, ostensibly as a social club for ex-Confederate soldiers. The Klan was structured like a fraternal organization complete with titles, costumes, and rituals. This seemingly benign purpose changed at some point during the tumultuous period of Radical Reconstruction in the South. At an organizational meeting in Nashville, Tennessee, in 1867, former Confederate General Nathan Bedford

Forrest was elected the first Imperial Wizard of the Order of the Ku Klux Klan. By this time, the masked members of the night-riding Klan were associated with intimidation, violence, and their distinctive white robes and hoods. Similar groups existed, such as the White Camelia, the White Brotherhood, the White League, and the '76 Association, but the Klan gained the most notoriety. The goal of all of these groups was to facilitate the restoration of power to white Democrats and a return to prewar society as they had known it. Thus, their tactics were directed at Southern Republicans—Scallywags, Carpetbaggers, and freed slaves. By the late 1870s, the Democratic party had regained political control in the South. Black Codes and Jim Crow laws were instituted to enforce a system of strict racial segregation. The practice of segregation was later upheld by the Supreme Court (*Plessy v. Ferguson* [1896]) in a ruling that would stand until the mid-1950s (*Brown v. Board of Education of Topeka, Kansas* [1954]). According to Balkin (2002), during this time "The Court drastically limited Congress's civil rights power by narrowly interpreting the Fourteenth Amendment, striking down many Reconstruction era civil rights laws, and looking the other way as Southern state governments systematically oppressed blacks" (Balkin 44). The KKK, having met its goals, had nearly disappeared by this time.

Anti-Klan Legislation

Congress enacted legislation in the early 1870s in response to the Klan's intimidation of newly-freed slaves. The First Enforcement Act (1870) was enacted to protect the voting rights of former slaves, making it a federal offense to interfere with voting rights. In 1871, following investigative hearings regarding the violent activities of the Klan, Congress passed the Second Enforcement Act, also known as the Klan Act. This act gave the president the power to suspend the writ of habeas corpus in cases involving conspiracy, and the power to declare a state of martial law. In response to lax or nonexistent protection of civil rights at the state and local level, this law made civil rights violations federal crimes under the Fourteenth Amendment. The new law was put to use later that year when President Ulysses S. Grant sent federal troops to stop Klan violence in South Carolina. Just over a decade later, however, parts of the Klan Act were declared unconstitutional in *U.S. v. Harris* (1883). In an appeal of a case involving a lynch mob, the Court ruled that the Fourteenth Amendment only authorized federal action against state violations of the amendment. The amendment did not apply to the acts of individuals.

1915–1945

The second appearance of The Klan in Atlanta, Georgia, in 1915, under the leadership of William J. Simmons, coincided with the release of D.W. Griffith's film *Birth of a Nation*, which glorified and romanticized the Reconstruction-era activities of the Klan. In its second incarnation the Klan, which was popular in the Midwest as well as in the South, vilified Roman Catholics, Jews, African Americans, Asians, immigrants, and organized labor. Simmons introduced cross burning as a Klan activity. The group increased its membership during the 1928 presidential campaign of Alfred E. Smith, who was Catholic. During the Great Depression in the 1930s, membership declined, and by 1944, the organization had disbanded.

1960s–2005

The Klan, or at least its practices and sentiments, resurfaced again in opposition to the Civil Rights Acts of the 1960s. Today there are various, marginalized white supremacist groups such as the Imperial Klans of America, the American Knights of the Ku Klux Klan, Aryan Nations, the National Alliance, and the Silent Brotherhood. In their official materials, these groups ban acts of violence and other illegal activities: These remnants of the KKK continue to spread a message of hatred and intolerance on their Web sites and at rallies and marches.

The Klan and the First Amendment

While the message of white supremacist groups such as the Klan is offensive to all but a few in contemporary American society, the American Civil Liberties Union (ACLU) has consistently supported the First Amendment rights of the KKK, and the courts have consistently upheld these rights.

In 1969, the Supreme Court reversed the conviction of a KKK leader who had conducted a televised rally and declared Ohio's Criminal Syndicalism Act unconstitutional. According to the Court's opinion in *Brandenburg v. Ohio,* the statute "purports to punish mere advocacy and to forbid, on pain of criminal punishment, assembly with others merely to advocate the described type of action." With its decision in *Brandenburg,* the Court ruled that the First Amendment protected advocacy and protest, however offensive, unless it promoted "imminent lawless action." With this decision, the Court significantly broadened the standards of protection set in earlier cases. In 2004, the group's right to hold a rally was upheld, but they were forbidden to wear hoods, an act prohibited by an 1845 New York law banning public gatherings by people wearing hoods and masks. The Supreme Court rejected an appeal by the Klan of a decision by the U.S. Court of Appeals for the Second Circuit upholding the 1845 law (see *Church of the American Knights of the Ku Klux Klan v. Kerik*).

One recent case upheld The Klan's right to participate in an activity that would publicize the group's name—and thus its message. In 2001, the Supreme Court refused to review a lower court decision affirming the right of the KKK to participate in Missouri's "adopt-a-highway" program in which volunteers clean roadside trash in an area designated by a sign identifying the group (see *Robb v. Hungerbeeler,* 2004). The state of Missouri had claimed that recognizing the Klan with a sign in its honor was in violation of laws prohibiting racial discrimination in federally funded programs.

See also American Civil Liberties Union; Black Codes; *Brandenburg v. Ohio* (1969); *Brown v. Board of Education* (1954;1955); Catholicism and Anti-Catholicism; Civil Rights Act of 1870; Civil Rights Act of 1871; Civil Rights Movement; Clear and Present Danger Doctrine; Criminal Syndicalism; First Amendment; Hate Crimes; Hate Speech; Jim Crow laws; *Pierce v. Society of Sisters* (1925); *Plessy v. Ferguson* (1896); Speech, Freedom of

Bibliography

Balkin, Jack M. 2002. "History Lesson." *Legal Affairs* (July/August): 44–49.

Gay Henry Lyons

KUNSTLER, WILLIAM (1919–1995)

William Moses Kunstler was born on July 7, 1919, to a middle-class Jewish physician and his wife in New York City. He majored in French literature at Yale, became a decorated army officer in World War II, and earned a law degree from Columbia. During the 1950s Kunstler handled mundane cases, taught, and wrote. Beginning in the 1960s and continuing to the end of his life, Kunstler practiced civil rights law, winning repute as a "radical" lawyer with controversial clients. William Kunstler died of heart failure on September 4, 1995, in New York City, leaving behind several books about his work.

In the early 1960s, Kunstler began to travel around the South as an ACLU attorney representing Freedom Riders. In the late 1960s, Kunstler represented Martin Luther King, Jr., the Black Panthers, H. Rap Brown, Stokely Carmichael, Adam Clayton Powell, Lenny Bruce, student demonstrators, and many others. He arranged to defend Lee Harvey Oswald and then defended Oswald's killer, Jack Ruby. Other notable cases of this period included 1967's *Hobson v. Hanson,* which became a step toward desegregation of the District of Columbia school system; *Palmer v. Thompson* (1971), in which the Supreme Court refused to force a Mississippi town to operate an integrated municipal pool system; and, shortly before Watergate, *United States v. United States District Court* (1972), in which the Supreme Court ruled that a "national security" exemption to the warrant requirement for wiretaps was unconstitutional.

In 1969, Kunstler participated in representing the Chicago Seven, on trial for disrupting the 1968 Democratic National Convention. The Seven and Kunstler turned the courtroom into a well-publicized platform for defense of the entire radical movement. Kunstler was cited for contempt, but the Seven eventually were cleared of charges. The tactics adopted by Kunstler during and after the Chicago Seven trial were representative of what is referred to as "radical" lawyering. The radical lawyer uses the court as a forum for airing the political viewpoints of his clients, criticizing the government or society at large, charging governmental agents or agencies with wrongdoing, and encouraging publicity in order to turn a trial into a public education tool. (Vile 2001, 441) Kunstler himself refers to this practice, learned from the Black Panthers' counsel Charles Gerry (Kunstler 1994, 193), as "movement law": "In the past, lawyers ... viewed the law as sacred and inviolate. But movement law considered the system as something to be used or changed, in order to gain the political objectives of the clients in a particular case" (Kunstler 1994, 105).

Kunstler continued to participate in liberal causes. In 1973, leaders of the American Indian Movement were tried for taking over Wounded Knee, South Dakota, in a 10-week siege. At the trial, Kunstler convinced the court of gross prosecutorial misconduct, and the charges were dropped. Again, in 1975, he helped to win the acquittal of two of three Lakota Indians accused of murdering two FBI agents. In 1989 and 1990, Kunstler contributed to a legal effort that won Supreme Court rulings in which burning an American flag was held to be speech protected by the First Amendment (see *Texas v. Johnson,* 1989; *United States v. Eichmann,* 1990).

In the 1980s and 1990s, Kunstler took on controversial clients having varying amounts of political cache or, in some cases, none at all. Kunstler defended or handled appeals for mobsters, mutinous inmates at Attica, one of the men originally convicted in the Central Park Jogger case, and Larry Davis, accused of shooting police officers in New York City. He created a sensation by introducing a "black rage" defense in the murder trial of Colin Ferguson; angered many by defending El Sayyid Nosair, accused of assassinating Rabbi Meir Kahane; and was excoriated for representing several of the men convicted in the 1993 World Trade Center bombing. Toward the end of his life, Kunstler adopted the cause of Muslim Americans, whom he perceived as oppressed by a society panicked about terrorism, and the attorney seemed proud to be representing a new crop of "politically unacceptable outcasts" (Kunstler 1994, xiii).

See also American Civil Liberties Union; The Chicago Seven; Civil Rights Movement; Contempt, Power of; Federal Bureau of Investigation (FBI); Flag Burning; Freedom Riders; Terrorism, War on

Bibliography

Kunstler, William. *My Life as a Radical Lawyer.* New York: Birch Lane Press, 1994.

Vile, John R. *Great American Lawyers.* Santa Barbara, CA: ABC-CLIO, 2001.

Rachel Pearsall

L

LATINO AMERICANS, CIVIL RIGHTS OF

It is difficult to say when the struggle for Latino American civil rights began in earnest. While the most famous early events occurred during the Civil Rights Movement of the 1960s, Latino Americans have publicly struggled for rights from the mid-1800s (Rosales 1996). As a minority group in the United States, Latino Americans enjoy the same legal protections afforded to other minority groups by federal legislation, constitutional amendments, and Supreme Court decisions. The movement for specific recognition of Latino American civil rights, however, has been primarily shaped at the grassroots level. Historically, the federal government has not been as focused on the civil rights of Latino Americans as it has been on the rights of African Americans and Native Americans.

One of the reasons that Latino Americans have not had a single concerted civil rights movement is because they are an ethnically diverse group. Typically, these loosely connected ethnic groups have struggled for civil rights in isolation from the broader Latino American population. The United States has seen robust Mexican American civil rights efforts in Southwestern states such as Texas and California. Campaigns in New York City, on the other hand, have had more of a Puerto Rican and Dominican focus. Supporters of Cuban American civil rights have been influential in Miami, Florida. The federal government has only recently begun to develop civil rights strategies for Latino Americans as a single group.

Latino Americans, like other minorities, have experienced discrimination in a number of areas—among them housing, employment, distribution of federal benefits and services, education, voting, and the administration of criminal justice (Hero 1992). Latino Americans have also struggled with linguistic barriers and difficulties in finding bilingual support in the government and the private sphere. Moreover, many Latino Americans must also contend with immigrants' rights issues.

The Mexican American struggle for civil rights is the oldest, broadest, and most visible facet of the Latino American equality campaign. The Mexican American, or Chicano, Civil Rights Movement (*El movimiento*) dates back to 1848, when the Treaty of Guadalupe Hidalgo was signed. As part of the treaty, Mexican nationals who remained in certain newly acquired American territory were given the option to accept American citizenship and were promised equal civil and property rights. Those promises, however, often went unfulfilled. This story was repeated across the Southwest as Anglo Americans and the United States government used and exploited land laws to deprive Mexican Americans of their property rights.

The ratification of the Fourteenth Amendment in 1868 gave many Mexican Americans newfound hope that they would receive full protections as

American citizens. Others, however, remained skeptical of Anglo American society and its supposed racial and cultural tolerance. Mexican Americans who adhered to the *México lindo* ideology saw themselves as Mexicans in America and did not look to the United States for support or direction.

This attitude fed and was fed by the widespread anti-Mexican sentiment of the mid-to-late nineteenth and early twentieth centuries. In the early 1900s, Congress responded to Americans' broad-based xenophobia by restricting the flow of immigrant labor even as the economy and demand for workers skyrocketed. Mexican laborers, however, were only marginally excluded in comparison to other nationals such as Chinese and Eastern Europeans. As a result, the numbers of Mexicans who legally and illegally came to the United States looking for work swelled, drawing the hostility of anti-immigrant Americans.

Alarmed by the growing Mexican American population and threatened by many immigrants' unwillingness to assimilate, a small but vocal political faction initiated an effort to bar the entry of Mexicans into the United States. In 1929, Congress passed legislation that severely restricted the immigration of Mexicans into the United States. The 1929 act marked the most restrictive piece of legislation affecting the immigration of Mexicans up to that point in American history (Rosales 1996).

During this time, Mexican Americans formed various organizations designed to combat defamation and legal abuses, protect refugees, fight capital punishment and segregation, and preserve the Spanish language press (Rosales 1996). In 1929, the League of United Latin American Citizens (LULAC) was created. Today, it stands as one of the most successful and prominent Latino American civil rights organizations. As a direct result of LULAC's work, several successful Latino-based civil rights programs have been initiated. In 1948, the American GI Forum (AGIF) was founded by Dr. Hector P. Garcia to uphold the rights of Latino war veterans. Another notable Latino American civil rights organization is the Mexican American Legal Defense and Education Fund (MALDEF).

MALDEF was founded to provide educational outreach and serve as the political and legal voice of the Latino community (Ortiz 1999).

By the 1950s, *México lindo* ideology was challenged by a newfound nationalism rooted in the belief that Mexicans were indeed Americans and not temporary visitors in the United States. This philosophy, referred to as Mexican Americanism, was founded on the belief that Mexican Americans were entitled to the same citizenship as white Americans were and that they should be treated equally under the law. Spurred by this belief, Mexican Americans fought legal efforts designed to subject them to Jim Crow segregation laws. This strategy was only partially successful, however, because the racial hues among Mexican Americans varied significantly and the language and cultural characteristics of the population manifested themselves so strongly. From the late 1950s and into the 1960s, Mexican Americans abandoned their campaign to be classified as white and instead began to emulate the African American Civil Rights Movement (Rosales 1996).

The Civil Rights Movement of the 1960s focused most broadly and prominently on African American concerns. The Latino American struggle for rights during this time was being fought one battle at a time on a much smaller scale. Mexican American youth, as well as some older Mexican Americans, were instrumental in mobilizing their peers to join in the cause. Latino American leaders, such as Rodolfo "Corky" Gonzales, Luis Valdez, and César Chávez, championed the cause of Latinos in the United States (largely in the Southwest) by publishing literature and poetry (e.g., Gonzales' "I am Joaquín") as well as organizing marches and conferences. In 1970, Rodolfo Gonzales was instrumental in helping organize a Latino American-based political party, La Raza Unida, whose aim was to provide a viable option for Latino American participation in the American electoral system. César Chávez was instrumental in organizing political protests by farm workers in central California in an effort to achieve farm worker self-determination. Chávez' tactics emphasized nonviolence and spiritual guidance, much like the strategies successfully employed by African American civil rights leaders (Rosales 1996).

Today, Latino Americans still face many obstacles in achieving full enfranchisement in American society. One of the major challenges to such progress is the English Only movement that began in the early 1980s. Advocates of the movement would like to make English the only language used by the government. In 2002, the No Child Left Behind Act effectively killed Title VII of the Elementary and Secondary Education Act (more commonly known as the Bilingual Education Act). No Child Left Behind calls for rapid acclimatization to English language instruction in lieu of extensive native-language instruction. Many Latino Americans see these efforts as an affront to their culture and fundamental civil rights.

Family reunification is another major area of concern. Many Latino Americans are calling for the relaxation of rules that make it difficult for family members living outside of the United States to come to America. In the wake of the terrorist attacks of 9/11, it has become even more difficult to obtain entry into the United States even for such seemingly innocuous purposes as reuniting families. In addition, advocates of Latino American civil rights have also pushed Congress to rethink its approach towards the deportation of legal residents who have committed past petty offenses, limits on health and nutritional services for legal immigrant children, and protection for refugees attempting to escape political persecution.

See also Asylum, Right to; Bilingual Education; Citizenship; Civil Rights Movement; Diversity; Employment Discrimination; Equal Protection Clause; Equal Protection Jurisprudence; Fourteenth Amendment (1868); Group Rights; Housing, Discrimination in; Immigrants and Aliens, Rights of; Interest Groups; Jim Crow Laws; Segregation, De Facto and De Jure; Vote, Right to

Bibliography

Acuña, Rodolfo. 1972. *Occupied America: The Chicano's Struggle Toward Liberation.* San Francisco: Canfield Press.

Grebler, Leo. 1966. *Mexican Immigration to the United States.* Los Angeles: University of California Press.

Hero, Rodney. 1992. *Latinos and the U.S. Political System: Two Tiered Pluralism.* Philadelphia: Temple University Press.

Rosales, F. Arturo. 1996. *Chicano! The History of the Mexican American Civil Rights Movement.* Houston: Arte Público Press.

Samora, Julian, and Patricia Vandel Simon. 1993. *A History of the Mexican-American People.* South Bend, IN: University of Notre Dame Press.

Richard T. Middleton, IV

LAWRENCE V. TEXAS (2003)

On June 26, 2003, the United States Supreme Court, by a six-to-three margin, struck down a Texas sodomy statute that prohibited any person from engaging in "deviate sexual intercourse with another individual of the same sex." The case, *Lawrence v. Texas,* marks an extremely important development as the war over gay rights continues to play itself out in the judicial system and American society at large. Many opponents feared that the Court's decision in *Lawrence* would lead to its acceptance of gay marriage and other protections for homosexuals. To date, the Supreme Court has shown no inclination to move in this direction, but its decision in *Lawrence* was a hopeful signal to the homosexual rights movement and its supporters.

On September 17, 1998, Harris County Sheriff's Deputy Joseph Quinn entered the apartment of John Lawrence in response to a weapons disturbance complaint. Deputy Quinn discovered Lawrence engaging in private, consensual homosexual sex with Tyron Garner. Both were arrested and charged under Texas' antisodomy law for "deviate sexual intercourse."

Lawrence and Garner eventually pled no contest to the charges and were fined $125 each. A three-judge panel of the Texas Court of Appeals reversed the lower court's decision by a 2–1 margin, agreeing with the defendants that their convictions violated the 1972 Equal Rights Amendment to the Texas Constitution barring discrimination on the basis of sex, race, color, creed, or national origin. The entire

Texas Court of Appeals reversed the panel's decision and rejected the defendants' arguments that the statute violated both the Due Process Clause and the Equal Protection Clause of the Fourteenth Amendment to the United States Constitution. The Texas Court of Criminal Appeals denied review and the case subsequently reached the United States Supreme Court on a writ of certiorari.

Writing for the majority, Justice Anthony Kennedy asserted that the sexual behavior in question was protected by the Due Process Clause of the Fourteenth Amendment. Homosexuals had a fundamental liberty interest that allowed them to engage in consensual sexual behavior. In support of his argument, Justice Kennedy pointed to the fact that in recent years, states had moved away from criminalizing consensual sexual acts by adults in the privacy of their own homes. Texas was one of only a handful of states that still banned same-sex sodomy.

One major hurdle for Justice Kennedy was the Supreme Court's prior decision in *Bowers v. Hardwick* (1986). The Court in *Bowers* had addressed many of the same issues raised in *Lawrence* and reached starkly different conclusions. In upholding Georgia's sodomy statute, Justice Byron White flatly stated on behalf of the Court's majority that there was no constitutional right to engage in homosexual sodomy. Consensual, private homosexual conduct could be regulated and punished by sodomy laws. Justice Kennedy noted that *Bowers* had suffered "serious erosion." Thus he accorded "criticism from other sources greater significance." The Supreme Court rarely explicitly overturns its prior decisions but the majority of the Court in *Lawrence* did just that. In support of the decision to overrule *Bowers,* Justice Kennedy asserted that: "To say that the issue in *Bowers* was simply the right to engage in certain sexual conduct demeans the claim the individual put forward, just as it would demean a married couple were it to be said marriage is simply about the right to have sexual intercourse."

Justice Sandra Day O'Connor concurred with the majority's ruling but for a different reason. She thought that the Texas statute violated the Equal Protection Clause of the Fourteenth Amendment because it targeted a group of people as opposed to a specific act. In other words, without good reason, the Texas law prohibited one group of people (homosexuals) from engaging in sodomy while allowing another group of people (heterosexuals) to engage in such behavior without penalty.

Justice Antonin Scalia was joined in his strongly worded dissenting opinion by Chief Justice William Rehnquist and Justice Clarence Thomas. Speaking for the Court's most consistently conservative voting bloc, Justice Scalia sharply attacked the Court's majority opinion on three main points.

First, he criticized the majority's characterization that the Court's holding in *Bowers* had been eroded and that this was a reason for overturning it. He wrote that many other Court opinions had been "eroded" over time (including, notably, *Roe v. Wade*) without being overturned. Many judicial decisions had been based on *Bowers* and to overturn it would upset settled law in this area.

Second, Justice Scalia claimed that only fundamental liberty interests were protected by the Due Process Clause of the Fourteenth Amendment. Consensual homosexual conduct could hardly be characterized as a "fundamental" interest that is deeply rooted in the country's history. Scalia would have subjected the Texas statute to the less strenuous rational basis test. Did the state have a rational basis for enacting the sodomy statute? Scalia argued that a state's interest in regulating the morality of its citizens was a justifiable ground for enacting such a statute. He pointed to other statutes prohibiting bigamy, incest, and fornication as examples of the power of the state in this area. Finally, Justice Scalia argued that the majority had inappropriately "taken sides in the culture war" and "signed on to the so-called homosexual agenda" by overruling a constitutional, democratically enacted state statute.

In a separate, two-paragraph dissent, Justice Clarence Thomas called the Texas statute "uncommonly silly" and indicated that if he were in the Texas legislature he would vote to repeal it. He voted as a Justice of the Supreme Court to uphold the statute, though, simply because it was constitutional. In his view, there was no constitutional right to privacy that protected this type of behavior from government regulation.

The Court's decision in *Lawrence* is just one important milestone in a long line of cases that attempt to determine the extent to which government can regulate the sexual behavior of consenting adults in the privacy of their own homes. Since laws regulating such behavior are still very important to many Americans, the Court is likely to continue to be involved in such issues.

See also Due Process Clauses; Due Process, Substantive; Equal Protection Clause; Fourteenth Amendment (1868); Fundamental Rights; Gay Rights Movement; Kennedy, Anthony; Liberty; Marriage, Rights Pertaining to; O'Connor, Sandra Day; Privacy, Constitutional Right of; Rational Basis Test; *Roe v. Wade* (1973); Same-Sex Marriage and Civil Unions; Scalia, Antonin; Strict Scrutiny; Thomas, Clarence; White, Byron R.

Darren A. Wheeler

LDS CHURCH. *See* Church of Jesus Christ of Latter-day Saints

LEGISLATIVE INVESTIGATIONS

Both Congress and the state legislatures have an inherent power to investigate. Obviously, this power is an indispensable prerequisite to the drafting and enactment of informed legislation. The Supreme Court has long recognized the essential connection between investigation and legislation and has placed few restrictions on the investigative power beyond the basic requirement that it be linked to some "identifiable legislative purpose," however broadly defined.

In exercising their power to investigate, Congress and state legislatures may subpoena records and other documents and, perhaps more significantly, may subpoena witnesses and order them to testify at hearings conducted by legislative committees. If an uncooperative witness refuses to testify by invoking the constitutional right against compulsory self-incrimination, legislatures may override this right by granting immunity from prosecution based on the witness's testimony before the committee. If further resistance is encountered, legislatures may invoke the power to hold witnesses in contempt, possibly resulting in their imprisonment.

The significance of a legislative grant of immunity from prosecution is illustrated by the case of Lt. Col. Oliver North, who was granted immunity in exchange for his congressional testimony as to the Iran-*Contra* Scandal of the mid-1980s. Although North was convicted of several federal crimes for his role in the scandal, the convictions were reversed because the Court of Appeals found that they were partly based on his immunized testimony before Congress (see *United States v. North*, 1990).

Although it is essential to performance of the legislative function, the power to investigate is certainly subject to abuse. During the Red Scare of the 1950s, the House Un-American Activities Committee (HUAC) and Senator Joseph McCarthy's Committee on Government Operations sought to expose communist infiltration and subversion by subjecting suspected communists to far-ranging and probing questions about their beliefs, affiliations, activities, and relationships. Individuals who invoked their constitutional immunity against compulsory self-incrimination in refusing to answer the committee's questions were branded "Fifth Amendment Communists." In a climate of near-hysteria, any sense of the proper scope and function of the investigatory power was all but forgotten.

In *Watkins v. United States* (1957), the Supreme Court reversed a conviction for contempt of Congress in a case where a witness had refused to answer questions put to him by HUAC. John Watkins answered questions about his own beliefs and activities but refused to "name names" of other suspected communists. The Supreme Court reversed Watkins's conviction primarily on procedural grounds, holding that he had been denied due process of law. The Court also expressed concern that First Amendment values were being threatened by HUAC's public hearings. Writing for the Court in *Watkins*, Chief Justice Earl Warren observed:

The mere summoning of a witness and compelling him to testify, against his will, about his beliefs, expressions or associations is a measure of governmental interference. And when those forced revelations concern matters that are unorthodox, unpopular, or even hateful to the general public, the reaction in the life of the witness may be disastrous. This effect is even more harsh when it is past beliefs, expressions or associations that are disclosed and judged by current standards rather than those contemporary with the matters exposed. Nor does the witness alone suffer the consequences. Those who are identified by witnesses and thereby placed in the same glare of publicity are equally subject to public stigma, scorn and obloquy. Beyond that, there is the more subtle and immeasurable effect upon those who tend to adhere to the most orthodox and uncontroversial views and associations in order to avoid a similar fate at some future time. That this impact is partly the result of non-governmental activity by private persons cannot relieve the investigators of their responsibility for initiating the reaction.

Critics of HUAC hoped the Court's decision in *Watkins* signaled a desire to limit congressional investigations on First Amendment grounds. In Congress, however, critics of *Watkins* and similar Warren Court decisions introduced legislation to remove the Court's appellate jurisdiction in cases where persons are held in contempt of Congress. A majority of the Court evidently took note of these efforts and soon backed away from First Amendment concerns regarding congressional investigations. In *Barenblatt v. United States* (1959), the Court in a sharply divided decision upheld a conviction for contempt of Congress, holding that the public interest in exposing Communist infiltration outweighed a witness's First Amendment rights in refusing to answer questions. The *Barenblatt* decision went a long way toward deflating Court-curbing efforts and rehabilitating the Court's standing in Congress. In the ensuing years, the Court continued to show deference to congressional investigations and generally refused to allow uncooperative witnesses to invoke the protections of the First Amendment (see, for example, *Wilkinson v. United States*, 1961).

Despite the *Barenblatt* ruling, the First Amendment does provide some degree of protection from legislative investigations. During the early 1960s,

several Southern state legislatures sought to harass and intimidate the National Association for the Advancement of Colored People (NAACP). When the Florida legislature investigated the NAACP and subpoenaed its membership list, the Supreme Court held that the legislature had violated NAACP members' freedom of association. Writing for the Court in *Gibson v. Florida Legislative Committee* (1963), Justice Arthur Goldberg observed that:

an adequate foundation for inquiry must be laid before proceeding in such a manner as will substantially intrude upon and severely curtail or inhibit constitutionally protected activities or seriously interfere with similarly protected associational rights. No such foundation has been laid here. The … Committee has failed to demonstrate the compelling and subordinating governmental interest essential to support direct inquiry into the membership records of the NAACP.

In 1970, at the height of the anti-Vietnam War protests, the U.S. Senate's Subcommittee on Internal Security began an investigation of the United States Servicemen's Fund, Inc. (USSF), a not-for-profit private corporation. When the committee sought to subpoena the organization's bank records, USSF sought an injunction in federal court. Although the district court refused to issue the injunction, the Court of Appeals reversed, noting that "[t]he right of voluntary associations, especially those engaged in activities which may not meet with popular favor, to be free from having either state or federal officials expose their affiliation and membership absent a compelling state or federal purpose has been made clear a number of times." In *Eastland v. United States Servicemen's Fund* (1975), the Supreme Court reversed the Court of Appeals, holding that the actions of the Senate subcommittee and its individual members were "immune from judicial interference" by virtue of the Speech or Debate Clause found in Article I, Section 6 of the Constitution. That clause provides that "for any Speech or Debate in either House, [Members of Congress] shall not be questioned in any other Place." The Court interpreted the language of the Clause broadly to preclude judicial review of members' actions that fall within the "sphere of legitimate legislative activity." The Court found that the actions of committee members in issuing the subpoena fell within that sphere and thus held that the federal courts should refrain from enjoining the subpoena, even though First Amendment rights might be at stake.

The Supreme Court has never clearly described the circumstances in which congressional immunity under the "speech or debate" clause would be trumped by an assertion of individual rights. Like communicative testimony, the coercive power of the investigating committee to compel the production of documents is limited in theory but virtually unrestricted in practice.

See also Association, Freedom of; Communist Party USA; Contempt, Power of; Due Process, Procedural; Fifth Amendment; First Amendment; Goldberg, Arthur; House Un-American Activities Committee (HUAC); McCarthy, Joseph R.; National Association for the Advancement of Colored People (NAACP); Self-Incrimination Clause; Speech, Freedom of; Warren, Earl

Bibliography

Lytle, Clifford. 1968. *The Warren Court and Its Critics.* Tucson: University of Arizona Press.

Shapiro, Martin. 1966. *Freedom of Speech: The Supreme Court and Judicial Review.* Englewood Cliffs, NJ: Prentice Hall.

Stephens, Otis H., and John M. Scheb II. 1988. *American Constitutional Law: Essays and Cases.* San Diego: Harcourt Brace Jovanovich.

Otis H. Stephens, Jr. and John M. Scheb II

LEMON TEST. *See Lemon v. Kurtzman*

LEMON V. KURTZMAN (1971)

Lemon v. Kurtzman (1971) marked the U.S. Supreme Court's first consideration of the constitutionality of state programs providing financial aid to church-affiliated elementary and secondary schools. It also can be viewed as the high-water mark in the Supreme Court's interpretation of the Establishment Clause of the First Amendment as mandating a strict separation between church and state. Finally, *Lemon* announced a three-pronged test for determining whether government actions had violated the Establishment Clause. This test remained influential on the Court for more than two decades.

In *Lemon* the Court addressed the constitutionality of two state programs of aid to nonpublic schools, including church-affiliated schools. Under the Pennsylvania program, the state purchased educational services from nonpublic schools by reimbursing them for the cost of textbooks and instructional materials in various secular subjects, as well as teachers' salaries when the teachers were engaged in teaching secular subjects such as mathematics and science. Under the Rhode Island program, the state paid teachers of secular subjects in nonpublic schools a supplement of 15 percent of their annual salary. Speaking for an eight-member Court majority, Chief Justice Warren E. Burger held that both programs violated the Constitution.

To survive constitutional scrutiny under the Establishment Clause, Burger insisted, state statutes had to meet three criteria. First, the statute had to have a secular legislative purpose; second, its primary effect could not be to advance or inhibit religion; and third, the statute could not foster an excessive government entanglement with religion. Applying this test to the Pennsylvania and Rhode Island programs, Burger concluded that both fostered an excessive government entanglement with religion. The Court noted that the Constitution forbids the use of public funds to support religious teaching. Given the pervasively religious educational mission of church-affiliated schools, state officials would be obliged to conduct "comprehensive, discriminating, and continuing surveillance" to ensure that teachers did not engage in religious instruction while their salaries were being paid by the state. This pervasive monitoring would create an excessive administrative entanglement. In addition, according to the Court, "political divisiveness along religious lines was one of the principal evils against which the First Amendment was intended to protect." However, a program of aid to church-affiliated schools would encourage political divisions along religious lines, as proponents and opponents of religious education clashed, thus producing an excessive political entanglement of government and religion. Thus, both programs were unconstitutional.

The three-pronged test enunciated in *Lemon* proved difficult to apply. In *Tilton v. Richardson* (1971), decided the same day as *Lemon*, the justices split five-to-four in upholding a federal statute under which private (including church-related) universities received federal grants and loans to construct buildings to be used solely for secular purposes. The justices also splintered badly in applying the *Lemon* test in subsequent cases involving less direct forms of state aid to nonpublic schools. By the early 1990s the Court had largely abandoned the effort to apply the three-pronged test enunciated in *Lemon*, preferring to examine whether government enactments violated the neutrality between religion and nonreligion required by the Establishment Clause.

In *Zelman v. Simmons-Harris* (2002), a five-member majority of the Supreme Court explicitly repudiated *Lemon*. Speaking for the Court, Chief Justice William Rehnquist concluded that in evaluating programs of governmental aid, the Court should apply only the first two criteria enunciated in *Lemon* (a secular purpose and a primary effect that neither advances nor inhibits religion), thus jettisoning the excessive-entanglement criterion. In addition, the Court held, in contrast to *Lemon*, that the religious mission of the schools receiving aid was not decisive. As long as a statute did not use religion as a criterion in determining what schools or students received aid, it could not be condemned as having the primary effect of advancing religion. This outcome, in direct conflict with the Court's position in *Lemon*, demonstrates that *Lemon v. Kurtzman* is no longer a persuasive precedent to a majority of the Supreme Court.

See also Burger, Warren E.; Establishment Clause; First Amendment; Religion, Freedom of; Rehnquist, William H.; Religious Schools, Government Aid to; Separation of Church and State

G. Alan Tarr

LEWIS, JOHN. *See* Student Nonviolent Coordinating Committee

LIBEL. *See* Defamation

LIBERALISM

Although there are scholars, such as Leo Strauss and Eric Havelock, who contend that liberalism rightly understood is rooted in the classical philosophy of the ancient Greeks, it is more commonly understood as the product of modern political thought—especially that of the seventeenth-century English political philosopher John Locke. For it is in Locke's *Second Treatise of Government* that one finds the five essential tenets of liberalism from which it emerged as a political philosophy, ideology, and movement: (1) society is the product of a voluntary compact among individuals who are equal in the state of nature; (2) people consent to the social contract, and form government as the most practical way to better secure their natural rights; (3) these natural rights, more commonly conceived after the nineteenth century as *human* rights, include the rights of life, liberty, and property; (4) the protection and promotion of these natural rights, through the enforcement of the contract upon individuals and groups, is the cardinal purpose of government; (5) rulers hold their authority only in trust from the people, and when that trust is violated by governors, a people may rise in opposition to the government and undo tyranny.

From Locke's basic tenets, liberalism was shaped and reshaped from the eighteenth through the early twentieth century by such prominent thinkers as Montesquieu, Adam Smith, Thomas Jefferson, Jeremy Bentham, John Stuart Mill, T. H. Green, and L. T. Hobhouse, into an ideology devoted to human progress through the maximization of individual freedom and choice, representative political institutions, equality of rights (social, economic, and civil), religious tolerance, and the amelioration of deplorable social conditions through moderate political reform. Buffeted by radical ideologies promising revolutionary transformations of society, liberalism faltered in the first half of the twentieth century. From the totalitarian ideological challenges of communism and fascism, however, a new liberalism encompassing social duty and the common good—yet rooted in the individual right to choice and freedom—emerged and remains vibrant.

The development of civil rights and liberties in the United States, indeed the development of law generally, is closely tied to the evolution of liberalism as a political and philosophical tradition. At the risk of oversimplification, we can identify three distinct phases in the development of liberalism: classical, modern, and postmodern. In each of these phases liberalism has produced a new understanding of the meaning of human freedom and equality.

Classical Liberalism

Following John Locke, eighteenth-century liberals advocated the abolition of monarchy and the establishment of republican government. Classical liberals espoused limited government, the rule of law, the separation of church and state, and individual freedom, all of which were fairly radical ideas in the eighteenth century. Because they believed, in the words of Thomas Jefferson, that "Governments are instituted among Men, deriving their just powers from the consent of the governed," they believed in the right of the people to "alter" or "abolish" an existing government in favor of one "most likely to effect their Safety and Happiness." Thus classical liberalism was a revolutionary ideology, which was used to justify revolutions in America and France as well as dramatic political changes in Britain and throughout Europe.

Published in the same year that Jefferson penned the Declaration of Independence, Adam Smith's *The Wealth of Nations* is another seminal work of classical liberalism. Smith believed that individuals were capable of determining their own economic fortunes and, if permitted to act freely in the marketplace, would produce greater wealth and advance social welfare far in excess of what could be achieved by governmental management of the economy. Thus Smith advocated the economic policy of *laissez-faire* under which government plays only a minimal role in creating the conditions necessary

for free commerce. This doctrine comported nicely with the classical liberal emphasis on individualism and limited government. Smith's ideas took hold in the United States more than anywhere else and contributed to the tremendous growth of the American economy.

Classical liberal ideas exerted profound influence on the Framers of the United States Constitution and the Bill of Rights. Certainly the classical liberal demand for limited government is evident in the Framers' design for the new federal government. And the liberal emphasis on individual freedom, most notably Locke's "natural rights" of "life, liberty and property," is manifested in the Bill of Rights.

In the early nineteenth century, liberal thought focused on the meaning of liberty. In England, Herbert Spencer and John Stuart Mill, and in America Henry David Thoreau, advocated the principle that individuals should be free to do as they please as long as they do not infringe on anyone else's freedom. It was in this conception of freedom that liberalism opposed not only despotic governments, but all institutions that stifled human freedom. Thus began the liberal assault on religion, the family, and on traditional moral codes from which emerged such ideologies and movements as secularism and feminism.

One of the distinguishing features of liberalism in all its phases is an underlying faith in human potential and respect for human dignity. Thus, liberal thinkers of the late eighteenth and early nineteenth centuries were troubled by the existence of human slavery in the American South. It was impossible to reconcile slavery with the liberal credo that "all men are created equal" and that each has a natural right to "life, liberty and the pursuit of happiness." By the mid-nineteenth century, most Americans with liberal sentiments came to support the movement to abolish slavery. Of course, a bloody civil war would be required to achieve that end.

After the Civil War, American liberal thought focused heavily on the meaning of equality and the amelioration of the deplorable conditions produced by massive and unprecedented immigration, urbanization, and industrialization. Liberals became champions of public education, social reform, and civil rights, especially for the newly freed former slaves, and later for women.

Modern Liberalism

Modern liberalism was a reaction to the dislocations of the Industrial Revolution as well as the rise of communism and other radical ideologies. As the twentieth century dawned, liberals came to believe that society must take responsibility for providing basic levels of opportunity, security, and education. Thus liberals advocated a positive role for government, an idea that gave rise to the innovations of the Progressive Era, the New Deal, and the Great Society. The historian H.W. Brands describes modern liberalism as "a prevailing confidence in the ability of government, preeminently the federal government, to accomplish substantial good on behalf of the American people." Regardless of what one thinks of the economic policies that flowed from modern liberalism, it must be conceded that these policies deprived the socialist and communist left of considerable public support in the United States. Under modern liberalism, policies once advocated only by radicals, such as social security and collective bargaining, became part of the political mainstream. This in turn stimulated an intellectual movement to return liberalism to its "rightly understood" classical tradition. Thus, Ludwig von Mises and others vigorously sought to return liberalism to its original emphasis on "the harmony of the rightly understood interests of all members of a free society founded on the principle of private ownership of means of production;" That is, a consensual society based on private property, free markets, and limited government in the service of individual choice and freedom.

Another distinguishing feature of modern liberalism is its solicitude for the civil rights of minorities. Modern liberal jurisprudence calls for strict judicial scrutiny of policies that adversely affect discrete and insular minorities (see *United States v. Carolone Products,* 1946). Politically speaking, it was the Democratic Party and the Civil Rights

Movement that achieved the striking civil rights gains for African Americans in the 1960s, but the rhetoric supporting these accomplishments was drawn from the lexicon of modern liberalism.

A major debate has developed among democratic theorists between those who call themselves *liberals* and those who call themselves *communitarians.* In the communitarian critique offered by thinkers such as Michael Sandel and Amitai Etizoni, liberalism overemphasizes the individual to the detriment of the community; that is, liberal ideology sows the seeds of its own destruction in promoting an asocial individualism. The communitarian critique of liberalism focuses on the increasingly profound divisions among individuals in society engendered by (1) expanding emphasis on the civil liberties and rights of racial, ethnic, and life-style minorities; (2) overemphasis on individual and group rights at the expense of civic obligation; and (3) an expanding sense of self-isolation and abandonment of community values as citizens adopt radical individualism. To overcome these divisions communitarians advocate focusing on the community rather than the individual. They envision a social order in which individuals are bound together by common values that foster communal bonds. Communitarians seek ways to embed individuals into a network of relations, which imbues them with unifying beliefs that promote individual obligation and commitment to civic engagement. This is to be accomplished with moral socialization through education, leadership, formation of consensus-building groups, peer pressure, exhortation, and support for moral voices in communities.

Liberals respond that the communitarians misrepresent liberalism and the communitarian alternative threatens to destroy tolerance and eventually liberty. Thus, for example, Kautz argues that communitarians are simply unable or unwilling to directly confront the intolerance that truly communitarian societies inevitably foster; that is, the communitarian correction to the flaws of liberalism is excessive and eventually must destroy the values it seeks to promote. It is better, he contends, to rely upon the liberal tradition of Locke and the American founders, which effectively incorporates the need for virtue and commitment to community, but is arrived at by free, rational individuals.

Postmodern Liberalism

The New Left, a term often used to categorize the radical politics of the 1960s, was notoriously impatient with democratic procedures and intolerant of disagreement. In these respects its temperament was profoundly illiberal, and accordingly, should not be regarded as a form of liberalism. However, a number of scholars are now recognizing a "postmodern" phase of liberalism and the New Left certainly influenced this development. Influenced by existentialism as well, postmodern liberalism eschews the rationalism and universalism of classical liberalism and is distinguished by its embrace of relativism and its celebration of "diversity." Postmodern liberals reject traditional values and institutions, such as the nuclear family, the church, and heterosexual marriage as needless restraints on individual freedom and self-discovery. They also reject efforts to introduce American or Western notions of freedom and equality to the rest of the world as cultural imperialism. Postmodern liberalism has been criticized harshly by thinkers of a more classical bent as providing inadequate moral foundations for claims of rights and even of being nihilistic.

Conclusion

The resilience and durability of liberal political thought over the course of four centuries is remarkable indeed. It is perhaps a testament to the solid, pragmatic grounding of its social and political doctrine in the autonomous human being and the right of individuals freely to express their minds and to direct their own lives. From this perspective springs a realistic but relatively positive view of human nature, faith in human potential, belief in the power of reason, and, ultimately, optimism about the possibility of social progress within free well-ordered societies. Liberalism endeavors to maximize individual liberty through rights guaranteed by contract and law. It envisions a society characterized by free action within a strong but limited framework of government. This framework is generally seen to include a pluralistic representative system of government, the rule of law, the free exchange of ideas, and economic competition. The tradition of liberalism stresses individual freedom and this emphasis on liberty is the major thread in all liberal thought.

See also Aristotle; Bentham, Jeremy; Bill of Rights; Communist Party USA; Conservatism; Declaration of Independence; Constitutional Democracy; Dewey, John; Economic Freedom; Equality; Free Marketplace of Ideas; Individualism; Jefferson, Thomas; Libertarianism; Liberty; Locke, John; Natural Law and Natural Rights; New Deal; Plato; Pluralism; Progressive Era; Property Rights; Rawls, John; Representative Democracy; Roosevelt, Franklin D.; Slavery; Thoreau, Henry David; United States Constitution; *United States v. Carolene Products* Footnote 4; Warren Court

Bibliography

Brands, H. W. 2003. *The Strange Death of American Liberalism.* New Haven, CT: Yale University Press.

Etzioni, Amitai. 1993. *The Spirit of Community: Rights, Responsibilities, and the Communitarian Agenda.* New York: Crown.

Gray, John. 2002. *Two Faces of Liberalism.* New York: The New Press.

Hartz, Louis. 1955. *The Liberal Tradition in America.* New York: Harcourt Brace.

Havelock, Eric A. 1957. *The Liberal Temper in Greek Politics.* New Haven, CT: Yale University Press.

Hobhouse, L. T. 1964. *Liberalism.* New York: Oxford University Press.

Kautz, Steven. 1995. *Liberalism and Community.* Ithaca, NY: Cornell University Press.

Kautz, Steven. 1996. "Postmodern Liberalism and the Politics of Liberal Education." *Social Philosophy and Policy* 13: 164–89.

Locke, John. 1988. *Two Treatises of Government.* Cambridge: Cambridge University Press.

Mill, John Stuart. 1976. *On Liberty.* New York: Penguin Books.

Rawls, John. 1993. *Political Liberalism.* New York: Columbia University Press.

Rorty, Richard. 1983. "Postmodernist Bourgeois Liberalism." In *Pragmatism: A Reader*, 329–36. New York: Vintage Books1997.

Sandel, Michael. 1996. *Democracy's Discontent: America in Search of a Public Philosophy*. Cambridge, MA: Harvard University Press.

Smith, Adam. 1982. *The Wealth of Nations*. Indianapolis, IN: Liberty Fund.

Strauss, Leo. 1968. *Liberalism Ancient and Modern*. Chicago: University of Chicago Press.

Von Mises, Ludwig. 2005. *Liberalism: The Classical Tradition*. Indianapolis, IN: Liberty Fund.

Michael R. Fitzgerald and John M. Scheb II

LIBERTARIANISM

Rooted in classical liberalism, libertarianism holds that law and public policy should maximize individual freedom and minimize the scope of government, which libertarians view as the chief threat to liberty. Accordingly, libertarians are strong advocates for the freedoms enshrined in the Bill of Rights. They also favor private property rights and economic freedom and object to high rates of taxation, economic regulation, and redistribution of wealth. Believing in unrestricted market competition, libertarians typically oppose any effort by government to manage or subsidize particular industries. And because they believe that each individual should be responsible for his or her own welfare, libertarians also object to social welfare programs and even compulsory education. Although libertarians profess belief in legal and political equality, they strongly oppose governmental efforts to foster social or economic equality through "social engineering."

The English philosopher John Stuart Mill is one of the classical liberals whose ideas, at least with regard to social policy, profoundly influenced libertarianism. In his influential essay *On Liberty* (1859), Mill argued that " … there is a sphere of action in which society, as distinguished from the individual, has, if any, only an indirect interest; comprehending all that portion of a person's life and conduct which affects only himself, or if it also affects others, only with their free, voluntary and undeceived consent and participation." Adopting this principle, libertarians favor strong privacy rights and oppose legislation they believe is designed only to foster traditional morality. In the libertarian view, the legitimate role of government

is protection of individuals from one another, not from their own vices or bad judgment. Thus, libertarians object to laws regulating sexual conduct, living arrangements, the private use of drugs—and even to laws mandating that motorists use seat belts. Perhaps the ultimate libertarian position is opposition to the criminal law against suicide. In the libertarian view, the individual has the right to make basic decisions regarding his or her own life—or death.

The idea that each individual should be considered an autonomous actor with respect to personal matters has become increasingly prevalent among Americans, especially younger people. In the late 1960s and throughout the 1970s, a large number of people began to question the authority of government to regulate the private lives of individuals in the name of traditional morality. Today, many Americans hold libertarian views with respect to sociomoral issues, but relatively few subscribe to the libertarian philosophy with respect to economic freedom and property rights. True libertarians espouse the classical liberal maxim, "That government is best which governs least." In postmodern America, only a small minority of citizens believes that restoration of "limited government" is possible or desirable. For those that do, the Libertarian Party (online at www. lp.org) offers an attractive alternative to the Democratic and Republican parties.

See also Conservatism; Drugs, Private Use of; Economic Freedom; Equality; Liberalism; Liberty; Privacy, Constitutional Right of; Property Rights; Right to Die; Seat Belt Laws; Zoning

Bibliography

Boaz, David, ed. 1997. *The Libertarian Reader*. New York: The Free Press.

Murray, Charles. 1997. *What It Means to be a Libertarian*. New York: Broadway Books.

Rothbard, Murray. 1978. *For a New Liberty: The Libertarian Manifesto*. New York: Collier Books.

John M. Scheb II

LIBERTY

The word "liberty" is perhaps the most frequently used element of the American political lexicon. Some of the most memorable statements ever uttered by American leaders invoke this most powerful theme of American political culture. A few well-known examples will suffice:

"They that can give up essential liberty to obtain a little temporary safety deserve neither liberty nor safety."—Benjamin Franklin (1759)

"Is life so dear, or peace so sweet, as to be purchased at the price of chains or slavery? Forbid it, Almighty God! I know not what course others may take but as for me; give me liberty or give me death!"—Patrick Henry (1775)

"The tree of liberty must be refreshed from time to time with the blood of patriots and tyrants."—Thomas Jefferson (1787)

"The greatest dangers to liberty lurk in insidious encroachment by men of zeal, well-meaning but without understanding."—Louis D. Brandeis (1928)

"Let every nation know, whether it wishes us well or ill, that we shall pay any price, bear any burden, meet any hardship, support any friend, oppose any foe to assure the survival and the success of liberty."—John F. Kennedy (1961)

The word *liberty* is associated with some of our most cherished national symbols: the Liberty Bell, the Statue of Liberty, and Lady Freedom atop the Capitol dome. The term *liberty* is also enshrined in our nation's most basic documents. The Declaration of Independence proclaims liberty, along with "life" and "the pursuit of happiness," to be an "unalienable" right. The Preamble to the Constitution states that one of the basic purposes of framing that great charter was to "secure the Blessings of Liberty to ourselves and our Posterity…" The Bill of Rights, specifically the Fifth Amendment, provides that "no person shall be deprived of life, *liberty* or property without due process of law …" {emphasis added} The Fourteenth Amendment likewise mentions "liberty" in enjoining the States against deprivations of rights without due process.

In *The Spirit of the Laws,* a book well known to the founders of the American Republic, Montesquieu observed, "No word has received more different significations and has struck minds in so many ways as has liberty." This article briefly examines the meaning of the term *liberty* in the context of American constitutionalism.

The Etymology of *Liberty*

The English word *liberty* derives from the Middle French *liberty* and ultimately from the Latin *libertas.* The Latin root *liber* means "free." Accordingly, *liberty* is often used synonymously with *freedom,* although some commentators have tried to distinguish between the two. In this article and, indeed, throughout this encyclopedia, we use these terms interchangeably.

We can begin by dispensing with the definitions of liberty that are not relevant to this project. One definition of liberty is: a breach of what is deemed proper or acceptable, as in "taking liberties." Another meaning has relevance to the military service, and in particular the Navy. Sailors are given "liberty" when they are permitted to go ashore for a short time while their ship is in port. Another less common meaning of liberty is the taking of unnecessary risks. Obviously, none of these meanings of liberty is relevant here.

A clearly relevant, albeit insufficient, definition of liberty is "the condition of being free from confinement, servitude, or forced labor." By this definition, anyone who is not imprisoned, indentured, or forced into slavery can be said to enjoy liberty. Arguably, those who wrote the Due Process Clauses of the Fifth and Fourteenth Amendments were using *liberty* in this narrow sense when they prohibited the federal and state governments, respectively, from depriving persons of their "liberty" without due process of law. But clearly, the "blessings of liberty" invoked by the Preamble to the Constitution involve much more than the protection against unjust incarceration. And when President Kennedy spoke of "the survival and success of liberty," obviously he was talking about something much broader than a guarantee against wrongful imprisonment.

Liberty and Democracy

One strain of political thought and commentary that was extant at the time of the American

Revolution equated *liberty* with the overthrow of despotic regimes and their replacement by representative institutions chosen in free and fair elections in which all citizens were afforded the right of participation. But for most Enlightenment thinkers, democracy was not to be equated with liberty, nor was it a sufficient guarantor thereof. Without proper legal, cultural, and institutional constraints, democracy can degenerate into "mob rule" or the "tyranny of the majority." In defining liberty, at least within the liberal tradition, one must focus on the rights and duties of the individual and most especially on the protection of the individual from unjust or improper governmental action. Certainly that was the approach taken by Thomas Jefferson, James Madison, and the other great architects of the American experiment.

All of the provisions of the Bill of Rights deal with some aspect of individual liberty, such as freedom of speech, the right to keep and bear arms, and the freedom from unreasonable searches and seizures. In all of these instances, the purpose of the provision is to protect the individual from some improper action on the part of the federal government. Although the Ninth Amendment indicates that the enumeration of such rights is not to be taken as an exhaustive catalog of individual freedoms, nowhere in the Bill of Rights is there given an overarching definition of liberty.

Expanding Notions of Freedom

Historically many Americans equated liberty with the right of the individual to engage in unfettered economic activity. This circumscription of liberty as economic freedom was widely accepted during the Victorian Era, which placed a premium on social conformity and convention. Indeed, the U.S. Supreme Court seemed to endorse this conception of liberty in its economic due process decisions in the late nineteenth and early twentieth centuries. In these decisions the Court adopted a somewhat strained interpretation of the Constitution to thwart legislation regulating business.

Without question, a landmark in the evolution of the idea of liberty was the publication of John Stuart Mill's celebrated essay *On Liberty* in 1859. Mill succeeded in broadening the pervasive Victorian notions of freedom from the economic realm to the intellectual, spiritual, and personal realms. Presaging the contemporary libertarian notion of freedom, Mill argued that " … there is a sphere of action in which society, as distinguished from the individual, has, if any, only an indirect interest; comprehending all that portion of a person's life and conduct which affects only himself, or if it also affects others, only with their free, voluntary and undeceived consent and participation."

Dissenting in *Olmstead v. United States* (1928), Justice Louis D. Brandeis endorsed Mill's expanded conception of personal freedom as well as his emphasis on individual autonomy and privacy:

The makers of our Constitution undertook to secure conditions favorable to the pursuit of happiness. They recognized the significance of man's spiritual nature, of his feelings and his intellect. They knew that only a part of his pain, pleasure, and satisfactions of life are to be found in material things. They sought to protect Americans in their beliefs, their thoughts, their emotions and their sensations. They conferred, as against the Government, the right to be let alone—the most comprehensive of rights and the right most valued by civilized men.

Today, while there is disagreement over the relationship between economic freedom and other aspects of liberty, there is a general acceptance of the proposition that liberty involves the entire range of human thought, activity, and expression.

Liberty as the Absence of Governmental Restraint

In conceptualizing the freedom of the individual, some define liberty rather casually as "the right to do as one pleases." Most commentators would probably reject that definition out of hand since it fails to acknowledge any limits on one's freedom or any obligation to respect the rights of others. Indeed, the notion that one may do entirely as one pleases is closer to the concept of *license,* which can be defined as the abuse of liberty or the employment of liberty in disregard for law, morality, or the rights of others.

A more defensible definition of liberty might be something like "the absence of unjust or undue governmental control of one's thoughts, words or actions." This approach is consistent with the widely held view that freedom is not absolute, but rather must be exercised within just and reasonable limits imposed by law. As Katharine Lee Bates wrote in the second verse of *America the Beautiful* (1913), "America! America! God mend thine every flaw, Confirm thy soul in self-control, Thy liberty in law!"

In the American political and constitutional traditions, liberty is defined negatively—that is, as the absence of illegitimate governmental controls on the individual. In other political traditions, most notably socialism, liberty tends to be defined as the power of the individual to achieve his or her goals. Thinkers in the socialist tradition point out that the absence of overt governmental control means nothing unless the individual actually has the means to achieve goals. Thus, for socialists, it is facile, even meaningless, to assert that the poor or politically powerless enjoy liberty. The socialist ideal is that all citizens should be equally "free," that is, empowered, to pursue happiness, which requires the equalization of material conditions throughout society. Of course, to achieve this equality socialists prescribe considerable government controls on everyone, at least with regard to the acquisition and use of property. Thus, to be "liberated" means in many instances to be compelled to do things against one's own will and interests. Suffice it to say that the socialist conception of freedom is far removed from the mainstream of American political thought and culture.

In the American liberal tradition, then, freedom is defined as the absence of unjust or undue governmental restrictions. Of course, this definition of liberty is but the beginning of the real problem—determining what government controls are unjust or undue. It is here that the real controversy over the meaning of American liberty continues to flourish.

Evolving Judicial Perspectives on Freedom

Courts have long held that no liberty is absolute, but the unmistakable trend over the last century has been for courts to adopt broader conceptions of the individual rights enumerated in the federal and state constitutions. Invoking the freedoms of speech and press enshrined in the First Amendment, courts in the latter decades of the twentieth century provided increased constitutional protection for the freedom of expression, making it much more difficult for governments at all levels to stifle expression deemed to be offensive, profane, indecent, inflammatory, subversive, or defamatory. Indeed, in the decades following the Great Depression, expressive freedom came to replace economic freedom at the apex of the hierarchy of judicially protected liberties.

Writing for the Court in *Palko v. Connecticut* (1937), Justice Benjamin Cardozo characterized freedom of speech as "the matrix, the indispensable condition, of nearly every other form of freedom." During the 1940s several members of the Supreme Court went so far as to suggest that the First Amendment freedoms of speech and press enjoy a "preferred position" in relation to other constitutional guarantees (see, for example, Justice William O. Douglas's majority opinion in *Murdock v. Pennsylvania,* 1943).

Until the late twentieth century, the view that dominated American law and political culture was that individual freedom could be limited by laws expressing traditional moral values and aesthetic sensibilities. Thus it was not considered unjust or an undue restriction of liberty for the law to forbid polygamy, sodomy, adultery, pornography, gambling, prostitution, and all sorts of "sins" and vices. With the increasing secularization and diversification of society, the idea that law may restrict an individual's choices in such matters has increasingly fallen into disfavor.

In the last half of the twentieth century, the libertarian conception of freedom gained widespread acceptance in the United States. Simply stated, that conception is that government and society have no right to regulate the decisions or activities of the individual that affect only that individual or others who are involved only by their own consent. In this conception of liberty, it is not the proper business of society or government to protect the individual against his or her vices or poor judgments.

Reflecting the changing mores of the country, state legislatures have liberalized laws affecting marriage and divorce. Ancient laws forbidding adultery and fornication were repealed or fell into disuse. Laws prohibiting gambling were also liberalized and one state, Nevada, even legalized prostitution by local option.

Under the aegis of the so-called constitutional right of privacy, American courts invalidated laws restricting sexual and reproductive choices. In the seminal case in this area, *Griswold v. Connecticut* (1965), the Supreme Court struck down a state law prohibiting the use of birth control devices as applied to married couples. Seven years later, in *Eisenstadt v. Baird,* the Court extended the ruling to cover singles as well, in effect recognizing a broad personal right to make one's own decisions in matters of sex and reproduction. It was this broad right that supplied the basis for *Roe v. Wade* (1973), effectively legalizing abortion, and more recently, *Lawrence v. Texas* (2003), which held that states could not criminalize private homosexual conduct between consenting adults. Writing for the Court in *Lawrence,* Justice Anthony Kennedy opined as to the nature of constitutional liberty:

Liberty protects the person from unwarranted government intrusions into a dwelling or other private places. In our tradition the State is not omnipresent in the home. And there are other spheres of our lives and existence, outside the home, where the State should not be a dominant presence. Freedom extends beyond spatial bounds. Liberty presumes an autonomy of self that includes freedom of thought, belief, expression, and certain intimate conduct. The instant case involves liberty of the person both in its spatial and more transcendent dimensions.

Two Faces of Liberty?

Despite (or perhaps due to) the expansion of personal liberty in the realms of lifestyle and expression, Americans have come to accept considerable governmental regulation of their economic activity. Although Americans are increasingly hostile to efforts to "legislate morality," they appear increasingly willing to accept restrictions on their acquisition and use of private property to promote social justice, environmental protection, and the public health and safety.

Both of the major ideological orientations in contemporary American politics, namely liberalism and conservatism, stress different facets of liberty. Conservatives prize economic freedom but stress the need for conformity to social norms. Liberals extol the values of free expression and lifestyle privacy but seem almost oblivious to property rights and economic liberty. From a truly libertarian point of view, both conservatives and liberals have crabbed conceptions of liberty.

The quest for liberty is at the heart of the American experiment, but the struggle to define that quintessential American value will go on indefinitely.

See also Accused, Rights of the; Association, Freedom of; Bill of Rights (American) (1789); Brandeis, Louis B.; Democracy, Constitutional; Due Process, Procedural; Due Process, Substantive; Economic Freedom; Fourteenth Amendment (1868); *Griswold v. Connecticut* (1965); Jefferson, Thomas; Kennedy, Anthony; *Lawrence v. Texas* (2003); Madison, James; Marriage, Rights Pertaining to; *Palko v. Connecticut* (1937); Police Power; Press, Freedom of the; Privacy, Constitutional Right of; Property Rights; Religion, Freedom of; Reproductive Freedom; *Roe v. Wade* (1973); Speech, Freedom of

Bibliography

Banning, Lance. 1998. *The Sacred Fire of Liberty: James Madison and the Founding of the Federal Republic.* Reprint ed. Ithaca, New York: Cornell University Press.

Berlin, Isaiah. 2002. *Liberty.* 2nd ed. Edited by Henry Hardy. New York: Oxford University Press.

Fischer, David Hackett. 2004. *Liberty and Freedom: A Visual History of America's Founding Ideas.* New York: Oxford University Press.

Friedman, Milton. 2002. *Capitalism and Freedom.* 40th Anniversary Edition. Chicago: University of Chicago Press.

Mill, John Stuart. 1998. *On Liberty and Other Essays.* New York: Oxford University Press.

Sharansky, Natan. 2004. T*he Case For Democracy: The Power of Freedom to Overcome Tyranny and Terror.* New York: Public Affairs

John M. Scheb II and Otis H. Stephens, Jr.

LIBRARY RECORDS, CONFIDENTIALITY OF.

See Privacy, Informational

LIFE, RIGHT TO. *See* Pro-Life Movement; Pro-Life Position on Abortion

LIMITED GOVERNMENT. *See* Liberalism; Libertarianism

LINCOLN, ABRAHAM (1809–1865)

Abraham Lincoln served as president at the moment of the nation's greatest peril, the Civil War. To handle the crisis, Lincoln wielded wide-ranging emergency powers. Lincoln's critics, both at the time and in the decades since, have charged that some of his wartime actions—particularly suspending the writ of habeas corpus and using military courts to try civilians—violated the Constitution's protection of individual civil liberties. Yet Lincoln also vastly improved the civil rights of African Americans through winning the Civil War, issuing the Emancipation Proclamation, and supporting the adoption of the Thirteenth Amendment. Today, most scholars rank Lincoln as the nation's greatest president.

Article I, Section 9 of the Constitution specifies that "the Writ of Habeas Corpus shall not be suspended, unless when in Cases of Rebellion or Invasion the public Safety may require it." In other words, persons who are arrested and detained have the right to a court appearance to determine whether their confinement is lawful and to release if it is not. Shortly after the Civil War began, Lincoln—without consulting Congress—suspended the writ of habeas corpus around the important route between Washington, D.C., and Philadelphia. Eventually, Lincoln suspended the writ throughout the country. This enabled the military to identify

and arrest suspected Confederate sympathizers and imprison them indefinitely, without charges being brought or a trial being conducted. Lincoln also directed that, for certain crimes that supported the rebellion, civilians could be tried by military courts. Lincoln saw both these measures as helping protect the Union by increasing the government's authority to fight the rebellion.

Lincoln's actions sparked controversy not only because they curtailed important civil liberties of persons accused of crimes, but because it was unclear whether the president had the power to take those steps on his own authority. Roger Taney, the chief justice at the time, strongly believed that Lincoln had overstepped his bounds. Taney, in his capacity as circuit court judge, issued a writ of habeas corpus for a man named John Merryman, who had been arrested for trying to organize a militia unit in Maryland to join the Confederacy. When his writ was not honored, Taney published a scathing opinion in which he asserted that "the people of the United States are no longer living under a government of laws." Lincoln simply ignored Taney and the opinion, and in 1863 Congress affirmed Lincoln's steps with the Habeas Corpus Act.

Lincoln has also been criticized for suppressing the press during the war. Many newspaper editors were arrested simply because they published stories critical of Lincoln or the war. Most of the suppression took place in the occupied South or in border states, however, a forceful opposition press operated in the North. Lincoln also ordered the censorship of the mail and of telegraph communications.

Despite Taney's opinion of Lincoln, during the war the Supreme Court as a whole narrowly sustained the president's actions. Only after the war was over, and Lincoln was dead, did the Court rule against him. In *Ex parte Milligan* (1866), the Court decided that the president did not have the authority to direct that civilians be tried in military courts in areas where the civilian courts were operating.

Lincoln admitted that his actions were drastic but argued that they were warranted in the context of the national crisis. Preserving the union, and the government upon which it was based, was his overriding goal. In a July 4, 1861, message to Congress, Lincoln justified suspending habeas corpus. He asked, "Are all the laws *but one* to go unexecuted, and the Government itself go to pieces lest that one be violated?" In an 1864 letter to a newspaper editor, Lincoln expanded his argument that he had acted for the greater good. "Was it possible," Lincoln asked, "to lose the nation and yet preserve the Constitution? By general law, life and limb must be protected, yet often a limb must be amputated to save a life; but a life is never wisely given to save a limb. I felt that measures otherwise unconstitutional might become lawful by becoming indispensable to the preservation of the nation."

Lincoln's approach to emancipation and reconstruction—like his actions on habeas corpus and military trials of civilians—stemmed from a combination of principle and practical politics. Lincoln had long regarded slavery as immoral, but he also believed that the Constitution protected slavery where it existed. He justified his Emancipation Proclamation as a war measure. Issued in its final form on January 1, 1863, the proclamation freed slaves only in the unconquered areas of the Confederacy. Many in Congress and some of Lincoln's own Cabinet members considered the proclamation too cautious a step, but Lincoln did not want to abolish slavery by executive decree. Instead, he advocated that slavery be abolished through an amendment to the Constitution.

With Lincoln's support, the 1864 Republican national convention adopted a platform favoring an amendment to ban slavery. After his reelection, Lincoln worked hard to persuade members of Congress to approve the amendment; its passage, he told one congressman, "will clinch the whole subject; it will bring the war, I have no doubt, rapidly to a close." The Senate passed the proposal with the required two-thirds vote in 1864; the House followed suit in 1865. Later that year, the required number of states ratified the measure and the Thirteenth Amendment went into effect.

Lincoln's presidency vividly illustrates a law of American politics: in times of crisis, especially war, the power of the president increases. That leads to another fact: increased presidential power can threaten the civil liberties of individual citizens. The challenge that confronted Lincoln, as well as later wartime presidents, was how to balance national security with the rights of individuals. Lincoln himself wondered if this problem inevitably came with democratic government. In his July 1861 message to Congress, he asked: "Is there in all republics this inherent and fatal weakness? Must a government of necessity be too *strong* for the liberties of its own people, or too *weak* to maintain its own existence?" Nearly a century and a half later, that question still resonates.

See also Abolitionist Movement; Civil Rights and Liberties During Wartime; Dred Scott Case; Emancipation Proclamation; Habeas Corpus; Lincoln-Douglas Debates; Military Tribunals; *Milligan, Ex Parte;* Reconstruction; Slavery; Taney, Roger B.; Thirteenth Amendment

Bibliography

Donald, David Herbert. 1995. *Lincoln*. New York: Simon & Schuster.

Neely, Mark E., Jr. 1991. *The Fate of Liberty: Abraham Lincoln and Civil Liberties*. New York: Oxford University Press.

Nelson, Michael, ed. 2002. *Guide to the Presidency*. 3rd ed. Washington, DC: CQ Press.

Paludan, Phillip Shaw. 1994. *The Presidency of Abraham Lincoln*. Lawrence: University Press of Kansas.

Mark Byrnes

LINCOLN-DOUGLAS DEBATES (1858)

Seven formal debates took place between the Democratic nominee for the U.S. Senate from Illinois, the incumbent Stephen A. Douglas, and the Republican candidate, Abraham Lincoln, in August, September, and October 1858. The candidates discussed only one issue—the extension of slavery to the western territories. Although Douglas won the election (at that time state legislatures selected senators), the debates made Lincoln a national figure and made possible his election to the presidency of the United States two years later. Lincoln's victory precipitated the secession of 11 southern states and the ensuing Civil War, which resulted in the end of slavery and the granting of citizenship to African Americans.

African slavery was an important part of British imperial policy toward its North American colonies. When 13 of the colonies declared their independence from the British Crown in 1776, seven of the new states abolished slavery within a few years. The principle was established that states could choose for themselves whether to recognize the right of whites to own Negro slaves. In 1787, however, Congress, under the Articles of Confederation, passed the Northwest Ordinance prohibiting slavery in the territory north of the Ohio River, which soon became the states of Ohio, Michigan, Indiana, Illinois, and Wisconsin. The constitution that replaced the articles the following year authorized Congress to stop the importation of slaves from Africa, a step Congress took 20 years later. The purchase from France in 1803 of the Louisiana Territory, an immense tract of land watered by the Mississippi and Missouri Rivers, offered Congress the opportunity to emulate the Northwest Ordinance. The antislavery forces, however, lacked sufficient power, and in the Missouri Compromise of 1820 Congress admitted Missouri as a slave state but banned slavery in the territory west and north of Missouri's southern border. Congress compromised again in 1850 when it admitted California as a free state but allowed slavery in the other territory acquired in the war with Mexico in 1846–1847. The Wilmot Proviso, a bill that would have banned slavery from the acquired territory, passed the House but failed in the Senate.

The Democratic Party, however, abandoned the Missouri Compromise in a bill introduced by Douglas, who had aspirations for the presidency and needed Southern support. The Kansas-Nebraska Act of 1854 lifted the ban on slavery in the territory west of Missouri and left it to the legislature of each territory whether to petition Congress for admission as a free or slave state, a principle Douglas termed "popular sovereignty." The Republican Party was formed two months later to bring about the repeal of this legislation. The Supreme Court dealt another blow to the Missouri

Compromise in 1857 in the Dred Scott Case, when it ruled that Congress could not exclude slaves from the territories, on the ground that the constitution protected slaveholders' property rights.

Lincoln sought to discredit both the doctrine of popular sovereignty and the Dred Scott decision in his debates with Douglas. First, he pointed out that the framers of the Declaration of Independence and the Constitution regarded slavery as a moral evil. Douglas's doctrine of popular sovereignty, however, treated slavery as morally neutral. Without a regular supply of new slaves from Africa and without the ability for slavery to move west with the settlers, they expected the institution gradually to wither away. Secondly, the fathers of the republic, said Lincoln, did not regard slaves simply as property. The constitution, for example, counts slaves in determining the population of each state for purposes of allocating seats in the House of Representatives and always uses the term "persons" rather than "slaves" to describe bondsmen. Free blacks, Lincoln pointed out, could own property, vote, and hold office in some of the states at the time of independence and the ratification of the Constitution.

Douglas attempted to paint Lincoln as an abolitionist and a proponent of Negro equality. Many of the settlers in Illinois, including Lincoln and his family, had migrated from the South and had strong prejudices against blacks. Furthermore, they disliked the willingness of abolitionists to break the law in order to dramatize their opposition to slavery and their attitude of moral superiority to Southerners. Lincoln responded by saying that he would do nothing to disturb slavery in the states where it existed while opposing its expansion to new states. He said that he supported the rule of law and regarded the white race as superior to the black. Ironically, Douglas's predictions in the debates that Lincoln's policies would lead to civil war, the emancipation of the slaves, and citizenship for blacks did in fact come to pass.

Lincoln accused Douglas of participating in a conspiracy with President James Buchanan, former President Franklin Pierce, and Supreme Court Chief Justice Roger Taney to nationalize slavery. He expected the Supreme Court to issue a second Dred Scott decision saying that the constitution protected white Americans' right to own slaves anywhere in the Union. In the second debate at Freeport, Illinois, in answer to a question from Lincoln, Douglas admitted that his doctrine of popular sovereignty conflicted with Taney's ruling in Dred Scott because it allowed the people of a territory to exclude slavery. The Freeport Doctrine, as it came to be known, split the Democratic Party into a northern and southern faction. In the 1860 presidential election, Douglas, the nominee of the northern wing of the party, won only 12 electoral votes, while John C. Breckinridge, the choice of the southern splinter, carried 72 votes. The division of the Democratic vote allowed the Republican nominee, Lincoln, to win with 180 electoral votes, even though he received fewer popular votes than Douglas and Breckinridge combined. John Bell, a fourth-party candidate, won 39 electoral votes.

The heart of the issue between Lincoln and Douglas was whether slavery was a moral or a political issue. If slavery were evil, argued Lincoln, then the law should not support it, no matter how profitable or popular it might be. Lincoln and Douglas also differed on the nature of the Founding. In Lincoln's view, the primary purpose of the establishment of the United States was to secure liberty. Democracy was secondary. The majority has no right to treat individuals unjustly. Slavery is wrong, said Lincoln, following the Declaration of Independence, because it violates the truth that all men are created equal and that all government must be based on the consent of the governed. Slaveholding, moreover, observed Lincoln, turns whites into petty tyrants, rendering them unfit for self-government. Lincoln's message was that natural rights and liberties are based in moral imperatives and cannot justly be abridged even when public opinion supports doing so.

See also Abolitionist Movement; Articles of Confederation; Constitutional Democracy; Declaration of Independence; Dred Scott Case; Equality; Lincoln, Abraham; Representative Democracy; Slavery; Taney, Roger B.

Bibliography

Angle, Paul, ed. 1991. *Complete Lincoln-Douglas Debates of 1858.* Chicago: University of Chicago Press.

Bartanen, Michael D., and Frank, David A. 1994. *Lincoln Douglas Debate.* Lincolnwood, IL: National Textbook Co.

Fehrenbacher, Don E. 1970. *Prelude to Greatness: Lincoln in the 1850's.* Stanford, CA: Stanford University Press.

Jaffa, Harry. 1999. *Crisis of the House Divided: An Interpretation of the Issues in the Lincoln-Douglas Debates.* Chicago: University of Chicago Press.

Wiese, Jeffrey. 2000. *Lincoln-Douglas Debate: Values in Conflict.* Topeka, KS: Clark.

Kenneth Holland

LINEUPS AND IDENTIFICATION PROCEDURES

Police use a number of different procedures in which crime victims and witnesses attempt to identify perpetrators. The classic procedure is the "lineup," in which a victim or witness is asked to identify the actual perpetrator from among a group of possible perpetrators. Similar procedures include *photo packs,* which are sets of "mug shots" shown individually to the victim or witness, and *showups,* where the police take the victim to the suspect to determine if the victim can make an identification. Police rely heavily on forensic evidence taken from a suspect compared with that found at a crime scene. All of these procedures are extremely important in police work, but each poses unique legal problems.

Lineups

In a lineup, a group of individuals, one of whom is the suspect in custody, appears before a victim or witness, who is usually shielded from the suspect's view. Often, the individuals in the lineup are asked to walk, turn sideways, wear certain items of clothing, or speak to assist the victim or eyewitness in making a positive identification. One might think that being required to appear in a lineup would be considered a form of self-incrimination in violation of the Fifth Amendment. However, in *United States v. Wade* (1967), the U.S. Supreme Court held that there is no Fifth Amendment immunity against being placed in a lineup. This is because the protection against self-incrimination applies to testimonial or communicative evidence and not to physical evidence. Nevertheless, courts must guard against the possibility that identification procedures, especially lineups, are unfair when a victim or witness is prompted to identify a particular suspect as the perpetrator (see, for example, *Foster v. California,* 1969). Obviously, if the perpetrator is known to be black, it is impermissibly suggestive for police to place one African-American suspect in a lineup with five white individuals. In practice, however, the more subtle suggestiveness of lineups causes problems for the courts. To avoid such problems, police should place several persons with similar physical characteristics in a lineup.

In *United States v. Wade* (1967), the Supreme Court held that once an accused has been formally charged with an offense a lineup is considered "a critical stage of the proceedings" which affords the accused a Sixth Amendment right to have counsel present. To ensure that police and prosecutors honor that right, the Court held in *Gilbert v. California* (1967) that a pretrial identification obtained in violation of the right to counsel is per se inadmissible at trial. On the other hand, in *Neil v. Biggers* (1972), the Court held that a pretrial identification obtained through impermissibly suggestive identification procedures is not per se inadmissible. Instead, such an identification may be introduced into evidence if the trial judge first finds that the witness's in-court identification is reliable and based on independent recall. In making this determination, the trial judge must consider: (1) the opportunity of the witness to view the accused at the time of the crime; (2) the witness's degree of attention; (3) the accuracy of the witness's prior description of the accused; (4) the level of certainty demonstrated at the confrontation; and (5) the time that elapsed between the crime and the confrontation.

After *United States v. Wade* it was unclear whether a suspect who was not formally charged with an offense had a constitutional right to have counsel present at a lineup. In *Kirby v. Illinois* (1972), a plurality opinion of the Supreme Court held that a lineup conducted before a suspect is charged with an offense is not "a critical stage of the proceedings." Therefore, a suspect not charged has no right to have counsel present at a lineup. States, of course, can grant greater protection under their constitutions. Indeed, some state courts grant a suspect the right to have counsel present at police lineups conducted prior to formal charges being initiated.

Photo Packs

As noted above, a photo pack is simply a set of mug shots shown individually to the victim or eyewitness in the hope of being able to identify the perpetrator. To produce a reliable, hence admissible, identification, the presentation of the photo pack should include several photos and should not emphasize one photo over the others. The words and actions of the officers making the presentation must manifest an attitude of disinterest. In analyzing a defendant's claim of being the victim of an impermissibly suggestive photo pack identification, courts generally apply a two-part test. First, did the photo array present the defendant in an impermissibly suggestive posture? Second, if so, under the totality of circumstances, did the procedure give rise to a substantial likelihood of misidentification?

The Sixth Amendment, according to the decision handed down in *United States v. Ash* (1973), does not grant an accused the right to have counsel present at a photographic display containing a picture of the accused and conducted to assist a witness to attempt to identify a suspect. This is true irrespective of whether an accused has been formally charged with an offense.

Showups

The showup is a frequently used method of identification of a suspect. In a showup, the police usually take the victim to view the suspect to determine if the victim can make an identification. At least one state supreme court has held that police may transport a person for an investigatory stop a short distance for purposes of a showup. Because the suspect has not been charged with an offense the Sixth Amendment right to counsel does not apply.

In *Wise v. United States* (1967), the U.S. Court of Appeals for the District of Columbia Circuit approved the use of showups, commenting, "[W]e do not consider a prompt identification of a suspect close to the time and place of an offense to diverge from the rudiments of fair play that govern the due balance of pertinent interests that suspects be treated fairly while the state pursues its responsibility of apprehending criminals."

In *Stovall v. Denno* (1967), the Supreme Court recognized that a defendant has a due process right to exclude identification testimony that results from unnecessarily suggestive procedures that may lead to an irreparably mistaken identification. Stovall was brought to the eyewitness victim's hospital room in handcuffs and was identified by the victim, who was in failing health. The Court ruled that although suggestive, under the circumstances this procedure was not "unnecessarily" suggestive. This form of "on-the-scene" confrontation between an eyewitness and a suspect is inherently suggestive because it is apparent that when law enforcement officers take a victim for a showup of a suspect, they usually believe they have caught the offender. Therefore, courts review identification testimony carefully to make sure a witness's identification testimony is not based on impermissibly suggestive identification procedures. In making such a determination courts often look to the length of time between the crime and the confrontation and the level of certainty demonstrated by the witness at the confrontation.

Although critics complain of the use of showups, such a confrontation may be justified by the necessity to preserve a witness's memory of a suspect before the suspect has had an opportunity to alter his or her clothing and appearance. Appellate courts consistently admonish caution in the use of showups; however, they generally approve of their use when the identification occurs shortly after the crime has been committed and the showup is conducted near the scene of the crime under circumstances that are not unduly suggestive. In approving showups some courts have pointed out that a victim's or eyewitness's on-the-scene identification is likely to be more reliable than a later identification because the memory is fresher. Courts form their judgments on the reliability of showups based on many factors and circumstances.

Forensic Methods

Forensic methods involve the application of scientific principles to legal issues. In the context of police work, forensic methods commonly include fingerprint identification, comparison of blood samples, matching of clothing fibers, head and body hair comparisons, identification of semen, and, more recently, DNA tests. When these methods are conducted by qualified persons, the results are usually admissible in evidence. Indeed, in *Schmerber v. California* (1966), the U.S. Supreme Court ruled that obtaining such physical evidence from suspects does not violate the constitutional prohibition against compulsory self-incrimination.

In *Gilbert v. California* (1967), the Supreme Court held that a suspect could be compelled to provide a handwriting exemplar, explaining that it is not testimony but an identifying physical characteristic. Similarly, in *United States v. Dionisio* (1973), the Court held that a suspect could be compelled to provide a voice exemplar on the ground that the recording is being used only to measure the physical properties of the suspect's voice, as distinct from the content of what the suspect has said.

In *Rochin v. California* (1952), the Supreme Court said that police may not use methods that "shock the conscience" in obtaining physical evidence from suspects. Courts will scrutinize closely procedures that subject the suspect to major bodily intrusions. For example, in *Winston v. Lee* (1985), the prosecution sought a court order requiring a suspect to have surgery to remove a bullet lodged in his chest. The prosecution believed that ballistics tests on the bullet would show that the suspect had been wounded during the course of a robbery. The Supreme Court, weighing the risks to the suspect against the government's need for evidence, and noting that the prosecution had other evidence against the suspect, disallowed the procedure. The Court declined to formulate a broad rule to govern such cases. Rather, courts must consider such matters on a case-by-case basis, carefully weighing the interests on both sides.

Defense lawyers can attack the methodology of forensic procedures as well as the qualifications of those administering them. If the evidence is inherently unreliable, it is inadmissible regardless of whether there were violations of the suspect's constitutional rights. In 1996 the FBI crime laboratory was criticized for allegedly sloppy procedures in the conduct of DNA and other forensic tests. This encouraged defense lawyers to challenge the reliability of the evidence in several cases where prosecutors were using evidence analyzed by the FBI crime lab.

With the rapid progress of science and technology, forensic procedures are constantly evolving and new procedures becoming available to the police. Evidence obtained through scientific and technological innovations can be both relevant and probative in a criminal case. Yet care must be taken to ensure that a new method is clearly supported by research.

Until recently, federal and state courts followed the test articulated by the U.S. Court of Appeals for the D.C. Circuit in *Frye v. United States* (1923), and admitted scientific evidence only if it was based on principles or theories generally accepted in the scientific community. In *Daubert v. Merrell Dow Pharmaceuticals* (1993), the Supreme Court held that the Federal Rules of Evidence supersede *Frye* and govern the admissibility of scientific evidence in the federal courts. This approach causes admissibility of scientific evidence to hinge on such factors as whether the evidence can be tested and whether it has been subjected to peer review. It remains to be seen whether state courts will continue to follow the *Frye* test.

See also Accused, Rights of the; Counsel, Right to; Critical Pretrial Stages; Due Process, Procedural; Fifth Amendment; Interrogation and Confessions; Self-Incrimination Clause; Sixth Amendment

Bibliography

Priest, Pat. 2002. "Eyewitness Identification and the Scientific Method." *Texas Bar Journal* 65: 974.

Scheb, John M., and John M. Scheb II. 2006. *Criminal Procedure.* Belmont, CA: Thomson/Wadsworth.

Wells, Gary L., and Eric P. Seelau. 1995. "Eyewitness Identification: Psychological Research and Legal Policy on Lineups." *Psychology, Public Policy, and Law* 1: 765.

Hon. John M. Scheb and John M. Scheb II

LITERACY TESTS

Discrimination against African Americans in the post-Civil War South extended to all parts of life, but particularly to the practice of voting. In the Civil War Amendments (the Thirteenth through Fifteenth Amendments to the Constitution) offered as part of the incentive to end postwar military occupation of the South, two amendments were intended to prevent the very discriminatory practices that former Confederate states put in place. The Fourteenth Amendment empowered the federal government to force states to honor Bill of Rights protections to the states, and the Fifteenth Amendment extended the voting franchise to the newly freed slaves (which the Thirteenth Amendment codified). Despite the Civil War Amendments, though, states particularly in the South found numerous ways to deny African Americans the right to vote. None of the amendments prohibited the states from creating onerous qualifications that would prevent many African Americans from the franchise.

White primaries, grandfather clauses, poll taxes, and racial gerrymandering all limited the ability of African Americans to vote, joining the literacy tests as ways around the intent of the Civil War Amendments. Literacy tests were a particularly effective form of disenfranchisement, as they tended to prevent African Americans from registering to vote and thereby rendered them unable to cast votes in any election at all. An African American who wanted to vote had to go to a county clerk's office and fill out a multipage registration form with various loyalty oaths and plentiful personal information that the applicant had to swear was accurate under penalty of perjury. Beyond the form, applicants had to prove that they could read and write, hence the literacy test.

The Alabama literacy test may be the most famous of all, because one state Senator, E. C. "Bud" Boswell, proposed the test to specifically disenfranchise black registration applicants. The test existed in three parts: First, the Registrar would provide a section of the Constitution that the applicant had to read aloud to the Registrar's satisfaction in Part A. Parts B and C asked intricate questions of current-day politics and Constitutional interpretation. Registration applicants were required to name the sitting Attorney General of the United States, identify the number of people that must testify against a defendant in treason cases, and the time of day on January 20 that a new President is inaugurated. An applicant to register had to take the literacy test and answer 90 percent of its 20 questions correctly to be eligible to vote, meaning that any applicant who missed more than two questions would not be allowed to register. As the test went far beyond basic standards for literacy, the test invalidated many legitimate attempts to register to vote, though rarely for white applicants as the grandfather clause allowed them to register without taking or even after failing the test.

During the Civil Rights Era of the 1950s and 1960s, a reaction against the tests began to build. In *Davis v. Schnell* (1949), a federal district court invalidated Alabama's literacy test as an unconstitutional denial of African-American voting rights. However, a 1959 Supreme Court case, *Lassiter v. Northampton Election Board*, ruled that a literacy test was not unconstitutional on its face. Instead, the Court upheld the North Carolina test since the Court found that the state applied the test equally to all applicants regardless of race. Six years later, Congress would pass the Voting Rights Act of 1965, which once and for all outlawed literacy tests as a precondition of registering or voting.

See also Fifteenth Amendment; Fourteenth Amendment (1868); Grandfather Clause; Poll Tax; Racial Gerrymandering; Voting Rights Act of 1965; White Primary

Bibliography

Denvir, John. 2001. *Democracy's Constitution: Claiming the Privileges of American Citizenship.* Champaign: University of Illinois Press.

Keyssar, Alexander. 2000. *The Right to Vote.* New York: Basic Books.

Chapman Rackaway

LITTLE, MALCOLM. *See* Malcolm X

LITTLE ROCK CRISIS (1957)

In the wake of the United States Supreme Court's rulings in *Brown v. Board of Education I* (1954) and *Brown II* (1955), many Southern states engaged in massive resistance, refusing to comply with the Court's directive requiring desegregation of public schools. According to Richard Kluger in his monumental study *Simple Justice,* "[t]hroughout the Fifties, the South interpreted 'all deliberate speed' to mean 'any conceivable delay,' and desegregation was far more a figment in the mind of the Supreme Court than a prominent new feature on the American social landscape" (Kluger 1975, 753). Resistance to *Brown* was fueled by the lack of support for the Court's decision by both Congress and the president.

In 1956, 101 Congressmen from the former Confederate states issued the Southern Manifesto (the only Southern senators who did not sign it were Lyndon Johnson of Texas, and Estes Kefauver and Albert Gore, Sr. of Tennessee) in which they criticized the Court's perceived abuse of judicial power and pledged to reverse the ruling in *Brown* (Kluger 1975, 752). President Eisenhower's reluctance to endorse *Brown* was evident in many public comments that he made about the ruling. In fact, he refused to say whether he even agreed with the Court's opinion (Kluger 1975, 753). Even though he had signed off on the Justice Department's brief to the Court arguing that it should overturn *Plessy v. Ferguson*, Eisenhower believed that law itself was not able to overcome prejudice (Urofsky and Finkelman 2002, 790). As chief executive, it was the president's responsibility to enforce the law, but Eisenhower refused to intervene in February 1956, when the University of Alabama would not admit Autherine Lucy, an African American, despite a federal court order requiring the university to do so.

Regardless of his misgivings over integration, Eisenhower was forced to act in the fall of 1957 when Arkansas Governor Orval Faubus called out the National Guard to prevent nine African American students, the "Little Rock Nine" as they came to be called, from integrating Central High School in Little Rock, Arkansas. In order to comply with the Court's initial ruling in *Brown*, the Little Rock school board instituted a desegregation plan that would go into effect on September 3, 1957 at Central High School. A day before the plan was to begin, Faubus called out the National Guard claiming that the troops were needed to quell imminent public disturbances. A district court ordered the school board and the superintendent to proceed with the planned integration. Faubus, however, was unyielding. For three weeks, the National Guard unit was stationed at the school to prevent desegregation. After the district court issued an injunction barring the use of the troops by the governor to thwart integration, the National Guard was removed and the city police were left to maintain order. As the African American students were taken into the school on September 23, a disturbance broke out when the officers were unable to contain protestors who had gathered at the school to express their animosity towards integration. The children were quickly removed from the building and driven away in police cars.

President Eisenhower concluded that he could not allow this blatant disregard of federal law and on September 25 he called 1,000 paratroopers into Little Rock. He also federalized 10,000 Arkansas national guardsmen to protect the Little Rock Nine and to maintain order (Urofsky and Finkelman 2002, 790). At the end of the school year, the Little Rock school board asked for and received from a federal district court a two-and-a-half year delay in implementing desegregation. This action was challenged by the NAACP in *Cooper v. Aaron* (1958).

In this case, the Supreme Court addressed two central issues: whether the constitutional rights of the African American students were violated by a delay in the implementation of desegregation plans, and whether state officials were bound by the Court's ruling in *Brown*. The Court took the unusual step of issuing a unanimous opinion signed by all nine justices. In its ruling, the Court held that the constitutional rights of the students could not be infringed by actions of the state in defiance of *Brown*, and that a delay in *Brown*'s implementation would deny them their rights. The Court also made it clear that the local school board was an agent of the state for purposes of the Fourteenth Amendment; therefore, it could not discriminate against the African American students. With regard to whether the governor and the legislature were required to follow *Brown*, the Court felt compelled to offer a brief civics lesson on the fundamental principles of the United States Constitution. It noted that the Supremacy Clause makes the Constitution the "supreme Law of the Land." Moreover, the Court quoted Chief Justice John Marshall's well-known adage from *Marbury v. Madison* that "[i]t is emphatically the province and duty of the judicial department to say what the law is." Based on these precepts, the state could not deny the rights of African American students without violating the Constitution and their own oath to support it.

This decision only engendered more hostility and Southerners remained adamantly opposed to integration. Governor Faubus shut down the Arkansas public schools to halt integration; a tactic also employed by other states. Until the Civil Rights Movement gained momentum in the 1960s and the Civil Rights Act of 1964 (which cut off funds to public institutions that were segregated) was passed, the judiciary was the only branch of the federal government committed to upholding the principle of equality established in *Brown v. Board*.

See also *Brown v. Board of Education* (1954; 1955); Civil Rights Act of 1964; Civil Rights Movement; *Cooper v. Aaron* (1958); Fourteenth Amendment (1868); Marshall, John; National Association for the Advancement of Colored People (NAACP); *Plessy v. Ferguson* (1896); Segregation, De Facto and De Jure; Segregation in Public Education; State Action Doctrine

Bibliography

Kluger, Richard. 1975. *Simple Justice: The History of Brown v. Board of Education and Black America's Struggle for Equality*. New York: Vintage Books.

Urofsky, Melvin, and Paul Finkelman. 2002. *A March of Liberty: A Constitutional History of the United States*. Vol. 2, *From 1877 to the Present*. 2nd ed. New York: Oxford University Press.

Kara E. Stooksbury

LIVING ARRANGEMENTS. *See* Privacy, Constitutional Right of

LIVING CONSTITUTION

In March 2000, during a debate with other Democratic candidates for president, Vice President Al Gore was asked what kind of justices he would place on the Supreme Court if given the opportunity. Gore responded, "I would look for justices of the Supreme Court who understand that our Constitution is a living and breathing document, that it was intended by our Founders to be interpreted in the light of the constantly evolving experience of the American people." Gore's answer provided a nice definition of the notion of the "living Constitution," a notion that has been widely adopted in both popular and scholarly discussions of constitutional interpretation. It has even been embraced by Justices of the Supreme Court, most notably the late William J. Brennan, who once wrote:

Current justices read the Constitution in the only way that we can: as twentieth-century Americans. We look to the history of the time of the framing and to the intervening history of interpretation. But the ultimate question must be: What do the words of the text mean in our time? (Brennan 1986, 438)

Proponents of the living Constitution often cite Chief Justice John Marshall's dictum in *McCulloch v. Maryland* (1819) that the Constitution was "intended to endure for ages to come, and, consequently, to be adapted to the various crises of human affairs...." However, it is unlikely that Marshall meant this statement as a justification for the judicial revision of the Constitution (even though Jeffersonians accused Marshall of doing precisely that in a series of decisions expanding the powers of the federal government). Certainly, Chief Justice Marshall realized the need for judicial interpretation of the Constitution, but he also stressed the need for judicial fidelity to the essential principles of the document. In *Marbury v. Madison* (1803), Marshall insisted that "the framers of the Constitution contemplated that instrument as a rule for the government of *courts,* as well as the legislature" (emphasis added).

Of course, the application of constitutional principles to specific legal questions is fraught with uncertainty. The broad phraseology of the document (e.g., "due process of law," "equal protection of the laws," "commerce among the states," etc.) easily lends itself to differing interpretations. The intentions of those who wrote these phrases are not easy to discern and, indeed, the framers were not in complete agreement as to what these provisions should mean. This uncertainty lends credence to the idea of the living Constitution, in which the meaning of constitutional provisions necessarily evolves over time through judicial interpretation (Tribe and Dorf 1991).

The idea of a living Constitution has been criticized by those who believe that the purpose of the Constitution is to provide immutable principles of government and law (see, e.g., Belz 1998; Meese 1986; Rehnquist 1976; Scalia 1997). Among the more vocal critics of the idea is Robert H. Bork, who President Ronald Reagan attempted (unsuccessfully) to place on the Supreme Court in 1987. In his public speeches and writings, Bork has argued strenuously for judges to confine themselves to the "original understanding" of the Constitution lest they transform themselves into lawmakers:

The judiciary's great office is to preserve the constitutional design. It does this not only by confining Congress and the President to the powers granted them by the Constitution and seeing that the powers granted are not used to invade the freedoms guaranteed by the Bill of Rights, but also, and equally important, that the democratic authority of the people is maintained in the full scope given by the Constitution. (Bork 1990, 4)

Much of the contemporary debate over the living Constitution has focused on the Supreme Court's recognition of a constitutional right of privacy, a right nowhere mentioned in the text of the Constitution. Dissenting in *Griswold v. Connecticut* (1965), the seminal case in this area, Justice Hugo L. Black made clear his disdain for the notion of the living Constitution:

I realize that many good and able men have eloquently spoken and written, sometimes in rhapsodical strains, about the duty of this Court to keep the Constitution in tune with the times. The idea is that the Constitution must be changed from time to time and that this Court is charged with a duty to make those changes. For myself, I must with all deference reject that philosophy. The Constitution makers knew the need for change and provided for it. Amendments suggested by the people's elected representatives can be submitted to the people or their selected agents for ratification. That method of change was good enough for our Fathers, and being somewhat old-fashioned I must add it is good enough for me.

Much of the controversy over President Reagan's attempt to place Robert Bork on the Supreme Court centered around the fact that Judge Bork essentially agreed with Justice Black that the Supreme Court had erred in recognizing a right of privacy as implicit in the Bill of Rights. And, of course, if there is no such constitutional right, then there is no basis for the Court's 1973 decision in *Roe v. Wade* effectively legalizing abortion. It was precisely this concern that led supporters of abortion rights to mobilize so effectively against the Bork nomination. It is a concern that continues to haunt every nomination to the Supreme Court, but especially nominations by Republican presidents who are known to be pro-life in their views on abortion.

Some commentators viewed the Senate's rejection of the Bork nomination as a reflection of the public's acceptance of the idea "that the Constitution is a commitment that certain areas of public life should be governed by unelected judges with the authority to decide what values are so important that they should be protected from majority rule" (Chemerinsky 1989, 36). It is fair to say most members of the attentive public understand that the Constitution is not written with the precision of statutes and that judges inevitably understand the majestic phrases of the Constitution in light of their own experience and values. But recent political conflict over judicial activism suggests that the "living Constitution" must not evolve at a rate too much greater than that of the societal consensus, lest the legitimacy of the courts' constitutional interpretations be called into question. It is important that the public not come to perceive the "living Constitution" as merely a rhetorical device for legitimizing the enactment of a political agenda by unelected, life-tenured federal judges.

See also Bill of Rights (American) (1789); Black, Hugo L.; Bork, Robert H.; Brennan, William J.; *Griswold v. Connecticut* (1965); Judicial Activism; Judicial Restraint; Marshall, John; Meese, Edwin III; Privacy, Constitutional Right of; Pro-Life Position on Abortion; Scalia, Antonin

Bibliography

Belz, Herman. 1998. *A Living Constitution or Fundamental Law? American Constitutionalism in Historical Perspective.* Lanham, MD: Rowman and Littlefield.

Bork, Robert H. 1990. *The Tempting of America: The Political Seduction of the Law.* New York: Touchstone.

Brennan, William J., Jr. 1986. "The Constitution of the United States: Contemporary Ratification." *South Texas Law Review* 27: 433.

Chemerinsky, Erwin. 1989. "The Constitution Is Not 'Hard Law': The Bork Rejection and the Future of Constitutional Jurisprudence." *Constitutional Commentary* 6: 29.

Farber, Daniel A. 1989. "The Originalism Debate: A Guide for the Perplexed." *Ohio State Law Review* 49: 1085.

Meese, Edwin III. 1986. "The Supreme Court of the United States: Bulwark of a Limited Constitution." *South Texas Law Review* 27: 455.

Rehnquist, William H. 1976. "The Notion of a Living Constitution." *Texas Law Review* 54: 693.

Reich, Charles A. 1963. "Mr. Justice Black and the Living Constitution." *Harvard Law Review* 76: 673.

Scalia, Antonin. 1997. *A Matter of Interpretation: Federal Courts and the Law.* Princeton, NJ: Princeton University Press.

Tribe, Laurence H., and Michael C. Dorf. 1991. *On Reading the Constitution.* Cambridge, MA: Harvard University Press.

John M. Scheb II and Otis H. Stephens, Jr.

LIVING WILL

Advances in medical technology have developed sophisticated life-prolonging procedures that can keep a person's body alive long after he or she is determined to be brain-dead. Treatment may be undesirable as it may only artificially prolong the process of dying rather than restore the person to an acceptable quality of life. The legislatures in several states have taken the position that one has a fundamental right to self-determination regarding decisions pertaining to his or her own health care. A competent adult may execute a *living will* in which he or she gives advance directives as to future care. A common provision in a living will is that in the event the principal is incapacitated and is suffering from a terminal illness from which there is no expectation of recovery and death is imminent, or the person is in a persistent vegetative state from which there is no reasonable expectation of recovery, life-preserving treatment is to be withheld or discontinued. It is the intent of the person executing the advance care document that the directives contained therein be honored and followed by his or her family and physician as the final expression of his or her wishes and desires.

On the other hand, the declarant may appoint a surrogate in the living will or other document to make the necessary medical decisions based upon the facts and circumstances existing at the time. The surrogate acting as a proxy or power of at-torney has the authority to make all decisions as to the rendering or withholding of medical treatment, to give informed consent, and to make any other relevant decisions that do not conflict with the principal's specific expression of directives.

The physician can follow the dictates in the living will only if the person does not have the capacity to make an informed decision and does not have a reasonable medical probability of recovering capacity. Furthermore, the person must have a terminal condition, or an end of state condition, or be in a persistent vegetative state. In the event the declarant is able to make an informed decision, his or her wishes will override any conflicting directives stated in the living will.

States have different requirements that must be met in order for a living will to be honored. Therefore, to insure the validity of a living will document, it must meet all the requirements listed above, as well as comply with the laws and statutory requirements of the applicable state.

See also Right to Die; Medical treatment, Right to Refuse; Privacy, Constitutional right of; Doctor-Assisted Suicide

Bibliography

Shenkman, Martin M., and Patti S. Klein. 2004. *Living Wills & Health Care Proxies: Assuring That Your End-of-Life Decisions Are Respected.* Tenafly, NJ: Law Made Easy Press.

Terry Dillon

LOCHNER V. NEW YORK (1905)

Because it epitomizes a controversial approach to constitutional interpretation, the U.S. Supreme Court's 1905 ruling in *Lochner v. New York* is among the most intensely debated of the Court's decisions. Although substantive due process can be traced as far back as the Supreme Court's decision in the *Dred Scott* case of 1857, *Lochner* provided the clearest and most influential application of this concept in the judicial invalidation of a state regulatory law. The law in question and the Court's opinion are best understood against the backdrop of the industrial conflict that pitted the emerging labor movement against the entrenched prerogatives of management around the turn of the twentieth century. The specific substantive content imported in *Lochner* and similar cases of the era is the doctrine of "liberty of contract," which asserts a constitutional right to enter into lawful contracts without unreasonable interference by government. In *Lochner,* the Court held that a state law limiting bakery employees to a 60-hour workweek infringed on the liberty of contract of both employers and employees.

New York justified the limitation on working hours as a public health measure and thus a valid exercise of the state's police power. But Justice Rufus Peckham, writing for a sharply divided Supreme Court, found no such justification for the law. "To the common understanding," Peckham opined, "the trade of a baker has never been regarded as an unhealthy one." Clearly, however, the Court's fundamental objection to the law was that it was a "meddlesome interference" with business. The majority regarded the law as an unjustified infringement on "the right to labor, and with the right of free contract on the part of the individual, either as employer or employee." It is worth noting that the majority gave no consideration whatsoever to the relative bargaining power of employers and employees in the industry.

Justices John M. Harlan (the elder) and Oliver Wendell Holmes, Jr., issued powerful dissents. While Harlan pursued a conventional line of analysis, stressing the reasonableness of the state regulation, Justice Holmes attacked the majority for reading *laissez-faire,* unimpeded free market economic theory into the Constitution:

This case is decided upon an economic theory which a large part of the country does not entertain. If it were a question whether I agreed with that theory, I should desire to study it further and long before making up my mind. But I do not conceive that to be my duty, because I strongly believe that my agreement or disagreement has nothing to do with the right of a majority to embody their opinions in law.

Constitutional scholars have widely accepted Justice Holmes' charge that the ruling in *Lochner*

was little more than an expression of the policy preferences of the Court's majority. In recent years, however, revisionist scholars have challenged the Holmesian view. Howard Gillman (1993), for example, argues that the *Lochner* decision "represented a serious principled effort to maintain one of the central distinctions in nineteenth-century constitutional law—the distinction between valid economic regulation, on the one hand, and invalid class legislation on the other—during a period of unprecedented class conflict." Thus, in Gillman's view, the Court invalidated the statute in *Lochner* not because it regulated business per se, but because it took sides in an emerging class conflict.

The philosophical perspective underlying *Lochner* remained influential for years, but its practical effect was short-lived. In *Muller v. Oregon* (1908), the Court upheld a law limiting the workday to 10 hours for women working in "any mechanical establishment, or factory, or laundry." In 1917, in *Bunting v. Oregon,* the Court extended the *Muller* precedent in upholding a similar statute extending maximum hours protection to men working in mills, factories, and manufacturing establishments. Even though *Bunting* had the practical effect of overruling *Lochner v. New York,* the Court did not explicitly repudiate that decision. Moreover, in striking down a federal minimum-wage law for women on Fifth Amendment due process grounds in *Adkins v. Children's Hospital* (1923), the Supreme Court relied on the *Lochner* rationale. Eventually, however, the Supreme Court came to accept a broad role for government in the regulation of the terms and conditions of employment (see *West Coast Hotel Company v. Parrish,* 1937).

The modern Supreme Court has repudiated the notion of "liberty of contract" (see *Ferguson v. Skrupa,* 1963). Substantive due process lives on, however, in the Supreme Court's recognition of a constitutional right of privacy, which places certain limits on state regulatory power. This right of privacy encompasses the liberty to make intensely personal decisions, such as those regarding abortion or sexual orientation (see, e.g., *Roe v. Wade,* 1973; *Lawrence v. Texas,* 2003).

See also Due Process Clauses; Due Process, Substantive; Economic Freedom; Fourteenth Amendment (1868); Harlan, John Marshall; Holmes, Oliver Wendell, Jr.; Individualism; Judicial Activism; Judicial Restraint; *Lawrence v. Texas* (2003); Liberty; New Deal; Privacy, Constitutional Right of; Property Rights; *Roe v. Wade (1973)*

Bibliography

Gillman, Howard. 1993. *The Constitution Besieged: The Rise and Decline of Lochner Era Police Powers Jurisprudence.* Durham, NC: Duke University Press, 1993.

Kens, Paul. 1990. *Judicial Power and Reform Politics: The Anatomy of* Lochner v. New York. Lawrence: University Press of Kansas.

Keynes, Edward. 1996. *Liberty, Property, and Privacy: Toward a Jurisprudence of Substantive Due Process.* University Park: Pennsylvania State University Press.

Otis H. Stephens, Jr. and John M. Scheb II

LOCKE, JOHN (1632–1704)

John Locke's influence on American political and constitutional thought was and remains considerable. Revolutionary pamphleteers from James Otis to Thomas Jefferson drew from Locke's political writings. And Lockean commitments and themes manifest constitutionally in many ways. Examples include the individual and constitutional rights to free exercise of religion, to due process, to freedom from search and seizure absent a showing of probable cause, to just compensation for private property taken for public use, and to those unenumerated rights "retained by the people," as well as the constitutional provisions mandating republican forms of state government, legislative primacy, and an independent judiciary. Locke continues to be cited in U.S. Supreme Court decisions regarding many of these matters.

The relationship between Lockean political philosophy and American political and constitutional thought and practice is, however, complex. The American Founders were a diverse lot and they drew their inspiration as well as particular doctrines from a wide and varied range of political and legal thinkers, including Aristotle, Greek and Roman Stoics, Sidney, Blackstone, Burlamqui, and others, in addition to Locke. Further, the American Founders were already far removed from the time, place, and circumstances to which Locke's political writings were in many ways a response and analysis. Contemporary American political and constitutional theorists and actors are even further removed from the context of Locke's work since few share the deeply religious outlook and assumptions from which Locke's political views grew and to which they gave expression. Further, they have access not just to Locke's work, but also to several centuries of criticism of Locke's work. Nevertheless, Locke's writings were well known to many of the American Founders and remain well known to contemporary American political and constitutional theorists and actors, and his political philosophy remains a touchstone in any serious discussion of American constitutional and civil rights.

Locke's Life and Works

John Locke was born in 1632 and died in 1704. He was born to parents of modest but independent means and deep Puritan convictions. His life may be divided into three periods. The first ranges over his childhood and early education during the years of the English Civil War and the Commonwealth. In 1647 Locke left home to attend Westminster school and later Christ Church, Oxford. He found Oxford dominated by a petrified scholasticism for which he had little patience or affection. Rejecting a clerical career, he pursued medical studies instead. But this did not prevent him from writing on political topics. His *Two Tracts on Government* (1660) and *Essay on Toleration* (1667) date from this period. (These works are not to be confused with the later *Two Treatises on Government* and *Letter on Toleration.*)

The second period in Locke's life begins with his relationship to Lord Ashley, later first Earl of Shaftesbury. Locke entered Shaftesbury's household in 1668. Shaftesbury was first an influential member and then, after 1675 or so, an aggressive critic of the Court of Charles II. Through his association with Shaftesbury, Locke found opportunities to participate in and learn about government, as both an insider and outsider. He served on the Council of Trade during Shaftesbury's chancellorship, and later found himself during the so-called Exclusion Crisis in close association with key members of a national opposition political movement to which Shaftesbury was by then committed. In 1683 he fled to Holland, where he remained until after William of Orange took the throne in 1688. It was during this second period that Locke wrote his *Two Treatises on Government* (1689), though scholars continue to debate when exactly he wrote various portions of this classic text. The *Two Treatises* were published shortly after Locke's return to England and constitute his most enduring contribution to American political and constitutional thought and practice.

Locke's return to England marks the beginning of the third period of his life. In addition to the *Two Treatises,* he published also in 1689 his *Letter on Toleration* and his *Essay Concerning Human Understanding.* It is in these works that Locke expresses his mature views with respect to the two questions around which his philosophical reflections were organized: How can men know? And how ought men live? For the next 15 years, Locke devoted himself to a wide range of projects, some practical and political and some philosophical. He died in 1704 among the most famous men of his day, not just in England but in Europe generally.

A complete review of Locke's contribution to American political and constitutional thought and practice is a task unrealizable within the scope of a short article. Three contributions merit special attention, however. The first concerns Locke's account of legitimate political authority, the second his account of property rights, and the third his account of religious liberty.

Locke on Political Authority

Locke's views on legitimate political authority and property rights are expressed most fully in his *Two Treatises.* Locke distinguished between the right of rulers to rule and the duty of subjects to obey. He did so because he was sure that the latter did not entail or establish the former. The subjects of an absolute but benevolent monarch have a duty to obey because resistance to such a monarch, assuming his or her benevolence, would do more harm than good. But an absolute monarch, no matter how benevolent, has no legitimate political authority, no right to rule, and rules by power alone. It follows that a malevolent or tyrannical absolute monarch is one both without legitimate political authority to rule and with respect to whom subjects owe no obedience. Locke's recognition and analysis of the possibility of the illegitimacy of existing and benevolent political authority is what set him apart from other theorists of his day, such as Filmer and Hobbes (neither of whom recognized this possibility).

The right to rule, or legitimate political authority, arises, Locke argues, out of a limited delegation by the ruled of natural right to the body politic as sovereign on conditions of trust. The right to govern entails the duty to govern in the interests of the governed. This is a complex claim that needs unpacking. The place to start is Locke's state of nature.

The state of nature is, in Locke's view, simply the condition men find themselves in in the absence of political authority. In this condition men are subject only to the natural law, the moral law as given by God and discoverable by reason. The two most basic natural laws are, first, to preserve oneself, and, second, to preserve others. In the absence of political authority and subject only to the natural law, men confront one another as free equals. But they confront one another as free equals possessed of certain natural rights. The most basic or important of these are the right to possess their own bodies and thoughts, to appropriate natural resources for personal use, and to enforce the natural law against those who violate it. These rights impose corresponding duties on others. Thus, while in the absence of political authority men confront one another politically as free equals, they remain bound by the demands of morality or natural law. In the state of nature, liberty is not license, as Locke famously says.

Whether or not men ever existed in a state of nature, it is obvious, Locke argues, that the state of nature is or would be a state of inconvenience. One reason for this is that the natural law is itself incomplete in the absence of conventional rules. Another is that men are not particularly good judges of their own causes and are also limited in their abilities and resources to enforce the natural law against one another individually. Yet another is that the natural law permits large inequalities in private property. These give rise to new temptations and conflicts and, given the nature of men, to increased violations of the moral or natural law. Thus, as the "rational and industrious" come to possess privately most productive property and vastly greater amounts of commodities or nonproductive property, the inadequacy of securing general compliance with the natural law through individuals exercising their own natural right to enforce it is likely to grow. In the state of nature, then, the natural law is not likely to be executed in a regular, reliable, and equitable fashion. And completing it through an enforceable regime of conventional rules is likely to be difficult.

Because of these inevitable inconveniences, men in a state of nature will each and all find it rational to constitute themselves as a corporate body politic, or civil society, empowered to enforce the natural law. This they do by delegating to themselves as a corporate body their individual rights to execute the natural law. The corporate body politic so constituted must possess the power to establish a fixed and known law and to adjudicate disputes arising under it. And so it acquires also the power to legislate and to adjudicate (as well as a federative power to make war, peace, alliances, etc.). But it acquires these powers, and the political authority they embody and serve, only on conditions of trust. The inconveniences of the state of nature make it rational for men to give up not all their natural rights but only their natural right to execute the natural law, and not absolutely or unconditionally, but rather provisionally and subject to terms. The powers and authority acquired by the corporate body politic, then, are acquired on the condition that they

be exercised so as to secure for all those subject to them the goods put at risk by the inconveniences of the state of nature, namely the goods of life, liberty, and estate within a stable moral order. Legitimate political authority depends, then, first on a unanimous delegation of authority by (or consent from) the governed, and, second on its being exercised in a manner consistent with the purposes for which it is constituted. Legitimate political authority is always limited, always constitutional, and never justified by power alone. Political authority regularly exercised in a manner hostile to the purposes for which it is always and everywhere constituted is illegitimate, and in serious cases citizens may be free, perhaps even duty bound, to resist it.

The American revolutionaries thought themselves in just such a circumstance—British subjects with respect to whom the British Crown regularly acted over an extended period of time and without remedy in a manner hostile to the purposes for which its authority was constituted. In the minds of the revolutionaries, it was not they who initiated a state of war against the Crown, it was rather the Crown that initiated a state of war against them by violating the terms of trust upon which its claim to legitimate political authority over them rested. While the Declaration of Independence evidences clear debts to Locke's political thought, it is unclear what Locke himself would have thought of the American Declaration. In 1698, William Molyneux, a friend of Locke's and member of the Irish Parliament, argued in a book later central to the Irish Nationalist cause that England could not legislate for Ireland with the aim of protecting English industry. There is no evidence that Locke was himself sympathetic to this position.

For Locke, only the unanimous consent of the governed can legitimate the political authority over them of the corporate body politic to which they belong. A corporate body politic is not, however, a government. And a government, a particular institutional arrangement, is what it needs to secure more fully the natural law for its members. Locke recognized this and argued that once a people constitutes itself as a corporate body politic, it may as a corporate body politic adopt for itself a particular institutional form, or government. To form a government, the corporate body politic needs, however, not the unanimous consent of all its members, but rather only the consent of the majority of its full or active members. These are those members (typically few) who expressly consent to their membership in the body politic and its authority over them. Locke distinguishes active members from those (typically many) who only tacitly consent to their membership in the body politic and its authority over them. Those who belong to the body politic by tacit consent alone need play no role in the formation of a government.

Those full or active members who, by the will of their majority, determine the structure of the body politic's governing institutions may adopt any number of possible constitutional forms. They need not create a democracy or adopt universal suffrage. So long as the government they create acts in a manner consistent with the people's trust governing its authority, its authority legitimately extends to all those who belong to the body politic.

Locke on Property Rights

Among these terms of trust is the requirement that political authority preserve men in their natural property rights. On Locke's view, all of creation belongs ultimately to God. But to all men in common God gives the natural world, and to each man individually God gives a body and a will. Because men are obligated to preserve themselves and others under the natural law, they are morally free to appropriate from the natural world held in common by all men so long as they leave enough and as good for others and do not allow that which they appropriate to spoil. In making any such appropriation, a man must inevitably mix some of his labor (the product of the body and will given to him individually by God) with part of the natural world. Assuming that his appropriation leaves enough and as good for others and that he does not allow that which he appropriates to spoil, the mixing of his own labor vests him with a claim to that which he appropriates sufficient to defeat any counterclaims

by others (who have by his appropriation presumably been left no worse off). To possess such a claim is to possess, for Locke, a natural property right. Since such rights depend only on the natural law, they constitute a moral constraint on the legitimate use of political authority. Thus, a government has no right to tax its subjects without their direct or indirect (through their representatives) consent, as constitutionally expressed.

It is the introduction of money as a placeholder for value that makes possible the vast inequalities in private property that Locke assumes to be a major source of inconvenience in the state of nature. This money does by rendering otiose the two provisos that serve as moral constraints on the individual right to appropriate from the natural world initially held in common by all men. Money does not spoil, so its introduction renders otiose the spoilage proviso. And money makes possible a commercial economy organized around the acquisition of exchange value. Since Locke thought it obvious that even the worst off in such an economy (the landless laborer in London) is better off than the best off in an economy without money (Locke's example is a "king [Chief] in North America" where he assumed natural resources were still held in common and there was no commercial economy), the introduction of money renders otiose also the "leave enough and as good for others" proviso.

And so it is that Locke argues that an individual might possess a natural right to a large estate (against a background of substantial inequalities of wealth) beyond the reach of legitimate political authority. Indeed, political authority may be legitimately asserted with respect to individual property rights only to secure them more fully. Property may be taxed (if legislatively authorized) to support those institutions necessary to secure property rights, and it may be taken (through the executive power) for public purposes only if just compensation is made. Still, it is important here to remember that which many contemporary libertarian defenders of property rights as a constraint on legitimate political authority too often forget. That is that Locke always insisted that individual property rights never trump a man's natural right to subsistence. There is no natural right to property where others are left without "enough and as good" or where the assertion of such a right is incompatible with the second fundamental law of nature, to preserve others.

Locke on Religious Liberty

Locke's views on religious liberty developed over time. In the early *Two Tracts on Government* (1660), he addressed himself primarily to the authority of the state to regulate religious practice. He argued that with respect to "matters indifferent" (that is, those matters of religious practice with respect to which neither reason nor revelation spoke unambiguously) the state may and indeed ought to act in the interests of order and stability, and citizens ought to obey, though they were free to believe whatever they liked. Locke modified this position only slightly in his *Essay on Toleration* (1667). There he emphasized that those exercising the power of the state must use wisely their discretion to regulate "matters indifferent" and ought generally to tolerate (within the general confines of Protestant Christianity) those practices that posed no direct threat to moral order or political stability. Notably, atheists and Catholics posed such threats in Locke's view: the former because they rejected the basis of all moral obligation, the latter because they subordinated political authority to the authority of the Papacy. While citizens remained bound always by the authority of the state, they were entitled to their own judgment with respect to the wisdom of civil regulations of "matters indifferent" and in any case could never abdicate their responsibility for their own salvation.

By 1689, and his *Letter on Toleration*, Locke's approach to questions of religious liberty had shifted. Whereas he had previously approached such questions from the point of view of the state's legitimate interest in order and stability, he approached them in the *Letter* from the points of view of religious doctrine and the natural rights of individual. With respect to religious doctrine, he maintained that it was blasphemously presumptuous for the state to interfere with religious belief or practice, since each man was responsible for his own salvation, and salvation could never be won apart from a voluntarily given inward faith. From the point of view of the church, Locke maintained, there is no religious reason to seek to use the power of the state to coerce confessions of faith or compliance with religious mandates. With respect to the rights of individuals, Locke argued that since no individual possessed any natural right over the soul of another, individuals could never delegate to the body politic any authority to care for the souls of others. The care of men's souls belongs first to them as individuals and second to the church. But the authority of the church over men's souls was necessarily constrained by legitimate political authority. Thus, while the church could withhold religious benefits from or even excommunicate persons who failed to act as required by the salvation of their souls, it could not alter their political, civil, or legal status. Here Locke argues from both religious and political considerations for an early version of what today is called separation of church and state. Locke did not think, of course, that any of the foregoing entailed commitments to freedom from religion or to the exclusion of religious considerations from political judgment.

In *Letter* Locke also emphasizes the ideal of religious toleration. He notes that believing in the orthodoxy of one's own church is never a sufficient reason for intolerance of others, since all believers think their own church orthodox. Further, the powers delegated to political officials are limited to the task of securing for all the earthly goods of life, liberty, and estate, and other constitutive elements of the public good. Accordingly, political officials possess no power to regulate religious matters of no direct consequence for the realization of these goods. Political officials may regulate religion, however, when religion does threaten these goods. Thus, they may regulate intolerant religious sects, sects that refuse to admit the separation of religious and political authority, and sects that refuse to admit the existence of the Christian God. In the end, it is toleration for and between Protestant Christians that Locke argues for. Nevertheless, Locke's *Letter* provides the inspiration and many of the arguments for the more wide-ranging conceptions of religious tolerance typically defended today.

Conclusion

Locke is in many ways a transitional figure in the history of political thought. He is simultaneously the last great exponent of early modern natural law theory as well as the first great exponent of a constitutional republicanism broadly tolerant and rooted in the ideal of citizens as free equals. His work remains influential in American political and constitutional thought and practice and likely will so remain for the next century.

See also Aristotle; Blackstone, William; Constitutional Democracy; Declaration of Independence; Due Process Clauses; Fourth Amendment; Hobbes, Thomas; Jefferson, Thomas; Just Compensation Clause; Liberalism; Natural Law and Natural Rights; Probable Cause; Property Rights; Religion, Freedom of; Rousseau, Jean Jacques; Separation of Church and State; Universal Suffrage

Bibliography

Dunn, John. 1984. *Locke*. New York: Oxford University Press.

Simmons, A. J. 1993. *On the Edge of Anarchy: Locke, Consent and the Limits of Society*. Princeton, NJ: Princeton University Press.

Tully, James. 1980. *A Discourse on Property: John Locke and his Adversaries*. Cambridge: Cambridge University Press.

Waldron, Jeremy. 2002. *God, Locke and Equality: Christian Foundations of John Locke's Political Thought*. Cambridge: Cambridge University Press.

David A. Reidy

LOITERING. *See* Vagrancy and Loitering

LOUIMA, ABNER. *See* Force, Use of by Law Enforcement

LOVING V. VIRGINIA (1967)

In *Loving v. Virginia* (1967) the United States Supreme Court considered the constitutionality of a state policy prohibiting interracial marriages.

The statutes, known as antimiscegenation laws, were a remnant of the colonial era. From 1661 until *Loving* was decided, at least 41 states had enacted antimiscegenation laws. The punishment for breaking the law varied by state, but typically there were both criminal and civil penalties. Some states treated the offense as a felony while others punished it as a misdemeanor. From the civil perspective, most states voided the marriage, which had severe consequences for several areas of marital rights including inheritance, workman's compensation, and the legitimacy status of children produced from those unions. State judges in all but two states had upheld the constitutionality of antimiscegenation statutes. The United States Supreme Court had declined to review the constitutionality of antimiscegenation laws in 1954, 1955, and again in 1964 (Nolan 1998). Ultimately the Court invalidated laws prohibiting interracial marriage in the *Loving* decision.

Two Virginia residents, Richard Loving, a white male, and Mildred Jeter, an African American female, were married in Washington, D.C. Shortly thereafter, they returned to Virginia to live. The Lovings were arrested and charged with violating Virginia's ban on interracial marriages, a felony offense punishable by up to five years' imprisonment. The couple pleaded guilty and was sentenced to one year in jail. The trial judge, however, agreed to suspend the sentence for 25 years based on two conditions: that they leave the state and that they agree not to return to Virginia together for 25 years. They moved to Washington, D.C., and in 1963 challenged their convictions on the grounds that the Virginia antimiscegenation laws violated the Fourteenth Amendment. The Virginia Supreme Court of Appeals upheld the statutes because they served several legitimate purposes such as preserving the "racial integrity" of its citizens, and preventing "the corruption of blood, a mongrel breed of citizens, and the obliteration of racial pride." That court also held that marriage was an activity regulated by the states, not the federal government, under the Tenth Amendment.

Chief Justice Earl Warren, writing for a unanimous court, observed that the state does have the authority to regulate marriage; however, those regulations must comport with the requirements of the Fourteenth Amendment. The state argued that the Equal Protection Clause only required that whites and African Americans be punished equally for violating the law. Warren rejected that argument and wrote that "[t]he mere fact of equal application does not mean that our analysis of this statute should follow the approach we have taken in cases involving no racial discrimination." The state had argued that the framers of the Fourteenth Amendment did not intend for the amendment to prevent the state from outlawing interracial marriage. Warren countered that while historical sources may cast light on the problem, they are insufficient to resolve the problem due to their inconclusive nature. The state further attempted to justify the law on the basis of a prior U.S. Supreme Court ruling, *Pace v. Alabama* (1882). In that case the Court upheld a conviction on the basis of an Alabama law that prohibited "adultery or fornication between a white person and a Negro" even though the penalty under that law was greater than the penalty applied to members of the same race who engaged in those activities. Warren dismissed that argument by pointing out that *Pace* had not withstood analysis in subsequent decisions of the Court.

Because Virginia's antimiscegenation statutes were based upon racial classifications, they were subjected to strict scrutiny analysis. According to Warren, under that method of inquiry, the only way for a statute based on racial classifications to stand is if it is necessary to the accomplishment of a permissible state objective independent of racial discrimination. Warren concluded that there "is patently no legitimate overriding purpose independent of invidious racial discrimination which

justices this classification." The Virginia statutes were intended to maintain "White Supremacy" and thus violated the Equal Protection Clause. Warren also addressed the importance of marriage and the freedom of choice in the decision to marry. He wrote, "[t]o deny this fundamental freedom on so unsupportable a basis as the racial classification embodied in these statutes ... is surely to deprive all the State's citizens of liberty without due process of law." Thus marriage, a fundamental right, cannot be restricted by the state on account of race.

As a result of the Court's decision, the Lovings' convictions were overturned, and laws in 16 states prohibiting interracial marriage were nullified. More significantly, it was the first case to develop equal protection jurisprudence as it relates to marriage and equality (Nolan 1998). This aspect of the opinion is cited by advocates of gay marriage as a legal basis for homosexual unions. The use of strict scrutiny by the Court is also significant, particularly Warren's comment reflecting the views of two of his brethren that it would be almost impossible for any law discriminating on the basis of race to survive strict scrutiny.

See also Due Process Clauses; Due Process, Substantive; Equal Protection Clause; Fourteenth Amendment (1868); Fundamental Rights; Interracial Marriage; Jim Crow Laws; Liberty; Marriage, Rights Pertaining to; Same-Sex Marriage and Civil Unions; Strict Scrutiny; Tenth Amendment; Warren, Earl

Bibliography

Nolan, Laurence C. 1998. "The Meaning of *Loving*: Marriage, Due Process, and Equal Protection (1967–1990) as Equality and Marriage, from *Loving* to *Zablocki*." *Howard Law Journal* 41(2): 245–70.

Kara E. Stooksbury

M

MACHIAVELLI, NICCOLÒ (1469–1527)

Niccolò Machiavelli was an Italian statesman and political thinker, often praised or blamed as the founder of modernism and realism in politics. Born to a poor branch of a prominent Florentine family, Machiavelli was appointed at age 29 to a high diplomatic post when Piero Soderini assumed power in Florence. Thereafter, Machiavelli became Soderini's right-hand man, "the ruling intelligence in Florentine affairs." In 1512, however, Soderini and Machiavelli were ousted when Lorenzo de Medici took power. Suspected of conspiracy against Lorenzo, Machiavelli was imprisoned and tortured, but soon set free with restrictions under an amnesty. Unemployed, he retired to a small estate in Sant'Andrea inherited from his father, where he studied and wrote. In 1513, Machiavelli produced *The Prince*, in which he distilled in sparse prose the lessons he had learned as a diplomat. He dedicated and presented his book to Lorenzo de Medici in the hope of regaining a post in his beloved Florentine politics, but it was not to be. After Lorenzo's death five years later, Machiavelli was appointed historiographer of Florence, yet never regained the power he once had.

The Prince is among the most influential books ever written on politics, rivaling Plato's *Republic* and Aristotle's *Politics*. Machiavelli counseled the "new prince," whose power lacked a basis in tradition, history, and custom, on the rules for acquiring and keeping political power. Like the Greeks, Machiavelli took human nature as the foundation of politics, but unlike them, he took an essentially pessimistic view of human nature. He likened it to that of animals, driven primarily by fear and appetite, and so counseled the Prince to be able to behave like an animal himself when necessary. This entails *virtu*, the freedom to alternate virtue with vice as the situation requires. If the Prince allows civil rights and liberties at all, then, it is only as required to secure his power, and not on any independent moral basis like the inherent dignity or natural rights of his subjects.

By many accounts, Machiavelli was an ardent nationalist who hated the French and Spanish occupations of Italy. In the Prince, he exhorted Lorenzo to seize the historical moment and liberate the fatherland from the barbarians. Ultimately, however, such liberation was to be but the means to founding a "new order," a republic of citizens worthy of freedom. This is among the great themes of the *Discourses on Livy*, in which Machiavelli clearly values liberty as man's natural state, at least where civilization prevails. Where the Prince is pessimistic about human nature, then, the Discourses embody the optimism of Machiavelli's fellow Italian humanists, a belief in the magnificence of man and a revival of the ancient faith in his ability, if free, to govern himself intelligently.

Yet we are still far removed from American civil rights and liberties. To be sure, the Prince's influence on modern liberalism, that is, the lowering of expectations of human behavior for political purposes, is indisputable. Yet the liberty celebrated in the *Discourses* is not the consumer-based negative liberty of American liberalism. It is rather an ancient, positive liberty, the freedom to master oneself in order to fulfill the duties of a citizen and soldier of a free republic. Like the Greeks, Machiavelli recognized that political liberty is short-lived and meaningless unless citizens discharge the responsibilities that come with such liberty. Despite their differences, then, both Machiavelli and the Socratics would reject much of the American regime of civil rights and liberties.

See also Aristotle; Liberalism; Liberty; Natural Law and Natural Rights; Plato

Bibliography

Bondasera, Peter, and Mark Musa, eds. 1979. *The Portable Machiavelli.* New York: Penguin Books.

Burkhardt, Jacob. 1990. *The Civilization of the Renaissance in Italy.* New York: Penguin Books.

Machiavelli, Niccolò. 1998. *The Discourses on Livy.* Translated and edited by Harvey Mansfield. Chicago: University of Chicago Press.

Machiavelli, Niccolò. 2004. *The Prince.* Translated and edited by William J. Connell. New York: Bedford/St. Martin's Press.

Viroli, Maurizio. 2002. *Niccolo's Smile: A Biography of Machiavelli.* Translated by Antony Shugaar. New York: Farrar, Straus and Giroux.

Martin Carcieri

MADISON, JAMES (1751–1836)

Political theorist, Virginian, statesman, and fourth president of the United States, James Madison was the enemy of political tyranny in all its forms and a vigilant defender of the people's liberties. Madison was the indefatigable proponent of ordered liberty during the creation and formative years of the American Republic. He is regarded by scholars as the principal architect of the United States Constitution and its first 10 amendments, known collectively as the Bill of Rights. Madison's contribution marks him as preeminent among the men who shaped, explained, and won the ratification of the Constitution. Throughout a brilliant public life, Madison sought to reconcile liberty, order, and popular government. However imperfect or flawed his reconciliation at any given point in his career, Madison nonetheless provided a dynamic vision of liberty and order unsurpassed by any other political thinker or politician in the history of the Republic—one rivaled perhaps only by Abraham Lincoln.

Madison's reputation rests largely on his talents as a political thinker, primarily due to his contribution to the *Federalist* papers. In these essays, written to explain and defend the framework of government he had played such a large role in writing at the Constitutional Convention of 1787, Madison argued that liberty, order, and popular government could be rendered compatible in an extended republic wherein a vast multiplicity of interests prevented any one faction from producing a tyrannical political minority or majority.

Madison's great contribution to civil liberty in the United States is apparent in three distinct periods of his career: first, in vigorously promoting religious freedom, tolerance, and the separation of church and state in Virginia; second, in his role in producing the national Bill of Rights; and third, in Madison's recognition during the late 1790s that external checks on government power were required to prevent incipient tyranny in the fledgling republic—checks only possible through the vigorous use of the liberties explicitly provided for in a Bill of Rights that he had originally considered superfluous.

In 1785, Patrick Henry proposed in the Virginia General Assembly a tax for the state support of the teachers of the Christian religion. Madison considered the proposal an egregious violation of the essential separation of church and state that assured citizens' natural and unalienable right to freedom of religion. In mobilizing popular opposition to Henry's bill, Madison produced one of the most powerful declarations for religious liberty and freedom of conscience to be found in American political thought, *The Memorial and Remonstrance of*

1785. Ultimately, Madison's arguments succeeded in turning popular sentiment against Henry's bill and removed roadblocks that had obstructed the passage of Thomas Jefferson's bill for religious liberty, which had languished in the assembly for six years. Upon defeating Henry's bill, Madison then brilliantly steered the passage of the Virginia Statute for Religious Freedom in 1786.

In 1788, Madison moved beyond his central role in shaping the Constitution, to lead the difficult, but ultimately successful, campaign to persuade the states to ratify the Constitution. Madison was convinced the proposed Constitution offered a structure of government more than sufficient to protect individual liberty from national or state government oppression through complex internal checks and balances and federalism. Madison argued that the new government was strong enough to maintain order, stability, and justice, but sufficiently limited and divided in its powers as to constitute no threat in its citizens' natural rights. To win ratification, however, Madison promised to promote amendments to the Constitution to protect individual civil liberties against the new central government. It was in the fulfillment of this pledge that Madison made his most widely recognized contribution to American civil liberty, the Bill of Rights. Although steadfast in his view that a written list of individual freedoms against government was unnecessary, and still certain that internal checks on oppression were far more reliable than "parchment barriers" to tyranny, Madison nonetheless felt duty-bound during the First Congress to produce the constitutional amendments that eventually became the Bill of Rights.

As the first decade of government under the fledgling Constitution unfolded, Madison grew increasingly anxious about what he viewed as "usurpations" in federal authority at the hands of the executive and judicial departments during the Washington and Adams Administrations. The creation of the first Bank of the United States, Chief Justice John Marshall's sweeping assertion and powerful application of judicial review, and the Alien and Sedition Acts, Madison believed threatened to transform the "essential character of a [central] government ... composed of limited and enumerated powers" into an engine of power and privilege-producing tyranny. Thus, allied with Thomas Jefferson, Madison endeavored to establish a counterbalance to excessive centralization of authority in the form of an opposition political party, a partisan press, and the reassertion of states' rights.

Madison's vision of limited government originally was based on the tempering influences of separated institutions sharing power in an extended republic where no faction could concentrate sufficient power to impose despotism over time. Eventually, Madison extended this vision to encompass the promulgation of a Bill of Rights further to protect liberty from tyrannical government. Among the most powerful remedies to government tyranny ever invented is the removal, or at least the potential removal, of public officials at the next election. During the first decade of the young republic, Madison and his political compatriots in the legislative chambers of the nation and the states, as well as in a series of election campaigns, energetically employed their constitutional right to form a mass political party, which rose to challenge the Washington and Adams Administrations—legally and peacefully as a "loyal opposition." Madison's greatest contribution to civil rights and civil liberties might best be illustrated by the victory of the Republican Party in the presidential election of 1800, in which a free people, without having to draw the sword, successfully removed a government it found wanting, in large measure due to its attempt to restrict civil liberties with the despised Alien and Sedition Acts.

Finally, Madison's deep and abiding devotion to liberty was manifest during his presidency when during the War of 1812, unlike other wartime presidents, he did not stretch the Constitution or invade civil liberties during the crisis.

See also Alien and Sedition Acts; Bill of Rights (American) (1789); Civil Rights and Liberties During Wartime; Jefferson, Thomas; Liberalism; Liberty; Lincoln, Abraham; Marshall, John; Memorial and Remonstrance; Natural Law and Natural Rights; Press, Freedom of the; Religion, Freedom of; Separation of Church and State; States' Rights, Doctrine of; United States Constitution;

Bibliography

Banning, Lance. 1995. *The Sacred Fire of Liberty: James Madison & the Founding of the Federal Republic.* Ithaca, NY: Cornell University Press.

Matthews, Richard K. 1995. *If Men Were Angels: James Madison & the Heartless Empire of Reason.* Lawrence: University Press of Kansas.

Rakove, Jack N., ed. 1999. *James Madison: Writings.* New York: Library of America.

Rutland, Robert Allan. 1955. *The Birth of the Bill of Rights: 1776–1791.* Chapel Hill: University of North Carolina Press.

Rutland, Robert Allan. 1997. *James Madison: The Founding Father.* Columbia: University of Missouri Press.

Wills, Garry James. 2002. *James Madison.* New York: Times Books.

Michael R. Fitzgerald

MAGNA CARTA (1215)

Magna Carta, the Great Charter, is the legendary document England's King John was compelled to sign on June 15, 1215, to forestall the loss of the throne at the hands of rebellious noblemen. In the great meadow at Runnymede the barons of John's realm extracted his reluctant consent to the terms upon which he would keep the Crown. The Charter itself is a redress of feudal grievances extorted from the King by members of the discontented ruling class. Although most of the articles of the Great Charter lost their significance with the passing of feudalism, the fundamental principle of Magna Carta, though not explicitly stated in the document, has endured through the ages. The principle is the supremacy of law.

At Runnymede in the thirteenth century, the sovereign of England assented to the principle that words on parchment bound him to specific conditions and limits that, upon pain of forfeiture of his throne were he to violate them, he was bound to respect and obey. This contract, among the most powerful in the realm, produced the principle that

there were laws upon which all citizens might rely and to which even the most powerful must submit. Moreover, in the submission of the King to the authority of his subjects rooted in contract, one finds the first stirrings of representation. The barons, in terms that applied to all within the realm, were holding the sovereign accountable to his subjects.

Thus began the long, arduous, uneven, and sometimes bloody process by which absolute government was to become limited by the rule of law. As Magna Carta was confirmed, often with great reluctance and a degree of compulsion, by King John's successors, English constitutionalism took hold and then radiated throughout the West and beyond.

Regarded as the foundation of the English constitutional tradition, Magna Carta was an important milestone in the advancement of constitutionalism generally. Within its 38 chapters are provisions guaranteeing the rights of the King's subjects, restricting the Crown's power to tax without consent of Parliament, and guaranteeing the authority of the church. In recognizing basic rights, limitations on governmental power, and the obligation of government to protect the rights of all, Magna Carta is the basis for the Virginia Declaration of Rights and the Declaration of Independence. It is the foundation of the U.S. Constitution and Bill of Rights, and other constitutions of the modern era. When President Lincoln sought to forestall succession in 1861 by calling his southern brethren not to break the "mystic cords of memory" that bound the Union—he was referring in part to the sacred principle of respect for the law of the land that reached back in the Anglo-Saxon tradition to Runnymede. Tragically, the leaders of the South invoked the same tradition to justify breaking the bonds of a federal Union, which they asserted no longer recognized or protected their rights.

By far the most important provision of Magna Carta in terms of the advancement of the rule of law is that which states: "No Freeman shall be taken, or imprisoned, or be disseised of his Freehold, or Liberties, or free Customs, or be outlawed, or exiled, or any otherwise destroyed; nor will we pass upon him, nor condemn him, but by lawful Judgment of his Peers, or by the Law of the Land."

This is the direct historical antecedent of the Due Process Clauses of the United States Constitution and similar clauses in all 50 state constitutions. In fact, in stating this principle, Article I, Section 8 of the Tennessee Constitution (adopted 1870) uses language very similar to that of Magna Carta: "That no man shall be taken or imprisoned, or disseised of his freehold, liberties or privileges, or outlawed, or exiled, or in any manner destroyed or deprived of his life, liberty or property, but by the judgment of his peers or the law of the land." Due process of law, or "the law of the land," requires government to treat citizens fairly and reasonably and to follow the applicable procedures of law when taking action that adversely affects life, liberty, or property. In short, due process encapsulates the fundamental American ideal of the rule of law.

Magna Carta is more significant for what it *began* than for what it specifically provided at the time. As Sir Winston Church observed: "In future ages it was to be used as the foundation of principles and systems of government of which neither King John nor his nobles dreamed." By establishing the sovereignty of law, the Great Charter began the conversion of a feudal principle, invoked to protect the privilege of a small ruling class, into a doctrine of legitimate government to which free peoples around the globe continue to rally whenever their rights and liberties are threatened, abused, or denied.

See also Bill of Rights (American) (1789); Bill of Rights (English) (1689); Common Law Background of American Civil Rights and Liberties; Cruel and Unusual Punishments Clause; Due Process Clauses; Due Process, Procedural; Due Process, Substantive; Grand Jury; Habeas Corpus; Habeas Corpus, Federal; Jury, Trial by; Liberalism; Massachusetts Body of Liberties; Petition, Right of; Property Rights; Sentencing, Proportionality in; Star Chamber; United States Constitution

Bibliography

Churchill, Winston S. 1956. *A History of the English-Speaking Peoples: The Birth of Britain.* Vol. 1. New York: Barnes and Noble Books.

Holt, J. C. 1992. *Magna Carta.* Cambridge: Cambridge University Press.

Kirk, Russell. 2003. *The Roots of American Order.* 4th ed. Wilmington, DE: ISI Books.

Smith, Goldwin. 1955. *A Constitutional and Legal History of England.* New York: Charles Scribner's Sons.

Michael R. Fitzgerald and John M. Scheb II

MALAPPORTIONMENT. *See* Reapportionment

MALCOLM X (1925–1965)

Malcolm X (born Malcolm Little, a.k.a. El Hajj Malik El-Shabazz) is among the most controversial and misunderstood figures in American history. He is reviled as an outspoken advocate of violence, black separatism, and hatred of the white race. He is celebrated as an unswerving advocate of black self-reliance and an eloquent critic of white supremacy. In truth, Malcolm X was a complicated person whose political views were more nuanced than either his critics or his acolytes acknowledge. As the now deceased Ossie Davis said in his 1965 eulogy of the assassinated Malcolm: "[He} was most meticulous in his use of words. Nobody knew better than he the power words have over the minds of men."

Malcolm was born to Earl and Louise Little on May 19, 1925. Louise was mother to eight children. Earl, a Baptist preacher, was active in the United Negro Improvement Association, a civil rights organization founded by Marcus Garvey, and was targeted by white supremacist hate groups like the Ku Klux Klan and Black Legion. Before Malcolm turned fourteen in 1939, he was, for all practical purposes, orphaned—his father's mutilated dead body having been found sprawled across trolley tracks and his mother having been committed to an asylum for her subsequent emotional breakdown. Malcolm spent the next seven years of his life shuffled among various foster and detention homes, working at diverse blue collar jobs, moving from place to place, and committing different petty and felonious crimes. In January 1946, he was convicted in Massachusetts of grand larceny, breaking and entering, and was sentenced to seven years in prison.

During Malcolm's incarceration, his siblings Reginald and Ella introduced him to the teachings of Elijah Muhammad, leader of the Nation of Islam (NOI), which Malcolm, always a conscientious student, examined assiduously. This immersion changed his life.

Malcolm was paroled in August 1952. By then he had become a loyal follower of Elijah Muhammad, was an active NOI member and, having rejected his surname as a "slave name," had adopted X to symbolize his lost African tribal name. Over the next decade, Malcolm X's star within NOI rose, while his relationship with Elijah Muhammad deteriorated from that of devoted protégé to that of disillusioned rival. NOI membership mushroomed from 500 in 1952 to 30,000 in 1963, largely through Malcolm X's public lecturing, writing, and electronic media appearances as an NOI minister. He burst on the public stage in a television documentary, titled "The Hate that Hate Produced," aired between July 13 and 17, 1959, during which he was interviewed by Mike Wallace and Louis E. Lomax. Malcolm X's tumultuous relationship with Elijah Muhammad culminated in Malcolm renouncing the NOI leader, breaking with that organization, and his founding of the Organization Afro-American Unity-Muslim Mosque (OAAU) in March 1964. As Malcolm X's relations with NOI worsened, he was the object of frequent assassination threats. The house he and his wife, Betty Shabazz, shared with their four daughters was fire-bombed on February 14, 1965. One week later, while addressing an OAAU rally at the Audubon Ballroom in Manhattan, he was shot dead by three men—all NOI members.

Ten months prior to his murder, Malcolm X had gone on his obligatory pilgrimage to Mecca (called the Hajj). His journey was a pivotal transition in a life of transitions. Malcolm X spoke of his transition in his *Autobiography*: "I was trying to turn a corner … I was no less angry than I had been, but at the same time the true brotherhood I had seen in the Holy World had influenced me to recognize that anger can blind human vision."

Bibliography

Bagwell, Orlando. 1995. *American Experience: Malcolm X—Make It Plain.* Orland Park, IL: MPI Home Video.

Baldwin, Lewis V. 2002. *Between Cross and Crescent: Christian and Muslim Perspectives on Malcolm and Martin.* Gainesville: University Press of Florida.

Cone, James H. 1992. *Malcolm & Martin & America: A Dream or A Nightmare.* Maryknoll, NY: Orbis Books.

Dyson, Michael Eric. 1995. *Making Malcolm: The Myth and Meaning of Malcolm X.* New York: Oxford University Press.

Malcolm X. 1965. *The Autobiography of Malcolm X.* With the assistance of Alex Haley. New York: Grove Press.

James C. Foster

MANDATORY MINIMUM SENTENCING. *See* Definite and Determinate Sentencing; Drugs, War on; Habitual Offender Laws; "Three Strikes" Laws

MAPP V. OHIO (1961)

Mapp v. Ohio is one of the Supreme Court's most important contributions to the field of criminal justice. In this landmark decision, the Court held that evidence obtained in violation of the Fourth Amendment prohibition against unreasonable searches and seizures is inadmissible in state criminal trials. Since *Weeks v. United States* (1914), the federal courts had observed this rule. *Mapp v. Ohio* is very significant because it extended the Fourth Amendment exclusionary rule to the state courts via the Due Process Clause of the Fourteenth Amendment.

In May 1957 following the bombing of the home of Don King, who would become famous as a boxing promoter, police received a tip from an informant indicating that the perpetrator was hiding in the home of Dollree Mapp. Ms. Mapp lived with her 15-year-old daughter in the second-floor flat of a two-story duplex in Cleveland. Police arrived at Mapp's home in the early afternoon of May 23 and requested permission to enter the premises. Mapp contacted her attorney, who advised her to deny admittance unless the police had a search warrant.

Since they had no warrant, police contacted their headquarters and continued to keep the house under surveillance.

Additional officers arrived about three hours later and police once again knocked and asked for admittance; when Mapp did not open the door quickly, the officers forcibly opened one of the doors. Ms. Mapp's attorney arrived but was refused permission to enter the house or to see his client. Mapp demanded to see a warrant and was shown a piece of paper that she grabbed "and placed in her bosom." A struggle ensued as police sought to repossess the paper and Ms. Mapp was handcuffed. Ms. Mapp was forcibly taken to her bedroom where police searched furniture and personal papers. At the trial no evidence of a warrant was ever introduced.

Continuing their search of the house, police uncovered what they believed to be pornographic materials in a trunk in the basement. In his concurring opinion in *Mapp v. Ohio*, Justice William O. Douglas characterized these materials as "four little pamphlets and a pencil doodle." Nevertheless, Mapp was arrested and charged with "unlawfully and knowingly having in her possession certain lewd and lascivious books, pictures, and photographs ... being so indecent and immoral ... that some would be offensive to the Court and improper to be placed in the records thereof." Thus, what began as the investigation of a house-bombing would become an obscenity trial. Mapp was convicted and was sentenced to serve up to seven years in the Ohio Reformatory for Women. After the Ohio Supreme Court upheld the conviction and sentence, the Supreme Court agreed to review the case.

As Justice John M. Harlan (the younger) noted in his dissenting opinion, the Supreme Court ultimately ignored the constitutional question raised by the defendant: whether the Ohio obscenity statute was consistent with the First Amendment. The Ohio Supreme Court had dealt with the statute's constitutionality. There, only four members of the court had concluded that the statute was invalid, while Ohio law required the vote of at least six members of the court to declare a statute unconstitutional.

Rather than address the First Amendment question, which was the principal issue briefed by the parties to the case, the Supreme Court turned its attention to a question raised by the American Civil Liberties Union. This was the first time the American Civil Liberties Union was granted oral argument as amicus curiae. The ACLU's brief framed the issue as follows:

This case presents the issue of whether evidence obtained in an illegal search and seizure can constitutionally be used in a State criminal proceeding. We are aware of the view that this Court has taken on this issue in *Wolf v. Colorado*. It is our purpose by this paragraph to respectfully request that this Court re-examine this issue and conclude that the ordered liberty concept guaranteed to persons by the due process clause of the Fourteenth Amendment necessarily requires that evidence illegally obtained in violation thereof, not be admissible in state criminal proceedings.

In the *Wolf* decision in 1949, the Court had held that although the Fourth Amendment right of the people to be secure "in their persons, houses, papers, and effects against unreasonable searches and seizures" applied to the states through the Fourteenth Amendment, the states were not required to exclude illegally obtained material from criminal trials. During oral argument, Justice Felix Frankfurter inquired whether the Court was being asked to overturn the opinion he wrote in *Wolf v. Colorado*. Ultimately, with respect to his refusal to extend the exclusionary rule to the states, that was precisely what the *Mapp* majority did.

Justice Tom Clark's opinion for the Court in *Mapp* held that "all evidence obtained by searches and seizures in violation of the Constitution is, by that same authority, inadmissible in a state court." In the Court's view, "[t]o hold otherwise is to grant the right but in reality to withhold its privilege and enjoyment." Clark opined that "the purpose of the exclusionary rule is to deter—to compel respect for the constitutional guaranty in the only effectively available way—by removing the incentive to disregard it." But he also made the case that the exclusionary rule is consistent with judicial integrity:

There are those who say, as did Justice (then Judge) Cardozo, that under our constitutional exclusionary doctrine "(t)he criminal is to go free because the constable has blundered." In some cases this will undoubtedly be the result.... The criminal goes free, if he must, but it is the law that sets him free. Nothing can destroy a government more quickly than its failure to observe its own laws, or worse, its disregard of the charter of its own existence. As Mr. Justice Brandeis, dissenting, said in *Olmstead v. United States,* "Our government is the potent, the omnipresent teacher. For good or for ill, it teaches the whole people by its example.... If the government becomes a lawbreaker, it breeds contempt for law; it invites every man to become a law unto himself; it invites anarchy."

Interestingly in 1973 Dollree Mapp was found guilty of drug possession in New York City and served more than nine years in prison before being paroled and having her sentence commuted. She continued to claim innocence after her release.

See also Accused, Rights of the; American Civil Liberties Union (ACLU); Clark, Tom C.; Douglas, William O., Due Process Clauses; First Amendment; Fourteenth Amendment (1868); Fourth Amendment; Frankfurter, Felix; Harlan, John Marshall, II; Obscenity and Pornography; Search Warrants

Bibliography

Stewart, Potter. 1983. "The Road to Mapp v. Ohio and Beyond: The Origins, Development and Future of the Exclusionary Rule in Search-and-Seizure Cases." *Columbia Law Review* 83: 1365.

Caryl Segal

MARRIAGE, RIGHTS PERTAINING TO

In 1923, the Supreme Court issued its decision in *Meyer v. Nebraska.* Justice James C. McReynolds, writing for the majority, stated that: "While this court has not attempted to define with exactness the liberty thus guaranteed [by the Due Process Clause of the Fourteenth Amendment], the term has received much consideration.... Without doubt, it denotes not merely freedom from bodily restraint but also the right of the individual ... to marry, establish a home and bring up children ... and generally to enjoy those privileges long recognized at common law as essential to the orderly pursuit of happiness by free men." This decision affirmed the right to marry as an unwritten freedom guaranteed through the Constitution. In its later decision of *Skinner v. Oklahoma ex rel. Williamson* (1942), the Court, in an opinion by Justice William O. Douglas, reiterated this position by describing the institution of marriage as "one of the basic civil rights of man" and "fundamental to the very existence and survival of the race." While marriage has long been an institution regulated by state control (as recognized in the 1888 case of *Maynard v. Hill*), governmental power in this area is not unlimited.

The Right to Marital Privacy

In *Griswold v. Connecticut* (1965), the Court recognized a "penumbral" right to privacy within the marital relationship through elements of the First, Third, Fourth, Ninth, and Fourteenth Amendments in conjunction with common-law values. In his opinion for the Court, Justice Douglas stated: "We deal with a right of privacy older than the Bill of Rights—older than our political parties, older than our school system. Marriage is a coming together for better or for worse, hopefully enduring, and intimate to the degree of being sacred. It is an association ... for as noble a purpose as any involved in our prior decisions." The Court affirmed this decision in the 1972 case of *Eisenstadt v. Baird,* in which Justice William Brennan noted in his opinion for the majority that: "If the right of privacy means anything, it is the right of the individual, married or single, to be free from unwarranted governmental intrusion into matters so fundamentally affecting a person as the decision as to whether to bear or beget a child." This right to privacy was later upheld and expanded in several famous Court decisions on reproductive freedom.

Reproductive Rights

In *Meyer* the Court recognized a couple's right to marry and have children. Utilizing the newly recognized "right to privacy," the Court decided *Roe v. Wade* (1973), which granted women the right to terminate a pregnancy by abortion. Three years later in *Planned Parenthood of Central Missouri v. Danforth* (1976), the Court was faced with reviewing a Missouri law that required spousal consent for elective abortions. By a vote of six-to-three the Court overturned the state's law. Justice Harry Blackmun noted: "…we recognize that the decision whether to undergo or to forgo an abortion may have profound effects on the future of any marriage…. Notwithstanding these factors, we cannot hold that the State has the constitutional authority to give the spouse unilaterally the ability to prohibit the wife from terminating her pregnancy, when the State itself lacks that right."

The Right to Marry Spouse of Choice

In 1967, the Court banned states from outlawing interracial marriages in *Loving v. Virginia*. In his opinion for the Court Chief Justice Earl Warren noted: "The Fourteenth Amendment requires that the freedom of choice to marry not be restricted by invidious racial discriminations. Under our Constitution, the freedom to marry, or not marry, a person of another race resides with the individual and cannot be infringed by the State." The Court affirmed this decision in *Bob Jones University v. United States* (1983) by upholding the IRS's decision to revoke the tax-exempt status of Bob Jones University for prohibiting interracial dating and marriage within the student body. The Court found the university's practice to be a violation of "fundamental national public policy."

In *Turner v. Safley* (1987) the Court ruled that prisoners have a constitutional right to marry during their incarceration. Justice O'Connor noted that an inmate's decision to marry "is a completely private one" and is a right that cannot be restricted.

In *Zablocki v. Redhail* (1978) the Court overturned a Wisconsin law that required citizens to obtain permission of a court to marry if they were under obligations to pay child support from previous relationships. In his opinion for the Court Justice Thurgood Marshall noted: "It is not surprising

that the decision to marry has been placed on the same level of importance as decisions relating to procreation, childbirth, child rearing, and family relationships…. The woman whom appellee desired to marry had a fundamental right to seek an abortion of their expected child … Surely, a decision to marry and raise the child in a traditional family setting must receive equivalent protection. And, if appellee's right to procreate means anything at all, it must imply some right to enter the only relationship in which the State of Wisconsin allows sexual relations legally to take place."

While these cases have allowed most citizens to marry the spouse of their choice, the Supreme Court has thus far declined to consider whether homosexual couples have the right to marry. As of this writing, Massachusetts has legalized the process and Vermont has instituted civil unions for same-sex couples. Although the Court has not yet ruled on a case involving homosexual marriage, in *Lawrence v. Texas* (2003), it overturned a Texas law that made homosexual sodomy a criminal offense. Here the Court overruled its controversial 1986 decision in *Bowers v. Hardwick,* which had upheld a Georgia law criminalizing sodomy. Writing for the Court in *Lawrence,* Justice Anthony Kennedy asserted that: "The petitioners are entitled to respect for their private lives. The State cannot demean their existence or control their destiny by making their private sexual conduct a crime." Over a century ago, the Court ruled on another form of nontraditional marriage: polygamy. In *Reynolds v. United States* (1878), the Court held that the First Amendment's Free Exercise of Religion Clause did not bar the federal government from making polygamy a crime. Chief Justice Morrison R. Waite argued that permitting marriage of polygamists "would be to make the professed doctrines of religious belief superior to the law of the land, and in effect to permit every citizen to become a law unto himself. Government could exist only in name under such circumstances."

The Right to Divorce

States regulate not only the marriage process between couples, but divorce proceedings as well.

Although the law of divorce has changed substantially over the years, couples retain the right to divorce and cannot be denied such a right due to financial constraints. See, for example, *Atherton v. Atherton* (1901), *Haddock v. Haddock* (1906), *Williams v. North Carolina* (1942), *Williams v. State of North Carolina* (1945), and *Boddie v. Connecticut* (1971).

See also Bill of Rights, American; Blackmun, Harry A.; *Bob Jones University v. United States* (1983); Brennan, William J., Jr.; Common Law Background of American Civil Rights and Liberties; Douglas, William O.; Due Process Clauses; Due Process, Substantive; First Amendment; Fourteenth Amendment (1868); Fourth Amendment; Free Exercise Clause; Gay Rights Movement; *Griswold v. Connecticut* (1965); Individual Rights; Internal Revenue Service (IRS); Interracial Marriage; Kennedy, Anthony; *Lawrence v. Texas* (2003); *Loving v. Virginia* (1967); Marshall, Thurgood; McReynolds, James Clark; *Meyer v. Nebraska* (1923); Ninth Amendment; Privacy, Constitutional Right of; Religion, Freedom of; *Reynolds v. United States* (1879); *Roe v. Wade* (1973); Same-Sex Marriage and Civil Unions; Third Amendment; Waite, Morrison Remick; Warren, Earl

Bibliography

Cott, Nancy F. 2002. *Public Vows: A History of Marriage and the Nation.* Cambridge, MA: Harvard University Press.

Hartog, Hendrik. 2000. *Man and Wife in America: A History.* Cambridge, MA: Harvard University Press.

Wallenstein, Peter. 2002. *Tell the Court I Love My Wife: Race, Marriage, and Law—An American History.* New York: Palgrave MacMillan.

Chaya Chandrasekaran

MARSHALL, JOHN (1755–1835)

John Marshall was the fourth Chief Justice of the United States and by most accounts the greatest justice to have served on the nation's highest court. He is credited with transforming the Supreme Court of the United States into an active, independent, and coequal branch of the federal government. By force of his powerful intellect, precise and eloquent reasoning, and embracing personality, Marshall established the Court as the primary arbiter and interpreter of the U.S. Constitution. The landmark decisions he delivered set the country's constitutional jurisprudence on a strongly nationalist course in accordance with his Federalist sympathies. Under Marshall's deft leadership, the Court laid and cemented some of the major cornerstones of the U.S. Constitutional order: the exercise of judicial review; the supremacy of federal law over state law; the implied powers of Congress, ensuring an expansive reach of federal governmental authority; and the recognition and enforcement of constitutional rights.

Born near Germantown, Virginia, at the foot of the Blue Ridge Mountains, John Marshall grew up along Virginia's frontier. He was the oldest of the 15 children of Thomas Marshall, an ascendant planter, and Mary Keith Marshall, a clergyman's daughter related to the state's eminent Randolph and Lee families. Raised in a culture marked by sophistication and rusticity, Marshall absorbed in his youth both the habits of gentrified life and the liberties of careless dress and informal manners that became characteristic of his adult comportment. Young Marshall received a limited education—only two years of formal study—before going off to fight and receive the practical education of an officer in the American Revolution. The war, which took him through engagements at Brandywine, Germantown, Monmouth among others, and the harsh winter at Valley Forge, molded and solidified Marshall's nationalist convictions. "I was confirmed," he said, "in the habit of considering America as my country, and Congress as my government."

Marshall was admitted to the bar in 1780 after briefly studying law with the distinguished patriot George Wythe at the College of William and Mary. He next settled into an increasingly prominent and lucrative legal practice in Richmond. He married Mary Willis Ambler, the daughter of a prominent Virginia family, in 1783. They had 10 children, only 6 of whom survived to adulthood. As his legal reputation waxed, so did his involvement in Virginia politics and Federalist causes. He was elected at various intervals to Virginia's House of Delegates (1782-1785, 1787-1791, and 1795-1797), served on the state's Council of State (1782-1784), and was elected to Virginia's ratification convention of 1788. Marshall strongly supported the approval of the U.S. Constitution and gave voice to what many Federalists believed to be an implied and important component of the proposed governmental arrangement: judicial review. A law of Congress "not warranted by any of the powers enumerated," he argued, "would be considered by the judges as an infringement of the Constitution.... They would declare it void."

Marshall repeatedly had declined to serve in the new national government for personal financial reasons, but finally, in 1797, he accepted President John Adams' appointment to a temporary commission, dispatched to Paris to repair deteriorating U.S. relations with France. The mission failed to resolve matters between the two countries, but Marshall emerged from the so-called XYZ Affair a national hero for his steadfast refusal to accede to French bribery demands. In 1799, at George Washington's urging, Marshall ran for and won a seat in the House of Representatives, where he quickly became a staunch backer of the Adams Administration. In a famous speech successfully defending Adams' controversial decision to extradite a British criminal suspect under the Jay Treaty, Marshall brilliantly identified and articulated what are now recognized as central constitutional propositions: the distinction between political and judicial questions, and the president's special responsibilities as "the sole organ of the nation in its external relations, and its sole representative with foreign nations." Following a cabinet shake-up in the waning days of his administration, Adams promoted Marshall to Secretary of State for his loyalty and support.

Fortuitous circumstances propelled Marshall to become chief justice of the United States. Following the resignation of Chief Justice Oliver Ellsworth in December 1800, President Adams nominated Marshall after John Jay refused the assignment. Jay, the nation's first chief justice, saw little future in regaining his old seat in "a system so defective" and bereft of "energy, weight, and dignity" and lacking "public confidence and respect." Marshall saw the office he assumed on February 4, 1801, differently. In the Supreme Court, he perceived the possibility of creating a vigorous, coequal branch of government energized by the grand purpose of laying the legal groundwork for an effective national government. Under his steady leadership—Marshall's tenure lasted 34 years, more than three times the combined length of service of his three predecessors—the Supreme Court's voice became more focused in purpose, content, and manner. Marshall solidified the practice of assigning a single "opinion of the Court" rather than following the custom of allowing each justice to issue a separate opinion.

Marshall's most important contribution to U.S. constitutional jurisprudence was his authorship of the fountainhead decision, *Marbury v. Madison* (1803). Using the force of logic ("If ... the constitution is superior to any ordinary act of the legislature ... the constitution, and not such ordinary act, must govern the case to which they both apply"), Marshall embraced the doctrine of judicial review—the right of the judiciary to strike down a law as unconstitutional—and secured the Court's major role in governing the country, arbitrating disputes between the branches of government, and delineating the boundaries of individual rights. *Marbury* used judicial review to invalidate a law of Congress. A subsequent decision, *Fletcher* v. *Peck* (1810), extended the reach of the doctrine to nullify state statutes incompatible with the Constitution. Two other Marshall Court cases, *Martin v. Hunter's Lessee* (1816) and *Cohens v. Virginia* (1821), established the authority of the Court to review state court judgments touching constitutional or federal law questions. These decisions placed the Supreme Court at the pinnacle of a legal order capable of maintaining national unity, national authority, and national standards.

In *McCulloch v. Maryland* (1819), Marshall began to develop doctrines for fully empowering the national government. In this case he reasoned that implied powers, deducible from the enumerated powers of Congress and a broad reading of the Necessary and Proper Clause, justified the creation of the Bank of the United States. In addition, he maintained that the Supremacy Clause, enshrining the primacy of national law over state law, mandated that federal government operations remain free of state obstructions, such as taxation by Maryland. In *Gibbons v. Ogden* (1824), Marshall adopted an expansive interpretation of Congress's Commerce Power to invalidate a state-authorized monopoly on steamboat navigation. His conception of "commercial intercourse between nations, and parts of nations, in all its branches" laid the constitutional foundations for developing a broad national market and creating government institutions capable of regulating the interstate economy.

Marshall's vision of a politically and economically strong national government intersected perfectly with his deep respect for private property. In the Contract Clause of the Constitution, which bars the states from impairing the obligation of contracts, Marshall saw a promising instrument to both limit the power of the states and champion what he considered the individual's fundamental right of property. In the 1810 *Fletcher* decision, Marshall placed public contracts—or the agreements between a state and private parties—under the clause's ambit and forbade Georgia from rescinding a public sale of land to private buyers. Later in *Dartmouth College v. Woodward* (1819), he applied the Contract Clause's guarantees to corporate charters and prevented New Hampshire from unilaterally changing Dartmouth College's governing structure from that of a private school to that of a public institution. Both decisions operated to minimize state control over private property, private enterprises, and ultimately the private free market system. But the Marshall opinions also set a momentous precedent for American law. They established the Supreme Court as the nation's preeminent authority for identifying, defining, and protecting the fundamental individual rights contained in the U.S. Constitution.

Marshall died in office on July 6, 1835. His achievements in forging a national union through law had been remarkable. They prompted John Adams to comment in 1826 near his own end: "My gift of John Marshall to the people of the United States was the proudest act of my life."

See also Contracts Clause; Fundamental Rights; Madison, James; Precedent, Doctrine of; Property Rights; Treason, Constitutional Limits on

Bibliography

Baker, Leonard. 1974. *John Marshall: A Life in Law.* New York: Macmillan Publishing Co.

Beveridge, Albert J. 1916–1919. *The Life of John Marshall.* 4 vols. Boston: Houghton Mifflin.

Hobson, Charles F. 1996. *The Great Chief Justice: John Marshall and the Rule of Law.* Lawrence: University Press of Kansas.

Newmyer, R. Kent. 2001. *John Marshall and the Heroic Age of the Supreme Court.* Baton Rouge, LA: Louisiana State University Press.

Smith, Jean Edward. 1996. *John Marshall: Definer of a Nation.* New York: Henry Holt and Company.

Stites, Francis N. 1981. *John Marshall: Defender of the Constitution.* New York: HarperCollins Publishers.

Alain L. Sanders

MARSHALL, THURGOOD (1908–1993)

Thurgood Marshall was born in Baltimore, Maryland on July 2, 1908. This was a tumultuous time in American history for African Americans, filled with both extreme racial violence and strict segregation. Marshall faced a sizable challenge based on his race alone. Born the second of two sons, some of his in-laws had premonitions that a "great man had been born" (Rowan 1993, 23). In his favor was the fact that all four of his grandparents were free, literate, politically active citizens. This was somewhat rare for the time period. Marshall's parents were upstanding, respectable people within the community who supported equal rights (Bland 1973, 3–4). His mother, a schoolteacher, envisioned a career in dentistry for her son because it would be a lucrative career for a Baltimore African American. His father, a part-time writer, would often visit the local courtrooms to see what types of cases were being tried, then return home to challenge his family to argue their views concerning the cases (Rowan 1993, 34). This structured, stable family setting provided the foundation for an upstanding and respectable man who would go on to have a brilliant legal career.

Marshall received his elementary and high school education in Baltimore public schools. He was said to be an average student who had a reputation as a cut-up. He continued his education at Lincoln University, enrolling in the fall of 1925 with the intention of studying dentistry. Lincoln had the reputation of being one of the finest African American universities in America. Before he began his junior year at Lincoln, Marshall met his future wife, and also abandoned the idea of becoming a dentist. He graduated in 1930 with a degree in humanities, with honors, and was determined to pursue a career in law. The University of Maryland was his first choice for law school, but because it was an all-white school, his application was denied.

Marshall graduated as valedictorian from Howard University Law School in 1933. He moved back to Baltimore and set up a general private practice. In the beginning, clients were few and far between, so Marshall began doing pro bono work primarily for the experience. His pro bono endeavors led him to employment with the National Association for the Advancement of Colored People (NAACP) (Bland 1973, 5–8). Dr. Charles Hamilton Houston, one of Marshall's law professors at Howard and his mentor, was also a member of the NAACP. Dr. Houston and Marshall, along with the rest of the NAACP, developed a long-range plan to bring down the doctrine of separate but equal. They concentrated primarily on educational centers and worked from top to bottom, beginning at the collegiate level. They believed that the American legal system would be more likely to treat those African Americans who were striving to achieve higher education as equals rather than subservient citizens. Their hypothesis proved correct. Marshall and the NAACP gained victory after victory in the court system, including an early decision requiring the desegregation of the University of Maryland Law School. They then set their sights on elementary and high schools. Marshall's struggle culminated with the famous

Supreme Court case, *Brown v. Board of Education* (1954). After original argument, and re-argument, the Court unanimously struck down the doctrine of separate but equal. Of his 29 victories before the Supreme Court, this was Marshall's most noteworthy (Delon 1994, 5–7).

Shortly after *Brown*, Marshall left the NAACP. He saw the Civil Rights Movement shifting from courtroom activities and litigation toward sit-ins and demonstrations. He was not going to participate in the latter, and was quoted as saying he had "outlived [his] usefulness" as an advocate (Tushnet 1997, 3). In 1961, he accepted an appointment to the United States Court of Appeals for the Second Circuit. Although he endured a somewhat confrontational confirmation, Marshall went on to write over 100 opinions for the court. After serving four years on the Court of Appeals, Marshall was nominated for and accepted a position as Solicitor General of the United States, where he won 14 of the 19 cases he argued. He served in that role for two years until 1967, when President Lyndon Johnson nominated him for a seat on the Supreme Court. Marshall was confirmed as the first African American Supreme Court Justice on August 30, 1967. Marshall's appointment as Justice Tom Clark's successor moved the Court in a slightly more liberal direction, but this trend was short-lived, as Chief Justice Burger's appointment in 1969 prompted a change to a more conservative Court (Tushnet 1997, 28). Marshall, always a steadfast liberal, quickly found himself in an unfamiliar place on the Court, often defending minority opinions. Unfortunately for Marshall, the Court held onto its conservative majority for the remainder of his tenure (Goldman and Gallen 1992, 252).

In 1991, Marshall retired from the Court, and died two years later in 1993 at the age of 84. His years as an NAACP advocate and a Supreme Court justice gained him a reputation as one of the most forthright proponents of civil rights that America has ever seen. Marshall believed that some things are worth fighting for, and his battles for equity between the races will be long remembered and respected.

See also *Brown v. Board of Education* (1954; 1955); Burger Court; Burger, Warren E.; Civil Rights Movement; Clark, Tom C.; Equal Protection Jurisprudence; Jim Crow Laws; Liberalism; National Association for the Advancement of Colored People (NAACP); Segregation, De Facto and De Jure; Warren Court

Bibliography

Bland, Randall. 1973. *Private Pressure on Public Law— The Legal Career of Justice Thurgood Marshall.* Port Washington, NY: National University Publications.

Delon, Floyd. 1994. The Legacy of Thurgood Marshall. *Journal of Negro Education* 63: 278.

Goldman, R. and Gallen, D. 1992. *Thurgood Marshall— Justice For All.* New York: Carroll and Graf.

Rowan, Carl. 1993. *Dream Makers, Dream Breakers— The World of Justice Thurgood Marshall.* Boston: Little, Brown and Company.

Tushnet, Mark. 1997. *Making Constitutional Law— Thurgood Marshall and the Supreme Court, 1961– 1991.* New York: Oxford University Press.

Seth Johnson and Ronald Stidham

MASSACHUSETTS BODY OF LIBERTIES

Having received its royal charter in 1629, the Massachusetts Bay Company was an established self-governing New World colony by 1634. Colonial law in these early years was both nonsystematic and nonreferential to either king or common law. Decisions were an autocratic matter, guided by Scripture and the private conscience and reason of magistrates.

In 1635, deputies in the General Court called for a promulgated code of law, in an attempt to diminish the magistrates' discretionary control. By 1639 two models had been offered to a standing committee of the General Court, headed by Governor John Winthrop and charged to "peruse all those models which have been, or shall be, further presented to the court." The first, the work of John Cotton, later entitled *Moses his Judicials*, was heavily referenced to the Old Testament. The second, by Nathaniel Ward, relied less on scripture and more on the Magna Carta and the common law of England (see Hart and Channing for these influences). Ward's

code was chosen, circulated to the various towns for suggestions and emendations, reduced to 100 items (98 propositions, a preamble and a close), and adopted by the General Court in December 1641 as the *Massachusetts Body of Liberties.*

Ward, a Puritan Minister and lawyer, was, perhaps, the best-trained legal mind in New England at that time. Born in 1578 in Haverhill, England, he studied law at Emmanuel College, Cambridge. He was a practicing barrister, and had traveled extensively on the continent, when, finally, had entered the ministry. He immigrated to the Massachusetts colony in 1634. Although a convinced Puritan, Ward, nonetheless, authored a document far in advance of his day.

The *Massachusetts Body of Liberties* speaks of fundamental rights and guarantees—liberties rather than restrictions. In Puritan religious terms, *liberty* connoted the freedom to construct a pure church and a holy commonwealth. Also, in practical terms, framing the code as "*Liberties,*" instead of laws, was intended to reduce the possibility of making a law directly opposed to the Crown, one of the conditions of self-government stated in the charter.

The code's preamble plus sections 1 through 17 anticipate our American Bill of Rights, stating fundamental principles relating to fairness, the value of life, property, one's reputation, and one's liberty. Sections 18 through 57 discuss the general rules and conditions for judicial proceedings. The following sections then enumerate the liberties and duties of free men (20 sections), of women (2 sections), of children (4 sections), of servants (4 sections), of foreigners and strangers (3 sections) and, most remarkably, perhaps the world's first laws that protected animals in the service of man (2 sections). Section 94 delineates 12 capital crimes. Only the twelfth, insurrection against the commonwealth, town, or government, is not referenced to the Old Testament. The final four sections reveal liberties God gave his churches. Finally, the closing paragraph gives the General Court sole power to interpret the code.

The *Body of Liberties* was replaced in 1648 by the more comprehensive and influential *Book of the General Lawes and Liberties.* Nathaniel Ward returned to England in 1647, where he died in 1652.

See also Bill of Rights, American; Common Law Background of American Civil Rights and Liberties; Fundamental Rights; Liberty; Magna Carta; Property Rights; Religion, Freedom of

Bibliography

Dean, John Ward. 1868. *A Memoir of the Rev. Nathaniel Ward, A.M.* Albany, NY: J. Munsell.

Hart, Albert Bushnell, and Edward Channing. 1896. *American History Leaflets No. 25, The Earliest New England Code of Laws, 1641.* Chicago: A. Lovell.

Palfrey, John Gorham. 1890. *History of New England.* Vol. 2. New York: Little, Brown.

Kevin Collins

MCCARDLE, EX PARTE (1869)

After the Civil War, Congress passed the Reconstruction Acts, which, among other things, imposed military rule on most of the southern states formerly comprising the Confederacy. As part of this program, military tribunals were authorized to try civilians who interfered with Reconstruction. William H. McCardle, editor of the *Vicksburg Times,* published a series of editorials highly critical of Reconstruction. Consequently, he was arrested by the military and held for trial by a military tribunal. McCardle sought release from custody through a petition for habeas corpus in federal court. Congress in 1867 had extended federal habeas corpus jurisdiction to cover state prisoners, which applied to McCardle, since he was in the custody of the military government of Mississippi. The 1867 Act also provided a right of appeal to the Supreme Court. Having lost his bid for relief in the lower court, McCardle exercised his right to appeal.

After the case was argued in the Supreme Court, Congress enacted legislation withdrawing the Supreme Court's appellate jurisdiction in habeas corpus cases. The legislation went so far as to deny the Court's authority to decide a case already argued. The obvious motive was to prevent the Court from ruling on the constitutionality of the Reconstruction Acts, which McCardle had challenged in his appeal. The Court could have declared unconstitutional this blatant attempt to prevent the Court

from exercising its power of judicial review, but the Court chose to capitulate. By acquiescing in the withdrawal of its jurisdiction in *McCardle,* the Court avoided a direct confrontation with Congress at a time when that institution was dominant in the national government.

In a footnote to his dissenting opinion in *Glidden Co. v. Zdanok* (1962), Justice William O. Douglas, joined by Justice Hugo Black, wrote, "There is a serious question whether the *McCardle* case could command a majority view today." The modern view is that Congress cannot exercise its power to regulate the Supreme Court's appellate jurisdiction so as to seriously curtail the Court's ability to protect the fundamental rights of citizens. Of course, in a crisis produced by, for instance, a wave of terrorism, the contemporary Supreme Court might acquiesce to Congress, much as did the Court during Reconstruction.

See also Black, Hugo L.; Douglas, William O.; Fundamental Rights; Habeas Corpus, Federal; Military Tribunals; Reconstruction

John M. Scheb II and Otis H. Stephens, Jr.

MCCARTHYISM. *See* McCarthy, Joseph R.

MCCARTHY, JOSEPH R. (1908–1957)

Republican Senator Joseph McCarthy's desire to purge the United States and its government of suspected communists during the beginning of the Cold War era gained him considerable notoriety among the American public. His specious allegations against government officials and other individuals were ultimately discredited; however, his views and tactics, now labeled "McCarthyism," provide strong evidence that mass paranoia can lead to infringements on civil liberties and civil rights.

Joseph McCarthy was born on November 14, 1908, in Grand Chute, Wisconsin. At the age of 14, McCarthy quit school and started a business raising chickens. The business was profitable for a few years, but ultimately failed. As a result, McCarthy finished his high school education and went on to earn a law degree from Marquette University in 1935. Shortly thereafter, McCarthy became interested in politics and won his first office, a state judgeship, after lying about his opponent's age (Matusow 1970). He made a spectacle of himself as a judge by holding court until midnight and granting "quickie" divorces. He left the post to serve in World War II, later exaggerating his contributions to the war effort to the Wisconsin media by referring to himself as a "tailgunner" (even though he was only allowed to sit in the passenger seat next to a tailgunner in a limited number of missions). In 1944 while he was still in the service, he launched a Senate campaign that was unsuccessful in the short term, but brought attention that would help him win a senatorial election in 1947 (Matusow 1970).

McCarthy gained little attention in the Senate until he made a speech in Wheeling, West Virginia on February 9, 1950, where he claimed to have in his hand a list of 205 State Department employees who were Communist Party members. The outrageous claim gained media attention and resonated with the American public at a time when Americans were becoming increasingly concerned about Soviet aggression in Europe and the Communist takeover of China; moreover, the claims were made two weeks after Alger Hiss, a high-ranking State Department official, was convicted of perjury amid allegations that he was a communist spy for the Soviet Union. After the invasion of South Korea by communist North Korea in June 1950, McCarthy's allegations garnered more interest and helped the Republican Party in the presidential and congressional elections of 1952.

After easily winning reelection in 1952, McCarthy became chair of the Senate Committee on Government Operations, a position he used to blatantly accuse Americans of being communists. Those who were called before the committee to testify and invoked their Fifth Amendment right against self-incrimination were accused of being traitors. McCarthy's tactics were initially backed by other Republicans, even when he demanded information on employees in the executive branch. President Eisenhower refused "in the most absolute assertion of the presidential right to withhold

information from Congress that had ever been uttered in American history" (Urofsky and Finkelman 2002, 765). Without the information, McCarthy could not support his assertions that there were communists in the executive branch.

McCarthy's influence began to wane after his tactics were exposed in 1954 by respected newsman Edward R. Murrow. McCarthy's decision to investigate communism within the armed services ultimately served to discredit him. The fully televised Army-McCarthy hearings ran from April 22 to June 17, 1954, and allowed the American public to see and hear what they had only been told about through newspapers and television newscasts. Americans were able to witness his disrespect for Senate rules as well as his abominable treatment of the witnesses testifying before the committee. The tide of public opinion turned against him and on December 2, 1954, the Senate voted to censure McCarthy for bringing disrespect upon the chamber. He died of alcoholism on May 2, 1957, without ever uncovering a communist in the United States government.

See also Communist Party USA; Fifth Amendment; House Un-American Activities Committee (HUAC); Legislative Investigations; Self-Incrimination Clause; Smith Act

Bibliography

Griffith, Robert. 1987. *The Politics of Fear: Joseph R. McCarthy and the Senate.* 2nd ed. Amherst: University of Massachusetts Press.

Matusow, Allen, ed.1970. *Joseph R. McCarthy.* Englewood Cliffs, NJ: Prentice-Hall.

Morgan, Ted. 2004. *Reds: McCarthyism in Twentieth Century America.* New York: Random House.

Reeves, Thomas C. 1997. *The Life and Times of Joe McCarthy.* Reprint ed. Lanham, MD: Madison Books.

Schrecker, Ellen. 2002. *The Age of McCarthyism: Brief History with Documents.* 2nd ed. Boston: Bedford/ St. Martin's.

Urofsky, Melvin I., and Paul Finkelman. 2002. *A March for Liberty: A Constitutional History of the United States.* Vol. 2: *From 1877-Present.* New York: Oxford University Press.

Kara E. Stooksbury

MCNABB-MALLORY RULE. *See* Interrogation and Confessions

MCREYNOLDS, JAMES CLARK (1862–1946)

In some ways James Clark McReynolds seemed the model of a Supreme Court justice. His appearance was likened to a Roman senator, and his dress was characterized as impeccable; in demeanor he was confident. To those gazing on the figure of McReynolds as he strode to Court with his walking stick, he clearly looked the part of a justice. Yet his personal attitudes revealed a character ill-suited for long-term service on a collegial bench, particularly a diverse bench riven by partisan and philosophical differences. Personally, he was a fairly reclusive man, careful in his choice of society. He is, of course, best known for his staunch defiance of the New Deal, strong stand in favor of liberty of contract, and belief in substantive due process. He is infamous for his racial prejudice, anti-Semitism, and his snubs of colleagues; few know of his generous support of the Save the Children charity during its early years. Assuredly, McReynolds' contributions to our current conceptions of civil rights and liberties are less substantial than many other justices even though he was on the bench during the period of incorporation of the First Amendment. Yet this reactionary, intolerant, and irascible justice played an important role in the development of the right to privacy.

James Clark McReynolds was born in Elkton, Kentucky, on February 3, 1862, close to the border with Tennessee. McReynolds clearly identified himself as a Southerner—growing up in an affluent family on a plantation. Although most of his childhood took place after the conclusion of the Civil War, his upbringing clearly reflected the antebellum and fundamentalist Christian values espoused by his Campbellite parents. McReynolds' father was a small town doctor who was dogmatic—a characteristic the doctor clearly passed along to his son.

McReynolds was a bright and successful student, graduating as valedictorian from Vanderbilt in 1882 and earning his law degree from the University of Virginia in little over a year in 1884.

He then entered into private practice in Nashville after graduation and served as professor at Vanderbilt's School of Law. True to his past, he was a conservative Democrat and could not abide by the 1896 Silver Platform. He therefore joined the Gold Democrats and ran unsuccessfully for Congress.

In 1903, the Kentuckian left the ivory tower and came to Washington to apply his talents to the antitrust campaigns of Theodore Roosevelt's presidential administration. Though McReynolds was a Southerner, his antitrust efforts even included the tobacco industry. Given his personal opinion of smoking—he would not tolerate smoking or tobacco use in his presence—perhaps this is less than surprising.

After serving four years in Washington as an assistant attorney general, McReynolds returned to private practice, joining a prestigious firm in New York City. He then reprised his role as assistant U.S. attorney general for one year (1910–1911) before returning to New York. He remained in private practice there for only a few short years until 1913, when his reputation as a trust-buster led President Woodrow Wilson to name McReynolds the Attorney General. Wilson soon found McReynolds difficult and took an early opportunity in 1914 to elevate him to the High Court to succeed Horace H. Lurton; McReynolds served as Attorney General for only one year and was 52 when he assumed his position as an associate justice.

Once on the Court, McReynolds remained a conservative Southern Democrat, allying himself most closely with Justices Van De Vanter, Butler, and Sutherland. Indeed, these four justices became known as the "four horsemen" for their stubborn refusal to accept the constitutionality of President Franklin D. Roosevelt's New Deal programs. Dissenting from the Supreme Court's decision upholding the Social Security program (*Steward Machine Co. v. Davis,* 1937), McReynolds lamented the "coercion" involved in requiring employers to participate in the system and concluded that "our federate plan of government confronts an enlarged peril." In many ways, McReynolds' upbringing as a staunch southerner of the old school played out in his later years on the Court as he spent his last years in dissent speaking as the lone voice of a bygone era—the last of the four horsemen to retire and provide FDR with another seat to fill on the Supreme Court.

McReynolds' work on the Court was rarely considered distinguished. Indeed, in 1970 a survey of experts ranked McReynolds as one of eight failures among the first 100 justices. He kept his opinions brief and terse; he had little of the flair for writing displayed by such colleagues as Holmes, Hughes, and Cardozo. He also wrote fewer opinions than some of his brethren. One of his clerks often remarked in his diaries during the momentous year of 1936 that McReynolds seemed to write fewer opinions because working on multiple opinions simultaneously seemed to irritate him. McReynolds was not ashamed of his anti-Semitic views and these views were well known to those on the Court. McReynolds did not attend social functions where either Brandeis or Cardozo was present. He refused to sign a letter of regret from the Court to Louis Brandeis upon the latter's retirement. He did not allow any fraternization between his African American household staff and himself or his white law clerks. For McReynolds, the Constitution provided little foundation for large extensions of rights for either African Americans or women. As demonstrated by his dissenting opinions in *Berger v. United States* (1921) and *Aldridge v. United States* (1931), McReynolds did not believe that a judge, openly hostile to the national origin, or a juror showing prejudice toward the race of the defendant was necessarily a hindrance to due process, and he issued the only dissenting opinion in the first Scottsboro case, which was joined by Justice Butler (see *Powell v. Alabama,* 1932). Had McReynolds lived, clearly he would not have supported the Warren Court's expansion of federal power, or civil rights and liberties.

Yet, whether he intended to or not, McReynolds did have an important impact on the development of the right to privacy through his opinions dealing with incorporation and the First Amendment. In 1923, McReynolds wrote the majority opinion in *Meyer v. Nebraska,* which concerned a state law

prohibiting the teaching of any modern language to children prior to the eighth grade. To McReynolds, this law was a clear violation of a core liberty that includes the right to contract, to learn, to marry and rear children, and to worship without undue interference from the state. Similarly, in *Pierce v. Society of Sisters,* McReynolds wrote that "Under the doctrine of *Meyer v. Nebraska,* ... we think it entirely plain that the Act of 1922 (providing for compulsory *public school* attendance) unreasonably interferes with the liberty of parents and guardians to direct the upbringing and education of children under their control." Forty years later, Justice Douglas relied on the language of these two decisions in support of his majority opinion in *Griswold v. Connecticut:*

By *Pierce v. Society of Sisters* ... the right to educate one's children as one chooses is made applicable to the States by the force of the First and Fourteenth Amendments. By *Meyer v. Nebraska* ... the same dignity is given the right to study the German language in a private school. In other words, the State may not, consistently with the spirit of the First Amendment, contract the spectrum of available knowledge.

Indeed, Justice Arthur Goldberg, writing for himself, Chief Justice Earl Warren, and Justice William J. Brennan, uses the same writings of McReynolds to establish a constitutional right to privacy. Thus, this pair of opinions by Justice McReynolds—a conservative, anti-Semitic, racially prejudiced, and patriarchal man—provided the liberal and progressive Douglas and Goldberg with precedents to buttress a landmark in the area of personal liberties. McReynolds retired at the age of 79 on February 1, 1941; he was the last of the four horsemen to leave the bench. Five years later, McReynolds contracted pneumonia, then died on August 24, 1946. He was buried in his hometown of Elkton. He left a substantial estate, most of which he bequeathed to charities aiding children.

See also Bill of Rights, Incorporation of; Brandeis, Louis D.; Brennan, William J., Jr.; Cardozo, Benjamin N.; Conservatism; Due Process, Substantive; First Amendment; Goldberg, Arthur; *Griswold v. Connecticut* (1965); Holmes, Oliver Wendell,

Jr.; Liberty; *Meyer v. Nebraska* (1923); The New Deal; *Pierce v. Society of Sisters* (1925); *Powell v. Alabama* (1932); Privacy, Constitutional Right of; Roosevelt, Franklin D.; Warren, Earl

Bibliography

Bond, James E. 1992. *I Dissent: The Legacy of Justice James Clark McReynolds.* Lanham, MD: George Mason University Press.

Cushman, Clare, ed. 1995. *The Supreme Court Justices.* 2nd ed. Washington, DC: Congressional Quarterly.

Friedman, Leon, and Israel, Fred L., eds. 1969. *The Justices of the United States Supreme Court 1789–1969.* Vol. 3. New York: Chelsea House Publishers.

Hall, Kermit L., ed. 1992. *The Oxford Companion to the Supreme Court of the United States.* New York: Oxford University Press.

Knox, John. 2002. *The Forgotten Memoir of John Knox: A Year in the Life of a Supreme Court Clerk in FDR's Washington.* Edited by Dennis J. Hutchinson and David J. Garrow. Chicago: University of Chicago Press.

McGurin, Barrett. 1997. *America's Court.* Golden, CO: Fulcrum.

Rorie Spill Solberg

MEDICAL TREATMENT, RIGHT TO REFUSE

Among the most serious decisions anyone will make are those concerning medical treatment for oneself and one's dependents. The right to refuse medical treatment for oneself is deeply rooted in the English common law. At common law, a doctor who performed medical treatment on a patient without that patient's "informed consent" had committed the tort of battery. Writing for the U.S. Supreme Court in *Union Pacific R.R. Co. v. Botsford* (1891), Justice Horace Gray observed that "[n]o right is held more sacred, or is more carefully guarded by the common law, than the right of every individual to the possession and control of his own person, free from all restraint or interference of others, unless by clear and unquestionable authority of law."

American courts have consistently protected this right to bodily integrity by maintaining the common-law doctrine of informed consent. In *Schloendorff v. Society of New York Hospital* (1914),

the New York Court of Appeals reviewed a case where a woman sued a hospital for performing an operation without her consent. Judge Benjamin Nathan Cardozo, who would go on to serve as an associate justice of the U.S. Supreme Court, wrote the opinion in *Schloendorff,* saying:

Every human being of adult years and sound mind has a right to determine what shall be done with his own body, and a surgeon who performs an operation without his patient's consent commits an assault, for which he is liable in damages. This is true except in cases of emergency where the patient is unconscious and where it is necessary to operate before consent can be obtained.

As the U.S. Supreme Court observed in *Cruzan v. Director, Missouri Department of Health* (1990), "The informed consent doctrine has become firmly entrenched in American tort law." And, as the Court also noted, "The logical corollary of the doctrine of informed consent is that the patient generally possesses the right not to consent, that is, to refuse treatment." In the *Cruzan* case, the Supreme Court also recognized a constitutional basis for the refusal of medical treatment. Writing for the Court, Chief Justice William H. Rehnquist stated, "The principle that a competent person has a constitutionally protected liberty interest in refusing unwanted medical treatment may be inferred from our prior decisions." Thus statutes interfering with the right to refuse medical treatment are subject to judicial review.

The most difficult medical decisions are those involving extraordinary means of life support. Since it was first recognized in the Karen Quinlan case in 1976, the right of a competent adult to require the removal of life support systems has become well established in law, both through court decisions and legislative enactments. In cases where the patient is unable to communicate such directives, the right can be exercised through surrogates under the doctrine of substituted judgment. Today, a competent adult can make advance directives concerning medical care through use of a living will, a durable power of attorney, and through appointment of surrogates.

Where a person has not executed an advance directive and is unable to assert a right to refuse medical treatment, the substituted judgment doctrine allows that person's spouse or guardian to assert that right. Parents and guardians are accorded this right for their children. If, however, a parent or guardian of a child refuses medical treatment for a child on religious grounds, courts will intervene, and if medical treatment is necessary to save a child's life, or even where treatment can insure the child's well-being and involves a relatively small risk, courts often find that the state's interest in safeguarding the welfare of children justifies overriding refusal by parents or guardians. Courts, however, have divided on whether to compel a parent or guardian who, on religious grounds, refuses to abide by a statutory requirement that a school-age child be vaccinated.

In some instances state statutes expressly provide for refusal to accept medical treatments. Courts are reluctant to become involved in health care decisions; however, they will intervene in situations where there is a conflict among decision makers (physicians, hospitals, family members, guardians, etc.) concerning refusal to allow medical treatment.

See also Cardozo, Benjamin N.; Right to Die; Due Process, Substantive; Jehovah's Witnesses; Liberty; Living Will; Parental Rights; Privacy, Constitutional Right of; Rehnquist, William H.; Substituted Judgment, Doctrine of

Bibliography

Cohen, B. D. 1991. *The Essential Guide to a Living Will: How to Protect Your Right to Refuse Medical Treatment.* New York: Simon & Schuster.

Grisso, Thomas, and Paul S. Applebaum. 2004. *Assessing Competence to Consent to Treatment: A Guide for Physicians and Other Health Professionals.* New York: Oxford University Press.

Scheb, John M., and John M. Scheb II. 2002. *An Introduction to the American Legal System.* Albany, NY: Delmar.

John M. Scheb II and Otis H. Stephens, Jr.

MEESE, EDWIN, III (1931–)

Born in Oakland, California, in 1931, Edwin Meese III graduated from Yale University in 1953 and earned a law degree from the University of California, Berkeley in 1966. After several years in private practice, he became deputy district attorney for Alameda County, California. In 1969, he was appointed as executive assistant and chief of staff to California Governor Ronald Reagan, holding that post through 1974. In 1980 Meese directed Reagan's postelection presidential transition team, then served as counselor to the president from 1981 to 1985. In that capacity he was responsible for interdepartmental relations with the White House, cabinet administration, and daily operations of the executive branch. Meese also headed the Office of Policy Development, where he played an important role in the August 1981 enactment of the Economic Recovery Act, the tax cut centerpiece of what became known as "Reaganomics."

In February 1985, Edwin Meese was named as the 75th U.S. Attorney General, replacing William French Smith; he served in this office until August 1988. Shortly after this appointment, a series of related events occurred that involved arms sales to Iran, release of American hostages in Lebanon, and diversion of funds to exile forces attempting to overthrow the Ortega government in Nicaragua. This policy became the subject of the November 1987 *Report of the Congressional Committees Investigating the Iran-Contra Affair* in which Attorney General Meese was prominently mentioned. According to the report, at the January 7, 1986, National Security Council meeting, having just been appointed a nonstatutory member by Reagan, Meese was asked by the President for a legal opinion regarding the ongoing arms sales to Iran. The Attorney General indicated that, drawing upon a 1981 assessment by his predecessor Smith, conducting this transfer under the Economy Act rather than the Arms Export Control Act would not require notification to Congress for up to 60 days. Reagan then signed a Presidential Finding to cover the plan retroactively; however, this never was reported to Congress.

When the Iran arms sales arrangement became known publicly in November 1986, it triggered a 12-day period of conflicting statements by the administration. On November 13 President Reagan made a televised address to deny the trade of arms for hostages and the failure to give Congress adequate notice of the covert operation. At the subsequent November 19 press conference, the President's comments varied from his address six days earlier. Thus at a November 21 meeting with President Reagan, Chief of Staff Don Regan, and National Security Advisor Admiral John Poindexter, Meese suggested that to clear up confusion over the various plan elements he should "develop a coherent overview of the facts" for public dissemination by the administration. He reported back to Reagan on November 24 not only on the arms sales, but also about the previously secret funds transfer to the *contras* by NSC staff member Oliver North.

President Reagan began a press conference on November 25 with a short statement that he had not been fully informed on all aspects of the operation, then turned over the podium to the Attorney General to handle the briefing. Meese described the arms sales, attempts to secure hostage releases, and the previously undisclosed funds transfer to the *contras*. Both the congressional report and a 1991 book by Theodore Draper indicated that Meese's statements were contrary to information he had gathered over the previous week. On November 26, President Reagan named a Special Review Board, headed by former senator John Tower, to make a complete review of National Security Council procedures, followed on December 19 by appointment by a three-judge panel. Lawrence E. Walsh was appointed as the independent counsel to investigate the matter. Mr. Meese addressed this entire episode in his book *With Reagan: The Inside Story*, published in 1992.

Beyond his role in the Iran-*Contra* Affair, Ed Meese became well known for his advocacy of a conservative view of constitutional interpretation and the judicial role (see Meese 1986). In a series of public speeches in 1985 Meese castigated the modern Court for ignoring the intentions of the framers of the Constitution and grafting its own policy preferences onto the document. Meese's attacks on judicial activism were very similar to those made by Judge Robert Bork, another vocal critic of the modern Court. As Attorney General, Meese was a strong supporter of President Reagan's ill-fated nomination of Bork to the United States Supreme Court.

In the 1990s and the first decade of the 21st century, Meese continued his attacks on modern constitutionalism and the "imperial judiciary." In testimony before the Senate Judiciary Committee on June 11, 1997, Meese urged the Senate not to confirm "activist judges" nominated by President Bill Clinton. Claiming that "the federal judiciary has strayed far beyond its proper functions," Meese called on Congress to curtail the jurisdiction of the federal courts. During his remarks, Meese telegraphed his general political conservatism by stating, "We will never return the federal government to its proper role in our society until we return the federal judiciary to its proper role in our government."

Since his retirement from government, Meese has been affiliated with a number of influential organizations, including the Heritage Foundation, the Hoover Institution, the Capitol Research Center, and the Federalist Society. In the summer of 2005, Meese again stepped into the political arena to champion President George W. Bush's nomination of Judge John Roberts to succeed Chief Justice William H. Rehnquist on the U.S. Supreme Court.

See also Bork, Robert H.; Conservatism; Judicial Activism; Judicial Restraint; Liberalism; O'Connor, Sandra Day; Original Intent, Doctrine of; United States Supreme Court

Bibliography

Draper, Theodore. 1991. *A Very Thin Line: The Iran-Contra Affairs*. New York: Touchstone Books.

Meese, Edwin III. 1986. "The Supreme Court of the United States: Bulwark of a Limited Constitution." *South Texas Law Review* 27: 455.

Meese, Edwin III. 1992. *With Reagan: The Inside Story*. Washington, DC: Regnery Gateway.

James Gilchrist

MEGAN'S LAW

In 1994, 7-year-old Megan Kanka was raped and strangled to death by her neighbor, Jesse

Timmendequas, who had two previous convictions for sexually assaulting children. Public furor over the young girl's murder was exacerbated by the fact that Timmendequas' neighbors had been unaware of his history of sex offenses. The legislation precipitated by Kanka's death, Megan's Law, provided the catalyst for the sex offender registration movement in the United States (Logan, 1999). Officially recognized as the Sex Offender Registration Act, Megan's Law was initially passed by the New Jersey Legislature in 1994. All 50 states, the District of Columbia, and the federal government have now adopted some version of the sex offender registration requirement (Logan, 1999).

Megan's Law is not the first legislative effort to control convicted sex offenders within the United States. Some of the earliest "sexual psychopath" laws established to supervise sex offenders originated during the 1930s. Under such laws, people convicted of sexual offenses were subjected to indefinite civil commitment in mental hospitals (Johnson, 1996). A more contemporary predecessor to Megan's Laws, the Jacob Wetterling Act, was passed by Congress in 1994. Eleven- year-old Jacob Wetterling was abducted from his Minnesota home in 1990, and he and his abductor have never been found (White, 1998). The Wetterling Act ordered states to establish registries of sexually violent offenders, including those offenders who had victimized children, and provided guidelines for the state programs. The purpose of these registries was to facilitate the annual monitoring of offenders' residences for a minimum of 10 years following their release from prison (Welchans, 2005). Moreover, this law requires that convicted sex offenders register with local police departments whenever they relocate to a new neighborhood. Any state that failed to adopt programs conforming to this legislation's requirements by 1997 lost 10 percent of its federal anticrime funding (White, 1998). But while the Wetterling Act required law enforcement to compile information on released sex offenders and *permitted* the release of such information, it did not *require* that the registration information be released to the public.

Megan's Laws go beyond the minimums required under the Wetterling Act by mandating that states establish procedures to inform the public about sex offenders living in close proximity. New Jersey Representative Dick Zimmer sponsored a Megan's Law type amendment to the Wetterling Act in 1995, following Megan Kanka's death (Welchans, 2005). This bill was signed into law by President Bill Clinton in 1996. Although the federal government requires that registrants' information be disseminated to the public, the states exercise considerable discretion in terms of which offenders will be subjected to disclosure, the type of information collected, and what standards and procedures will be used to make such determinations (Logan, 1999). Commonly used methods of community notification include "press releases, flyers, phone calls, door-to-door contact, neighborhood meetings, and Internet Web sites" (Matson and Leib 1996, cited in Levenson and Cotter 2005, 50).

Sex offender registration and community notification laws have faced constitutional challenges. The U.S. Supreme Court, however, has been seemingly unmoved by offenders' claims. (Logan, 1999). The two most common challenges to sex offender and notification laws include purported violations of the Due Process and Ex Post Facto Clauses of the Constitution. In 1997, the Court ruled in *Kansas v. Hendricks* that civil commitment of "sexually violent predators" who had completed prison terms for their sexual offenses did not violate the offenders' due process rights nor did such commitments constitute double jeopardy. In the 2003 decision of *Connecticut Department of Public Safety v. Doe* the Court, again, determined that Megan's Law does not violate an offender's due process rights. In this case, the Court asserted that people convicted of sexual offenses and subjected to Connecticut's version of Megan's Law are not entitled to a hearing prior to the disclosure of their registration information to the public. An ex post facto argument regarding sex offender registration was presented in the 2003 case of *Smith v. Doe*. Ex post facto laws, which only criminalize a person's conduct "after the fact," deny defendants their due process protections and are unconstitutional. In *Smith*, the Court concluded that Alaska's version of Megan's Law can be applied retroactively without violating the Ex Post Facto Clause of the Constitution because the law serves a regulatory and not a punitive function.

The impact of Megan's Laws on both offenders and the communities being warned has yet to be fully determined. Despite uncertainty regarding the laws' effectiveness, they have received tremendous popular support (Levenson and Cotter 2005). Some critics maintain that Megan's Laws do not make for sound crime control policy. Rather than reducing sexual offenses, these laws may be little more than "feel-good legislation" with far-reaching and dire consequences (Freeman-Longo 1996). The viability of Megan's Laws has been questioned in several ways. Such laws may encourage vigilante acts from incensed community members. In cases of incest, the victim's identity is conceivably divulged along with the offender's. The public exposure of their loved ones may impair the quality of life of the innocent spouses and relatives of registered offenders. Registration and community notification laws also struggle to deal equitably with aging offenders. A precise cutoff age for sex offender registration has not been ascertained. There has also been controversy over whether juvenile sex offenders should be subjected to registration. Moreover, the effectiveness of Megan's Laws remains in question. Parents in larger communities may not be able to keep track of all the offenders in close proximity. Offenders also may visit other towns where they are not required to register. Finally, the penalties offenders face for failing to register are inconsistent from jurisdiction to jurisdiction.

See also Accused, Rights of the; Due Process Clauses; Equal Protection Clause; Ex Post Facto Laws; Privacy, Informational; Sex Offenders, Rights of

Bibliography

Freeman-Longo, Robert. 1996. "Prevention or Problem." *Sexual Abuse: A Journal of Research and Treatment* 8: 91.

Johnson, Marna J. 1996. "Minnesota's Sexual Psychopathic Personality and Sexually Dangerous Person Statute: Throwing Away the Key." *William Mitchell Law Review* 21: 1139.

Levenson, Jill S., and Leo P. Cotter. 2005. "The Effect of Megan's Law on Sex Offender Reintegration." *Journal of Contemporary Criminal Justice* 21: 49.

Logan, Wayne A. 1999. "Liberty Interests in the Preventive State: Procedural Due Process and Sex Offender Community Notification Laws." *Journal of Criminal Law and Criminology* 89: 1167.

Welchans, Sarah. 2005. "Megan's Law: Evaluations of Sexual Offender Registries." *Criminal Justice Policy Review* 16: 123.

White, Whitney L. 1998. "Punishment or Protection: Does Community Notification of Released Sex Offenders Violate the Double Jeopardy Clause?" *Criminal Law Bulletin* 34: 185.

Christine Ivie Edge

"MEMORIAL AND REMONSTRANCE" (1785)

"Memorial and Remonstrance," written anonymously by James Madison in 1785, is one of the most eloquent arguments for religious liberty ever penned by an American. In addition, because James Madison also drafted the federal Bill of Rights, many Supreme Court justices and scholars have looked to the Memorial and Remonstrance for guidance in interpreting the religion clauses of the First Amendment.

It was a conflict over religious liberty in Virginia that prompted Madison to write "Memorial and Remonstrance." In 1784, Patrick Henry introduced a bill in the Virginia Assembly that would have established a property tax whose proceeds would be used to support "teachers of the Christian religion." Each taxpayer would determine the denomination to which his taxes would go, so no one would be forced to support a church not of his own choice. Although the measure enjoyed broad support initially, Madison and other opponents of the bill were able to postpone enactment until after a legislative adjournment, so that legislators could survey the views of their constituents. "Memorial and Remonstrance" was written to persuade Virginians to oppose Henry's bill, and it succeeded. After the

Virginia Assembly reconvened, Henry's bill was defeated, and Thomas Jefferson's Bill for Establishing Religious Freedom was enacted in its place.

Although the product of a particular dispute, many of Madison's arguments in "Memorial and Remonstrance" apply equally to all efforts to enlist government in promoting religion. The religious assessment proposed by Henry may seem only a minimal intrusion on religious liberty, but Madison insisted that "it is proper to take alarm at the first experiment on our liberties." Moreover, the assessment implicated fundamental principles. Madison insisted that the right of every human being to the free exercise of religion in line with the dictates of his conscience is an "unalienable right." Thus, government has no authority to regulate religious belief, to compel religious observances, or to underwrite religious institutions. Madison claimed that government does not need the support of religious institutions for its survival. In fact, a government that protects the religious liberty of all will create a firm foundation of popular support, whereas one that meddles in religion will likely promote disharmony and conflict. Conversely, religion does not need the support of government in order to flourish. To assume otherwise is to assume that religion is a human creation, not ordained by God. In practice, religions have typically fared better when they were not beholden to government, as governmental support tends to corrupt and enervate religious institutions instead of making them effective advocates of religious truth. Madison thus concludes that religion must remain a voluntary, private affair, so that every man may "render to the Creator such homage and such only as he believes to be acceptable to him."

See also Bill of Rights (American) (1789); Establishment Clause; First Amendment; Free Exercise Clause; Jefferson, Thomas; Madison, James; Religion, Freedom of; Separation of Church and State

Bibliography

Curry, Thomas J. 1986. *The First Freedoms: Church and State in America to the Passage of the First Amendment.* New York: Oxford University Press.

Miller, William Lee. 2003. *The First Liberty: America's Foundation in Religious Freedom.* Rev. ed. Washington, DC: Georgetown University Press.

Stokes, Anson Phelps. *Church and State in the United States.* Rev. ed. Westport, CT: Greenwood Press, 1975.

G. Alan Tarr

MENTAL INCOMPETENCE. *See* Death Penalty and Mental Incompetence

MEREDITH, JAMES (1933–)

On October 1, 1962, James Meredith became the first African American student to register at the University of Mississippi (Ole Miss). This landmark victory in the struggle for civil rights in America was achieved only after a legal and political battle that involved the NAACP, the governor of Mississippi, President John F. Kennedy, the federal courts, the U.S. Marshals Service, and even the U.S. Army.

Before entering Ole Miss, Meredith was a student at Jackson State University, which was at that time an exclusively black institution. In January 1961, Meredith applied to Ole Miss but was turned down, even though he met the academic standards for admission. In May 1961, the NAACP Legal Defense Fund brought a federal lawsuit on Meredith's behalf. The district court in Mississippi denied relief, but the U.S. Court of Appeals for the Fifth Circuit reversed and ordered that Meredith be admitted to Ole Miss (see *Meredith v. Fair,* 1962). Ross Barnett, the governor of Mississippi, became personally involved in the case and refused to allow the University to admit Meredith.

On September 28, the Fifth U.S. Circuit Court of Appeals found Barnett in contempt and ordered that unless James Meredith was registered by October 2, the governor would be taken into custody and fined $10,000 for each day thereafter that he blocked Meredith's registration. Two days later, after an unsuccessful attempt to persuade Barnett to back down, President Kennedy issued an executive order directing the U.S. Marshals Service to effect James Meredith's registration. That evening federal marshals accompanied Meredith to the Ole Miss campus, where he was housed in a dormitory room reserved for him. The following morning, in the presence of federal authorities, the University effected Meredith's registration. When word of this got out, a riot broke out on campus. Three thousand people, including but not limited to Ole Miss students, attacked the marshals with bricks, bottles, and even homemade bombs. President Kennedy then dispatched 20,000 U.S. Army soldiers to the scene and order was soon restored, but the riot resulted in the deaths of two people and left 60 marshals injured. The nation was shocked by the violence; indeed the nation's conscience was galvanized. After decades of indifference, the attitudes of the white majority, even in the South, were changing.

In August of 1963 James Meredith graduated from the University of Mississippi. Three years later he published *Three Years in Mississippi,* recounting his ordeal at Ole Miss. Shortly after the book was published, Meredith was shot by a sniper during a civil rights march from Memphis, Tennessee to Jackson, Mississippi. He recovered from his wound and was able to rejoin the march three weeks later, accompanied by Dr. Martin Luther King, Jr., and other civil rights leaders. In 1968, Meredith received his law degree from Columbia University. He went on to become a stockbroker, a Republican, and a conservative, and even served for a year on the staff of Senator Jesse Helms, a conservative Republican from North Carolina.

See also Baker Motley, Constance; Civil Rights Movement; Evers, Medgar; National Association for the Advancement of Colored People; U.S. Marshals Service

Bibliography

Doyle, William. 2001. *An American Insurrection: The Battle of Oxford, Mississippi, 1962.* New York: Doubleday.

Meredith, James. 1966. *Three Years in Mississippi.* Bloomington, IN: Indiana University Press.

John M. Scheb II

MERIT SYSTEMS PROTECTION BOARD (MSPB)

Created by Reorganization Plan Number 2 in 1978, the Merit Systems Protection Board (MSPB) is an independent agency responsible for maintaining the integrity of federal merit systems and protecting the rights of federal employees who work within the merit system. The Civil Service Reform Act of 1978 abolished the Civil Service Commission established by the Pendleton Act of 1883 and designated the newly established Merit Systems Protection Board and the Office of Personnel Management as its successors. While the original functions of the Civil Service Commission were transferred to the Office of Personnel Management, the MSPB was established to monitor all federal merit systems and to judge appeals.

The Board is headquartered in Washington D.C. with field offices in major cities. Members of the MSPB include a chairman, a vice-chairman, and one other member. No more than two members may be chosen from the same political party. Each board member is appointed by the president and confirmed by the Senate. The seven-year terms overlapping and are not renewable. Members may only be dismissed by the president for reasons of inefficiency, neglect of duty, or malfeasance in office. The Special Counsel of the Board is also appointed by the president and confirmed by the Senate. This individual is responsible for protecting federal employees from prohibited personnel practices cited in the Civil Service Reform Act. Also, the Special Counsel of the Board prosecutes disciplinary charges before the Board against federal, state, and local officials and employees who violate certain civil service laws and regulations. Thirdly, the Special Counsel may be involved with certain types of whistleblower allegations.

The MSPB hears most federal employee appeals with the exception of cases concerning examination ratings, classification decisions, insurance carrier decisions, and discrimination complaints involving no other issues. The Board also hears and decides cases brought by the Special Counsel concerning alleged, prohibited personnel practices as defined in Title 5, Section 2303 of the United States code. In addition, studies of personnel practices within the Civil Service and other merit systems in the executive branch are conducted by the MSPB. The majority of cases brought before the Board involve federal employee appeals of agency suspensions of more than 14 days, removals, reductions in grade or pay, and furloughs of 30 days or less. The Board also hears appeals regarding performance-based removals or reductions in grade, reduction in work force actions, OPM employment practices and suitability determinations, and demands of restoration or reemployment rights. Complaints of alleged violations of the Uniformed Services Employment and Reemployment Rights Act, the Veterans Employment Opportunities Act, and the Presidential and Executive Office Accountability Act may also be brought before the MSPB.

Since its inception in 1978, the Merit Systems Protection Board has developed a comprehensive body of unified, civil service law that guides agencies, employees, and their respective agents in pursuing and challenging unfavorable personnel actions. Judicial review of decisions made by the Merit Systems Protection Board is usually conducted by the Court of Appeals for the Federal Circuit.

See also Civil Service Reform Act of 1978; Due Process, Procedural; Public Employees, Constitutional Rights of; United States Courts of Appeals

Bibliography

Ingraham, Patricia W., and David H. Rosenbloom. 1992. *The Promise and Paradox of Civil Service Reform.* Pittsburgh: University of Pittsburgh Press.

Merit Systems Protection Board. 1979. *Questions and Answers on the Merit Systems Protection Board.* Washington, DC: Merit Systems Protection Board.

P. Edward French

MEYER V. NEBRASKA (1923)

In 1919, the Nebraska legislature enacted a law prohibiting the teaching of modern foreign languages to children who had not yet completed the eighth grade in school. Meyer, a teacher in a Lutheran school, was convicted of violating the law for teaching in the German language to a 10-year-old child. The state's justification was that the prohibition was necessary to encourage immigrants to learn the English language to promote their social integration. In upholding the statute, the Nebraska Supreme Court noted that the state legislature "had seen the baneful effects of permitting foreigners, who had taken residence in this country, to rear and educate their children in the language of their native land."

In reviewing the case, the United States Supreme Court reversed Meyer's conviction and struck down the statute on which it was based. The Court recognized that citizens have the right to study foreign languages in private schools, state statutes to the contrary notwithstanding. In the Court's view, the statute interfered both with the right of teachers to pursue a theretofore innocent occupation and the right of parents to control the education of their children.

The Supreme Court's decision in *Meyer v. Nebraska* was based on the Due Process Clause of the Fourteenth Amendment, which prohibits states from depriving persons of life, liberty, or property without due process of law. Writing for the Court, Justice James C. McReynolds observed that the "liberty" protected by the Fourteenth Amendment "denotes not merely freedom from bodily restraint but also the right of the individual to contract, to engage in any of the common occupations of life, to acquire useful knowledge, to marry, establish a home and bring up children, to worship God according to the dictates of his own conscience, and generally to enjoy those privileges long recognized at common law as essential to the orderly pursuit of happiness by free men." McReynolds asserted that "this liberty may not be interfered with, under the guise of protecting the public interest, by legislative action which is arbitrary or without reasonable relation to some purpose within the competency of the State to effect." In McReynolds' view, the state lacked a sufficient rational basis for prohibiting the teaching of foreign languages.

Dissenting along with Justice George Sutherland, Justice Oliver Wendell Holmes, Jr., argued that "a teacher might be forbidden to teach many things, and the only criterion of his liberty under the Constitution that I can think of is 'whether, considering the end in view, the statute passes the bounds of reason and assumes the character of a merely arbitrary fiat.' " In Holmes' view, the Nebraska statute was not merely arbitrary; it had a rational basis in the state's legitimate interest in fostering a common language. Arguing for judicial restraint in such matters, Holmes wrote: "I think I appreciate the objection to the law but it appears to me to present a question upon which men reasonably might differ and therefore I am unable to say that the Constitution of the United States prevents the experiment being tried."

Meyer v. Nebraska is rightly regarded as an example of the doctrine of substantive due process. According to this doctrine, the Due Process Clause provides more than merely procedural protections against deprivations of liberty; it prohibits the state from enacting laws that unduly interfere with liberty, broadly defined. *Meyer* is also justly regarded as an important precursor to the constitutional right of privacy recognized in *Roe v. Wade* and other cases involving reproductive rights.

See also Due Process Clauses; Due Process, Substantive; Fourteenth Amendment (1868); Holmes, Oliver Wendell, Jr.; Judicial Activism; Judicial Restraint; Liberty; McReynolds, James C.; Parental Rights; *Pierce v. Society of Sisters* (1925); Privacy, Constitutional Right of; Reproductive Freedom; *Roe v. Wade* (1973).

John M. Scheb II and Otis H. Stephens, Jr.

MILITARY CONSCRIPTION

Military conscription, better known as the draft, is a system of compulsory service in a nation's armed forces. The modern form of military conscription can be traced back to the Roman Empire, when in its latter days the empire utilized conscription to fill its military's ranks fending off the Germanic barbarians. In 1798 France instituted the first modern conscription law, and from 1800 to 1812 some 2,600,000 men were drafted into Napoleon's armies. Great Britain employed "impressment," a system of draft it utilized in the latter 1700s and early 1800s to provide the crews necessary to maintain its large navy. In each of these systems compulsory service pertained only to male citizens. The United States draws its tradition of military conscription from these earlier examples.

During the American Revolution there was a widely held belief that any form of forced military service was contrary to the principles of individual rights and personal freedom. Also the frequent wars in Europe caused Americans to have a deep distrust of professional standing armies. They felt a citizen-militia should make up the backbone of the country's defenses. Even when George Washington proposed a compulsory national militia to fight the British, the idea was quickly rejected by leaders in the various states. In June 1775 the Continental Congress did authorize a multistate army, which remained in place until the war was over. The Continental Army was composed only of paid volunteers, and the entire army was decommissioned on June 2, 1783, leaving only 86 persons to guard various U.S. weapons depositories.

Article I, Section 8, of the United States Constitution, ratified in 1788, gave the Congress authority to "raise and support armies." However, a controversy soon arose as to whether the Constitution actually grants the federal government the authority to require military service of its male citizens. Some argue that the Constitution makes a clear distinction between the individual states' right to maintain militias, and Congress's authority to declare war and raise armies. The argument denies that Congress has any constitutional authority to use forced conscription to raise or maintain an army. Others contend that it is well within Congress's implied powers in light of the "raising and supporting of armies" provision within the Article I. Section 8. The controversy persists today; however, the Supreme Court ruled in *Arver v. United States* (1918) that Congress is within its constitutional limits in passing legislation requiring military service.

The first actual proposal for a national draft came during the War of 1812. James Monroe, then President Madison's Secretary of War, encouraged the Congress to pass legislation creating a system of military conscription. In 1814, with relatively few men voluntarily enlisting in the armed forces, a bill was introduced into the House Committee on Military Affairs to establish a plan whereby eligible men between the ages of 18 and 45 would be on call to serve in the military. The war ended in February 1815 without the bill ever coming out of the House committee.

The Civil War saw the first utilization of a national military draft. During the early stages of the war volunteers rushed to join the armies of the North and the South, but by 1862 the Confederacy had implemented a system of military conscription. The U.S. Congress passed the Enrollment Act of 1863 establishing a military draft in February, and President Lincoln signed the bill into law in March of that year. While the bill was being debated in Congress, Supreme Court Chief Justice Roger B. Taney in a private letter wrote that the conscription measure before the Congress was certainly unconstitutional. The question of the constitutionality of the Enrollment Act never reached the Supreme Court during the war. There was a provision in the act that allowed a draftee to hire a substitute or to pay $300 and avoid service. The provision led to the claim that the war was "a rich mans war, but a poor man's fight." The Enrollment Act met with much dissent all across the north. There were riots protesting the draft in Boston, Albany, New York City, Portsmouth, New Hampshire, Wooster, Ohio, and in other cities and towns. By far the worst of the riots was in New York City. On the morning of July 13, 1863, thousands of poor and working-class people rioted through the streets of New York, burning the draft headquarters, and setting hundreds of other fires. They ransacked the homes of many wealthy and prominent citizens, including the mayor's house. The crowds also unleashed their anger against blacks living in the city, lynching a number of black men. The worst rioting in American history raged for four days and estimates of those killed went as high as 1,200, with millions

of dollars in property damage. The federal government was forced to send six regiments of soldiers from Gettysburg, Pennsylvania to restore order. The last call for United States draftees was on December 18, 1864. Military conscription ended with the conclusion of the war and was not reinstituted until after the United States entered World War I.

The United States entered World War I on April 6, 1917. The following day, the Wilson administration asked Congress to pass legislation authorizing a direct federal draft. The controversy over whether the federal government had the constitutional authority to create and enforce such laws had not been settled during the Civil War, and a fierce debate erupted in the Congress. One of the Senators leading the resistance to a draft, Charles F. Thomas of Colorado, declared:

Opposition to compulsory military service is characteristic of every government fit to be called a democracy.... Democracies abhor the principle of compulsory service. The exercise of which menaces and may destroy their liberties.... We are now told that compulsory military service is democratic. Mr. President, that is a libel and a reproach upon the name of democracy. It is as repugnant to democracy as any despotic principle which can be conceived.

The debate continued for several weeks, with the Congress eventually passing the Selective Service Law and President Wilson signing the act on May 18, 1917. The act authorized a draft of all male citizens between the ages of 18 and 45. It allowed exemptions for ministers, divinity students, certain public officials, and conscientious objectors, who were excused if they were members of a recognized sect that forbade its followers to engage in war. Unlike the Civil War, this act did not allow for substitutions or the paying of fees to avoid service, and all soldiers would have to serve for the duration of the war. This would be the first war in which the vast majority of the American forces were comprised of soldiers that had been drafted rather than had willingly joined. During the Civil War volunteers made up more than 92 percent of U.S. forces, while in World War I, 72 percent of the forces were draftees.

The new military conscription act was immediately challenged in the courts, with several cases reaching the Supreme Court. The Court combined the cases, which became known as the "selective draft law cases." In *Arver v. United States* (1918), the official name for the combined cases, the Supreme Court affirmed the constitutionality of the act, upholding the government's authority to establish a direct federal draft. At the end of World War I the United States ended military conscription, returning to a volunteer army; some 3.5 million male citizens were drafted during the war.

The first peacetime conscription was adopted in 1940 with the Selective Training and Service Act, and because of strong dissent within Congress it was passed for one year only. Many in the Congress saw compulsory selective service as a move on the part of the Roosevelt administration to prepare the United States for involvement in the war raging in Europe. In August of 1941 the act was narrowly extended, with the House voting 203 to 202 in favor of extending the draft. The act stated that all men ages 18 to 45 were eligible, and required all eligible men to register for the draft. As the United States entered World War II, the need to field a large number of troops quickly forced the government to greatly increase the number of men selected for service. More than 10,000,000 men were drafted into the armed forces before the act expired on March 31, 1947.

After a Soviet-backed military coup in Czechoslovakia, the U.S. Congress reinstated military conscription in June of 1948. The draft was continually renewed until the end of the Vietnam War in 1973, when it was allowed to expire. The Vietnam War divided the country, with a large number of citizens, especially the young, opposing it. This made the draft very unpopular and the Nixon administration along with a majority in the Congress advocated a return to an all-volunteer army; the last man inducted entered the Army on June 30, 1973. The Soviet invasion of Afghanistan in 1980 prompted the Carter administration to reactivate the draft registration system. The Congress agreed with President Carter's decision but did not enact one

of his requests. Carter had asked that the compulsory registration include females as well as males. The registration was challenged in the courts by a number of men claiming it violated the Due Process Clause in the Fifth Amendment and was therefore unconstitutional. The Supreme Court in *Rostker v. Goldberg* (1981) ruled that male-only compulsory registration was not a violation of the Due Process Clause. The Court found that because of combat restrictions on women, men and women were not "similarly situated" for the purposes of draft registration. In 1982, the Reagan administration purposed the continuation of compulsory draft registration, which is still in effect as of this writing. From its introduction in World War I to its expiration in 1973, more than 16,000,000 males were inducted into the military through compulsory conscription. Military registration is mandatory for all males between the ages of 18 and 26 years of age. Failure to register can result in not being eligible to receive any government-backed loans, and forfeiture of job opportunities that might be available within the government. Today the attitude of the country still reflects its original convictions that compulsory military conscription is not in keeping with the ideals of constitutional democracy and should be utilized only in time of national emergency.

See also Constitutional Democracy; Due Process Clauses; Fifth Amendment; Gender-Based Discrimination; Lincoln, Abraham; Madison, James; Roosevelt, Franklin D.; Second Amendment; Taney, Roger B.; Third Amendment

Bibliography

Anderson, Martin, ed. 1982. *The Military Draft: Selected Readings on Conscription.* Stanford, CA: Hoover Institution Press.

Carper, Jean. 1967. *Bitter Greetings: The Scandal of the Military Draft.* New York: Grossman Publishers.

Chambers, John Whiteclay, II. 1987. *To Raise an Army: The Draft Comes to Modern America.* New York: The Free Press.

Graham, John Remington. 1971. *A Constitutional History of the Military Draft.* Minneapolis: Ross & Haines.

Leach, Jack Franklin. 1952. *Conscription in the United States: Historical Background.* Rutland, VT: Charles E. Tuttle Publishing Company.

Risley, Ford. 2004. *The Civil War: Primary Documents on Events from 1860 to 1865.* Westport, CT: Greenwood Press.

Michael Haynes

MILITARY SERVICE, CIVIL RIGHTS AND LIBERTIES IN

Historically, few of the civil rights of ordinary citizens were recognized for members of the American military. Soldiers and sailors were bound to serve for the term of their induction, were not free to leave or come and go as they pleased, and were subject to strict rules of discipline and obedience to the orders of superiors. These rules were enforced by a separate system of justice, the court-martial, which was viewed as an arm of the command and in which many of the due process rights accorded in civilian courts were not available. Individual rights, such as privacy and free speech, were forfeited upon enlistment.

This restricted view of the civil rights of service members was altered in the late twentieth century, affected by reforms in military justice and civilian civil rights movements. But induction into the military still represents a legal change in status and materially reduced civil rights.

One must look to many sources for defining the civil rights of service members. Congress has the authority under Article I, Section 8, of the Constitution to make rules for the regulation of the land and naval forces. This authority has been exercised by the passage of the Articles of War (since 1950, the Uniform Code of Military Justice [UCMJ]) that defines offenses punishable by court-martial and governs the practice of military justice.

Congress has also passed numerous statutes relating to the armed forces, although they do not generally regulate with precision the day-to-day conduct of service members. Day-to-day conduct is governed by a plethora of executive directives, military regulations, command orders and standing operating procedures, and individual commander discretion.

The president, as commander-in-chief, has the power to adopt rules and regulations governing the armed forces, which are exercised by executive directives and regulations of the Departments of Defense and the services. Individual rights are rarely addressed, and then usually in terms of procedures and the operation of the chain of command.

Throughout the nineteenth and the first half of the twentieth century, it was generally believed that the Bill of Rights did not apply to service members. The due process and other rights of an accused were replaced by congressional acts governing military justice and by executive and administrative regulations. However, the Court of Military Appeals (since 1994, called the Court of Appeals for the Armed Forces) that was created by the UCMJ for civilian review of courts-martial held that the protections of the Bill of Rights, "except those which are expressly or by necessary implication, inapplicable," are available to service members (*United States v. Jacoby,* 1960).

Which constitutional rights are necessarily inapplicable is the crux issue. Most of the basic constitutional rights in criminal courts apply in military justice proceedings, either through provisions of the UCMJ or the administrative Manual for Courts Martial, or by decisions of the military or civilian courts. This includes the right against self-incrimination, unreasonable searches and seizures, and double jeopardy and the right to counsel, a speedy trial, discovery of evidence, and a public trial and transcript. In some cases court-martial rights exceed the scope of the constitutional right, for example, Article 31 of the UCMJ prohibits even nonverbal self-incrimination, which is not guaranteed by Fifth Amendment precedents.

As extensive as procedural rights are in courts-martial, the structure of the court-martial leaves service members subject to a more disciplinarian and command-dominated court system. The UCMJ left intact command control; individual commanders decide whether to court-martial, appoint counsel and court members, and can approve or disapprove findings and sentences. "Command influence" in attempting to affect the outcome of a court-martial is prohibited, but command control still leaves considerable powers in commanders. There is also no right to a jury of peers; courts are selected from officers, except that enlisted personnel can request that one-third be enlisted persons of higher rank.

Another feature of the UMCJ also compares unfavorably with civilian due process. There are a number of vague offenses, such as the "general article" that prescribes "conduct of a nature to bring discredit upon the armed forces" and "disorders and neglects to the prejudice of good order and discipline," and the article forbidding "conduct unbecoming an officer and a gentlemen." Although the Manual for Courts-Martial provides specifications with advance warning that certain acts are covered, these vague offenses are open-ended.

Civil rights outside of military justice are still considerably restricted. The Vietnam War witnessed attempts to service members to assert First Amendment rights, and the military reacted harshly to criticism of the war.

The Supreme Court upheld the "general article" in the conviction of an army doctor who criticized the war to subordinates (*Parker v. Levy,* 1974). The Court of Military Appeals upheld the court-martial conviction of black marines for criticizing the war as a "white man's war" in a bull session in Vietnam. It found a "clear and present danger" from the speech in this context, but said "the right to believe in a particular faith or philosophy and the right to express one's opinions or to complain about real or imaginary wrongs are legitimate activities in the military community as much as they are in the civilian" (*United States v. Daniels,* 1970). Army regulations on "Guidance on Dissent" (1970) slightly liberalized the right of service members to criticize the war and the military in proper circumstances.

Rights to privacy have been given little attention in the military. However, as living and housing conditions in the volunteer military have improved, service members often have separate rooms with some latitude for decoration, at least when not in a combat zone or basic training. On many military installations, service personnel live off-post with little regulation of their private lives, although they remain subject to the UCMJ even off-post and off-duty.

The "don't ask, don't tell" policy regarding homosexuality has been criticized, but the military remains firmly committed to discharging persons who reveal a homosexual orientation. Since it was instituted in 1994, over 10,000 persons have been discharged for homosexual orientation, including a number with highly specialized assignments such as linguists and nuclear warfare experts. Constitutional challenges that the policy infringes the right to individual attitudes, irrespective of conduct, have not been successful.

Article 125 of the UCMJ criminalizes sodomy, whether heterosexual or homosexual or consensual or not. Serious doubts have been raised as to its constitutionality since the Supreme Court held state sodomy laws unconstitutional in *Lawrence v. Texas* (2003). The Pentagon has proposed that Article 125 be removed, but that sodomy could still be prosecuted under the general article prohibiting "disorders and neglects to the prejudice of good order and discipline."

Equal opportunity rights have been officially respected in the military about as well as in any American institution. Following serious racial conflict during the Vietnam War, the military undertook training of all personnel concerning its nondiscriminatory policies and established informal channels for complaints. The military is highly racially integrated, and although charges of race discrimination still arise, there are extensive military regulations governing race discrimination and race relations.

Integration of women into the armed forces has progressed rapidly in the last couple of decades, but problems remain. A 1992 presidential commission rejected the proposal that women be allowed to serve in all positions, including combat. Women are excluded from direct ground combat positions, although many have served in auxiliary positions in combat zones in the Afghan and Iraqi hostilities.

Complaints that women have been subjected to sexual harassment and sexual assaults have been raised in many commands, including the service academies. Although there have been claims that women fear retaliation for making complaints and that their complaints are often ignored by commanders, there have been a number of military investigations, some of which have resulted in reprimands of superiors. Directives aimed at making women safer in the military environment, including amnesty for making complaints, have been adopted in the service academies and considered for the general forces.

See also Accused, Rights of the; Bill of Rights (American) (1789); Civil Rights Movement; Counsel, Right to; Courts-Martial; Discrimination; Double Jeopardy, Prohibition of; Due Process, Procedural; First Amendment; Fourth Amendment; Gender-Based Discrimination; *Lawrence v. Texas* (2003); Military Conscription; Military Tribunals; Privacy, Constitutional Right of; Public Trial, Right to a; Religious Freedom in Military Service; Self-Incrimination Clause; Sexual Orientation, Discrimination Based on; Speech, Freedom of; Speedy Trial, Right to; Travel, Right to; Uniform Code of Military Justice (UCMJ)

Bibliography

Blaustein, Alfred, Donald Zillman, and Edward Sherman. 1978. *Cases and Materials on Military Law: The Scope of Military Authority in a Democracy.* New York: Matthew Bender.

Fidell, Eugene R., and Dwight H. Sullivan. *Evolving Military Justice.* 2002. Annapolis, MD: Naval Institute Press.

Edward F. Sherman

MILITARY SERVICE, COMPULSORY. *See* Military Conscription

MILITARY TRIBUNALS

The term *military tribunal* has been used for centuries to refer to bodies appointed by commanders, or pursuant to military or executive regulations, to try persons accused of violations of military law. The most prominent are courts-martial, which in the United States were originally governed by the Articles of War (replaced by the Uniform Code of Military Justice, or UCMJ, passed by Congress in 1950).

The term has also been used to refer to *military commissions,* which in the United States were first formally created during the Mexican War to try violations of the laws of war and of proclamations and orders in foreign territory occupied by American forces.

Finally, the term is sometimes used to describe informal "boards of officers" and "courts or boards of inquiry" that have been appointed to advise commanders or officials as to particular charges or matters, but which, unlike courts-martial or military commissions, do not adjudge guilt and punishment but only make recommendations to the commander.

Courts-martial are the principal legal instrument for enforcing the requirements of military law. Historically courts-martial functioned as a system of justice separate from civilian courts. They were considered an arm of the commander to enforce order and discipline; the commander had broad powers to convene a court, appoint the members, oversee the proceedings, and approve or disapprove findings and sentences. At its most basic level, courts-martial meted out "drum head justice," convened in the field with a drum as a desk, to make a quick determination as to charges so the force could quickly get back to the tasks at hand. There was, however, a hierarchy of tribunals ranging from the general court-martial for the most serious offenses and offering greater formality, to the special, and finally the summary, court-martial, which had declining formalities and potential sentences.

Public outcry against the harshness of military justice after World War I led to the amendment of the Articles of War with some broader due process rights. Further denunciations of military justice arose out of World War II. when millions of drafted service members were subjected to harsh discipline and penalties, including a sizable number of death sentences. Congress responded with the passage of the UCMJ in 1950. It left command control of court-martial processes and appointments intact, but accorded broader procedural rights to the accused.

The UCMJ also created a civilian Court of Military Appeals (since 1994 called the Court of Appeals for the Armed Forces), providing for the first time for civilian judicial monitoring and review of courts-martial. The Court is composed of five civilian judges appointed for 15-year terms by the president with the advice and consent of the Senate.

In its early years, the Court interpreted its role as going beyond review of court-martial records; it took a proactive role in interpreting statutes, executive orders, and regulations. and in applying constitutional standards to courts-martial, even striking down procedures prescribed by the administrative Manual for Courts-Martial. The Court hears cases appealed from the intermediate military appellate courts, the Courts of Criminal Appeals in each service, whose judges are primarily military officers. In 1983, Congress authorized direct appeal to the Supreme Court of certain cases decided by the Court of Military Appeals, but the number has been small.

Military justice was again subjected to public scrutiny during the Vietnam War as drafted civilians criticized the high degree of command control and the harsh reaction to dissent within the military. The Military Justice Act of 1968 further "judicialized" courts-martial, creating "military judges" to preside at general courts-martial, and subsequent directives and regulations removed military defense counsel from the supervisory and rating authority of commander convening authority.

A petition for habeas corpus in federal courts has provided consideration of deprivation of constitutional rights that the military manifestly refused to consider. It was especially used to challenge the imposition of court-martial jurisdiction. The Supreme Court ruled in *Burns v. Wilson* (1957) that court-martial jurisdiction could not be asserted over a civilian defendant abroad. In *Solorio v. United States* (1987) it upheld court-martial jurisdiction over service members even off-post and off-duty. A difficult issue that arose in the aftermath of the Afghanistan and Iraq hostilities has been whether jurisdiction can be asserted over civilian contractors and employees who accompany the troops.

The term *military commission* was first used by General Winfield Scott in 1847 to deal with violations of the law of war and of military proclamations in occupied Mexico by American service members and Mexican civilians. Military commissions were needed since the Articles of War only prescribed military offenses (which was changed at a later time and in the UCMJ), leaving civilian offenses to the civil courts, which were not adequately functioning in Mexico. Military commissions were used in over 4,000 trials during the Civil War and some 1,500 during reconstruction, leading to a postwar Supreme Court case (*Ex parte Milligan*, 1866) that held they could not be used to try a civilian in a border state when the civilian courts were functioning.

Military commissions were revived in World War II, to try saboteurs set ashore by a German submarine (*Ex parte Quirin*, 1942) and enemy commanders and combatants after the war (*In re Yamashita*, 1946) for violations of the law of war. Although upheld by the Supreme Court, the commissions have been heavily criticized for their lack of due process and failure to comply even with the standards required of courts-martial.

In November 2001, President George W. Bush resurrected the military commission, authorizing by executive directive their use to try suspected terrorists. Prescribed procedures that lacked certain safeguards provided in courts-martial and civilian courts were criticized. In 2004, the Supreme Court ruled, in cases involving "enemy combatants" captured in the Afghan conflict, that detention must comport with due process, backed by judicial review. Those opinions did not address whether the president can create military commissions or the scope of presidential powers in the context of the conflict against al Qaeda. By late 2005, no commission trials had been held.

See also Accused, Rights of the; Courts-Martial; Due Process, Procedural; Habeas Corpus; Military Service, Civil Rights and Liberties in; *Milligan, Ex parte* (1866); *Quirin, Ex parte* (1942); Terrorism, War on; Uniform Code of Military Justice

Bibliography

Lurie, Jonathan. 2001. *Pursuing Military Justice: The History of the United States Court of Appeals for the Armed Forces, 1951–1980.* 2nd ed. Princeton, NJ: Princeton University Press.

Rant, James, and Jeffrey Blackett, eds. 2003. *Courts Martial, Discipline, and the Criminal Process in the Armed Forces.* 2d ed. New York: Blackstone.

                                        Edward F. Sherman

MILITIA MOVEMENT. *See* Arms, Right to Keep and Bear

MILL, JOHN STUART. *See* Bentham, Jeremy; Liberalism; Libertarianism; Rousseau, Jean-Jacques

MILLER V. CALIFORNIA (1973)

In *Roth v. United States* (1957), the Supreme Court upheld the constitutionality of a federal obscenity statute against a challenge based on the First Amendment. Writing for the Court in *Roth,* Justice William Brennan observed that "implicit in the history of the First Amendment is the rejection of obscenity as utterly without redeeming social importance."

In *Miller v. California* (1973), the Court reaffirmed the central holding of *Roth* that obscenity is beyond the pale of the First Amendment, but it also delineated a new three-part definition of obscenity. Writing for the Court, Chief Justice Warren E. Burger stated that "the basic guidelines for the trier of fact" in obscenity cases are: "(a) whether 'the average person, applying contemporary community standards' would find that the work, taken as a whole, appeals to the prurient interest, ... (b) whether the work depicts or describes, in a patently offensive way, sexual conduct specifically defined by the applicable state law, and (c) whether the work, taken as a whole, lacks serious literary, artistic, political, or scientific value."

In *Miller* the Court specifically rejected the notion traceable to *Roth* and adopted by a plurality of justices in *Memoirs v. Massachusetts* (1966) that, to be obscene, a particular work must be "*utterly* without redeeming social value." In his majority

opinion, Chief Justice Burger claimed that to adopt this test would saddle prosecutors with a "burden virtually impossible to discharge under our criminal standards of proof."

The Court in *Miller* also held that obscenity is to be determined by applying "contemporary community standards" rather than national standards. Conceding that "First Amendment limitations on the powers of the States do not vary from community to community," Chief Justice Burger insisted nevertheless that "our nation is simply too big and too diverse for this Court to reasonably expect that such standards could be articulated for all 50 States in a single formulation, even assuming the prerequisite consensus exists."

In a passionate dissent, Justice William O. Douglas argued that allowing prosecutors to effectively "ban publications that are 'offensive' to some people puts an ominous gloss on freedom of the press." Douglas characterized laws proscribing obscenity as "a regime of censorship, which, if adopted, should be done by constitutional amendment after full debate by the people." Justice William Brennan, joined by Justices Potter Stewart and Thurgood Marshall, also dissented in *Miller*. In Brennan's view, the state law under which Miller was convicted was "unconstitutionally overbroad, and therefore invalid on its face."

The dissenting justices and many commentators interpreted the Court's embrace of "community standards" as a green light for criminal prosecutions in the obscenity field. Yet the following year the Court made clear that this was not the case. In *Jenkins v. Georgia* (1974), the Court reversed the conviction of an Albany, Georgia theater manager who had been prosecuted after showing the movie *Carnal Knowledge*. The Court's opinion made clear that only material showing "patently offensive hard core sexual conduct" could be proscribed under the test delineated in *Miller v. California*. In light of the development of the video industry, digital photography and the Internet, and the resulting ability of individuals to easily disseminate hard-core pornography, including what might be legally defined as obscenity, throughout the world, the continuing relevance of the Supreme Court's obscenity standards as set forth in *Miller* is highly questionable.

See also Brennan, William J., Jr.; Burger, Warren E.; Censorship; Douglas, William O.; First Amendment; Marshall, Thurgood; Obscenity and Pornography; Overbreadth, Doctrine of; Press, Freedom of the; Speech, Freedom of; Stewart, Potter.

> *John M. Scheb II and Otis H. Stephens, Jr.*

MILLIGAN, EX PARTE (1866)

Ex Parte Milligan is the most important Supreme Court decision involving the suspension of the writ of habeas corpus, which William Blackstone in his *Commentaries on the Laws of England* calls "the most celebrated writ in the English law." Habeas corpus is an order that a court issues to an official who is holding another person to deliver that person to the court so that it may determine whether the detention has a legal basis. It is used most often by persons who are held in custody by the criminal justice system, and it can lead to their release. At a minimum, it precludes incarceration for an indefinite time period with no chance for redress. Thus, this writ is a bulwark of a free society.

Article I, section 9, clause 2 of the United States Constitution provides that "the privilege of the writ of habeas corpus shall not be suspended, unless when in cases of rebellion or invasion the public safety may require it." The governor of the Philippines, using the authority of a federal statute, suspended the privilege in 1905, and the governor of Hawaii, acting under another federal statute, suspended it during World War II. The most famous suspension was effected by President Abraham Lincoln during the Civil War. He acted under the authority of a federal statute that authorized suspension, under certain limits, during the war. One limit was that all persons, other than prisoners of war, who were charged with violating a federal law must be released upon the dismissal of the pertinent grand jury. That suspension and that statute led to *Ex Parte Milligan*.

Milligan, a resident of Indiana, belonged to the Sons of Liberty, a secret society that, according to the charges against him, worked to overthrow the United States government. In the time when the writ was suspended, he was brought before a military tribunal and charged with conspiracy, aiding the Confederacy, inciting insurrection, disloyal practices, and violation of the laws of war. The tribunal convicted him and sentenced him to be hanged. In *Ex Parte Milligan* the Supreme Court held that the tribunal's proceedings were not authorized by law, that the suspension of the writ did not apply to Milligan because the grand jury that would have heard his case had been dismissed and that, therefore, he must be set free.

At first glance, this case seems to involve nothing more than statutory interpretation. However, it is important for three reasons. The first is that it specified the effect of a suspension of the writ of habeas corpus. Proper invocation of the constitutional provision does not stop courts from issuing the writ. Rather, it orders custodians of persons who are in custody temporarily to disregard those writs. In other words, a chief executive (in the three instances of suspension a governor or a president suspended the writ, either before or after the relevant legislative body authorized it) may not use the constitutional provision to usurp the authority of courts by nullifying one of their traditional functions. After the Civil War ended and the statutory right to suspend the writ lapsed, it was again available to Milligan to challenge his sentence.

The second reason follows from the first. If courts have inviolate functions, such as issuing writs, and under the doctrine of separation of powers cannot be foiled willy-nilly by other branches of government, they certainly cannot be circumvented entirely. That is, suspending the writ does not force persons into another legal system, such as a military tribunal. That result also follows from other constitutional provisions, such as the right to a jury trial under the Sixth Amendment. The court in this case recognized the centrality of that issue: "the controlling question in the case is this: upon the facts stated and the exhibits filed, had the military commission mentioned in it jurisdiction, legally, to try and sentence him?" The court not only answered that under the relevant statute the commission did not have jurisdiction but also generalized, stating succinctly and clearly that "martial rule can never exist where the courts are open, and in the proper and unobstructed exercise of their jurisdiction." That is, suspending the writ does not authorize military arrests and trials.

The third reason is evident in that statement by the court. That reason is the great force with which the court upheld such fundamental rights as the right to a trial by jury, even during times of national trauma, when the temptation to whittle away at civil rights is most severe. Very early in its opinion the court made clear its position: "the importance of the main question presented by this record cannot be overstated; for it involves the very framework of the government and the fundamental principles of American liberty." The court knew what it was defending and what it was withstanding: "by the protection of the law human rights are secured; withdraw that protection, and they are at the mercy of wicked rulers or the clamor of an excited people." Although it recognized the need for and legitimacy of properly circumscribed martial law, the court also recognized that during a war rights were more likely to be abridged by a military court than by a nonmilitary court.

Ex Parte Milligan is thus a classic civil rights case. In it the court—ironically, while setting free a perpetrator of unseemly deeds—in majestic language enunciated rights that all citizens of this country should treasure.

See also Blackstone, William; Common Law Background of American Civil Rights and Liberties; Grand Jury; Habeas Corpus; Jury, Trial by; Lincoln, Abraham; Military Tribunals; Reconstruction; Sixth Amendment

Bibliography

Rehnquist, William H. 1998. *All the Laws But One: Civil Liberties in Wartime.* New York: Alfred A. Knopf.

Jack Stark

MILTON, JOHN. *See* "Areopagitica"

MIRANDA V. ARIZONA (1966)

In the landmark decision of *Miranda v. Arizona* (1966), the United States Supreme Court promulgated a set of procedural requirements that must be met before the prosecution can introduce into evidence confessions or other statements made by a suspect in response to police interrogation. The broad ruling in *Miranda* actually covered four cases—three coming from state courts and one originating in a federal court. All of these cases centered on the admissibility of statements obtained as a result of police interrogation, and all were characterized either by failure of the police to advise suspects of their constitutional rights or by the absence of a "knowing and intelligent" waiver of those rights. By reviewing state and federal convictions in a single decision, the Supreme Court removed important differences that previously existed between interrogation requirements at these distinct levels of government.

In an elaborate opinion representing the views of five members of the Court, Chief Justice Earl Warren laid down a set of requirements that must be satisfied before police may interrogate a suspect in private. According to Warren, "The prosecution may not use statements, whether exculpatory or inculpatory, stemming from custodial interrogation of the defendant unless it demonstrates the use of safeguards effective to secure the [Fifth Amendment] privilege against self-incrimination."

These safeguards may be briefly stated as follows: "Prior to any questioning, the person must be warned that he has a right to remain silent, that any statement he does make may be used as evidence against him, and that he has a right to the presence of an attorney, either retained or appointed." Warren went on to explain that a suspect may waive these rights but that "a heavy burden rests on the government to demonstrate" that the suspect has done so "knowingly and intelligently." Finally, the suspect may stop the questioning at any time either by asserting the right to remain silent or by requesting the assistance of counsel.

As previously noted, the *Miranda* decision was based on the Fifth Amendment's protection against self-incrimination. Warren maintained that a suspect's statements, made in the absence of warnings, were not the product of free choice. Accordingly, such statements were deemed involuntary and therefore inadmissible.

Warren discussed at length traditional interrogation techniques and the atmosphere of coercion presumed to pervade incommunicado detention. By the 1960s, approved methods of police interrogation no longer included the "third degree" tactics of physical coercion prevalent in the 1920s and 1930s. However, subtler forms of psychological coercion persisted. These included isolation of the suspect from counsel and family members, deprivation of sleep, threats, deception, and intimidation. In a long line of confession cases dating from the mid-1940s and culminating in *Miranda,* the Court attempted to mitigate the coercive effects of these and related forms of police pressure. Drawing from police manuals widely used at the time of *Miranda,* Warren elaborated on the various methods of psychological coercion. He concluded that even when these tactics are not used, "custodial interrogation exacts a heavy toll on individual liberty and trades on the weakness of individuals."

To mitigate the coercive effects of interrogation on a suspect, the Court set forth the "*Miranda* warnings," reasoning that an accused person, duly informed of his or her rights, would be less likely to be coerced than an uniformed person.

Each of the defendants whose convictions were reviewed in *Miranda* was deprived of the knowledge of his rights. All of them, according to the Court, were "thrust into an unfamiliar atmosphere and run through menacing police interrogation procedures ... in none of these cases did the officers undertake to afford appropriate safeguards at the outset of the interrogation to insure that the statements were truly the product of free choice." Miranda, an indigent Mexican defendant with a mental illness, was interrogated in a special interrogation room and not informed either of his right to have counsel present, or his privilege against self-incrimination. The second defendant, Vignera, was questioned twice without being apprised of

his right to have counsel present or his right to remain silent. Westover (the third defendant) was interrogated for a lengthy period, first by police and then by the FBI, without knowingly waiving his right to remain silent or his right to consult with counsel. And Stewart, an indigent black man who had dropped out of school in the sixth grade, was held for five days and interrogated nine separate times before he confessed. He was advised neither of his right to remain silent nor of his right to counsel. "The current practice of incommunicado interrogation is at odds with one of our Nation's most cherished principles—that the individual may not be compelled to incriminate himself. Unless adequate protective devices are employed to dispel the compulsion inherent in custodial surroundings, no statement obtained from the defendant can truly be the product of his free choice." According to the majority opinion, the Fifth Amendment privilege against self-incrimination is as applicable to in-custody interrogation as it is to testifying at trial.

The Court maintained that the requirements it prescribed should not be overly problematic for the government to institute. Indeed, the FBI had been issuing similar warnings for years with continued success, as had investigators in England. The Uniform Code of Military Justice also mandated warnings regarding silence, and the right to have an attorney present had been recognized by military tribunals. Other countries, such as Scotland and India, had entirely banned confessions made only to police. None of these examples resulted in a diminished capacity to enforce the law. The Court did not expect that the *Miranda* requirements would adversely affect efforts to control crime in the United States either.

In response to Warren's majority opinion, Justices Harlan and White filed lengthy dissents. (Justice Clark filed a three-page opinion dissenting in large part, but concurring in one of the four judgments rendered by the Court.) The dissenters argued that the new rule fashioned by the majority was too rigid and would impair criminal investigations by discouraging confessions. Indeed, Justice White said, "I have no desire whatsoever to share the responsibility for any such impact on the present criminal process." He found some pressure on suspects to be appropriate and nonmalicious and felt that the Court had exaggerated current police practices in making its sweeping and negative claims about what happens during interrogation. Justice Harlan maintained that the rule was not properly based on the Fifth Amendment. He insisted that the protection against self-incrimination applied only to trial and not to interrogation. The dissenters contended that the presence of a lawyer during interrogation was an unwarranted extension of the Sixth Amendment right to counsel. They also insisted that none of the foreign jurisdictions mentioned by the Court as exemplars of police interrogation practices went as far as the Court did in *Miranda*. Finally, the dissenters agreed that the traditional case-by-case determination of voluntariness—the Court's due process approach to state confession cases prior to *Miranda*—was preferable to the imposition of uniform interrogation requirements. Miranda represented a new approach to the constitutional problems presented by police interrogation.

Miranda was not well received by either those in law enforcement or by the public. Many feared that its consequences would be detrimental to law enforcement. Time has shown these consequences to be minimal.

In an ironic twist of fate, Miranda, after having served his sentence (because he was still convicted without his confession), was killed in a bar fight. His assailants were arrested and read their *Miranda* rights.

See also Accused, Rights of the; Counsel, Right to; Fifth Amendment; Interrogation and Confessions; *Miranda v. Arizona*, Exceptions to; Self-Incrimination Clause; Uniform Code of Military Justice (UCMJ); Warren, Earl

Bibliography

Grano, Joseph D. 1993. *Confessions, Truth and the Law.* Ann Arbor: University of Michigan Press.

Stephens, Otis H. 1973. *The Supreme Court and Confessions of Guilt.* Knoxville: University of Tennessee Press.

Stuart, Gary L. 2004. *Miranda: The Story of America's Right to Remain Silent.* Tucson: University of Arizona Press.

Sara Benesh

MIRANDA V. ARIZONA, EXCEPTIONS TO

In 1966, the United States Supreme Court decided *Miranda v. Arizona,* the landmark case in which it delineated procedural requirements for the use of a confession. To wit, the suspect in custody must be advised of the right to remain silent; that anything said by the suspect can and will be used by the prosecution as evidence; that the suspect has a right to an attorney; and that if the suspect cannot afford an attorney, one will be provided at the expense of the government. At any time during questioning, the suspect can assert either the right to remain silent or the desire for counsel; in that case questioning must cease. The *Miranda* decision also provides that a suspect may waive these rights and submit to questioning, provided the waiver is "knowing and voluntary." The *Miranda* decision was quite controversial at the time and many called for its overruling. While the Supreme Court has recently reaffirmed the principles in *Miranda* and its constitutional basis (*Dickerson v. United States* [2000]), Courts subsequent to the Warren Court (which decided *Miranda*) have consistently narrowed the decision's application. This entry discusses those cases and considers the health of *Miranda* as a precedent given subsequent exceptions.

The Warren Court, in its decision in *Miranda,* noted the inherent coerciveness of the interrogation atmosphere. Therefore, according to that Court, a confession obtained through custodial interrogation could not stand without informing the accused of his or her rights under the Constitution. This information, they reasoned, would serve to mitigate the power differential between the police and the accused. They did not, however, go so far as to allow the *Miranda* decision to apply retroactively, which would have greatly increased the scope of the decision (*Johnson v. New Jersey* [1966]).

Later Courts, disagreeing with the Warren Court on the *Miranda* decision, allowed for many uses of confessions without full *Miranda* warnings. Additionally, *Miranda* left open the question of what constitutes the two core conditions of the decision: custody and interrogation. The strength of the *Miranda* decision as precedent depends in some ways on how custody and interrogation are defined and those definitions came from Courts subsequent to the Warren Court.

In 1971, the Burger Court decided *Harris v. New York,* in which it ruled that statements obtained without *Miranda* warnings, while inadmissible as evidence at trial, could nonetheless be used to impeach testimony by the accused in his or her defense. In that case, the accused provided an alibi, while under oath, which was contradictory to the statement he had provided police without the benefit of *Miranda* warnings. The Court ruled that that contradiction could be raised at his trial.

In *Michigan v. Tucker* (1974) the Court recognized an exception to *Miranda* that applied to witnesses obtained via information provided in an unwarned statement. In *Tucker,* a rape suspect made a statement to police without the benefit of *Miranda* warnings, in which he argued that he was with a friend at the time of the crime. Police then questioned this friend who denied being with the accused during that timeframe. The Court found that the reliability of the witness's statement had nothing to do with the failure of the police to warn the suspect of his rights, and so that testimony could be used even though the police may never have talked with the witness were it not for the accused's unwarned statements.

The question of whether an assertion of the right to silence invalidates any subsequent interrogations was at issue in *Michigan v. Mosley* (1975). In that case, an accused, after having been advised of his rights under *Miranda,* was interrogated about some robberies. He invoked his right to silence and the officer immediately ceased the interrogation. Several hours later, in a different place, another officer advised him of his *Miranda* rights and began to question him about an unrelated murder. The accused chose this time to talk and made some incriminating statements, which were used against him. The Supreme Court found that this police behavior was acceptable since warnings were given twice, his right to stop the questioning was honored, and there was a significant time lapse between the two interrogation sessions.

New York v. Quarles (1984) provides a public safety exception to the *Miranda* requirements. In that case, police were in pursuit of a suspect in a grocery store and, when they apprehended him, saw that he was wearing an empty holster. The police immediately asked him where the gun was and the suspect revealed where he had dropped it. That he revealed the location of the gun before being warned of his right to remain silent and to have an attorney is not a problem to the Court; rather, the police were justified in their actions because they were attempting to protect the safety of those in the store.

Also in 1984, the Burger Court created an "inevitable discovery" exception (in *Nix v. Williams*), which holds that, if evidence obtained illegally would have nonetheless been discovered even without the constitutional violation, provided the prosecutor presents a preponderance of evidence to support that claim, it is admissible. In the case, Williams (the accused) was in a police car traveling to meet with his attorney in another town when one of the officers discussed how important it would be to find the body of the victim before an ensuing snow storm so that her family, from whom the young girl had been taken on Christmas Eve, could have a Christian burial. The accused directed police to the body and was later convicted of the young girl's murder. He won the first appeal of his conviction, arguing that his statements were impermissibly obtained without the presence of his attorney (*Brewer v. Williams,* 1977) and was retried. In his second Supreme Court appeal, he argued that because his statement leading to the body was deemed to be inadmissible by the Supreme Court in *Brewer,* the body itself and the condition thereof should also be inadmissible as evidence against him. However, because search teams were within two and one-half miles of the girl's body and the location of the body was within the area to be searched, the state claimed that the body would have been found shortly after the accused brought them to it, in the same condition as it was when the accused brought them to it, even without his help. The Court agreed.

In 1985, the Court decided that, while statements made before the advice as to rights is given are inadmissible, statements made later after said rights are read are admissible. In *Oregon v. Elstad,* the suspect made an incriminating statement before being read his rights and was later given his warnings at the police station, at which time he confessed to a burglary. The first unwarned statement, according to the Court, does not taint the later statement made with full knowledge of his rights.

When a defendant knowingly waives his or her rights, statements obtained may be used against him or her in court as well. In *Moran v. Burbine* (1986) the Court held that, even though the defendant's attorney had contacted police wishing to speak to his client, the defendant's waiver of his right to remain silent and to have an attorney present during interrogation was knowing. His statement, therefore, could be used against him.

In *New York v. Harris* (1990) a confession obtained after an illegal search was at issue. The police entered the home of a murder suspect without a search warrant or permission from anyone in the house. The suspect was arrested and taken to the station where he was advised of his *Miranda* rights and made a confession. The Court found that the fact that the police illegally entered his home did not taint the subsequent confession since *Miranda* warnings were given.

Also in 1990, the Court made clear that *Miranda* did not apply to standard booking proceedings. In *Pennsylvania v. Muniz,* the accused was arrested for drunk driving and his booking was videotaped. Because he was not given his *Miranda* warnings until after the booking, he argued that the tape of his booking, which demonstrated his intoxicated state, was inadmissible against him. The Court disagreed, arguing that even though his speech was slurred and that was evident on the tape, the questions posed as

part of a routine booking do not constitute an interrogation (except for a question about the date of the accused's sixth birthday). The videotaped booking, therefore, was admissible under *Miranda* and his conviction for drunk driving was upheld.

The harmless error rule was at issue in *Arizona v. Fulminante* (1991). In that case, an officer posing as an inmate offered protection from other inmates to the accused, in exchange for an admission about a murder. The Court held that this admission could not be entered into evidence against the accused since it was coerced by the threat of physical attack by the other inmates. In a badly fractured decision, Chief Justice Rehnquist spoke for five members of the Court in holding that "harmless error analysis" was appropriate in this case. This technical point, however, did not answer the ultimate question of whether the conviction should be reversed. Justice White, writing for a different five-member majority (only Justice Scalia joined both groups), provided the answer: "Because a majority of the Court has determined that Fulminante's confession to Anthony Sarivola was coerced and because a majority has determined that admitting this confession was not harmless beyond a reasonable doubt, we agree with the Arizona Supreme Court's conclusion that Fulminante is entitled to a new trial at which the confession is not admitted."

The question of what constitutes interrogation, mentioned above, also formed the basis of some exceptions to *Miranda* warnings. When a suspect does not know that the person to whom he is talking, for example, is a police officer, that person does not suffer from the coerciveness inherent in police questioning and so does not need to be apprised of his Miranda rights. In *Illinois v. Perkins* (1990) an undercover police agent, acting as a fellow inmate, obtained incriminating statements about a crime for which the accused was not incarcerated. The Court ruled that said statements could be used against him. Additionally, in *Rhode Island v. Innis* (1980), the Court allowed the statement of an accused who was riding in the back of the police car while the police were discussing how sad it would be were a child to find the murder weapon. The suspect spoke up and told them where it was and the police found the weapon and used his admission against him. The Court found that this was appropriate even under *Miranda* because he was not being interrogated. The police officers did not perceive their conversation to be reasonably likely to elicit a response from the accused (cf., *Brewer v. Williams* [1977] where the Court ruled that they did perceive their conversation likely to elicit response).

Finally, in a recent decision, the Court ruled that a gun obtained via an unwarned but voluntary admission could be used against the accused and was not the fruit of the illegally obtained confession (*U.S. v. Patane* [2004]). The plurality reasoned that while the accused's confession could not be used against him, the physical evidence obtained there from does not violate the protections afforded by the Fifth Amendment's protection against self-incrimination. That this decision was made the same day the Court invalidated a confession for lack of *Miranda* warnings (*Missouri v. Seibert,* 2004) makes it all the more peculiar (although in the latter case, the police admitted to intentionally avoiding the warnings in order to obtain a confession). Overall though, as noted by the Court in *Dickerson, Miranda* remains good law. Exceptions to it, however, abound and may indeed continue to accumulate.

Bibliography

Bateman, Connor G. 2002. "*Dickerson v. United States: Miranda* is Deemed a Constitutional Rule, but Does It Really Matter?" *Arkansas Law Review* 55: 1277.

Dripps, Donald A. 2000. "Is Miranda Caselaw Really Inconsistent? A Proposed Fifth Amendment Synthesis." *Constitutional Commentary* 17: 19.

Kamisar, Yale. 1980. *Police Interrogation and Confessions: Essays in Law and Policy.* Ann Arbor: University of Michigan Press.

Klein, Susan R. 2001. "Miranda's Exceptions in a Post-Dickerson World." *Journal of Law & Criminology* 92: 567.

Stuart, Gary L. 2004. *Miranda: The Story of America's Right to Remain Silent.* Tucson: The University of Arizona Press.

White, Welsh S. 2001. *Miranda's Waning Protections: Police Interrogation Practices After Dickerson.* Ann Arbor: University of Michigan Press.

Sara Benesh

MISCEGENATION LAWS. *See* Interracial Marriage

MISSOURI COMPROMISE. *See* Abolitionist Movement; Dred Scott Case

MOMENT OF SILENCE LAWS

Moment of silence laws developed as a response to the Supreme Court's decisions in *Engel v. Vitale* (1962) and *Abington School District v. Schempp* (1963), where government-written prayers and state-sponsored Bible readings in public schools were struck down as violating the Establishment Clause of the First Amendment. Seeking to avoid compliance with these decisions and to promote prayer in public schools, 25 states enacted "moment of silence" laws either permitting or mandating teachers to observe a moment of silence prior to the high court's consideration of the constitutionality of such enactments in *Wallace v. Jaffree* (1985).

Generally, the state statutes enacted prior to *Jaffree* fell into two categories: those that permitted or required a moment of silence at the beginning of the school day for silent meditation and prayer and those that simply set aside a moment for silent meditation or contemplation without a prayer option. Lower federal courts were divided on the validity of laws containing the prayer option. In *Gaines v. Anderson* (1976), for example, a federal district court in Massachusetts upheld a state law that mandated a moment of silence for "meditation or prayer," finding that it was consistent with the test established by the Supreme Court in *Lemon v. Kurtzman* (1971) to resolve Establishment Clause disputes. According to the *Lemon* test, a statute must have a valid secular legislative purpose, a primary effect that neither advances nor inhibits religion, and avoidance of "excessive entanglement" with religion to pass constitutional muster.

However, most lower courts came to opposite conclusions prior to using the same *Lemon* test. In

Beck v. McElrath (1982), for example, a Tennessee law that mandated a moment of silence, not to exceed one minute, for "meditation or prayer or personal beliefs" was held unconstitutional by a federal court in that state. Likewise struck down were a New Mexico law that permitted and a West Virginia law that required a moment of silence for "contemplation, meditation or prayer" (see *Duffy v. Las Cruces Public Schools,* 1983; *Walter v. West Virginia Board of Education,* 1985). Finally, in *May v. Cooperman* (1983) a federal district court struck down a New Jersey statute, which required a daily moment of silence for "contemplation or introspection." Although it lacked a specifically religious option, the court found that the legislative history indicated that the real purpose of lawmakers was to return prayer to the public schools.

Given the widespread criticism, noncompliance, and proposals to reverse the Supreme Court's school prayer decisions, perhaps it is not surprising that the Supreme Court waited until 1985 before deciding whether silent moment laws violated the Establishment Clause. In *Wallace v. Jaffree,* a six-justice majority decided that an Alabama law authorizing public schools to set aside a one-minute period of silence for "meditation or voluntary prayer" was unconstitutional. Writing for the Court, Justice John Paul Stevens held that this law violated the first two prongs of the *Lemon* test. The real purpose of this enactment, explained Stevens, was not secular; rather, it was to return prayer to the state's public schools. Moreover, the primary effect was to advance religion since prayer was declared a favored practice.

However, *Jaffree* did not necessarily invalidate all moment of silence laws. In *dicta,* the Court noted that another Alabama law, one that only mentioned meditation, already protected every student's right under the First Amendment to engage in voluntary silent prayer during an appropriate moment in the school day. In a concurring opinion Justice Sandra Day O'Connor went even further, suggesting that even a "silent moment with prayer" law might pass constitutional muster if it could be demonstrated in the text, legislative history, and implementation

that there was no intended state "endorsement" of prayer in public schools.

Although the Supreme Court has not addressed the issue since *Jaffree,* 29 states either permit or require a moment of silence at the beginning of the school day. While some statutes continue to refer to a prayer option, the majority enacted since 1998 seek to avoid a finding of unconstitutionality by avoiding any mention of prayer in either the legislative history or the text of the law. Removing the prayer option, however, has led to contradictory results in the U.S. courts of appeal. In *Bown v. Gwinnet County School Board* (1997), for example, the Eleventh U.S. Circuit Court of Appeals upheld a Georgia law that specifically stated that its silent moment was intended to allow students to collect their thoughts at the start of the school day and not be conducted as a "religious service." Yet, it also stated that student-initiated voluntary prayers were permissible at school-related events. An opposite conclusion was reached in *May v. Cooperman* (1985), when the Third U.S. Circuit Court of Appeals, using all three prongs of the *Lemon* test, found that the secular purposes identified by the legislature were merely a "pretext" for returning prayer to the state's public school classrooms.

Other states have been bolder, continuing the pre-*Jaffree* trend of specifically including a prayer option and with the same contradictory results. In *Brown v. Gilmore* (2001), for example, the Fourth U.S. Circuit upheld a Virginia statute allowing a moment for meditation, prayer, or any other silent activity. Acknowledging that the legislature, by joint resolution, had declared its opposition to the Supreme Court's decision in *Engel,* the Fourth U.S. Circuit said it was permissible for there to be both a secular and a religious purpose to pass muster under the Establishment Clause. This was especially true when a statute sought to promote the values of the free exercise of religion by students. However, a different conclusion was drawn regarding a valid secular purpose when, in *Doe v. School Board* (2001), the Fifth U.S. Circuit Court of Appeals struck down a Louisiana statute that had been amended twice to allow prayer, including vocal prayer, as part of its silent moment legislation.

Proponents of allowing voluntary prayer in public schools argue that the addition of more accommodationist justices on the Supreme Court, modifications of the *Lemon* test in *Agostini v. Felton* (1997) and later Establishment Clause decisions, the ambiguities of *Jaffree,* and a changing political environment might result in a more permissive outcome should the high court revisit the constitutionality of silent moment laws. Others, favoring a stricter separation between church and state, note that any change is unlikely since the Supreme Court continues to consistently oppose prayer in public schools. This is evident in its decisions both in *Lee v. Weisman* (1992), the graduation prayer case, and *Santa Fe Independent School District v. Doe* (2000), the student-initiated prayers at high school football game case. In both cases, the justices remain concerned about the dangers caused by state promotion and endorsement of religion and the problem of coercion of public school children to conform to dominant religious ideas through student peer pressure.

See also Establishment Clause; First Amendment; Free Exercise Clause; O'Connor, Sandra Day; Religion, Freedom of; School Prayer Decisions; Separation of Church and State; Stevens, John Paul

Bibliography

Alley, Robert S. 1988. *The Supreme Court on Church and State.* New York: Oxford University Press, 1988.

Grunes, Rodney A. 1986. "Prayer in the Public Schools: Getting Around the Supreme Court." *Politics and Policy* 6: 17.

Kaminer, Debbie. 2002. "Bringing Organized Prayer in Through the Back Door." *Stanford Law & Policy Review* 13: 267.

Walsh, Elizabeth Anne. 2004. "Note: Shh! State Legislators Bite Your Tongues: Semantics Dictate the Constitutionality of Public School 'Moment of Silence' Statutes." *The Catholic Lawyer* 43: 225.

Witte, John Jr. 2005. *Religion and the American Constitutional Experiment.* 2nd ed. Boulder, CO: Westview Press.

Rodney Grunes

MONTGOMERY BUS BOYCOTT. *See* Boycotts; Civil Rights Movement; King, Martin Luther, Jr.; Parks, Rosa

MORAL INDIVIDUALISM. *See* Individualism

MORMON CHURCH. *See* Church of Jesus Christ of Latter-day Saints (LDS Church)

MOTION PICTURE ASSOCIATION OF AMERICA (MPAA)

The Motion Picture Association of America is an outgrowth of a movie industry trade association started in 1922 when Hollywood faced legal, political, and social challenges. Two 1915 developments increased pressure for changes. D.W. Griffith released *The Clansman,* later retitled *The Birth of a Nation,* to acclaim for its technological advancements but to widespread criticism and violent protests for its white supremacist viewpoint toward African Americans. That same year in *Mutual Film Corp. v. Industrial Commission of Ohio* the U.S. Supreme Court denied First Amendment protection to motion pictures, characterizing the industry as pure entertainment, a business distinct from the press. In addition, Hollywood sex scandals and offensive film content—some based on award-winning novels—provoked indignation and calls for censorship among many Americans and organized groups. Industry leaders worried also that the government might bring antitrust actions against the vertically organized studios, which monopolized production, distribution, and exhibition.

Hollywood began an aggressive public relations campaign, hiring former U.S. Postmaster General Will H. Hays to direct the new Motion Picture Producers and Distributors of America, Inc. (MPPDA), build the industry's image, and appease the most vocal critics by working closely with them. In 1930 the organization sanctioned the Motion Picture Production Code, written by a Catholic priest. The self-imposed and voluntary code, setting forth standards of "good taste" and laying out specific content regulations, became effective in 1934 and continued for more than 30 years. Referred to as the

Hays Code, it said little about violence, but specifically prohibited sexual content, such as passionate scenes not essential to the plot, excessive and lustful kissing, lustful embracing, suggestive postures and gestures, seduction or rape, miscegenation, and venereal diseases. Unless used in a reverent manner, words like God, Lord, Jesus, and Christ were to be avoided, and profane or vulgar expressions could not be used in any circumstances, the code mandated. Evil could never triumph over good in films. Enforcement came by withholding the Production Code Seal, and thus distribution, from films that fell short of the morality standards. Vertical integration of the studios mandated compliance.

Finally, in 1966 the code was relaxed as social mores had changed and the Supreme Court had extended First Amendment protection to film and refined the definition of obscenity. Starting in 1968, with Jack Valenti as MPAA executive director, a rating system was created to categorize films according to suitability for children. The original four categories were as follows: G (general audiences; all ages admitted); PG (All ages admitted but parental guidance suggested); R (Restricted; under 17 admitted only if accompanied by parent or adult guardian); X (No one under 17 admitted). Eventually, two other categories were added: PG-13 (Parental guidance suggested; Some material may be inappropriate for children under the age of 13) and NC-17 (No children under 17). Producers and distributors do not have to submit their films for rating. The rating system has its own critics, including some parents and religious organizations, plus those who say economic incentives to win the most inclusive rating possible stifles artistic creativity.

In the mid-1940s the MPPDA changed its name to the Motion Picture Association of America. According to its Web site, MPAA and its international counterpart, the Motion Picture Association (MPA), "serve as the voice and advocate of the American motion picture, home video and television industries, domestically through the MPAA and internationally through the MPA. Today, these associations represent not only the world of theatrical film, but serve as leader and advocate for major producers and distributors of entertainment programming for television, cable, home video and future delivery systems not yet imagined."

MPAA operates offices in Los Angeles and Washington, D.C., and among its board of directors are the chairmen and presidents of the seven major producers and distributors of motion picture and television programs in the United States. In recent years, unauthorized copying of movies facilitated by new technology—first video recording of movies from television broadcasts and then peer-to-peer file sharing via the Internet—has dominated the legal landscape for MPAA, as it seeks to protect copyrights and explores alternative distribution methods.

See also First Amendment; Internet, Free speech on; Obscenity and Pornography; Prior Restraint, Doctrine of

Bibliography

Katz, Ephraim (revised by Fred Klein and Ronald Dean Nolen). 2001. *The Film Encyclopedia.* 4th ed. New York: HarperResource.

Maltby, Richard. 1992. "To Prevent the Prevalent Type of Book: Censorship and Adaptation in Hollywood, 1924–1934." *American Quarterly* (December): 544–83.

Dorothy Bowles

MOTT, LUCRETIA. *See* Seneca Falls Declaration (1848)

MPAA. *See* Motion Picture Association of America

MSPB. *See* Merit Systems Protection Board

N

NAACP. *See* National Association for the Advancement of Colored People

NAACP V. ALABAMA (1958)

In the middle of the twentieth century, advocates of civil rights grew more determined and forceful and began taking their fight to the courts. One of the more important cases decided in that period is *N.A.A.C.P. v. Alabama* (1958). It merits close analysis because of its groundbreaking precedential value and its effect on the Civil Rights Movement.

By 1958, the Alabama NAACP had helped African Americans who sought admittance to the University of Alabama and had supported a boycott of Montgomery's bus line. The state of Alabama countered the NAACP's growing influence by demanding that the organization comply with a state law requiring the registration of non-Alabama corporations. Specifically, the statute required that a corporation must file its charter and designate a place of business and an agent to receive court documents. Pursuant to this law, an Alabama court issued a broad order for the NAACP to make extremely revealing disclosures about its operations in the state. The NAACP substantially complied with the state's orders, but it refused to disclose its membership list and sought an injunction to prevent the state from obtaining that information. The NAACP's plea for injunctive relief eventually went before the U.S. Supreme Court.

The primary constitutional argument advanced by the organization's attorneys (one of whom was future Supreme Court Justice Thurgood Marshall) was that the state's demands on the organization interfered with the liberty interest protected by the Due Process Clause of the Fourteenth Amendment. In his opinion for the Court, Justice John Marshall Harlan (the younger) went well beyond an inquiry into that issue. First, he agreed with the NAACP that a forced disclosure of its membership lists would "abridge the rights of its rank-and-file members to engage in lawful association." That abridgment, he added, was a diminution of liberty. Moreover, he noted the connection between association and advocacy and, in particular, between those freedoms and the freedom of speech. He declared that there is an implied freedom of association in the Constitution and analogized that freedom to the First Amendment freedoms of speech, of the press, and of assembly. At one point he referred to "these indispensable liberties, whether of speech, press, or association" as if all three were of equal constitutional weight.

A few of the Court's arguments are open to question. Some critics object to the Court's conflation of assembly, association, and advocacy and the way it grounded its arguments partly on freedom of speech and freedom of the press cases. At one point, the Court made reference to "a requirement that adherents of particular religious faiths or political parties wear identifying arm-bands," facts that were not at issue in the NAACP's case. That reference tends to inflame passions. The court also used mere dicta from a concurring opinion as a precedent. The Court had trouble reconciling this decision with an earlier case in which it upheld a statute requiring the Ku Klux Klan to provide certain information, including its membership lists, to governmental officials. The Court managed to differentiate the two cases by contrasting the peaceful methods of the NAACP with the violent, dangerous tactics of the KKK.

Although the Court's legal reasoning is somewhat flawed in places, certain facts of the case make its holding compelling. While the lower court's order for the production of the membership lists does not directly abridge the right of association, it does so indirectly. If publicly identified, members could have been abused and dissuaded from participating in the organization by anti-civil-rights individuals and groups. In fact, the court cited loss of employment and threats of physical harm as examples of the intimidation that some known members of the NAACP had suffered. In light of this danger, the court held that the right of association includes a right of privacy, a right to shield one's membership from public exposure.

Second, the state had argued that it had a compelling interest in ensuring the compliance of foreign corporations with Alabama law—an interest that overrode the members' privacy concerns. However, Justice Harlan stated that the organization had openly verified its operation in the state and had complied with the lower court's disclosure requirements except for producing its membership list. Hence, there was no compelling state interest in conflict with the members' privacy interest.

In addition to its value to NAACP members in Alabama, the decision in this case laid the foundations for future groundbreaking developments in civil rights and liberties law. The most important effect of *N.A.A.C.P. v. Alabama* was the establishment of a First Amendment right of association, a right that is incorporated as one of the liberty interests protected by the Due Process Clause of the Fourteenth Amendment. More specifically, this case ensured that organizations could preserve the privacy of their members by refusing to name them. In the context of the Civil Rights Movement, this case made it easier for groups to oppose powerful interests and harder to harass and intimidate people with unpopular views. This freedom of association in turn furthered the cause of civil rights.

See also Association, Freedom of; Civil Rights Movement; First Amendment; Fourteenth Amendment (1868); Harlan, John Marshall, II; Ku Klux Klan; Marshall, Thurgood; National Association for the Advancement of Colored People (NAACP); Speech, Freedom of

Jack Stark

NARAL. *See* National Abortion Rights Action League

NATIONAL ABORTION RIGHTS ACTION LEAGUE (NARAL)

The National Abortion Rights Action League (NARAL) was founded in 1969 by Dr. Bernard Nathanson with cooperation from Lawrence Lader and Betty Friedan. Dr. Nathanson, an obstetrician and gynecologist by training, was disturbed by the effects of "back-alley" abortions on the health of women he treated, and founded the organization as a grassroots lobbying effort to legalize abortion nationwide; although he would later change his mind and adopt a pro-life view on the issue. The organization was originally named the National Association for the Repeal of Abortion Laws during a time when abortion was illegal in most states. The group changed its name after the *Roe v. Wade* decision in 1973 to the National Abortion and Reproductive Rights Action League; later changing that name to its present form, NARAL ProChoice America.

NARAL actually consists of three organizations: NARAL Pro-Choice America, Inc., and the NARAL Pro-Choice America Foundation are not-for-profit corporations devoted to lobbying, public education, and grassroots organizing. NARAL Pro-Choice America PAC is a political action committee that supports pro-choice candidates. NARAL's Web site is located at www.naral.org.

NARAL has opposed a number of state and federal laws and rules that have, in the years since *Roe v. Wade* (1973), restricted access to abortion for some groups of women. NARAL has also opposed laws that prohibit Medicaid recipients from receiving funding for abortions, require that pregnant minors receive parental consent before receiving an abortion, and outlaw abortions after a certain point in gestation. NARAL promotes policies that it believes would reduce the need for abortions, such as better access to contraception, health care, and sex education.

Above all, NARAL is concerned that political changes could lead to the overturning of *Roe v. Wade;* thus the organization is active in supporting pro-choice candidates, monitoring the finances of pro-life candidates, and voicing opinions on presidential appointees, especially those to federal judgeships. In 1987, the organization played a prominent role in the defeat of Robert Bork's nomination to the U.S. Supreme Court.

See also Abortion, Public Funding of; Abortion, Right to; Bork, Robert H.; Feminist Movement; Interest Groups; Pro-Choice Position on Abortion; *Roe v. Wade* (1973)

Bibliography

Jost, Kenneth. 2003. "Abortion Debates." Retrieved October 29, 2005, from CQ Researcher Database. http://www.cq.com/.

Staggenborg, Suzanne. 1994. *The Pro-Choice Movement: Organization and Activism in the Abortion Conflict.* New York: Oxford University Press.

Kara E. Stooksbury

NATIONAL ASSOCIATION FOR THE ADVANCEMENT OF COLORED PEOPLE (NAACP)

The National Association for the Advancement of Colored People (NAACP) is a nonprofit organization dedicated to using democratic processes to enact and enforce civil rights laws in the United States and throughout the world. This approach has led some critics to view the NAACP as a passive organization. Yet, as the oldest and largest civil rights organization in the United States, the NAACP has made a lasting impact on civil rights policy.

The brainchild of William English Walling, the NAACP was founded on February 12, 1909 (President Abraham Lincoln's 100th birthday) following the 1908 lynching of two African Americans in Springfield, Illinois (Kellogg 1973). Early members such as Ida Wells-Barnett, W.E.B. DuBois, Dr. Henry Moscowitz, Mary White Ovington, Oswald Garrison Villiard, Rev. Francis J. Grimke, and Rabbi Emil G. Hirsch urged political action to remedy the injustices committed against persons of African descent.

Among the first actions of the organization was "The Call" for a conference to address issues such as electoral disfranchisement, the Jim Crow laws, inadequate educational opportunities, and anti-black violence. The call itself was signed by over 60 prominent blacks and whites, approximately a third of whom were women.

W.E.B. Du Bois was among those who signed "The Call." As editor of the NAACP's journal *The Crisis* from its founding in 1910 until 1934, Du Bois broadened the focus of the organization's stance on race relations (Kellogg 1973). Meanwhile, the organization increased its membership tenfold between 1916 and 1920 under James Weldon Johnson, the organization's first black Executive Secretary. Johnson's focus on lobbying and litigation efforts against disenfranchisement, peonage (involuntary servitude to pay off debt), U.S. actions in Haiti, and lynching are believed to be responsible for turning the organization into a powerful political player.

The NAACP found its greatest successes under the auspices of its legal department (created in 1935) and Legal Defense and Educational Fund (founded in 1940). Under leaders such as Charles Hamilton Houston and Thurgood Marshall, the NAACP won significant legal victories, including *Brown v. Board of Education* (1954) and many lesser known judicial decisions enhancing the rights of minorities. However, not all of the NAACP's successes involved the judicial process. In 1941, the NAACP's Washington Bureau was created to lobby the legislative and executive branches. Victories resulting from the bureau's work included an executive order to ban discrimination in the federal government, the passage of the Civil Rights Act of 1964, the Voting Rights Act of 1965, and the Fair Housing Act of 1968.

Delays in enforcing these new laws resulted in organizations such as the Southern Christian Leadership Conference and Student Non-Violent Coordinating Committee criticizing the NAACP as too passive. Civil rights leaders, including Rev. Martin Luther King, Jr., became critical of the NAACP's strategy and favored instead direct action and mass mobilization to achieve change. Still, it is the insider strategy of the NAACP that has ensured that civil rights endure, backed by law, into current times, despite the decline of public interest in the issue.

In addition to its efforts in the United States, the NAACP also continues to maintain a commitment to civil rights throughout the world. Most of its attention to matters abroad has involved governments run by blacks, decolonization, and U.S. relations with African nations. It also encompasses issues of prejudice in countries such as China, Indonesia, and India. The NAACP has even supported the plight of Catholics in Northern Ireland and Israel while simultaneously supporting Palestinian self-determination (Miller 2002).

Some commentators, such as Robert C. Smith (2002), believe the influence of the NAACP has waned in recent years. They believe Republican control of Congress, a more conservative federal judiciary, a shift away from overt to more covert forms of racism, and the limited resources of the NAACP have all hampered the effectiveness of its "insider" strategy. However, even these scholars concede that the NACCP continues to impact policy. Smith, for instance, notes that while efforts in the late 1980s to block judicial nominees were largely unsuccessful, they did lead to the selection of more moderate and lesser known nominees (Smith 2002).

Governed by a 64-member board of directors and possessing a half-million members in 2005, the NAACP has worked within the political process to become a formidable advocate of civil rights in the United States and abroad. With a history of legal victories and leaders such as Daisy Bates, Medgar Evers, Benjamin Hooks, Thurgood Marshall, Rosa Parks, Jackie Robinson, Joel Spingarn, Arthur Spingarn, Walter White, Roy Wilkins, Margaret Bush Wilson, and Myrlie Evers-Williams, even its critics cannot deny the impact the organization has had on public policy.

See also *Brown* v. *Board of Education* (1954; 1955); Civil Rights Act of 1964; Civil Rights Movement; Evers, Medgar; Fair Housing Act (1968); Interest Groups; Jim Crow Laws; King, Dr. Martin Luther, Jr.; Marshall, Thurgood; Parks, Rosa; Southern Christian Leadership Conference; Student Nonviolent Coordinating Committee; Voting Rights Act of 1965

Bibliography

Kellogg, Charles Flint. 1973. *NAACP: A History of the National Association for the Advancement of Colored People.* Vol. 1. Baltimore: John Hopkins University Press.

Miller, Jake C. 2002. "The NAACP and Global Human Rights." *Western Journal of Black Studies* 26 (Spring): 22–32.

Smith, Robert C. 2002. "The NAACP in the Twenty-first Century." In *Black Political Organizations*, ed. Ollie A. Johnson III and Karin L. Stanford, 28–39. New Brunswick, NJ: Rutgers University Press.

Jennifer R. Woodward

NATIONAL ASSOCIATION FOR THE DEAF. *See* Disability Rights Organizations

NATIONAL COUNCIL ON INDEPENDENT LIVING. *See* Disability Rights Organizations

NATIONAL FEDERATION OF THE BLIND. *See* Disability Rights Organizations

NATIONAL LABOR RELATIONS ACT. *See* Labor, Rights Pertaining to; The New Deal

NATIONAL ORGANIZATION FOR WOMEN (NOW)

The National Organization for Women (NOW) was established by attendees of the Third National Conference of the Commission on the Status of Women, June 28–30, 1966. Among NOW's 28 founders was Betty Friedan, author of *The Feminine Mystique* (1963). The organization was founded on the philosophy of "tak[ing] action to bring women into full participation in the mainstream of American society now, exercising all privileges and responsibilities thereof in truly equal partnership with men" (NOW 1966 Statement of Purpose, www.now.org/history/purpos66.htm, April 27, 2006).

Today, NOW consists of three major arms: NOW, Incorporated; the NOW Foundation; and the NOW Political Action Committee (NOW/PAC). NOW, Incorporated, is a national membership organization dedicated to grassroots political action on behalf of women's rights. As a nonprofit corporation, it receives all its operating funds from private donations and membership dues. NOW, Inc. is the largest feminist organization in the United States. The organization was founded June 30, 1966, in Washington, DC, where it maintains its national headquarters.

NOW has 500,000 contributing members and 550 chapters in all 50 states and the District of Columbia. NOW state and chapter organizations are subunits of NOW and serve as the building blocks of NOW. The NOW Foundation, the education and legal arm of NOW, conducts policy and advocacy work on an international level. Finally, the electoral politics arm of NOW consists of NOW/PAC and NOW Equality PAC (NEP). Although NOW/PAC endorses and supports feminist candidates for federal office, NOW/PAC is nonpartisan and will support anyone, male or female, with a feminist agenda. Pursuant to Federal Election Commission (FEC) rules, only NOW members may contribute to NOW/PAC. At the local level, NEP supports the election of feminist candidates for state and local offices around the country such as governor, state legislature, or city council. Anyone may contribute to NEP. Many individual NOW chapters also form their own separate PACs to support local candidates. NOW, the NOW Foundation, and NOW/PAC share priorities: pressing for an amendment to the U.S. Constitution that will guarantee equal rights for women; achieving economic equality for women; championing abortion rights, reproductive freedom, and other women's health issues; supporting civil rights for all and opposing racism; opposing bigotry against lesbians and gays; and ending violence against women. However, NOW, the NOW Foundation, and NOW/PAC are separate entities.

NOW, through the NOW Foundation and the NOW/PAC, engages in extensive electoral and lobbying work and litigation. In addition to these methods, the NOW organization organizes mass marches, rallies, pickets, and nonviolent civil disobedience. The organization is especially proud of its mobilization efforts in support of passage of an Equal Rights Amendment (ERA).

Researchers can obtain additional information about NOW, the NOW Foundation, and NOW PAC at the organization's website, www.now.org. Other sources of information include the NOW Foundation's *Annual Report* and the organization's communications publication, the National NOW Times.

See also Abortion, Right to; Equal Rights Amendment; Feminist Movement; Gender-Based Discrimination; Interest Groups; Reproductive Freedom

Bibliography

Hernandez, Aileen, and Letitia P. Sommers. 1971. *The First Five Years, 1966–1971*. Chicago: National Organization for Women.

National Organization of Women Foundation. 2001. *Annual Report*. Washington, DC: National Organization for Women.

National Organization for Women. 2003. *History and Frequently Asked Questions*. Washington, DC: National Organization for Women.

Urban, Dennis. 2002. *"Women of SNCC: Struggle, Sexism and the Emergence of Feminist Consciousness, 1960–1966."* International Social Science Review 77: 185.

Kimberly L. Douglass

NATIONAL RIFLE ASSOCIATION. *See* Arms, Right to Keep and Bear; Interest Groups

NATIONAL RIGHT TO LIFE COMMITTEE (NRLC)

The National Right to Life Committee (NRLC) (on the Web at www.nrlc.org) is an organization formed in response to the U.S. Supreme Court's decision in *Roe v. Wade* (1973). In June of 1973 a group of pro-life leaders created the organization in order to lead the opposition to the Court's ruling, which prevented states from prohibiting abortion. The NLRC is the largest anti-abortion grassroots organization. According to the NLRC, there are currently over 3,000 local chapters in all 50 states. Although the group's primary goal is to overturn *Roe v. Wade*, it has also taken positions on other issues affecting human life including the abortion pill, RU-486, human cloning, euthanasia, physician-assisted suicide, and stem cell research. Its involvement in these issues is due to their belief that life, from conception to natural death, should be protected by law.

NLRC is composed of several departments to carry out three basic objectives: education, legislation, and political action. The major components of the NRLC include: (1) The National Right to Life Educational Trust Fund, which develops fact sheets and advertising; (2) the NRL Political Action Committee, which has the responsibility of identifying and providing support to pro-life candidates; (3) the federal and state legislative offices lobby lawmakers; (4) the Medical Ethics office, concerned primarily with issues that affect the elderly, such as euthanasia; and (5) the General Counsel, which has the responsibility of defending pro-life legislation and filing litigation to get abortion rights legislation overturned.

More specifically, the NLRC has been instrumental in the passage of federal legislation prohibiting partial birth abortions. It has also been an advocate of Supreme Court nominees who are in favor of overturning *Roe v. Wade* and has sponsored advertisements to that end. It has opposed U.S. funding for international family planning because

it views it as an attempt to legalize and promote abortion-on-demand in developing countries. The organization has also been opposed to the Equal Rights Amendment, which has been reintroduced in Congress on multiple occasions since its defeat, because it believes that such an amendment would prohibit limitations on abortion. NLRC also lobbied Congress to include a provision in a Medicare bill that would ensure that senior citizens were not subjected to medical rationing, which it characterizes as involuntary euthanasia. The NLRC opposed bipartisan campaign finance reform legislation because it believed that such legislation prohibited its freedom of speech and would cripple the pro-life movement.

See also Abortion, Right to; Campaign Finance Reform; Equal Rights Amendment; Pro-Life Movement; Pro-Life Position on Abortion; Reproductive Freedom; *Roe v. Wade* (1973); Speech, Freedom of; Suicide, Doctor Assisted

Bibliography

Carney, Eliza Newlan. 1997. "Abortion Foes Fight the Speech Police." *National Journal* 29: 2378.

Feldman, Linda. 1997. "Debate Reviving Over Funds for Global Family Planning." *Christian Science Monitor* 89: 3.

Kara E. Stooksbury

NATION OF ISLAM (NOI)

Often referred to as the "Black Muslims," the Nation of Islam (NOI) is a religious group composed of black Americans. The NOI gained national attention during the 1950s and 1960s for its rejection of the goal of racial integration and its advocacy of black nationalism.

In the 1930s in Detroit, a mysterious man usually known as Wallace D. Fard became the root of what would become the NOI. Fard sold silks door-to-door and talked with his customers about Islam and his idea that black Americans were descendants of Asiatic Muslims. Fard believed the original man, created by Allah, was black. Whites were devils, bred into being thousands of years ago by an evil scientist named Yacub. Allah planned to reinstall blacks as the superior race at Armageddon. Blacks, Fard taught, should reject Christianity as the religion of slaveholders and seek to develop self-contained territory. Fard disappeared without explanation in 1934. Subsequently Fard's protégé, Elijah Muhammad, began to refer to himself as the Messenger or Prophet of Allah. While Fard's birthday was and is celebrated each year by the NOI as Savior's Day, Elijah Muhammad would become and remain the organization's central personality.

Muhammad was born Elijah Poole in Sandersville, Georgia, in 1897, to a poor sharecropper who was also a Baptist minister. Elijah moved his family to Detroit in 1923 and there heard Fard speak in 1931. Fard taught his followers to cast off their European surnames or "slave names" and granted new surnames to the faithful. Poole first became Elijah Karriem and then, as a sign of his importance to Fard, Elijah Muhammad. Muhammad helped to found Detroit's Temple Number One and, in 1932, Chicago's Temple Number Two, which would become the headquarters of the NOI. Muhammad served a four-year prison term for interfering with the World War II draft. He did not value participation in the existing political system; the NOI leader repeatedly demanded that the United States cede one or more states for an all-black nation within a nation. He also admonished his followers to refrain from inciting violence but to defend themselves at all costs if attacked. NOI members identified strongly with all non-European ethnic groups and especially with Arabs; the organization was vehemently anti-Zionist.

The NOI's belief that the white race was the devil on earth resonated deeply with many black Americans who had experienced institutional racism and individual acts of racism. The NOI grew to possibly between 50,000 and 100,000 members at its height (Lincoln 1982, 241). Its standards were strict: NOI members were to be dignified, disciplined, prayerful, and faithfully unquestioning of Muhammad's teachings; they must refrain from alcohol, drugs, smoking, promiscuity, dancing, swearing, and certain foods. Muhammad taught

that men and women had preordained roles, with men as the natural heads of households, but that women should be educated and respected. A society known as the Fruit of Islam (FOI), sometimes referred to as a paramilitary organization, drew the most able men of the NOI for security work, rigorous study, martial arts training, and keeping order within the NOI. The NOI founded schools, addiction treatment programs, newspapers, farms, and other businesses.

Muhammad's right hand during the 1950s and early 1960s was the controversial Malcolm X, born Malcolm Little in Omaha, Nebraska in 1925, to a Baptist minister and his wife. A street hustler and thief as a young man, Malcolm X converted to Muhammad's brand of Islam in prison, and after his release in 1952 became an influential spokesperson and founder of new temples across America. His prominence fueled internal strife in the NOI, and in 1963 Malcolm X was suspended from the organization. He became interested in orthodox Islam during a 1964 trip to the Middle East and subsequently renounced the NOI's absolutist condemnation of whites. He was assassinated in 1965.

Louis X, minister of the important Harlem Temple Number Seven, became Muhammad's next protégé and the NOI's chief spokesperson. Louis X, now known as Louis Farrakhan, was less aggressive than Malcolm X but has enjoyed his share of controversy since his ascendancy. Born Louis Eugene Walcott in Roxbury, Massachusetts, in 1933, Louis Farrakhan grew up in the Episcopal church and attended the Winston-Salem Teachers College in North Carolina. As a young man, he made his living as a calypso singer named the "Charmer." He converted to the NOI after hearing Muhammad speak in 1955. Shortly thereafter, he became a minister, and rose to national prominence.

After Muhammad's death in 1975, his son, Wallace Deen Muhammad, attempted to bring his father's organization in line with orthodox Islam. Farrakhan led a segment of the group to reject this trend, and the movement split, with Farrakhan taking the name "Nation of Islam" for his splinter group. Wallace Deen Muhammad's organization dropped that name and has garnered much less publicity than his father's movement. As of this writing, the aging Farrakhan remains the leader of the Nation of Islam.

The NOI, and especially the Fruit of Islam, have been heavily monitored by the FBI. The organization and its leaders have been accused not only of anti-white racism but also of anti-Semitism and of advocating or instigating violence. They have been denounced as thugs and accused of receiving funds from Middle Eastern governments. The NOI's activities today receive a lesser amount of public attention. Two exceptions include the Million Man March in Washington in 1995, which was intended to counter negative portrayals of black men in the media, and a sensational interpersonal conflict between Farrakhan and Malcolm X's survivors.

See also Federal Bureau of Investigation; Malcolm X; Discrimination; Religion, Free Exercise of

Bibliography

Lincoln, C. Eric. 1982. *The Black Muslims in America.* Rev. ed. Westport, CT: Greenwood Press.

Malcolm X. 1965. *The Autobiography of Malcolm X.* With Alex Haley. New York: Ballantine Books.

Rachel Pearsall

NATIVE AMERICAN CHURCH

The term *Native American Church* "Native American Church" may refer to a network of loosely affiliated Native American religious groups or to individual groups not connected to a larger organization (Stewart 1997, 240). These groups share a sense of pan-tribal commonality and the peyote ritual. A number of syncretistic and intertribal religions spread among Native Americans in the nineteenth century. The most durable of these began among the tribes of the Great Plains and centered on the ritual consumption of peyote (Slotkin 1956, 18–19). Peyotist groups in Oklahoma incorporated as the Native American Church in 1918. Native American Church members nationwide may have numbered upward of 200,000 in the mid-1990s (Stewart 1997, 327).

The peyote ritual usually takes place throughout Saturday night and involves meditation, song, and the consumption of peyote. Native American Church members refer to peyote as a sacrament and believe that it brings them closer to the deity, identified with Jesus or with a figure from tribal religion. The religion has a strong ethical emphasis.

Beginning in the early part of the twentieth century, state governments began to ban peyote use, and First Amendment challenges to these laws began to appear in state courts with varying results. In 1970, Congress's Comprehensive Drug Abuse Prevention and Control Act listed peyote and mescaline as Schedule I hallucinogenic drugs—drugs with no safe or accepted medical use and a high potential for abuse—but federal regulations exempted Native American Church members from enforcement of the federal law. In 1978, Congress' American Indian Religious Freedom Act articulated a protective policy toward traditional native religious practices but did not specifically mention peyote or countermand state drug laws.

In 1990, two Oregon men were denied unemployment compensation because they had been fired for ritual peyote use. The two sued, claiming a violation of their First Amendment free exercise rights. In *Employment Division v. Smith,* the U.S. Supreme Court ruled six-to-three that the state might enforce its own drug laws regardless of the religious context of the drug use. *Smith* undercut a longstanding constitutional doctrine that a state must have a "compelling interest" for any action—even a law of general application—that burdened a religious practice (see *Sherbert v. Verner,* 1963). The Religious Freedom Restoration Act, passed by Congress in 1993, attempted to reestablish the "compelling interest" doctrine and was considered a victory by the Native American Church and many other diverse groups. However, in *Boerne v. Flores* (1997) the Supreme Court declared the law unconstitutional on the ground that Congress had intruded on the Supreme Court's power to interpret the Constitution.

Notwithstanding the Supreme Court's decision in *Employment Division v. Smith,* Native American practitioners of peyotism gained protection under the American Indian Religious Freedom Act Amendments of 1994, which read in part: "[T]he use, possession or transportation of peyote by an Indian for bona fide traditional ceremonial purposes in connection with the practice of a traditional Indian religion is lawful, and shall not be prohibited by the United States or any State." There is controversy over whether nonnative converts to the Native American Church should be entitled to a similar exemption.

See also *Employment Division, Department of Human Resources of Oregon v. Smith* (1990); First Amendment; Free Exercise Clause; Fundamental Rights; Native Americans, Civil Rights of; Religion, Freedom of; Religious Freedom Restoration Act; Strict Scrutiny

Bibliography

Slotkin, J. S. 1956. *The Peyote Religion: A Study in Indian-White Relations.* Glencoe, IL: The Free Press.

Stewart, Omer. 1997. *Peyote Religion: A History.* Norman: University of Oklahoma Press, 1997.

Rachel Pearsall

NATIVE AMERICANS, CIVIL RIGHTS OF

To understand the complex dynamics affecting the civil rights of Native Americans, it is important to first differentiate between Native American ancestry and tribal membership. Typically, "Native American" (as well as "Indian" or "American Indian") has come to refer to an individual indigenous person of the United States. "Tribe" (as well as "tribal nation," "Indian tribe," and "indigenous nation") is most commonly used to describe indigenous peoples of the United States in the aggregate sense (Wilkins 2002). Native Americans have rights as individuals and rights that arise from their tribal memberships. Historically, these rights have been determined by the federal government (as a party to treaties, the trustee of Indian interests, and the holder of plenary constitutional power to legislate Indian issues) and by the sovereign tribes.

Congress and the Bureau of Indian Affairs (BIA) have the power to confer legal status (federal recognition) on Indian tribes, although prior to 1978, federal recognition was also sometimes granted by court rulings and administrative orders. Federally recognized tribes are considered "domestic dependent nations" and their rights to tribal sovereignty are acknowledged by the federal government (see *Cherokee Nation v. State of Georgia,* 1831). The concept of tribal sovereignty refers to a tribe's right to define its membership, govern itself, regulate tribal relations, and manage tribal property (Olsen 1997). As a result of tribal sovereignty, most tribes are exempt from state tax laws and are not subject to most of the same constitutional constraints as are the federal and state government (Wilkins 2002).

Early in the history of federal relations with Native Americans, the U.S. government entered into treaties with Indian tribes. The legislative and executive branches regarded tribes as independent nations, analogous to a nation like France or England, and used their constitutional powers to ratify treaties with them. Native Americans were viewed as citizens of their respective tribes and their tribes were subject to the provisions of these treaties. Eventually, the federal government began to waver in its view of Indian tribes as absolute sovereign entities. Beginning in the 1820s, a number of Court decisions and federal statues articulated the earliest version of this new doctrine. In the case of *Cherokee Nation v. State of Georgia* (1831), the Court decided that Indian tribes were not truly sovereign and independent nations, but were "domestic, dependent nations."

In *Johnson and Graham's Lessee v. M'Intosh* (1823), the Supreme Court decided the question of who had clear title to disputed tribal land. The plaintiff, a non-Indian, had gained title from Native Americans who had previously occupied the land. The defendant, also a non-Indian, had gained title from U.S. land grants. In deciding the case, the Court used the notion of "discovery" to determine the rightful source of title to the land. According to the Court, when a European nation discovered land not already claimed by another European nation, "[the original inhabitants'] power to dispose of the soil at their own will, to whomsoever they pleased, was denied by the original fundamental principal that discovery gave exclusive title to those who made it." Therefore, Great Britain took title to land by discovering and conquering it. When America won its independence, the new government took Great Britain's right to transfer and govern all land within American borders, including land still occupied by Indians (Olson 1997). Indians retained only the right to occupy the land.

The federal government strengthened its control over Indian affairs during the era of the Trail of Tears. Congress passed the Indian Removal Act of 1830, which required that large numbers of Indians in the eastern United States move to reservations west of the Mississippi River. Legislators worried that refugee Indians might commit crimes against American citizens in the states they crossed, leading to a conflict of authority between federal and local law. Accordingly, Congress passed the Indian Country Crimes Act of 1834, which gave the federal government exclusive jurisdiction over Indians in such instances. This law did not, however, apply to crimes committed by Indians against other Indians' persons or property (Olsen 1997).

The Supreme Court was confronted with the issue of Indian on Indian crime in the landmark case of *Ex Parte Crow Dog* (1883). In this case, Crow Dog, an Indian who had killed another Indian, was punished according to tribal law. Local non-Indian authorities thought that the reparations were inadequate, however, and that Crow Dog should have been more severely punished. As a consequence, Crow Dog was arrested and convicted of first-degree murder. The Supreme Court, in reviewing the case, reaffirmed the idea of tribal jurisdiction over crimes committed by one Indian against another Indian in tribal territory. In *Crow Dog*, the Court defined Indian tribes as "semi-independent nations" that were exempt from certain federal laws because of treaty rights (Olsen 1997). The Court asserted that Indians could be subject to federal jurisdiction only if Congress specified their accountability in the federal code. As a result,

Congress passed the Major Crimes Act of 1885. The act extended federal criminal jurisdiction over major felonies committed against both Indians and non-Indians alike. The Supreme Court upheld the Act in *U.S. v. Kagama* (1886).

During a period in American history frequently referred to as the "age of assimilation," Congress passed the Indian Appropriations Act of 1871 (Olsen 1997). Under this act, the federal government refused to contract with Indian tribes as sovereign or domestic dependent nations deserving treaty rights. Instead, Congress promulgated rules for tribes, and the federal government administered programs through the Department of the Interior. This, in effect, ended the U.S. government's practice of making treaties with Native American tribes. Moreover, the Indian Appropriations Act stripped tribes of their sovereign status, while leaving tribe members without U.S. citizenship. In *Elk v. Wilkins* (1884), the Supreme Court ruled that Indians "assimilated into white society" were not citizens of the United States because they had not been naturalized. As such, they did not enjoy voting rights. While they were subject to the laws of the country, the protections afforded under the rights of citizenship did not apply to them, unless they were granted those rights through a process known as allotment. Congress enacted the General Allotment Act in 1887, which granted citizenship to Indians who received land allotments and voluntarily took up residence apart from their tribes.

As a result of judicial decisions that nonallotted Indians were not citizens and tribes were not sovereign nations, the government was required to maintain a trust relationship with tribal nations and individual Indians. Reserved tribal lands have been held in trust by the federal government for various tribes. The United States, in its role as trustee, has taken on the responsibility to protect these lands and the natural and cultural assets of the tribes (Wilkins 2002). The Supreme Court, in a series of cases, recognized that the federal government had a responsibility to protect the rights of Indians as well as to honor agreements and treaties. For example, in *Winters v. United States* (1908), the Supreme Court decided that governmental creation of agricultural reservations implied that Indians would have a sufficient amount of water for irrigation of those lands. The debate over whether Native Americans were citizens of the respective states where they resided was ultimately put to rest with the passage of the Indian Citizenship Act of 1924, making them legal citizens of the United States.

More recently, Congress has returned to a heightened recognition of tribes as semisovereign entities. Only for a brief period in the 1950s did this wane when Congress revisited the idea of Indian assimilation. From the late 1960s to the 1980s, Congress began to take additional steps to protect the integrity of Indian civil rights. One such measure was Congressional prohibition on dismembering and assimilating tribes, or tribal termination, without the express written consent of the tribe. Another major hallmark in the Native American civil rights movement was Congress's passage of the Indian Civil Rights Act of 1968. This act required that tribal governments recognize a myriad of civil rights and liberties, most of which are contained in the Constitution's Bill of Rights and Fourteenth Amendment.

The enumeration of rights in the Indian Civil Rights Act of 1968 differed in some respects from constitutional rights as interpreted by the Supreme Court. For example, the 1968 act did not prohibit a tribe from establishing a religion, require it to provide free legal counsel to a defendant who could not afford it, or provide a jury trial in all criminal cases. More recently, Congress has adopted a policy of fostering tribal self-governance. Around 1988, Congress began to shift administrative responsibility for many services and programs from the Bureau of Indian Affairs (BIA) to the tribes themselves. The Indian Self-Determination Act Amendments of 1988 called for a five-year project ("Tribal Self-Governance Demonstration Project") designed to transfer autonomy to select tribes for the decision making and control of various federal programs. This initiative was bolstered by the Tribal Self-Governance Act of 1994, which allowed for a yearly increase in the number of tribes that could participate in the self-governance program.

See also Bill of Rights (American) (1789); Citizenship; Civil Rights Movement; Diversity; *Employment Division, Department of Human Resources of Oregon v. Smith;* Fourteenth Amendment, Section 5 of the; Group Rights; Native American Church

Bibliography

Egan, Timothy. 1999. "Poor Indians on Rich Land Fight a U.S. Maze." *New York Times,* (9 March): A20.

Evans, Suzanne E. 1996. "Voting." In Frederick E. Hoxie, ed. *Encyclopedia of North American Indians: Native American History, Culture, and Life From Paleo-Indians to the Present.* Boston: Houghton Mifflin Co.

Johansen, Bruce E. 1998. *The Encyclopedia of Native American Legal Tradition.* Westport, CT: Greenwood.

Olsen, James S., ed. 1997. *Encyclopedia of American Indian Civil Rights.* Westport, CT: Greenwood.

Wilkins, David. E. 2002. *American Indian Politics and the American Political System.* 2002. Lanham, MD: Rowman and Littlefield.

Richard T. Middleton, IV

NATURAL LAW AND NATURAL RIGHTS

In proclaiming that "all men are created equal" and "that they are endowed by their Creator with certain unalienable rights," the Declaration of Independence (1776) reflects the theory of natural rights that characterized much of Enlightenment thought. Paraphrasing John Locke, the Declaration goes on to identify the natural, or "unalienable," rights of man as "life, liberty and the pursuit of happiness." For Enlightenment thinkers from Locke to Jefferson, these basic rights emanate from "the Laws of Nature and of Nature's God," again using the language of the Declaration of Independence. Thus the concept of "natural rights" is inseparable from the larger notion of "natural law."

The concept of natural law is deeply rooted in Western political and legal thought. It has been invoked, discussed, and debated by lawyers and philosophers since ancient times. Yet the concept is, ultimately, an elusive one. Natural law is a set of precepts that is presumed to flow from man's "nature" and apply in even the social conditions existing prior to the emergence of government. Natural law is sometimes used to refer to universal principles of morality and justice; however, precisely what those principles are is subject to conflicting interpretations.

Even so, there is considerable agreement at the most general level about what positions comprise a natural law theory. Most natural law theorists generally accept the following propositions: (1) moral principles are either objectively true or objectively false (i.e., true independently of what any particular person or group of persons believes); (2) the content of a moral principle is determined by the facts of human nature; and (3) the principles of this natural law morality can be discerned by reason.

In the Judeo-Christian tradition, natural law is ultimately linked to divine ordinance. In his *Summa Theologica,* the medieval philosopher Thomas Aquinas (1224–1274) defined natural law as the "participation in the Eternal Law by rational creatures." In his celebrated *Commentaries on the Laws of England* (1765–1769), William Blackstone wrote that man "must necessarily be subject to the laws of his creator, for he is entirely a dependent being." In Blackstone's view, the "will of his maker is called the law of nature." While God's ordinances reflect the facts of a human nature that is itself the product of divine choices, the natural law, on this view, is ultimately authoritative in virtue of God's will.

In secular formulations, natural law is based entirely on the rational nature of human beings. In *De Republica,* the ancient Roman orator Cicero (106–43 b.c.) defined natural law as "right reason in agreement with nature." Similarly, the seventeenth-century Dutch jurist Hugo Grotius defined natural law as rules of human conduct that can be discovered solely by the use of reason; they are accessible to reason because the facts of human nature are accessible to reason.

Perhaps the most important contemporary natural law theorist is John Finnis. Finnis's theory of natural law begins with an explanation of the concept of law. In Finnis's view, the natural law consists of basic principles of "practical reasonableness." Finnis grounds these basic principles of natural law in empirical observations of what is universally valued as basic goods. For example, he notes that all human societies "show a concern for the value of human life; ... regard the procreation of a new human life as a good thing[;] ... restrict sexual activity; ... display a concern for truth[;] ... know friendship[;] ... have some conception of ... property[;] [and] ... value play ..." (Finnis 1980, 83) These universal basic goods define certain principles of practical reasonableness that obligate all human beings.

The influence of natural law theory has been widespread. Even today, legal theorists, lawyers, lawmakers, and judges sometimes invoke natural law. But natural law as such is distinct from positive law (i.e., law that originates from human beings in legislative, judicial, or quasi-legislative acts) and, indeed, is rarely enforced by Western legal systems as law. It is a philosophical/ethical theory—the idea that there is a set of principles of morality and justice that transcends the positive law. Natural law and divine law continue to be important because they provide a basis upon which to judge the positive law. In the absence of higher law, government is, from the standpoint of morality, free to proclaim the law to be anything that those in power wish it to be.

If natural rights flow from natural law, and if natural law is viewed as corresponding with traditional Judeo-Christian notions of morality (an equation made by some, but not all natural law theorists), then it becomes difficult to justify certain contemporary rights, most notably abortion and the "right to die." In defending these rights, one can challenge the equation of natural law and Judeo-Christian morality. Indeed, there are secular formulations of natural law that lend support to these controversial rights. Alternatively, one can reject altogether the notions of natural law and natural rights. But one should be aware that to do so breaks with the prevailing ideas of the founders of the United States.

See also Abortion, Right to; Blackstone, William; Common Law Background of American Civil Rights and Liberties; Declaration of Independence;

Right to Die; Equality; Individual Rights; Jefferson, Thomas; Liberalism; Libertarianism; Liberty; Locke, John; Property Rights

Bibliography

Budziszewski, J. 1997. *Written on the Heart: The Case for Natural Law.* Downers Grove, IL: InterVarsity Press.

Finnis, John. 1980. *Natural Law and Natural Rights.* Oxford: Clarendon Press.

Maritain, Jacques. 2001. *Natural Law: Reflections on Theory and Practice.* South Bend, IN: St. Augustine's Press.

Kenneth Einar Himma and John M. Scheb II

NATURAL RIGHTS. *See* Natural Law and Natural Rights

NEAR V. MINNESOTA EX REL. OLSON (1931)

In this seminal First Amendment decision the U.S. Supreme Court struck down a state law that permitted public officials to seek an injunction to stop publication of any "malicious, scandalous and defamatory newspaper, magazine or other periodical." The statute was invoked to suppress publication of a small Minneapolis newspaper, the *Saturday Press,* which had strong anti-Semitic overtones and maligned local political officials, particularly the chief of police. This law provided that once a newspaper was enjoined, further publication was punishable as contempt of court. Writing for the Court, Chief Justice Charles Evans Hughes characterized this statute "the essence of censorship" and declared it unconstitutional:

The fact that for approximately one hundred and fifty years there has been almost an entire absence of attempts to impose previous restraints upon publications relating to the malfeasance of public officers is significant of the deep-seated conviction that such restraints would violate constitutional right. Public officers, whose character and conduct remain open to debate and free discussion in the press, find their remedies for false accusations in actions under libel laws providing for redress and punishment, and not in proceedings to restrain the publication of newspapers and periodicals.

With its decision in *Near v. Minnesota,* the Court incorporated the First Amendment freedom of the press into the Due Process Clause of the Fourteenth Amendment, thus making it fully applicable to the states. The doctrine of prior restraint recognized in *Near* was the basis for the Supreme Court's landmark decision in *New York Times v. United States* (1971), where the Court refused to allow the Nixon Administration to prevent publication of the Pentagon Papers.

See also Anti-Semitism; Bill of Rights, Incorporation of; Defamation; Due Process Clauses; First Amendment; Fourteenth Amendment (1868); Hughes, Charles Evans; Injunction; *New York Times v. Sullivan; New York Times v. United States;* Press, Freedom of the; Prior Restraint, Doctrine of

Bibliography

Friendly, Fred. 1981. *Minnesota Rag: Scandal Sheet that Shaped the Constitution.* New York: Random House.

John M. Scheb II and Otis H. Stephens, Jr.

THE NEW DEAL

Franklin D. Roosevelt (FDR) won the presidency in 1932 by promising the American people a "New Deal" to cope with the extreme hardships wrought by the Great Depression. The American public, still shocked by the stock market crash of 1929, and reeling from massive unemployment and the widespread failures of banks, farms, and other enterprises, was ready for a new approach. Under the New Deal, FDR and the Democratic Congress established public works programs such as the Civilian Conservation Corps (CCC) and the Works Progress Administration (WPA), as well as a variety of regulatory programs affecting agriculture, banking, mining, manufacturing, telecommunications, utilities, and the stock market. Under the New Deal, workers gained the right to unionize and bargain collectively with management. And for the first time, workers were guaranteed a minimum wage. Perhaps the most important achievement from the standpoint of average Americans was the enactment of the Social Security Act of 1935, which really represents the beginning of the modern welfare state. In many ways, the New Deal represents the triumph of modern liberalism.

Conservatives were alarmed by the scope of the New Deal and in particular by its interference with economic freedom as the concept was traditionally understood, as well as the centralization of power in the Executive Branch. Some conservatives argued that the New Deal represented a significant step toward the implementation of socialism. Defenders of the New Deal argued that to rely on the traditional laissez-faire approach in the face of a calamity of the magnitude of the Great Depression would simply pave the way for a more radical and authoritarian system on the model of Hitler's Germany or the Soviet Union. The New Deal was thus defended as a pragmatic alternative to communism or fascism.

Conservatives were not convinced. During the first Roosevelt Administration (1933–1936), they found a powerful ally in the United States Supreme Court. After adverse decisions struck down key elements of the New Deal, Roosevelt began to refer to the Supreme Court as the "nine old men" and characterized them as out of touch with modern economic problems. FDR even proposed a plan by which he would be able to "pack" the Court with justices who would support his ideas. Although FDR's court packing plan was never adopted by Congress, it clearly got the Court's attention.

In the spring of 1937, the Court changed direction dramatically by upholding a Washington state minimum wage law on March 29, the National Labor Relations Act on April 12, and the Social Security Act on May 24. The National Labor Relations Act was one of the most important legislative accomplishments of the New Deal. Writing for the Supreme Court in *N.L.R.B v. Jones & Laughlin Steel Corporation* (1937), Chief Justice Charles Evans Hughes recognized that "the right of employees to self-organization and to have representatives of their own choosing for the purpose of collective bargaining is often an essential condition of industrial peace." In dissent, Justice James C. McReynolds argued that the new law infringed on economic freedom and property rights:

The right to contract is fundamental and includes the privilege of selecting those with whom one is willing to assume contractual relations. This right is unduly abridged by the act now upheld. A private owner is deprived of power to manage his own property by freely selecting those to whom his manufacturing operations are to be entrusted.

The Court's decision in the *Jones & Laughlin Steel* case signaled the beginning of a virtual constitutional revolution via judicial interpretation. FDR's four-term presidency saw almost complete turnover in the membership of the Supreme Court, as FDR was able to appoint eight new justices to the Court. The Roosevelt Court, as it came to be known, firmly established the legitimacy of the modern regulatory state as well as the primacy of the presidency in the scheme of national governance. With landmark decisions like *West Virginia State Board of Education v. Barnette* (1943), the Roosevelt Court also set the stage for the judicial expansion of civil rights and liberties in the latter half of the twentieth century. Two of FDR's appointments to the Supreme Court, Hugo Black and William O. Douglas, played enormous roles in that process.

See also Black, Hugo L.; Douglas, William O.; Economic Freedom; Liberalism; McReynolds, James C.; Roosevelt, Eleanor; Roosevelt, Franklin D.; *West Virginia State Board of Education v. Barnette* (1943)

Bibliography

Goodwin, Doris Kearns. 1994. *No Ordinary Time*. New York: Simon and Schuster.

Leuchtenberg, William E. 1963. *Franklin D Roosevelt and the New Deal*. New York: Harper and Row.

Pritchett, C. Herman. 1948. *The Roosevelt Court*. New York: Macmillan.

John M. Scheb II and Otis H. Stephens, Jr.

NEW JUDICIAL FEDERALISM

The new judicial federalism refers to a practice that dates from the 1970s when state courts, relying on state bills of rights, began to provide broader protection for rights than was available under the federal Constitution.

The new judicial federalism rests on three legal principles. First, both federal and state bills of rights protect against the violation of rights by state governments. This was not always the case. Initially, state bills of rights protected against state violations, and the federal Bill of Rights against federal violations. Relying on the Due Process Clause of the Fourteenth Amendment, the U.S. Supreme Court began early in the twentieth century to extend the protections of the federal Bill of Rights to prohibit state violations of rights. By the 1960s, this process of "selective incorporation" had made almost all the guarantees of the Bill of Rights applicable against both state governments and the federal government. Thus, the actions of a state government can violate either the federal Constitution or the state constitutions (or both), and the actions of a state government can be challenged in either federal or state court.

Second, each state supreme court serves as the ultimate interpreter of its state's law, including its state constitution. The U.S. Supreme Court can review the rulings of state supreme courts whenever federal law is involved. However, when a case involves no claim under the federal constitution or when a state court ruling is based exclusively on state law, on what is referred to as "independent and adequate state grounds," the decision of the state supreme court interpreting state law, including the state bill of rights, is final and not subject to review by a federal court.

Third, federal law is supreme within its sphere, so when federal law and state law conflict, federal law prevails. States and state courts, therefore, cannot recognize less in the way of rights for their residents than is required by federal law. Federal law thus creates a national minimum of rights. But states and state courts can provide more protection for rights than is required as a matter of federal law. Since the early 1970s, that is precisely what the states have done.

From 1950 to 1969, in only 10 cases did state judges rely on state guarantees of rights to afford greater protection than was available under the federal Constitution. However, since 1970 they have done so in more than one thousand cases. This dramatic change is closely linked to changes in personnel on the U.S. Supreme Court, best symbolized by the appointment of Warren Burger in 1969 to succeed Earl Warren as chief justice. These personnel changes alarmed civil-liberties advocates, who expected that the reconstituted Supreme Court would erode the gains they had made during the Warren Court era, particularly with regard to the rights of defendants in criminal cases. In retrospect, these fears were exaggerated: the Burger Court, while narrowing some of the Warren Court's restrictions on the use of evidence in criminal prosecutions, did not launch a full-scale assault on *Mapp v. Ohio, Miranda v. Arizona,* or other landmark Warren Court rulings. Yet what is crucial is that these fears led civil-liberties groups to seek alternative means to safeguard rights, a search that led them eventually to embrace state bills of rights.

On initial inspection, this must have seemed an odd choice. State bills of rights protect many of the same set of fundamental rights—the freedoms of speech and of the press, religious liberty, and protections for defendants—that are found in the federal Bill of Rights, and state courts had historically not been aggressive in enforcing those guarantees. Nevertheless, rights advocates recognized that state judges interpreting state bills of rights are not obliged to conform their interpretations to the rulings of federal courts interpreting analogous federal provisions. Even when the language is identical or nearly identical, state judges are interpreting a unique document, with a unique history, and this uniqueness may justify a different interpretation. Moreover, even if the federal courts have interpreted an identical provision in a nearly identical case, the federal ruling is not binding—states are the ultimate interpreters of their state constitutions, and they may simply disagree. They need not assume that the federal interpretation is the best legal interpretation.

In addition, even when the state guarantees are analogous to those found in the federal Bill of Rights—for example, state guarantees of freedom of speech and of religious liberty—they are often framed in distinctive language. In particular, they are often more specific than their federal counterparts. For example, in addition to prohibiting governmental establishment of religion, 19 states specifically bar religious tests for witnesses or jurors, and 35 prohibit expenditures for "any sectarian purpose." These textual differences may provide the basis for interpretations diverging from those emanating from the U.S. Supreme Court.

Many state declarations of rights also contain additional protections that have no federal analogue. For example, 39 states guarantee access to a legal remedy to those who suffer injuries, 11 expressly protect a right to privacy, and 17 expressly protect gender equality. Thus, these constitutions offered the prospect of extending rights protections beyond those recognized by the Warren Court.

Most important, under the doctrine of "independent and adequate state grounds," rulings based solely on state law are not subject to federal scrutiny. This means that expansive state rulings, if based on state rights guarantees, are insulated from reversal by the Supreme Court. Thus, the shift to state bills of rights represented a tactical maneuver by groups eager to evade what they perceived as a less hospitable federal constitutional law.

When litigants first advanced state constitutional claims in the early 1970s, the supreme courts in California, New Jersey, New York, and a few other states were immediately responsive to their arguments. Their pioneering rulings encouraged other state courts to look more closely at their state bills of rights. Over time, what began as a reaction in a few state supreme courts has become a national phenomenon. Moreover, the focus has shifted. The new judicial federalism originated in reaction to the rulings–or anticipated rulings—of the Burger Court, particularly in the criminal justice area. Thus, during the 1970s most rulings under the new judicial federalism involved the rights of defendants. Other early new-judicial-federalism rulings involved the reform of public school finance, which itself became a state constitutional issue after the U.S. Supreme Court in *San Antonio Independent School District v. Rodriguez* (1973) foreclosed consideration of the

issue under the federal Constitution. Finally, the issue of free-speech rights on private property, such as shopping malls, arose as an important issue under state constitutions, once again emerging after the U.S. Supreme Court ruled that the First Amendment did not protect such speech. What these examples illustrate is that the new judicial federalism began as a fall-back position, a second-best approach, when the preferred approach of federal constitutional protection was unavailable, and the state constitutional agenda was largely determined, ironically enough, by the adverse decisions of the U.S. Supreme Court.

More recently, important state constitutional issues have arisen that do not reflect disappointment about the judicial decisions emanating from the nation's capital. One such issue involves the right of gay and lesbian couples to marry. This issue has never been specifically addressed by the U.S. Supreme Court, but state courts, relying on state constitutions, have weighed in on the issue. In 1993, the Hawaii Supreme Court ruled that denying marriage licenses to gay and lesbian couples violated the state constitution. Five years later, an Alaska court concluded that marriage was a fundamental right and that barring same-sex marriages amounted to sex discrimination in violation of the Alaska Constitution. In 1999, the Vermont Supreme Court ruled that the state constitution guaranteed gay and lesbian couples the same legal rights and benefits of marriage enjoyed by heterosexual couples, and it ordered the Vermont legislature to craft a law that would satisfy the ruling, either by legalizing gay marriage or by creating an equivalent partnership structure. More recently, the Massachusetts Supreme Judicial Court ruled in 2003 that denying marriage licenses to same-sex couples violated the state's constitution, prompting a number of states to adopt constitutional amendments affirming that marriage in their states would be limited to one male and one female.

Another emerging area in state constitutional law, likewise one in which the U.S. Supreme Court has played no role, involves the intersection of constitutional law and tort law. Business interests, insurance companies, and the medical profession have long complained that tort-law legal doctrines unduly favor plaintiffs, and that juries in tort cases, especially when those cases pit ordinary citizens against large corporations, tend to award compensatory and punitive damages that are arbitrary and excessive. Whatever the validity of those charges, they have led state legislators to enact tort-reform statutes designed to shift the balance of power between plaintiffs and defendants. These statutes in turn have been challenged as violative of state constitutional guarantees, such as the right to a jury trial and the right to a redress of grievances. In several states–including Illinois, Ohio, and Oregon—these challenges have succeeded. However, the issue is far from settled, as new reform statutes are likely to spawn new litigation in state after state, making tort reform the most important state constitutional issue of the early twenty-first century.

The states' experience with regard to same-sex marriages and tort reform highlights a key feature of the new judicial federalism—it is intimately bound up with the political process in the states. The federal Constitution is difficult to amend, and on only five occasions has it been altered to overturn rulings of the United States Supreme Court. In contrast, voters can quite easily amend their state constitutions, even their state declarations of rights, to overturn judicial decisions with which they disagree. Hawaii and Alaska did so in the 1990s with regard to gay marriage, adopting amendments confirming that marriage was confined to heterosexual couples, thereby overturning their previously noted, respective state supreme courts' decisions to the contrary. Massachusetts and California did so earlier with regard to state constitutional rulings invalidating the death penalty, and California and Florida did so to counter expansive interpretations of the rights of defendants under state constitutions. Controversial state constitutional rulings may thus start, rather than conclude constitutional debates, and the participants in those debates are likely to include legislators, interest groups, and ordinary citizens, as well as judges.

By the early twenty-first century, the new judicial federalism has become an established feature of civil-liberties litigation. Citizens and officials might disagree with particular new-judicial-federalism rulings, but the legitimacy of relying on state bills of rights is no longer questioned. The federal Bill of Rights continues to provide the primary protection for rights, but state guarantees provide an important supplementary protection under the new judicial federalism.

See also Bill of Rights (American) (1789); Bill of Rights, Incorporation of; Burger Court; Burger, Warren E.; Death Penalty and the Supreme Court; Due Process Clauses; Federalism and Civil Rights and Liberties; First Amendment; Fourteenth Amendment (1868); Jury, Trial by; *Mapp v. Ohio* (1961); *Miranda v. Arizona* (1967); Same-Sex Marriage and Civil Unions; Speech, Freedom of; Warren Court; Warren, Earl

Bibliography

Tarr, G. Alan. 1998. *Understanding State Constitutions.* Princeton, NJ: Princeton University Press.

Williams, Robert F. 1999. *State Constitutional Law: Cases and Materials.* 3rd ed. Charlottesville, VA: Lexis Law Publishing.

G. Alan Tarr

NEW LEFT. *See* The Chicago Seven; Civil Rights Movement; Counterculture; Free Speech Movement; Liberalism; Students for a Democratic Society

NEW PROPERTY

The Fifth Amendment prohibits the federal government from taking private property without due process of law; the Fourteenth Amendment imposes the same prohibition on the states. Traditionally, "property" within the meaning of the Due Process Clauses was defined as real estate, personal property, money, and intangible assets. When the government sought to deprive an owner of these types of property rights, there was no question that due process had to be observed. On the other hand, as the Supreme Court recognized in *Bailey v. Richardson,* 341 U.S. 918 (1951), government jobs, benefits, licenses, and grants were viewed as privileges that could be revoked without notice or hearing. As the scope of government grew in the modern era, more and more of the country's wealth was linked to government benefits, leading some commentators to call for due process protection for this "new property" (Reich 1964). In 1965, Professor Charles Reich, a leading advocate of this position, wrote:

Society today is built around entitlement.... Many of the most important of these entitlements now flow from government: subsidies to farmers and businessmen, routes for airlines and channels for television stations; long term contracts for defense, space, and education; social security pensions for individuals. Such sources of security, whether private or public, are no longer regarded as luxuries or gratuities; to the recipients they are essentials, fully deserved, and in no sense a form of charity. It is only the poor whose entitlements, although recognized by public policy, have not been effectively enforced. (Reich 1965, 1255)

In *Goldberg v. Kelly* (1970), the Supreme Court adopted the new property thesis by extending due process protections to welfare beneficiaries. In a footnote to his opinion for the Court, Justice William J. Brennan noted, "It may be realistic today to regard welfare entitlements as more like 'property' than a 'gratuity.' Much of the existing wealth in this country takes the form of rights that do not fall within traditional common-law concepts of property."

In succeeding years, courts at all levels would recognize a variety of government benefits as property interests entitled to due process protections. Although the term *the new property* has fallen into disuse, the concept has been fully incorporated into constitutional law as courts today typically take a broad view of property interests when considering governmental actions that adversely affect individuals.

See also Brennan, William J., Jr.; Due Process Clauses; Due Process, Procedural; Fifth Amendment; Fourteenth Amendment(1868); Property Rights;

Bibliography

Monaghan, Henry Paul. 1977. "*Of 'Liberty' and 'Property.*'" Cornell Law Review 62: 405.

Reich, Charles A. 1964. "*The New Property.*" Yale Law Journal 73: 733.

Reich, Charles A. 1965. "*Individual Rights and Social Welfare: The Emerging Legal Issues.*" Yale Law Journal 74: 1245.

John M. Scheb II and Otis H. Stephens, Jr.

NEW YORK TIMES V. SULLIVAN (1964)

New York Times v. Sullivan is one of the Supreme Court's most well known, most cited, and most important First Amendment cases. For the defamation lawyer, there is perhaps no more important case. But, *New York Times v. Sullivan* also is important because of its significance to the American Civil Rights Movement. L. B. Sullivan, one of the elected commissioners of the City of Montgomery, sued the *New York Times,* contending that a full-page advertisement published in the *New York Times* in 1960 had libeled him. The advertisement was entitled, "Heed Their Rising Voices." It had called for Americans to take note of: the Civil Rights Movement, the brave role African-American students were playing in the movement through nonviolent demonstrations, and the "wave of terror" facing civil rights proponents in the American south. The ad appealed for funds to support the students, the right to vote campaign, and the legal defense of Dr. Martin Luther King, Jr., one of the movement's leaders. The advertisement's text was followed by the names of 64 famous Americans and then another line providing: "We in the South who are struggling daily for dignity and freedom warmly endorse this appeal.... " Thereunder appeared the names of 16 other individuals, 14 of whom were identified as clergy in various southern cities.

Critically, the advertisement made several statements that were not factually accurate descriptions of events as they had occurred in Montgomery. For instance, the advertisement stated that Dr. King had been arrested seven times when he had been arrested only four times. There were certain other factual inaccuracies as well.

Sullivan sued *The Times* and the alleged signatories, contending that the factual inaccuracies in the ad harmed his reputation, that is, they defamed him. Although Sullivan was not named in the advertisement, he contended that a person could read the false statements of fact as referring to him because he was the Commissioner of Public Affairs whose duties included supervision of the police department. Thus, any criticism of the police department could be construed as a statement of and concerning, Sullivan—an element of Sullivan's Alabama common-law libel claim. The jury that heard the case in the circuit court of Montgomery County awarded Sullivan $500,000 in damages, although he had not pointed to any particular pecuniary loss. The $500,000 award did not differentiate between compensatory and punitive damages. The trial judge rejected the defendants' arguments that the decision abridged their rights to freedom of speech and freedom of the press under the First and Fourteenth Amendments to the United States Constitution. On appeal, the Supreme Court of Alabama affirmed. On the First Amendment issue, the Alabama Supreme Court summarily stated that the First Amendment did not protect libelous publications and that the Fourteenth Amendment was directed against state action and not private action. The United States Supreme Court granted certiorari. In the United States Supreme Court, the *New York Times* position was argued by legendary Columbia Law Professor Herbert Wexler, who had also played an instrumental role in writing the *Times* brief.

Justice William Brennan wrote the majority opinion for the Court and turned first to the plaintiff's argument that the Alabama decision was not state action. He noted:

Although this is a civil law suit between private parties, the Alabama courts have applied a state rule of law which petitioners claim to impose invalid restrictions on their constitutional freedoms of speech and press. It matters not that the law has been applied in a civil action and that it is common law only, though supplemented by statute.... The test is not the form in which state power has been applied but, whatever the form, whether such power has in fact been exercised.

Thus, the Court had held that a state court decision, applying state tort law—here, defamation—was state action for purposes of the Fourteenth Amendment. The Court then turned to the argument that the First Amendment was inapplicable because the statement was published as part of a commercial advertisement. Rejecting that argument, Justice Brennan stated that the publication at issue was not a purely commercial advertisement. Rather, it "communicated information, expressed opinion, recited grievances, protested claimed abuses, and sought financial support on behalf of a movement whose existence and objectives are matters of the highest public interest and concern." Any other conclusion would adversely affect a newspaper's willingness to carry an editorial advertisement and would "shackle the First Amendment" and place "a handicap upon the freedoms of expression.... "

Then, Justice Brennan turned to the crux of the opinion as most have come to know it. Brennan noted that under Alabama law at the time, once a statement was deemed libelous per se—that is, that it would tend to injure a person and his reputation or bring him into public contempt—the defendant effectively had no defense unless it could prove that the statement was true in all its particulars. Justice Brennan went on to boldly and clearly state why, in the Court's opinion, Alabama law, as applied, was unconstitutional. Libel, he said, "can claim no talismanic immunity from constitutional limitations. It must be measured by standards that satisfy the First Amendment." Justice Brennan then cited numerous authorities proclaiming the value of free expression on public questions as guaranteed by the First Amendment. He noted that "debate on public issues should be uninhibited, robust, and wide-open, and that it may well include vehement, caustic, and sometimes unpleasantly sharp attacks on government and public officials." The advertisement at issue in the case was a statement of "grievance and protest on one of the major public issues" of the time. Did it lose its First Amendment protection because some of the factual statements were false and it allegedly defamed the plaintiff? Brennan quoted James Madison as follows: "Some degree of abuse is inseparable from the proper use of everything, and in no instance is this more true than in that of the press." Justice Brennan relied upon the Court's previous decisions in cases involving criminal contempt arising from criticism of a judge for the proposition that damage to official reputation was not a grounds for repressing otherwise free speech. Thus, Brennan concluded that "neither factual error nor defamatory content suffices to remove the constitutional shield from criticism of official conduct.... " Likewise, "the combination of the two elements is no less inadequate."

As further support for his conclusions, Justice Brennan related the controversy arising from the Sedition Act of 1798, which the Court had never considered or declared unconstitutional. However, protest against the act had been pronounced and persuasive and the attack on the Sedition Act had "carried the day in the court of history." But, returning to a variance of the Fourteenth Amendment state action theme, was there a difference between a criminal statute proscribing speech and a judgment in a common-law libel action? In response, Justice Brennan pointed out that concern over a potential damage award in a tort case "may be markedly more inhibiting than the fear of prosecution under a criminal statute." The various protections afforded to a defendant in a criminal law case are not available in a civil case and thus the civil case may have a severe chilling effect upon the defendant's willingness to speak.

But, what about the defense of truth? Did the defense of truth save Alabama's libel law? Not according to Justice Brennan and the United States Supreme Court. "A rule compelling the critic of official conduct to guarantee the truth of all his factual assertions—and to do so on pain of libel judgments virtually unlimited in amount—leads to ... self-censorship." Placing the burden of proving truth on the defendant may chill true speech, not just false speech. To that extent, Alabama's rule was inconsistent with the First and Fourteenth Amendments.

Thus, the Court held that Alabama's application of its defamation law was unconstitutional, but would it pronounce a rule for the future? The answer to this important question was yes. Critically, Justice Brennan stated:

The constitutional guarantees require, we think, a federal rule that prohibits a public official from recovering damages for a defamatory falsehood relating to his official misconduct unless he proves that the statement was made with "actual malice"—that is, with knowledge that it was false or with reckless disregard of whether it was false or not.

Thus, according to the Court, a public official plaintiff in a defamation case would be required to prove that any statement was made with "actual malice." Here, actual malice did not mean "ill-will" or "evil motive," as the term is used at common law. Instead, it had a special constitutional meaning—"actual malice" after *The New York Times Co. v. Sullivan* meant "knowledge of falsity" or "reckless disregard of the truth."

While the Court's statement that actual malice would be required in a suit by a public official, the Court's opinion had two and possibly three *other* constitutional aspects to it. First, the Court required that the public official plaintiff satisfy his burden of proof not by a mere preponderance of the evidence (more likely than not) but with "convincing clarity." Convincing clarity may be read as an analogous standard to proof by clear and convincing evidence. Second, the Court held that from a constitutional perspective the statements in the advertisement were not sufficiently "of and concerning" the plaintiff. In a defamation case, the plaintiff must establish that the false statements of fact were made about him, that is, of and concerning him. Here, the Court noted that there was no reference to Sullivan in the advertisement either by name or official position. If the Constitution allowed such vague references as those in the ad to be read as referring to Sullivan, then any criticism of the government could be translated into criticism of individual governmental officers. Such a state of affairs would unduly chill defendants' rights to free speech. Consequently, upholding a libel judgment for the plaintiff was constitutionally suspect. Critically, the Court neither did nor has provided a clear constitutional standard for what a plaintiff must show regarding the "of and concerning" requirement. Third, the Court refused to hold that the *Times* had knowledge that some of the facts in "Heed Their Rising Voices" were false even though the *Times'* news files contained stories against which those facts could have been checked. Arguably, this aspect of the case has some constitutional dimension to it—limiting inconsistent state law on imputed knowledge or vicarious liability in cases like *New York Times*.

Justice Black concurred and Justice Douglas joined in his concurrence. Justice Black would have recognized that the *Times* and the individual defendants "had an absolute, unconditional constitutional right to publish in the Times advertisement their criticisms of the Montgomery agencies and officials." Justice Goldberg also concurred. He, too, was joined by Justice Douglas. Like Justice Black, Goldberg thought that the *Times* was afforded even greater protection than the majority's absolute malice rule.

Thus, *New York Times Co. v. Sullivan* was a major victory for the proponents of the Civil Rights Movement. It took away a state's ability to frustrate the progress of the movement through its common law of defamation. By the time the decision was published, there were numerous other suits against the *New York Times* alleging defamation, and the victory was a significant one both in principle and because of the negative financial impact of liability on the press.

Moreover, the case was a victory for the First Amendment. It established the press's right in cases filed by public officials to be free from state common law defamation liability that had bordered on strict liability. The decision also recognized that the right to comment and criticize the government and government officials included a limited right to publish false statements of fact that may, from the common law perspective, be defamatory.

The Court's opinion balanced the critic's First Amendment right to speak against the state's interest to protect its citizens' reputations and to articulate and apply its own law of defamation. In the context of the public official, the First Amendment right

was paramount. As a result, for the Civil Rights Movement and for the media, *New York Times v. Sullivan* is a great and significant decision. Indeed, more than 40 years after its decision, it remains a great and significant decision today. But, critically, the Court's judicial regulation of the common law of defamation did not stop with *New York Times*. Thus, it is appropriate now to turn to discuss *some* of the development and accompanying confusion that the Court wrought in the wake of *New York Times*. This discussion is by no means complete but attempts to highlight the significant jurisprudential development.

First, the Court extended *New York Times'* actual malice requirement from suits by "public officials" to suits by "public figures" in *Curtis Publishing Co. v. Butts,* 388 U.S. 130 (1967). Additionally, the Court wrestled with the meaning of actual malice and what was required to prove it. In one case, the Court said that proof of constitutional actual malice would require a "high degree of awareness of … probable falsity" (*Garrison v. Louisiana,* 379 U.S. 64 [1964]). Later, in *St. Amant v. Thompson,* 390 U.S. 727 (1968), the Court said that actual malice would require either actual knowledge of falsity or that the defendant entertained serious doubts about a statement's truth. Thus, the Court seemed to articulate a subjective standard for actual malice. The Court continues to wrestle with the meaning of actual malice, and state courts wrestle with the overlap between *New York Times* constitutional (actual) malice and common law malice, which also may be relevant in a defamation case. Indeed, the U.S. Supreme Court has gone so far as to say that it might be preferable to jettison the phrase "actual malice" altogether because of the confusion it has created (*see Masson v. New Yorker Magazine,* 1991).

In *Rosenbloom v. Metromedia, Inc.* (1971), a badly divided Court indicated that *The New York Times* standard may apply to any case in which the speech involved was a matter of public concern or interest. Seemingly backing away from *Rosenbloom,* the Court in *Gertz v. Robert Welch, Inc.* (1974), noted the difficulty of deciding whether speech was a matter of public interest or not. In *Gertz,* the Court faced a situation where the plaintiff, a lawyer, was suing a publisher who had allegedly made false statements about his membership in various communist or Marxist organizations and his participation in an alleged conspiracy to undermine local police. The Court, in an opinion by Justice Powell, refused to apply *The New York Times* standard. The Court stated that where the plaintiff was not a public official or a public figure, but rather a private figure, the state's interest in protecting the reputation of its citizens and in articulating its law of defamation did not require application of *The New York Times* standard. While First Amendment values of free speech were still important in such a case, they were not as important as in the *New York Times* context. Consequently, the Court said that a state was free to apply a less demanding standard than *New York Times* as long as it did not impose liability without fault. Consequently, *Gertz* seemed to hold that constitutionally a private figure plaintiff had to establish at least negligence regarding the truth or falsity of the statement in order to recover. On a related subject involving damages, the *Gertz* Court held that a private figure could not recover without a showing of some actual injury unless the private figure made a showing of *New York Times* actual malice. If the plaintiff proved *New York Times* actual malice then personal and punitive damages were constitutionally permissible.

But who was a private figure and who was a public figure? The *Gertz* Court noted that there were two types of public figures: universal public figures and vortex public figures. The universal public figure was someone who had gained such notoriety as to be a public figure for all purposes. The more common (or vortex) public figure was someone who had thrust herself into the limelight of some public controversy. As noted, the Court felt *The New York Times*' standard was applicable to a public figure because the public figure had greater access to the media than the private figure, and the public figure, from a normative standpoint, had voluntarily entered the field of public debate.

Gertz signaled a major modification of *New York Times v. Sullivan*. It held that the rule or standard of *New York Times v. Sullivan* did not apply in a case involving a private figure. However, the Court imposed (or seemed to impose) significant limitations on the private figure's right to recover in a defamation action. The private figure had to establish at least negligence, and had to establish actual injury unless he or she proved *New York Times* actual malice, in which case presumed and punitive damages would be constitutionally permissible.

The Court did not stop with *Gertz*. After *Gertz*, in *Philadelphia Newspapers, Inc. v. Hepps* (1986), the Court held that a private plaintiff in a defamation case must prove falsity. The state could not allocate the burden of proof to the defendant to prove truth.

Critically, in *Dunn & Bradstreet, Inc. v. Greenmoss Builders, Inc.* (1985), the Court revived the matter of public concern or interest criteria. In *Greenmoss*, the Court held that Vermont's interest in protecting the reputation of its citizens and in articulating its own law of defamation justified a Vermont court awarding presumed damages to a private figure even when *New York Times* actual malice was not proved because the speech was *not* a matter of public concern. One may wonder if a state would be free, in the wake of *Greenmoss*, to return to a strict liability standard in a defamation case as long as the speech did not relate to a matter of public concern. Additionally, could the state in such a case make truth a defense, rather than making falsity an element of plaintiff's prima facie case? Does the First Amendment have *any* significant role in such a case?

Moreover, the Court has considered cases involving opinion versus fact in defamation cases (see *Milkovich v. Lorain Journal Co.*, 1990), and the constitutional relevance of altering quotations (see *Masson v. New Yorker Magazine*, 1991). And, the Court has extended *New York Times* (and its progeny) to tort cases other than defamation such as the right to privacy (see *Time, Inc. v. Hill*, 1967), and even intentional infliction of emotion distress (see *Hustler Magazine v. Falwell*, 1988). Yet, it has not extended it in cases involving promissory estoppel (see *Cohen v. Cowles Media Co.*, 1991), or appropriation (see *Zacchini v. Scripps-Howard Broadcasting Co.*, 1977).

Thus, *New York Times* and its progeny have created a hodgepodge of constitutional defamation (and other tort) law, and state defamation (and other tort) law, where the appropriate standard depends upon state law as well as whether the plaintiff is a public official, a public figure, or a private figure, and whether the relevant speech involves a matter of public concern. In addition, in cases not discussed in great detail herein, the Court has extended the *New York Times* actual malice standard to cases involving invasion of privacy and intentional infliction of emotional distress; has articulated rules regarding standards of review and summary judgment in the defamation context; and has decided defamation cases involving opinions and quotations. The point is that *New York Times* has spawned a somewhat confusing, not always consistent, and intellectually burdensome set of rules and decisions. Perhaps, this patchwork of state law, constitutional law, and procedural law is an inevitable result of life in a federal system.

See also Alien and Sedition Acts; Brennan, William J., Jr.; Civil Rights Movement; Common Law Background of American Civil Rights and Liberties; Defamation; Federalism, Civil Rights and; First Amendment; Goldberg, Arthur; King, Dr. Martin Luther, Jr.; Madison, James; Press, Freedom of the; Privacy, Invasion of; Warren Court

Bibliography

Lewis, Anthony. 1992. *Make No Law: The Sullivan Case and the First Amendment*. New York: Random House.

McWhorter, Diane. 2001. *Carry Me Home; Birmingham, Alabama—The Climactic Battle of the Civil Rights Revolution*. New York: Touchstone.

Smolla, Rodney. 2001. *Law of Defamation*. 2nd ed. St. Paul, MN: West.

Thomas C. Galligan, Jr.

NEW YORK TIMES V. UNITED STATES. *See* Pentagon Papers Case (*New York Times v. United States*)

NINETEENTH AMENDMENT. *See* Women's Suffrage

NINTH AMENDMENT (1791)

Adopted as part of the Bill of Rights in 1789 and ratified by the states in 1791, the Ninth Amendment provides: "The enumeration in the Constitution, of certain rights, shall not be construed to deny or disparage others retained by the people." James Madison, the principal author of the Bill of Rights, drafted this amendment to make clear that the specification of liberties in the preceding amendments was not to be interpreted as an exhaustive inventory of constitutional rights. As Abramson, Pinkerton, and Huppin (2003, 2) have pointed out, the Ninth Amendment is "an explicit acknowledgment that the Bill of Rights does not, and cannot, comprehensively encompass all foreseeable fundamental rights."

The Ninth Amendment reflects the "natural rights" philosophy embraced by late-eighteenth-century Americans. In this view, individual rights precede and transcend the power of government; individuals possess all rights except those that have been surrendered to government for the protection of the public good. Yet prior to 1965, the Ninth Amendment had little significance in constitutional law. In the words of Justice Potter Stewart, dissenting in *Griswold v. Connecticut* (1965),

[t]he Ninth Amendment, like its companion the Tenth, which this Court has held "states but a truism that all is retained which has not been surrendered, ... " was framed by James Madison and adopted by the States simply to make clear that the adoption of the Bill of Rights did not alter the plan that the Federal government was to be a government of express and limited powers, and that all rights and powers not delegated to it were retained by the people and the individual States.

Despite Justice Stewart's objections, the Court in *Griswold* relied in part on the Ninth Amendment in recognizing for the first time a constitutional right of privacy. In this landmark case, the Court invalidated a Connecticut statute that made it a crime to use birth control devices. In his concurring opinion, Justice Arthur Goldberg stressed the importance of the Ninth Amendment in creating a firm constitutional foundation for the newly declared right of privacy:

To hold that a right so basic and fundamental and so deep-rooted in our society as the right of privacy in marriage may be infringed because that right is not guaranteed in so many words by the first eight amendments to the Constitution is to ignore the Ninth Amendment and to give it no effect whatsoever. Moreover, a judicial construction that this fundamental right is not protected by the Constitution because it is not mentioned in explicit terms by one of the first eight amendments or elsewhere in the Constitution would violate the Ninth Amendment.

In his dissenting opinion, Justice Stewart insisted that "the idea that a federal court could ever use the Ninth Amendment to annul a law passed by the elected representatives of the people of the State of Connecticut would have caused James Madison no little wonder."

Although federal and state courts have seldom relied explicitly on the Ninth Amendment, they have over the years recognized a number of rights that Americans take for granted but which are not specifically enumerated in the Constitution. The Supreme Court has recognized the right to marry (see *Loving v. Virginia,* 1967), the right to determine how one's children are to be reared and educated (see *Meyer v. Nebraska,* 1923), the right to travel freely across state lines (see *Shapiro v. Thompson,* 1969), and the right to refuse life-sustaining medical treatment (see *Cruzan v. Missouri Health Department,* 1990) as being implicit in the "liberty" guaranteed by the Due Process Clauses of the Fifth and Fourteenth Amendments.

See also Bill of Rights; Due Process Clauses; Due Process, Substantive; Federalist Papers; Fifth Amendment; Fourteenth Amendment (1868); Fundamental Rights; Goldberg, Arthur; *Griswold v. Connecticut* (1965); Liberty; *Loving v. Virginia* (1967); Madison, James; Marriage, Rights Pertaining to; *Meyer v. Nebraska* (1923); Natural Rights; Privacy, Constitutional Right of; Reproductive Freedom; Right to Die; Stewart, Potter; Travel, Right to

Bibliography

Abramson, Paul R., Steven D. Pinkerton, and Mark Huppin. 2003. *Sexual Rights in America: The Ninth Amendment and the Pursuit of Happiness.* New York: New York University Press.

    John M. Scheb II and Otis H. Stephens, Jr.

Massey, Calvin R. *Silent Rights: The Ninth Amendment and the Constitution's Unenumerated Rights.* Philadelphia: Temple University Press.

NO CONTEST PLEA. *See* Pleas in Criminal Cases

NOI. *See* Nation of Islam

NOT GUILTY, PLEA OF. *See* Pleas in Criminal Cases

NOTICE, RIGHT TO. *See* Due Process, Procedural

NOW. *See* National Organization for Women

NRLC. *See* National Right to Life Committee

NUDITY. *See* Public Nudity

NULLIFICATION, DOCTRINE OF. *See* States' Rights, Doctrine of

O

OBSCENITY AND PORNOGRAPHY

The First Amendment is the cornerstone of the Bill of Rights and the foundation of our civil liberties. Without the freedom of speech and press along with religious freedom and the right to assemble and petition government, the United States would be a vastly different country—a country most Americans would neither recognize nor one in which they would want to live. But First Amendment freedoms encompass a vast spectrum of rights and almost all Americans recognize that these freedoms have some limits. With freedom of expression, the nature and extent of those limits are the meat and potatoes of First Amendment law.

Freedom of speech and press can be analytically differentiated to distinguish three types of expression: political speech; commercial speech; and artistic expression. We consider artistic expression here and it should be noted that artistic speech covers a wide variety of communication media, including the written word, the spoken word, photography, motion pictures, television, the Internet, records/CDs/tapes, theater, dance, music, painting, drawing, and sculpture.

Freedom of political expression goes to the heart of a democratic political order and that right is strained to the limit when exercised by those who would deny such freedom to others or whose written or oral message is that of hate and violence. Commercial freedom of expression focuses on the economic order and is strained to the limit when exercised in a misleading, false, or fraudulent manner. Artistic free expression, on the other hand, is concentrated on cultural and moral order and touches the order's raw nerves particularly in its representation of sex and sexual behavior. For artistic expression the fear is not debasing the political system or undermining the economic system, but debasing and undermining society's ethics, morals, and culture in terms of how people treat each other and themselves.

Those who want society to be protected against what they consider to be unbridled immorality and sexism have favored censorship and the suppression of certain sexually oriented material they consider to be obscene. But this has also meant that First Amendment questions are ultimately raised because censorship and the suppression of expression run counter to the philosophy of the First Amendment, which values complete freedom of thought and the free trade in ideas with the faith that in the contest of ideas the vile, false, and the hateful will ultimately be rejected.

Defining Obscenity

Obscenity has long been an issue in Anglo-American law. The leading English case in the nineteenth century was *Regina v. Hicklin* (1868), which allowed written material to be judged by the effect of an isolated excerpt upon the most weak-minded member of the community susceptible to lustful thoughts. American courts adopted the *Hicklin* standard and utilizing it legitimized censorship including the banning of such literary classics as Theodore Dreiser's *An American Tragedy* and D.H. Lawrence's *Lady Chatterly's Lover*. It was not until the attempt to suppress another literary master-piece, James Joyce's *Ulysses,* that American courts moved away from the severe *Hicklin* standard. In *United States v. One Book called "Ulysses,"* (1934), the new standard became how the average man (not just those most susceptible to lustful thoughts) reacts to the material. Furthermore, the standard required the entire book to be considered and not just isolated passages.

The U.S. Supreme Court first confronted the is-sue of artistic freedom of expression in *Mutual Film Corporation v. Ohio Industrial Commission* (1915). In that case the Court determined that motion pic-tures were not part of the press and thus were not entitled to First Amendment protection. Not until *Burstyn v. Wilson* (1952) did the Court extend the scope of the First Amendment to cover motion pic-tures. Although the Court dealt with a censorship law that included obscenity, the *Burstyn* case con-cerned a violation of the "sacrilegious" provision of the New York law under challenge; thus the Court did not specifically grapple with obscenity.

In *Roth v. United States* (1957), the Court explicitly ruled that the First Amendment does not protect obscenity. However the Court also sought to define obscenity in a way that would not unduly inhibit legitimate artistic expression in the sexual realm. Justice Brennan, writing for the Court, made it clear that sex and obscenity, indeed nudity and obscenity, are not synonymous. The portrayal of sex and nudity in art, literature, and scientific works itself is not a sufficient reason to deny such mate-rial the protection of the First Amendment. Rather, what makes a work obscene is the use of sex, includ-ing nudity, in a manner that appeals to a prurient interest—that is, it excites lustful thoughts and is physiologically sexually arousing. The standard, then, is whether "to the average person, applying contemporary community standards, the dominant

theme of the material taken as a whole appeals to a prurient interest." Justice Brennan noted that the First Amendment is not absolute.

Traditionally, certain types of speech, such as libel and obscenity, were not intended by the Fram-ers to be protected by the First Amendment. But Brennan added: "All ideas having even the slightest redeeming social importance—unorthodox ideas, controversial ideas, even ideas hateful to the pre-vailing climate of opinion—have the full protection of the guaranties unless excludable because they encroach upon the limited area of more important interests. But implicit in the history of the First Amendment is the rejection of obscenity as ut-terly without redeeming social importance." Thus, obscenity is, by definition, "utterly without redeem-ing social importance ... [and] is not within the area of constitutionally protected speech or press."

In a subsequent case, *Jacobellis v. Ohio* (1964), a plurality ruled that a national standard is to be used in determining "contemporary community stan-dards" to ascertain if the work appeals to a prurient interest. Applying the broad definition of obscenity in specific instances, however, proved troublesome for the Court. Indeed, in the *Jacobellis* decision, an exasperated Justice Stewart admitted that he could not define hard core pornography, "but I know it when I see it.... " By the mid-1960s in order for a work of art, a book, a magazine, or motion picture to be adjudged obscene by the Supreme Court it had to be shown that the work was utterly or completely without redeeming social value, something quite difficult to demonstrate.

The Court's more permissive approach was noted in *Memoirs v. Massachusetts* (1966) in which the book *Fanny Hill: Memoirs of a Woman of Plea-sure,* written by John Cleland in the eighteenth cen-tury, was found to contain some socially redeeming value (e.g., it shed light on the culture and sexual mores of a segment of eighteenth-century society). Justice Brennan, in his opinion for a plurality, made it clear that three characteristics of a disputed work must be present before that work can be adjudged obscene: (1) the dominant theme appeals to a pru-rient interest in sex; (2) sex is treated in a manner that is patently offensive by contemporary national standards; and (3) the work is utterly without redeeming social value.

But on the same day that *Memoirs* was handed down, the Court also ruled in *Ginzburg v. United States* (1966) that when there was doubt as to whether a work was legally obscene, evidence of the merchandising or advertising would then be examined to determine whether or not there was sexual pandering. If sexual pandering was determined, then the work would not receive any benefit of the doubt.

The 1960s was a decade of massive social change, and part of that change included the liberalization of artistic standards in terms of representation of sex, sexual behavior, and language. The strict privately enforced codes that governed motion pictures were abandoned and replaced by a movie rating system in which R-rated films could have uncensored language and some nudity along with simulated sex acts. By the end of the decade, books no longer were self-censored or subject to prosecution because written descriptions of sex and sexual behavior appeared to have absolute constitutional protection. Photographic representations of sex, although somewhat more troublesome, passed the muster of the Warren Court's looser standards.

In one of the last decisions of the Warren Court, *Stanley v. Georgia* (1969), the Court for the first time gave obscenity some constitutional protection. In that decision the Court found that one may possess legally obscene matter in the privacy of one's own home and that it is none of the government's business what any individual reads. This was modified in later years to allow states to prohibit the possession of child pornography.

Redefining Obscenity

The Burger Court of the 1970s undertook to reverse the Warren Court's liberal stance on obscenity. The Court's new policy was stated in two major obscenity cases, *Miller v. California* (1973) and *Paris Adult Theatre v. Slaton* (1973), both decided on the same day. Under the Court's new standards concerning obscenity, local communities could impose

their criteria as to what representations of sex, taken as a whole, appealed to the prurient interest. State statutes were directed to be explicit and precise as to the representations of sex to be considered patently offensive. Furthermore, the Court directed that no longer must the challenged work be utterly without redeeming social value. Rather, a work can be considered legally obscene if the work, taken as a whole, lacks serious literary, artistic, political, or scientific value. No longer, for example, could one hour of explicit copulation in a motion picture be redeemed by including a ten-minute segment of political discussion about censorship.

The new standards caused some initial confusion that the Court found necessary to correct the following year in *Jenkins v. Georgia* (1974). *Jenkins* concerned the acclaimed Hollywood film (nominated for several Academy Awards) "Carnal Knowledge" that the Georgia Supreme Court, ostensibly applying the criteria spelled out in *Miller* and *Paris,* found to be obscene. The U.S. Supreme Court reversed the Georgia high court and made it clear that objective measures of serious artistic value must control the application of *Miller* and *Paris.* "Carnal Knowledge," although focused on sex and sexual mores, was assuredly a serious artistic work and the prudery of the Georgia justices could not justify the violation of the First Amendment.

In practice, the Court seemed to be limiting obscenity to "hard-core pornography." The Court clearly was more supportive of efforts to suppress certain sexually oriented material but the Court's policy did not, in fact, result in a nationwide crackdown on the billion-dollar pornography industry. But the legal tools were made available to prosecutors in the event they wished to stifle hard-core pornography and were willing to undertake extensive litigation in which the challenge would be to differentiate between "soft-core" and "hard-core."

More Recent Trends

In 1986, the Court was supportive of local officials who used zoning laws to contain and regulate pornography shops and theaters (*City of Renton v. Playtime Theatres, Inc.*). The Court found the zoning ordinance at issue to be content-neutral and a valid time-place-and-manner regulation. The Court also found in *New York v. P.J. Video Inc.* (1986) that the probable cause standard used to evaluate warrant applications was the same regardless of whether the evidence was presumptively protected by the First Amendment. In *Barnes v. Glen Theatre, Inc.* (1991) the Court upheld an Indiana public decency statute that required dancers to wear pasties and a G-string. This statute was found to not violate the First Amendment rights of the dancers or anyone else. And in *Arcara v. Cloud Books, Inc.* (1986), the Court upheld a New York statute under which an "adult" bookstore was closed for one year when the premises were found to be a public nuisance because they were used for prostitution and lewd behavior (such as masturbation in the "private" projection booths). The Court found that this activity had no element of protected expression and justified the closing of a bookstore.

However, in *Fort Wayne Books, Inc. v. Indiana* (1989), the Rehnquist Court found that the First Amendment was violated when an adult bookstore was padlocked and the contents were seized prior to a trial determination that the materials were obscene or that racketeering violations had occurred. The Rehnquist Court's overall take on artistic free expression in the sexual realm was suggested by its decision in *National Endowment for the Arts v. Finley* (1998). In that decision the Court did not find a First Amendment violation in the congressional directive to the National Endowment for the Arts that required the consideration of "general standards of decency and respect for the diverse beliefs and values of the American public" in awarding grants. The majority on the Rehnquist Court has been sensitive to First Amendment concerns, but is unwilling to give sexual expression the benefit of the doubt in the gray areas.

With the rise of the women's movement, the obscenity issue assumed a new perspective. The hard-core sex industry has been accused of shamelessly exploiting and degrading women's bodies, often merging sex and violence. Some civil libertarians have rethought their position on censorship

as it applies to these materials and have sought to distinguish erotic, nonsexist sexual material from exploitative, sexist, violent pornography. But this distinction has met with objections from unyielding defenders of the First Amendment such as the American Civil Liberties Union, who are fearful that censors are unable to make such distinctions (one person's erotica is another's pornography) and believe, furthermore, that adult members of society should be free to decide for themselves what they wish to read, see, or hear as long as they are not imposing their choices on others or otherwise impinging on another's rights.

Broadcast Media and Telephone Communication

There should also be mention of the special status of the broadcast media (radio and television) as distinct from the print media and also from live theater or from motion pictures that are theatrically exhibited. Although the broadcast media, including cable television, have First Amendment protection, the airwaves are subject to some regulation by the Federal Communications Commission (FCC) in the realm of sex and language. In *FCC v. Pacifica Foundation* (1978), the Court upheld government regulation of the content of broadcasts found by the FCC to be "indecent but not obscene." The FCC was empowered by Congress in 1988 to crack down on the dial-a-porn industry and this led to the decision in *Sable Communications of California, Inc. v. FCC* (1989) in which the Court allowed regulation of obscene phone messages but not "indecent" ones. In *Denver Area Educ. Telcom. Consortium v. FCC* (1996), the Court also handed down a divided ruling. The Court upheld the provision of the Cable Television Consumer Protection and Competition Act that permits (but does not require) the cable company to prohibit obscene or indecent programming on leased access channels. However, public access channels may not be subject to such censorship and cable operators may not be required to segregate and block patently offensive leased access channel programming.

In *United States v. Playboy, Inc.* (2000), the Court invalidated a provision of the Telecommunications Act of 1996 requiring cable companies to fully block sex-oriented adult cable television to homes from the hours of 6:00 A.M. to 9:00 P.M. to protect children from indecent programming. Justice Kennedy, writing for the majority, pointed out that this was a content-based restriction aimed at suppressing certain speakers. It was not the least restrictive way to protect children. He noted: "The objective of shielding children does not suffice to support a blanket ban if the protection can be obtained by a less restrictive alternative." An obvious less restrictive measure would be for individual cable subscribers to be able to have adult channels completely blocked so that they would not be received in their homes while those desiring to receive such channels would be able to continue receiving them.

Protecting Children

As the cases described in the previous section suggest, the protection of children is very much an issue in the obscenity field, indeed it can be argued that it has become THE issue. The Court, in *New York v. Ferber* (1982), treated sympathetically a New York law aimed at the so-called kiddie-porn industry that punished the distributors of sexually oriented materials that used children under the age of 16. The materials involved did not have to meet the legal definition of obscenity in order for them to be regulated. In *U.S. v. X-Citement Video, Inc.* (1994), the Court upheld a conviction under the Protection of Children Against Sexual Exploitation Act of 1977 and interpreted the statute as requiring that the accused know that one of the performers was a minor—something that was not explicit in the law. Possession of child pornography in the privacy of one's home may be made a state crime, ruled the Court in *Osborne v. Ohio* (1990). In this case, the Court made a major exception to the *Stanley v. Georgia* (1969) policy that placed privacy values on a higher plane than regulation of obscenity.

The more recent Rehnquist Court, however, has made some important distinctions designed to protect the First Amendment rights of adults. The Court struck down certain provisions of the Communications Decency Act of 1996 that sought to protect minors from harmful sexual material on the Internet. The law criminalized the knowing transmission of obscene or indecent messages to those under the age of 18 and prohibited the knowing sending or displaying of any message to those under 18 "that in context depicts or describes, in terms patently offensive as measured by contemporary community standards, sexual or excretory activities or organs." A sender could avoid prosecution if the sender demonstrated a good-faith effort to screen out minors by requiring proof of age before transmitting the material. The lower court issued an injunction against enforcement of these provisions with regard to "indecent" but not "obscene" material. In *Reno v. American Civil Liberties Union* (1997) the Court affirmed the lower court and ruled that the challenged provisions were content-based, were not time-place-manner restrictions, and were facially overbroad in violation of the First Amendment.

Congress has enacted other measures geared to protect children. The Child Pornography Prevention Act of 1996 banned virtual child pornography, that is, computer-generated images or pictures that appear to be depicting a minor engaging in sexually explicit conduct but were produced by means other than using real children, for example, using youthful-looking adults or computer-generated technology. The Court in *Ashcroft v. Free Speech Coalition* (2002) ruled that this ban was overbroad and thus violated the First Amendment. No real children were involved. Material using computer-generated images of children or young-looking adults made to look underage cannot be treated the same way as material using real underage persons.

In a more conciliatory decision, *Ashcroft v. American Civil Liberties Union* (2002), the Rehnquist Court ruled that the 1998 Child Online Protection Act's reference to contemporary community standards in defining what was harmful to minors did not itself render the Act unconstitutionally overbroad under the First Amendment. However, when the case returned to the Supreme Court in 2004, the Court ruled that enforcement of the Act was correctly enjoined by the Third Circuit because the statute likely violated the First Amendment.

Of even greater significance was the Court's decision in 2003 in *U.S. v. American Library Association, Inc.* In that case the Court upheld the constitutionality of the Children's Internet Protection Act of 2000, which requires public libraries, as a condition for receiving federal subsidies, to use internet filters to screen out indecent and obscene material. Congress can set such conditions for receiving federal funds without violating the First Amendment.

Conclusion

The current state of obscenity law can be summarized as follows: Obscenity is not protected by the First Amendment; however, the private possession in one's home of pornography depicting adults has constitutional protection. The definition of obscenity is not easy but the standards enunciated in *Miller v. California* (1973) still hold today. The focus of statutes and prosecutorial activity is to protect minors from being exploited by the sex industry and to protect them from exposure to indecent and obscene material. The Supreme Court has tended, with only few exceptions, to give greater leeway to adult access to sexually oriented material depicting adults.

See also American Civil Liberties Union; Ashcroft, John D.; Bill of Rights; Burger Court; Child Pornography; Commercial Speech; Decency, Standards of; Douglas, William O.; First Amendment; Internet, Free Speech on the; Kennedy, Anthony; *Miller v. California* (1973); Overbreadth, Doctrine of; Petition, Right of; Press, Freedom of the; Privacy, Constitutional Right of; Rehnquist Court; Religion, Freedom of; *Reno v. American Civil Liberties Union* (1997); Speech, Freedom of; Stewart, Potter; Time, Place, and Manner Restrictions; Warren Court

Bibliography

Harrison, Maureen, and Steve Gilbert, eds. 2000. *Obscenity and Pornography Decisions of the United States Supreme Court.* Carlsbad, CA: Excellent Books.

Hixson, Richard F. 1996. *Pornography and the Justices: The Supreme Court and the Intractable Obscenity Problem.* Carbondale: Southern Illinois University Press.

Sheldon Goldman

O'CONNOR, SANDRA DAY (1930–)

Sandra Day O'Connor burst onto the national scene when she became the first woman appointed to the Supreme Court of the United States. For 24 years, O'Connor occupied a position of prominence at the heart of the Supreme Court, a voice of moderation and compromise between her liberal and conservative colleagues.

O'Connor was born on March 26, 1930. After graduating third in her class from Stanford Law School, O'Connor encountered difficulty in finding a job that matched her talents. At that time the law was the exclusive domain of men and few women were welcomed into the fraternity. Those women who did practice were often relegated to less prestigious jobs than similarly skilled male classmates. For a decade O'Connor raised her family and practiced law in a number of settings, ranging from a county attorney's office to a private firm. She held a position as Assistant Attorney General of Arizona in the late 1960s, which led to service in the Arizona Senate in the early 1970s. In 1975, O'Connor sought a new challenge and found it in her election as judge of Maricopa County Superior Court. Governor Bruce Babbitt appointed O'Connor to the Arizona Court of Appeals in 1979.

When Justice Potter Stewart retired from the United States Supreme Court in 1981, a newly elected President Ronald Reagan was placed in a position of delivering on a campaign promise to appoint a woman to the high court. Sandra Day O'Connor was selected and joined a court that included her old Stanford Law School classmate, William Rehnquist. Initially observers thought that O'Connor would share Rehnquist's conservative inclinations, but with every passing year she became more independent and more moderate.

This increasing moderation is reflected in a number of her most influential opinions. Early in her tenure O'Connor stood as the key vote on an otherwise evenly divided Supreme Court in the case of *Lynch v. Donnelly*. At issue was whether a nativity scene in a city park in Pawtucket, Rhode Island constituted a violation of the First Amendment's Establishment Clause. A majority opinion written by Chief Justice Warren E. Burger rejected the challenge, arguing that "To forbid the use of this one passive symbol—the crèche—at the very time people are taking note of the season with Christmas hymns and carols in public schools and other public places, and while the Congress and legislatures open sessions with prayers by paid chaplains, would be a stilted overreaction contrary to our history and to our holdings." Writing for the four dissenters, Justice William Brennan argued that "The essence of the crèche's symbolic purpose and effect is to prompt the observer to experience a sense of simple awe and wonder appropriate to the contemplation of one of the central elements of Christian dogma—that God sent His Son into the world to be a Messiah." Justice O'Connor refused to adopt either of these approaches, rejecting the majority's willingness to defer to tradition and the dissenters' eagerness to find a violation of the First Amendment. O'Connor wrote separately "to suggest a clarification of our Establishment Clause doctrine" and proposed a test based on whether the governmental action in question constituted an endorsement of religion. Ultimately she employed this test to conclude that "the government's display of the crèche in this particular physical setting is no more an endorsement of religion than such governmental 'acknowledgements' of religion as legislative prayers of the type approved in *Marsh v. Chambers,* printing 'In God We Trust' on coins and opening court sessions with 'God save the United States and this honorable Court.'"

O'Connor's tendency to occupy the center was demonstrated clearly in the case of *Employment Division v. Smith* (1990), in which the Court ruled that the First Amendment's Free Exercise Clause does not protect the religiously inspired use of the hallucinogen peyote. Justice Antonin Scalia's majority opinion established that the government simply had to pass a rational basis analysis before it could intrude upon religiously motivated violations of the law, a standard that provided great deference to the government. Not surprisingly, Scalia concluded that this standard was satisfied in *Smith.* Justice Harry Blackmun's dissent presented a stark contrast, arguing that the appropriate standard for measuring the government's action was the more demanding compelling state interest test. Blackmun concluded that the government's attempt to characterize the ingestion of peyote as unacceptable failed to meet this compelling state interest analysis. Justice O'Connor provided a compromise between these two positions, agreeing with Blackmun that governmental interference with religious practices must be measured against the more demanding standard of the compelling state interest test. She disagreed with Blackmun about the importance of curbing illegal drug use, however, asserting that the state of Oregon did in fact have a compelling interest in preventing its citizens from possessing and using peyote.

Perhaps the ultimate example of O'Connor's pragmatism came in *Planned Parenthood of Southeastern Pennsylvania v. Casey* (1992), a case in which the justices reconsidered the intensely controversial decision of *Roe v. Wade.* The conservative justices sought to overturn the decision of *Roe v. Wade* and set the stage for states to restrict or even prohibit abortion, while the liberal justices wanted to restate a commitment to *Roe* and insist that state restrictions on abortion be subjected to the strictest level of scrutiny. Again, O'Connor constructed a middle-ground approach, rejecting the arguments of both warring camps. With Justices Anthony Kennedy and David Souter, O'Connor crafted an opinion that rejected the trimester approach of *Roe v. Wade* and substituted an analysis of whether the fetus had reached the point of viability. However, *Roe*'s fundamental assertion that the Constitution protects a woman's decision to terminate her pregnancy was not rejected: "No change in *Roe*'s factual underpinnings has left its central holding obsolete, and none supports an argument for overruling it." Yet Justice O'Connor did not consider a woman's right to terminate a pregnancy absolute: "The woman's liberty is not so unlimited, however, that from the outset the State cannot show its concern for the life of the unborn, and at a later point in fetal development the State's interest in life has sufficient force so that the right of the woman to terminate the pregnancy can be restricted." Under O'Connor's framework, courts now ask whether a governmental restriction creates an undue burden on a woman's right to obtain an abortion prior to the point of viability.

Some see Sandra Day O'Connor's quest for moderation as a Solomon-like rejection of extremism. Those who bristle at members of the Supreme Court operating from either fringe find much to appreciate about her approach to constitutional decision making. Yet by occupying the center, O'Connor has exposed herself to criticism from both flanks. Some conservatives see her approach as naive, preaching the necessity of limiting individual liberty while creating tests that will allow societal norms and preferences to be thwarted. Some liberals perceive O'Connor's approach as hypocritical, paying lip service to the minority while finding ways to tilt the board in the direction of the majority and the government. While the wisdom of her approach is perhaps debatable, the result is not. Sandra Day O'Connor's moderation and pragmatism placed her in a position to determine the direction of the Supreme Court in case after case, term after term, decade after decade.

See also Abortion, Right to; Blackmun, Harry A.; Brennan, William J., Jr.; Burger Court; Burger, Warren E.; Conservatism; *Employment Division, Department of Human Resources of Oregon v. Smith* (1990); Establishment Clause; First Amendment; Free Exercise Clause; Gender-Based Discrimination; Kennedy, Anthony; Liberalism; Rational Basis Test; Rehnquist Court; Rehnquist, William H.; *Roe v. Wade* (1973); Scalia, Antonin; Souter, David H.

Bibliography

Maveety, Nancy. 1996. *Justice Sandra Day O'Connor: Strategist on the Supreme Court.* Lanham, MD: Rowman and Littlefield.

O'Connor, Sandra Day, and H. Alan Day. 2002. *Lazy B: Growing Up On a Cattle Ranch in the American Southwest.* New York: Random House.

O'Connor, Sandra Day. 2003. *The Majesty of the Law: Reflections of a Supreme Court Justice.* New York: Random House.

Van Sickel, Robert W. 1998. *Not a Particularly Different Voice: The Jurisprudence of Sandra Day O'Connor.* New York: Peter Lang Publishing.

Anthony Simones

OCR. *See* Office for Civil Rights

OFFICE FOR CIVIL RIGHTS (OCR)

Located within the U.S. Department of Education, the Office for Civil Rights (OCR) enforces federal laws that prohibit discrimination based on race, color, national origin, sex, age, or disability in all educational programs that receive financial support from the federal government. OCR is responsible for resolving complaints relating to discrimination towards students, as well as looking for systemic solutions to civil rights problems. In addition, OCR assists institutions in achieving voluntary compliance with the rules it is required to enforce.

In recent years, Congress has enacted several regulations to protect students from different types of discrimination in educational institutions receiving federal funding. The No Child Left Behind Act, signed into law on January 8, 2002, contains specific provisions for the prevention of discrimination against students. Previous laws aimed at ensuring equal access to public education were: (1) Title VI of the Civil Rights Act of 1964 (race, color, and national origin discrimination); (2) Title IX of the Education Amendments of 1972 (sex discrimination); (3) Section 504 of the Rehabilitation Act of 1973, and Title II of the Americans with Disabilities Act of 1990 (disability discrimination); and (4) The Age Discrimination Act of 1975 (age discrimination).

While OCR enforces various laws related to discrimination on the basis of race, color, national origin, sex, and age, it also attempts to prevent discrimination in programs or activities funded by the Department of Education. Another of OCR's enforcement responsibilities, the Boy Scouts of America Equal Access Act, states that no educational institution that allows one or more outside youth or community groups to meet on its premises or at its facilities before or after school hours may deny equal access or a fair opportunity to meet to any youth group listed in Title 36 of the United States Code as a patriotic society. The Boy Scouts of America are included in this group.

To accomplish its multiple goals, OCR has 12 enforcement offices around the country located in: Boston, New York, Philadelphia, Seattle, Atlanta, Dallas, Cleveland, Chicago, Kansas City, Denver, San Francisco, and Washington, DC. Depending on their location, these offices are grouped into four divisions: Eastern, Southern, Midwestern, and Western divisions. There are also two Enforcement Directors that supervise and coordinate the activities of the four divisions. OCR's headquarters in Washington, DC, provides administrative support, policy development, and overall coordination of efforts.

One important administrative tool is the Complaint of Discrimination, a formal document stating that an educational institution that receives federal funding has discriminated against an individual. Complaints of discrimination can be lodged with OCR, either on paper or through an online complaint form on OCR's website (www.ed.gov/about/offices/list/ocr/index.html). There are several important aspects of the complaint process. First, the complaint form should contain the name of the educational institution, the name of the person who has been discriminated against, the date of the discrimination, and the name, signature, and contact information of the person filing the complaint. Second, the complaint must be filed within 180 days after the alleged discrimination. Within seven days, OCR will call the individual who filed the complaint to acknowledge that the organization has received the complaint. Within 30 days, OCR will contact the complainant to inform him or her whether it will continue with the complaint process. OCR is neutral in its assessment of the facts and does not advise either party. Finally, OCR cannot proceed with a discrimination complaint when another agency or school is dealing with the same case; for example, through their formal grievance procedure. In most cases an individual can file a claim in court without resorting to the OCR complaint process. However, in the case of age discrimination, an individual is required to file with the OCR before filing a claim in court.

See also Civil Rights Act of 1964; Title IX of the Education Amendments of 1972

J. Ramon Gil-Garcia

OPEN FIELDS DOCTRINE

English common law famously held that "a man's home is his castle." The Fourth Amendment to the U.S. Constitution, which prohibits "unreasonable searches and seizures," specifically mentions the people's right to be secure in their houses as well as their persons, papers, and effects. Because, as the Supreme Court recognized in *United States v. United States District Court* (1972), the "physical entry of the home is the chief evil against which the wording of the Fourth Amendment is directed," a person in his or her home enjoys the maximum protection the Constitution affords with respect to searches and seizures.

The term *curtilage*, which comes from the English common law, refers to the enclosed space of ground surrounding a dwelling. In *Hester v. United States* (1924), the Supreme Court held that the Fourth Amendment provides the same protection to the curtilage as to the house itself. On the other hand, the "open fields" surrounding the house and curtilage are not entitled to Fourth Amendment protection. Writing for the Supreme Court in *Hester,* Justice Oliver Wendell Holmes noted that "the special protection accorded by the Fourth Amendment ... is not extended to the open fields. The distinction between the latter and the house is as old as the common law."

In *Oliver v. United States* (1984), the Supreme Court reaffirmed the open fields doctrine. In that case, narcotics officers acting on a tip entered the defendant's land by going around a locked gate and ignoring the posted "No Trespassing" signs. When agents observed a field of marijuana, they arrested the owner of the property for manufacturing a controlled substance. On appeal, the Supreme Court upheld the search because it concluded that the Fourth Amendment did not apply to the open fields around the defendant's home, despite his attempt to protect it by posting signs. Writing for the majority in *Oliver*, Justice Lewis Powell observed that:

open fields do not provide the setting for those intimate activities that the Amendment is intended to shelter from government interference or surveillance. There is no societal interest in protecting the privacy of those activities, such as the cultivation of crops, that occur in open fields. Moreover, as a practical matter these lands usually are accessible to the public and the police in ways that a home, an office, or commercial structure would not be. It is not generally true that fences or "No Trespassing" signs effectively bar the public from viewing open fields in rural areas.... For these reasons, the asserted expectation of privacy in open fields is not an expectation that "society recognizes as reasonable."

In his dissenting opinion, Justice Thurgood Marshall insisted that Oliver had a reasonable expectation of privacy in his lands:

Privately owned woods and fields that are not exposed to public view regularly are employed in a variety of ways that society acknowledges deserve privacy. Many landowners like to take solitary walks on their property, confident that they will not be confronted in their rambles by strangers or policemen. Others conduct agricultural businesses on their property. Some landowners use their secluded spaces to meet lovers, others to gather together with fellow worshippers, still others to engage in sustained creative endeavor. Private land is sometimes used as a refuge for wildlife, where flora and fauna are protected from human intervention of any kind. Our respect for the freedom of landowners to use their posted "open fields" in ways such as these partially explains the seriousness with which the positive law regards deliberate invasions of such spaces, ... and substantially reinforces the landowners' contention that their expectations of privacy are "reasonable."

In *United States v. Dunn* (1987), the Supreme Court again reaffirmed the open fields doctrine, holding that "there is no constitutional difference between police observations conducted while in a public place and while standing in the open fields." In *Dunn*, agents of the Drug Enforcement Administration, acting without a warrant, went onto the defendant's land because they suspected he was operating an illegal methamphetamine lab. Led by telltale odors to his barn, they peered inside and observed what appeared to be a meth lab. With that information they secured a search warrant, which they executed and made an arrest. Speaking through Justice Byron White, the Supreme Court held that the DEA agents "lawfully viewed the interior of respondent's barn, and their observations were properly considered by the Magistrate in issuing a search warrant for respondent's premises." In dissent, Justice William Brennan argued that "the agents infringed upon Dunn's reasonable expectation of privacy in the barn and its contents."

Although the open fields doctrine remains controversial, it appears to be firmly established in the Supreme Court's Fourth Amendment jurisprudence.

See also Brennan, William J.; Castle Doctrine; Common Law Background of American Civil Rights and Liberties; Fourth Amendment; Holmes, Oliver Wendell, Jr.; Marshall, Thurgood; Powell, Lewis F. Jr.; Privacy, Reasonable Expectations of; White, Byron R.

Bibliography

Scheb, John M., and John M. Scheb II. 2006. *Criminal Procedure*. Belmont, CA: Thomson/Wadsworth.

John M. Scheb II and Otis H. Stephens, Jr.

OPERATION RESCUE

Since the United States Supreme Court's ruling in *Roe v. Wade* (1973), which held that the constitutional right to privacy was broad enough to encompass a woman's decision to terminate her pregnancy, abortion providers have been the object of protests by those who believe that abortion is morally wrong. During the mid- to late 1980s, increased extremism in anti-abortion protests was attributed in part to Operation Rescue (OR), a group founded by militant pro-lifer Randall Terry in 1986. Operation Rescue's strategy was primarily to target the women attempting to receive abortions instead of the legal and political institutions that permitted abortion. The group considered that a "rescue" was accomplished each time they succeeded in dissuading a woman from going through with an abortion (Toner 1993). Operation Rescue had a pervasive Christian religious tone.

OR's tactics involved blockading the entrances to abortion clinics and directly interacting with women who sought to enter those clinics. The blockades were composed of protestors who would stand, sit, or sometimes lie down in tight groups in front of clinic doors. These protesters were supplemented by picketers, often shouting loudly and carrying signs bearing slogans or, in some cases, pictures of healthy or dead fetuses. OR counselors took up posts outside clinics and then approached women going into the clinics. These counselors would then aggressively exhort the women to carry their pregnancies to term. The counselors often handed women folders containing information about abortion alternatives, dramatic (and some argue exaggerated) information about frightening medical complications of abortion, written testimonials by women who had had abortions and regretted them, and sometimes gruesome pictures of whole or partial dead fetuses.

In 1988, OR staged a large protest they called the "Siege of Atlanta," during which many members were arrested and jailed, and the organization gained national attention. Randall Terry was among those jailed and subsequently became a highly visible figure, especially when he was prosecuted in 1992 for planning, in violation of a federal injunction, to thrust a dead fetus in the face of then-Governor Bill Clinton at the 1992 Democratic National Convention (Sullivan 1992). After the Atlanta protest, OR attempted to stage large protests in several other cities over the next few years. OR's activities prompted abortion services providers nationwide to develop defense strategies, which in various

cases included erecting fences, training "defenders" to form protective human barriers around clinics, or recruiting "escorts" to see women safely in and out of clinic doors.

By the early 1990s, uproar over OR's tactics led to the passage of several state and local laws that prohibited blocking access to the entrances of health care facilities and to a federal law, the Freedom of Access to Clinic Entrances Act of 1993. FACE makes blocking a clinic entrance or threatening people who try to enter the clinic a federal crime with penalties of up to $10,000 in fines or six months in jail for a first offense.

OR was sued twice for extortion under the federal RICO statute; the claims rested on the assertion that OR had committed extortion by depriving women of abortion services and that the organization was corrupt. In both cases, these claims were unsuccessful. The Supreme Court ruled in *Scheidler v. National Organization for Women, Inc.* (2003) that Operation Rescue had not obtained property from women at clinics and therefore had not committed extortion as defined by the RICO Act.

After the legal battles in the early 1990s, Operation Rescue went bankrupt and disbanded. Today there are many groups bearing the name "Operation Rescue," including autonomous local groups and Operation Rescue West, which runs the web site www.operationrescue.org. Another group, Operation Save America, led by a former prominent OR member, the Rev. Flip Benham, may be the most direct descendant of the original Operation Rescue (Barry 2001). Randall Terry is no longer involved in any of the organizations, having disappeared from public life.

Operation Rescue's association with anti-abortion violence is a debated issue. In 1988, when Terry was arrested in Atlanta, some of his fellow arrestees included James Kopp, who went on to kill an abortion provider, Dr. Barnett Slepian, in 1998, and Shelley Shannon, who was convicted of killing a doctor in 1993 in Wichita (Risen 1998). Operation Rescue spokesperson Wendy Wright countered accusations of violence by stating in

1993 that the group had seen 72,000 arrests and not one conviction of a violent act by a pro-lifer (Toner 1993).

See also Abortion, Right to; Freedom of Access to Clinic Entrances Act; National Organization for Women; Planned Parenthood; Pro-Life Movement; Pro-Life Position on Abortion; *Roe v. Wade* (1973)

Bibliography

Barry, Dan. 2001. "Icon for Abortion Protesters Is Looking for a Second Act." *New York Times* (20 July): A1.

Risen, James. 1998. "Tracing the Path of a Hard-Line Foe of Abortion." *New York Times* (6 November): B5.

Sullivan, Ronald. 1992. "U.S. Prosecutor Declines Case Against Operation Rescue Chief." *New York Times* (5 August): B3.

Toner, Robin. 1993. "Minneapolis Clinics Brace for Siege: Operation Rescue's on the Way." *New York Times*. (6 July): A8.

Rachel Pearsall

OPPORTUNITY, EQUALITY OF. *See* Equality

ORIGINAL INTENT, DOCTRINE OF

"Original intent" is a method of constitutional interpretation in which the Constitution is interpreted according to its understanding by the framers. Proponents of original intent ("originalists") believe that clear evidence of the framers' intent governs any undecided question of constitutional law.

How should the Constitution be interpreted? This important question has long been the subject of debate. In 1985, that debate was fueled by Attorney General Edwin Meese, who began giving speeches on constitutional jurisprudence. According to Meese (1986), the Constitution should be interpreted according to the text and the framer's original intent. If the Constitution were interpreted this way, decisions would be made in a neutral manner, "not … tainted by ideological predilection" (Meese 1986, 464). The argument for original intent focuses on the fact that the Constitution would lose its force as binding law if the intent

of the framers can be avoided for policy reasons. Courts would be above the Constitution, which would jeopardize our system of government.

In response to Meese, William J. Brennan, Associate Justice of the United States Supreme Court, argued that we should not be ruled by the dead hand of the past. He stated that "[i]t is arrogant to pretend that from our vantage we can gauge accurately the intent of the Framers on application of principle to specific, contemporary questions" (Brennan, 1986, 435). Thus, Brennan is a "nonoriginalist," which means that he believes in a "living Constitution" that grows from generation to generation and allows judges to determine the current needs of society. According to Brennan, "Current justices read the Constitution in the only way that we can: as twentieth-century Americans. We look to the history of the time of the framing and to the intervening history of interpretation. But the ultimate question must be: What do the words of the text mean in our time?" (Brennan 1986, 438). Thus, for Justice Brennan and other nonoriginalists, the choice is between being ruled by the dead hand of the past or by the current living. For Meese and other originalists, the choice is between courts that say what the law is, which is their proper role, and courts that make law and policy, which is the function of the legislature (Farber 1989).

Many scholars have criticized Meese's view that the Constitution should be interpreted according to the original intentions of its framers (Powell 1985; Brest 1980). One problem is that the framers of the Constitution and Bill of Rights did not discuss many of the issues that we are confronted with today. Another problem is that the documentary evidence from which to glean the intentions of the framers is sketchy at best. Indeed, James Madison recorded only 10 percent of debate that took place at the Constitutional Convention. Yet another problem is the difficulty of determining a collective "intent" from the various and often conflicting intentions of individuals who participated in the framing of the Constitution (Farber 1989). Another criticism of original intent is that the framers represented only white males. Thus, if the Constitution is based on popular sovereignty, the framers could not bind those who were not included in the political community at the time the Constitution was adopted. Furthermore, some would argue that the framers themselves did not believe in interpreting the Constitution according to their intent, but intended future generations to adapt the Constitution to their own needs.

In recent years, originalism has evolved from "original intent" to "original meaning" (Barnett 1999). Now originalists are seeking the original meaning of the text instead of seeking the subjective intent of the framers. Two proponents of this new form of originalism are Robert Bork and Antonin Scalia. According to Robert Bork (1990), if someone finds a letter from George Washington to Martha that explains what he meant by the power to lay taxes, that does not change the meaning of the Constitution. Thus, it does not matter what George Washington meant, or what anyone else meant. "When lawmakers use words, the law that results is what those words ordinarily mean" (Bork 1990, 144). Justice Scalia has written that "[w]e look for a sort of 'objectified' intent—the intent that a reasonable person would gather from the text of the law, placed alongside the remainder of the *corpus juris*...." (Scalia 1997, 17) In Scalia's view, judges should look for "the original meaning of the text, not what the original draftsmen intended" (Scalia 1997, 38). According to Scalia, the whole purpose of a Constitution is to prevent change—to keep certain rights that cannot be taken away except by amending the Constitution. Those who believe in a living Constitution have changed constitutional interpretation into a common law method of adjudication.

Robert Bork has argued that judges who do not interpret the Constitution according to the original intent of the framers "will, in truth, be enforcing their own morality upon the rest of us and calling it the Constitution" (Levy 1988, xiii). Furthermore, Bork has stated that "[t]he originalist attempts to discern the principles the [framers] enacted, the values they sought to protect" (Perry 1991, 684, n. 46).

Although the debate continues, scholars have argued that this move from specific intentions

to general principles actually eliminates any real difference between originalism and nonoriginalism (Solum 1989).

See also Bork, Robert H.; Brennan, William J., Jr.; Common Law Background of American Civil Rights and Liberties; Living Constitution; Madison, James; Meese, Edwin III; Scalia, Antonin

Bibliography

Barnett, Randy E. 1999. "An Originalism for Nonoriginalists." *Loyola Law Review* 45: 611.

Bork, Robert H. 1990. The *Tempting of America: The Political Seduction of the Law*. New York: Touchstone.

Brennan, William J., Jr. 1986. "The Constitution of the United States: Contemporary Ratification." *South Texas Law Review* 27: 433.

Brest, Paul. 1980. "The Misconceived Quest for the Original Understanding." *Boston University Law Review* 60: 204.

Farber, Daniel A. 1989. "The Originalism Debate: A Guide for the Perplexed." *Ohio State Law Review* 49: 1085.

Levy, Leonard W. 1988. *Original Intent and the Framers' Constitution*. New York: Macmillan.

Meese, Edwin III. 1986. "The Supreme Court of the United States: Bulwark of a Limited Constitution." *South Texas Law Review* 27: 455.

Perry, Michael J. 1991. "The Legitimacy of Particular Conceptions of Constitutional Interpretation." *Virginia Law Review* 77: 669.

Powell, H. Jefferson. 1985. "The Original Understanding of Original Intent." *Harvard Law Review* 98: 885–948.

Scalia, Antonin. 1997. *A Matter of Interpretation: Federal Courts and the Law*. Princeton, NJ. Princeton University Press.

Solum, Lawrence B. 1989. "Originalism as Transformative Politics." *Tulane Law Review* 63: 1599.

Pamela Corley

OVERBREADTH, DOCTRINE OF

Overbreadth is a controversial First Amendment doctrine used to invalidate governmental restrictions on free expression. A law is fatally overbroad if, in addition to proscribing unprotected speech, it prohibits constitutionally protected speech as well. The overbreadth doctrine is an exception to the general rule that one person is not allowed to invoke the constitutional rights of any other person. Defendants in First Amendment cases are allowed to challenge laws that might be unconstitutional *as applied to other people* engaged in free speech activities. The stated purpose of the overbreadth doctrine is to prevent a "chilling effect"—discouraging people from speaking or expressing themselves due to fear of prosecution or uncertainty about the scope of the law. The chief criticism of the overbreadth doctrine is that it allows "guilty" defendants to escape punishment—often a politically unpopular result.

The doctrine is closely related to the use of "strict scrutiny" in cases involving infringement on fundamental rights, a test that requires the government to demonstrate a compelling purpose justifying the infringement and to choose least restrictive or narrowly-tailored means to achieve the governmental purpose. If the defendant shows that expression protected by the First Amendment is within coverage of the law, the government must demonstrate an interest in or purpose for the law that is sufficient to justify the broad wording of the prohibition. If the governmental interest is insufficient or there is a less restrictive way of achieving that interest, that is, by wording the statute more narrowly, the defendant wins, and the statute is declared to be invalid *on its face* or *per se.*

To illustrate the application of overbreadth doctrine, suppose that a defendant is arrested for distributing videos that meet the *Miller v. California* (1973) definition of obscenity. The defendant is charged with violation of a statute that is a general prohibition on the distribution of pornography. The overbreadth doctrine allows the defendant to challenge the law *on its face,* instead of its application to his activities. The law could not validly apply to bookstore owners selling books that contain pornographic passages, but are not obscene, because pornography is protected First Amendment expression. In this case, the law would be declared invalid and the defendant could not be convicted, because the law is overbroad. The broad wording

of the statute punishes protected expression, and the government could easily have drafted a narrowly worded prohibition on the distribution of obscene materials.

The Supreme Court employed the overbreadth doctrine in *Reno v. ACLU* (1997) to strike down provisions of the Communications Decency Act of 1996 (CDA). Congress enacted the CDA to protect minors from exposure to harmful material on the Internet. The Court said: "Under the CDA, a parent allowing her 17-year-old to use the family computer to obtain information on the Internet that she, in her parental judgment, deems appropriate could face a lengthy prison term. Similarly, a parent who sent his 17-year-old college freshman information on birth control via e-mail could be incarcerated even though neither he, his child, nor anyone in their home community, found the material 'indecent' or 'patently offensive,' if the college town's community thought otherwise." The Court concluded that it was possible for Congress to draft more narrowly tailored provisions, so that legitimate speech would not fall within the prohibitions of the law.

More recently, in *Ashcroft v. Free Speech Coalition* (2002), the Supreme Court found the "virtual pornography" provisions of the Child Pornography Prevention Act of 1996 invalid because computer-generated "virtual" child pornography, unlike real child pornography, was not intrinsically related to the sexual abuse of children and because some works banned by the statute might have significant literary or artistic value. The court emphasized that "the Government may not suppress lawful speech as the means to suppress unlawful speech."

An overbroad state statute can be "cured" by interpretation of state courts, narrowing the applicability of the language used in the law to comply with the First Amendment requirement that laws regulating free speech be "narrowly tailored."

See also Ashcroft, John; Child Pornography; First Amendment; First Amendment, Interpretation of; Fundamental Rights; *Miller v. California* (1973);

Obscenity and Pornography; *Reno v. American Civil Liberties Union* (1997); Speech, Freedom of; Strict Scrutiny

Bibliography

Chen, Alan K. 2003. "Statutory Speech Bubbles, First Amendment Overbreadth, and Improper Legislative Purpose." *Harvard Civil Rights-Civil Liberties Law Review* 38: 31.

Cummins, Brendan D. 1996. "The Thorny Path to *Thornhill:* The Origins at Equity of the Free Speech Overbreadth Doctrine." *Yale Law Journal* 105: 1671.

Carolyn P. Johnson

P

PAINE, THOMAS (1737–1809)

Thomas Paine was born on January 29, 1737, at Thetford, England, the son of a Quaker corseter and Anglican mother. At age 12, Paine failed out of school. At 13, he became an apprentice to his father, who was a stay maker, but Thomas disliked the trade and, at 19, he went to sea aboard a privateer. In 1768, after a short series of adventures, Paine returned to England and held various jobs, eventually becoming an excise officer, collecting taxes from smugglers he tracked down. Paine failed at this job as well. He was discharged from his post twice in four years. His final discharge came in 1772 after he published a pamphlet calling for a pay increase for excise officers in order to prevent corruption in government service.

In 1774, he met Benjamin Franklin in London while Franklin was serving as a representative of the American colonies in Great Britain. Paine and Franklin became friends, and Franklin wrote letters of recommendation to help Paine immigrate to Philadelphia.

Paine arrived in Philadelphia on November 30, 1774. He began his new life as a publicist. In 1775, he anonymously published *African Slavery in America,* in which he argued that slavery was unjust and inhumane. During this period, Paine also became coeditor of the *Pennsylvania Magazine.* Upon his arrival, Paine sensed that a rebellion was imminent because of taxation in the colonies.

On January 10, 1776, Paine anonymously published *Common Sense,* a 50-page pamphlet advocating independence from England. Paine argued that Great Britain exploited the colonies, and that there was no advantage in maintaining ties with the mother country, particularly given the lack of colonial representation. Paine's pamphlet also called for the establishment of a republican form of government in America. To Paine, government was a necessary evil. As long as it was representative and frequently checked with elections, it could be safe. Government's only responsibility was to regulate; therefore, it should be as simply structured as possible. *Common Sense* helped stimulate political debate throughout the colonies and influenced the adoption of the Declaration of Independence. *Common Sense* eventually sold more than 500,000 copies. Paine donated all proceeds from the pamphlet to the revolutionary cause.

During the Revolutionary War, Paine volunteered in the Continental Army. Between 1776 and 1783, Paine wrote a series of widely read pamphlets entitled *The American Crisis,* one of which contained Paine's most famous first line: "These are the times that try men's souls." George Washington ordered that Paine's pamphlets be read to his troops to inspire their revolutionary fervor and bolster their morale.

Paine had grand visions for reshaping society. He opposed slavery and was one of the first to advocate the creation of a world peace organization and social security for the poor and elderly. Despite his lack of income, Paine created a fund to support needy soldiers. His own financial situation forced Paine to apply for financial aid from Congress. His opponents turned down his plea. However, Pennsylvania and New York willingly assisted Paine in his finances. New York even gave him a farm in New Rochelle.

Paine possessed a wide array of interests. Thus, instead of continuing the revolutionary cause, he returned to Europe in 1787 to pursue his interests in invention and engineering. Unfortunately, Paine could not find financial backers for his smokeless candle and a design for a single-arch iron bridge in Europe.

In 1791 and 1792, Paine published the two-part treatise *The Rights of Man,* a reply to Edmund Burke's *Reflections Upon the French Revolution* (1790). Burke argued that France should not partake in revolution, but instead reform the existing government. Paine, on the other hand, believed the French Revolution would create democracy in Europe similar to that of the United States. He also analyzed European society and exposed its weaknesses, including monarchical governments, lack of a progressive income tax, illiteracy, poverty, unemployment, and war. *The Rights of Man* sold a million and a half copies in England alone. Because of his negative comments concerning the monarchy, England eventually banned the book and charged Paine with seditious libel. France, on the other hand, voted Paine an honorary citizen of the French republic. In December 1792, England tried Paine in absentia, because he had left for France.

Paine was imprisoned during the "Reign of Terror" that gripped France in the wake of the French Revolution. Despite entreaties to the U.S. government, officials in Washington denied Paine's claim to be an American citizen. His radical politics caused concern within the Federalist Party. James Monroe, U.S. minister to France, secured Paine's freedom in November 1794, just before Paine was to be executed.

While still in prison, Paine published Part 1 of *The Age of Reason* (1794–1796). He published Part II in 1795 and a portion of Part III in 1807. The book praised the achievements of the Age of Enlightenment. Many misinterpreted Paine's work as a promotion of atheism, but Paine only objected to organized religion and not religion itself. This misinterpretation led to a bad reputation for Paine, and he suffered from alienation by old friends because of it. Paine remained in Europe until 1802, at which time he returned to the United States at the invitation of President Thomas Jefferson. By this time, Paine was a rapidly aging man suffering from alcohol abuse. Because of his association with atheism, many Americans dismissed his contributions to the American Revolution. He died in New York City on June 8, 1809. Sadly, his reputation had been completely destroyed, and only a handful of people attended his funeral. In 1819, the English radical William Cobbett took Paine's remains so that they could be buried in England as a symbol of democratic reform. Great Britain would not allow this, and Paine's remains mysteriously disappeared. The whereabouts of his remains are still unknown.

See also Conservatism; Declaration of Independence; Jefferson, Thomas; Liberalism; Quakers; Slavery

Bibliography

Foner, Eric. 1977. *Tom Paine and Revolutionary America.* New York: Oxford University Press.

Keane, John. 1995. *Tom Paine: A Political Life.* New York: Grove Press.

Ann M. Bennett

PALKO V. CONNECTICUT (1937)

Palko v. Connecticut (1937) is a key case in the line of Supreme Court decisions developing the doctrine of incorporation, the means by which most provisions of the Bill of Rights have been held enforceable against state and local governments. The doctrine originated in the late nineteenth century and was first espoused by the Supreme Court in *Chicago, Burlington and Quincy Railroad Co.*

v. City of Chicago (1897). In that case the Court held that the Just Compensation Clause of the Fifth Amendment was applicable to state and local governments via the Due Process Clause of the Fourteenth Amendment.

In the 1920s and 1930s, the Court held that the First Amendment freedoms of speech, press, assembly, and religion were likewise incorporated into the Fourteenth Amendment's broad restrictions on state action (see, respectively, *Fiske v. Kansas,* 1927; *Near v. Minnesota,* 1931; *DeJonge v. Oregon,* 1937; and *Hamilton v. Board of Regents,* 1934). On the other hand, the Court had previously refused to incorporate the Grand Jury Clause of the Fifth Amendment (see *Hurtado v. California,*1884), the Self-Incrimination Clause of the Fifth Amendment (see *Twining v. New Jersey,* 1908), or the Sixth Amendment right to trial by jury (see *Maxwell v. Dow,* 1900).

In *Palko v. Connecticut* the Court attempted to reconcile what many perceived to be a contradiction by adopting a test for the *selective* incorporation of the Bill of Rights. To merit incorporation, said Justice Benjamin N. Cardozo, a provision of the Bill of Rights must be essential to "a scheme of ordered liberty." The specific question in the *Palko* case was whether the Fifth Amendment protection against double jeopardy would apply to the states via the Fourteenth Amendment. After a jury trial in a Connecticut court, Frank Palko had been convicted of second-degree murder and sentenced to life in prison. As allowed by Connecticut law at the time, the prosecution appealed to the state supreme court, arguing that procedural errors in the trial had prevented a conviction for murder in the first degree. The state supreme court agreed and ordered a new trial, whereupon Palko was convicted of first-degree murder and sentenced to death. In reviewing the case, the U.S. Supreme Court found it unnecessary to determine whether this procedure would constitute double jeopardy, because it held that the Double Jeopardy Clause did not apply to the state courts.

Justice Cardozo's majority opinion in *Palko* suggested that the Double Jeopardy Clause lay on

"a different plane of social and moral values" than the First Amendment freedoms that had been previously incorporated. The protection against double jeopardy was not "of the very essence of a scheme of ordered liberty." To abolish it, in Cardozo's view, would not violate a "principle of justice so rooted in the traditions and conscience of our people as to be ranked as fundamental." In retrying Palko, the state of Connecticut was asking "no more than this, that the case against him shall go on until there shall be a trial free from the corrosion of substantial legal error."

In 1969, the holding that the Double Jeopardy Clause does not apply to state criminal prosecutions was overturned by the Supreme Court in *Benton v. Maryland.* But the doctrine of selective incorporation that emerged from *Palko* has never been repudiated by the Court.

See also Bill of Rights, Incorporation of; Cardozo, Benjamin N.; *Chicago, Burlington and Quincy Railroad Co v. City of Chicago* (1897); *Hamilton v. Board of Regents of the University of California (1934); Near v. Minnesota ex rel. Olson* (1931); Self-Incrimination Clause

John M. Scheb II and Otis H. Stephens, Jr.

PARENS PATRIAE, DOCTRINE OF

The doctrine of *parens patriae* was adopted by the United States from English common law and is Latin for "parent of the country." Under the common law system the Crown utilized the doctrine to assume guardianship over "infants, idiots, [and] lunatics ... " as mentioned in the case of *Cary v. Bertie* (1696). In the United States today, states have the authority to invoke *parens patriae* most notably to protect minors and the mentally ill/disabled. In *Mormon Church v. United States* (1890) the Supreme Court stated,

This prerogative of *parens patriae* is inherent in the supreme power of every state, whether that power is lodged in a royal person, or in the legislature, and has no affinity to those arbitrary powers which are sometimes exerted by irresponsible monarchs to the great detriment of the people, and the destruction of their liberties. On the contrary, it is a most beneficent function, and often necessary to be exercised in the interests of humanity, and for the prevention of injury to those who cannot protect themselves.

Juveniles

Over the years the acceptable use of *parens patriae* has been limited and more clearly defined through landmark Supreme Court cases. One of the first limitations came through *Pierce v. Society of Sisters* (1925) in which the Court ruled that states could not invoke the doctrine to require children to attend public rather than private school between the ages of 8 and 16. While this ruling gave parents the right to choose between public and private school education, *Prince v. Massachusetts* (1944) ruled that "the state as *parens patriae* may restrict the parent's control by requiring school attendance" even if the "parent grounds his claim to control the child's course of conduct on religion or conscience." This decision was distinguished but not overruled almost 30 years later in *Wisconsin v. Yoder* (1972), which ruled that the Freedom of Religion Clause of the First Amendment outweighed the state's interest in mandating school attendance past eighth grade.

The next major limitation to the state's power in invoking the doctrine came in 1966 through *Kent v. United States*, in which Justice Abe Fortas stated: "The State is *parens patriae*, rather than prosecuting attorney and judge. But the admonition to function in a 'parental' relationship is not an invitation to procedural arbitrariness." This decision, coupled with *In re Gault* (1967), helped begin the reform of the juvenile justice system, which had previously denied minors a fair trial process. The *Gault* decision prohibited states from using *parens patriae* to deny due process rights to minors.

Another limitation to the use of the doctrine came through *Stanley v. Illinois* (1972), in which the Court decided that the state could not invoke *parens patriae* to deny due process in order to keep a biological father (not married to the mother) from gaining custody of his children upon the death of the mother. Affirmation of this decision came in

Santosky v. Kramer (1982), in which Justice Harry Blackmun ruled: "Before a State may sever completely and irrevocably the rights of parents in their natural child, due process requires that the State support its allegations by at least clear and convincing evidence." The limitations imposed by these cases have helped put in place safeguards against unconstitutional use of the doctrine.

Since *Santosky* the use of the doctrine in regard to minors was reaffirmed through *Schall v. Martin* (1984) in which Chief Justice William H. Rehnquist noted: "Children, by definition, are not assumed to have the capacity to take care of themselves. They are assumed to be subject to the control of their parents, and if parental control falters, the State must play its part as *parens patriae*." The Court also affirmed the use of the doctrine to deny Fourth Amendment rights to minors in public schools in *New Jersey v. TLO* (1985) and *Vernonia School District v. Acton* (1995), in which the Court decided students could be searched and tested for drugs during school if reasonably deemed necessary.

Mentally Ill/Disabled Persons

In the case of those who are mentally ill/disabled, the Court has made a wide variety of decisions on the proper use of *parens patriae* by the states. In *Addington v. Texas* (1979) the Court ruled that only a standard of "clear and convincing evidence" is needed to commit someone to a mental facility due to the state's interest in protecting its mentally ill citizens from themselves and others. Along the same lines of community protection, *Jones v. United States* (1983) affirmed states' use of *parens patriae* to keep a criminal defendant (who claims "not guilty" by reason of insanity) in a mental facility as long as it takes for the patient to be no longer a danger to society. This decision was later affirmed in *Foucha v. Louisiana* (1992) in which the Court ruled that the state may not invoke *parens patriae* to keep a committed criminal defendant in a mental institution if he or she no longer proves to be insane.

In *Cruzan v. Director, Missouri Department of Health* (1990) the Court ruled that family members cannot decide the fate of a close relative in a vegetative state without presenting clear and convincing evidence that the patient would have wanted to end his or her life. Without that evidence the state can invoke *parens patriae* to protect the life of the patient. Another decision regarding a patient's body came in *Washington v. Harper* (1990), in which the Court ruled that the state could utilize *parens patriae* to treat mentally ill patients against their will without a hearing based on the judgment of a doctor. To this Justice Anthony Kennedy stated: "Where an inmate's mental disability is the root cause of the threat he poses to the inmate population, the State's interest in decreasing the danger to others necessarily encompasses an interest in providing him with medical treatment for his illness." More than 10 years later in *Sell v. United States* (2003), the Court ruled that states may invoke *parens patriae* to administer antipsychotic medications to mentally ill criminal defendants against their will in order to render them competent to stand trial.

Utilizing *Parens Patriae*

While the Supreme Court has placed a number of limitations on the use of *parens patriae,* the doctrine is still invoked regularly by state and national governments today. In addition to being utilized to protect juveniles and the mentally ill/disabled, the doctrine is also used by Native American tribes to protect their members and by the state and national governments to protect the health and welfare of citizens.

See also Blackmun, Harry A.; Common-Law Background of American Civil Rights and Liberties; Due Process, Procedural; First Amendment; Fortas, Abe; Fourth Amendment; Free Exercise Clause; Insanity Defense; Juvenile Justice; Kennedy, Anthony; Medical Treatment, Right to Refuse; Native Americans, Civil Rights of; *Pierce v. Society of Sisters* (1925); Religion, Freedom of; Right to Die; Substituted Judgment, Doctrine of; *Wisconsin v. Yoder* (1972)

Bibliography

Arrigo, Bruce A. 1996. *The Contours of Psychiatric Justice: A Postmodern Critique of Mental Illness,* *Criminal Insanity, and the Law (Current Issues in Criminal Justice).* New York: Garland Publishing.

Brewer, Holly. 2005. *By Birth or Consent: Children, Law, and the Anglo-American Revolution in Authority.* Williamsburg, VA: Omohundro Institute of Early American History and Culture.

Chaya Chandrasekaran

PARENTAL RIGHTS

The Right to be a Parent

Case law has helped define the rights of parents in the parent-child relationship where the U.S. Constitution has not. In 1923, the Supreme Court ruled in *Meyer v. Nebraska* that citizens have an unwritten right, among other things, to "establish a home and bring up children," protected by the Due Process Clause of the U.S. Constitution. This right was reiterated through *Eisenstadt v. Baird* (1972) in which Justice William Brennan stated: "If the right of privacy means anything, it is the right of the individual, married or single, to be free from unwarranted governmental intrusion into matters so fundamentally affecting a person as the decision whether to bear or beget a child." Although citizens have the right to bring children into the world and raise them, the state, through the doctrine of *parens patriae,* can assume custody of children or direct their interests if deemed necessary. However, the use of this doctrine is not unlimited and the Court has reiterated the importance of keeping the parent-child relationship intact, unless absolutely necessary, through cases over the years.

Even when the Court has invoked the doctrine of *parens patriae,* it has gone out of its way to show deference to parental rights. For example, in *Prince v. Massachusetts* (1944), where the Court upheld a child labor regulation against a mother's claim that it violated her First Amendment right to the free exercise of religion, Justice Wiley Rutledge wrote for an eight-member majority, stating: "It is cardinal with us that the custody, care and nurture of the child reside first in the parents, whose primary function and freedom include preparation for obligations the state can neither supply nor hinder." This sentiment was reiterated almost 60 years later in *Troxel v. Granville* (2000) in which Justice Sandra Day O'Connor stated: "[T]he interest of parents in the care, custody, and control of their children—is perhaps the oldest of the fundamental liberty interests recognized by this Court." Although *parens patriae* has been successfully invoked in certain areas to serve the child's best interests, the courts have long recognized the important liberty and privacy concerns embodied in the parent-child relationship.

Education

In *Pierce v. Society of Sisters* (1925) the Court examined Oregon's Compulsory Education Act of 1922, which required parents to send their children to public, as opposed to private, school between ages 8 and 16. In response to this intervention by the state, Justice McReynolds said: "[W]e think it entirely plain that the Act of 1922 unreasonably interferes with the liberty of parents and guardians to direct the upbringing and education of children under their control: as often heretofore pointed out, rights guaranteed by the Constitution may not be abridged by legislation which has no reasonable relation to some purpose within the competency of the State." The Court ruled once again in favor of parents' rights in *Wisconsin v. Yoder* (1972) when it decided that the religious rights of Old Order Amish parents outweigh the state's interest in requiring children to attend school past the eighth grade.

Custody

In *Stanley v. Illinois* (1972) the Court ruled that, without a hearing, the state could not keep an unwed biological father from gaining custody of his children, after the mother died or lost the ability to care for the children. Similarly in *Lassiter v. Department of Social Services* (1981), the Court ruled that states must adhere to the Due Process requirements of the Constitution when terminating a parent-child relationship. One year later the Court reviewed *Santosky v. Kramer* (1982), in which Justice Harry Blackmun noted: "Before a State may sever completely and irrevocably the rights of parents in their natural child, due process requires that the State support its allegations by at least clear and convincing evidence." In 1984 the Court ruled in favor of the mother in the case of *Palmore v. Sidoti*, in which a state awarded custody to a father after the mother engaged in an interracial relationship with an African American man. In reference to the racial prejudices exposed by the case, Chief Justice Warren E. Burger stated: "The Constitution cannot control such prejudices, but neither can it tolerate them. Private biases may be outside the reach of the law, but the law cannot, directly or indirectly, give them effect."

In another case involving removal of a child from its guardians, *Reno v. Flores* (1993), the Court noted: "'The best interest of the child,' a venerable phrase familiar from divorce proceedings, is a proper and feasible criterion for making the decision as to which of two parents will be accorded custody. But it is not traditionally the sole criterion.... Even if it were shown, for example, that a particular couple desirous of adopting a child would best provide for the child's welfare, the child would nonetheless not be removed from the custody of its parents so long as they were providing for the child adequately." Three years later the Court ruled six to three in favor of the mother in the case of *M.L.B. v. S.L.J.* (1996), in which a state revoked custody of children from the mother after she was unable to pay record preparation fees. To this Justice Ruth Ginsburg stated: "We place decrees forever terminating parental rights in the category of cases in which the State may not 'bolt the door to equal justice' recognizing that parental termination decrees are among the most severe forms of state action." One case in which the Court ruled in favor of the state instead of the parent was *Quilloin v. Walcott* (1978), which affirmed the state's right to "deny an unwed father authority to prevent adoption of his illegitimate child," especially if the father has never wished for or does not wish for custody of his children.

Reproductive Rights of Minors

In *Planned Parenthood of Central Missouri v. Danforth* (1976) the Court overturned a state policy requiring the consent of at least one parent or guardian before a child could have an abortion, affirming a minor's right to privacy. *Bellotti v. Baird* (1979) allowed states to require parental consent before a minor has an abortion as long as the minor has a chance to bypass consent judicially. If the minor proves to be mature enough to make a decision then the Court must allow the bypass to occur. *Planned Parenthood v. Casey* (1992) affirmed this decision.

Commitment of Child to Mental Institution

In *Parham v. J.R.* (1979) the Court decided that children do not have to be afforded due process before being committed to a mental institution since fit parents act in their child's best interest. To this the Court noted: "In defining the respective rights and prerogatives of the child and parent in the voluntary commitment setting, we conclude that our precedents permit the parents to retain a substantial, if not the dominant, role in the decision, absent a finding of neglect or abuse, and that the traditional presumption that the parents act in the best interests of their child should apply. We also conclude, however, that the child's rights and the nature of the commitment decision are such that parents cannot always have absolute and unreviewable discretion to decide whether to have a child institutionalized."

See also Blackmun, Harry A.; Brennan, William J., Jr.; Burger, Warren E.; Due Process Clauses; Due Process, Procedural; Due Process, Substantive; *Eisenstadt v. Baird;* Fourteenth Amendment (1868); Free Exercise Clause; Fundamental Rights; Ginsburg, Ruth Bader; Marriage, Rights Pertaining to; *Meyer v. Nebraska* (1923); O'Connor, Sandra Day; *Parens Patriae,* Doctrine of; *Pierce v. Society of Sisters* (1925); Privacy, Constitutional Right of; Religion, Freedom of; Rutledge, Wiley; *Wisconsin v. Yoder* (1972)

Bibliography

Harris, Leslie J. J., and Teitelbaum, Lee E. 2002. *Children, Parents and the Law*. New York: Aspen Publishers, Inc.

Peters, Shawn Francis. 2003. *The Yoder Case: Religious Freedom, Education, and Parental Rights (Landmark Law Cases and American Society)*. Lawrence: University Press of Kansas.

Stanley, Jacqueline D. 2002. *Unmarried Parents' Rights*. Naperville, IL: Sourcebooks.

Chaya Chandrasekaran

PARKS, ROSA (1913–2005)

Rosa Louise McCauley was born on February 4, 1913, in Tuskegee, Alabama. Despite receiving an education in the segregated public schools of Tuskegee and Montgomery and at the historically black university, Alabama State College (now known as Alabama State University), Parks worked as a seamstress—one of the only jobs available to African American women at the time. In 1932, she married Raymond Parks, a barber. Both worked for the Montgomery chapter of the National Association for the Advancement of Colored People (NAACP), with Rosa eventually serving as secretary and youth council adviser.

The Montgomery City Lines bus system, like most in the Deep South, adhered to strict policies requiring the racial segregation of passengers. Approximately 75 percent of local bus patrons were African Americans who were prohibited from sitting in sections reserved for whites. Black and white passengers could neither sit on the same row nor could black patrons stand next to rows occupied by white passengers. Black passengers had to enter through the front door, pay, get off the bus, and reenter through the back door. When buses were crowded, they had to forfeit seats in the rear "colored" section to whites as well. Besides the segregated bus policy, black patrons also endured abusive language and threats from drivers—many of whom carried guns (Williams 1987, 61).

Rosa Parks was the symbol of a boycott that would change her life, but was not the first African American to refuse to surrender a seat on a Montgomery bus to a white passenger. Early in 1955, 15-year-old Claudette Colvin was dragged from a bus by local policemen and arrested after she refused to give up her seat. Representatives from the NAACP, activist E. D. Nixon, Jo Ann Robinson of the Women's

Political Council, and Parks as NAACP youth council adviser wanted to file a federal lawsuit on Colvin's behalf questioning the constitutionality of segregated buses (Williams 1987, 63). However, shortly before their first court date, Colvin, who was unmarried, discovered that she was pregnant. Fearing that the press would portray her as a troublemaker, Parks and the NAACP decided to withdraw the lawsuit until a person with a flawless background was found to serve as plaintiff.

Shortly before her arrest, Parks attended a workshop on race relations at the Highlander Folk School in Monteagle, Tennessee, which trained poor people in the South to empower themselves and their communities (Williams 1987, 66). On December 1, 1955, as she was riding home from work, Parks was ordered by bus driver James F. Blake to forfeit her seat to a white passenger. After she refused, she was arrested and fined $14. Eleven years earlier in 1943, Blake had prohibited Parks from boarding a bus because of her refusal to reenter through the back door (Williams 1987, 66). Ironically, Blake was the driver of the bus on December 1. After refusing to give up her seat, Parks was arrested and charged with violating the law banning integration. She was the ideal person to sustain a test case against bus segregation. The members of the Women's Political Council, a local political and civic group, developed and distributed 35,000 flyers in one day publicizing a boycott of segregated buses on the day of Parks' arrest (Williams 1987, 69). An unknown but charismatic young minister, Martin Luther King, Jr., became its primary spokesperson. For approximately 13 months, black citizens, and their white supporters, transported boycotters to and from work. The boycott ended after 382 days on December 21, 1956, when the Supreme Court ruled that segregation on city buses was unconstitutional. Because of her role in the boycott, Parks became known as the "mother of the civil rights movement."

Because of the harassment she and her family received during and after the boycott, they moved to Detroit, Michigan, in 1957. For several decades, Parks worked in the office of Congressman John Conyers and continued to be involved in the civil rights struggle by giving speeches and attending marches and demonstrations. From 1955 on, Parks received numerous accolades, including the Martin Luther King, Jr., Nonviolent Peace Prize. In 1987, Rosa and Raymond Parks founded the Rosa and Raymond Parks Institute of Self Development in Detroit, which has a special program called Pathways to Freedom for children between ages 11–18. Children in the program travel across the country tracing the Underground Railroad, visiting the scenes of critical events in the civil rights movement and learning aspects of America's history. Rosa Parks died of natural causes at her home in Detroit, Michigan, on October 24, 2005. She was 92 years old.

See also Boycotts; Civil Rights Movement; Jim Crow Laws; King, Dr. Martin Luther, Jr.; National Association for the Advancement of Colored People (NAACP)

Bibliography

Parks, Rosa, and J. Haskins. 1999. *Rosa Parks: My Story.* New York: Puffin Books.
Williams, Juan. 1987. *Eyes on the Prize: America's Civil Rights Years, 1954–1965.* New York: Penguin Books.
    Sharon D. Wright Austin

"PAROCHIAID." *See* Religious Schools, Government Aid to

PAROLE. *See* Probation and Parole

PARTIAL-BIRTH ABORTION. *See* Abortion, Right to

PATRIOT ACT. *See* USA PATRIOT Act (2001)

PENTAGON PAPERS CASE (*NEW YORK TIMES V. UNITED STATES*)

In June 1971, with the nation immersed in rancorous debate about the Vietnam War, the government ordered *The New York Times,* the country's "newspaper of record," to cease publishing a series of articles based on classified Pentagon documents. It was the first time in more than two centuries of U.S. history that the government had exercised prior restraint on the press in the name of national security. For the next 15 days, citizens followed a mesmerizing series of court maneuvers as the constitutionality of the restraining order fast-tracked its way through the judicial system, culminating in a Supreme Court decision invalidating the government's action and upholding the right to publish.

The story of how the *Times* came to possess the Pentagon papers and to decide to publish them is much like the history of U.S. foreign policy in Vietnam: complex, convoluted, and wrought with indecision and trepidation. By the late 1960s, many people who had spent time in Vietnam—soldiers, military consultants, and reporters—detected growing discrepancies between what they saw there and what they heard Washington leaders say about the war. One of those people was Daniel Ellsberg, a middle-class Midwesterner who attended Harvard University on a scholarship and graduated third in his class in 1952. He joined the Marines for two tours of duty before returning to Harvard to earn a doctorate, specializing in the theory of bargaining and earning the admiration of Professor Henry Kissinger, who in 1969 would become President Richard Nixon's national security adviser. Ellsberg's expertise and intelligence was in demand throughout the Defense Department where he held top security clearances and worked with people at the highest level of foreign policy decision making. He returned to Vietnam in 1965 as a State Department civilian and frequently joined Marine and Army units in field operations, carrying a carbine and reportedly risking his life several times.

Ellsberg was a "hawk" in every sense of the word for much of the war, until he began to sense that elected leaders were misleading citizens about the likelihood of U.S. success. Also, atrocities committed by soldiers and the failure of the military to hold them responsible for their conduct disillusioned him. Despite his growing sense of unease about the war's conduct, Ellsberg agreed to work for the RAND Corporation to compile a study secretly commissioned by Secretary of Defense Robert McNamara on the history of U.S. decision making in Vietnam.

McNamara's purpose for ordering the massive study in 1967 remains uncertain. Once it became public, he said that he wanted to preserve a record for historians; others have speculated that McNamara realized the futility of the war effort and hoped the study would affect policy changes within the administration; President Johnson and Secretary of State Dean Rusk indicated their suspicion that McNamara wanted to help Robert Kennedy in his bid for the 1968 presidential nomination. The Vietnam History Task Force completed its assignment in early January 1969, producing some 7,000 pages in 47 volumes, titled *History of U.S. Decision Making Process on Vietnam Policy,* and stamping it "top secret—sensitive." By that time, McNamara was no longer a cabinet member, Kennedy was dead, and Richard Nixon was just days from moving into the White House. Of the 15 copies printed, two remained at the RAND Corporation's Washington office, and others were dispersed to outgoing officials and to Nixon's incoming defense secretary, Melvin Laird, and Henry Kissinger, national security adviser. Apparently no one paid much attention to the huge document.

Ellsberg, meanwhile, had left the Vietnam History Task Force project before its completion, and his attitude had moved even further away from his once hawkish position on the war. When Kissinger, as part of the Nixon transition team, contracted with RAND for another Vietnam-related project, the president of RAND, a former Pentagon official, hired Ellsberg for the task. As part of this work, Ellsberg requested and received permission to study the complete work of the History Task Force. By the fall of 1969 the Nixon administration had demonstrated little inclination to end the stalemate in Vietnam, and Ellsberg began to sneak out portions of the secret document and spend all night photocopying pages. He eventually contacted Senator J. William Fulbright, chairman of the Foreign Relations Committee, and urged him to release them as part of a congressional hearing. Fulbright wrote to Secretary of Defense Laird and asked that the history be declassified and released to the Foreign Relations Committee. Laird refused.

After more than a year of unsuccessfully trying to persuade other members of Congress and his former Harvard colleague Henry Kissinger—all of whom had security clearances—to release the documents, Ellsberg decided to talk with the press, a move several senators had suggested. In February 1971, Ellsberg contacted *New York Times* reporter Neil Sheehan, whom he had known in Vietnam, who seemed exceptionally knowledgeable about Vietnam policy, and who had written an opinion piece calling for an investigation into alleged military atrocities. It took at least another month for Sheehan to convince his editors that the material was authentic and worth examining. In mid-March, Sheehan met Ellsberg in Boston to acquire the documents. Ellsberg withheld four volumes that he thought particularly sensitive and also footnotes so as not to compromise intelligence sources.

Sheehan and one *Times* editor spent two weeks in Washington studying the documents and deciding they warranted publication. Then the material was taken to New York where several other *Times* writers and editors studied it further, taking care not to include military details in their articles. To safeguard the documents, the small task force worked in secret at the Hilton Hotel for another three weeks. Once the *Times* committed to publishing, the newspaper's attorney, James Goodale, was brought into the process. Despite the advice of more experienced legal colleagues who cautioned against publishing, Goodale studied the federal espionage statutes and told editors that the *Times* had a First Amendment right to publish. At the same time, the law firm that had served the newspaper for 25 years and represented it in the landmark *New York Times v. Sullivan* (1964) libel case told publisher Arthur Ochs Sulzberger that it would not defend the paper if court action resulted.

On Sunday, June 13, 1971, on a front page dominated by a photo of Tricia Nixon and her father President Nixon at her wedding in the Rose Garden, appeared a story spread across four columns with a headline in rather small one-third inch type: "Vietnam Archive: Pentagon Study Traces 3 Decades of Growing U.S. Involvement." The second installment of the planned 10-part series appeared the following day. By then the Nixon administration, at Henry Kissinger's urging, had queried its Office of Legal Counsel, directed by William Rehnquist, about the legality of an injunction against the *Times*. Despite a telephoned warning from an administration official that a court order would be forthcoming if the newspaper continued the series, the *Times* published a third installment on Tuesday.

The government received a temporary restraining order from Judge Murray Gurfein, a Nixon-appointed judge who was serving his first day on the bench. An evidentiary hearing was set for June 18, a day that dawned with excerpts from the secret documents appearing in the *Washington Post.*

Whereas the *Times* had spent at least three months poring over the papers, the *Post,* eager to be perceived as competitive with the *Times,* had received the multivolume set from Ellsberg only 14 hours before publication. Publisher Katharine Graham approved publication despite the fear of *Post* executives and lawyers about the fate of the company's television station licenses. As the *Times* company owned no television stations, this was not a concern in its decision to publish.

Professor Alexander M. Bickel of the Yale Law School represented the *Times* before Judge Gurfein at the hearing. Another First Amendment scholar from Yale Law, Thomas Emerson, spoke first, representing almost 30 members of Congress who sought to intervene in the case on behalf of the *Times*. Gurfein denied the request as well as intervention requests from various civil liberties groups. Throughout the day and continuing until almost midnight, with part of the hearing closed to the public, *Times* and government lawyers argued their positions. By mid-afternoon the following day, a Saturday, Gurfein delivered his opinion, refusing to accept the government's espionage law argument and holding that "no cogent reasons were advanced as to why these documents, except in the general framework of embarrassment previously mentioned, would vitally affect the security of the nation." Additionally, Gurfein affirmed the values of free expression and the public's right to know about the affairs of government.

This decision did not clear the way for the *Times* to continue publishing the Pentagon Papers, however, because an appeals court judge was standing by to hear oral arguments immediately. By the end of that rare Saturday proceeding, Judge Irving Kaufman continued the restraining order until Monday, the day that another federal court judge in Washington would hear evidence in the government's temporary restraining order against the *Post*. The temporary order against the *Post* was not issued in time to prevent further reports from the documents in Saturday editions.

During the next several days government lawyers argued on two geographical fronts for prior restraint: before district court Judge Gerhard Gesell and all nine judges of the D.C. U. S. Circuit Court of Appeals in Washington and before eight Second U.S. Circuit Court of Appeals judges in New York. All proceedings were expedited, with lawyers and judges working nights and weekends, indicative of the extreme importance they accorded the highly unusual restraint of the press. The Second Circuit judges permitted government lawyers to submit documents not introduced before Judge Gurfein, apparently based on the argument that the *in camera* part of the evidentiary hearing had been unduly rushed. That court, by a five to three decision, remanded the case to Judge Gurfein and gave him 10 days to decide it. On the same day, the appeals court in Washington voted seven to two to confirm Judge Gesell's order that would allow the *Post* to publish when the restraining order ended on June 25. The *Times* might have to wait until July 4 to continue publishing stories based on the Pentagon Papers. The Nixon Administration appealed the *Post* case to the Supreme Court, and the *New York Times* petitioned the same court for certiorari, listing five reasons for granting immediate review.

The High Court, about to recess for the summer, was faced with the specter of both papers being restrained until the Court reconvened in October or immediately hearing oral arguments. Public interest was high and other newspapers reportedly had received copies of the Pentagon Papers and were preparing articles based on them. The Court scheduled oral arguments for Saturday, June 26. The Court denied the government's request to hear part of the arguments in secret but agreed that parts of the briefs could be sealed.

Before a packed courtroom on Saturday, Solicitor General Erwin Griswold argued that the First Amendment did not prohibit all prior restraints, a point that the *Times* and *Post* had conceded all along. In addition to objecting to the haste of the multiple judicial proceedings, he also argued that in order for the president to perform his constitutional duties effectively, courts should accept executive branch judgments that further disclosures from the Pentagon Papers would compromise national security. Griswold claimed that the proper legal standard should be whether further publication would cause "grave and irreparable" harm to national security, and he asserted that harm to diplomatic relations contemplated in the future would meet that standard.

Professor Bickel, speaking for the *Times,* used a separation of powers argument—that no statute existed authorizing the president to exercise prior restraint and that, absent statutory authority, the government had submitted insufficient evidence to warrant such restraint. In response to a question by Justice Harry Blackmun, Bickel agreed that prior restraint was a proper response to prevent the death of soldiers but claimed that the government's evidence pointed instead to a vague fear of potential harm to diplomatic relations. In answer to Justice Byron White's question about the standard of proof required, Bickel said the harm had to be a "grave" danger to the nation and that the link between publication and the danger must be "direct and immediate and visible." Although the Pentagon Papers were classified, Bickel argued that they contained no information that would meet this legal standard. The *Washington Post* lawyer, William R. Glendon, was likewise asked to state the legal standard he thought should apply. He used the test the D.C. Circuit instructed Judge Gesell to apply: whether further publication would "so prejudice the defense interests of the United States or result in such irreparable injury" as to justify prior restraint. The government's evidence, Glendon said, was only "conjecture and surmise." Further, he argued that, as the title of the classified documents indicated, the collection was only a history and included nothing that would endanger national security or threaten the lives of soldiers.

By the time the Supreme Court announced its decision four days later on June 30, the secret Pentagon Papers had not remained secret, as *The Chicago Sun-Times, Los Angeles Times, St. Louis Post-Dispatch, Christian Science Monitor* and Knight newspapers had published original stories based on the documents. The Court issued a per curiam opinion, and all nine justices filed individual opinions. The Court's opinion said: "Any system of prior restraints of expression comes to this Court bearing a heavy presumption against its constitutional validity [citing *Bantam Books, Inc. v. Sullivan*, 1963, and *Near v. Minnesota*, 1931]. The Government thus carries a heavy burden of showing justification for the imposition of such a restraint [citing *Organization for a Better Austin v. Keefe*, 1971]. The District Court for the Southern District of New York in the *New York Times* case and the District of Columbia Circuit in the *Washington Post* case held that the Government had not met that burden. We agree."

Six of the justices wrote concurring opinions. Chief Justice Warren E. Burger as well as Justices Harlan and Blackmun wrote dissenting opinions, objecting to the "frenzied train of events" that left inadequate time for careful considerations of all the "difficult questions of fact, of law, and of judgment" that they thought the situation should have addressed. The dissenters wrote that "the scope of the judicial function in passing upon the activities of the Executive Branch of the Government in the field of foreign affairs is very narrowly restricted" under the concept of separation of powers. They disagreed that the lower courts were sufficiently deferential to the executive branch.

The government never invoked criminal sanctions against the newspapers. For revealing the documents to the press, Ellsberg was indicted on charges of violating the Espionage Act and for stealing government documents, but the government dropped the case after it became known that the White House "plumbers unit" had broken into Ellsberg's doctor's office, seeking information that might discredit him.

The legal significance of the case is that it establishes that the government cannot silence the press on mere allegations of harm to national security; instead, the government must present sufficient evidence to prove that publication will cause direct, immediate, and irreparable damage. Risks are inherent in a democracy, and the Supreme Court decided that a free press presented less danger to a strong democracy than government censorship. As Justice Potter Stewart wrote in his concurring opinion and the *New York Times* quoted in an editorial the following day, "Without an informed and free press, there cannot be an enlightened people." Beyond its legal significance, some scholars and presidential staff members of that era connect the dramatic Pentagon Papers episode directly to the infamous White House plumbers unit's burglary of the Democratic National Committee at the Watergate complex and, ultimately, to the downfall of the Nixon presidency.

See also Blackmun, Harry A.; Burger, Warren E.; First Amendment; Harlan, John Marshall, II; *Near v. Minnesota ex rel. Olson* (1931); *New York Times Co. v. Sullivan* (1964); Press, Freedom of the; Prior Restraint, Doctrine of; Stewart, Potter; White, Byron R.

Bibliography

Halberstam, David. 1979. *The Powers That Be.* New York: Alfred A. Knopf.

Powe, Lucas A. Jr. 1991. *The Fourth Estate and the Constitution: Freedom of the Press in America.* Berkeley: University of California Press.

Rudenstine, David. 1996. *The Day the Presses Stopped: A History of the Pentagon Papers Case.* Berkeley: University of California Press.

Dorothy Bowles

PEOPLE FOR THE AMERICAN WAY (PFAW)

People for the American Way (PFAW) was founded in 1980 by television producer Norman Lear (of "All in the Family" fame) and a small group of individuals he recruited, including Barbara Jordan (first African American woman elected to Congress), Father Theodore Hesburgh (then president of Notre Dame University), Andrew Heiskell (philanthropist and former chairman/CEO of Time Inc.), and the Rev. William Howard (then president of the National Council of Churches). Lear had become alarmed by the increasing influence of the religious right, particularly the mix of compelling religious exhortation and right-wing politics in the messages of televangelists, whom he believed to be browbeaters. Lear said at the time: "People … were being led to believe that they were bad Christians if they didn't have certain views about gay rights, abortion, the recognition of Taiwan, the E.R.A." (Schwartz 1981, D1).

PFAW's first nationwide action was a series of television commercials featuring prominent personalities, such as Goldie Hawn and Muhammad Ali, discussing the value of diversity. According to Lear: "What we've discovered is something that Reverend Falwell and the new right realized a long time ago: The way to people's heads these days is through their hearts. It's hard to touch people with rhetoric, but there's still an avenue open—through their emotions and their viscera" (Schwartz 1981, D1).

PFAW is considered a liberal civil rights organization and is often compared in philosophy with the American Civil Liberties Union. Like the ACLU, PFAW supports strict separation of church and state, although PFAW is more explicit in defining itself as the political opponent of the religious right. Like the ACLU, PFAW takes a strong view of the freedom of expression and resists any governmental efforts to restrict speech or access to information.

And like many other civil rights groups, PFAW takes a strong stand in favor of women's rights, gay rights, the rights of racial minorities, and affirmative action.

PFAW's primary political activities are public education, lobbying, and get-out-the-vote efforts, especially among young people. The PFAW Foundation is a separate nonprofit corporation, which primarily disseminates information and provides legal and voting support services. Attorneys working in the interests of PFAW causes may be compensated by the PFAW Legal Defense Fund.

Shortly after its founding, PFAW became involved with the issue of religion in public education and still describes this as one of its main areas of work. The group's efforts have targeted the exclusion of evolution from school curricula, the teaching of the Bible in history classes in public schools, and efforts by parents and others to exclude certain texts from classrooms. In the early 1980s, the Legal Defense Fund participated in the successful defense of schools in Church Hill, Tennessee, when a group of parents represented by lawyers from the Concerned Women for America sued to have many of the school's texts removed from the curriculum because they conflicted with their families' religious beliefs. In *Mozert v. Hawkins County Public Schools* (1984), the federal district court agreed that requiring students to read textbooks that offended their parents' religious views violated the Free Exercise Clause of the First Amendment. But the Sixth U.S. Circuit Court of Appeals reversed, holding that the parents had "failed to establish the existence of an unconstitutional burden" on their free exercise of religion (see *Mozert v. Hawkins County Public Schools,* 1987). The U.S. Supreme Court denied certiorari, leaving the Sixth Circuit's ruling intact.

The PFAW Foundation and Legal Defense Fund are most frequently involved in litigation as amici curiae. Relying on a network of more than three hundred affiliated lawyers, PFAW routinely files amicus briefs in state and federal cases involving First Amendment, privacy, and equal protection issues. Prominent U.S. Supreme Court cases in which PFAW has filed amicus briefs include *Stenberg v. Carhart* (2000), in which the Court struck down a Nebraska law criminalizing partial birth abortion; *Lawrence v. Texas* (2003), in which the Court struck down a Texas statute prohibiting private homosexual conduct; and *McCreary County v. ACLU* (2005), in which the Court invalidated the public display of the Ten Commandments in several Kentucky courthouses. In each of these cases, the position advocated by PFAW prevailed in the high court. The PFAW website explains that the purpose of its litigation efforts is to "defend our constitutional and civil liberties and fight the Religious Right around the country."

PFAW has also played a significant role in the federal judicial nomination process. The involvement of PFAW and other liberal groups in the 1987 defeat of President Ronald Reagan's Supreme Court nominee, Judge Robert Bork, helped to change the way judges are vetted in Senate hearings. Partly because of the activism of such groups, prospective federal judges are now grilled about their positions on civil rights issues, and the public now views judicial nominations as having a direct effect on civil rights. In 2005, PFAW was among the most vocal opponents of President George W. Bush's nomination of Judge John Roberts to succeed William H. Rehnquist as Chief Justice of the Supreme Court. Although PFAW did not succeed in preventing Judge Roberts' confirmation as Chief Justice, it remains one of the most powerful players in the legal and political arenas in which battles over civil rights and liberties are waged.

See also Abortion, Right to; Affirmative Action; American Civil Liberties Union; Bork, Robert H.; Concerned Women for America; Equal Protection Clause; Evolution/Creationism Controversy; First Amendment; Flag Burning; Free Exercise Clause; Gay Rights Movement; Interest Groups; Liberalism; Rehnquist, William H.; Religion, Freedom of; Religious Right; Separation of Church and State; Ten Commandments, Public Display of the; Terrorism, War on

Bibliography

People for the American Way, www.pfaw.org/general. Accessed June 15, 2004.

Schwartz, Tony. 1981. "In the Kingdom of Video." *New York Times* (22 March): D1. People for the American way, www.pfaw.org/pfaw/general. Accessed June 15, 2004.

Rachel Pearsall and Kara E. Stooksbury

PEOPLE FOR THE ETHICAL TREATMENT OF ANIMALS (PETA)

Founded in 1980, People for the Ethical Treatment of Animals (PETA), is a nonprofit organization established to protect the rights of all animals. With over 800,000 members, PETA remains the largest animal rights organization in the world. The organization's official website (www.peta.org) claims, "PETA educates policymakers and the public about animal abuse and promotes an understanding of the right of all animals to be treated with respect."

Most PETA members consider eating, wearing the skins of, and conducting experiments using animals to be both inhumane and unethical. They also condemn those who exploit animals in entertainment arenas and focus primarily on this industry as well as factory farms, laboratories, and fur trade businesses. Thus, by contrast with animal welfare groups that simply seek humane animal treatment, PETA epitomizes an animal rights organization that opposes any use of nonhuman animals by humans (Guither 1997, 9).

Cofounder Ingrid Newkirk launched PETA, advancing the view that "animals have a worth in and of themselves, that they are not inferior to human beings but rather just different from us and they really don't exist for us nor do they belong to us" (Newkirk 1990, xiv). Newkirk's opinion came to represent the philosophy of the organization. While she and cofounder Alex Pacheco sought activists eager to spread the animal rights message, Newkirk penned a how-to manual for adults interested in involvement, *Save the Animals!* With a growing adult membership, PETA also reached out to America's youth with both elementary campaigns and children's books (Guither 1997, 48).

PETA won its initial victory when the U.S. Supreme Court handed down a decision favorable to animals in laboratories. Beginning with a 1981 raid at a Maryland laboratory, the Silver Spring monkey case, *Primate Protection League v. Tulane Ed. Fund* (1991), resulted in the United States charging its first experimenter with cruelty to animals. Other victories include the cessation of cosmetic animal testing and the reduction of animal-involved drug research. Most importantly, however, PETA victories seek to improve and save animals' lives.

In 1993, PETA began its tactics of investigative work, congressional involvement, consumer boycotts, and media coverage on an international level. One example of the organization's investigative work involves uncovering the inhumane killing methods used on fur ranches. Many teams found that smaller fur businesses kill the animals via suffocation (Williams 1991, 111). From a finding such as this, PETA utilizes the media to broaden awareness of the cruelty and works with legislatures to prohibit abuse of this type. These advertising campaigns and lobbying efforts establish PETA as a both a legitimate force in policy making and an influential stakeholder in governing (Nibert 2002, 177).

Quite possibly, PETA's famed status rests with its celebrity endorsements and campaigns. From models such as Christy Turlington and Tyra Banks posing nude in the "I'd Rather Go Naked Than Wear Fur" campaign to actors Jennie Garth and Alicia Silverstone actively promoting PETA positions, these headliners made PETA a household name. On the other hand, some critics maintain that Newkirk and PETA supporters' strong animal rights beliefs often hinder the animal rights movement (Cohen and Regan 2001, 35). Whether a benefit or a hindrance to the animal rights movement, PETA remains the largest and most prominent animal rights organization in the world.

See also Animal Rights; Interest Groups

Bibliography

Cohen, Carl, and Tom Regan. 2001. *The Animal Rights Debate*. Lanham, MD: Rowman and Littlefield.

Guither, Harold D. 1997. *Animal Rights: History and Scope of a Radical Social Movement*. Carbondale: Southern Illinois University Press.

Newkirk, Ingrid. 1990. *Save the Animals!: 101 Easy Things You Can Do*. New York: Warner Books.

Nibert, David. 2002. *Animal Rights/Human Rights: Entanglements of Oppression and Liberation*. Lanham, MD: Rowman and Littlefield.

Williams, Jeanne, ed. 1991. *Animal Rights and Welfare*. New York: H.W. Wilson.

Krissy Gladders

PEREMPTORY CHALLENGES TO PROSPECTIVE JURORS

Prior to every jury trial, potential jurors are gathered at the courthouse, and the judge and the attorneys ask questions about the jurors' views and experiences. At this stage of jury selection, known as *voir dire*, attorneys seek to uncover biases and prejudices that might make it difficult for a juror to render a fair, impartial judgment. Jurors are often asked if they know any of the parties involved in the case, including the attorneys and even the judge. Jurors are generally asked if they have an opinion on the case or, more generally, its subject matter. In criminal proceedings, potential jurors are often asked if they have ever been a victim of such a crime or if any of their family or friends has been so victimized. If an attorney does not want a juror to become a member of the final jury panel, that attorney may challenge the juror.

An attorney may challenge a potential juror in three ways. First, the attorney may object to the entire jury pool, alleging that it does not fairly represent the defendant's peers. For example, an all-white jury pool in a criminal case would be subject to challenge by the attorney of a black defendant. Second, a potential juror may be challenged "for cause." In this instance, the attorney must explain to the court the reason for disqualifying the potential juror. If the attorney's argument is accepted, the juror is struck from the jury pool. If the judge rejects the argument, the attorney may pursue a third alternative, the peremptory challenge.

A peremptory challenge is an attorney's demand to excuse a potential juror without explanation. Peremptory challenges are often employed when an attorney suspects that a potential juror may not be fair and unbiased in spite of the juror's answers to the questions. These challenges may be based on anything from intuition to the slant of a juror's eyebrows. Peremptory challenges, by contrast with challenges "for cause," are limited in number. No more than three peremptory challenges are typically permitted in civil cases. In criminal cases potentially resulting in prison sentences, as many as 20 peremptory challenges may be permitted.

Although the Supreme Court has clearly stated that a defendant has no constitutional right to be tried by jurors of his own race, it has held that the systematic exclusion of such persons violates the Equal Protection Clause of the Fourteenth Amendment (*Strauder v. West Virginia*, 1879). In *Swain v. Alabama* (1965), the Supreme Court suggested that the State's "systematic striking" of African Americans from a trial jury "raises a *prima facie* case under the Fourteenth Amendment." The Court, nevertheless, placed such a heavy burden of proof on the defendant to establish that the peremptory challenge system had been perverted that prosecutors remained largely free from constitutional scrutiny in exercising their peremptory challenges.

The court revisited this issue in the important 1986 case of *Batson v. Kentucky*. The Court held, among other things, that "the State's privilege to strike individual jurors through peremptory challenges, is subject to the commands of the Equal Protection Clause." *Batson* identified three steps to guide a trial court's constitutional review of peremptory challenges. First, the defendant must make out a *prima facie* case "by showing that the totality of the relevant facts gives rise to an inference of discriminatory purpose." Second, once the *prima facie* case is established, the "burden shifts to the state to explain adequately the racial exclusion." Finally, "if a race-neutral explanation is tendered, the trial court must decide ... whether the opponent of the strike has proved purposeful racial discrimination." If convinced that it is racially

motivated, the trial judge may deny the use of a peremptory challenge.

Powers v. Ohio broadened the *Batson* rule in 1991, making it clear that a defendant need not be of the same race as the excluded juror to successfully challenge the juror's exclusion. The Court in the same year also extended *Batson* to civil trials as well (*Edmondson v. Leesville Concrete Company*). In the 1992 decision of *Georgia v. McCollum* the Court further extended the *Batson* rule by holding that a defendant's exercise of peremptory challenges was state action, and that the Equal Protection Clause prohibits defendants from engaging in purposeful discrimination on the basis of race. In spite of these decisions, trial judges still have wide discretion in reviewing racially motivated peremptory challenges. In the 1995 case of *Purkett v. Elem*, for example, the Supreme Court itself construed the *Batson* rule narrowly by holding that a trial judge is not required to reject a peremptory challenge even if the lawyer making the challenge gives an implausible nonracial explanation for excluding a black person from the jury. Ten years later the Court interpreted the *Batson* rule more broadly as a basis for limiting racially motivated peremptory challenges. By an eight-to-one majority, the Court in *Johnson v. California* (2005) held that California's "more likely than not" standard was more onerous and therefore inconsistent with the requirements for a prima facie case outlined in *Batson*. Anticipating the problems that the Court would encounter in attempting to give effect to the *Batson* rule, Justice Thurgood Marshall, concurring in that case, had predicted that "the decision today will not end the racial discrimination that peremptories inject into the jury-selection process. That goal can be accomplished only by eliminating peremptory challenges entirely."

Concurring in a companion case to *California v. Johnson* (*Miller-El v. Dretke*, 2005), Justice Stephen G. Breyer echoed Marshall's criticism. Breyer called for reconsideration of the *Batson* test and "the peremptory challenge system as a whole."

In 1994 the Supreme Court resolved a conflict among the federal circuits by holding that the Equal

Protection Clause prohibits gender-based peremptory challenges (*J.E.B. v. Alabama ex rel. T.B.*). Writing for the majority, Justice Harry Blackmun emphasized the relationship between racially based and gender-based peremptory challenges, observing that "[f]ailing to provide jurors the same protection against gender discrimination as race discrimination could frustrate the purpose of *Batson* itself." Blackmun's conclusion reinforces the views of Justices Marshall and Breyer regarding the perceived shortcomings of peremptory challenges. Many trial lawyers have come to believe that this system is too deeply flawed to survive much longer.

See also Accused, Rights of the; Blackmun, Harry A.; Breyer, Stephen G.; Challenges for Cause; Counsel, Right to; Equal Protection Clause; Equal Protection Jurisprudence; Fourteenth Amendment (1868); Gender-Based Discrimination; Jury, Trial by; Marshall, Thurgood

Margaret Ryniker

PETA. *See* People for the Ethical Treatment of Animals

PETITION, RIGHT OF

The First Amendment to the United States Constitution explicitly protects the right "to petition government for a redress of grievances." Writing for the Supreme Court in *United States v. Cruikshank* (1876), Chief Justice Morrison R. Waite observed: "The very idea of a government, republican in form, implies a right on the part of its citizens to meet peaceably for consultation in respect to public affairs and to petition for a redress of grievances."

The right of petition is deeply rooted in Anglo-American legal and political traditions. Chapter 61 of the Magna Carta (1215) articulated the right of a baron whose rights were transgressed by the Crown to "petition to have that transgression redressed without delay." The Petition of Right (1628) asserted the right of Parliament to petition the Crown for the redress of grievances. By the late seventeenth century, the right of petition had been extended to all subjects. In 1669, the House of Commons

adopted a resolution affirming the inherent right of all English subjects to petition that body "in case of grievance." The English Bill of Rights of 1689 provided that "it is the right of the subjects to petition the King, and all commitments and prosecutions for such petitioning are illegal."

In the American context, the Massachusetts Body of Liberties (1641) was the first royal charter expressly to protect the right of petition: "Every man whether Inhabitant or foreigner, free or not free shall have libertie to come to any publique Court, Councel or town meeting, and either by speech or writeing to move any lawfull, seasonable, and materiall question, or to present any necessary motion, complaint, petition, Bill or information." The right of petition was universally recognized and widely exercised throughout the colonies.

The right of petition is assumed by the Declaration of Independence (1776). In detailing grievances against the Crown, Thomas Jefferson wrote: "We have Petitioned for Redress in the most humble terms: Our repeated Petitions have been answered only by repeated injury." In the decade that followed the American Revolution, many of the new state constitutions contained explicit references to the right of petition. For example, Article XI of the Maryland Declaration of Rights (1776), stated that "every man hath a right to petition the Legislature, for the redress of grievances, in a peaceable and orderly manner."

The Petition Clause of the First Amendment refers to the right to petition "government," not merely the "legislature." In the debate in the House of Representatives leading up to the adoption of the Bill of Rights, James Madison made it clear that the Petition Clause would enable the people to "communicate their will" to their elected representatives in Congress as well as to executive officials. Madison did not mention the right to petition "the judiciary," but modern judicial interpretations of the Petition Clause incorporate the courts as well. For example, in *California Transport v. Trucking Unlimited* (1972), the Supreme Court recognized that the right of petition includes the right of access to courts and to executive agencies. However, in *Bill*

Johnson's Restaurants, Inc. v. National Labor Relations Board (1983), the Court said that "baseless litigation is not immunized by the First Amendment right to petition." And in *Bush v. Lucas* (1983), the Court held that federal employees do not have a constitutional right to sue in the courts to redress First Amendment violations allegedly committed by their agency-employers as long as Congress has provided an adequate administrative remedy.

In *DeJonge v. Oregon* (1937), the Supreme Court held that the First Amendment freedoms of assembly and petition, which the Court viewed as closely related, are among those fundamental rights protected against abridgement by the states by the Due Process Clause of the Fourteenth Amendment. Since then, in numerous cases involving freedom of assembly, the Court has noted the close connection between that freedom and the right of petition. For example, in *Edwards v. South Carolina* (1963), the Court held that in arresting a group of civil rights protesters on the grounds of the state capitol, "South Carolina infringed the petitioners' constitutionally protected rights of free speech, free assembly, and freedom to petition for redress of their grievances."

Congress and all the state legislatures have rules governing the receipt of petitions. And most states (but not the federal government) have some form of initiative and referendum—procedures by which requisite numbers of citizens can bring policy measures directly to the voters. But the right of petition embraces not only formal petitions submitted to legislatures, but direct citizen contact with representatives and executive officials through meetings, letter-writing, and e-mail. As *Edwards v. South Carolina* demonstrates, it also includes the right of groups to assemble for the purposes of demonstration and protest. And, as noted by the Supreme Court in *California Transport v. Trucking Unlimited* (1972), it also includes the right to sue in the courts. Although the Supreme Court has not explicitly acknowledged this, it can be argued that the right of petition encompasses lobbying and related interest group activities.

It should be noted that the right of petition does not include the right to express "damaging falsehoods" when exercising that right. Writing for the Supreme Court in *McDonald v. Smith* (1985), Chief Justice Warren E. Burger pointed out that "[a]lthough the values in the right of petition as an important aspect of self-government are beyond question, it does not follow that the Framers of the First Amendment believed that the Petition Clause provided absolute immunity from damages for libel." In rejecting the claim that the Petition Clause absolutely immunizes the author of a petition from being sued for defamation, Chief Justice Burger concluded: "The right to petition is guaranteed; the right to commit libel with impunity is not."

Today, the right of petition is understood broadly to include any and all lawful demands made by citizens on any and all agencies of government, as long as the means by which those demands are communicated are also lawful.

See also Assembly, Freedom of; Bill of Rights, American; Bill of Rights, English; Bill of Rights, Incorporation of; Burger, Warren E.; Civil Rights Movement; Declaration of Independence; Defamation; Due Process Clauses; *Edwards v. South Carolina* (1963); First Amendment; Fourteenth Amendment (1868); Jefferson, Thomas; Madison, James; Magna Carta; Massachusetts Body of Liberties; Representative Democracy; Waite, Morrison Remick

Bibliography

Higginson, Stephen A. 1986. "A Short History of the Right to Petition Government for a Redress of Grievances." *Yale Law Journal* 96: 142.

Mark, Gregory A. 1998. "The Vestigial Constitution: The History and Significance of the Right to Petition." *Fordham Law Review* 66: 2153.

John M. Scheb II and Otis H. Stephens, Jr.

PFAW. *See* People for the American Way

PHYSICIAN-ASSISTED SUICIDE. *See* Right to Die; Doctor-Assisted Suicide; Privacy, Constitutional Right of

PICKETING

The Supreme Court of the United States has long recognized that picketing—that is, physically demonstrating at a particular location—is a time-honored method of expressing a message, especially for those persons who may feel disenfranchised, cannot afford other means of expressing themselves, or are aiming their messages at a narrow problem. For those reasons, the Court has granted broad protection to picketers, while balancing their rights against the rights of other individuals and against public peace and safety. The Court has held that picketers may not be required to secure licenses, that restrictions on picketing must be content neutral, and that picketing cannot be banned from public property.

A key ruling on picketing came near the middle of the last century. In *Thornhill v. Alabama* (1940), the Court struck down a state law prohibiting picketing a place of business, noting that freedom of speech and press "are among the fundamental personal rights and liberties which are secured to all persons" by the Constitution, and that picketing was one of the activities that "may enlighten the public on the nature and causes" of public debate.

This is not to say that picketing may never be restricted, but the validity of restrictions often depends upon where the picketing occurs and the rationale for imposing restrictions. Picketing in an area designated as public forum—like a park or sidewalk—is almost always protected, for example, if the picketing is peaceful and does not interfere with other valid uses of the forum. The Court held in *Board of Airport Commissioners v. Jews for Jesus* (1987), for example, that absolute bans on First Amendment activity, including picketing, are nearly always unconstitutional.

Picketing on private property is more problematic. The Court has recognized that owners have certain rights over their property. When that property is used for a public purpose, however, and when it's obvious that picketers are expressing their own viewpoints and are not speaking for the property owners, the Court has struck down restrictions on picketing, as it did in *Pruneyard Shopping Center v. Robins* (1974), *Amalgamated Food Employees Union v. Logan Valley Plaza* (1968), and other cases.

In a related matter, the Court held in 2002 that the government may not require persons wanting to distribute information door-to-door first to secure licenses. A scheme in which a town required a person to secure a "Solicitation Permit" was struck down in *Watchtower Bible and Tract Society of New York v. Village of Stratton,* even though the issuance of the permit was pro forma. The Court agreed with a group of Jehovah's Witnesses that the process of applying for the permit infringed their First Amendment rights.

On the other hand, the Court has also allowed some picketing—in shopping malls and at private residences, for example—to be restricted. And, in *Greer v. Spock* (1976), the Court also ruled that the military could restrict picketing and the distribution of literature on military bases—even those portions of the bases open to the public.

Finally, the Court has allowed restrictions on picketing near abortion clinics, particularly when the picketing includes attempts to prevent women from entering the clinics. In *Madsen v. Women's Health Clinic* (1994), it held that restrictions on picketing were not aimed at the anti-abortion message of the activists, but were aimed at conduct, that is, at efforts by the activists to interfere with people entering or leaving the clinics. The Court also upheld the use of zones in which picketing could be banned but held that 300-foot buffer zones were unreasonable and burdened more speech than necessary to serve the government's interest in guaranteeing the free flow of traffic. Three years later, the Court also held, in *Schenck v. Pro-Choice Network of Western New York,* that a so-called "floating buffer zone" requiring picketers to stay at least 15 feet from people or vehicles entering or leaving the clinics violated the First Amendment because it overburdened speech.

In a related matter, the Court held in 2003 that a First Amendment challenge to a law prohibiting trespassing could not stand absent a showing that freedom of speech was being inhibited. *Virginia v. Hicks* began when the city of Richmond and the Richmond Redevelopment and Housing Authority devised a plan to help reduce unwanted traffic in Whitcomb Court, a low-income housing project. The town gave to the housing authority the streets within and adjacent to the project, thereby closing those streets to public use. The housing authority then developed a set of rules governing foot traffic on those streets and authorized the Richmond Police Department to enforce the new trespass laws.

Kevin Lamont Hicks was convicted of violating the trespassing law and appealed his conviction on grounds that his First Amendment rights had been violated. He won in the lower courts, but the Supreme Court held that there was no evidence Hicks was attempting to speak. He had been barred from returning to the housing project, the Court noted, and, therefore, his challenge related solely to the rule that those barred could not reenter.

See also First Amendment; Fundamental Rights; Jehovah's Witnesses; Preferred Freedoms Doctrine; Property Rights; Public Forum; Speech, Freedom of; Speech/Conduct Distinction; Time, Place, and Manner Regulations

Bibliography

Arizmendi, Sylvia. 1994. "Residential Picketing: Will the Public Forum Follow Us Home?" *Howard Law Journal* 37: 495.

Landwehr, Hazel A. 1993. "Unfriendly Persuasion: Enjoining Residential Picketing." *Duke Law Journal* 43: 148.

Madinger, Lee B. 1989. "Free Speech in Public Places: Application of the *Perry* Analysis in Picketing." *Whittier Law Review* 11: 267.

W. Wat Hopkins

PIERCE V. SOCIETY OF SISTERS (1925)

In the early 1920s, the United States experienced an upsurge in "nativism," an antipathy toward people not thought to be "true Americans." This category of undesirables included commu-nists, Catholics, and immigrants. It was in this climate that the state of Oregon decided to outlaw private education and force all children to attend public schools. The Compulsory Education Act of 1922, adopted by referendum, provided:

Any parent, guardian or other person in the State of Oregon, having control or charge or custody of a child under the age of sixteen years and of the age of eight years or over at the commencement of a term of public school of the district in which the said child resides, who shall fail or neglect or refuse to send such child to a public school for the period of time a public school shall be held during the current year in said district, shall be guilty of a misdemeanor and each day's failure to send such child to a public school shall constitute a separate offense.

Supporters of the measure argued that requiring all children to attend public schools would foster good citizenship and democratic values and would facilitate the integration of immigrants into American culture. The measure was backed by the Ku Klux Klan and loudly touted by Walter Pierce, who was elected governor at the same time the referendum was conducted. Pierce was able to exploit politically the xenophobia and anticommunist hysteria that he, the KKK, and many of the state's newspapers had fanned. Many Oregonians had become convinced that private schools could be breeding grounds for "anti-American" ideologies such as papism, anarchism, and communism.

Not surprisingly, the Compulsory Education Act was opposed by Catholics, Jews, Seventh Day Adventists, and other minority religious groups that operated their own private schools. Immediately after its passage, two organizations that operated private schools, the Sisters of the Holy Names of Jesus and Mary and the Hill Military Academy, brought suit against Governor Pierce to challenge the constitutionality of the new law. The United States District Court in Oregon declared the act unconstitutional as an infringement both upon property rights and the rights of parents to determine the education of their children.

In a decision that made national news, the U.S. Supreme Court unanimously affirmed the ruling of the District Court. Writing for the Court, Justice James C. McReynolds concluded that the act "unreasonably interferes with the liberty of parents and guardians to direct the upbringing and education of children under their control." He also asserted that the act threatened the economic rights of the plaintiffs "through the unwarranted compulsion which appellants are exercising over present and prospective patrons of their school" and noted that "this court has gone very far to protect against loss threatened by such action." Relying on the doctrine of substantive due process, McReynolds and his colleagues assumed that the "liberty" protected against state action by the Due Process Clause of the Fourteenth Amendment subsumed the various rights infringed by the Compulsory Education Act.

Pierce v. Society of Sisters was viewed at the time as a victory both for parental rights and economic freedom. Eventually, it (along with *Meyer v. Nebraska*, 1923) came to be seen as an important precursor to the modern Supreme Court's tendency to recognize personal, noneconomic freedoms that are not specifically enumerated in the text of the Constitution. More specifically, Pierce helped to create the jurisprudential foundation for *Griswold v. Connecticut* (1965) and other Supreme Court decisions recognizing constitutional rights of privacy and personal autonomy.

See also Catholicism and Anti-Catholicism; Due Process Clauses; Due Process, Substantive; Economic Freedom; Fourteenth Amendment; Free Exercise Clause; *Griswold v. Connecticut* (1965); Ku Klux Klan (KKK); Liberty; McReynolds, James C.; *Meyer v. Nebraska* (1923); Privacy, Constitutional Right of; Property Rights; Religion, Freedom of

Bibliography

Mizia, Robert Louis. 2000. "Prejudice and Educational Choice: 75th Anniversary of *Pierce v. Society of Sisters.*" *Momentum* (April/May): 17–19.

Saalfeld, Lawrence. 1984. *Forces of Prejudice in Oregon, 1920–1925.* Portland, OR: University of Portland Press.

John M. Scheb II and Otis H. Stephens, Jr.

PINKERTON RULE. *See* Conspiracy

PLAIN VIEW DOCTRINE

American courts have consistently held that the Fourth Amendment to the United States Constitution expresses a strong preference for conducting searches and seizures pursuant to a warrant issued by a judge or magistrate. Yet the courts have also recognized a number of exceptions to the warrant requirement. One of these involves evidence in "plain view" to a police officer. In *Harris v. United States* (1968), the Supreme Court held that "objects falling in the plain view of an officer who has a right to be in the position to have that view are subject to seizure and may be introduced in evidence."

There are two applications of the plain view doctrine. One involves evidence that is exposed to public view. The Fourth Amendment does not apply to such evidence because there is no legitimate expectation of privacy with respect to property exposed to public observation. In *Katz v. United States* (1967), the Supreme Court observed that "a man's home is, for most purposes, a place where he expects privacy, but objects, activities, or statements that he exposes to the 'plain view' of outsiders are not 'protected' because no intention to keep them to himself has been exhibited." In *California v. Ciraolo* (1986) the Supreme Court upheld the use of evidence obtained through aerial observation of the defendant's fenced back yard, saying: "Nor does the mere fact that an individual has taken measures to restrict some views of his activities preclude an officer's observations from a public vantage point where he has a right to be and which renders the activities clearly visible."

The second and more difficult application of the plain view doctrine involves situations where police are engaged in a lawful search of an area that is not exposed to public view and come upon evidence they were not looking for. For example, police engaged in a legitimate warrantless search of a home in response to an emergency call might discover contraband in plain view as they enter the home. In *Coolidge v. New Hampshire* (1971), the Supreme

Court's plurality opinion observed: "Where, once an otherwise lawful search is in progress, the police inadvertently come upon a piece of evidence, it would often be a needless inconvenience, and sometimes dangerous—to the evidence or to the police themselves—to require them to ignore it until they have obtained a warrant particularly describing it."

Following *Coolidge v. New Hampshire,* federal and state courts generally required that evidence be discovered "inadvertently" during the course of a lawful search to be subject to the plain view exception. However, in *Horton v. California* (1990), a Supreme Court majority made clear that inadvertent discovery is not an essential element of the plain view doctrine. Nevertheless, some state courts have continued to insist that the inadvertence requirement is a limitation on the plain-view exception to the warrant requirement. State courts may do this by relying on search and seizure provisions of their respective state constitutions, which may provide greater (but not lesser) protection against police searches and seizures than is provided by the Fourth Amendment.

See also Emergency Searches; Fourth Amendment; Fourth Amendment Exclusionary Rule; Search Incident to a Lawful Arrest; Search Warrants; Warrantless Searches

John M. Scheb II and Otis H. Stephens, Jr.

PLANNED PARENTHOOD

The Planned Parenthood Federation of America, an affiliate of the International Planned Parenthood Federation, is an umbrella organization for the 123 independent organizations operating under the Planned Parenthood name. PPFA also incorporates affiliates whose purpose is to lobby and litigate in support of universal access to reproductive health services, most notably abortion, although Planned Parenthood clinics across the country also provide a number of other birth control options as well as prenatal care. The Planned Parenthood Action Fund is a nonprofit lobbying group.

Planned Parenthood descends from the American Birth Control League, founded by birth control pioneer Margaret Sanger in New York in 1921. Even the phrase *birth control* has been attributed to Sanger (Loth 1950, 95). Sanger, one of 18 children, aspired to become a doctor but instead trained as a maternity nurse and worked in the poorer neighborhoods of New York City. The effects of dangerous back-alley or self-conducted abortions on lower-income women distressed her, as did the medical community's aversion to discussing birth control and the state laws, known as Comstock laws, which outlawed the dissemination of information about contraception. In 1914 Sanger published an illegal pamphlet containing birth control information and fled the country under indictment. When she returned, her cause had gained enough media attention that the government declined to prosecute. Sanger opened her first birth control clinic in Brooklyn in 1916 and served 30 days in jail for doing so. She opened a second clinic in 1923. Funded by her second husband, oil millionaire J. Noah Slee, who would later finance the first American manufacture of diaphragms, Sanger led a lobbying and public education campaign against restrictions on birth control and held conferences on population growth and reproductive rights.

A series of court decisions in the late 1920s and 1930s progressively weakened the Comstock laws, and public opinion began to shift in favor of Sanger's work. In 1946 she cofounded the current organization, the International Planned Parenthood Federation. No small amount of controversy surrounded Sanger; the organization she was instrumental in founding has been mentioned in connection with eugenics and population control (see Gordon 1976, 341–90). These accusations faded away, however, as birth control became more widely accepted.

Prior to the Supreme Court's ruling in *Roe v. Wade* (1973), Planned Parenthood enjoyed support from both liberal and conservative individuals and politicians, and Congress began to include family planning in federal health care appropriations bills as contraceptive measures such as the birth control pill gained popular acceptance. Title X of the Public Health Service Act of 1970, signed into law by President Nixon, provided federal funding for birth control counseling and distribution in clinics, and Planned Parenthood was a major grantee under this provision.

After 1973, Planned Parenthood's endorsement of the *Roe* decision, its decision to provide abortion services in some of its clinics, and its opposition to limitations on the abortion right plunged the organization once more into large-scale controversy. Various state and federal laws, passed since *Roe,* have attempted partially to circumscribe abortion availability by, for example, requiring waiting periods for abortions, requiring spousal or parental notification for women seeking abortions, forbidding use of public funds for abortion services for poor women, or by other means. Planned Parenthood organizations (either local or national) have been involved in litigation aimed at undermining these laws.

Planned Parenthood of Missouri challenged a Missouri abortion law in *Planned Parenthood of Missouri v. Danforth* (1976). The law required spousal or parental notification procedures, outlawed one common procedure (saline amniocentesis) after the first 12 weeks, and included a provision that a physician performing an abortion "exercise professional care to preserve the fetus' life and health, failing which he is deemed guilty of manslaughter and is liable in an action for damages." The Supreme Court agreed with Planned Parenthood that these provisions were unconstitutional. However, other provisions requiring an informed-consent procedure and certain recordkeeping standards were upheld by the Court.

In *Planned Parenthood Federation v. Ashcroft* (1983), the Supreme Court also granted the organization another partial victory by striking down a portion of a Missouri law requiring that second-trimester abortions be performed in a hospital. However, Planned Parenthood's further request that a parental notification requirement be struck down was denied; the Court held that the Missouri law's

inclusion of a judicial bypass procedure satisfied the requirements of constitutionality.

Another partial victory fell to a local Planned Parenthood affiliate when the Court, in *Planned Parenthood of Southeastern Pennsylvania v. Casey* (1992), struck down a provision of the Pennsylvania law requiring married women to sign a statement that their husbands had been notified of their intent to obtain an abortion. Once again, the outcome was mixed from the perspective of Planned Parenthood: the Court upheld Pennsylvania's requirements for a waiting period, for parental notification with a judicial bypass, and for certain recordkeeping procedures.

It may be fair to say that the primary activities of Planned Parenthood clinics are medical rather than political. However, the nationwide group plays a major role in the controversy over abortion and other aspects of reproduction.

See also Abortion, Public Funding of; Abortion, Right to; *Griswold v. Connecticut* (1965); Interest Groups; Reproductive Freedom; *Roe v. Wade* (1973)

Bibliography

Gordon, Linda. 1976. *Woman's Body, Woman's Right: A Social History of Birth Control in America.* New York: Grossman Publishers.

Loth, David. 1950. "Planned Parenthood." *Annals of the American Academy of Political and Social Science* 272: 95.

Kara E. Stooksbury

PLANNED PARENTHOOD OF CENTRAL MISSOURI V. DANFORTH (1976). See Abortion, Right to

PLANNED PARENTHOOD OF SOUTHEASTERN PENNSYLVANIA V. CASEY (1992). See Abortion, Right to

PLANNED PARENTHOOD V. ASHCROFT (1983). See Abortion, Right to

PLATO (C. 427–347 B.C.)

In the late fifth century b.c., the Greek city-state of Athens was in crisis stemming from its defeat by Sparta in Peloponnesian War. One of the main figures to emerge during that crisis was the philosopher Socrates (c. 470–399 b.c.), a contemporary of the sophists Protagoras and Gorgias. While they had distinct agendas, Socrates and the sophists jointly turned intellectual inquiry away from its focus on natural philosophy and the physical world toward the human domain of ethics and politics.

As a follower of Socrates, Plato sided with philosophy, the quest for truth, and against sophistry, which embodied the skills of persuasion regardless of truth to exert influence in political and legal fora. In the aftermath of the war, however, Socrates was tried, convicted, and executed for religious nonconformism and corrupting Athenian youth. In the ensuing political instability, some of Socrates' followers left Athens for a time, and so Plato spent several years traveling the Mediterranean. Returning to Athens circa 487 b.c. he founded the Academy, the first university in the western world. The Academy sought to provide an advanced education for those who would be political leaders, and it remained in operation for nearly 900 years, until the fall of Rome. In 467 b.c., the eighteen-year-old son of the court physician of Philip of Macedon, father of Alexander the Great, came to study with Plato. This was Aristotle, Plato's greatest student, who studied and taught at the Academy for 20 years, until Plato's death in 347.

As suggested, Plato's great project was to show the superiority of philosophy to sophistry. In the process, he became the first European to articulate a comprehensive, architectonic philosophical system encompassing all of known and perceived reality. Beyond his philosophical depth and range, Plato possessed great literary gifts, creating the dialogue as a vehicle for gaining access to higher truth. The *Republic,* perhaps Plato's greatest dialogue, is nominally an inquiry into the nature of justice, but it grapples with questions of morals, politics, metaphysics, epistemology, psychology, education, and art.

Within the domain of politics and law, Plato would not have recognized, and indeed would have deplored, modern conceptions of civil rights and liberties. As a classical conservative, he embraced a collectivist rather than individualist view of society,

and some have seen in him the seeds of modern totalitarian thought. The Platonic view is thus the antithesis of liberal democracy, and Plato believed democracy (in the direct participatory form he observed in Athens) the worst possible form of constitution except for tyranny. In his view, politics and law should be based on higher philosophical truths, specifically the true nature of man. For Plato, the just soul and the just state have the same form, that is, one in which the different elements are in order, under the guidance of a rational principle. Since such truths and their political implications can be grasped only by a select few after decades of study and reflection, Plato argued that they alone, the "philosopher-kings," should have political power. This entailed writing the laws that the rest of society, for its own good, would live and work by, including its educational, occupational, and even mating possibilities.

Thus, while the great philosopher Socrates asked important questions about the proper character of social and political life, the great theorists Plato and Aristotle gave and defended elaborate answers to such questions. Constitutionalists and statesmen have been responding to their answers ever since.

See also Aristotle; Conservatism, Classical; Liberalism, Classical; Socrates

Bibliography

Klosko, George. 1986. *The Development of Plato's Political Theory.* New York: Routledge, 1986.

Kraut, Richard, ed. 1992. *The Cambridge Companion to Plato.* Cambridge: Cambridge University Press.

Plato. 1997. *Complete Works.* Edited by John M. Cooper. Indianapolis: Hackett Publishing Co.

Popper, Karl. 1962. *The Open Society and Its Enemies.* New York: Harper and Row.

Sacks, D. 1995. *The Oxford Dictionary of the Ancient Greek World.* Oxford: Oxford University Press.

Martin Carcieri

PLEA BARGAINING

Although the Sixth Amendment provides that, "In all criminal prosecutions, the accused shall enjoy the right to a speedy and public trial," more than 90 percent of all criminal cases in the United States are plea bargained. To entice an admission of guilt, the prosecutor agrees to certain concessions. Barely mentioned in the law, this informal process takes three forms. In count bargaining, the prosecutor drops some charges in exchange for a guilty plea to others. To make the offer more attractive, the charges dropped are often the most serious ones. Charge bargaining commonly involves replacing a felony charge with a misdemeanor. In sentence bargaining, the prosecutor promises to recommend a relatively light sentence, and judges are very likely to comply. Insofar as most defendants are especially concerned with avoiding jail time, a powerful and common promise is to recommend probation.

Some judges sit down with both sides and enter directly into plea bargaining. However, a large majority simply respond to the agreement once it has been worked out between the prosecution and defense. If the judge has reason to believe that an innocent defendant is pleading guilty, he or she is not supposed to accept the plea agreement, but in fact judges rarely reject negotiated pleas. If there is no trial, what basis does the judge have for believing the defendant is guilty? First, the prosecutor reads the "factual basis" (what he or she believes would be proven if the case went to trial and why). Second, the judge may have witnesses for the prosecution testify before he or she accepts the guilty plea. Because the acceptance of a plea bargain entails the waiver of constitutional rights associated with trial, the judge must ensure that the defendant has agreed to plead guilty intelligently and voluntarily (see *Boykin v. Alabama,* 1969).

Plea bargaining makes life easier for judges, prosecutors, public defenders, and private defense attorneys. Because bargaining takes much less time than a trial, it greatly lightens the often excessive caseloads of judges, prosecutors, and public defenders. Private defense lawyers frequently take cases for a flat fee, so bargaining enables them to rapidly close one case and move on to other cases and additional fees.

Defendants also benefit from plea bargaining. A bargained case is likely to get less publicity, and private attorneys sometimes charge less for a plea bargained case than for a case that goes to trial. Plea bargaining generally stops the investigation, which if continued might uncover additional crimes the defendant has committed. Moreover, sentences in plea bargained cases tend to be much lighter than those in cases where the defendant is convicted at trial.

Plea bargaining has its harsh critics. Because of the often markedly lighter sentences, bargaining may entice the innocent to plead guilty. It may demoralize police officers. Serious problems with the system, such as police brutality, which might come out at trial, never get discussed. A system in which justice is bargained may undermine public faith in the courts, and unless one has strong proof of being pressured into entering a guilty plea, successful appeal is virtually impossible even if evidence of innocence surfaces at a later time.

Despite these criticisms, many argue that on balance, plea bargaining is generally preferable to trial. Supporters of plea bargaining believe that most defendants are guilty, so trying them just further clogs already overburdened courts at unnecessary public expense. In response to claims that prosecutors often sell out victims with plea bargaining, prosecutors note that convictions at trial for some of the worst offenders are simply impossible, and the only hope for punishment lies in the defendants' admission of guilt. Examples include many rape cases and child sexual abuse cases, in which victims are unwilling to undergo still further trauma by testifying in court.

Three Supreme Court cases on plea bargaining are noteworthy. In *North Carolina v. Alford* (1970), the defendant claimed that he pled guilty to second-degree murder, while claiming innocence, in order to escape a likely death penalty if found guilty of first-degree murder at trial. The Supreme Court noted that inasmuch as there was strong evidence of guilt, his plea was uncoerced and constitutional even if entered out of fear.

In *Santobello v. New York* (1971), the prosecutor enticed Santobello into entering a guilty plea by agreeing to refrain from recommending a sentence (a signal to the judge that a light sentence was acceptable). At the sentencing stage several months later, a different prosecutor from the same office recommended the maximum sentence, which the judge imposed, while claiming to be uninfluenced by that recommendation. Santobello then tried unsuccessfully to withdraw his guilty plea in the trial court. The Supreme Court vacated Santobello's conviction and held that in such cases, the trial court must either assure that the prosecution keeps its promise or allow the defendant to withdraw the guilty plea.

In *Bordenkircher v. Hayes* (1978), the prosecutor offered to recommend a five-year sentence in exchange for a guilty plea, but if Hayes was unwilling to "save the court the inconvenience and necessity of a trial," he would seek his reindictment as a habitual criminal with a mandatory life sentence. Hayes rejected the offer and wound up with a life sentence. The defense told the Supreme Court that exercising his constitutional right to a trial had in effect increased his sentence from five years to life, but the Court held that recommending a much tougher sentence for those who go to trial is the prosecutor's prerogative.

See also Accused, Rights of the; Due Process, Procedural; Pleas in Criminal Cases; Probation and Parole; Sixth Amendment; Force, Use of by Law Enforcement

Bibliography

Carp, Robert A., Ronald Stidham, and Kenneth L. Manning. 2004. *Judicial Process in America.* 6th ed. Washington, DC: CQ Press.

George Kiser

PLEAS IN CRIMINAL CASES

Before a person accused of a crime can be found guilty and sentenced, the accused must be afforded an opportunity to enter a plea. In most jurisdictions, the accused has four options. The first is to plead not guilty, in which case the judge will schedule the case for trial. The second option is to plead guilty,

which is in fact what happens in the great majority of cases due in large part to the pervasive practice of plea bargaining. The third option is to plead "no contest" or *nolo contendere,* a plea that does not admit guilt but does not contest the charges. The no contest plea, although functionally equivalent to a guilty plea, provides the accused the advantage that it generally cannot be construed as an admission of guilt in a related civil suit. The final option is the so-called best interests plea, also known as an *Alford* plea because it was recognized by the Supreme Court in *North Carolina v. Alford* (1970). This is a plea of guilty containing a protestation of innocence, a plea that is made when the defendant rationally concludes that his or her best interests are best served by pleading guilty. Because a plea of guilty or no contest entails a waiver of the right to trial and other related constitutional protections, the Supreme Court held in *Boykin v. Alabama* (1969) that trial judges must determine that such pleas are entered intelligently and voluntarily.

See also Accused, Rights of the; No Contest Plea; Plea Bargaining

John M. Scheb II and Otis H. Stephens, Jr.

PLESSY V. FERGUSON (1896)

The Supreme Court's decision in the *Plessy v. Ferguson* (1896) is generally regarded as one of its most infamous rulings. This case provided the Court with a convenient opportunity to invoke the separate but equal doctrine, a formulation that legalized racial segregation in the United States and remained the law of the land until the mid-1950s. *Plessy v. Ferguson* is best understood in historical context. After the passage of the Civil War amendments, the Thirteenth (ending slavery), the Fourteenth (granting citizenship to all persons born or naturalized in the United States), and the Fifteenth (enfranchising African Americans), respectively, Southern citizens were embittered and emboldened to challenge the rights of the newly freed former slaves. The federal Congress attempted to end segregation in public places with the Civil Rights Act of 1875, but the Supreme

Court in the Civil Rights Cases of 1883 declared this legislation unconstitutional. In the meantime, the era of Reconstruction had ended, and the voting rights of former Confederates had been fully restored. Now sensing support from the staunchly conservative Court, Southern states began enacting so-called Jim Crow laws—legislation requiring strict racial segregation in all facets of social life. One such law was at the heart of the *Plessy v. Ferguson* case.

In Louisiana, segregation in public railroad cars was required by the state legislature. However, one man, Homer Plessy, decided to challenge Jim Crow by sitting in the passenger car for whites rather than in the section marked "colored only." Mr. Plessy was one-eighth black and could easily have sat in the white section without controversy, but he pointed out his black heritage to the train conductor in a deliberate effort to bring this case before the Supreme Court. This is often referred to as a test case.

The case did find its way to the high court, and Plessy's lawyer argued that the Louisiana law violated his client's civil rights on both Thirteenth and Fourteenth Amendment grounds. The Supreme Court ruled against Plessy in a seven-to-one decision. Justice Henry Billings Brown delivered the Court's opinion, and Justice John Marshall Harlan (the elder) penned a prophetic dissent that years later would provide the rationale for the majority opinion in *Brown v. Board of Education* (1954), in which the Supreme Court rejected the "separate but equal" doctrine as applied to public schools. In the *Plessy* decision Justice Brown spent little time discussing the Thirteenth Amendment challenge; he dismissed it as "too clear for argument." Brown and the majority had more difficulty in reaching the Fourteenth Amendment rationale. Indeed, they acknowledged that the "object" of this amendment was "to enforce the absolute equality of the two races before the law." Nevertheless, they felt that segregation was merely a part of the "nature of things." They maintained that segregated or separate accommodations were legal as long as they were equal. Moreover, they insisted that this practice did not "stamp the colored race with a badge of inferiority."

Justice Harlan rejected this convoluted rationale arguing simply: "our constitution is color-blind." He prophetically noted that the majority opinion would later "prove to be quite as pernicious as the decision made by this tribunal in the *Dred Scott Case*" Indeed, these two decisions are now considered among the most unfortunate in our nation's history. Clearly, the separate but equal doctrine did stamp a badge of inferiority on African Americans. Public accommodations remained separate in many states, but they were anything but equal.

As previously noted, almost 60 years later, the Supreme Court repudiated the *Plessy* rationale using Harlan's dissent as the basis for its new majority opinion in *Brown v. Board of Education*. In a unanimous ruling in 1954, the Court held that "In the field of public education the doctrine of 'separate but equal' has no place." This landmark decision was the beginning of the end for the Jim Crow laws.

See also *Brown v. Board of Education* (1954; 1955); The Civil Rights Cases; Dred Scott Case (1857); Equal Protection Clause; Fifteenth Amendment; Fourteenth Amendment (1868); Harlan, John Marshall; Jim Crow Laws; Public Accommodation, Places of; Reconstruction; Thirteenth Amendment

Bibliography

Epstein, Lee, and Thomas G. Walker. 2001. *Constitutional Law For A Changing America: Rights, Liberties, And Justice*. 4th ed. Washington DC: CQ Press.

Stephens, Otis H., Jr. and John M. Scheb II. 2003. *American Constitutional Law*. 3rd ed. Belmont, CA: Wadsworth.

Lori Maxwell

PLURALISM

We have become not a melting pot but a beautiful mosaic—different people, different beliefs, different yearnings, different dreams.

—*Jimmy Carter, 39th President of the United States*

Pluralism is a term that has slightly different meanings depending on the context in which it is being used or discussed, but the foundation of the concept is that a diversity of things (ideas, opinions, groups, individuals, values, etc.) ultimately enriches life and society. The concept of pluralism emerged in the United States in the early 1900s during a time of societal upheaval. America had witnessed the immigration of millions from Europe and Asia, the country was moving from an agrarian to an industrial society, and the increasing urbanization of the land had resulted in almost 600 new cities (pop. 10,000+) in just 40 years. This influx of new people, cultures, religions, politics, and social and ethical values created a more complicated, less homogenous society. This delighted many, but frightened many others, as American life and society changed forever.

William James, the American psychologist and philosopher (1842–1910), termed this emerging society a "Pluralistic Universe" (see James 1908; James 1909). James was enthusiastic about the possibilities such variety would bring to society and life. He influenced such individuals as Randolph Bourne, Margaret Mead, and W.E.B. DuBois. Bourne also felt it was best to enjoy the diversity and embrace the opportunity of a "boiling stew," versus the more popular, less volatile idea of a "melting pot." However, others, such as Jane Addams and John Dewey, who accepted the inevitability of change from diverse groups of people, also felt that time would change this diversity into unification (the "melting pot"), which they termed "Americanization."

By the 1960s, the civil rights movement and women's rights had come into the national spotlight, so pluralism in society turned to issues of race and gender. A call for minorities to hold on to and celebrate their heritage resulted in a new and somewhat controversial term, *multiculturalism*. This concept advocated celebration of differences and heritage and less willingness to become part of the melting pot.

In early twenty-first-century America, the notion of a pluralistic society continues to evolve and elicit discussion. Even Europe has had to begin to deal with its own pluralism. Unlike America, Europe has only recently experienced massive waves of immigrants from African and Islamic communities. These groups have been less willing to "melt" into their new landscape, which has led some to ask, "How far does one bend to accommodate the other?"

Columbia University humanities professor Giovanni Sartori has questioned the limits of pluralism. Characterizing entry into a new community as "a give and take affair," he observes, "Strangers who are unwilling to give in exchange for what they get, who wish to remain 'alien' to the point of challenging the very laws of the land that hosts them are bound to elicit fear, rejection and hostility…." (Sartori 1997, 68). The historian Arthur M. Schlesinger, Jr., puts the issue succinctly: "The question America confronts as a pluralistic society is how to vindicate cherished cultures and traditions without breaking the bonds of cohesion—common ideals, common political institutions, common language, common culture, common fate—that hold the republic together" (Schlesinger 1992, 138).

In contemporary America, areas of concern include the power of special interest groups and corporations. Power based in corporations or special interest groups has become more concentrated, so only time will tell if pluralism with its commitment to diversity and toleration of dissent can withstand these continued challenges. However, pluralism will remain a concept embraced by many as one which encourages diversity, dissent, and respect for other viewpoints with the hope that these differing perspectives will go beyond individual differences and create an accord of ideas and opinions that will ensure a vibrant future for all.

See also Civil Rights Movement; Diversity; Free Marketplace of Ideas; Immigrants and Aliens, Rights of

Bibliography

James, William. 1909. *A Pluralistic Universe.* New York: Longmans, Green & Company.

James, William. 1908. *Pluralism, Pragmatism and Instrumental Truth.* New York: Longmans, Green & Company.

Lustig, R. J. 1984. "Pluralism." In *Encyclopedia of American Political History: Studies of the Principal Movements and Ideas*, ed. J. P. Greene, 910–20. New York: Scribner's.

Sartori, Giovani. 1997. "Understanding Pluralism." *Journal of Democracy* 8: 58.

Schlesinger, Arthur M., Jr. 1992. *The Disuniting of America.* New York: W. W. Norton.

Nissa Dahlin-Brown

POE V. ULLMAN (1961)

In this case, which was a precursor to *Griswold v. Connecticut* (1965), the Supreme Court was asked to rule on the constitutionality of an 1879 Connecticut law proscribing the use of contraceptives. The Court declined the invitation, however, and dismissed the appeal.

The litigation began when a married couple going by the pseudonyms Paul and Pauline Poe brought suit in a Connecticut court to challenge the constitutionality of the Connecticut law, which prohibited the use of birth control devices, even by married couples. Pauline Poe had given birth three times, but all three infants had severe birth defects and died soon after delivery. Pauline's obstetrician and gynecologist, Dr. Buxton, concluded that the birth defects were congenital and advised her against becoming pregnant. Because Ullman, the state's attorney, had indicated his intention to prosecute those who violated the anticontraception law, the Poes filed suit to test the constitutionality of the statute. Dr. Buxton also filed suit, claiming that the statute interfered with his ability to practice medicine. A third lawsuit was filed by "Jane Doe," an anonymous married woman who was also Dr. Buxton's patient. In her complaint Doe claimed that she had become extremely ill during a recent pregnancy and that Dr. Buxton had advised her that becoming pregnant again would be life-threatening.

All three complaints relied on the Fourteenth Amendment; all claimed that enforcement of the statute would deprive plaintiffs of "liberty" without "due process of law." After both suits proved unsuccessful in the Connecticut courts, the plaintiffs appealed to the U.S. Supreme Court. Dividing five-to-four, the Court dismissed their appeals, ruling that they did not present a "justiciable" question. There was no majority opinion, but Justice Felix Frankfurter, writing for the plurality, noted that "[t]he lack of immediacy of the threat described by these allegations ... raise[s] serious questions of non-justiciability of appellants' claims." Frankfurter characterized the plaintiffs' purported fear of prosecution as "chimerical" because the law had "so many years gone uniformly and without exception unenforced." Justice William Brennan, concurring in the judgment, agreed that the appeal should be "dismissed for failure to present a real and substantial controversy which unequivocally calls for adjudication of the rights claimed in advance of any attempt by the State to curtail them by criminal prosecution."

Dissenting, Justices Hugo Black and Potter Stewart indicated their view that the Court was incorrect in dismissing the appeals, but they indicated nothing as to their views on the merits of the case. In his dissenting opinion, Justice William O. Douglas insisted that the Court was wrong "to turn [the appellants] away and make them flout the law and get arrested to have their constitutional rights determined." But Douglas also left no doubt as to his view of the constitutional question raised by the appeal:

Can there be any doubt that a Bill of Rights that in time of peace bars soldiers from being quartered in a home "without the consent of the Owner" should also bar the police from investigating the intimacies of the marriage relation? The idea of allowing the State that leeway is congenial only to a totalitarian regime.

Justice John Marshall Harlan (the younger) also produced a forceful dissenting opinion, but one that was much more analytical than Douglas' passionate dissent. Harlan argued that the Fourteenth Amendment protects sexual privacy within marriage, and that accordingly, the Connecticut law should be invalidated insofar as it applied to married couples. But he distinguished sexual activity outside marriage, which he believed was subject to the police power of the state:

Adultery, homosexuality and the like are sexual intimacies which the State forbids altogether, the but intimacy of husband and wife is necessarily an essential and accepted feature of the institution of marriage, an institution which the State not only must allow, but which always and in every age it has fostered and protected. It is one thing when the State exerts its power either to forbid extra-marital sexuality altogether, or to say who may marry, but it is quite another when, having acknowledged a marriage and the intimacies inherent in it, it undertakes to regulate by means of the criminal law the details of that intimacy.

A few months after the Supreme Court handed down *Poe v. Ullman,* Estelle Griswold opened a Planned Parenthood Clinic in New Haven. After she was convicted of violating the anticontraception statute, the Supreme Court was ready to address the constitutional question it avoided in *Poe v. Ullman. Griswold v. Connecticut* (1965) would become one of the most important, and most controversial, decisions of the Warren Court.

See also Bill of Rights (American) (1789); Black, Hugo L.; Douglas, William O.; Due Process Clauses; Due Process, Substantive; Fourteenth Amendment (1868); Frankfurter, Felix; *Griswold v. Connecticut* (1965); Harlan, John Marshall, II; Liberty; Marriage, Rights Pertaining to; Planned Parenthood; Privacy, Constitutional Right of; Stewart, Potter; Warren Court

Bibliography

Friendly, Fred W., and Martha J. H. Elliot. 1984. *The Constitution: That Delicate Balance.* New York: Random House.

Johnson, John W. 2005. *Griswold v. Connecticut: Birth Control and the Constitutional Right of Privacy.* Lawrence: University Press of Kansas.

John M. Scheb II and Otis H. Stephens, Jr.

POLICE BRUTALITY. *See* Force, Use of by Law Enforcement

POLICE POWER

The term *police power* was coined by the English common law to denote the power of the Crown, and later the Parliament, to enforce restrictions on society for the maintenance of the common good. In the late eighteenth century, Sir William Blackstone's *Commentaries on the Laws of England* defined the police power as "the due regulation and domestic order of the kingdom, whereby individuals of the state, like members of a well-governed family, are bound to conform their general behavior to the rules of propriety, good neighborhood and good manners: and to be decent, industrious, and inoffensive in their respective stations."

In the American legal tradition, the definition of police power is somewhat more confined. It refers to the inherent authority of state legislatures to enact laws restricting personal freedom and the use of property in order to safeguard the public health, safety, order, and welfare. The supposed origin of this inherent power was the transfer of sovereignty from the Crown to the newly established state governments after the Declaration of Independence. In *Gibbons v. Ogden* (1824), Chief Justice John Marshall described the police power of state governments as "that immense mass of legislation, which embraces everything within the territory of a State, not surrendered to the general government."

The Framers of the Constitution did not vest the Congress with the police power. As James Madison wrote in *Federalist No. 45,* "The powers delegated by the proposed Constitution to the federal government are few and defined. Those which are to remain in the State governments are numerous and indefinite." However, through broad interpretation of its power to regulate interstate commerce, Congress in the modern era has asserted a degree of legislative authority approaching the plenary power of state legislatures. Much of the federal law in the fields of environmental protection, civil rights, and criminal justice is based explicitly on the Commerce Clause. Still, the courts maintain the view (some would say "fiction") that Congress is not vested with the police power. For example, in striking down a far-reaching exercise of congressional power under the Commerce Clause, the Supreme Court in *United States v. Lopez* (1995) observed, "To uphold the Government's contentions here, we would have to pile inference upon inference in a manner that would bid fair to convert congressional authority under the Commerce Clause to a general police power of the sort retained by the States."

Although the police powers of the states are broad and formidable, they are subject to limitations imposed on the states via the Fourteenth Amendment. In *Lochner v. New York* (1905), the Court recognized that "property and liberty are held on such reasonable conditions as may be imposed by the governing power of the state in the exercise of those powers, and with such conditions the 14th Amendment was not designed to interfere." At a minimum, an exercise of the state's police power must be rationally related to a legitimate governmental interest. Because the Fourteenth Amendment has been held to incorporate most of the provisions of the Bill of Rights, states may not exercise their police powers so as to intrude on these fundamental freedoms in the absence of a compelling governmental interest. As the Supreme Court recognized in *Snyder v. Massachusetts* (1934) and many times since, the Due Process Clause of the Fourteenth Amendment also incorporates other liberty interests "so rooted in the traditions and conscience of our people as to be ranked as fundamental."

Traditionally, the police power of the state was thought to extend to the regulation of immoral conduct. In *Bowers v. Hardwick* (1986), the Supreme Court observed that law "is constantly based on notions of morality, and if all laws representing essentially moral choices are to be invalidated under the Due Process Clause, the courts will be very busy indeed." Concurring in *Barnes v. Glen Theatre, Inc.* (1991), Justice Antonin Scalia observed: "While there may be great diversity of view on whether various of these prohibitions should exist... there is no doubt that, absent specific constitutional protection for the conduct involved, the Constitution does not prohibit them simply because they regulate 'morality.'"

While states certainly maintain broad authority to regulate indecent behavior in public places, and may use zoning laws to regulate the location of adult-oriented businesses, private, consensual sexual conduct is no longer considered a valid object of the police power. For example, in *Lawrence v. Texas* (2003) the Supreme Court struck down a state law prohibiting private, consensual homosexual conduct. Writing for the Court, Justice Anthony Kennedy concluded that the challenged law "furthers no legitimate state interest which can justify its intrusion into the personal and private life of the individual."

See also Blackstone, William; Due Process Clauses; Due Process, Substantive; Fourteenth Amendment (1868); Kennedy, Anthony; *Lawrence v. Texas* (2003); Liberty; *Lochner v. New York* (1905); Marshall, John; Morality; Privacy, Constitutional Right of; Scalia, Antonin; *United States v. Lopez* (1995); Zoning

Bibliography

Dubber, Markus Dirk. 2004. "'The Power to Govern Men and Things': Patriarchal Origins of the Police Power in American Law." *Buffalo Law Review* 52: 1277.

Freund, Ernst. 1904. *The Police Power, Public Policy and Constitutional Rights.* Chicago: Callaghan.

John M. Scheb II and Otis H. Stephens, Jr.

POLL TAX

A poll tax, generally defined, is a small amount of money that a person is required to pay in order to be able to vote. In the United States, poll taxes have a dual legacy. They were once considered a major step in extending the right to vote to many, while at the same time they were imposed to prevent the poor, and especially African Americans, from exercising the franchise. With ratification of the Twenty-Fourth Amendment in 1964, the poll tax was abolished in federal elections in the United States. Two years later, in *Harper v. Virginia Board of Elections* (1966), the Supreme Court extended this ban by holding that poll taxes in state elections violated the Equal Protection Clause of the Fourteenth Amendment.

At the time of America's independence in 1776, many of England's legal practices were adopted, including the rules regarding who could vote. In many states the voting franchise was limited to male adults who owned a certain amount of property or land. The belief was that property ownership was a sign of the owner's independence and his investment in the community. Paupers, it was thought, did not have enough at stake in society and therefore should not be allowed to vote.

When the United States Constitution was adopted in 1787, it was silent about who could vote, leaving it up to the states to determine qualifications for the franchise. Many of the Framers, including James Madison, advocated the retention of property qualifications for voting, again claiming that ownership of land assured both independence and a commitment to the community. Many states incorporated these beliefs into their laws. Maryland, South Carolina, and Virginia required an individual to own 50 acres of land to be able to vote, whereas Rhode Island and Connecticut required an estate worth at least 40 shillings per year. None of these were trifling sums.

But property qualifications began to disappear in the early nineteenth century. They did so for at least two reasons. First, voting came to be regarded as a natural right (at least for white males) and the growing population of wage earners began to demand this right even though most of them could not afford to own real estate. Thus, changes in the economy necessitated a different way to demonstrate independence and a stake in a community, besides actually owning land.

The second reason property qualifications disappeared is that they were often replaced with a poll tax. This tax, whether it was a payment of a small sum at the time of voting, or a demonstration that one had paid local taxes, indicated that one was wealthy enough to be independent and have a stake in the community. States such as New Hampshire had a poll tax as early as 1784. Delaware, Maine, and Mississippi required either the payment of annual or local taxes or a fee at the time of voting. The replacement of property requirements with a poll tax was seen as an important reform that extended franchise rights in the pre–Civil War period.

Poll taxes took on a new meaning after the Civil War, especially in the South. During Reconstruction the Republicans in Congress passed numerous civil rights bills, extending political rights to the former slaves. In addition to the Thirteenth Amendment (which abolished slavery) and the Fourteenth Amendment (which, among other things, extended citizenship to all persons born or naturalized in the United States), the adoption of the Fifteenth Amendment in 1870 made it illegal to deny citizens the right to vote based on race. The impact of these amendments, as well as many of the civil rights laws passed by Congress during Reconstruction, led to the enfranchising of many former slaves who voted and often elected African Americans to Congress and state legislatures in the south. Reconstruction ended in 1877, following the controversial election of Rutherford B. Hayes as president. As a result, federal enforcement of civil rights laws in the South came to an end.

Southern states then constructed a variety of schemes to deny African Americans their voting rights. One way was for the Ku Klux Klan to lynch, threaten, or harass former slaves who attempted to vote. Another mechanism was to pass laws that would make it more difficult for these individuals to vote. Still another device was the introduction of a poll tax. Even though the tax was small, one or two dollars, it was allowed to accumulate if unpaid and imposed a significant economic burden on many African Americans. The poll tax, along with grandfather clauses and literacy tests, was part of what came to be known as the Jim Crow laws that effectively denied all but a few African Americans in the south the right to vote.

Poll taxes, besides suppressing the voting rights of African Americans, also suppressed those of poor whites who could not afford these fees. Starting during the Great Depression of the 1930s, when many whites could not afford to vote, states such as North Carolina and Florida repealed their poll taxes. In addition, the National Association for the Advancement of Colored People (NAACP) began to attack many of the Jim Crow laws, including the poll tax. Unfortunately, in *Breedlove v. Suttles* (1937) the Supreme Court unanimously upheld the Georgia poll tax. Efforts to abolish the poll tax in Congress, at least for federal elections, were stymied until the 1960s.

As a result of pressure brought by the civil rights movement and demonstrations in the 1960s, Congress passed, and the states ratified, the Twenty-Fourth Amendment in 1964. This amendment, however, abolished the poll tax only in federal elections. As previously noted, the Supreme Court in *Harper v. Virginia Board of Elections* (1966) recognized that voting was a fundamental right and that poll taxes in state elections violated the Equal Protection Clause of the Fourteenth Amendment.

See also Civil Rights Movement; Equal Protection Clause; Fifteenth Amendment; Fourteenth Amendment (1868); Fundamental Rights; Jim Crow Laws; Ku Klux Klan; National Association for the Advancement of Colored People (NAACP); Representative Democracy; Twenty-Fourth Amendment; Universal Suffrage; Vote, Right to

Bibliography

Keyssar, Alexander. 2000. *The Right to Vote: The Contested History of Democracy in the United States.* New York: Basic Books.

Stephenson, Donald Grier Jr. 2004. *The Right to Vote: Rights and Liberties under the Law.* Santa Barbara, CA: ABC-CLIO.

David Schultz

POLYGAMY. *See* Church of Jesus Christ of Latter-day Saints (LDS Church); Marriage, Rights Pertaining to; *Reynolds v. United States*

POLYGRAPH TESTING

There is no scientific evidence that a polygraph machine can reliably distinguish between a subject who is lying and one who is not. The National Academy of Sciences maintains that the polygraph machine is not effective at discerning between truth and falsehood. And yet polygraph machines,

also called lie detectors, have been in use in the United States since the 1930s. When evaluating the merits of using polygraph machines and other technologies, two questions need to be posed. The first question is whether gathering and using this kind of evidence is acceptable within our constitutional framework of rights and liberties. The second question involves the reliability and accuracy of the test. The first question was originally answered in *Frye v. United States* (1923) with revisions made in the Federal Rules of Evidence, as well as in the *Daubert* and *Scheffer* cases. The second has been answered by several scientific tests, starting in the early 1950s.

Evolution of Admissibility

William Marston, a psychologist, invented the first mechanical lie detector around 1917. The machine purportedly ferreted out lies by measuring the subject's systolic blood pressure. Marston worked diligently to get polygraph results accepted as evidence in court cases. Revisions to both the device and testing procedure theoretically increased the accuracy of the test to the point that its use in law enforcement became commonplace. It was not until 1923, however, that the courts formulated a test to determine whether a given technology could be used to obtain evidence. In *Frye v. United States* (1923), the D.C. U.S. Circuit Court of Appeals held that polygraph evidence was not admissible in court because it was not "sufficiently established to have gained general acceptance in the particular field in which it belongs." The "general acceptance" criterion became known as the *Frye* test and was applied to all instances of novel scientific evidence until the Federal Rules of Evidence were created.

The Federal Rules of Evidence, instituted in 1975, should have eliminated all questions over the admissibility of polygraph evidence in the courts. Some courts, however, continued to follow the test from *Frye.* Two cases in particular concern admissibility of polygraph evidence post-1975, *Daubert* and *Scheffer.* The first dealt with the new rules in terms of *Frye*'s framework, while the second tested the military's per se exclusion of polygraph evidence.

Daubert v. Merrell Dow Pharmaceuticals (1993) ostensibly addressed the question of whether Bendectin (a medicine prescribed to pregnant women) was a teratogen; the deeper question, however, involved admissibility rules for scientific evidence in court. The defendant's experts showed that all scientific research had failed to establish a connection between Bendectin and birth defects in humans. The claimant's experts demonstrated that several studies found Bendectin to cause birth defects in animals, in both in vitro and in vivo studies. Justice Harry Blackmun agreed with the original court, which held that the testimony of the claimant's experts was not admissible in court because the effects on animals were not relevant to the case. The *Daubert* decision upheld the Federal Rules of Evidence in replacing *Frye's* "general acceptance from the scientific community" test with an independent judicial assessment. In other words, scientific testimony that is both relevant and reliable must be included, and testimony that is irrelevant and/or unreliable must be excluded. This finding was later upheld in an opinion by Chief Justice William H. Rehnquist in *General Electric Co. v. Joiner* (1997). Thus, according to *Daubert*, scientific evidence (including polygraph evidence) could be admitted at trial, as long as the judge found it both reliable and relevant.

United States V. Scheffer (1998) specifically addressed evidentiary standards with respect to polygraph machines. The U.S. Court of Appeals for the Armed Forces held that Military Rule of Evidence 707, a blanket ban on all use of polygraphs by military courts, was a violation of both the Fifth and Sixth Amendments, and was as such unconstitutional. The Supreme Court disagreed. Reviewing the studies on polygraph reliability, the Supreme Court decided to leave the decision as to whether or not to admit polygraph evidence up to each jurisdiction. That is, each jurisdiction could decide to exclude it per se or to evaluate it case by case in accord with *Daubert*. Thus, while *Daubert* allowed the admission of polygraph evidence, *Scheffer* stopped short of requiring it. Today, 27 states

exclude polygraph evidence, 22 allow it if both parties agree, and New Mexico routinely allows it.

The Polygraph at Work

Court cases represent one common use for polygraph tests, and employment decisions represent another. While usually not admissible in courts, from the 1950s until 1988, polygraph tests were commonly given for employment screening. In 1988, through the efforts of the American Civil Liberties Union and other privacy-rights organizations, Congress passed the Federal Employee Polygraph Protection Act (EPPA), which generally banned employers from using the polygraph on their employees. Some exceptions were allowed. For example, in cases where the employer provides clear documentation of his or her suspicions regarding the conduct of the employee, and the employer has not fired the employee based solely on the results of the polygraph examination, use of the test is permissible. The polygraph, however, cannot be required as a condition of employment in most workplaces. Employers exempted from EPPA provisions include state and local governments, companies that manufacture or dispense controlled substances, and companies that do sensitive work on government contracts.

Reliability of the Polygraph

Perhaps the most important question has yet to be answered here. Under *Daubert*, scientific evidence can be admitted as long as the judge believes it is both relevant and reliable. But are polygraph examinations reliable? That is, are polygraph machines really lie detectors? The answer depends on who is asked. Some advocates of the polygraph claim accuracy rates as high as 99 percent, while others, such as the National College of DUI Defense, estimate that the machines are between 70 percent and 90 percent accurate. However, scientific, double-blind studies have never come close to that level. The first scientific tests, those performed in the 1950s, found that polygraphs were no more accurate than guessing. A 1981 study found error rates between 18 percent and 55 percent, and a third study found that false positives were much more frequent than false negatives; that is, a truthful person would be found lying at a higher rate than a deceitful person would be found telling the truth. Thus, while advocates continue pushing for admissibility, science has found the accuracy of the polygraph machine wanting.

And so, even in light of *Daubert,* polygraph evidence may never be acceptable in court. As Justice Clarence Thomas wrote in *Scheffer,* "there is simply no way to know in a particular case whether a polygraph examiner's conclusion is accurate, because certain doubts and uncertainties plague even the best polygraph exams."

See also American Civil Liberties Union (ACLU); Blackmun, Harry A.; Fifth Amendment; Sixth Amendment; Stevens, John Paul; Thomas, Clarence

Bibliography

Kleinberg, Murray, ed. 2002. *Handbook of Polygraph Testing.* San Diego: Academic Press.

Ole J. Forsberg

PORNOGRAPHY. *See* Child Pornography; Obscenity and Pornography

POSITIVISM, LEGAL. *See* Hart, H.L.A.

POSTCONVICTION RELIEF

Until fairly recently the only way that a state prisoner who had exhausted the ordinary appeals process could secure additional review of a conviction or sentence was to seek a writ of habeas corpus in a state or federal court. Today, most states have enacted laws or rules of judicial procedure allowing prisoners, under appropriate circumstances, to challenge their convictions or sentences even after their ordinary appeals have been exhausted. Because access to federal habeas corpus review has been constrained by federal legislation and judicial decisions, these state-level postconviction review procedures have taken on great importance in the administration of justice.

Most state postconviction relief rules allow a prisoner to challenge a conviction on the ground that it was obtained in violation of the federal or state constitution, which allows a prisoner to litigate constitutional issues of criminal procedure. Some state statutes and rules refer to "prisoners" or "persons in custody" but courts often interpret these terms to allow a defendant on probation to seek postconviction relief.

In addition to imposing time limits for filing, to promote finality in judicial proceedings courts usually recognize a number of procedural bars to postconviction relief. For example, a defendant seeking postconviction relief ordinarily may not relitigate a claim previously decided nor assert a new claim or a claim that could have been raised on direct appeal. A common exception is where a state prisoner challenges a conviction on the basis of ineffective assistance of counsel, which does not usually lend itself to be raised as an appellate issue because it is not an issue ordinarily preserved at trial. And some courts have made exceptions where constitutional issues have not been raised at the trial level.

State rules also typically allow prisoners to assert that evidence is available which was unknown or unavailable to the defendant at trial and which has a direct and material bearing on the defendant's guilt or innocence. This is particularly significant in light of the Supreme Court's controversial decision in *Herrera v. Collins* (1993), which held that federal habeas corpus review is not the proper mechanism for litigation of belated claims of actual innocence brought by persons convicted in state courts. In recent years, there has been a flurry of cases where prisoners were exonerated through postconviction review based on DNA evidence that was not available at trial. Since 2000 many states have adopted statutes and procedural rules to provide for postconviction DNA testing. These measures usually require a convicted defendant to allege that he or she was not previously tested for DNA or, if previously tested, that subsequent testing techniques will likely produce a definitive result, which would exonerate the defendant or mitigate his or her sentence.

Rule 3.850 of the Florida Rules of Criminal Procedure is fairly typical of state postconviction relief procedures. Rule 3.850 recognizes six grounds for postconviction relief:

1. The judgment was entered or sentence was imposed in violation of the Constitution or laws of the United States or the State of Florida.
2. The court did not have jurisdiction to enter the judgment.
3. The court did not have jurisdiction to impose the sentence.
4. The sentence exceeded the maximum authorized by law.
5. The plea was involuntary.
6. The judgment or sentence is otherwise subject to collateral attack.

There are time limits on filing for postconviction relief. Florida Rule 3.850 allows a motion to vacate a sentence that exceeded statutory limits to be filed at any time, but places a two-year limit on other motions for postconviction relief in no capital cases and a one-year limit on other motions in capital cases. Rule 3.853, which provides for postconviction DNA testing, imposes a similar time limit.

Rule 3.850 also bars many successive petitions for postconviction review by providing: "A second or successive motion may be dismissed if the judge finds that it fails to allege new or different grounds for relief and the prior determination was on the merits or, if new and different grounds are alleged, the judge finds that the failure of the moving or the attorney to assert those grounds in a prior motion constituted an abuse of the procedure governed by these rules."

See also Accused, Rights of the; Appeal, Right of; Due Process, Procedural; Habeas Corpus; Habeas Corpus, Federal

Bibliography

Schacht, Barry, Peter Neufeld, and Jim Dwyer. 2000. *Actual Innocence: Five Days to Execution, and Other Dispatches From the Wrongly Convicted.* New York: Doubleday.

Scheb, John M., and John M. Scheb II. 2006. *Criminal Procedure.* 4th ed. Belmont, CA: Thomson/Wadsworth.

Swafford, Tara. 1995. "Responding to *Herrera v. Collins:* Ensuring that Innocents are not Executed." *Case Western Law Review* 45: 603.

John M. Scheb II

POWELL, LEWIS F., JR. (1907–1998)

Lewis F. Powell, Jr. was born into a comfortable middle-class existence in Suffolk, Virginia. He graduated from Washington and Lee College in 1929 and received his law degree from Harvard in 1932. In private practice in his home state of Virginia, Powell achieved national prominence as a corporate lawyer and served as president of the American Bar Association 1964–1965. Powell refused President Richard Nixon's first attempt to nominate him to the U.S. Supreme Court in 1971. Only the next year, after the Senate had rejected Nixon's first two Southern nominees, did Powell reluctantly agree to the nomination at the age of 64. He was part of a package, with William Rehnquist, nominated to replace Hugo Black and John M. Harlan. Despite some opposition from liberal groups, Powell was confirmed easily, receiving only one negative vote in the Senate.

Powell's 16 years on the Court nearly coincided with the era of Chief Justice Warren E. Burger. Though his rulings were in many ways conservative, Powell was one of the Burger Court's centrists, benefiting from the fact that, in judicial and parliamentary politics alike, who controls the center controls the outcome. Powell thus often cast the deciding vote in major cases by articulating a compromise or moderate position between liberals like William Brennan and Thurgood Marshall on the left and Rehnquist and Burger on the right. Space constraints limit us to a consideration of his constitutional rather than statutory jurisprudence, and three themes clearly emerge: conservatism, liberalism, and pragmatism—Powell's capacity to forge a creative third way.

To begin with procedural issues rooted in Article III case or controversy limitations, Powell sided with the conservatives in standing cases, that is in favor of tightening the requirements for access to federal courts. In *Wrath v. Seldom* (1975), for example, Powell held for the Court that to establish standing a plaintiff must carry the burden of plausibly alleging injury, causation, and redress, which he held not satisfied in that case. This rule was reinforced in *Allen v. Wright* (1984), in which Powell joined the majority. In *Goldwater v. Carter* (1979), moreover, Powell concurred in Rehnquist's ruling that a challenge by U.S. Senators to President Carter's abrogation of a U.S. treaty without submitting it to the Senate for ratification presented no case or controversy. Where Rehnquist based his ruling on the political question doctrine, however, Powell rested on grounds of ripeness: since Congress had not yet formally challenged Carter's action, the problem might still be resolved within the political branches, and should be allowed to do so, if possible, without judicial intervention. In this way, Powell would have avoided burdening political question jurisprudence with an unnecessary ruling.

As for issues of legislative power, Powell concurred in *INS v. Chadha* (1983), in which the Chief Justice held for the majority that since the legislative veto attempts to make law without comporting with Article I requirements of bicameralism and presentment, it unconstitutionally violates the no delegation principle. Though Powell shared the concern in Justice White's dissent over the sweeping decision's impact on over 200 statutory schemes, Powell concurred on the narrower ground that the legislative veto amounted to a bill of attainder, an attempt by a legislature to perform a judicial function. As for Congress's commerce power, Powell dissented vigorously from the majority opinion in *Garcia v. SAMTA* (1985), which held the application of federal Fair Labor Standards Act provisions to a local transit authority beyond Congress's authority. Writing for Burger, Rehnquist, and Sandra Day O'Connor, Powell emphasized conservative themes of stare decisis, framers' intent, and a dual federalist conception of the Tenth Amendment. As for the

"dormant" Commerce Clause, notwithstanding his inclination for deference to the states, Powell held for the majority in *Kassel v. Consolidated Freightways* (1981) that Iowa's limits on truck lengths on state highways exceeded the state's power. Brennan and Marshall concurred, finding Iowa's intent to discriminate against out-of-state interests a per se violation of the Commerce Clause. Powell, however, struck the law as an impermissible means of state action, both because it discriminated in effect and because upon close scrutiny the law undermined public safety more than it advanced it. Justices Rehnquist, Burger, and PotterStewart dissented, holding that the law could not, under the deferential standard appropriate in such cases, be judged an irrational means of advancing safety.

Powell's conservatism is also evident in his First Amendment jurisprudence, though this has involved rulings both for and against government. In *Young v. American Mini-Theatres* (1976), for example, Powell joined John Paul Stevens' opinion upholding a "skid row" zoning ordinance against a claim that it impermissibly regulated conduct protected by the Free Speech Clause. Deferring to local government, Powell sought to enable its efforts to protect public health and morals under the police power. In *First National Bank of Boston v. Bellotti* (1978), by contrast, Powell held for the majority that a state law prohibiting corporate contributions or expenditures intended to influence the vote on issues not materially affecting the corporation's interests violates the First Amendment. If this opinion was conservative in the sense of favoring corporate power, it was still a ruling against government, and so reflected a libertarian rather than an authoritarian conservatism.

As for criminal law and procedure, Powell's inclination to defer to the states is again evident. In *Stone v. Powell* (1976), over a vigorous dissent by Brennan and Marshall, Powell held for the Court that since the exclusionary rule is a judicially created remedy rather than a constitutional right, and since federal review on writ of habeas corpus is limited to examining whether a state has denied U.S. constitutional rights, federal courts are not required on habeas corpus to reexamine a state court's application of the exclusionary rule. As for capital punishment, writing for Burger, Rehnquist, and Harry Blackmun, Powell dissented from the Court's ruling in *Furman v. Georgia* (1972) that, as applied, the death penalty constituted cruel and unusual punishment in violation of the Eighth Amendment. Powell was thus vindicated in *Gregg v. Georgia* (1976), writing for the majority that so long as procedures satisfying the concerns of Furman are in place, a state's imposition of the death penalty does not necessarily violate the Eighth Amendment. In *McCleskey v. Kemp* (1987), further, Powell held for a bare majority that a study showing a much higher risk of imposition of the death penalty on blacks than whites convicted of first-degree murder in Georgia was insufficient to overturn a death sentence imposed upon a particular black defendant.

McCleskey also involved an equal protection challenge, and Powell is probably best known for his Fourteenth Amendment jurisprudence. In *Mathews v. Eldridge* (1976), for example, Powell established the modern rule of administrative due process, a pragmatic balancing of individual and community interests with attention to the efficiency of the administrative process. In *San Antonio Independent School District v. Rodriguez* (1973), further, Powell held for a five to four majority that the Texas public school financing formula, which allocated over twice as much money per pupil in wealthy as in poor school districts, did not violate equal protection. In reaching this decision, Powell ruled that wealth is not a suspect classification and that education is not a fundamental interest for purposes of equal protection analysis. He thus applied mere rational basis scrutiny, which the Texas public school financing scheme survived. In this way, Powell deferred to state flexibility and avoided the prospect of federal judicial oversight of another aspect of public education beyond racial integration.

Mathews and *Rodriguez* are cautious, compromise opinions, yet Powell's Fourteenth Amendment jurisprudence also reveals his liberal streak. In *Bowers v. Hardwick* (1986), to be sure, he reluctantly

gave the conservatives the fifth vote they needed to uphold Georgia's antisodomy statute against substantive due process challenge (which statute the Georgia Supreme Court has since struck down under its state constitution). Not only did Powell later express regret over his decisions in both *McCleskey* and *Bowers,* however, but he also joined Blackmun's opinion in *Roe v. Wade* (1973), one of the Court's most liberal rulings, establishing a limited right of abortion under privacy and substantive due process. Powell's liberalism is further evident in his most famous ruling, *University of California Regents v. Bakke* (1978). In *Bakke,* Powell held that diversity is a compelling state interest justifying the use of race or ethnicity as one of many factors in public university admissions under the Equal Protection Clause. While both diversity and privacy are core liberal values, it should be noted, privacy is a mere negative liberty, a fundamental right which individuals may use as a shield against governmental intrusion, forcing strict judicial scrutiny of that state action. Diversity, by contrast, is a weapon that government can wield against an individual challenging its use of race preferences against him. Thus, liberal as *Bakke* is, it still charted a middle ground between allowing racial quotas, as the liberal wing of the Court sought to do, and invalidating any use of race in the admissions process, as the conservatives sought to do.

John C. Jefferies (1994) has called *Bakke* "an intellectual muddle but a political masterpiece," and this ruling again illustrates Powell's capacity for the creative third way. However one characterizes it, *Bakke* was the key opinion on which the Supreme Court relied when, 25 years after *Bakke,* it finally revisited the question in *Grutter v. Bollinger* and *Gratz v. Bollinger* (2003) whether race preferences in public university admissions violates the Equal Protection Clause. The influence of the Burger Court's great centrist thus continues.

See also Affirmative Action; Black, Hugo L.; Blackmun, Harry A.; Brennan, William J., Jr.; Burger Court; Burger, Warren E.; Conservatism; Diversity; Due Process, Procedural; Due Process, Substantive;

Eighth Amendment; Equal Protection Clause; First Amendment; Fourteenth Amendment; Fundamental Rights; *Furman v. Georgia* (1972); *Gregg v. Georgia* (1976); Group Rights; Habeas Corpus, Federal; Harlan, John Marshall, II; Individual Rights; Liberalism; Liberty; Marshall, Thurgood; Police Power; Precedent, Doctrine of; Privacy, Constitutional Right of; Rational Basis Test; Rehnquist, William H.; *Roe v. Wade* (1973); Speech, Freedom of; State Action Doctrine; Strict Scrutiny; Tenth Amendment; White, Byron R.

Bibliography

Carcieri, Martin D. 2000. "The Wages of Taking *Bakke* Seriously: The Untenable Denial of the Primacy of the Individual." *Tennessee Law Review* 67: 949.

Jefferies, John C. 1994. *Justice Lewis F. Powell, Jr.* New York: Charles Scribner's Sons.

Kahn, Paul W. 1987. "The Court, the Community, and the Judicial Balance: The Jurisprudence of Justice Powell." *Yale Law Journal* 97: 1.

Urofsky, Melvin, 1984. "Mr. Justice Powell and Education: The Balancing of Competing Values." *Journal of Law and Education* 13: 581.

Martin Carcieri

POWELL V. ALABAMA (1932)

Also known as the first of the Scottsboro Cases, *Powell v. Alabama* was among the most important Supreme Court decisions of the early twentieth century with respect to the rights of the accused. In addition, the case graphically illustrated the depth and intensity of white racism in the American South heightened by the economic class conflict engendered by the Great Depression.

Ozie Powell and eight other young, out-of-work African American males were arrested following a fight with seven white males on a freight train traveling through northern Alabama on the morning of March 25, 1931. Powell and his companions were accused of raping two white girls who were present at the time of the altercation and who remained on the train after the white males were allegedly forced off.

Word of the fight and the allegation of rape spread quickly and a growing crowd of angry whites was flocking to Scottsboro, the county seat, by the time the nine suspects were brought to the jail that afternoon. By 8:30 that evening a mob had gathered at the jail and was demanding the release of the nine prisoners into their "custody." After attempting unsuccessfully to remove the prisoners to a more secure jail in a nearby town, the county sheriff contacted the Alabama governor and requested that units of the state militia be dispatched to Scottsboro to guard the prisoners and maintain order. The request was granted, and the prisoners remained under military guard until after the completion of their trials on the ninth day of April.

On March 31, six days after their arrests, Powell and his companions were formally indicted, and their trials were set to begin on the following Monday, April 6, 1931. The defendants, who were poor, uneducated, and far removed from friends and family, were tried hurriedly without any truly meaningful assistance of counsel. Milo C. Moody, an elderly member of the local bar, and Stephen L. Roddy, a Chattanooga attorney, provided limited assistance to the defendants at trial. Neither attorney, however, was given a sufficient opportunity to prepare an adequate defense. Two of the defendants were tried individually, two were tried jointly, and the remaining five were tried as a group—all this over a four-day period. All-white juries sentenced each of the youthful defendants to death with the exception of 13-year-old Roy Wright, whose case was declared a mistrial. By a margin of six to one, the Alabama Supreme Court affirmed seven of these convictions but granted a new trial for Eugene Williams on the ground that he was allegedly a juvenile at the time of his conviction.

The Scottsboro case drew major national attention, especially from the International Labor Defense (ILD), the legal arm of the American Communist Party. This advocacy group upstaged the National Association for Advancement of Colored People (NAACP) in defending the "Scottsboro boys" and succeeded in petitioning the U.S. Supreme Court for review in 1932.

In a seven-to-two decision, the Supreme Court reversed the seven remaining convictions, holding that the defendants had been denied due process of law as required by the Fourteenth Amendment. Writing for the Court, Justice George Sutherland concluded:

In the light of the facts outlined in the forepart of this opinion—the ignorance and illiteracy of the defendants, their youth, the circumstances of public hostility, the imprisonment and the close surveillance of the defendants by the military forces, the fact that their friends and families were all in other states and communication with them necessarily difficult, and above all that they stood in deadly peril of their lives—we think the failure of the trial court to give them reasonable time and opportunity to secure counsel was a clear denial of due process.

Sutherland's majority opinion stopped well short of saying that all indigent defendants must be provided with meaningful representation in all felony cases. Nor did it say that the Sixth Amendment right to counsel is incorporated into the Due Process Clause of the Fourteenth Amendment. It merely held that "in a capital case, where the defendant is unable to employ counsel, and is incapable adequately of making his own defense because of ignorance, feeble-mindedness, illiteracy, or the like, it is the duty of the court, whether requested or not, to assign counsel for him as a necessary requisite of due process." Nevertheless, the opinion, despite its cautious and somewhat patronizing tone, was an important step toward the recognition of meaningful representation by counsel as an essential element of due process, a right that the Court formally recognized some 30 years later in the landmark case of *Gideon v. Wainwright* (1963).

In the decade that followed the Supreme Court's decision, there would be seven retrials involving the Scottsboro defendants. In the final trial, conducted in 1937, four defendants received life sentences while charges against the other five were dismissed. A letter written in 1932 by Ruby Bates, one of the alleged victims in the case, admitted that none of the Scottsboro defendants had raped her. Today, it is widely acknowledged that the Scottsboro defendants were falsely accused. In 1976, Clarence Norris, the only surviving Scottsboro defendant, was pardoned by Alabama Governor George Wallace.

See also Accused, Rights of the; Bill of Rights, Incorporation of; Communist Party USA; Counsel, Ineffective Assistance of; Counsel, Right to; Due Process Clauses; Due Process, Procedural; Fourteenth Amendment (1868); *Gideon v. Wainwright* (1963); National Association for the Advancement of Colored People (NAACP); Sixth Amendment

Bibliography

Carter, Dan T. 1979. *Scottsboro: A Tragedy of the American South.* Baton Rouge: Louisiana State University Press.

Goodman, James E. 1994. *Stories of Scottsboro.* New York: Vintage Books.

Patterson, Haywood, and Earl Conrad. 1950. *Scottsboro Boy.* Garden City, NY: Doubleday.

Otis H. Stephens, Jr. and John M. Scheb II

PRECEDENT, DOCTRINE OF

American law developed based on the English common law where the doctrine of courts following precedent became an overriding characteristic. A page of history is essential to understand the role the common law plays in the American legal system.

Until the Norman Conquest in 1066 a.d., English law developed on the basis of unwritten decisions of people's courts. After the Norman Conquest, law came to be administered by the king's courts, which endeavored to make the law common to the country, hence the designation *common law.* In the late thirteenth century clerks began writing down the rulings of the common-law courts, and by the fourteenth century these decisions were serving as precedents to guide judges in similar cases. This doctrine of following precedent is known as *stare decisis et non quieta movere* (to adhere to decisions and not to disturb what is settled.). Usually referred to as *stare decisis,* the doctrine became well established with the development of the printing press in the fifteenth century.

The common law developed as an adversarial model and stare decisis led courts to reason by analogy, often termed the "greatest tool of the judiciary." Following precedent led to consistency and predictability in the law, but there is a danger that a particular precedent might have developed in too narrow a factual scenario or may not have been formulated with sufficient reasoning. Thus, the doctrine holds that a court should follow the principle of law enunciated in previous decisions by the highest court within its jurisdiction, assuming that the principle is relevant to the current decision and makes sense in contemporary circumstances. This stands in sharp contrast to the civil law, which is based on codes and allows limited interpretation by courts.

Under stare decisis, the precedents of higher courts are binding on lower courts within their jurisdiction. For example, the decisions of the North Carolina Supreme Court are binding on all courts within the North Carolina state court system. On the other hand, the decisions of an appellate court with jurisdiction over a particular geographical region are not binding on sister courts in other regions. This is because stare decisis is a vertical concept. Likewise, decisions of the United States Court of Appeals for the Fifth Circuit, while binding on federal courts within that circuit, are not binding on the federal courts located within the other circuits. Nevertheless, other circuits may choose to follow the Fifth Circuit and thus adopt its precedent as binding. This is sometimes termed horizontal stare decisis.

In his dissenting opinion in *Burnett v. Coronado Oil Co.* (1932), Justice Louis D. Brandeis observed that "*Stare decisis* is usually the wise policy, because in most matters it is more important that the applicable rule of law be settled than that it be settled right." Justice Felix Frankfurter was less sanguine about the doctrine when, in *Helvering v. Hallock* (1940), he observed, "We recognize that *stare decisis* embodies an important social policy. It represents an element of continuity in law, and is rooted in the psychologic need to satisfy reasonable expectations. But *stare decisis* is a

principle of policy and not a mechanical formula of adherence."

In *Flagiello v. Pennsylvania Hospital* (1965), Justice Musmanno of the Supreme Court of Pennsylvania provided an interesting metaphor:

Stare decisis channels the law…. The ships of jurisprudence must flow that well defined channel which, over the years, has been proved to be secure and trustworthy. But it would not comport with wisdom to insist that, should shoals rise in a heretofore safe course and rocks emerge to encumber the passage, the ship should nonetheless pursue the original course, merely because it presented no hazard in the past. The principle of *stare decisis* does not demand that we follow precedents which shipwreck justice.

Although the doctrine of *stare decisis* applies to American constitutional law, it is not uncommon for the Supreme Court to depart from precedent. Perhaps the most famous reversal is *Brown v. Board of Education* (1954), in which the Supreme Court repudiated the "separate but equal" doctrine of *Plessy v. Ferguson* (1896) and ruled that racial segregation in the public schools is unconstitutional. The separate but equal doctrine had legitimized racial segregation in this country for nearly six decades. Beginning with the *Brown* decision, official segregation was invalidated as a denial of the equal protection of the laws.

Devotion to precedent is considered a hallmark of judicial restraint. Following precedent limits a judge's ability to determine the outcome of a case in a way that he or she might choose if it were a matter of first impression. In 1973, the Supreme Court's seven-to-two decision in *Roe v. Wade* legalized a woman's right to an abortion. *Roe v. Wade* has broad moral and legal ramifications and has generated strong views. Should justices who joined the Court after the *Roe* decision and who believe it was incorrectly decided vote to overrule it, or should the principle of *stare decisis* be observed? The issue came into sharp focus in *Planned Parenthood v. Casey* (1992), when the Supreme Court divided five-to-four in reaffirming *Roe v. Wade*. Justices Sandra Day O'Connor, Anthony Kennedy, and David Souter discussed the factors to be taken into account when the Court reconsiders a constitutional decision:

[W]hen this Court reexamines a prior holding, its judgment is customarily informed by a series of prudential and pragmatic considerations designed to test the consistency of overruling a prior decision with the ideal of the rule of law, and to gauge the respective costs of reaffirming and overruling a prior case. Thus, for example, we may ask whether the rule has proven to be intolerable simply in defying practical workability, ... whether the rule is subject to a kind of reliance that would lend a special hardship to the consequences of overruling and add inequity to the cost of repudiation, ... whether related principles of law have so far developed as to have left the old rule no more than a remnant of abandoned doctrine, ... or whether facts have so changed, or come to be seen so differently, as to have robbed the old rule of significant application or justification.

Applying these considerations, Justices O'Connor, Kennedy, and Souter joined two of their colleagues (John P. Stevens and Harry Blackmun) in concluding that *Roe* should be upheld. Speaking for the four dissenters, Chief Justice Rehnquist made clear his view that "Roe was wrongly decided, and ... can and should be overruled consistently with our traditional approach to *stare decisis* in constitutional cases."

More than a decade after *Casey,* the question of whether *Roe v. Wade* should be overturned by the Supreme Court dominates the politics surrounding appointments to the High Bench. Members of the Senate Judiciary Committee wasted no time in putting this question to Judge John Roberts during the September 2005 hearing on his nomination to succeed William H. Rehnquist as Chief Justice of the United States. In answering the question, Roberts talked about the importance of stare decisis, saying, "It is not enough that you may think the prior decision was wrongly decided." But he refused to say whether, if confirmed as the nation's 16th Chief Justice, he would vote to overturn *Roe v. Wade.* Nevertheless, by a wide margin of votes, the U.S. Senate confirmed his appointment as Chief Justice.

Today, *stare decisis* remains an important component of both the English and American legal systems. It leads to stability and predictability in the law; yet it allows the courts to fill in the gaps that inevitably appear in the statutory law and leaves open an opportunity to depart from precedent based on contemporary circumstances. Alternatives to following precedent would allow courts to exercise unbridled discretion in decision making or require the legislative branches of federal and state governments to adopt all encompassing codifications of laws.

See also Abortion, Right to; Blackmun, Harry A.; Brandeis, Louis D.; *Brown v. Board of Education* (1954; 1955); Common Law Background of American Civil Rights and Liberties; Equal Protection Clause; Fourteenth Amendment (1868); Judicial Restraint; Kennedy, Anthony; *Miranda v. Arizona* (1967); O'Connor, Sandra Day; *Plessy v. Ferguson* (1896); Rehnquist, William H.; *Roe v. Wade* (1973); Souter, David H.; Stevens, John P.

Bibliography

Cooper, Charles J. 1988. "*Stare Decisis:* Precedent and Principle in Constitutional Adjudication." *Cornell Law Review* 73: 401.

Maltz, Earl M. 1980. "Some Thoughts on the Death of Stare Decisis in Constitutional Law." *Wisconsin Law Review* 1980: 467.

Monaghan, Henry P. 1988. "*Stare Decisis* and Constitutional Adjudication." *Columbia Law Review* 88: 723.

Powell, Lewis F., Jr. 1991. "*Stare Decisis* and Judicial Restraint." *Journal of Supreme Court History* 1991: 13.
                    Hon. John M. Scheb and John M. Scheb II

PREFERENCES, RACIAL. *See* Affirmative Action

PREFERRED FREEDOMS DOCTRINE

The preferred freedoms doctrine refers to a ranking or hierarchy of constitutional rights. The preferred freedoms approach sought to distinguish the standards used in evaluating cases on the basis of the issue at hand. The specific form this tool took in the twentieth century was a preference for individual liberties and civil rights. Thus, the Supreme Court would use more exacting standards in assessing alleged infringements on individual liberties and civil rights than the typical deferential rational basis or reasonableness tests used in evaluating economic issues.

The first explicit mention of this hierarchical ordering of rights came in Justice Benjamin Cardozo's majority opinion in *Palko v. Connecticut* (1937). But Oliver Wendell Holmes, Jr. may have established the concept when he suggested that the Supreme Court should not substitute its judgment for that of the legislature in economic matters but formulated the clear and present danger test in *Schenck v. United States* (1919), which recognized the primacy of the First Amendment. It was left to Justice Cardozo in *Palko* to argue that Americans have a handful of fundamental rights. Cardozo argued that these fundamental rights were the "very essence of a scheme of ordered liberty." Included within those fundamental rights were freedom of speech, freedom of the press, and freedom of religion. The Court would periodically add different rights to the list. When the Court identified a right as fundamental, it would subject the state's restriction to strict scrutiny and ignore the normal presumption of constitutionality.

In footnote four of his *United States v. Carolene Products* (1938) opinion, Justice Harlan Fiske Stone suggested that the Court adopt a variant of the preferred freedoms doctrine. Stone argued that when the Court evaluated economic issues, it should adopt a relaxed presumption of constitutionality. The Court should presume that such issues rest on a rational basis and defer to the legislature. On the other hand, when legislation affected fundamental rights or singled out discrete and insular minorities for unequal treatment, the Supreme Court should assume the laws are unconstitutional. Thus, in Stone's words, civil rights and individual liberties should occupy a "preferred position" in the Court's consideration.

The preferred position doctrine, which argued for a judicial double standard, worked its way from a footnote to a dissent and eventually attracted majority support. Justice Felix Frankfurter was critical

of the attempt of the Court to create a hierarchy of rights. He argued that such an ordering of rights was not part of the Constitution, but rather was a reflection of the personal values of the justices. He feared that the Court would expose itself to the same type of problems that had led President Franklin Roosevelt to threaten the institution with the Court-packing plan in 1937.

The preferred freedoms doctrine has been a recipe and a justification for selective judicial activism in dealing with individual liberties and civil rights. The doctrine has been offered as the standard justification for the very existence of an unelected branch of government in an otherwise majoritarian political system. It is the sole means, some argue, of protecting the rights of minorities from the potential tyranny of the majority. The preferred freedoms or preferred position doctrine became an accepted doctrine and has been absorbed into the tests and precedents that the Court relies on in a number of different issue areas. The creation of and the addition to the catalogue of fundamental rights, the creation of strict and moderate scrutiny to deal with questions of discrimination, and the process of selective incorporation of the Bill of Rights to the states all reflect the recognition that some rights and liberties receive a higher level of protection than others.

The Warren Court animated the preferred position doctrine, expanding the protection for civil liberties and civil rights. The Burger Court trimmed the sails a bit, but expanded rights and liberties in some areas (like gender equality and reproductive rights) and generally kept the preferred freedoms doctrine alive. The Rehnquist Court, on the other hand, has been more decisive in rejecting the double standard, by implication, treating all issues by the same basic standards. Some critics charge that the Rehnquist Court, in fact, placed economic issues on a higher level than individual liberties and civil rights. Thus, they claim that the Rehnquist Court adopted a double standard and a preferred freedoms doctrine, but it was a preference for property rights rather than individual liberties.

See also Bill of Rights; Bill of Rights, Incorporation of; Burger Court; Cardozo, Benjamin N.; Clear and Present Danger Doctrine; First Amendment; Fundamental Rights; Holmes, Oliver Wendell, Jr.; Judicial Activism; Judicial Restraint; *Palko v. Connecticut* (1937); Property Rights; Rational Basis Test; Rehnquist Court; Roosevelt, Franklin D.; *Schenck v. United States* (1919); Speech, Freedom of; Stone, Harlan Fiske; Strict Scrutiny; Warren Court

Bibliography

Abraham, Henry, and Barbara Perry. 2003. *Freedom and the Court.* 8th ed. Lawrence: University Press of Kansas.

Pacelle, Richard L., Jr. 2002. *The Role of the Supreme Court in American Politics: The Least Dangerous Branch?* Boulder, CO: Westview Press.

Richard L. Pacelle, Jr.

PRELIMINARY HEARING

In a preliminary hearing in a criminal prosecution, a judge or magistrate examines the state's case to determine whether there is probable cause to bind the accused over to the grand jury or, in the absence of a grand jury requirement, hold the accused for trial. In *Gerstein v. Pugh* (1975), the U.S. Supreme Court held that when an arrest is made without a warrant, a preliminary hearing is constitutionally required in the absence of grand jury review to determine the sufficiency of the charges. However, in *Gerstein* the Court did not require preliminary hearings to be full-blown adversarial proceedings. Writing for the majority, Justice Lewis Powell noted, "There is no single preferred pretrial procedure and the nature of the probable cause determination usually will be shaped to accord with a State's pretrial procedure viewed as a whole." Powell also noted that "the probable cause determination is not a 'critical stage' in the prosecution that would require appointed counsel." Nevertheless, most states do provide for adversarial hearings in open court with both parties represented by counsel.

Typically, in a preliminary hearing the defense has the privilege of cross-examining witnesses for the prosecution and can learn the details and strengths of the state's case. The state can preserve testimony of witnesses who may balk at testifying at the trial. Thus, the preliminary hearing serves the interests of both the prosecution and the defense by providing an inquiry into probable cause for arrest and detention, a screening device for prosecutors, and an opportunity for the defense to discover the prosecutor's case. For these reasons, civil libertarians generally prefer the preliminary hearing to the ancient grand jury mechanism as a means of protecting persons against unwarranted criminal prosecution.

See also Accused, Rights of the; Critical Pretrial Stages; Due Process, Procedural; Fourth Amendment; Grand Jury; Warrantless Arrest

Bibliography

Scheb, John M., and John M. Scheb II. 2006. *Criminal Procedure.* 4th ed. Belmont, CA: Thomson/Wadsworth.

John M. Scheb II and Otis H. Stephens, Jr.

PRESENTENCE INVESTIGATION REPORTS (PSIR)

Sentencing is a critical stage in a criminal prosecution, and in every jurisdiction in the United States sentences for adults convicted of crimes are imposed in open court. Federal Rule of Criminal Procedure 32 requires that a United States probation officer conduct a presentence investigation and prepare and submit to the court a Presentence Investigation Report (PSIR) before the court sentences a defendant. There are exceptions to the requirement: if a federal statute requires otherwise, or if the court finds that the information in the record enables it to meaningfully exercise its sentencing authority and the court explains its finding on the record.

Most states have statutes or court rules that require (or in some instances authorize at request of a sentencing judge) the preparation and submission to the court of a PSIR. The requirements vary considerably, often applying only to a defendant convicted of a felony. In Connecticut, if a defendant is convicted of a crime other than a capital felony, the punishment for which may include imprisonment for more than one year, a PSIR is required, and the judicial authority may, in its discretion, order a presentence investigation for a defendant convicted of any crime or offense. Under the Florida Rules of Criminal Procedure, where the court has discretion as to what sentence to impose, it may require a PSIR. However, no sentence other than probation can be imposed on a defendant guilty of a first felony, or for committing a felony while under 18 years of age, until after a PSIR has been considered by the sentencing judge.

At the federal level, Rule 32 requires that the PSIR include information about a defendant's physical, mental, and emotional health, education and vocational skills, employment history, and financial condition, that is, any circumstances affecting the defendant's behavior that may be helpful in imposing sentence or in correctional treatment. It also mandates that PSIRs exclude diagnostic opinions, if the opinions might "seriously disrupt a program of rehabilitation," any sources of information obtained upon a promise of confidentiality, and any other information that, if disclosed, might result in physical or other harm to the defendant or others. At the state level the information to be included in a PSIR varies but is generally similar to the federal requirements.

In *Gardner v. Florida* (1977), a trial court judge had sentenced a defendant to death, based partly on confidential information in the PSIR, but never disclosed to the defendant. In rejecting the defendant's death sentence, a plurality of the U.S. Supreme Court held that withholding information relied on in sentencing, which the defendant had no opportunity to controvert or explain, denied the defendant due process of law. Thereafter the federal presentencing guidelines were amended to assure a defendant access to any confidential information used by the court in determining a sentence. States have varying requirements but usually make some provision for disclosure of contents of a PSIR to defendants.

Making sure the information in a PSIR is correct is especially important considering that the great majority of defendants plead guilty pursuant to plea bargaining, in which case the court does not have the advantage of hearing information at trial concerning the defendant, information that has been tested in the crucible of the adversarial process. Rule 32 now requires the probation officer to give the PSIR to the defendant, the defendant's attorney, and an attorney for the government well in advance of scheduled sentencing. This enables these interested parties to file objections to information included in or omitted from the PSIR. After receiving objections, the probation officer investigates further and may revise the report as appropriate before submitting it to the court. The sentencing judge rules on any unresolved objections unless the judge determines a ruling is unnecessary either because the matter will not affect sentencing, or because the court will not consider the matter in sentencing. Finally, the defendant may raise objections to the PSIR at the sentencing hearing, at which time the sentencing judge may allow the parties to introduce testimony or other pertinent evidence. This is vital at the federal level where the Bureau of Prisons may use the PSIR to determine the defendant's place of incarceration in order to place a defendant in the least restrictive facility.

See also Adversary System of Justice; Due Process, Procedural; Plea Bargaining; Sentencing Hearing

Hon. John M. Scheb

PRESS, FREEDOM OF THE

The First Amendment explicitly protects freedom of the press. Although the freedoms of speech and press are often subsumed under the broader principle of freedom of expression, freedom of the press has its own distinctive characteristics, and its constitutional development may be distinguished analytically from that of other First Amendment protections. While the Framers of the Bill of Rights conceived of freedom of the press in terms of the right to publish newspapers, books, pamphlets, and other writings, the concept has taken on a larger meaning with the advent of electronic media.

The constitutional commitment to freedom of the press has its roots in English common law and in colonial experience, especially during the decades immediately preceding the American Revolution. The mass media of that period, consisting of small independent newspapers and pamphlets, played a vital role in facilitating political debate as well as in disseminating information. It is worth recalling in this context that the ratification of the Constitution was vigorously debated not only in the state ratifying conventions but in the press as well. The collection of essays known as *The Federalist Papers* first appeared as a series of newspaper articles analyzing and endorsing the new Constitution. Anti-Federalists also made wide use of newspapers in expressing opposition to ratification.

Prior Restraint

The primary contribution of the English common law to development of freedom of the press in the United States consists of the rule against prior restraint. In his *Commentaries on the Laws of England,* William Blackstone stated the rule in the following language: "The liberty of the press is indeed essential to the nature of a free state; but this consists in laying no previous restraints upon publications, and not in freedom from censure for criminal matter when published." This concept has been of great importance to the Supreme Court in defining freedom of the press under the First Amendment, but it has not been applied as an absolute guarantee or regarded as a complete statement of freedom of the press (see *Near v. Minnesota,* 1931; *New York Times v. United States,* 1971; *Nebraska Press Association v. Stuart,* 1976).

A Fundamental Freedom

In *Near v. Minnesota* (1931), the Supreme Court held that freedom of the press is among the fundamental rights protected by the Fourteenth Amendment against state action, but it also noted, "Liberty of speech and of the press is not an absolute right, and the state may punish its abuse." Historically, courts have recognized various limitations on the freedom of the press by holding that the First Amendment does not protect libel, obscenity, invasion of privacy, or clear and present dangers to the national security. However, the tendency of the Supreme Court in the modern era has been to expand freedom of the press by narrowing these exceptions to the First Amendment.

Libel

Libel consists of injuring someone's reputation by reporting falsehoods about that person. It is not a crime, but a tort, the remedy for which is a civil suit for damages. Libelous publications have traditionally been outside the scope of First Amendment protection. However, in *New York Times Co. v. Sullivan* (1964) and subsequent decisions, the Supreme Court has made it easier for defendants in libel suits brought by public officials and public figures to avoid libel judgments by requiring that plaintiffs prove the defendants' "actual malice." In so doing, the Court substantially expanded First Amendment freedom in an area traditionally controlled by principles of tort law. This development reflects what the late Justice William J. Brennan described in the *Sullivan* decision as "a profound national commitment to the principle that debate on public issues should be uninhibited, robust, and wide-open."

Invasion of Privacy

Closely related to libel is the concept of invasion of privacy. Many jurisdictions have laws permitting private individuals to sue the press for unwarranted invasions of their privacy. Following its decision in *New York Times v. Sullivan,* the Supreme Court began to restrict such lawsuits. In *Time, Inc. v. Hill* (1967), the Supreme Court said that the First Amendment "preclude[s] the application of [an invasion of privacy] statute to redress false reports of matters of public interest in the absence of proof that the defendant published the report with knowledge of its falsity or in reckless disregard of the truth."

In a similar vein, the Supreme Court has blocked efforts to restrict the press from reporting the identities of crime victims. In *Cox Broadcasting v. Cohn* (1975), the Court reversed a judgment for the plaintiff in a case in which a television station reported the name of a rape victim. Similarly, in *The Florida Star v. B.J.F.* (1989), the Court overturned a verdict against a newspaper that reported the name of a rape victim. These decisions reflect a commitment to the principle that the press has the right to report information that it lawfully obtains.

The Free Press/Fair Trial Dilemma

The courts have long recognized that media coverage of a sensational criminal case may be prejudicial to the right of the defendant to receive a fair trial by an unbiased jury. In exceptional circumstances a court may depart from the prior restraint doctrine by restricting news coverage of a criminal case. Appellate courts will scrutinize such restrictions very closely, however, to insure that they are narrowly tailored and do not unduly restrict the right of the press to inform the public about the criminal justice system. The U.S. Supreme Court has emphasized the severe limitations against prior restraints, even in the context of a sensational criminal trial. Writing for the Court in *Nebraska Press Association v. Stuart* (1976), Chief Justice Warren E. Burger noted that "the barriers to prior restraint remain high and the presumption against its use remains intact."

Access to Information

There is little doubt that the press has a constitutional right to publish information about government activities, subject to narrow exceptions based on national security. But the Supreme Court has never recognized a constitutional right to obtain government information, as distinguished from the right to publish information already obtained. On the other hand, Congress has created, through enactment of the Freedom of Information Act, a statutory right of public access to much of the information collected by government agencies. Clearly, FOIA has proven to be a major asset to reporters seeking to cover the activities of government.

Confidential Sources

Aside from the First Amendment and FOIA, the reporter's greatest asset is the confidential source.

The institutionalized media therefore argue strenuously that the First Amendment gives reporters an absolute privilege to maintain the confidentiality of their sources, a privilege similar to that claimed by lawyers with respect to their clients. On the other hand, prosecutors tend to argue that the public interest in finding the truth in a criminal prosecution outweighs a reporter's interest in maintaining the confidentiality of sources. While some states have shield laws protecting journalists in such situations, others permit reporters to be held in contempt and confined for refusing to divulge their sources.

In *Branzburg v. Hayes* (1974), the Supreme Court confronted a situation in which a newspaper reporter subpoenaed to appear before a grand jury refused to identify certain persons he had seen using and selling illicit drugs. The reporter had observed the illegal activities during an undercover investigation of the local drug scene. Citing the First Amendment, he refused to disclose his confidential sources to the grand jury. The Supreme Court rejected the First Amendment argument, saying that it "cannot seriously entertain the notion that the First Amendment protects a newsman's agreement to conceal the criminal conduct of his source, or evidence thereof, on the theory that it is better to write about crime than to do something about it."

Broadcast Media

The Framers of the First Amendment could not have foreseen the invention of radio and television, let alone the prevalence of these electronic media in contemporary society. Nevertheless, because television and radio are used to express ideas in the public forum, most observers would agree that the electronic media deserve First Amendment protection, at least to some extent. Yet since their inception, radio and television have been regulated extensively by the federal government.

In order to operate a television or radio station, one must obtain a license from the Federal Communications Commission (FCC); to broadcast without a license from the FCC is a federal crime (as operators of "pirate" radio stations have often discovered). In granting licenses, the FCC is authorized to regulate the station's frequency, wattage, and hours of transmission. To a lesser extent, it also has the power to regulate the content of broadcasts. For example, the FCC has developed regulations to keep the airwaves free of obscene or indecent programming, and these rules have been upheld by the courts (see *FCC v. Pacifica Foundation,* 1978). Moreover, station licenses come up for renewal every three years, and the FCC is invested with tremendous discretion to determine whether a given station has been operating in the public interest. Clearly, government regulations that apply to the electronic media in the private sector would be unconstitutional if applied to the print media. The more permissive approach to government regulation of television and radio is predicated on the "scarcity theory," which holds that due to the limited number of available broadcast channels, the government must allocate this scarce resource in the public interest.

Widespread access to cable and satellite TV, not to mention the Internet, raises serious questions about the continued validity of the scarcity theory. Currently, cablecasts (as distinguished from broadcasts) are not subject to FCC content regulations. Thus, what may not be shown on NBC or one of the other broadcast networks may be shown on HBO, which is available exclusively to cable subscribers who must pay an additional premium for this service. Increasingly, there are calls for greater government regulation of cable and satellite TV, especially with regard to sexually oriented programming.

Conclusion

Freedom of the press is far more than a felicitous phrase contained in the First Amendment. It represents a basic national commitment to the idea that a free press is essential to the survival of constitutional democracy. Although the American people often find fault with the mass media, most people understand and support the press in its "watchdog" role. For its part, the Supreme Court has buttressed the role of the media by erecting a high barrier against prior restraint and scrutinizing closely any form of press censorship. Yet, like all constitutional rights, freedom of the press is neither absolute nor unlimited. It must be balanced against the government's responsibility to protect national security, the interest of the criminal justice system in ferreting out crime, and society's interest in maintaining a modicum of public decency. Freedom of the press must also be weighed against the rights of individuals to be treated fairly and maintain a degree of personal privacy. The Supreme Court has shown that it is willing to circumscribe to some extent the First Amendment guarantee of freedom of the press in order to protect these other values.

See also Bill of Rights, Incorporation of; Blackstone, William; Burger, Warren E.; Common Law Background of American Civil Rights and Liberties; Defamation; Federal Communications Commission; Federalist Papers; First Amendment; Free Press/Fair Trial Issue; Freedom of Information Act; Gag Orders; Grand Jury; *Hustler Magazine v. Falwell* (1988); Internet, Free Speech on the; Privacy, Invasion of; *Near v. Minnesota ex rel. Olson* (1931); *New York Times v. Sullivan* (1964); Obscenity and Pornography; Prior Restraint, Doctrine of; Speech, Freedom of; Zenger, John Peter

Bibliography

Friendly, Fred W. 1976. *The Good Guys, the Bad Guys and the First Amendment.* New York: Random House.

Levy, Leonard W. 1985. *Emergence of a Free Press.* New York: Oxford University Press, 1985.

Lewis, Anthony. 1992. *Make No Law: The Sullivan Case and the First Amendment.* New York: Random House.

Lofton, John. 1981. *The Press as Guardian of the First Amendment.* Columbia: University of South Carolina Press.

O'Brien, David. 1981. *The Public's Right to Know: The Supreme Court and the First Amendment.* New York: Praeger.

Powe, Lucas. 1987. *American Broadcasting and the First Amendment.* Berkeley: University of California Press.

Otis H. Stephens, Jr. and John M. Scheb II

PRESUMPTION OF INNOCENCE

In the Anglo-American legal tradition, a person accused of a crime is presumed innocent until proven guilty beyond a reasonable doubt. William Blackstone, the great commentator on English common law, is credited with the oft-quoted maxim: "Better that ten guilty persons escape than that one innocent suffer."

In *Commonwealth v. Webster* (1850), the Supreme Judicial Court of Massachusetts stated: "All the presumptions of law independent of evidence are in favor of innocence; and every person is presumed to be innocent until he is proved guilty." And in *Coffin v. United States* (1895), the U.S. Supreme Court asserted: "The principle that there is a presumption of innocence in favor of the accused is the undoubted law, axiomatic and elementary, and its enforcement lies at the foundation of the administration of our criminal law." In *Coffin,* the Court defined the presumption of innocence as "a conclusion drawn by the law in favor of the citizen, by virtue whereof, when brought to trial upon a criminal charge, he must be acquitted, unless he is proven to be guilty."

Today, the idea that one accused of a crime is presumed innocent is widely accepted, not just in the United States, but also in democratic societies around the world. Article 11 of the Universal Declaration of Human Rights proclaims: "Everyone charged with a penal offence has the right to be presumed innocent until proved guilty according to law in a public trial at which he has had all the guarantees necessary for his defence." Similarly, Article 6.2 of the Convention for the Protection of Human Rights and Fundamental Freedoms of the Council of Europe, which is binding on all members of the European Union, states: "Everyone charged with a criminal offence shall be presumed innocent until proved guilty according to law."

While the presumption of innocence is solidly grounded in law and philosophy, in practice it can be a difficult norm to implement. Communities confronted by brutal and senseless crimes exert strong pressures on the criminal justice system to identify and punish perpetrators. When there is extensive pretrial publicity surrounding the arrest of a suspect, and most especially if there are reports that police have obtained a confession or other incriminating evidence, the community is likely to forget the presumption of innocence. Of course, defendants are not to be tried in the media or in the court of public opinion. Judges are obligated to provide every accused who pleads not guilty a fair trial. In a jury trial, judges must allow extensive questioning of prospective jurors (known as *voir dire*) and dismiss those who exhibit bias. In extreme cases, judges will grant motions to change the venue of the trial. In a criminal case that has attracted national attention, it may be difficult to find a community where most prospective jurors have not already formed an opinion of the defendant based on media coverage of the case. Most judges believe that voir dire is the most effective means of securing an unbiased juror. In all criminal cases being tried by jury, judges must instruct jurors that the defendant is presumed innocent until proved guilty beyond a reasonable doubt.

See also: Accused, Rights of the; Blackstone, William; Due Process, Procedural; Reasonable Doubt Standard; Venue, Change of

John M. Scheb II and Otis H. Stephens, Jr.

PRETRIAL DETENTION

Pretrial detention refers to the confinement of a defendant in a local jail facility pending trial. Those held in pretrial detention fall into two general categories: persons who are *unable* to post bail for financial reasons and persons who were *denied* bail. Bail is usually not an option for defendants who are deemed unlikely to appear as scheduled at court, nor is it available to those who might threaten the community if released.

The detrimental impact of pretrial detention on case outcomes has been documented in myriad studies. Caleb Foote's seminal research on bail in Philadelphia during the 1950s is generally recognized as the first such study. His research revealed that defendants who were denied bail were more likely to be both convicted and incarcerated. Rankin found in 1964 that pretrial detention significantly increased the likelihood of a defendant's conviction. Though Goldkamp (1979) did not find a prejudicial effect with regard to rates of conviction, he did note that pretrial detention appeared to negatively affect defendants in terms of placement in diversion programs and sentence severity.

Many theories have been suggested to explain the harmful impact of pretrial detention on defendants' cases. Those held before their trials are unable to fully assist in their own defense, since their confinement prevents them from locating witnesses on their own behalf and otherwise contributing to their cases. Furthermore, even those who maintain their innocence may feel compelled to plead guilty as a means to end their indefinite pretrial confinement. Finally, since they can return to court well-groomed and escorted by family, those who post bail are able to present themselves more favorably to the judge or jury.

To address problems posed by the money bail system, ROR (release on recognizance) was introduced. The 1966 federal Bail Reform Act mandated that the federal courts develop ROR procedures, allowing defendants to be released without any financial consideration. Numerous states also implemented their own versions of ROR, as well as 10 percent bail plans. Under such plans, defendants are permitted to post 10 percent of their formal bail amounts (Walker, 2001).

By the 1980s, however, nearly all states had been prompted by the war on drugs to pass preventive detention laws. These laws enable judges to deny some defendants bail on the basis of a perceived likelihood that they would harm others in the community. In addition to raising constitutional questions, preventive detention laws have undoubtedly contributed to the considerable increase in pretrial incarceration.

On any given day, more than half of those who are in jail are being detained prior to trial. Jail overcrowding, an ongoing problem in the United States,

has been exacerbated by the increased use of pretrial detention (Austin, Krisberg, and Litsky, 1985; Walker, 2001). Facility overcrowding coupled with deficient government funding has led to diminished basic services and worsening conditions in America's jails (McConville, 1995).

The use of alternatives to pretrial detention (other than traditional ROR) may prove helpful in reducing the problems associated with the practice. One such alternative is Supervised Pretrial Release (SPR). Defendants released under SPR agree to abide by closely monitored, court-ordered conditions that are more rigorous than those conditions stipulated by ROR (Austin, Krisberg, and Litsky 1985). Defendants selected for this type of pretrial release are those who are deemed not to be trustworthy candidates for ROR, but who are capable of coexisting within the community if provided with appropriate supervision and services.

Bibliography

Austin, James, Barry Krisberg, and Paul Litsky. 1985. "The Effectiveness of Supervised Pretrial Release." *Crime and Delinquency* 31: 519.

Foote, Caleb. 1954. "Compelling Appearance in Court: Administration of Bail in Philadelphia." *University of Pennsylvania Law Review* 102: 1031.

Goldkamp, John. 1979. *Two Classes of Accused: A Study of Bail and Detention in American Justice.* Cambridge, MA: Ballinger.

McConville, Sean. 1995. "Local Justice: The Jail." *The Oxford History of the Prison: The Practice of Punishment in Western Society.* In Norval Morris and David J. Rothman, eds. New York: Oxford University Press.

Rankin, Anne. 1964. "The Effects of Pretrial Detention." *New York University Law Review* 39: 641.

Walker, Samuel. 2001. *Sense and Nonsense about Crime and Drugs: A Policy Guide.* Belmont, CA: Wadsworth.

Christine Ivie Edge

PRETRIAL DISCOVERY

Pretrial discovery refers to disclosure before trial of evidence in the hands of adverse parties or others. The objective is to allow access to evidence or facts leading to relevant evidence. This can encourage pleas in criminal cases or settlements in civil litigation. And, where a trial becomes necessary, pretrial discovery assists the parties in preparing their cases by preventing surprises at trial, or as lawyers sometimes quip, "to prevent trial by ambush."

Counsel conduct pretrial discovery by taking oral or written depositions of parties and witnesses, by requiring production of documents or tangible articles, and by requiring physical or mental examinations of parties.

There is no general constitutional right to discovery in criminal cases. The *Jencks* Act, codified at 18 U.S.C. sec. 3500, provides some limits on discovery in federal criminal cases. It provides a defendant is not entitled to inspect a statement or report prepared by a government witness "until said witness has testified on direct examination in the trial of the case." However, in *Brady v. Maryland* (1963) the Supreme Court ruled that the Due Process Clause of the Fourteenth Amendment of the U.S. Constitution requires the prosecution to disclose evidence favorable to an accused upon request. Federal Rule of Criminal Procedure 16 expands the scope of pretrial discovery and vests broad discretion in trial judges to allow discovery by the prosecution and defense. The rule permits the defense to discover a defendant's written or recorded statements and prior criminal record. It also provides for reciprocal discovery by the prosecution and defense of certain other documents and reports. Rules of discovery, however, do not grant the prosecution the right to depose a criminal defendant.

Most states have liberal rules of discovery that enable the prosecution and defense to gain access to evidence in the hands of opposing parties. These rules typically vest broad discretionary authority in trial judges to regulate the conduct and scope of discovery and authorize sanctions against parties who violate rules or court orders.

Discovery procedures in civil litigation often enable parties to arrive at a resolution of issues without a trial. Rule 26 of the Federal Rules of Civil Procedure provides extensive rules governing the duty and scope of disclosure and methods of pursuing discovery in civil litigation. Many state rules of civil procedure providing for discovery are patterned after the federal rules. Both federal and state rules of civil procedure provide for liberal discovery. Litigants can discover from adverse parties or witnesses any information, not privileged, that is relevant or may lead to relevant evidence concerning issues in a lawsuit. Where pretrial discovery does not lead to a settlement, the process is designed to narrow issues and enable parties to prepare their cases for trial. Trial judges are given broad discretion to regulate the processes of discovery and to issue protective orders to prevent abuses and to prevent inquiry in certain areas, such as trade secrets.

See also Accused, Rights of the; Adversary System of Justice; Counsel, Ineffective Assistance of; Counsel, Right to; Due Process Clauses; Due Process, Procedural; Exculpatory Evidence, Disclosure of; Fourteenth Amendment; *Jencks* Act (1957)

Bibliography

Scheb, John M., and John M. Scheb II. 2006. *Criminal Procedure*. Belmont, CA: Thomson/Wadsworth.

Hon. John M. Scheb

PRETRIAL MOTIONS. *See* Continuance, Motion for; Exculpatory Evidence, Disclosure of; Pretrial Discovery; Venue, Change of

PRETRIAL PUBLICITY, PROBLEM OF. *See* Free Press/Fair Trial Problem

PRIOR RESTRAINT, DOCTRINE OF

Prior restraint is prepublication censorship of information by government and is the most dangerous form of censorship. If government can stop expression before it occurs, that is far more absolute control than the threat of postpublication punishment, as in the instances of defamation or obscenity. "If it can be said that the threat of civil or criminal sanctions after publication 'chills' speech," the Supreme Court wrote in *Nebraska Press Association v. Stuart* (1976), "prior restraint 'freezes' it." This ancient enemy of freedom continued to exist in the United States into the twenty-first century, if in somewhat attenuated form, despite the 1931 Supreme Court decision, *Near v. Minnesota.* In that landmark decision, the Court held that the core meaning of the First Amendment guarantees of speech and press freedom forbids prior restraint.

Near involved an injunction under a Minnesota nuisance statute that allowed a judge, sitting without a jury, to halt the publication of a "malicious, scandalous, or defamatory newspaper." The newspaper enjoined was J. M. Near and Howard Guilford's anti-Semitic, anti-Catholic, antilabor *Saturday Press.* An appeal to the Minnesota Supreme Court failed to dislodge the injunction, with that court declaring that principles of free expression did not protect scandalous and defamatory publications. Conservative *Chicago Tribune* publisher Robert R. McCormick provided the financial support for *Near*'s appeal to the U.S. Supreme Court (Friendly 1992, 66ff).

Writing for a five-to-four Court, Chief Justice Charles Evans Hughes crafted this most important First Amendment decision. *Near* nationalized the First Amendment. The *Near* majority not only declared the Minnesota "gag law" unconstitutional, the Court for the first time applied the powers of the First Amendment to halt a state effort to restrict expression. Chief Justice Hughes wrote that the Minnesota statute could not stand because "[I]t is no longer open to doubt that the liberty of the press ... is within the liberties safeguarded by the Fourteenth Amendment from invasion by 'state action.'"

The *Near* majority reinterpreted the writings of Sir William Blackstone, whose *Commentaries,* first published in England in 1765, were influential in the growth of American law in the nation's early years. Blackstone defined liberty of the press "as laying no previous restraints on publication, and not in freedom from censure from criminal matter when published" (Blackstone 1769, 4:151, 152).

Chief Justice Hughes then devised a double modification of Blackstonian free press theory. Unlike Blackstone, Hughes declared that in exceptional instances, prior restraint was permissible. Examples of allowable prior restraint included prevention of publication of sailing dates of troop transports or locations of troops in wartime or interference with military recruiting. To protect decency, obscene publications could be halted, and incitements to violence or overthrow of orderly government could be blocked to protect society. "The constitutional guaranty of free speech," Hughes wrote, " ... does not 'protect a man from an injunction against uttering words that may have all the effects of force.'"

Although Hughes made exceptions to Blackstone's sweeping "no previous restraint" principle, another Blackstonian declaration was liberalized. Blackstone had followed his definition of liberty of the press with the progovernment edict that press freedom did not consist "in freedom from censure from criminal matter when published" (Blackstone 1765, 4:152). So to Blackstone, liberty of the press meant only the outlawing of prepublication censorship. Criticism of government or government officials, in other words, could be punishable.

Hughes took issue with Blackstone, finding that the people and the press have the right to criticize government. He wrote that the growing complexity of government and opportunities for corruption "by unfaithful officials ... emphasizes the primary need of a vigilant and courageous press." Even if press freedom is abused by "miscreant purveyors or scandal[,] [that] does not make any the less necessary the immunity of the press from previous restraint dealing with official misconduct. Subsequent punishment for such abuses as may exist is the appropriate remedy, consistent with constitutional privilege."

Despite the narrow five-to-four vote margin in *Near,* this decision has withstood repeated challenges and has become a foundation of freedom, the key interpretation of the First Amendment in American legal history. Forty years after *Near,* the administration of President Richard M. Nixon went to court to stifle newspaper publication of excerpts from a top-secret 47-volume study of the war in Vietnam, *History of the United States Decision-Making Process on Vietnam Policy.* This 7,000-page leak of secret documents to *New York Times* reporter Neil Sheehan resulted, after three months' careful study by reporters and editors, in the *Times*'s publication, on June 13, 1971, of an article headlined "Vietnam Archive: Pentagon Study Traces 3 Decades of Growing U.S. Involvement." Less than 48 hours later, Attorney General John Mitchell sent a telegram to the *Times*, demanding that the articles cease to avoid "irreparable injury to the defense interests of the United States" (Pember, 404). The *Times* ignored that plea.

The Department of Justice then petitioned U.S. District Judge Murray Gurfein (serving his first day on the bench) to halt the articles, and he issued a temporary injunction on June 15. That may have halted the *Times*, but other excerpts from the top secret report then appeared in the *Washington Post* and a number of other major newspapers (Pember, 404–405). The U.S. Court of Appeals for the District of Columbia circuit responded to the newspapers' appeal by ordering a halt to further publication until the U.S. Supreme Court could hear the case. Moving with unprecedented haste, the Supreme Court on June 25 agreed to an expedited hearing, leaving the order against publication in force. Justices Hugo L. Black, William J. Brennan, Jr., William O. Douglas, and Thurgood Marshall protested the continuing prior restraint. *Times* columnist James Reston wrote on June 16, "For the first time in the history of the Republic, the Attorney General of the United States has tried to suppress documents he hasn't read about a war that hasn't been declared."

On June 30, 1971, voting six-to-three to refuse the Justice Department's petition for a permanent injunction against publication, the Supreme Court issued a short per curiam opinion (Kutler 1992, 588). The Court simply refused to continue the injunctions which the Justice Department had secured against *The New York Times* and *The Washington Post*. The per curiam opinion quoted the Court's 1963 decision in *Bantam Books v. Sullivan*: "Any system of prior restraints comes to this Court bearing a heavy presumption against its constitutional validity." The Court concluded that the government had not proved its case attempting to justify prior restraint. Under such extreme

haste, the Court produced a variety of concurring and dissenting opinions, but with enough votes to state clearly that the press could resume publication of the leaked documents. *Near v. Minnesota* still stood.

Battles against prior restraint are never won for all time. The Supreme Court in 1976 confronted "restrictive orders" (called "gag orders" by the media) laid on reporters covering a mass murder case in Nebraska. The reporters were ordered not to cover the existence or contents of the suspect's confession or other facts "strongly implicative" of the accused. In *Nebraska Press Association v. Stuart* (1976), the Supreme Court unanimously held these restrictive orders to be unconstitutional prior restraint.

A prior restraint case in the late 1970s involving *The Progressive*, a Madison, Wisconsin-based magazine, never reached the Supreme Court. This case, ultimately mooted by publication elsewhere, suggested that material classified top secret—and indeed all confidential or secret information—is slippery and hard to contain. In this instance, the federal government learned of the magazine's intention to publish an article by Howard Morland titled, "The H-Bomb Secret: How We Got It, Why We're Telling It." U.S. District Judge Robert Warren, although aware of the 1971 Pentagon Papers decision by the Supreme Court, issued the injunction. Judge Warren concluded that the publication could cause "grave, direct, immediate and irreparable harm to the United States." (United States v. Progressive, 1979)

Appealing the prior restraint order, *The Progressive* and Morland delayed publication of the article six months, arguing that the Atomic Energy Act was so sweeping that it could forbid even casual conversations about nuclear weapons and that no real secrets would be told by the article. But in mid-September, 1979, a letter to U.S. Senator Charles Percy from computer programmer Charles Hansen was published in *The Press Connection*, an 11,000-circulation daily being published during an American Newspaper Guild strike in Madison. The Hansen letter included a diagram of a hydrogen bomb and a list of key components. The government then moved to drop the injunction against *The Progressive,* where Morland's article finally was published. A year later, Judge Warren dismissed the case against the magazine. In 1996, the Sixth U.S. Circuit Court of Appeals overturned a temporary restraining order against *Business Week.* The magazine had acquired court-sealed documents in a lawsuit by manufacturing giant Procter & Gamble against Bankers Trust Co., but a federal district judge prohibited publication of an article based on the documents, asserting it would cause "irreparable harm." In *Procter & Gamble v. Banker's Trust Co.* (1996), the Sixth Circuit, however, declared that "prohibiting the publication of a news story ... is the essence of censorship and is allowed only under exceptional circumstances." Again, prior restraint was ruled unconstitutional.

Prior restraint goes back nearly to the origins of printing in England and can still be found in the United States in the twenty-first century. In sixteenth-century England, membership in the Stationers Company provided a kind of prepublication license needed for printers to escape imprisonment, mutilation, or even death by drawing and quartering for printing without permission. Powers of search for and seizure of unlicensed presses and printers were confirmed by Elizabeth I's Star Chamber Decree of 1586, which also set up a system of licensing that remained in effect well into the seventeenth century (Siebert 1952, 60–61.) Although print media may not be licensed in the United States, Congress requires that radio and television broadcasters be licensed by the Federal Communications Commission (see *National Broadcasting Co. v. United States,* 1943). Also, student publications in public high schools may be subjected to prepublication censorship when they are related to the schools' curricula (see *Hazelwood School District v. Kuhlmeier,*1988), and courts have upheld "time, place, and manner" regulations to control, for example, sound trucks emitting loud and raucous noises (see *Kovacs v. Cooper* 1949).

Courts allow prior restraint of criminal speech. In *United States v. Schiff* (2003), a federal district court upheld an injunction against Irving Schiff and two associates who operated Web sites and who published material touting a system for avoiding paying income taxes. The district court held, "This message is subject to injunction as false, misleading and deceptive speech, incitement, and aiding and abetting illegal conduct."

Although prior restraint is disfavored by courts, it continues to occur. Areas of law where prepublication injunctions can occur include commercial speech, defamation, invasion of privacy, copyright infringement, and access to government information.

Evolving communication technologies, however, make it more difficult to use prior restraint. During the Oklahoma City Bombing trial of 1997, the *Dallas Morning News* published a story on its Web site outlining a purported admission by suspect Timothy McVeigh that he was responsible for the explosion that killed 168 persons and injured hundreds more. *Playboy* magazine had developed a far more detailed version of the same information, but was under the threat of an injunction had it announced that it was planning to publish. But once the *Morning News* had committed the basic information to its Web site, *Playboy* could publish. Because Internet publication can occur instantaneously, government attempts at prior restraint can be evaded. Contempt citations or prosecutions for violating laws may occur, but only after the fact of publication.

Historically, when the United States is at war, prior restraint often is invoked in the name of national self-protection or national security. Before the Civil War, postmasters often refused to deliver publications of Northern antislavery societies, and Southern states passed laws forbidding circulation of such information (Nye 1963, 69–71). During the Civil War, President Abraham Lincoln ordered closure of several "Copperhead" (pro-Southern) newspapers (Stevens 1982, 41–43). During World War I, efforts to block antiwar sentiments (termed *sedition*) were frequent and energetic, including extensive revocations of mailing privileges (Peterson and Fite 1957). During World War II, voluntary self-censorship by the press was successful at home, although stringent military censorship was in place in battle zones (Stevens 1982, 54–56).

As held in *Near v. Minnesota* (1931), prior restraint is permissible in wartime when lives are at stake, and that includes the legal authority to control dispatches or broadcasts from a battle zone. Coverage of the Vietnam conflict in the 1960s and 1970s was open to the point that President Richard M. Nixon blamed the media, especially television coverage, for demoralization at home (Hallin 1989, 4). U.S. military policy makers, in the guise of cooperating with news media, devised press pools for the 1983 Grenada and 1989 Panama invasions. The pools did not aid press coverage, but instead had the general effect of keeping reporters away from the action (Garneau 1990; Buckley 1991).

During the first Persian Gulf War in 1991, rigid news-management of the images and accounts was the general rule. *New York Times* correspondent Malcolm W. Browne then wrote, "For the first time since World War II, correspondents must submit to near-total supervision of their work" (Browne 1991).

News coverage of Persian Gulf War II in 2003 was more extensive, thanks to a statement of principles developed by U.S. military and media representatives to allow greater battle coverage. More than 600 journalists were "embedded" with combat units, providing pictures and accounts of battles and on-the-record interviews with service members. This increased accommodation for the media occurred when evolving satellite and cellular camera phone technology also made military censorship of earlier times a practical impossibility. Reporters no longer needed military communication equipment to get their reports back to the United States (Dalglish 2003). Although prior restraint is still legally permissible in some circumstances, Internet and satellite communication technology increasingly trumps the effectiveness of prior restraint.

See also Bill of Rights, Incorporation of; Black, Hugo L.; Blackstone, William; Brennan, William J., Jr.; Defamation; Douglas, William O.; First Amendment; Gag Orders; Internet, Free Speech on the; Lincoln, Abraham; Marshall, Thurgood; *New York Times v. Sullivan* (1964); Obscenity and Pornography; Press, Freedom of the; Star Chamber; U.S. Department of Justice (DOJ)

Bibliography

Blackstone, Sir William. 1769. *Commentaries on the Laws of England*. Oxford: Clarendon Press.

Buckley, Kevin. 1991. *Panama*. New York: Simon & Schuster.

Browne, Malcolm W. 1991. "Conflicting Censorship Upsets Many Journalists." *New York Times* (21 January): A8.

Dalglish, Lucy. 2003. "We All Benefited from Embeds: So What Took So Long?" *The News Media and the Law* (Spring): 3.

Friendly, Fred W. 1992. *Minnesota Rag*. New York: Oxford University Press.

Garneau, George. 1990. "Panning the Pentagon." *Editor & Publisher* (31 March): 11.

Hallin, Daniel C. 1989. *The "Uncensored War": The Media and Vietnam*. Berkley: University of California Press.

Kutler, Stanley I. 1992. "*New York Times Co. v. U.S.*" in *The Oxford Companion to the Supreme Court or the United States*, ed. Kermit L. Hall, 588–89. New York: Oxford University Press.

Nye, Russel Blaine. 1963. *Fettered Freedom*. East Lansing: Michigan State University Press.

Pember, Don. 2004. *Mass Media Law, 14th edition*. New York: McGraw Hill.

Peterson, H.C., and Gilbert Fite. 1957. *Opponents of the War, 1917–1918*. Madison: University of Wisconsin Press.

Siebert, Fredrick Seaton. 1952. *Freedom of the Press in England, 1476–1776*. Urbana: University of Illinois Press.

Stevens, John D. 1982. *Shaping the First Amendment*. Beverly Hills: Sage.

Dwight L. Teeter, Jr.

PRISONERS' RIGHTS

Prior to the 1960s, prisoners' rights were limited due to an absence of procedural avenues to assert such rights. The federal courts had exercised a hands-off approach regarding the internal operations of prisons. Myriad reasons have been cited for the courts' previous refusal to intervene in prison matters. A widely advanced explanation for this judicial reluctance is the courts' belief that they did not have the authority to intercede. Premised on a "separation of powers" rationale, the courts maintained that they lacked judicial review of the prison system's administrative decisions, since prisons are housed under the authority of the attorney general. Further, judges insisted that their deficient professional expertise regarding prison life precluded them from making informed decisions concerning the management of prisons. Another contributing factor that worked to foster judicial indifference regarding the conditions and policies of prisons was the prevailing perception of prisoners as slaves of the state.

Although rejection of the hands-off doctrine occurred during the 1960s and 1970s and those are the years most associated with judicial activism regarding prisoners' rights, those decades do not represent the first time prisoners' rights were recognized and enforced by the judiciary. Multiple court cases during the late nineteenth and early twentieth centuries contradict the widely held belief that prisoners were without rights (Wallace 2001). Case law during this timeframe reveals that both civil and criminal cases involving unsanitary and unhealthy prison conditions and the use of corporal punishment were heard. Due to the absence of procedural protections afforded prisoners during the 1960s and 1970s through vehicles such as the revitalized Civil Rights Act, prisoners in the late nineteenth and early twentieth centuries relied on procurable remedies such as habeas corpus relief, contempt proceedings, and injunctive relief to address their grievances.

During the 1960s, the courts became increasingly involved in the management of prison affairs. The seminal 1964 court case, *Cooper v. Pate*, is frequently cited as the impetus for increased court involvement in prison matters, as it established prisoners' right to access the courts. An appeal from a lower court ruling, *Cooper v. Pate* involved prison officials' discretion to deny Muslim prisoners their Korans and the opportunity to worship. In this significant case, the United States Supreme Court ruled that state officials can be sued by prisoners in federal court for violating prisoners' constitutional rights.

Once the federal courts recognized prisoners as persons with veritable constitutional rights, the Prisoners' Rights movement began to proliferate. The Black Muslims in America's prisons and jails were instrumental in precipitating the expansion of prisoners' rights. In particular, the Muslims asserted their right to access religious literature and to worship as they desired. In addition to prisoners, the movement was joined by some within free society: attorneys and prison reform groups (Jacobs 2001).

Prisoners can now challenge various aspects of their incarceration. One area of litigation involves contesting the conditions of the prisoner's confinement. Such challenges have been particularly acute in older facilities where overcrowding and limited corrections funds have created Eighth Amendment claims regarding safety, sanitation, hygiene, nutrition, and medical care (Cooper 1988). Another area of litigation involves prisoner challenges to both the formal and informal procedures and rules observed by corrections staff. These challenges include alleged violations of due process (e.g., prison disciplinary practices), equal protection (e.g., racial discrimination), and First Amendment rights (e.g., religious freedom) (Cooper 1988).

Corrections populations have been differentially impacted by the efforts of the Prisoners' Rights movement. Jail inmates are more likely than those housed in prisons to encounter brutal conditions on account of the decentralized structure and rural locations of jails, which insulate them from scrutiny (Sturm 1993). Female prisoners did not begin to utilize litigation as a means to enact prison reform until the mid-1970s, and have not benefited from many rulings made in favor of male litigants and limited to conditions in specific prisons (Leonard 1983). Juvenile facilities remain rife with inadequate services for offenders; reform has been slower due to the lower likelihood that those living in juvenile justice institutions will challenge unsatisfactory conditions (Sturm 1993).

Though prisoners' rights have been acknowledged by the courts for several decades, judicial intervention on behalf of prisoners has arguably waned in recent years. Assorted explanations have been proffered for the reduction in judicial involvement. Since offender confinement is the paramount responsibility of prison administrators, the Supreme Court has generally held that prisoners' rights should be upheld only to the extent that institutional security is not compromised. Changes in the composition of the Supreme Court have also engendered decreased judicial intervention in prisons, as justices less sympathetic to prisoners' claims have been appointed. Further, both judges and legislators have become resistant to those prisoner lawsuits perceived as frivolous. DiIulio (1991) cites the emergence of AIDS cases in the nation's jails and prisons as being one reason for an increase in judicial willingness to defer to the expertise of on-site correctional personnel.

See also Criminal Confinement, Conditions of; Cruel and Unusual Punishments Clause; Due Process, Procedural; Eighth Amendment; First Amendment; Fourteenth Amendment (1868); Habeas Corpus; Judicial Activism; Religion, Freedom of; Section 1983 Actions

Bibliography

Cooper, Phillip J. 1988. "Prisons: The Cruel and Unusual Punishment Controversy." In *Incarcerating Criminals: Prisons and Jails in Social and Organizational Context,* eds. T. Flanagan, J. Marquart, and K. Adams, 59–70. New York: Oxford University Press.

DiIulio, John J. 1991. "Judicial Intervention: Lessons from the Past." In *Incarcerating Criminals: Prisons and Jails in Social and Organizational Context,* eds. T. Flanagan, J. Marquart, and K. Adams, 81–90. New York: Oxford University Press.

Jacobs, James B. 2001. "The Prisoners' Rights Movement and Its Impacts." In *Correctional Contexts: Contemporary and Classical Readings,* eds. E. Latessa, A. Holsinger, J. Marquart, and J. Sorensen, 211–228. 2nd ed. Los Angeles: Roxbury Publishing Company.

Leonard, Ellen. 1983. "Judicial Decisions and Prison Reform: The Impact of Litigation on Women Prisoners." *Social Problems* 31: 45.

Sturm, Susan. 1993. "The Legacy and Future of Corrections Litigation." *University of Pennsylvania Law Review* 142: 639.

Wallace, Donald H. 2001. "Prisoners' Rights: Historical Views." In *Correctional Contexts: Contemporary and Classical Readings,* eds. E. Latessa, A. Holsinger, J. Marquart, and J. Sorensen, 211–28. 2nd ed. Los Angeles: Roxbury Publishing Company.

Christine Ivie Edge

PRIVACY, CONSTITUTIONAL RIGHT OF

Although the term *privacy* is not found in the text of the United States Constitution, the courts have recognized a sphere of intimate personal conduct that is constitutionally protected from governmental interference. In *Griswold v. Connecticut* (1965), its first explicit recognition of this constitutional right, the U.S. Supreme Court struck down a state law restricting the use of contraceptive devices. As it has developed since *Griswold,* the right of privacy encompasses personal choices involving sex, reproduction, and end-of-life medical decisions. It has also been employed successfully with respect to surrogate motherhood, nontraditional living arrangements and, in at least one notable state court decision, the personal use of marijuana (see *Ravin v. State,* 1975).

Reproductive Freedom

In *Griswold* the Court invalidated a Connecticut statute making it a crime, even for married persons, to use contraceptives. In his opinion for the Court, Justice William O. Douglas asked, rhetorically, "Would we allow the police to search the sacred precincts of marital bedrooms for telltale signs of the use of contraceptives?" Douglas answered this question, saying, "The very idea is repulsive to the notions of privacy surrounding the marriage relationship." However, Justice Douglas was vague as to the constitutional locus of the right of privacy, invoking "penumbras" and "emanations" from the First, Third, Fourth, Fifth, and Ninth Amendments.

In an effort to buttress the constitutional foundation of the Court's decision, Justice Arthur

Goldberg's concurring opinion stressed the Ninth Amendment, which provides that "[t]he enumeration in the Constitution, of certain rights, shall not be construed to deny or disparage others retained by the people." In separate opinions concurring in the judgment, Justices John M. Harlan (the younger) and Byron White maintained that the Connecticut law infringed the "liberty" protected by the Fourteenth Amendment, a liberty that, in their view, transcends the particular protections of the Bill of Rights. In taking this course, Justices Harlan and White followed the "substantive due process" approach that had been employed in *Meyer v. Nebraska* (1923), *Pierce v. Society of Sisters* (1925), and other cases in which the Court had used the Fourteenth Amendment to strike down legislation that did not contravene explicit constitutional limitations.

In dissent, Justice Potter Stewart, joined by Justice Hugo Black, characterized the Connecticut statute as "an uncommonly silly law" and made clear that, in his personal view, "the use of contraceptives in the relationship of marriage should be left to personal and private choice, based upon the individual's moral, ethical, and religious beliefs." But, Stewart noted, "we are not asked in this case to say whether we think this law is unwise, or even asinine. We are asked to hold that it violates the United States Constitution. And that I cannot do." In a separate dissent, Justice Black made clear his disdain for the Court's freewheeling approach to constitutional interpretation:

I get nowhere in this case by talk about a constitutional "right of privacy" as an emanation from one or more constitutional provisions. I like my privacy as well as the next one, but I am nevertheless compelled to admit that government has a right to invade it unless prohibited by some specific constitutional provision.

The *Griswold* decision and the various opinions produced by the Justices in that case remain at the center of a ongoing dispute over constitutional interpretation. The Court's recognition of the right of privacy in *Griswold* exemplifies the "Living Constitution," kept "in tune with the times" by evolving judicial interpretations. In contrast, the dissenting opinions by Justices Stewart and Black in *Griswold* represent a stricter, more conservative approach to constitutional interpretation. In contemporary political discourse, these competing approaches are sometimes labeled "judicial activism" and "judicial restraint," and the *Griswold* decision is often held up as judicial activism par excellence.

In *Griswold* the Court was careful to invalidate the Connecticut law only insofar as it invaded marital privacy. But in *Eisenstadt v. Baird* (1972), the Court struck down a Massachusetts anticontraception statute on its face. Justice William Brennan's opinion for the Court in *Eisenstadt* defined the right of privacy as "the right of the individual, married or single, to be free from unwarranted governmental intrusion into matters so fundamentally affecting a person as the decision whether or not to beget a child." Having thus articulated a broad right protecting individual reproductive decisions, *Eisenstadt* paved the way for the most controversial Supreme Court decision in modern history: *Roe v. Wade* (1973).

In *Roe,* the Court held that the constitutional right of privacy "is broad enough to encompass a woman's decision whether or not to terminate her pregnancy." This seven-to-two decision invalidated the Texas anti-abortion statute and rendered unenforceable similar laws in most states. The essential holding in *Roe v. Wade* has been reaffirmed by the Supreme Court on several occasions, most recently in *Stenberg v. Carhart* (2000), where the Court invalidated a Nebraska law banning a procedure commonly described as partial-birth abortion. That questions about *Roe v. Wade* continue to dominate all new nominations to the Supreme Court attests to the extremely controversial nature of this decision and the right to privacy on which it is based.

Sexual Conduct

Prior to the 1960s, it was generally assumed that government had the authority to enforce traditional sexual mores through the criminal law. Even though laws against adultery, fornication, and sodomy were seldom enforced and had in fact been abolished in many states, few questioned the right of governments to enact and enforce such prohibitions. In the wake of *Griswold, Eisenstadt,* and *Roe,* commentators began to suggest that the right of privacy could be viewed as a shield against governmental interference with private sexual conduct between consenting adults. Beginning in the 1970s, activists in the gay rights movement sought to use the right of privacy to attack laws criminalizing homosexual conduct.

In *Bowers v. Hardwick* (1986) the Supreme Court declined to extend the right of privacy to protect homosexual conduct between consenting adults. However, a number of state courts invalidated sodomy laws on state constitutional grounds. For example, in *Powell v. State* (1998), the Georgia Supreme Court held that the same sodomy law upheld by the U.S. Supreme Court in *Bowers v. Hardwick* violated the right of privacy implicit in the Georgia state constitution.

In *Lawrence v. Texas* (2003), the Supreme Court revisited and overturned its decision in *Bowers v. Hardwick.* Writing for the Court, Justice Anthony Kennedy asserted that a Texas law criminalizing private, consensual homosexual conduct intruded upon personal liberty and autonomy without a sufficient justification. For Justice Kennedy and his colleagues in the majority, promotion of traditional moral standards was not sufficient justification for intruding on private sexual conduct. Although Kennedy did not use the term "right of privacy" per se, clearly the rights of personal liberty and autonomy infringed by the Texas statute bear close resemblance to the right of privacy expounded in *Griswold, Eisenstadt, Roe,* and the numerous state and federal judicial opinions based on those decisions.

Dissenting in *Lawrence v. Texas,* Justice Antonin Scalia argued that the Court's opinion had undercut the foundations of other long-standing criminal prohibitions such as those against incest, bestiality, bigamy, and obscenity. "If," Scalia reasoned, "the promotion of majoritarian sexual morality is not even a legitimate state interest, none of the above-mentioned laws can survive rational-basis review."

Whether Justice Scalia was correct as a matter of legal reasoning, it is unlikely that courts will interpret *Lawrence v. Texas* so as to shield these activities from the criminal law. It may well be that, as Robert Bork once predicted, the constitutional right of privacy "will turn out to protect those activities that enough Justices to form a majority think ought to be protected and not activities with which they have little sympathy" (Bork 1990, 99).

The Right to Die

Since the mid-1970s, the right of privacy has been successfully asserted in state courts as a basis for refusing extraordinary forms of medical treatment. It is now settled law that a competent adult with a terminal illness has the right to refuse medical treatment that unnaturally prolongs his or her life. Invoking the doctrine of "substituted judgment," courts now routinely allow the spouse or family of a comatose individual to direct removal of a life support system. Such decisions have touched off a national debate about the so-called right to die. In *Bouvia v. Superior Court* (1986), an oft-cited right-to-die case, a California appellate court noted that "a desire to terminate one's life is probably the ultimate exercise of one's right to privacy...." If the right of privacy allows an individual to make "fundamental life choices" and to decide what happens to his or her body, then how can laws that forbid suicide (or aiding and abetting another person's suicide) be constitutional?

For its part, the Supreme Court has treaded lightly in this field. In *Cruzan v. Director, Missouri Health Department* (1990), the Court recognized that the right of the individual to terminate life-prolonging treatment, but also determined that it is reasonable for states to impose legal safeguards against the abuse of the "substituted judgment" doctrine. And in *Washington v. Glucksberg* (1997), the Court upheld a state ban on doctor-assisted suicide, stressing the state's "unqualified interest in the preservation of human life" over the individual's rights of privacy and autonomy. Clearly, the tone of Chief Justice Rehnquist's opinion in *Glucksberg* contrasted sharply with Justice Harry Blackmun's opinion for the Court in *Roe v. Wade,* where privacy and personal autonomy were held to trump the state's interest in protecting the unborn.

Divergent Views of the Law

When the Supreme Court invoked the right of privacy to effectively legalize abortion in *Roe v. Wade,* it was giving expression to a sense of moral individualism that is deeply rooted in American culture. However, countervailing notions of traditional morality are also deeply ingrained in American society, as the relentless criticism of *Roe v. Wade* demonstrates. In no other area of constitutional law are individualism and traditional morality so sharply antagonistic as in the area of privacy rights.

The debate over the constitutional right of privacy is ultimately a debate between two divergent views of the law. In the libertarian view, the law exists to protect individuals from one another. In this view, morality is not in and of itself a legitimate basis for law. The classical conservative view, on the other hand, sees law and morality as inseparable and holds that the maintenance of societal morality is one of the essential functions of the legal system. In recent years these competing perspectives have become politicized, and courts of law adjudicating privacy issues have found themselves in the midst of a culture war.

See also Abortion, Public Funding of; Abortion, Right to; Bill of Rights; Black, Hugo L.; Blackmun, Harry A.; Bork, Robert H.; Brennan, William J., Jr.; Conservatism; Doctor-Assisted Suicide; Douglas, William O.; Drugs, Private Use of; Due Process, Substantive; Fourteenth Amendment; Gay Rights Movement; *Griswold v. Connecticut* (1965); Harlan, John Marshall, II; Judicial Activism; Judicial Restraint; Kennedy, Anthony; Liberalism; Libertarianism; Liberty; Living Constitution; Medical Treatment, Right to Refuse; Right to Die; *Meyer v. Nebraska* (1923); Ninth Amendment; *Pierce v. Society of Sisters* (1925); *Poe v. Ullman* (1961); Privacy, Invasion of; Rehnquist, William H.; Reproductive Freedom; Scalia, Antonin; Stewart, Potter; Surrogate Motherhood; White, Byron R.

Bibliography

Bork, Robert H. 1990. *The Tempting of America: The Political Seduction of the Law.* New York: Simon and Schuster.

DeRosa, Marshall. 1996. *The Ninth Amendment and the Politics of Creative Jurisprudence: Disparaging the Fundamental Right of Popular Control.* Somerset, NJ: Transaction Publishers.

McClellan, Grant S., ed. 1976. *The Right to Privacy.* New York: H.W. Wilson.

Murphy, Paul L. 1990. *The Right to Privacy and the Ninth Amendment.* New York: Garland Publishing.

O'Brien, David M. 1979. *Privacy, Law and Public Policy.* New York: Praeger.

Westin, Alan F. 1970. *Privacy and Freedom.* New York: Atheneum.

John M. Scheb II

PRIVACY, FINANCIAL. *See* Privacy, Informational

PRIVACY, INFORMATIONAL

In the Information Age, government agencies, insurance companies, banks, hospitals, schools, and numerous other public and private institutions collect and maintain enormous quantities of information about individuals. Failure to protect the confidentiality of these records can produce real harm. Without appropriate limits on the disclosure and sharing of personal information, people's reputations, finances, and security can be placed in jeopardy. Over the last several decades, Americans have become increasingly concerned about these issues. Congress and the state legislatures have responded by enacting significant statutory protections of informational privacy.

The Federal Privacy Act of 1974

The seminal legislation in this field is the federal Privacy Act of 1974, which requires that personal information files held by federal agencies are limited to those that are clearly necessary. The Privacy Act prohibits secret record-keeping systems. The law requires that individuals be afforded the opportunity to see what information about them is kept and to challenge the accuracy of such information. It also provides that personal information collected for one purpose will not be used for another purpose without the consent of the affected person. Finally, the Privacy Act requires that if agencies disclose personal information, they must inform the affected person as to whom the disclosure was made, for what purpose, and on what date.

The Privacy Act was amended in 1976 to require that social security numbers be kept confidential by the government agencies that collect them. This is of enormous importance today, as criminals often use social security numbers to commit "identify theft" or perpetrate fraudulent schemes of various kinds.

State Laws Protecting Informational Privacy

The federal Privacy Act applies only to agencies of the national government. However, most states have adopted laws paralleling the federal protections by limiting record keeping about individuals by state agencies. A good example of this is the Minnesota Government Data Privacy Act, which classifies information on individuals into three categories: confidential, private, and public. Confidential information is that which must remain inaccessible to the public and to the individual who is the subject of the information. Private information is that which is inaccessible to the public but is accessible to the individual subject. Lastly, public information is that which is accessible to everyone and indeed must be provided to a requesting party under the applicable state open records law. The law requires state agencies to inform individuals from whom private or confidential information is sought as to the purpose and intended use of the requested data, whether the individual is legally required to supply the information, and the identity of others who will have access to the information.

Privacy of Educational Records

The Family Educational Rights Privacy Act (FERPA), better known as the Buckley Amendment, protects the privacy of students' educational records. The law applies to all state and local educational institutions that receive federal funds and provides that federal funds are to be withheld from school districts that have a policy or practice of permitting the release of education records without the students' written consent, or parental consent of minor students. FERPA defines educational records as "records, files, documents, and other materials" containing information directly related to a student, which "are maintained by an educational agency or institution or by a person acting for such agency or institution."

FERPA authorizes the Secretary of Education to deal with violations of the act. To that end, the Department of Education has established the Family Policy Compliance Office (FPCO) to respond to written complaints of violations. FPCO investigates complaints and determines what steps are necessary to insure that violations no longer take place. Federal funds can be withheld unless and until educational institutions comply with these steps.

Lower federal courts have disagreed on whether one whose interests are adversely affected by violation of FERPA may bring a civil suit for damages in federal court. In *Gonzaga Univ. v. Doe* (2002) the Supreme Court held that FERPA does not provide private parties with a cause of action. Writing for the Court, Chief Justice Rehnquist concluded that "FERPA's nondisclosure provisions contain no rights-creating language, they have an aggregate, not individual, focus, and they serve primarily to direct the Secretary of Education's distribution of public funds to educational institutions."

Financial Privacy

In *United States v. Miller* (1976), the U.S. Supreme Court ruled that bank customers had no legal right to privacy in financial information held by financial institutions because these are the business records of the banks. In order to ameliorate the effect of that decision, Congress enacted the Right to Financial Privacy Act (RFPA) of 1978. The act defines *financial institution* broadly and states that no government authority may have access to, or obtain copies of, the information contained in the financial records of any customer from a financial institution unless the financial records are reasonably described and the customer authorizes access, or there is an appropriate administrative subpoena or summons (a search warrant, or subpoena, or other appropriate written request from an authorized government authority).

RFPA provides exemptions that allow disclosure to a federal agency of information not specifically related to an individual or in regard to a financial institution's interest concerning its loans and loan guarantees, and where federal agencies are conducting supervisory investigations of institutions. In addition, the IRS, which has its own statutory privacy protections, may obtain information from a bank about a customer without a summons or notice. Disclosures may be made pursuant to other federal statutes and, of course, in civil litigation information may be disclosed pursuant to Federal Rules of Civil Procedure. Finally, the federal government can obtain information if the institution's customer is suspected of terrorist action. The act requires the federal government to give an institution's customer notice when it is seeking disclosure in order to afford a person an opportunity to challenge such request.

Confidentiality of Health Records

Along with financial records, medical records are an essential element of a person's individual privacy, but historically the law has not recognized a person's right to privacy in such records. In *Whalen v. Roe* (1977) the U.S. Supreme Court recognized that disclosures of private medical information to doctors, hospital personnel, insurance companies, and public health agencies are often an essential part of modern medical practice even when the disclosure may reflect unfavorably on the character of the patient.

In recent years Congress has recognized this strong desire for privacy in medical records and when it enacted the Health Insurance Portability and Accountability Act of 1996 (HIPAA), it mandated that the Department of Health and Human Services (HHS) develop privacy standards to protect patients' medical records and other health information furnished to physicians, hospitals, and

other health care providers. HHS subsequently promulgated a Privacy Protection Rule that represents the first comprehensive federal protection for the privacy of patients' medical records and other individually identifiable information. The new rule covers such medical information, whether communicated electronically, on paper, or orally, that is used or disclosed by entities subject to the rule. It grants patients access to their records and requires that they consent before release or disclosure of protected information. For example, patients have to grant authorization before an entity subject to the rule can release a patient's medical records to a bank or life insurance company. Affected entities were required to comply with the new rule by April 14, 2003. Those who violate the rule are subject to civil and criminal penalties. HHS has announced that the new federal privacy standards simply set a national "floor" to protect persons and that any state law providing additional protections would continue to apply.

Confidentiality of Library Records

Nearly all the states have also adopted laws protecting the privacy of library records. The New York statute, codified at section 4509 of the New York Consolidated Laws, is fairly typical:

Library records, which contain names or other personally identifying details regarding the users of public, free association, school, college and university libraries and library systems of this state, including but not limited to records related to the circulation of library materials, computer database searches, interlibrary loan transactions, reference queries, requests for photocopies of library materials, title reserve requests, or the use of audio-visual materials, films or records, shall be confidential and shall not be disclosed except that such records may be disclosed to the extent necessary for the proper operation of such library and shall be disclosed upon request or consent of the user or pursuant to subpoena, court order or where otherwise required by statute.

The USA PATRIOT Act of 2001 made it easier for FBI agents to gain access to library records, including circulation records, Internet use records, and registration information. Under Section 215 of the act, to obtain the necessary surveillance warrant, agents do not have to demonstrate probable cause but only assert before a federal magistrate that the records sought are related to an ongoing investigation related to terrorism or counterintelligence. The American Civil Liberties Union (ACLU), the American Library Association (ALA), and other advocates of "the right to read" have voiced strong opposition to this section of the USA PATRIOT Act. The ALA's "Policy Concerning Confidentiality of Personally Identifiable Information about Library Users Existing ALA Policy states, "The government's interest in library use reflects a dangerous and fallacious equation of what a person reads with what that person believes or how that person is likely to behave. Such a presumption can and does threaten the freedom of access to information" (The ALA's "Policy Concerning Confidentiality of Personally Identifiable Information about Library Users).

Video Privacy

One of the strongest protections of informational privacy is found in the Video Privacy Protection Act of 1988. This federal statute prohibits "any person, engaged in the business … of rental, sale or delivery of prerecorded video cassette tapes or similar audiovisual materials" from disclosing "personally identifiably information" to someone other than the consumer without the consumer's written consent. This prevents others from finding out what videos people have been watching, which serves to protect them from embarrassment and abuse from those who disapprove of their private viewing habits. The statute provides a federal civil remedy to consumers whose rights are violated by improper disclosure of video rental information.

The Video Privacy Protection Act does not prohibit the disclosure of information that is subpoenaed by a court of law pursuant to a criminal prosecution or civil suit. However, the statute provides that the consumer is to be given fair notice and afforded the opportunity to contest the request in court. The act also makes an exception, of course, in cases where law enforcement officers, acting pursuant to judicial authorization, seek such information as part of a legitimate investigation. Under the statute the consumer whose records are sought is entitled to prior notice that law enforcement agents are seeking to obtain this information (although § 215 of the USA PATRIOT Act presumably creates an exception to this protection for investigations related to terrorism or counterintelligence).

Computer Privacy

Anyone who uses a computer that is connected to the Internet is well aware of the threats to privacy posed by hackers who find ingenious ways to purloin private information from other parties' computers. Although such activities are prohibited under state and federal laws, perpetrators are often difficult to identify. In most instances, victims do not even realize that they have been victimized. Increasingly, computer users are using antivirus programs, firewalls, and "spam" (junk e-mail) blockers to protect themselves from intruders. And parents are increasingly relying on filtering software to protect their children from Web sites and chat rooms that may harbor hidden dangers. What many computer users still do not realize is how much information is stored on their computer drives without their conscious effort to save such data. Files downloaded from the Internet are stored in caches that must be positively deleted. Even deleted files remain on hard drives unless and until they are overwritten by newly saved files. The only way to cover one's tracks, as it were, is to employ specialized software designed to expunge deleted files.

Not infrequently police seize computers and associated media to search for child pornography, incriminating e-mails, or other evidence of wrongdoing. Of course, to make such a seizure from the home or private office, police must have probable cause and, in most instances, a search warrant. However, in most instances employees do not enjoy the same Fourth Amendment protections in the workplace. Employers typically take the position that any computing done on their equipment is their intellectual property. The courts tend to agree and therefore are unsympathetic to claims that an employer committed an invasion of privacy by accessing files on an employee's computer. Today many employers routinely monitor their employees' e-mail transmissions and Internet activity. Currently, there are very few laws in effect to regulate this activity or protect workers' electronic privacy in the workplace.

Dissenting in *Olmstead v. U.S.* (1928), Justice Louis D. Brandeis expressed concern that the "progress of science" would lead to new ways in which a person's privacy could be compromised. Justice Brandeis' concern is more justified today than ever before.

See also American Civil Liberties Union; Brandeis, Louis D.; Foreign Intelligence Surveillance Act (FISA); Fourth Amendment; Freedom of Information Act (FOIA); Privacy, Constitutional Right of; Probable Cause; Search Warrants; Section 1983 Actions; USA PATRIOT Act (2001)

Bibliography

Branscomb, Anne Wells. 1995. *Who Owns Information? From Privacy to Public Access.* New York: Harper Collins Publishers.

Cate, Fred H. 1997. *Privacy in the Information Age.* Washington, DC: Brookings Institution Press.

Klosek, Jacqueline. 2000. *Data Privacy in the Information Age.* Westport, CT: Quorum Books.

John M. Scheb II

PRIVACY, INVASION OF

Privacy as a right has been slow in establishing itself in American law. Boston lawyers Samuel D. Warren and Louis D. Brandeis argued in 1890 for recognition of the invasion of privacy as a tort in the United States, but American courts were lukewarm in their initial response to this "right to privacy" proposal. It took 15 years for privacy to be accepted by a state supreme court as a legal right for individuals (see *Pavesich v. New England Life Ins. Co.* [Ga. 1905]).

At present privacy is recognized in nearly every jurisdiction either statutorily or in common law. Courts recognize four privacy torts:

- "intrusion upon the plaintiff's seclusion or solitude, or into his private affairs";
- "public disclosure of embarrassing private facts about the plaintiff";
- "publicity which places the plaintiff in a false light in the public eye"; and
- "appropriation, for the defendant's advantage, of the plaintiff's name or likeness."

Intrusion is similar to "trespass," or unauthorized entry onto someone's private property. The *Restatement (Second) of Torts* defines intrusion thus: "One who intentionally intrudes, physically or otherwise, upon the solitude or seclusion of another or his private affairs or concerns, is subject to liability to the other for invasion of his privacy, if the intrusion would be highly offensive to a reasonable person." Intrusion is different from the other types of invasion of privacy in that it does not require publication of information as a cause of action. Rather, the highly offensive conduct of news gathering is sufficient. However, as compared with other privacy torts, the impact of intrusion on news reporting has been limited largely because few reporters intentionally intrude upon another's private place in an outrageous manner.

In determining the intrusive action of news reporters or photographers, a court will ask whether the plaintiff(s) had a reasonable expectation of privacy. If a plaintiff was in a public place, the act of news gathering would not constitute an intrusion unless it was offensive enough to be labeled harassment. Surreptitious taping and filming may constitute intrusion, depending on how and where it is done and on applicable state law. Surreptitious taping of telephone conversations by a conversation participant is prohibited in 10 states.

However, the press can usually publish or broadcast illegal recordings made by third parties and provided to the journalists. The Supreme Court held in *Bartnicki v. Vopper* (2001) that news media cannot be held liable for publication of taped material if it concerns matters of public importance, if the media played no part in the illegal information-gathering, and if the media obtained the recording lawfully.

Disclosure of embarrassing private facts pertains to the content rather than the source of news stories. Many privacy claims have pressed this cause of action, but very few decisions have been rendered against respondents from news media. The private facts claim requires proof of four elements: (1) that facts were publicized; (2) that the facts were private facts concerning the plaintiff; (3) that the facts would be highly offensive to a reasonable person; and (4) that the subject matter of the facts published is not a matter of legitimate public concern.

Publicity is rarely difficult to prove because publication in a print or broadcast media or over the Internet meets this requirement. However, if the embarrassing facts about a person's life are already publicly known and in the public record, they are no longer private when published. In *Cox Broadcasting Corp. v. Cohn* (1975), the Supreme Court held that the States may not punish the press for publication of "truthful information" contained in court records open to the public.

The question of what kind of information would be highly embarrassing to a reasonable person is interwoven with whether publication of the embarrassing information lacks a legitimate public interest. News media are not necessarily liable for the disclosure of private facts merely because the facts lack news value. The Supreme Court held in *Florida Star v. B.J.F.* (1989) that news media can be punished for publishing truthful information only when the punishment advances a "state interest of the highest order."

False light privacy is often likened to defamation, but it is distinguishable. A false light action seeks to vindicate mental and emotional harm, while a defamation suit seeks compensation for injury to reputation. Further, a false light cause of action may arise even when truthful information has been published about an individual if it contains a false implication about the individual. By contrast, to be defamatory, a statement must be false, and respondents in defamations suits may defend themselves by proving the truth of their statements.

A false light suit must demonstrate: (1) publicity about a person, (2) which places that person in a false light, (3) which is highly offensive to a reason-

able person, and (4) under circumstances where the publisher or broadcaster had knowledge of, or acted in reckless disregard of, the falsity of the publicized matter and the false light in which the person would be placed.

False light claims arise from informational addition or omission from a story as well as from its embellishment. The Supreme Court decision in *Time, Inc. v. Hill* (1967) is a case in point. The James J. Hill family sued Time, Inc., for placing them in a false light when it published an article in *Life* magazine about their experiences while being held hostage by escaped convicts. The article carried staged photographs, which showed one of the sons being mistreated by a "brutish convict" and the daughter biting the hand of an abusive convict. The pictures were embellishments because Hill family members (or family was) were not abused by the convicts. While the Hill family won at trial, the Supreme Court reversed the damage award. The Court held that false light plaintiffs involved in matters of public interest must prove that the media defendant published falsehood either knowingly or with reckless disregard for the truth.

Appropriation is the unauthorized commercial use by the news media of an individual's name, picture, and similar personal traits. When celebrities are involved, appropriation is often referred to as a violation of the "right of publicity." News media are rarely sued for appropriation since they have the First Amendment right to publish stories, using names and pictures of those who are involved in news events—whether they are celebrities or not. No permission is required. Even when a newsmaker's picture is used by a television or radio station in advertising to promote itself and its news programs, that advertisement cannot be a cause of action for appropriation against the media outlet. Nonetheless, in its only appropriation case against the press thus far, the Supreme Court in *Zacchini v. Scripps-Howard Broadcasting* (1977) held that broadcasting the "entire act" of the "Human Cannonball," Hugo Zacchini, violated his right of publicity because it "poses a substantial threat to the economic value of that performance."

The press can use several defenses when it is sued for an invasion of privacy. Consent is the best defense, especially if it is valid and comprehensive enough to cover all possible situations. Newsworthiness is the most effective defense when disclosure of private facts is at issue. Courts tend to define newsworthiness or public interest of news reporting liberally. In the context of news reporting on government proceedings, the public's right to know may justify the media's publication of truthful information lawfully obtained from court records. Truth can be used as a defense against a false light claim, but in practice the First Amendment "actual malice" requirement (see *New York Times v. Sullivan*, 1964) is a better option for the media when their false stories relate to matters of public interest.

Bibliography

McCarthy, J. Thomas. 2005. *The Rights of Publicity and Privacy.* 2nd ed. St. Paul, MN: Thomson/West.

Kyu Ho Youm

PRIVACY, REASONABLE EXPECTATIONS OF

The Fourth Amendment prohibits unreasonable searches and seizures, but what constitutes a "search"? Historically, the prohibitions of the Fourth Amendment applied only to physical intrusions on someone's person or property. In *Olmstead v. United States* (1928), Chief Justice William Howard Taft opined that the Fourth Amendment was limited to searches "of material things—the person, the house, his papers, or his effects." Thus in *Olmstead* the Court refused to consider wiretapping a form of search within the meaning of the Fourth Amendment. Following that precedent, state and federal courts took the position that surveillance without physical contact with the suspect or the suspect's property fell outside the scope of the Fourth Amendment.

In *Katz v. United States* (1967), the Supreme Court overturned *Olmstead* and repudiated the so-called "trespass doctrine." Saying "the Fourth Amendment protects people, not places," the Court held that federal agents violated the Constitution when they planted a microphone in a public phone booth in order to listen in on the conversations of a suspected bookie. Because "bugging" the phone booth was a search within the meaning of the Fourth Amendment, and because the agents failed to obtain prior judicial authorization, the evidence they obtained through eavesdropping had to be suppressed. The *Katz* decision effectively brought wiretapping and other forms of electronic surveillance within the limitations of the Fourth Amendment.

The post-*Katz* approach to determining the scope of protected privacy under the Fourth Amendment was nicely stated in Justice John M. Harlan's concurring opinion in that case: "My understanding of the rule as it has emerged from prior decisions is that there is a twofold requirement, first that a person have exhibited an actual (subjective) expectation of privacy and, second, that the expectation be one that society is prepared to recognize as 'reasonable.'"

Potentially, the term *search* applies to any official invasion of a person's reasonable expectation of privacy as to one's person, house, papers, or effects. Currently, any means of invading a person's "reasonable expectation of privacy" is considered a search for Fourth Amendment purposes. The critical question that courts must address in reviewing cases where police conduct surveillance or eavesdropping without probable cause or prior judicial authorization is whether such surveillance intruded on a person's reasonable expectation of privacy.

In *Kyllo v. United States* (2001), the Supreme Court considered whether the use of a thermal imager by police was a search within the meaning of the Fourth Amendment. Thermal imagers have been in wide use by police around the country as means of detecting indoor marijuana growing operations. Because such operations require growing lights, they emit unusual levels of heat, which are visible using infrared imaging equipment. Prior to the Kyllo decision, police and prosecutors argued that thermal imaging is not a search within the meaning of the Fourth Amendment, since it only collects data on heat that is being released into the public space. In the *Kyllo* case police used the device to scan a home they suspected to be housing an indoor marijuana-growing operation. After detecting a high level of heat emerging from the home, they obtained a warrant to search the residence and seized more than 100 marijuana plants. In a five-to-four decision, the Supreme Court held that the initial use of the thermal imager without prior judicial authorization was in violation of the Fourth Amendment. Writing for the Court, Justice Antonin Scalia opined that "[w]here, as here, the Government uses a device that is not in general public use, to explore details of the home that would previously have been unknowable without physical intrusion, the surveillance is a search and is presumptively unreasonable without a warrant." In dissent, Justice John P. Stevens noted that "[a]ll that the infrared camera did … was passively measure heat emitted from the exterior surfaces of petitioner's home; all that those measurements showed were relative differences in emission levels, vaguely indicating that some areas of the roof and outside walls were warmer than others." In Stevens's view, the police did not significantly intrude on the privacy of the occupants.

The issue of what constitutes a reasonable expectation of privacy has been litigated in hundreds of cases in federal and state courts. However, the uniqueness of individual situations has resulted in disparate judicial results, with police frequently complaining that courts decisions fail to furnish "bright line" rules. In a number of well-defined situations, however, courts have upheld minimally intrusive suspicionless searches on the assumption that people's privacy expectations are significantly attenuated in such situations.

With increased concern over airplane hijacking and terrorism has come increased security at the nation's airports. Passengers attempting to board aircraft routinely pass through metal detectors; their carry-on baggage and checked luggage are routinely subjected to X-ray scans. Should these procedures suggest the presence of suspicious objects, physical searches are conducted to determine what the objects are. There is little question that such searches are reasonable, given their minimal intrusiveness, the gravity of the safety interests involved, and the reduced privacy expectations associated with airline travel. Indeed, travelers are often notified through airport public address systems and signs that all bags are subject to search. Such announcements place passengers on notice that ordinary Fourth Amendment protections do not apply.

See also Fourth Amendment; Harlan, John Marshall, II; *Katz v. United States* (1967); Precedent, Doctrine of; Taft, William Howard; Terrorism, War on

Bibliography

McWhirter, Darien A. 1994. *Search, Seizure, and Privacy.* Phoenix: Oryx Press.

Scheb, John M., and John M. Scheb II. 2006. *Criminal Procedure.* Belmont, CA: Thomson/Wadsworth.

Stephens, Otis H., Jr., and Richard A. Glenn. 2006. *Unreasonable Searches and Seizures: Rights and Liberties under the Law.* Santa Barbara, CA: ABC-Clio.

Westin, Alan F. 1966. "Science, Privacy, and Freedom: Issues and Proposals for the 1970's." *Columbia Law Review* 66: 1003.

John M. Scheb II and Otis H. Stephens, Jr.

PRIVACY ACT (1974)

The federal Privacy Act (codified at 5 U.S.C. § 552a) prohibits improper disclosure of personal information maintained by government agencies while ensuring the accuracy of the agency records about individuals. It provides for the right of U.S. citizens and lawfully admitted permanent residents to inspect federal government records, to prevent improper distribution of those records, and to correct errors in them, if necessary.

Those who have the right to access agency records under the Privacy Act do not have to explain why they want to see their files. It should be noted that foreign nationals cannot use the Privacy Act to access records about themselves or to correct them, although they can obtain access to agency records through the Freedom of Information Act (FOIA).

The Privacy Act covers records maintained, used, and disseminated by executive agencies of the federal government. Cabinet departments, military departments, government-controlled corporations, and independent regulatory agencies such as the

Federal Communications Commission and other agencies are subject to the act.

The Privacy Act applies only to the records that a government agency maintains in "a system of records." A system of records under the Act refers to a group of records from which personal information can be retrieved according to the name of the individual or by an identifying number or symbol assigned to the individual. If certain personal information about an individual is not kept in the system of records, the information falls outside the jurisdiction of the federal law. The Act proscribes release of government records "by any means of communication to any person or to any agency," except when the individual to which the record pertains requests or consents in writing to its release.

The federal law includes a number of exceptions—both general and specific. Two *general* exemptions are particularly noteworthy. First, all records maintained by the Central Intelligence Agency are exempt from disclosure. Second, selected records maintained by an agency whose principal function is to enforce criminal laws are not releasable because they may contain information identifying individual criminal offenders.

The Privacy Act provides for seven *specific* exemptions:

- Systems of records containing classified information relating to national defense or foreign policy;
- Systems of records containing investigatory material compiled for law enforcement purposes;
- Systems of records maintained in connection with Secret Service protection of the president of the United States or other individuals;
- Systems of records required by statute to be maintained and used solely as statistical records;
- Systems of records relating to investigatory material compiled solely to determine suitability, eligibility, or qualifications for federal civilian employment, military service, federal contracts, or access to classified information;
- Systems of records that contain testing or examination material used solely to determine individual qualifications for federal service, but only when disclosure would affect the testing or examination process;
- Systems of records containing confidential evaluation material used to determine potential for promotion in the armed services.

No government agency can use the Privacy Act's exemptions to deny access to records that are defined as public information under the FOIA. Also, government agencies are barred from using FOIA exemptions to withhold from a qualified individual access to government records under the Act.

The Privacy Act authorizes any eligible individual to request in writing correction of his or her record when that record is not accurate, relevant, timely, or complete. But the individual can correct only errors in the system of records that pertain to himself or herself.

While the federal law stipulates no administrative appeal of the denial of access to agency records, an administrative appeal is nonetheless often allowed. When an access request is denied under the Act, agencies usually inform the requester of any appeal process if it is available.

A government agency must acknowledge receipt of a request for correction of agency records within 10 working days. The agency must rule on the request "promptly." It must either make the corrections, as requested, or inform the individual as to whether his or her correction request has been denied. If the request for correction is denied, the government agency must notify the individual of its refusal of the request, the reason for refusing the request, and procedures for the individual to request a review of the denial.

If an individual disagrees with an agency's refusal to correct a file, he or she can request a review of the refusal. If the agency continues to deny a request for correction, the agency must inform the individual that the Act provides for judicial review of the agency's decision on the request.

The Privacy Act includes a civil enforcement provision whenever a government agency denies access to a record or refuses to correct the record. An individual can bring a civil action against the government agency by filing it in a federal district court in the district in which the individual lives, in which the records are located, or in the District of Columbia. The statute of limitations for Privacy Act lawsuits is two years from the date on which the basis for the lawsuit arose. But this limitation does not apply where an agency has materially and willfully misrepresented any information required to be disclosed to an individual and where the information so misrepresented is material to establishment of the liability of the agency to the individual. In cases of misrepresentation, an action may be brought at any time within two years after discovery by the individual of the misrepresentation.

The plaintiff can recover monetary damages for the agency's intentional violation of the law. Also, if the plaintiff substantially prevails, he or she may receive reasonable attorney fees and litigation costs, as determined by the court.

The Privacy Act authorizes sanctions against government officials for willfully disclosing personal records when they know that their release is not allowed. It also provides for a fine of up to $5,000 for maintaining a system of records without the notice requirement or for knowingly and willfully requesting or obtaining any record concerning an individual from a government agency under false pretenses.

In *Doe v. Chao* (2004), the Supreme Court held that a plaintiff must prove actual injury in order to recover damages under the Privacy Act. The Court stated that assertion of "adverse effect" with no proof of actual damage is insufficient for an award of civil damages.

The real impact of the Privacy Act remains to be seen. Congress revised the law in 1984 to prevent government officials from using it as an end-run around the FOIA on access to government records. But the federal statute tends to induce government agencies to err on the side of withholding information. This is especially true of governmental records that fall under an FOIA exemption and thus are not required to be disclosed. Withholding information that should be released cannot be punished under the FOIA unless the withholding is "arbitrary" or "capricious."

See also Freedom of Information Act; Privacy, Informational

Bibliography

Franklin, Justice D., and Robert F. Bouchard. 1986. *Guidebook to the Freedom of Information and Privacy Acts.* 2nd ed. New York: Clark Boardman.

Kyu Ho Youm

PRIVACY RIGHTS. *See* Abortion, Right to; Abortion, Public Funding of; Doctor-Assisted Suicide; Drugs, Private Use of; Due Process, Substantive; Fourteenth Amendment (1868); *Griswold v. Connecticut* (1965); *Lawrence v. Texas* (2003); Privacy, Constitutional Right of; Privacy, Informational; Privacy, Invasion of; Privacy, Reasonable Expectations of; Reproductive Freedom; Right to Die; *Roe v. Wade* (1973); Seat Belt Laws; Surrogate Motherhood

PRIVILEGES OR IMMUNITIES CLAUSE

Section 1 of the Fourteenth Amendment to the United States Constitution applies to the state governments and contains a number of important guarantees including citizenship, due process, and equal protection. It also contains a provision known as the Privileges or Immunities Clause, which provides that: "No state shall make or enforce any law which shall abridge the privileges or immunities of citizens of the United States." This clause came directly from the Privileges and Immunities Clause of Article IV, Section 2 of the Constitution, which stemmed from a provision in the Articles of Confederation. The framers of the Constitution included the clause to promote unity among the newly independent states (Davis and Peltason 2004). The author of Section 1, Representative John A. Bingham of Ohio, and Jacob Howard, who presented the amendment in the Senate, argued that the clause would apply the guarantees of the Constitution, including the Bill of Rights, to the states (Urofsky and Finkelman 2002, 445).

Justice Bushrod Washington's interpretation of the Privileges and Immunities Clause in Article IV was well known to the framers of the Fourteenth Amendment. In *Corfield v. Coryell* (1823), Washington asserted that the clause protected privileges and immunities "which are, in their nature, fundamental; which belong of right to the citizens of all free governments; and which have, at all times, been enjoyed by the citizens of the several states." Among those rights were "protection by the government; the enjoyment of life and liberty, with the right to acquire and possess property of every kind, to pursue and obtain happiness and safety; subject nevertheless to such restraints as the government may justly prescribe for the general good of the whole." The congressional debates concerning the Fourteenth Amendment echoed that interpretation of privileges and immunities. Moreover, some members of Congress indicated that they believed the clause in Article IV provided equal rights for all citizens, and that Congress had the authority to protect those rights in the Fourteenth Amendment (Davis and Peltason 2004). The supporters of the amendment believed that it would allow Congress to enforce existing constitutional protections against discriminatory action by the states.

The United States Supreme Court, however, took a more limited view of the clause and the Fourteenth Amendment generally. The Court had the opportunity to interpret the Fourteenth Amendment for the first time in the Slaughterhouse Cases (1873). This case was the combination of three lawsuits dealing with a Louisiana law that established a monopoly on the slaughter of animals by requiring butchers to undertake those activities in one location, New Orleans, to protect the public's health. The butchers argued that the law interfered with their right to engage in business without government interference. They asserted that the Privileges or Immunities Clause protected such a right. The Supreme Court, however, disagreed in a five-to-four ruling. At the outset, Justice Samuel Miller's majority opinion asserted that the amendment was

intended to apply to the newly freed slaves. Miller further argued that the Fourteenth Amendment was not intended to protect a citizen against legislative power from his own state, but served as a limit on the power of the federal government instead. To support that assertion, Miller pointed out that the clause itself states that privileges or immunities apply to the "citizens of the United States." Therefore, it was up to the state governments to determine what rights they might choose to grant to state citizens.

Justice Stephen Field's dissent countered that the clause protected the "natural and inalienable rights which belong to all citizens" from interference by the states. Field argued that any other interpretation of the meaning of the amendment was without merit. Why put such a clause in a new amendment, if the guarantees were identical to those already protected by the original Constitution?

In an opinion handed down a day after the Slaughterhouse Cases, the Court also had the opportunity to speak to the meaning of the Privileges or Immunities Clause. In *Bradwell v. Illinois* (1873), the Court, by a larger margin (eight-to-one), held that the Privileges or Immunities Clause did not prohibit a state from denying a woman a license to practice law. The Court reasoned "the right to control and regulate the granting of license to practice law in the courts of a State is one of those powers which are not transferred for its protection to the Federal Government, and its exercise is in no manner governed or controlled by citizenship of the United States."

Two years later in another case concerning women's rights, *Minor v. Happersett* (1875), the Court found that restricting suffrage to men was not a violation of the Privileges or Immunities Clause. Chief Justice Morrison Waite's majority opinion offered a very restrictive definition of citizenship and asserted that citizenship, in and of itself, does not confer a right to vote. Moreover, the Privileges or Immunities Clause did not impose a federal limitation on state control of voting rights.

There have been very few other cases involving the Privileges or Immunities Clause. In *Colgate v. Harvey* (1935), the Court held that the right to conduct interstate business dealings was protected by the Privileges or Immunities Clause. This ruling however was overturned five years later in *Madden v. Kentucky* (1940). More recently, the Court resurrected the Privileges or Immunities Clause in *Saenz v. Rose* (1999) in which it struck down a California policy limiting welfare benefits by requiring that individuals who lived in the state less than a year were only eligible to receive benefits equal to the amount they would have received in their prior state of residence. Justice John Paul Stevens relied in part on the Privileges or Immunities Clause, which required that newly arrived citizens be entitled to the same privileges and immunities of other citizens. Stevens quoted from both the majority and dissenting opinions in the Slaughterhouse Cases to support his rationale. Justice Miller's majority opinion recognized that one of the privileges conferred by this Clause "is that a citizen of the United States can, of his own volition, become a citizen of any State of the Union by a *bona fide* residence therein, with the same rights as other citizens of that State." Justice Bradley, in dissent, used even stronger language to make the same point:

A citizen of the United States has a perfect constitutional right to go to and reside in any State he chooses, and to claim citizenship therein, and an equality of rights with every other citizen; and the whole power of the nation is pledged to sustain him in that right. He is not bound to cringe to any superior, or to pray for any act of grace, as a means of enjoying all the rights and privileges enjoyed by other citizens.

Justice Clarence Thomas and Chief Justice William Rehnquist dissented because they feared that by relying on the Privileges or Immunities Clause, the Court could open the door to creating other constitutional rights.

The Court's early interpretation of the Privileges or Immunities Clause rendered it meaningless in protecting rights from encroachment by the state government. The intent of the framers of the Fourteenth Amendment was realized, however, when the Court began to incorporate provisions of the Bill of Rights into the Due Process Clause of the Fourteenth Amendment, which has required states to protect the rights of its citizens based on a national standard.

See also Bill of Rights, Incorporation of; Due Process Clauses; Equal Protection Clause; Fifth Amendment; Fourteenth Amendment (1868); Rehnquist, William H.; Stevens, John Paul; Thomas, Clarence; Waite, Morrison Remick

Bibliography

Davis, Sue, and J. W. Peltason. 2004. *Corwin and Peltason's Understanding the Constitution.* 16th ed. Belmont, CA: Wadsworth.

Urofsky, Melvin I., and Paul Finkelman. 2002. *A March for Liberty: A Constitutional History of the United States.* 2nd ed. Vol. 1, *From The Founding to 1890.* New York: Oxford University Press.

Kara E. Stooksbury

PROBABLE CAUSE

The Fourth Amendment to the United States Constitution, which prohibits unreasonable searches and seizures, states that "no Warrants shall issue, but upon probable cause …" The probable cause requirement was included in order to prohibit the "general warrants" that were anathema to the American colonists in the years leading up to the Revolution. Such warrants allowed law enforcement agents to arrest and search anyone merely on suspicion. Although courts permit certain types of searches on the lesser standard of "reasonable suspicion," searches and seizures (including warrantless arrests and searches) generally must be supported by probable cause in order to comply with the requirements of the Fourth Amendment.

Like many legal terms, "probable cause" is not amenable to precise definition. In *Locke v. United States* (1813), Chief Justice John Marshall wrote that "the term 'probable cause', according to its usual acceptation, means less than evidence which would justify condemnation…." Sixty-five years later, in *Stacey v. Emery,* the Supreme Court said, "If the facts and circumstances before the officer are such as to warrant a man of prudence and caution in believing that the offense has been committed, it is sufficient." In later years the years the Supreme Court would rely on this definition (see, e.g., *Carroll v. United States,* 1925). Justice Wiley Rutledge, writing for the Court in *Brinegar v. United States* (1949), observed:

In dealing with probable cause, ... as the very name implies, we deal with probabilities. These are not technical; they are the factual and practical considerations of everyday life on which reasonable and prudent men, not legal technicians, act. The standard of proof is accordingly correlative to what must be proved.

Thus for a police officer to make a warrantless arrest the facts and circumstances within the officer's knowledge and such reasonably trustworthy information available must establish that an offense is being or has been committed. An officer can establish probable cause by observation or by obtaining information from various sources.

Likewise, before issuing an arrest warrant or a search warrant a magistrate must determine that the affidavit in support of the warrant discloses probable cause to believe a named person has committed an offense or that search of identified premises will yield evidence of a crime. Often a police officer's affidavit to secure a search warrant is based on information supplied by informants who may be seeking favorable treatment from the police; thus their credibility may be questionable.

Justice John Marshall Harlan (the younger) had occasion to discuss the concept of probable cause to issue a search warrant in his opinion for the Court in *Spinelli v. United States* (1969). According to that opinion, "only the probability, and not a prima facie showing, of criminal activity is the standard of probable cause...." Harlan also noted that a magistrate's "determination of probable cause should be paid great deference by reviewing courts...." Nevertheless, in *Spinelli* the Supreme Court invalidated a search warrant, holding that the magistrate erred in finding probable cause because the officers' supporting affidavit did not set forth underlying circumstances to enable the magistrate to independently judge the informants'

basis of knowledge and reliability. The *Spinelli* decision made it difficult for police officers to obtain search warrants, particularly in the War on Drugs.

During the 1980s a more conservative Supreme Court concluded that the *Spinelli* approach was not a workable test. Writing for the Court in *Illinois v. Gates* (1983), Justice William H. Rehnquist observed that "probable cause is a fluid concept—turning on the assessment of probabilities in particular factual contexts—not readily, or even usefully, reduced to a neat set of legal rules." In *Gates,* the Court held that magistrates making probable cause determinations in response to police applications for search warrants should use a common-sense approach based on the totality of circumstances. In so holding, the Court rejected the test articulated in *Spinelli v. United States* and other previous cases that required an affidavit based on hearsay information to establish both the veracity and basis of knowledge of an informant before probable cause could be found.

Although state courts are free to impose a higher standard, most have followed the totality of circumstances approach. But some state courts have declined to follow the *Gates* approach and have opted to provide their citizens more protection than allowed by the federal view. In some instances, these state views result from linguistic variations in state constitutional counterparts to the Fourth Amendment. For example, in *Commonwealth v. Upton* (1985), the Massachusetts Supreme Court noted that its state constitution provides more substantive protection to criminal defendants than does the Fourth Amendment in the determination of probable cause. Thus, the court held that an affidavit based on a telephone tip from an anonymous informer whose veracity was not shown did not establish probable cause for issuance of a search warrant.

See also Fourth Amendment; Harlan, John Marshall, II; Informants, Anonymous and Confidential; Marshall, John; New Judicial Federalism; Reasonable Doubt Standard; Rehnquist, William H.; Search Warrants; Writs of Assistance and General Warrants

Bibliography

Kamisar, Yale. 1984. "*Gates,* 'Probable Cause,' 'Good Faith,' and Beyond." *Iowa Law Review* 69: 551.

Scheb, John M., and John M. Scheb II. 2006. *Criminal Procedure.* Belmont, CA: Thomson/Wadsworth.

Shapiro, B. J. 1991. *Beyond "Reasonable Doubt" and "Probable Cause": Historical Perspectives on the Anglo-American Law of Evidence.* Berkeley: University of California Press.

Stephens, Otis H., Jr., and Richard A. Glenn. 2006. *Unreasonable Searches and Seizures: Rights and Liberties under the Law.* Santa Barbara, CA: ABC-Clio.

John M. Scheb II and Otis H. Stephens, Jr.

PROBATION AND PAROLE

Probation and parole are alternatives to incarceration of persons convicted of crimes. Due to the rising costs of housing inmates in correctional facilities, both are important resources for the criminal justice system. Yet, for a number of reasons, both remain controversial.

The concept of probation is a relatively new development in the approach to corrections. In 1878, Massachusetts became the first state to establish a formal probation system. The federal government followed in 1927, passing the National Probation Act, which made provisions for hiring probation officers in the states. Other states passed similar legislation making provisions for probation agencies, including juvenile probation. By 1957, every state had some form of probation program for adult offenders.

Probation, as it exists now, is used extensively in the United States as a practical alternative to incarceration that is characterized as mostly fragmented and decentralized. The structure and duties of probation offices vary from state to state, but probation remains an integral part of the corrections system administered through the courts. Probation is a sanction that can take many forms because there are several combinations of conditions that can be associated with a probated sentence. For example, a probationer, as a condition of her probation, may be required to provide restitution to the victim, perform community service, pay probation fees,

and so forth. If one or more of these conditions are not met, the probationer may be facing revocation of probation.

There are two ways a probationer can violate the conditions of probation. One is a technical violation; the other is the commission of new crimes. A technical violation occurs where the probationer has violated the condition(s) of probation. Violation of probation, whether it is technical or involves breaking other criminal laws, will often result in imprisonment of the probationer for the balance of the sentence.

Probationers accused of violating probation must be afforded due process of law before probation can be revoked. In *Gagnon v. Scarpelli* (1973), the U.S. Supreme Court held that, before their probation can be revoked, probationers are entitled to a hearing in which they have the right to confront witnesses and have allegations against them presented in writing.

Unlike probation, parole is not a separate criminal sanction. Parole, a word originally meaning a promise made with or confirmed by pledge of one's honor, is currently defined as an early conditional release of a prison inmate. There are two basic forms of conditional release available, discretionary and mandatory. The discretionary release of an inmate involves a decision by a paroling authority based upon conditions and eligibility criteria. Discretionary release can also be a type of sentence reduction or emergency release where typically nonviolent and/or inmates nearing the end of their terms are released to make room for additional inmates. The mandatory release is an inmate's early release after a specified period of time, usually the result of good time credits.

Modern parole provisions derive from the eighteenth-century practice of transportation and exile, especially in the marks system developed in the 1840s by British Navy Captain Alexander Maconochie. With Maconochie's "marks of commendation," an inmate could earn his way to freedom by accumulating marks for good behavior. In 1854, the director of the Irish prison system, Sir Walter Crofton, adopted features of Maconochie's marks system while instituting his own concepts. The concepts developed by Crofton and Maconochie resemble many of the provisions of modern parole, such as refraining from violating additional criminal laws, reporting to officers, notification in change of residence, and avoiding associations with known criminals.

In 1876, New York's Elmira Reformatory became the first prison to implement a parole program. The program required inmates to be evaluated in three grades ranging from personal interview, work assignments, and an eventual parole hearing, provided the inmate earn an adequate number of marks. The overall development of parole programs in the United States was born out of necessity to alleviate turbulent prison conditions and overcrowding. At the onset, prison administrators favored the use of parole as a means to control the inmates by providing incentives to comply with prison regulations. The availability of parole, like probation, was also instrumental in reducing the burgeoning inmate population. Other professionals in the criminal justice profession supported parole because it made plea bargains more attractive and was far less expensive to taxpayers than incarceration.

The parole process begins with a parole eligibility date that is assigned at the beginning of an inmate's sentence. This date indicates the earliest an inmate can be released. Probably the most challenging aspect of the parole process is the problem of reentry of the inmate into the world outside the prison gates. All states provide some type of reentry orientation for those inmates who qualify for parole. These orientation programs, some more comprehensive than others, generally include job training, literacy skills, and counseling. The individual state's paroling authority, usually a parole board, makes the decision to parole. The parole applicant, institutional representatives, the board members, and sometimes those who oppose parole for that individual usually attend a parole hearing. If the applicant is granted parole, the board is typically responsible for setting the conditions of the individual's parole, providing reentry resources, and protecting the interest of the public while placing the individual. The pa-

rolee is still legally in state custody, but has been granted the privilege of living outside the prison in the community.

Recent studies have revealed that the recidivism rate is very high among those newly paroled. Parole revocation procedures are very similar to those associated with probation—parole can be revoked both for technical violations and for the commission of new crimes. In *Morrissey v. Brewer* (1972), the U.S. Supreme Court held that parolees are entitled to procedural due process before parole can be revoked.

Just as provisions for granting parole vary greatly from one state to the next, so does the practice of utilizing parole boards and revoking parole. In fact some states have eliminated these boards. In passing the Sentencing Reform Act of 1984, Congress abolished parole altogether in the federal system. Under so-called Truth in Sentencing laws, a number of states have likewise abolished or severely curtailed parole for state offenders. Of course, these policies only exacerbate the problems of overcrowding in the federal and state prisons.

See also Due Process, Procedural; House Arrest; Restitution; Sentencing, Eighth Amendment and; Three Strikes Laws; Truth in Sentencing

Bibliography

Carlson, Norman A., Karen M. Hess, and Christine M. H. Orthmann. 1999. *Corrections in the 21st Century, A Practical Approach.* Belmont, CA: West/Wadsworth.

Schmalleger, Frank, and John Ortiz Smykla. 2002. *Corrections in the 21st Century.* 2nd ed. New York: McGraw Hill.

Cassie Adams-Walls

PRO-CHOICE MOVEMENT. *See* Abortion, Right to; Interest Groups and Civil Rights and Liberties; National Abortion Rights Action League; National Organization for Women; Pro-Choice Position on Abortion

PRO-CHOICE POSITION ON ABORTION

The pro-choice position is primarily a normative position about the content of the law with respect to abortion (i.e., about what the law should be). On this view, the law ought to protect a "right to choose" that allows largely unrestricted access to abortions during, at least, the early stages of pregnancy. Laws that criminalize abortion are, on this view, illegitimate and hence, as a matter of political morality, impermissibly enforced by the state.

It is important to realize that the pro-choice position *per se* does not express or include any one view about the morality of having abortions; it is, again, a view about the moral legitimacy of legal restrictions on abortion, and not about the morality of a woman's having an abortion. Indeed, choice advocates themselves disagree on the morality of abortion and take a wide range of positions on this question. While some pro-choice advocates believe that having an abortion involves no moral badness or wrongness, many pro-choice advocates believe that abortion might frequently be wrong even during the early stages of pregnancy but that its wrongness does not rise to the level of murder because the fetus is not a moral person (i.e., not a being with fundamental moral rights) during these stages.

What unites all positions fairly characterized as pro-choice, however, is the claim that the law should generally allow, as a matter of "legal right," largely unrestricted access to abortion during some specified period, which includes, at the very least, the first trimester of pregnancy. More conservative (and common) pro-choice positions hold that this period ends when fetal consciousness begins (typically about 20 to 24 weeks into the pregnancy), while less conservative (and much less common) positions hold that this period includes the entire duration of pregnancy.

The pro-choice position is usually grounded in two moral claims—one about women and one about fetuses. The first is that women have a moral right (i.e., a right grounded in *moral* principles) to reproductive privacy that is primarily grounded in the special interest that women have in pregnancy and childbirth decisions. Since, as is evident, pregnancy can have a host of significant effects on a woman's physical, psychological, and financial health, it is morally problematic for the state in most circum-

stances to coercively interfere with a woman's decision to have—or not to have—a child. Accordingly, women have a moral right to reproductive privacy that, other things being equal, entitles women to freedom from coercive state interference in a woman's reproductive decisions (e.g., the decision to obtain and use contraceptives).

The second is a claim about the moral status of fetuses during a specified period. According to this view, the fetus is not a "moral person" during the relevant stage of pregnancy. It is important to distinguish moral personhood from genetic personhood. While the latter is a purely descriptive category concerned with whether the fetus is biologically human, the latter refers to a moral status. In particular, a moral person has a full set of fundamental moral rights, which would include most notably the right to life—though some of these cannot be exercised by even an infant, much less a fetus, and must be exercised on its behalf by some other party.

Choice advocates have offered a number of theories of personhood (i.e., theories that purport to explain the necessary and sufficient conditions for having the special status of being a "moral person") that deny the pro-life position that the fetus is a person from the moment of conception. Some theorists argue that the fetus does not have this moral status until viability, potential independence from the mother being thought to be a necessary condition for personhood. Some have argued that the fetus does not have this status until consciousness begins. Yet others have argued that the fetus cannot be a person until brain activity begins in the brainstem.

In any event, the pro-choice position is typically defended as follows. Since the fetus is not a person early in the pregnancy, it does not have a right to life and cannot, strictly speaking, be murdered. (Only something with the status of moral person can be murdered; nonhuman animals can be wrongly killed, but this does not rise to the level of murder). Since termination of the fetus's life does not amount to murder, it is not something that the state has moral obligation to prohibit. Since women have a right to reproductive freedom and since the state is not morally obligated to prohibit abortion for other reasons, the state is morally obligated to protect a legal right to abortions.

To understand the pro-choice position, it is absolutely crucial to note that someone who takes this position need not deny that abortion is morally wrong. Indeed, many abortion-rights advocates take the position that abortion is wrong because it terminates the life of something that will become a moral person, but that the wrongness of abortion does not rise to the level of murder—again, something that is legitimately prohibited. This is the position that is expressed by frequently heard and seemingly paradoxical remarks by choice advocates: "I don't agree with abortion, but I believe a woman has a right to choose."

It is true, of course, that some choice advocates believe that abortion is a morally neutral act (neither morally good nor morally bad), but this is a *minority* position. Most choice theorists believe that abortion is, at the very least, presumptively wrong. These choice advocates, then, agree with choice opponents that abortion is wrong but, again, disagree that the wrongness rises to the level of something, like murder, that should be legally prohibited.

Nevertheless, some choice advocates have argued that abortion ought to be permitted even if the early fetus is a moral person with a right to life. In one of the most famous and controversial papers in the applied ethics literature, Judith Jarvis Thomson argues that the mere claim that the fetus is a person does not imply that abortion is murder. She considers a situation in which one awakes to find that one has, against one's will, been plugged into a violinist. Even if the violinist needs use of one's body for nine months to survive, most people agree that it is morally permissible (and certainly not murder) to unplug from the violinist even though doing so results in the violinist's death. On Thomson's famous view, one person A must affirmatively do something to give another person B a right to use A's body—and merely having consensual intercourse, she argues, is insufficient to give the fetus a right to use the mother's body. Thus, she concludes that abortion is morally permissible and presumably ought to be legally permitted in most cases—even if it is sometimes "indecent."

See also Abortion, Right to; Liberty; Natural Law and Natural Rights; Privacy, Constitutional Right of; Pro-Life Position on Abortion

Bibliography

Boonin, David. 2002. *A Defense of Abortion*. Cambridge, MA: Cambridge University Press.

Dworkin, Ronald. 1994. *Life's Dominion*. Cambridge, MA: Harvard University Press.

Himma, Kenneth Einar. 2003. "What Philosophy of Mind Can Tell Us about the Morality of Abortion: Personhood, Materialism, and the Existence of Self." *International Journal of Applied Philosophy* 17: 73–93.

Thomson, Judith Jarvis. 1971. A Defense of Abortion. *Philosophy and Public Affairs* 1: 47.

Kenneth Einar Himma

PROFANITY

Historically, many states and cities maintained criminal prohibitions against public profanity. In *Chaplinsky v. New Hampshire* (1942), the U.S. Supreme Court indicated that such laws are constitutionally sound because profanity is beyond the pale of the First Amendment:

There are certain well-defined and narrowly limited classes of speech, the prevention and punishment of which have never been thought to raise any constitutional problem. These include the lewd and obscene, the profane, the libelous, and the insulting or "fighting" words—those which by their very utterance inflict injury or tend to incite an immediate breach of the peace. It has been well observed that such utterances are no essential part of any exposition of ideas, and are of such slight social value as a step to truth that any benefit that may be derived from them is clearly outweighed by the social interest in order and morality.

The Court's dictum in *Chaplinsky* reflected a more conservative era. In the 1960s, societal attitudes and tastes changed dramatically; profanity became more socially acceptable and certainly more prominent in the popular culture. Inevitably these societal changes impacted the way the courts viewed profanity. Thus, in *Cohen v. California* (1971), the Supreme Court invalidated the "offensive conduct" conviction of a man who entered a courthouse wearing a jacket emblazoned with the slogan "Fuck the Draft." Writing for the Court, Justice John M. Harlan (the younger) noted that "while the particular four-letter-word being litigated here is perhaps more distasteful than others of its genre, it is nevertheless often true that one man's vulgarity is another's lyric." Such a decision would have been unthinkable in the 1940s or 1950s.

Despite the Supreme Court's decision in *Cohen v. California,* a number of jurisdictions retain laws proscribing profanity. Such laws are seldom enforced and even more rarely challenged in court. A notable exception occurred in 1999 in the widely publicized case of the "cussing canoeist." When Timothy Boomer, age 25, fell out of his canoe and into the Rifle River in Michigan, he let loose a three-minute tirade of profanity. Two sheriff's deputies patrolling the river heard Boomer and ticketed him. Boomer was charged with violating an 1897 Michigan statute that provides: "Any person who shall use any indecent, immoral, obscene, vulgar or insulting language in the presence or hearing of any woman or child shall be guilty of a misdemeanor." A jury found Boomer guilty and the court sentenced him to four days' community service and imposed a $75 fine. In *People v. Boomer* (2002), the Michigan Court of Appeals reversed Boomer's conviction on vagueness grounds, noting that "it would be difficult to conceive of a statute that would be more vague…."

The *Boomer* and *Cohen* decisions, while not holding that profanity is per se protected by the First Amendment, suggest that convictions in this area are difficult to sustain on appeal. It may well be that profanity has acquired a sort of de facto constitutional protection, as evidenced by the rarity of prosecutions in this area.

John M. Scheb II

PROHIBITION (1917–1933)

The Prohibition Era, lasting from the establishment of the Eighteenth Amendment in 1917 and ending with its repeal in 1933, was as inevitable as its demise. An historical overview of the factors leading to prohibition as well as the political, constitutional, and societal factors contributing to its repeal show why the "noble experiment," so named by President Herbert Hoover in 1928, faltered and failed in the wake of unenforceable legislation, widespread noncompliance, shifting political agendas, the rise of organized crime, and constitutional dilemmas.

Temperance and prohibition of alcohol were not a new idea in the United States at the dawn of the twentieth century. Many groups and clubs had fostered the notion of abstaining from excessive alcohol consumption as far back as the American Revolution. Over time, the temperance movement curried favor among progressives as a grand experiment in social change, and later became a banner carried by conservatives in the face of perceived degeneration of moral values in the American public. A grain shortage during the First World War allowed Congress, comprised of a majority of prohibition supporters, the foothold necessary to pass a wartime prohibition on alcoholic beverages. Faced with the prospect of the return of a peacetime economy, which would include a return to free-flowing alcohol, the Republican majority in Congress proposed the Eighteenth Amendment on December 18, 1917.

While the amendment was on its way to eventual ratification, other legislation became necessary for prohibition to make a competitive bid for legitimacy. The language of the Eighteenth Amendment did not express a definition of alcoholic beverages, nor did it outlaw their consumption. The language merely prohibited the manufacture, sale, import, and export of intoxicating drink. Moreover, the amendment failed to specify a mode of enforcement or penalties and fines for violation. This was rectified by the National Prohibition Enforcement Act, better known as the Volstead Act after its author, passed by Congress on October 28, 1919.

The Volstead Act gave the Eighteenth Amendment the teeth it needed for enforcement. The act defined an alcoholic beverage as one which contained .5 percent alcohol or greater, as well as giving federal jurisdiction to the enforcement of prohibition laws. Though the act did allow for the prescription of alcohol by physicians for medical reasons and use of alcohol in religious sacraments, the Volstead Act, like the Eighteenth Amendment, did not prohibit the consumption of alcoholic beverages, but did prohibit their transport, sale, manufacture, import, and export. President Woodrow Wilson originally vetoed the Volstead Act. However, Congress overrode the veto and passed the measure into law. Because the final state had ratified the Eighteenth Amendment in January 1919, prohibition went into effect nationwide on January 17, 1920.

After the laws were in place, however, practical enforcement of prohibition became a larger challenge than anticipated. Popular acceptance of the law as justified was not extant. Thousands of speakeasies sprang up overnight to supply the public with beer and liquor, and government agencies shouldered with the responsibility of enforcing the laws found themselves overmatched in manpower and financing. Congress attempted to address the problem, beginning in 1927 with the establishment of the Bureau of Prohibition. In 1930, enforcement was transferred to the Department of Justice, directly under the supervision of the attorney general. None of these efforts appreciably changed the inability of the government to enforce prohibition. Since the legislation of prohibition was in large part a moral law, this fact was not enough to erode support for the Eighteenth Amendment. Other factors, including the rise of organized crime, individual rights violations, and religious concerns eventually changed the minds of lawmakers and the public to back away from prohibition.

With the manufacture of intoxicating drinks an illegal enterprise, organized crime became rampant in relation to prohibition. Huge amounts of money were available for those with the will, resolve, and power to flaunt the law for profit. In the face of organized crime syndicates protecting their investment with any force necessary, gun ownership became a hot-button issue. As a result of the struggle to enforce prohibition, gun laws were enacted for the first time on American soil. This sparked debate over the Second Amendment.

As the warrantless search and seizures necessary for enforcement of the Volstead Act came under fire by those interested in maintaining the civil liberties guaranteed under the Constitution, the Fourth Amendment became a focal point for conflict. While the government supported the idea of prohibition, authorities became frustrated that the same governmental body would not allow the measures deemed necessary for effective enforcement. The government refused to bend the rules for authorities, fearing intrusion into the private lives of innocent citizens. This impasse further eroded support for prohibition.

Additionally, the First Amendment was challenged as Roman Catholics argued that prohibition enacted a restraint on religious liberties. Since the proponents of prohibition were largely Protestant, Catholics argued that they were being singled out by Congress, and that the law deprived them of free exercise of their religious rights, despite the fact the wine for sacraments was omitted from prosecution. Catholics felt like they were being relegated to second class status due to their religious customs.

Due to the constitutional challenges posed by prohibition, coupled with the obvious sense of failure to effectively enforce the law and the explosion of organized crime, support for prohibition dwindled throughout the twenties and even shifted towards repealing the Eighteenth Amendment. It became obvious to most, even those in favor of prohibition, that the steps necessary to enforce the laws would irreparably damage the American tradition of individual liberty.

A Democratic majority, largely opposed to prohibition, was elected to Congress in 1932, signaling a political shift into what would become the New Deal Era. By February 1933, an amendment to repeal prohibition had been approved by Congress. Although Congress softened the Volstead Act by permitting the sale of 3.2 percent alcohol beer and wine, special ratifying conventions approved the Twenty-First Amendment repealing the Eighteenth in December 1933, thereby voiding both the Eighteenth Amendment and the Volstead Act.

Though the federal prohibition era came to a close in 1933, it remained within state jurisdictions to make their own laws regarding alcohol sale, distribution, and age limit. Many states, particularly those in the South, did just that for decades. Mississippi became the last state to abolish statewide prohibition laws in 1966. While many local areas still remain dry to this day in the United States, it is largely only a matter of convenience, as those looking for an intoxicating drink merely need drive across a county line to obtain legal purchase of such a beverage. Federal incentives, such as road monies, have encouraged all states to raise their legal drinking age to 21.

The road of prohibition has come full circle in the United States, all within the twentieth century. The temperance movement, espousing moderation and then abstention of alcohol, led to federal laws and a constitutional amendment. However, as organized crime increased with the new market in alcohol, enforcement of laws became impossible. Constitutional conflicts arose over the viability of prohibition, and a changing political landscape in the form of Roosevelt's New Deal Era lead to the repeal of the Eighteenth Amendment and the end of prohibition. While many remain opposed to the consumption of alcohol today, a more moderate climate is found that harkens back to the early temperance movements with groups such as Mothers Against Drunk Driving and Alcoholics Anonymous, warnings on advertisements, and the national alcoholism awareness campaigns espousing personal responsibility.

See also Catholicism and Anti-Catholicism; First Amendment; Fourth Amendment; Free Exercise Clause; The New Deal; Religion, Freedom of; Roosevelt, Franklin D.; Second Amendment; U.S. Department of Justice

Bibliography

Asbury, Herbert. 1950. *The Great Illusion: An Informal History of Prohibition.* New York: Doubleday.

Behr, Edward. 1996. *Prohibition: 13 Years that Changed America.* New York: Arcade.

Clark, Norman H. 1976. *Deliver Us from Evil: An Interpretation of American Prohibition.* New York: W.W. Norton.

Rumbarger, John J. 1989. *Profits, Power, and Prohibition: Alcohol Reform and the Industrializing of America 1800–1930.* Albany: State University of New York.

Sinclair, Andrew. 1962. *Prohibition: The Era of Excess.* Boston: Little, Brown.

A. J. Lepley

PRO-LIFE MOVEMENT

The pro-life movement is a network of activists and organizations dedicated to protecting the right to life, as they see it, from abortion, euthanasia, doctor-assisted suicide, and more recently stem-cell research. The movement, which has considerable grassroots support among Evangelical Christians and Roman Catholics, is connected ideologically and politically to the Religious Right and has strong influence within the Republican Party.

The movement embraces a number of organized groups, such as the National Right to Life Committee, Operation Rescue, and Rescue America. The National Right to Life Committee is a conventional interest group, committed to lobbying, litigation, and influencing elections. Rescue America and Operation Rescue are direct-action groups that picket and sometimes blockade abortion clinics. Critics charge that these groups harass women going to clinics seeking abortions and try to intimidate doctors and other clinic personnel. For its part, Operation Rescue argues that its actions are specifically protected by the First Amendment. Those on the other side of the issue believe that such actions constitute an interference with a woman's constitutional right to obtain an abortion.

In March 1993, the nation was shocked when Dr. David Gunn was shot and killed by an antiabortion protester outside a clinic in Pensacola, Florida. Since then there have been at least five murders of abortion providers and numerous instances in which abortion clinics have been bombed or vandalized, clinic staff members and doctors have been harassed, and women seeking abortions have been confronted. Indeed, antiabortion activities have been successful in closing down many abortion clinics throughout the country. Although most people on both sides of the abortion issue deplore the violence that has infected the struggle over abortion rights, the very nature of the issue increases the likelihood that protest will become violent.

In *Bray v. Alexandria Women's Health Clinic* (1993), the U.S. Supreme Court held that the Civil Rights Act of 1871 could not be used to prevent abortion protesters from blocking access to clinics. This, among other things, led Congress to enact the Freedom of Access to Clinics Entrances (FACE) Act of 1994, which prohibits the use or threat of force or physical obstruction for the purpose of injuring, intimidating, or interfering with a person seeking to obtain or provide reproductive health services. Although critics claim that FACE interferes with expressive freedoms protected by the First Amendment, a number of federal appeals courts have upheld the statute against constitutional challenges. The courts have held that FACE applies not to expressive conduct, but only to conduct that is not protected by the First Amendment (threats, assault, trespass, vandalism, etc.).

FACE also contains criminal sanctions. Although the number of criminal prosecutions and civil suits brought by the Department of Justice (DOJ) has been relatively small, the impact of DOJ's enforcement efforts appears to have been fairly appreciable. A report issued in 2000 by the Feminist Majority Foundation claimed that in 1994, 52 percent of abortion clinics were experiencing "severe violence" and that, as the result of FACE, the proportion declined to 20 percent in 1999.

In numerous cases courts have issued injunctions to regulate the time, place, and manner of anti-abortion protests. The U.S. Supreme Court has reviewed such restrictions in two important cases. In *Madsen v. Women's Health Center* (1994) the Court reviewed a Florida court's injunction that prohibited anti-abortion protesters from coming within a 36-foot buffer zone around the entrances

to an abortion clinic. The injunction also banned "singing, chanting, whistling, shouting, yelling, use of bullhorns, auto horns, sound amplification equipment or other sounds or images observable to or within earshot of the patients inside the clinic" between the hours of 7:30 a.m. and noon on Mondays through Saturdays. Writing for the Court in *Madsen,* Chief Justice William H. Rehnquist concluded that the 36-foot buffer zone "burdens no more speech than necessary to accomplish the governmental interest at stake." Rehnquist noted the state's interests in ensuring public safety and order, promoting the free flow of traffic along streets and sidewalks, protecting a woman's freedom to seek abortion and other pregnancy-related services, and protecting the property rights of all citizens. The Court also upheld the noise restrictions contained in the injunction, noting that "the First Amendment does not demand that patients at a medical facility undertake Herculean efforts to escape the cacophony of political protests." But the Court invalidated other parts of the injunction, holding that the state judge had gone too far in limiting expression. Six years later, in *Schenck v. Pro-Choice Network* (1997), the Court applied its *Madsen* rationale in upholding an injunction designed to keep demonstrators at least 15 feet from the doorways and driveways of clinics. Consistent with *Madsen,* the Court, however, struck down a provision of the injunction creating a "floating buffer zone" around clients and staff entering and exiting abortion clinics.

The Human Life Amendment

In President Ronald Reagan, the pro-life movement had a strong ally in the White House. Speaking at the Conservative Political Action Conference on February 26, 1982, President Reagan said, "We must with calmness and resolve help the vast majority of our fellow Americans understand that the more than one and one-half million abortions performed in America in 1980 amount to a great moral evil, an assault on the sacredness of human life." Throughout his presidency, Reagan repeatedly called for a "Human Life Amendment" to the Constitution. Since 1973, more than 300 such proposals have been introduced into Congress, but only once did such a measure come close to passage. In 1983, the Hatch-Eagleton Human Life Amendment, which stated that "[t]he right to an abortion is not secured by this Constitution," failed to pass the Senate by only one vote. Since 1983, the prospects for a Human Life Amendment have faded considerably. Amending the U.S. Constitution is extraordinarily difficult and requires a strong national consensus, which clearly does not exist with respect to abortion.

The Controversy Over Stem-Cell Research

In 2001, the pro-life movement focused on a new issue—stem-cell research. Pro-life activists opposed the use of stem cells obtained from human embryos, as they regard the destruction of any human embryo to be tantamount to homicide. In August 2001 President George W. Bush issued an executive order limiting the use of federal funds to support research in this area to the 78 embryonic stem cell lines then in existence. Opponents of the order insisted that new stem cell lines had to be created in order for research to progress. Stem cell research again became a national issue during the 2004 campaign as candidate John Kerry (as well as a number of celebrities) criticized President Bush's stand on the issue. Former First Lady Nancy Reagan also brought attention to the issue after the death of former President Ronald Reagan from Alzheimer's Disease; an ailment, it is argued, that could potentially be treated as a result of stem cell research.

Opposition to the Right to Die

One can argue that the right to life, assuming it belongs to the individual, implies the right to choose death through euthanasia or even suicide. The pro-life movement has been staunchly opposed to efforts to legalize euthanasia or doctor-assisted suicide. Sometimes their opposition to such measures has been expressed in terms of a desire to protect especially vulnerable persons from victimization by others whose motivations are questionable. But, ultimately, most in the pro-life movement

do not believe that individuals should have the right to cause or hasten their own death, even to escape pain and suffering. In their view, control over life and death should be left to God.

See also Abortion, Right to; Assembly, Freedom of; Catholicism and Anti-Catholicism; Conservatism; Doctor-Assisted Suicide; First Amendment; Freedom of Access to Clinic Entrances Act (FACE); Interest Groups; Pro-Choice Position on Abortion; Pro-Life Position on Abortion; Rehnquist, William H.; Religious Right; Right to Die; *Roe v. Wade* (1973); Speech/Conduct Distinction; Speech, Freedom of; Time, Place and Manner Regulations

Bibliography

Bader, Eleanor J., and Patricia Baird-Windle. 2001. *Targets of Hatred: Antiabortion Terrorism*. New York: Palgrave.

Gorney, Cynthia. 1998. *Articles of Faith: A Frontline History of the Abortion Wars*. New York: Simon and Schuster.

Wagner, Teresa R. 2003. *Back to the Drawing Board: The Future of the Pro-Life Movement*. St. Augustine's Press.

John M. Scheb II

PRO-LIFE POSITION ON ABORTION

The passionately contested abortion issue is principally an issue about whether and under what circumstances the law should permit a woman, in consultation with her physician, to obtain an abortion. Abortion-rights advocates (or "pro-choice" advocates) believe that the law should allow abortion during at least the early to middle stages of pregnancy, and some believe access to abortion should be a fundamental right. Abortion-rights opponents (or "pro-life" advocates) believe that abortion should be legally prohibited—indeed, criminalized—from the moment of conception.

Pro-life advocates disagree about whether there should be any exceptions to the legal prohibition on abortion. The most stringent pro-life position holds that abortion should never be permitted. A more moderate position holds that abortion should be permitted only when necessary to save the life of the mother. The most modest position holds that, in addition to these exceptions, abortion should be permitted to terminate pregnancies that result from rape or incest.

The view that abortion should be legally prohibited is usually (but not always) grounded in the claim that the fetus is a *moral person* from the moment of conception with a right to life. Since, according to this reasoning, the fetus is innocent of any wrongdoing, abortion violates the fetus's right to life (unless justified under some exception such as an exception to save the life of the mother) and is hence *murder*—something the state is morally obligated to prohibit by law.

The idea that the fetus is a moral person from the moment of conception is usually grounded in one of two views about personhood. According to the first, moral personhood begins at the moment of ensoulment (i.e., the moment the fetus acquires a human soul)—personhood being conceived as a causal composite of living human body and human soul. Since, on this largely religious view, ensoulment occurs at the moment of conception, the fetus is a moral person from the moment of conception.

According to the second position, every genetic person (i.e., living being with human DNA) is a moral person. Since the fetus is a genetic person from the moment of conception, it is a moral person from the moment of conception. This second position is frequently justified in explicitly religious terms: since God loves all living human beings, all have the special moral status associated with personhood and thus have an inalienable moral right to life. But this position need not be justified in religious terms. Some proponents (including those who deny the existence of souls) argue that simply being alive with human DNA is sufficient, without recourse to other considerations, to confer moral personhood on a being.

The view that abortion should be generally prohibited is sometimes grounded in the weaker position that we cannot justifiably rule out the possibility that the fetus is a moral person from the moment of conception. Since, according to this view, it follows

that we cannot justifiably rule out the possibility that abortion violates a right to life and hence constitutes murder, abortion should be legally prohibited. It is worth noting that some pro-life persons who take this position also oppose the death penalty on the ground that the state cannot justifiably rule out the possibility of executing an innocent person.

Intriguingly, some pro-life advocates attempt to justify criminalizing abortion without recourse to the position that the fetus is a moral person from the moment of conception. Marquis (1989) argues that abortion amounts to murder, regardless of whether the fetus is a person, because it deprives the fetus of a "future like ours." According to Marquis, what makes murder the gravest of moral wrongs is that it deprives a living human being of future enjoyment of the goods of a human life, which include, among other things, friendship, love, sex, knowledge, and aesthetic enjoyment—all the goods that make a human life worth living. Since abortion equally deprives a fetus of future enjoyment of all the goods that make a human life worth living, it is as grave a moral wrong as any other murder. Accordingly, Marquis concludes that the abortion issue does not turn on when the fetus becomes a moral person: abortion should generally be prohibited as murder from the moment of conception.

It is important to realize that the pro-life position is consistent with the idea that a woman has a morally protected interest, other things being equal, in reproductive privacy or autonomy (i.e., in being free from state interference with reproductive decisions). However, a pro-life advocate who takes this position would argue that while such an interest might imply that the state should allow access to contraceptives, it does not imply that the state should allow access to abortion because the mother's interest in reproductive privacy is outweighed by the moral wrong that is involved in killing a fetus—regardless of whether it is a person or simply a potential person with "a future like ours."

See also Abortion, Right to; Natural Law and Natural Rights; Privacy, Constitutional Right of; Pro-Choice Position on Abortion

Bibliography

Bennett, Belinda, ed. 2004. *Abortion*. Burlington, VA: Ashgate Publishing.

Brody, Baruch. 1974. *Abortion and the Sanctity of Human Life*. Cambridge, MA: MIT Press.

Marquis, Dan. 1989. "Why Abortion is Immoral." *Journal of Philosophy* 84: 183.

Kenneth Einar Himma

PROPERTY RIGHTS

In his *Second Treatise of Government* (1690), John Locke observed, "The great and chief end ... of Men's uniting into Commonwealths, and putting themselves under Government, is the preservation of their property." Certainly many of the founders of the American Republic agreed with Locke. In *The Federalist* No. 54 (1788), James Madison wrote, "Government is instituted no less for the protection of the property than of the persons of individuals." Writing in the *National Gazette* in March 1792, Madison defined a "just government" as one "which impartially secures to every man, whatever is his own."

The founders viewed private property as one of the natural rights of man and sought to protect property rights through the rule of law. The Framers of the U.S. Constitution sought to protect property rights by limiting the power of state legislatures to enact laws "impairing the Obligation of Contracts" (see Article I, §10, paragraph 1). The Fifth Amendment, ratified in 1791 as part of the Bill of Rights, provided that "private property [shall not] be taken for public use, without just compensation." Moreover, the Fifth Amendment prohibited the national government from depriving persons of property without "due process of law."

Private property is a value deeply ingrained in the American political culture. In the popular mindset, private property is closely associated with liberty, privacy, and personal autonomy. While many intellectuals on the political left downplay the linkage between private property and other freedoms, the Supreme Court has recognized the connection. In *Lynch v. Household Finance Corp.* (1972), the Court observed:

The right to enjoy property without lawful deprivation ... is in truth a personal right.... In fact, a fundamental interdependence exists between the personal right to liberty and the personal right in property. Neither could have meaning without the other. That rights in property are basic civil rights has long been recognized.

In his celebrated *Commentaries on the Laws of England*, William Blackstone wrote that the right of property "consists in the free use, enjoyment and disposal of all acquisitions, without any control or diminution, save only by the laws of the land." In the early days of the Republic, there was little demand for government to enact laws restricting the use of private property. But in the wake of the Industrial Revolution, the public came to demand government intervention into the economic realm to protect the interests of farmers, workers, consumers, and other afflicted segments of society. In the twentieth century the local, state, and national governments enacted numerous measures restricting the acquisition, use, and transfer of private property. Through zoning ordinances, building codes, antitrust laws, environmental regulation, civil rights statutes, and many other types of enactments, government today limits property rights in order to promote collective interests. And through an expanded definition of *public use,* government now exercises broad powers of eminent domain—taking private land for purposes deemed worthwhile by the people's elected representatives.

The Supreme Court long ago accepted the idea of legal restrictions on property rights, as seen in the following excerpt from the majority opinion in *Village of Euclid v. Ambler Realty Co.* (1926), where the Court upheld the power of local governments to regulate land use:

Regulations, the wisdom, necessity, and validity of which, as applied to existing conditions, are so apparent that they are now uniformly sustained, a century ago, or even half a century ago, probably would have been rejected as arbitrary and oppressive. Such regulations are sustained, under the complex conditions of our day, for reasons analogous to those which justify traffic regulations, which, before the advent of automobiles and rapid transit street railways, would have been condemned as fatally arbitrary and unreasonable. And in this there is no inconsistency, for, while the meaning of constitutional guaranties never varies, the scope of their application must expand or contract to meet the new and different conditions which are constantly coming within the field of their operation. In a changing world it is impossible that it should be otherwise.

While the constitutional issues involving property rights are by and large settled, the degree to which government should interfere with private property is a continuing source of political conflict in this country. Indeed, this is one of the principal cleavages between conservatives (and Republicans), who typically champion private property and the free enterprise system, and liberals (and Democrats), who tend to argue for government regulation to promote the public interest. However, these political arguments tend to be over the degree to which government should regulate private property, not whether government possesses such authority. Few today see property rights as absolute, although libertarians come closest to that view.

See also Conservatism; Contracts Clause; Economic Freedom; Just Compensation Clause; Liberalism; Libertarianism; Liberty; Locke, John; Madison, James; Natural Law and Natural Rights; Public Use Clause; Zoning

Bibliography

Anderson, Terry, and Fred S. McChesney, eds. 2003. *Property Rights: Cooperation, Conflict and Law.* Princeton, NJ: Princeton University Press.

John M. Scheb II

PSIR. *See* Presentence Investigation Reports

PUBLIC ACCOMMODATION, PLACES OF

A place of public accommodation is a business that opens its doors to the general public. This category of businesses includes restaurants, bars, hotels, theaters, amusement parks, retail stores, shopping malls, and many other types of businesses. Such businesses are subject to various legal restrictions, most notably labor laws and regulations affecting

the sale of alcohol and the preparation of food. Historically, these businesses were free to discriminate among their patrons on the basis of race, gender, or any other characteristic. In the modern era, places of public accommodation became the subject of civil rights laws designed to combat such discrimination.

The earliest congressional attempt to prohibit racial discrimination by places of public accommodation was the Civil Rights Act of 1875, passed during Reconstruction and based on Section 5 of the Fourteenth Amendment. This key provision gives Congress the power to enact "appropriate legislation" in the civil rights field. In the Civil Rights Cases of 1883, however, the U.S. Supreme Court struck down the principal provisions of the 1875 law, holding that the Fourteenth Amendment limits Congressional action to the prohibition of official, state-sponsored discrimination, as distinct from discrimination practiced by private establishments. This reading of the Constitution recognized an implicit private right to discriminate against individuals throughout the broad field of public accommodations, thus severely limiting the impact of the Fourteenth Amendment. It would be 80 years until Congress would again attempt to pass legislation outlawing such discrimination.

In the late nineteenth century, states began to enact statutes prohibiting racial discrimination in public accommodations. By 1964, 32 states had passed laws of this kind. But in the South, there were no such laws, and many restaurants, hotels, theaters, and other businesses refused service to African Americans or segregated them from other customers. Because Southern state legislatures were unwilling to address this discrimination, congressional action would be required.

Title II of the Civil Rights Act of 1964 prohibited racial discrimination by places of public accommodation that affect interstate commerce. In enacting Title II, Congress relied on its broad powers under the Commerce Clause of Article I, Section 8 of the Constitution. And in *Heart of Atlanta Motel v. United States* (1964), the Supreme Court unanimously upheld this enactment as a proper exercise of the commerce power. Because the Heart of Atlanta Motel served primarily interstate travelers, the Court ruled that its racially restrictive practices could impede the free flow of interstate commerce and could therefore be appropriately regulated by Congress. In *Katzenbach v. McClung* (1964), the Court went even further by recognizing the power of Congress under the Commerce Clause to bar racial discrimination in a restaurant patronized almost entirely by local customers. The Court found a sufficient connection with interstate commerce in the purchase of food and equipment from out-of-state sources.

In 1990, Congress enacted another landmark measure affecting access to public accommodations. Title III of the Americans with Disabilities Act provides, "No individual shall be discriminated against on the basis of disability in the full and equal enjoyment of the goods, services, facilities, privileges, advantages, or accommodations of any place of public accommodation." The statute defines "discrimination" as a "failure to make reasonable modifications in policies, practices or procedures" or "a failure to remove architectural barriers, and communication barriers." The ADA requires that all new construction of places of public accommodation be fully accessible to persons with disabilities.

States have enacted their own statutes affecting public accommodations, and many of them go beyond the requirements of federal law. For example, Section 106.52 of the Wisconsin Statutes prohibits denial of service or unequal treatment in service on the basis of sex, race, color, creed, disability, sexual orientation, national origin, or ancestry. Similarly, the King County, Washington Public Accommodations Ordinance (K.C.C. 12.22) forbids discrimination on the basis of sexual orientation. Federal law does not currently prohibit discrimination on the basis of sexual orientation.

In some states, agencies and courts have defined the term "public accommodation" very expansively to attack discrimination in organizations not traditionally considered to be places of public accommodation. For example, in *Roberts v. United States*

Jaycees (1984) the Supreme Court upheld a Minnesota law that was interpreted to require a civic organization to accept women as full members. Similarly, in *Rotary International v. Rotary Club of Duarte* (1987), the Court permitted the state of California, which characterized the Rotary Club as a "business establishment," to force that club to accept women as members. Likewise, in *New York Club Association v. City of New York* (1988), the Court upheld a New York City ordinance that required certain all-male social clubs to admit women.

On the other hand, in *Hurley v. Irish-American Gay, Lesbian and Bisexual Group of Boston* (1995), the Court held that the state of Massachusetts could not prohibit the organizers of the annual St. Patrick's Day parade from excluding a gay pride group that wished to participate in the parade. A state court had ruled that gay groups could not be excluded under Massachusetts' public accommodations statute. The Supreme Court reversed, holding that the First Amendment freedom of association barred the state from requiring the parade's organizers to allow participation by the gay and lesbian group. In *Boy Scouts of America v. Dale* (2000), the Supreme Court considered a more difficult case of discrimination on the basis of sexual orientation. The New Jersey Supreme Court had ruled that the Boy Scouts of America was covered by the New Jersey public accommodation law and thus could not deny membership to homosexual males. The U.S. Supreme Court held, however, that this was a "severe intrusion on the Boy Scouts' rights to freedom of expressive association." Thus, there are limits to the power of a state or local government to redefine organizations as public accommodations for the purpose of making them subject to antidiscrimination laws.

An emerging legal issue is whether an Internet service provider such as AOL or a commercial Web site such as Amazon.com is a place of public accommodation. If it is, then it is subject to ADA accessibility requirements. In 2002, a group called Access Now filed suit against Southwest Airlines, charging that its Web site denied access to the visually impaired. The gravamen of the complaint was that because the Southwest Web site was not compatible with the accessibility software available to the visually impaired, those users were unfairly denied the opportunity to purchase low-fare airline tickets and earn other benefits available only through the Internet. In *Access Now v. Southwest Airlines* (2002), a federal judge dismissed the case after finding that Web sites are outside the scope of the public accommodation provisions of the ADA, which apply only to "specific, physical, concrete space[s]." However, this decision is unlikely to be the last word on the matter, and Congress can, if it is so inclined, amend the ADA to apply to "virtual" public accommodations as well as physical ones.

See also Association, Freedom of; *Boy Scouts of America v. Dale* (2000); Civil Rights Act of 1964; Disabilities, Rights of Persons with; Discrimination; Economic Freedom; First Amendment; *Heart of Atlanta Motel v. United States* (1964); *Katzenbach v. McClung* (1964); Sexual Orientation, Discrimination Based on

Bibliography

Cortner, Richard C. 2001. *Civil Rights and Public Accommodations*. Lawrence: University Press of Kansas.

Otis H. Stephens, Jr. and John M. Scheb II

PUBLIC DEFENDER. *See* Counsel, Right to

PUBLIC EDUCATION, RIGHT TO

The constitutional right to a public education has been debated at both the federal and state levels of government. To understand these developments one must be familiar with the history of public support for education in the United States, which harkens back to the colonial era. Attitudes toward education in the New England colonies had a profound impact on later educational development in the United States. The Puritans were instrumental in the enactment of legislation providing for publicly supported schools as early as 1647. There was less interest in education in the Middle Colonies, although Latin grammar schools and certain types of vocational schools were established. Southern colonies showed the least interest because wealthy Southerners could send their sons back to England or provide private tutors. There was also a widespread belief that education was a private matter and therefore taxes which resulted in one man paying for the education of another's sons were unthinkable.

During the Revolutionary War the development of public education came to a halt. After the war, there were more pressing concerns than public education. Chief among them was the Constitution. Notably absent from the Constitution was any provision regarding public education. This omission is not surprising since education was still in many areas primarily a concern of the church. The First and Tenth Amendments ultimately changed that. The First Amendment's prohibition on the establishment of religion eventually ended public taxation for religious purposes, thereby laying the foundation for secular public schools. According to the Tenth Amendment any "powers not delegated to the United States by the Constitution, nor prohibited by it to the States, are reserved to the States respectively…" Control of education is one of these powers; therefore, each state is responsible for its own education system.

The role that the states have played has changed over time. Initially local school districts were given great latitude regarding public education. The states began to exert more control particularly in the 1980s as the release of such national reports as *A Nation at Risk,* issued in 1983, warned that the national economy could be jeopardized by a "mediocre" education system. Throughout the 1980s state legislatures introduced comprehensive reforms designed to improve the quality of education. The growth of the state role in education was also spurred by an inherent flaw of local control: the inability to equitably distribute resources. Schools were funded through revenue produced from property taxes. Local districts were limited in how much funding could be raised depending on the value of the property within the district. This resulted in funding disparities between districts. Little action was taken to change these funding schemes until lawsuits were filed arguing for equitable funding. It has been primarily in the context of these lawsuits that education rights have been defined.

Education finance litigation has proceeded in three waves. The first wave consisted of both state and federal court rulings that attempted to define education rights. As these courts reached differing conclusions concerning the extent to which the Constitution protected education rights, the U.S. Supreme Court ultimately settled the issue. In *San Antonio Independent School District v. Rodriguez* (1973), the Court reviewed a Texas funding scheme that resulted in funding disparities. Justice Lewis Powell's majority opinion asserted that there was no fundamental right to a public education because the Constitution contained no such guarantee and that the funding scheme did not work to the disadvantage of a particular class since some school children from poor families resided in property-rich districts. Powell also argued that lower levels of funding would not necessarily result in a lower quality of education. Because a fundamental right was not infringed by the funding scheme, the Court did not apply the highest standard of review, strict scrutiny, but rather the lowest standard, the rational basis test. The Court found that the Texas funding scheme furthered the legitimate state interest of fostering local participation in public education and it provided every child with a basic education; therefore, there was no violation of the Equal Protection Clause.

In dissent, Justice William Brennan argued that strict scrutiny should have been applied since education was linked to the meaningful exercise of other rights, such as voting. Justice Byron White argued that the Texas scheme failed the rational basis test because in reality property-poor districts had little control due to their inability to collect additional revenue. Justice Thurgood Marshall chastised the majority for backing away from the Court's commitment to equality of educational opportunity and echoed Brennan's rationale regarding strict scrutiny.

In the wake of *Rodriguez,* the issues of funding equity and education rights were left to state courts.

The second wave of litigation began shortly after the *Rodriguez* decision with a New Jersey case, *Robinson v. Cahill* (1973). The New Jersey Supreme Court invalidated the state's funding scheme and spawned a wave of cases in which state supreme courts relied on state equal protection clauses to invalidate funding schemes. The third wave of litigation began in 1989 with the Kentucky Supreme Court's decision in *Rose v. Council* in which it invalidated the entire system of common schools on the basis of the Kentucky Constitution's education clause. Several states have followed that line of constitutional interpretation and have expanded the right to an education in their respective states. Because these rulings are based entirely on state constitutions, federal courts may not review them.

In the only other U.S. Supreme Court ruling on the right to public education and school funding, *Plyler v. Doe* (1982), the Court invalidated a Texas law which withheld from local school districts any state funds for the education of illegal aliens and which authorized local school districts to deny enrollment to such children. Rather than apply the rational basis test, however, the Court employed a higher level of scrutiny, intermediate scrutiny, because education was more important than other social welfare benefits. The dissenters were critical of this standard of review because it had been established in *Rodriguez* that education was not a fundamental right. In 1988 the Court specifically refused to extend the rationale articulated in *Plyler v. Doe* beyond its unique circumstances in *Kadrmas v. Dickinson Public Schools* (1988). These decisions have left the definition of education rights almost exclusively to the states.

See also Establishment Clause; New Judicial Federalism; *Pierce v. Society of Sisters* (1925); Tenth Amendment; *Tinker v. Des Moines Independent Community School District* (1967)

Bibliography

Burrup, Percy, Vern Brimley, and Rulon Garfield. 1988. *Financing Education in a Climate of Change.* 4th ed. Boston: Allyn and Bacon.

Cubberly, Ellwood. 1919. *Public Education in the United States.* Boston: Houghton Mifflin.

Kara E. Stooksbury

PUBLIC EDUCATION, SEGREGATION IN. *See* Segregation in Public Education

PUBLIC EMPLOYEES, CONSTITUTIONAL RIGHTS OF

Because public employees are employed by government, rather than by private enterprise, they enjoy certain rights with respect to their employer that would not be available to employees in the private sector. Unlike private employers, government action is constrained by constitutional protections, such as those found in the First, Fourth, Fifth, and Fourteenth Amendments to the United States Constitution. Both state and federal employers are subject to these constraints (states via the Fourteenth Amendment), and state governments are also subject to protections of individual rights within their own state constitutions. That is not to say that employees in the private sector do not have significant rights, but those rights are often based on statutory law, such as Title VII of the Civil Rights Act of 1964 and similar antidiscrimination laws enacted by state and local governments.

First Amendment Rights

Employees in both the public and private sector may find that their employers impose limitations on their freedom of speech. Government employees retain First Amendment rights, but a governmental employer may nevertheless restrain certain types of speech even when such governmental restraints would be unconstitutional if applied to the general public. In particular, the U.S. Supreme Court has recognized employees' rights to speak on matters of "public concern," which typically involve issues related to government policies that are of interest to the general public (*Connick v. Myers,* 1983).

Government employees are uniquely qualified to comment on such topics and their employment may not be adversely affected when they do so. Thus, for example, the Court has held it impermissible for

a school district to dismiss a teacher because she openly criticized the Board of Education for its allocation of funds between athletics and academics. In *Pickering v. Board of Education* (1968), the Court established a balancing test for determining whether employee speech should be protected under the First Amendment, which requires courts to balance the interests of the employee in commenting upon matters of public concern against the interests of the government in promoting the efficiency of the public services it performs through its employees.

Where an employee's speech fails to raise matters of public concern, it may still be protected under the First Amendment in certain circumstances where such speech is not detrimental to the government employer's mission and function. When government employees use their own time to speak or write on topics unrelated to their employment, the employer may restrict such speech only on the basis of a justification that is "far stronger than mere speculation" that the speech would compromise the functioning of the government office (*United States v. Treasury Employees,* 1995). In such cases, the government bears a heavy burden to demonstrate that the challenged speech threatens immediate workplace disruption—a burden which is difficult for the government to meet if the speech is unrelated to the employee's position in the government service and does not infringe on his employer's mission or function. In *U.S. v. Treasury Employees,* for example, the Court held that the federal government could not impose certain monetary limitations on outside earnings from speaking or writing on a class of federal employees because the government had shown no justification for the outside salary limitations.

Due Process Protections

The Due Process Clause of the Fifth and Fourteenth Amendments prohibit government from depriving any individual of life, liberty, or property without due process of law. The Supreme Court has held that, where some restrictions exist on a manager's discretion to terminate or otherwise adversely affect a public employee's employment, a property interest exists in that employment, since in such circumstances the employee has more than a "unilateral expectation" that the employment will continue. Thus, for example, where an employee may be terminated only for "misfeasance, malfeasance or nonfeasance," he enjoys a property interest in his position and may not be terminated without due process of law (*Cleveland Board of Education v. Loudermill,* 1985). Another example includes situations in which a government employee is protected by an employment contract that ensures continued employment unless he or she engages in inappropriate action that is grounds for termination or demotion. Where an employee serves completely "at will"—that is, where no statutory, regulatory, or contractual restrictions exist to constrain managerial discretion regarding the conditions of employment—no property interest arises with respect to his position.

Where a property right does exist, the employee may not be terminated without "due process of law." In defining the process due, the Supreme Court has held that the employee is entitled to meaningful notification of the adverse employment and a reasonable opportunity to present his version of events prior to the actual termination or other adverse employment action. Such a hearing need not constitute a full evidentiary hearing with lawyers and witnesses. Rather, the employee need only be given information about the reasons for the adverse employment action and an opportunity to respond to that information. Following the employment action, however, due process may require a more elaborate evidentiary hearing at which the employee has rights to counsel, to cross-examine witnesses, and to a neutral decision maker (*Cleveland Board of Education v. Loudermill,* 1985).

Termination of government employment may implicate an employee's liberty interests as well. Thus, where the government terminates an employee in such a way as to limit the employee's ability to obtain future employment—such as by making false statements about the employee's shortcomings and thus undermining his reputation—it may implicate the employee's constitutional right to liberty. In *Paul v. Davis* (1976), the Supreme Court interpreted this right narrowly, however, by imposing the "stigma plus" test. To successfully argue that an adverse employment action has infringed liberty interests, the employee must show that there was a false statement that would be harmful to a person's reputation (the "stigma"), accompanied by an alteration or impairment of a right or status previously recognized by law (the "plus"). If the employee is able to make this showing, then he or she is entitled to a pretermination hearing to clear his name.

Fourth Amendment Concerns

Not only do public employees enjoy limited rights to due process and free speech in the workplace, but the Fourth Amendment also protects them from unreasonable searches and seizures in connection with their employment. In *O'Connor v. Ortega* (1987), the Supreme Court observed that "individuals do not lose Fourth Amendment rights merely because they work for the government instead of a private employer." However, the Fourth Amendment applies only where the employee has a "reasonable expectation of privacy," which must be assessed within the unique context of the employment relation. For example, an employee may have a reasonable expectation of privacy in the contents of his desk and file cabinets where the employer had established no policy or regulation discouraging employees from storing personal papers and effects in their offices (*O'Connor v. Ortega,* 1987). An employee would have no such expectation of privacy if the desk or cabinets were shared with other employees or if the employer had established a policy that office space was to be used for work purposes only and would be subject to intrusion by fellow employees or managers. Even when a reasonable expectation of privacy exists, however, the employer may conduct a search if the decision to do so is "reasonable." Whether a search is reasonable is determined by balancing the invasion of the employees' legitimate expectations of privacy against the government's need for supervision, control, and the efficient operation of the workplace.

In recent years, whether certain searches reasonably further the government's function or mission has arisen in cases involving employee urine and drug testing. Clearly, all employees have a reasonable expectation of privacy with respect to their bodily integrity, and blood, breath, and urine testing intrude in that private sphere. In the criminal context, such searches could not be accomplished absent probable cause to believe that a crime had been committed and a search warrant. Nevertheless, it may be reasonable for the government to regularly or randomly test its employees for drug or alcohol use without probable cause and a warrant when safety concerns mitigate in favor of the government's interest in a drug or alcohol-free workforce. For example, in *National Treasury Employees Union v. Von Raab* (1989), the Court upheld a drug-testing program requiring urine specimens from employees applying for Customs Service positions that involved interdiction of illegal drugs and the handling of firearms. According to the Court, "the Government's need to conduct the suspicionless searches required by the Customs program outweighs the privacy interests of employees engaged directly in drug interdiction, and of those who otherwise are required to carry firearms."

See also Bill of Rights, Incorporation of; Civil Rights Act of 1964; Drug Testing; Due Process Clauses; Due Process, Procedural; Employment Discrimination; Fifth Amendment; First Amendment; Fourteenth Amendment (1868); Fourth Amendment; Liberty; Privacy, Reasonable Expectations of; Privilege/Right Distinction; Property Rights; Speech, Freedom of

Bibliography

Arcila, Fabio, Jr. 2004. "Special Needs and Special Deference: Suspicionless Civil Searches in the Modern Regulatory State." *Administrative Law Review* 56: 1223.

Greenberg, Sanford N. 1989. "The Free Speech Rights of Public Employees." *George Washington Law Review* 57: 1281.

Singer, Craig D. 1992. "Conduct and Belief: Public Employees' First Amendment Rights to Free Expression and Political Affiliation." *University of Chicago Law Review* 59: 897.

Stefanie A. Lindquist

PUBLIC FORUM

By protecting the freedoms of speech and assembly, the First Amendment supports the right of individuals and groups to engage in expressive activities in the "public forum." As the Supreme Court said in *Perry Educational Association v. Perry Local Educators' Association* (1983), the public forum includes not only streets and parks but any property "opened for use by the public as a place for expressive activity." In *Hague v. CIO* (1939), Justice Owen Roberts observed that "[s]uch use of the streets and public places has from ancient times, been a part of the privileges, immunities, rights, and liberties of citizens."

The creation of a public forum does not require formal government action; a particular place may acquire the character of a public forum simply through use. For example, an area of a college campus that is used over the years by various groups for speeches and demonstrations with the tacit consent of the college administration becomes a de facto public forum, even though the administration never designates it as a place for assemblies and expressive activities. On the other hand, not every place open to the public constitutes a public forum. For example, in *Lloyd Corporation v. Tanner* (1972), the Supreme Court observed that a privately owned shopping center does not "lose its private character merely because the public is generally invited to use it for designated purposes.... " And not every place owned by the government qualifies as a public forum. In *Adderley v. Florida* (1966), the Supreme Court recognized that "[t]he State, no less than a private owner of property, has power to preserve the property under its control for the use to which it is lawfully dedicated." Thus, prisons, military reservations, government offices, and so forth are not available for the exercise of First Amendment rights and those who attempt to enter such premises are subject to prosecution for trespass.

The Supreme Court has identified three categories of public forum: (1) the "traditional" public forum, for example, streets and parks; (2) the "limited purpose" or state-created "semi-public" forum; and (3) public property not by tradition or designation a public forum (Tribe 1988, 987; Nowak and Rotunda 2004, 1324–25).

Restrictions on speech in the traditional public forum are subject to strict scrutiny by the courts, meaning that limitations on speech content do not offend constitutional standards if the state can demonstrate a compelling governmental interest in limiting the speech and the law limiting the speech is narrowly tailored. Reasonable time, place, and manner restrictions in these forums likewise do not offend constitutional standards so long as the restrictions are content-neutral and narrowly tailored to serve a significant governmental interest. In limited-purpose public forums, restrictions on speech are subject to the same analysis by the courts, but the state has the option to close such forums—unlike traditional public forums, there is no requirement that the state keep limited-purpose public forums open and operative indefinitely. Public property not by tradition or designation a public forum, such as the property at issue in *Adderley,* may be reserved by government for a certain purpose, and speech in these forums may be regulated so long as such regulation is reasonable and is not an attempt to suppress a certain viewpoint. Clearly restrictions of speech on property not by tradition or designation a public forum are subject to less exacting judicial review, which is to say that they are more likely to be upheld.

See also First Amendment; Kennedy, Anthony; Speech, Freedom of; Strict Scrutiny; Time, Place, and Manner Restrictions

Bibliography

Blakeman, John C. 2002. "Federal District Courts, Religious Speech, and the Public Forum: An Analysis of Litigation Patterns and Outcomes." *Journal of Church and State* 44: 93.

Casarez, Nicole B. 2000. "Public Forums, Selective Subsidies, and Shifting Standards of Viewpoint Discrimination." *Albany Law Review* 64: 501.

Kalven, Harry, Jr. 1965. "The Concept of the Public Forum: *Cox v. Louisiana.*" *Supreme Court Review* 1965: 1.

Krotoszynski, Ronald J., Jr. 1995. "Celebrating Selma: The Importance of Context in Public Forum Analysis." *Yale Law Journal* 104: 1411.

Leeper, Roy. 2000. "The Ku Klux Klan, Public Highways, and the Public Forum." *Communications and the Law* 22: 39.

McGill, Matthew D. 2000. "Unleashing the Limited Public Forum: A Modest Revision to a Dysfunctional Doctrine." *Stanford Law Review* 52: 929.

Nowak, John, and Ronald Rotunda. 2004. *Constitutional Law.* 7th ed. St. Paul, MN: Thomson/West.

Tribe, Laurence. 1988. *American Constitutional Law.* 2nd ed. New York: Foundation Press.

Otis H. Stephens, Jr., and John M. Scheb II

PUBLIC HEARING. *See* Hearing, Right to

PUBLIC NUDITY

Criminal laws in every state forbid public nudity, although certain communities have authorized "topless" or "clothing optional" beaches where the prohibition of public nudity is relaxed or inapplicable. Although the courts have never recognized that the prohibition of public nudity infringes any constitutional right, they have found that in certain contexts, nudity is entitled to protection under the First Amendment. As long as they are not obscene and do not involve child pornography, books, movies, and even stage plays featuring nudity are constitutionally protected.

A more difficult problem is posed by nude dancing in "gentleman's clubs" and other commercial establishments. Should it be treated as a form of public nudity and therefore not entitled to constitutional protection, or is it more akin to the artistic use of nudity in films and plays and therefore protected by the First Amendment?

The U.S. Supreme Court faced this issue most recently in *Erie v. Pap's A.M.* (2000). The case began when the operator of a nightclub featuring nude dancing challenged an Erie, Pennsylvania, ordinance that prohibited public nudity. The nightclub owner claimed that the ordinance infringed his First

Amendment free expression rights by prohibiting expressive conduct in the form of nude dancing. The Pennsylvania Supreme Court agreed, but the Supreme Court did not, finding the ordinance constitutional in a fractured vote.

Writing for four justices, Sandra Day O'Connor found that, since the ordinance prohibited all nudity, not just nude dancing, it was not a content-based restriction and was constitutional under the Court's intermediate scrutiny test. Justice O'Connor admitted that nude dancing is expressive conduct—though "it falls only within the outer ambit of the First Amendment's protection." The two justices who concurred in the judgment, thereby allowing the ordinance to stand, were not willing to go that far. Antonin Scalia, joined by Clarence Thomas, wrote that nude dancing could be regulated as conduct, unless there was evidence that an ordinance aimed at the dancing was aimed specifically at the "communicative character" of the dancing rather than the nudity itself.

Only Justices John Paul Stevens and Ruth Bader Ginsburg recognized that nude dancing is, indeed, expressive conduct, and regulations such as those enacted in Erie must face strict scrutiny. Discounting the Court's argument that the ban was aimed at the secondary effects of nude dancing—increased sex crimes, for example—Justice Stevens wrote that the Court held, for the first time, that such effects "may justify the total suppression of protected speech."

What seems clear from the Court's opinion in *Erie*—as well as earlier nude dancing cases (*Barnes v. Glen Theatre* [1991] and *Renton v. Playtime Theatres* [1986], for example)—is that members of the Court are willing to allow certain types of expressive conduct to be regulated, not because the conduct is not expressive, but because they do not approve of the method or content of the communication.

See also First Amendment; Ginsburg, Ruth Bader; O'Connor, Sandra Day; Obscenity and Pornography; Scalia, Antonin; Speech, Freedom of; Speech/ Conduct Distinction; Stevens, John Paul; Strict Scrutiny; Symbolic Speech; Thomas, Clarence; Time, Place, and Manner Regulations

Bibliography

Blasi, Vincent. 1992. "Six Conservatives in Search of the First Amendment: The Revealing Case of Nude Dancing." *William and Mary Law Review* 33: 611.

Goldstein, Robert J. 1971. "Topless Dancing as a Form of Expression and Communication." In *The Rhetoric of Nonverbal Communication*, ed. Haig A. Bosmajian. Glenview, IL: Scott, Foresman and Co.

Mitchell, Anne E. 2002. "Nude Dancing and First Amendment Scrutiny." *Urban Lawyer* 34: 277.

W. Wat Hopkins

PUBLIC SCHOOLS, FUNDING OF. *See* Public Education, Right to

PUBLIC SCHOOLS, SEARCHES AND SEIZURES IN

In *New Jersey v. T.L.O.* (1985), the United States Supreme Court first addressed the application of the Fourth Amendment in the school setting. The Court's ruling in *T.L.O.* firmly established the right of public school students to be free from unreasonable searches (and seizures) but it relaxed the usual probable cause standard to one of reasonable suspicion. In reaching this conclusion, the Court rejected the claim that the doctrine of *in loco parentis* relieves school authorities from the strictures of the Fourth Amendment. The Court conceded that the authority teachers and administrators exercise over students is partially justified by the doctrine of *in loco parentis,* but reasoned that teachers and school administrators are agents of the state charged with administering state educational policy. As state actors, the Fourth Amendment limits the way school officials can enforce school disciplinary and safety policies.

Although the Court held that school officials are bound by the Fourth Amendment, it added that the nature of public schooling—generally hundreds of students, sometimes thousands, brought together by compulsory education laws, supervised by teachers and administrators six or more hours a day for nine months a year—meant that students have less of an expectation of privacy than do ordinary citizens. With less of an expectation of privacy in the school setting, searches there are reasonable upon the existence of reasonable suspicion instead of the higher standard of probable cause that generally applies to searches in nonschool settings.

Determining whether reasonable suspicion exists for the search of a student or a student's possessions by school officials is a twofold inquiry: the search must be "justified at its inception" and it must be "reasonably related in scope" to the reason for the search. A search of a student is justified at its inception if school officials have reasonable grounds for suspecting that the search will uncover evidence that the student has broken the law or school rules. A search is reasonable in scope when conducted by means that are "reasonably related to the objectives of the search and [is] not excessively intrusive in light of the age and sex of the student and the nature of the infraction." By this standard, the search of the student's purse in *T.L.O.* was constitutionally permissible because school authorities had reasonable grounds for suspecting that the student had been smoking in violation of school policy and because the search of her purse might reasonably turn up evidence (cigarettes) that would tend to support the suspicion.

T.L.O. is one of three Supreme Court decisions involving students and the Fourth Amendment. The other two cases involved drug testing public school students, an issue the Court first addressed in *Vernonia School District 47J v. Acton* (1995). In this case, a school district with a pervasive drug problem among its students, particularly its student athletes, imposed a policy of random, suspicionless drug testing of all athletes. The Court upheld this policy based on the special needs exception to the Fourth Amendment's warrant requirement. Under this exception, traditional Fourth Amendment requirements are not necessary "in those exceptional circumstances in which special needs, beyond the normal need for law enforcement" make them unworkable. Therefore, the Court balances the government's special needs against the individual's privacy rights. In *Vernonia,* Justice Antonin Scalia argued that the school district had a legitimate interest in enacting this policy due to the danger that drug use

by athletes posed to their physical well-being. This interest was balanced against the limited expectation of privacy held by athletes due to the practices of communal undress and showers. The Court found that the drug testing policy was reasonable even though the searches were conducted without a warrant, probable cause, or individualized suspicion.

While the drug testing policy upheld in *Vernonia* was limited to student athletes, a drug testing policy of students involved in any extracurricular activity was challenged in *Board of Education v. Earls* (2002). The Tecumseh School district seemingly did not have a pervasive drug problem, but imposed the drug testing policy after several incidents indicating an increase in student drug use. Relying on the special needs exception, the Court upheld the policy. Justice Clarence Thomas reasoned that the school had a legitimate interest in preventing and detecting drug use among those who participated in extracurricular activities. He stated that a pervasive drug problem had never been required by the Court in order to justify suspicionless searches. Further, he emphasized that in *Vernonia,* the school's custodial role was more significant than the lower expectation of privacy of athletes; however, students' privacy interests were limited because drug testing was one of many other requirements imposed on students who participated in extracurricular activities. As in *Vernonia,* the Court found that the policy was reasonable given the importance of the state's interest.

While Supreme Court review of cases involving students and the Fourth Amendment has been limited, numerous lower courts have addressed the constitutionality of locker searches, strip searches, and the use of metal detectors and drug-sniffing dogs. Most courts that have addressed the constitutionality of locker searches have ruled that students have little to no reasonable expectation of privacy in their lockers, which means that school authorities need not possess individualized suspicion before conducting a locker search. The rationale for the conclusion that students have little to no expectation of privacy in their lockers varies, but generally focuses on one or more of the following rationales: (1) lockers are school property, not the students'; (2) school policies exist putting students on notice that lockers are not theirs but are the school's and are subject to entry at any time; (3) school authorities retain a master key or combination to open all lockers, or require students to give combinations to locks they place on the lockers to school authorities, thereby signaling to students that others will have access to the lockers; and (4) school officials routinely open lockers without notice to make repairs to them.

Because a strip search involves a high degree of intrusiveness upon a student's privacy interest, virtually all lower courts that have addressed the issue have ruled that strip searching students is not reasonable unless individualized suspicion exists. Additionally, strip searches must be conducted in a manner appropriate to the age and sex of the students searched.

The constitutionality of the use of drug-sniffing dogs depends on the object of the dog's sniff. Following Supreme Court precedent, all courts hold that a dog sniff of an inanimate object is not a search under the Fourth Amendment. Consequently, there need not be individualized suspicion before drug dogs are allowed to inspect lockers and automobiles. Lower courts are split, however, on whether reasonable or individualized suspicion must exist before a drug dog can sniff a student. In *Powers v. Plumas Unified School District* (1999), the U.S. Court of Appeals for the Ninth Circuit ruled that the level of intrusiveness upon a student's person during a dog sniff is of such a level as to require reasonable suspicion. However, in *Doe v. Renfrow* (1980), the Seventh Circuit held that students have no reasonable expectation of privacy in the air around themselves. Thus, a drug dog sniff of their persons was not a search under the Fourth Amendment.

Searching students with the aid of a metal detector appears to be an infrequently challenged procedure. Of the few jurisdictions that have addressed the issue, virtually all have ruled that individualized suspicion is unnecessary. The rationale for this conclusion is that metal detector searches are minimally intrusive in that they generally involve passing a hand-held wand over the exterior of a student's person. Given the minimal invasiveness of a metal detector, the school's interest in providing a safe learning environment has been held to outweigh a student's limited expectation of privacy.

While students are not without Fourth Amendment rights, the foregoing discussion illustrates the judiciary's exceptional deference to local communities' efforts to minimize drug use and violence in the nation's public schools.

See also Drug Testing; Drugs, War on; Fourth Amendment; *In Loco Parentis;* Privacy, Reasonable Expectations of; Probable Cause; Scalia, Antonin; Thomas, Clarence; Warrantless Searches

Bibliography

Russo, Charles J., and Ralph D. Mawdsley. 2004. *Searches, Seizures and Drug Testing Procedures: Balancing Rights and School Safety.* Horsham, Pennsylvania: LRP Publications.

Kevin Pybas

PUBLIC SUPPORT FOR CIVIL RIGHTS AND LIBERTIES

Civil rights and civil liberties claims now comprise a large part of the U.S. Supreme Court's docket and include many of the Court's best-known and most controversial rulings. At times, such as during the cold war era "red scare" of the 1940s and 1950s, American public opinion was quite opposed to legal claims by political leftists and accused communists (Murphy 1972). At that time some justices saw a hostile public opinion as pressuring the Court into decisions unfriendly to the legal positions of suspected leftists. As Justices Black and Douglas wrote in *Dennis v. U.S.* (1951): "Public opinion being what it is now, few will protest the conviction of these Communist petitioners. There is hope, however, that in calmer times, when present pressures, passions, and fears subside, this or some later Court will restore the First Amendment liberties to the high preferred place where they belong in a free society." Yet the "red scare" era of public hostility to claims for constitutional protection lasted only about a decade and includes but a handful of all the modern Supreme Court's many rulings on civil rights and civil liberties claims. This article examines public opinion support for a much larger number of civil liberties and civil rights claims since the New Deal era.

Since the origin of modern public opinion polling during the mid-1930s, pollsters have written many poll questions tapping American attitudes on civil rights and civil liberties issues in lawsuits that reached the U.S. Supreme Court. The 178 poll-to-ruling matches reported here are based on poll samples of national adults conducted at or about the time a legal dispute reached the U.S. Supreme Court. These 178 poll-to-ruling matches capture many of the highest-profile civil rights and civil liberties issues during the modern Supreme Court's history, and allow a reading of how fully public opinion has supported civil rights and civil liberties claims. For each poll-to-ruling comparison. public opinion was classified as either pro-claim, anti-claim, or (in a few cases) as unclear. The Supreme Court's ruling was also classified as either pro-claim or anti-claim.

As an example consider the Supreme Court's ruling in *Lawrence v. Texas* (2003). A six-to-three majority upheld a gay rights claim against a Texas law criminalizing homosexual relations, even those that were consensual and in private. A nationwide Gallup Poll taken six weeks before the *Lawrence* decision was announced reported that a 59-to-37 percent majority agreed that "homosexual relations between consenting adults should ... be legal." Here both American public opinion and the Court's ruling were counted as pro-claim.

By contrast a 74-to-23 percent poll majority opposed the *Lee v. Weisman* (1992) ruling to back a religious claim barring a rabbi's prayer at a public high school graduation ceremony. The Gallup Poll question was: "The U.S. Supreme Court has ruled that conducting religious prayers at any public school graduation ceremony is unconstitutional because it violates the First Amendment, which concerns the separation between church and state. Do you, yourself, believe that prayers should or should not be a part of public school graduation ceremonies?" Here American public opinion was

counted as anti-claim, but the Court's ruling was counted as pro-claim.

For a few decisions available polls were closely divided (within the .05 margin of error) or else available polls reported conflicting results; here American public opinion toward the claim was counted as unclear. For example, a 1965 Gallup Poll asked, "Some states have laws making it a crime for a white person and a Negro to marry. Do you approve or disapprove of such laws?" Nationwide 48 percent of respondents approved, 46 percent disapproved, and 6 percent reported no opinion. Here public opinion was classified as unclear, and the Supreme Court's *Loving v. Virginia* (1967) ruling striking down Virginia's antimiscegenation law was counted as pro-claim.

How often has American public opinion supported civil rights and liberties claims? Since the 1930s American attitudes toward civil rights and liberties claims have been quite mixed, but by no means wholly negative. Overall, American public opinion favored 35 percent of these 178 claims, opposed 57 percent of these claims, and was unclear on the remaining 8 percent of these claims.

These overall results obscure enormous variations in public opinion support for different types of civil rights and liberties claims. Public opinion support was much greater for some types of claims than for others. When at least 7 poll-to-ruling matches could be identified by topic, public opinion most often favored gay/lesbian claims or racial equality claims—doing so 63 percent and 58 percent of the time, respectively. At the other extreme the polls least often supported religious liberties claims, cold war/leftist claims, and student claims—doing so less than a quarter of the time (23 percent, 16 percent, and 14 percent respectively). Between these extremes falls poll support for medical privacy claims (polls were positive 46 percent of the time), sex and gender equality claims (42 percent), elections and voting claims (36 percent), abortion and reproductive rights claims (33 percent), death penalty (27 percent), other (non-death penalty) criminal claims (27 percent), and welfare and poverty claims (25 percent). This wide range in attitudes suggests that

American public opinion toward civil rights and liberties claims is quite mixed, but not wholly negative. Public opinion during the "red scare" period from the 1940s and 1950s certainly was not typical of American attitudes toward most other types of civil liberties and rights claims.

Perhaps surprisingly, poll support for civil liberties and rights claims does not vary as greatly over time as might have been expected. During the Hughes, Stone, and Vinson Courts, public opinion was favorable to about half (47 percent) of the few (only 15) civil rights and liberties claims for which polls are available. Thereafter the polls were favorable to these claims at very stable rates—33 percent of the time during the Warren Court, 32 percent of the time during the Burger Court, and 36 percent of the time during the Rehnquist Court era (on 21, 69, and 73 claims, respectively). Since the 1950s, then, public opinion poll majorities have supported civil rights and liberties claims about a third of the time, and opposed them slightly more than half the time (57 percent, 57 percent, and 62 percent of the time for the Warren, Burger, and Rehnquist Courts, respectively). This relative stability in public opinion support may be surprising given the great variation in the types of claims heard over time.

For this sample of 178 rulings, the Supreme Court supported the civil rights and liberties claim 42 percent of the time and opposed the claim 58 percent of the time. Overall, the modern Supreme Court has indeed more often supported civil liberties and rights claims than did American public opinion, but the difference is not large. Stated otherwise, public opinion *opposed* these claims 57 percent of the time, while the Supreme Court opposed these claims 58 percent of the time. By this apples-to-apples comparison, the modern Supreme Court was not much greater a champion of civil rights and liberties than was the American public.

The Supreme Court more often supported most, but not all types of civil rights and liberties claims than did American public opinion. For these 178 claims the Supreme Court was especially supportive of media claims, religious freedom claims, and

death penalty claims, at least compared to American public opinion. Here the Court supported claims 42 percent, 21 percent, and 20 percent more often, respectively, than did public opinion. Less dramatically, the Court also supported abortion, racial, and Cold War Era leftists' claims slightly more often than did public opinion (13 percent, 9 percent, and 8 percent more often, respectively).

In a few areas the Court supported rights claims as often as did public opinion poll majorities—for student-related claims and (non-death penalty) criminal claims. In some areas, however, the Court *less often* favored rights claims than did public opinion poll majorities. For sex and gender role claims, medical privacy claims, and gay and lesbian claims, American public opinion actually more often supported the claim than did the Supreme Court (9 percent, 15 percent, and 25 percent more often, respectively). In short, the modern Supreme Court has been friendlier than was American public opinion to some, but not all, claims.

For most, but not all, time periods the modern Supreme Court supported civil rights and liberties claims more often than did American public opinion. At the extreme stands the Warren Court. The Warren Court supported 71 percent of the claims reaching that Court, while public opinion supported only a third (33 percent) of these claims. During the Burger Court this sharp difference between the Court rulings and American public opinion began to shrink. The Burger Court supported only 46 percent of these claims, while public opinion supported 32 percent of these claims. During the Rehnquist Court era these differences completely disappeared. The Rehnquist Court (to date) supported slightly *fewer* rights claims than did public opinion—34 percent versus 36 percent, respectively. Constitutional law scholars should not simply assume that the Supreme Court always supports more civil rights and liberties claims than does American public opinion. The Court's record of supporting rights and liberties claims varies greatly across topic and time period.

The modern Court has also typically supported civil rights and liberties claims when the polls did or when the polls were unclear. When a public opinion poll majority favored the claim, the Court upheld the claim 57 percent of the time. When polls were closely divided or when different polls reported conflicting results, the Court upheld the claim 67 percent of the time. When a poll majority opposed the claim, however, the Court upheld the claim only 29 percent of the time. As these results suggest, the Court and American public opinion usually, although not inevitably, agree on civil rights and liberties claims.

Historically, politically liberal claimants raised most civil rights and liberties claims (Epstein 2003, 230). However, politically conservative claimants have also raised a still small but growing number of claims against a local, state, or federal law or regulation. Although few legal scholars have examined conservative claimants in the area of civil rights and liberties (but see Epstein 1985, 1993; Ivers and O'Connor 1987; Wilcox 1992, 1996), it is possible to compare public opinion polls versus Supreme Court support separately for liberal versus conservative claims. Examples of politically conservative claimants raising a civil rights or liberties claim against a federal, state, or local government during the Burger Court include *University of California Regents v. Bakke* (1978) or *Bob Jones University v. U.S.* (1983), and from the Rehnquist Court, *Adarand v. Pena* (1995), *Johnson v. Transportation Agency of Santa Clara County* (1987), *Nixon v. Shrink Missouri Government PAC* (2000), or *The Good News Club v. Milford Central Schools* (2001). How did politically conservative, versus liberal, claimants fare with American public opinion or with the Supreme Court?

Because very few conservative claimants filed claims prior to the Burger Court era, results are offered only for the Burger and Rehnquist Court eras when conservative claimants made up nearly one-sixth of all the claims in this sample. During the Burger Court era conservative claimants fared less well than liberal claimants either in terms of public opinion or Supreme Court support. At that time public opinion supported only 18 percent of conservative claimants, versus 34 percent of liberal claimants. The Burger Court itself voted in favor of

only 36 percent of conservative claimants, versus 48 percent of liberal claimants.

By the Rehnquist Court era, however, conservative claimants fared much better in terms of both American public opinion and at the Court itself. During the Rehnquist Court era American public opinion favored 53 percent of conservative claimants, versus only 31 percent of liberal claimants. The Rehnquist Court itself voted in favor of 47 percent of conservative claimants and only 31 percent of liberal claimants. That politically conservative claimants enjoyed greater success at the Rehnquist Court may be no surprise since a majority of the justices were appointed by conservative Republican presidents. That conservative claimants also enjoyed greater success with public opinion needs more explanation, and may be due to the conservative majority's docket control, to the growing success of liberals in state and local governments (including courts), to strategic appeals by conservative interest groups, or to the general conservative drift of American public opinion.

Not surprisingly, Republican and Democrat justices vote very differently on civil rights and liberties cases depending on whether they are brought by liberal or by conservative claimants. The modern Court's Republican justices voted for liberal claimants 42 percent of the time, but for conservative claimants 54 percent of the time. Yet more striking is the pattern found among Democrat justices, who voted for liberal claimants 68 percent of the time, but for conservative claimants only 18 percent of the time. These results suggest an intriguing possibility. If the number of conservative claimants heard by the Court steadily grows, many past conclusions about the Supreme Court's or individual justices' support for civil rights and liberties claims may change dramatically.

Supreme Court decisions on civil rights and civil liberties claims do not greatly influence American public opinion. In 28 instances identically worded poll questions have been available both before and after the Supreme Court announced a ruling on a civil rights and liberties issue (Marshall 1989, 2004). Across short periods of time the average poll shift from before to after a Court decision was only nine tenths of one percent, but the poll movement was *away from* the Court's ruling. Stated otherwise, when the Supreme Court announces a civil rights or liberties ruling, American public opinion on the average moves only slightly, but away from the majority's decision. When these poll shifts are broken down further, pre-to-post ruling poll shifts averaged only plus 1 percent for rulings in favor of the claimant, and only minus 3 percent for rulings against a claimant.

Taken together, the relationship between American public opinion and the Supreme Court's civil rights and liberties rulings is complex. By the available polling evidence extending over two thirds of a century, American public opinion supported about a third of civil rights and liberties claims, opposed about half the claims, and split evenly on the remainder. The "red scare" era of intense public hostility toward claims by leftists and accused communists during the 1940s and 1950s describes accurately only one specific time period during which public opinion was very hostile to rights claims. Yet it clearly does not accurately describe overall public opinion toward many other types of civil rights and liberties claims since the mid-1930s. Finally, whether the Supreme Court has been friendlier toward civil rights and liberties claims than public opinion depends on the type of case and the time period involved.

See also Abortion, Right to; Black, Hugo L.; *Bob Jones University v. United States* (1983); Burger Court; Communist Party USA; Conservatism; Death Penalty and the Supreme Court; Douglas, William O.; First Amendment; Gay Rights Movement; *Lawrence v. Texas* (2003); Liberalism; *Loving v. Virginia* (1967); The New Deal; Rehnquist Court; Religion, Freedom of; School Prayer Decisions; Separation of Church and State; Speech, Freedom of; Stone, Harlan Fiske; Warren Court; Welfare Rights

Bibliography

Epstein, Lee. 1985. *Conservatives in Court.* Knoxville: University of Tennessee Press.

Epstein, Lee. 1993. "Interest Group Litigation during the Rehnquist Court Era." *Journal of Law and Politics* 9: 639.

Epstein, Lee, Jeffrey A. Segal, Harold J. Spaeth, and Thomas G. Walker. 2003. *The Supreme Court Compendium: Data, Decisions, and Developments.* 3rd ed. Washington, DC: Congressional Quarterly.

Ivers, Gregg, and Karen O'Connor. 1987. "Friends as Foes: The *Amicus Curiae* Participation and Effectiveness of the American Civil Liberties Union and the Americans for Effective Law Enforcement in Criminal Cases, 1969–1982." *Law and Policy* 9: 161.

Marshall, Thomas R. 1989. *Public Opinion and the Supreme Court.* Boston: Unwin Hyman.

Marshall, Thomas R. 2004. "Public Opinion and Supreme Court Decisions: Reconsidering Legitimacy." Paper presented at the April 2004 annual meeting of the Midwest Political Science Association, Chicago, Illinois.

Murphy, Paul. 1972. *The Constitution in Crisis Times.* New York: Harper and Row.

Wilcox, Clyde. 1992. *God's Warriors: The Christian Right in Twentieth Century America.* Baltimore: Johns Hopkins University Press.

Wilcox, Clyde. 1996. *Onward Christian Soldiers: The Christian Right in Politics.* Boulder, CO: Westview Press.

Thomas R. Marshall

PUBLIC TRIAL, RIGHT TO A

The Sixth Amendment to the U.S. Constitution guarantees criminal defendants the right to a "public trial by an impartial jury." On the other hand, the First Amendment provides for freedom of the press. Consequently, a defendant's right to a fair trial and the news media's right to report trials clash because prejudicial publicity before and during the trial may violate the criminal defendant's due process.

Over the past 40-plus years, the Supreme Court has tried to balance the inherent conflict between a defendant's right to a fair trial and the media's right to cover criminal trial proceedings. In the 1960s, the Court made it clear that prejudicial media coverage could justify reversal of criminal convictions. In *Sheppard v. Maxwell* (1966), the Court stated:

Unfair and prejudicial news comment on pending trials has become increasingly prevalent. Due process requires that the accused receive a trial by an impartial jury free from outside influence. Given the pervasiveness of modern communications and the difficulty of effacing prejudicial publicity from the minds of jurors, the trial courts must take strong measures to ensure that the balance is never weighed against the accused.

Among the usual measures that trial judges use to handle prejudicial publicity are the following:

- Change of venue—moving a trial to a new location in which the publicity is not pervasive and prejudicial;
- Change of venire—importing jurors from another community where the publicity is less intense;
- Continuance—delaying a trial until the initial publicity surrounding the trial diminishes;
- Voir dire—rigorous questioning of prospective jurors to weed out potentially prejudiced jurors;
- Admonition—a judge's order to jurors to avoid media coverage of the trial and not to discuss the trial with anyone except other jurors;
- Sequestration—sheltering jurors from prejudicial publicity by isolating them in a place during the trial.

Notably the Supreme Court in *Sheppard* never suggested gag orders as an option for judges in preventing the media from publishing prejudicial information. In 1976, however, the Court considered for the first time whether a gag order can be issued by a trial judge to protect a defendant's right to a fair trial.

In *Nebraska Press Association v. Stuart* (1976), the Supreme Court, relying on a variation of the clear and present danger doctrine, said that the constitutionality of a gag order must be determined by evaluating the circumstances of a particular case and deciding whether "the gravity of the 'evil,' discounted by its improbability" justifies the gag order.

The Court required that a trial judge, before issuing a gag order, answer yes to each of the following questions: (1) Has there been intense and pervasive pretrial publicity that is likely to affect the fairness of the trial? (2) Are there no alternatives to a gag order that would mitigate the effects of the pretrial publicity? (3) How effectively will a gag order prevent the pretrial publicity from affecting a defendant's right to a fair trial?

And yet the public trial question under the Sixth Amendment—for whom is the right to a public trial?—remained to be resolved for a while. Initially the Supreme Court took a position that the Sixth Amendment on a public trial was for the accused only. But in *Richmond Newspapers, Inc. v. Virginia* (1980), the Court held that the First Amendment guarantees the press and the public a right to attend criminal trials. "Absent an overriding interest articulated in findings, the trial of a criminal case must be open to the public," the Court stated, because "the First Amendment can be read as protecting the right of everyone to attend trials so as to give meaning to those explicit guarantees [of free speech and free press]."

The post-*Richmond* Court has amplified the First Amendment right of access to criminal trials in the context of the press's right to gather news information. In *Globe Newspaper Co. v. Superior Court* (1982), the Court articulated the constitutionality of presumption against closure of criminal trials: Where the State tries to deny the press and the public access to a criminal trial, it must show that "the denial is necessitated by a compelling governmental interest, and is narrowly tailored to serve that interest."

The Supreme Court in *Press-Enterprise Co. v. Superior Court (Press-Enterprise I)* (1984), affirmed the exceptionality of closure of judicial proceedings. In reversing a trial court's closure of voir dire in a criminal trial, the Court observed that "closed proceedings, although not absolutely precluded, must be rare and only for cause shown that outweighs the value of openness."

The First Amendment right of access to trial proceedings has been expanded to cover preliminary hearings. The Court in *Press-Enterprise Co. v. Superior Court (Press-Enterprise II)* (1986), stated that the First Amendment proscribes closure of preliminary hearings unless specific on-the-record findings establish that closure was essential to protect a higher interest and it was narrowly tailored to serve that interest.

Does the *Richmond* principle on access to criminal trials apply to juvenile proceedings? The Supreme Court has yet to directly address the question. More often than not, however, lower courts have been reluctant to apply the First Amendment's sweeping right of access to criminal trials involving juveniles.

Another relevant question: Do the press and the public have a constitutional right of access to *civil* trials? Thus far the Supreme Court has had no opportunity to rule on the issue, although individual justices have indicated that history and rationale for openness of criminal trials should support access to civil trial. Lower courts have embraced the access rationales of *Richmond* and its progeny in varying degrees when they have dealt with the First Amendment access to civil trials.

Over the years television coverage of criminal trials has been a topic of contention amidst the debate about the news media's right to cover judicial proceedings. The Supreme Court in 1965 rejected an argument for telecasting trials as a First Amendment right. The use of cameras in the courtroom, the Court stated in *Estes v. Texas* (1965), "involves such a probability that prejudice will result that it is deemed inherently lacking in due process."

In the mid-1970s, however, several states, including Florida, allowed broadcasting of trials on an experimental basis. Televising of criminal trial proceedings was challenged as a violation of the Sixth Amendment right of the accused to a fair trial in *Chandler v. Florida* (1981). The Supreme Court held that televising criminal trials is not inherently prejudicial. It also said *Estes* was not "an absolute ban on state experimentation with an evolving technology" of mass communication relating to trial proceedings. Nonetheless, the Court cautioned that televising trials can violate due process if he can prove that cameras in the courtroom have impacted the jury or trial participants in his case so adversely that he has been denied due process.

At present every state allows television coverage of trials and appellate proceedings in varying degrees. But the District of Columbia continues to prohibit cameras from the courtroom. Likewise, the no-camera policy of federal courts remains, although in the early 1990s cameras were experimented with in federal courts. The Second and Ninth Circuits have authorized television coverage of court proceedings on a case-by-case basis.

The right to public trials is now firmly established in American law. Criminal (and civil) trials are presumptively open to the public because of the First Amendment guarantees of freedom of speech and the press. Hence, closure of trials is exceptional, and the State must document an overriding interest in closure. Cameras have become a fixture in state court proceedings during the past 20 years. In this light, federal courts will likely follow suit sooner or later.

See also Accused, Rights of the; Clear and Present Danger Doctrine; Continuance, Motion for; Due Process, Procedural; First Amendment; Free Press/ Fair Trial Problem; Jury, Trial by; Press, Freedom of the; Prior Restraint, Doctrine of; Sixth Amendment; Venue, Change of

Bibliography

Dienes, C. Thomas, Lee Levine, and Robert C. Lind. 2001. *Newsgathering and the Law.* 2nd ed. Charlottesville, VA: Lexis Law Publishing.

Kyu Ho Youm

PUBLIC USE CLAUSE

The Takings Clause of the Fifth Amendment to the Constitution limits the power of eminent domain by requiring that governmental taking of private property be for a public use. In *Chicago, Burlington, & Quincy Railroad Co. v. Chicago* (1897), the Supreme Court held that the same requirement applies to the states through the Fourteenth Amendment.

Initially, the courts considered the term "public use" to be synonymous with "use by the public," and they held the exercise of the power of eminent domain to be invalid if the property taken were conveyed to private individuals instead of being used, for example, for the construction of roads, schools, or parks. Beginning with *Clark v. Nash* (1905), however, the Supreme Court began to equate public use with any use conducive to the public interest or public welfare. The result has been that the public use limitation on governments' power of eminent domain no longer limits the uses for which governments can take private property.

In *Clark,* the Supreme Court held that Utah could authorize by statute an individual to condemn a right of way across his neighbor's land for the enlargement of an irrigation ditch, thereby enabling him to obtain water from a stream to irrigate his land, which otherwise would remain absolutely valueless. The Court held that "the validity of such statutes may sometimes depend upon many different facts, the existence of which would make a public use, even by an individual, where, in the absence of such facts, the use would clearly be private." The facts present in this case that convinced the Court that Utah's condemnation statute served the public interest—and therefore a public use—were the "climate and soil" of the "arid and mountainous States of the West" and the recognition by these states that "the cultivation of an otherwise valueless soil, by means of irrigation" was "absolutely necessary" for their "growth and prosperity."

Applying its equation of public use with the exercise of the police power in furtherance of the public interest, the Court has approved the widespread use of the power of eminent domain by federal and state governments in conjunction with private companies to facilitate urban renewal, destruction of slums, erection of low-cost housing in place of deteriorated housing, and the promotion of aesthetic values as well as economic ones. The leading modern case in this field is *Berman v. Parker* (1954). In it, the Court sustained a federal statute for the District of Columbia granting its redevelopment agency the power to acquire privately owned land in blighted areas by the use of eminent domain to eliminate slum and substandard housing conditions and to resell that land to other

private individuals subject to conditions designed to accomplish these purposes. A unanimous Court held that the judiciary's role in determining whether eminent domain is being used for a public purpose "is an extremely narrow one." Courts must defer to the legislature on questions of eminent domain no less than on all other exercises of the police power: "When the legislature has spoken, the public interest has been declared in terms well-nigh conclusive. In such cases, the legislature, not the judiciary, is the main guardian of the public needs to be served by social legislation."

Against the argument that the taking of an individual's property merely to develop a better balanced, more attractive community was not a proper public use, the Court in *Berman v. Parker* declared that the values by which governments can pursue their exercise of eminent domain "are spiritual as well as physical, aesthetic as well as monetary. It is within the power of the legislature to determine that the community should be beautiful as well as healthy, spacious as well as clean, well-balanced as well as carefully patrolled.... If those who govern the District of Columbia decide that the Nation's Capital should be beautiful as well as sanitary, there is nothing in the Fifth Amendment that stands in the way." And against the argument that there is no public use involved when government takes the private property of one individual only to sell it in turn to another, the Court again showed its deference to the legislative branches: Not only is the power of eminent domain "merely the means to the end," "but the means of executing the project are for Congress and Congress alone to determine, once the public purpose has been established."

Under the extraordinarily deferential standard laid down in *Berman v. Parker,* eminent domain can be exercised to achieve anything that is otherwise within the power of the legislature. *Hawaii Housing Authority* v. *Midkiff* (1984) and *Kelo v. City of New London* (2005) are the most important recent examples. In *Midkiff,* the Supreme Court unanimously upheld Hawaii's use of its power of eminent domain to acquire property from large landowners and transfer it to lessees living on single-family residential lots on the land. The purpose of this land condemnation scheme was to reduce the concentration of land ownership, and the Court declared that "our cases make clear that empirical debates over the wisdom of takings—no less than debates over the wisdom of other kinds of socioeconomic legislation—are not to be carried out in the federal courts." And in *Kelo,* a sharply divided Court upheld the use of eminent domain for economic development purposes in language so sweeping that the dissent declared that it had "effectively delete[d] the words 'for public use' from the Takings Clause."

See also Bill of Rights, Incorporation of; *Chicago, Burlington, & Quincy Railroad Co. v. Chicago* (1897); Due Process, Procedural; Due Process, Substantive; Fifth Amendment; Fourteenth Amendment; Just Compensation Clause; *Kelo v. City of New London* (2005); Property Rights

Bibliography

Epstein, Richard. 1989. *Takings: Private Property and the Power of Eminent Domain.* Cambridge, MA: Harvard University Press.

Garnett, Nicole Stelle. 2003. "The Public Use Question as a Takings Problem." *George Washington Law Review* 71: 934.

Ralph A. Rossum

PUNITIVE DAMAGES

Unlike compensatory damages that are designed to compensate the plaintiff for any actual injury suffered by the plaintiff as a result of the defendant's wrongful conduct, punitive damages serve the separate purpose of punishing the defendant for his or her malicious or reckless conduct and of deterring others from engaging in similar conduct in the future. Punitive damages are not available as a matter of right no matter how egregious the defendant's conduct. Rather, the decision to award punitive damages always lies within the discretion of the trier of fact. An award of compensatory damages is not a prerequisite to an award of punitive damages.

Given the punishment and deterrent purposes of an award of punitive damages, they must be assessed against each defendant individually. As the U.S. Court of Appeals for the Second Circuit recognized in *McFadden v. Sanchez* (1983), "The degree of appropriate punishment and the extent to which deterrence may be achieved at an individual's expense are obviously matters appropriate for individualized determination." Accordingly, punitive damages may not be assessed jointly against multiple defendants. Likewise, because the appropriateness of an award of punitive damages requires determination on an individual basis, the Supreme Court has articulated special rules that limit the circumstances under which a principal may be required to pay punitive damages for the act of its agent (see, for example, *Kolstad v. American Dental Association* [1999]).

Evidence of the defendant's net worth is relevant in assessing the amount of punitive damages. Punitive damages can be awarded, however, even without proof of the defendant's wealth. The defendant, not the plaintiff, carries the burden of introducing evidence of net worth if the defendant wishes that information to be considered by the trier of fact in awarding punitive damages.

The availability of punitive damages in civil rights actions depends upon the particular civil right statute upon which the plaintiff's claim is based. In the Civil Rights Restoration Act of 1991, Congress expressly authorized the award of punitive damages in actions alleging intentional employment discrimination in violation of Title VII of the Civil Rights Act of 1964 and Title I of the Americans with Disabilities Act. Punitive damages also are available in actions brought pursuant to 42 U.S.C. sec. 1981 (originally part of the Civil Rights Act of 1866), and 42 U.S.C. sec. 1983 (originally part of the Civil Rights Act of 1871). They are not available, however, in actions brought under Title VI of the Civil Rights Act of 1964, sec. 504 of the Rehabilitation Act, or Title II of the Americans with Disabilities Act.

Punitive damages are not available against all defendants. For example, in *City of Newport v. Fact Concerts, Inc.* (1981), the Supreme Court held that punitive damages are not available against local governmental entities sued in a section 1983 action. Likewise, when Congress authorized punitive damages in cases of intentional employment discrimination in the Civil Rights Restoration Act of 1991, it expressly excluded actions brought against "a government, government agency or political subdivision."

Even if punitive damages otherwise are available, not every deprivation of a federal right justifies a punitive damage award. In section 1983 actions, for example, the Supreme Court has held that punitive damages are appropriate only if the defendant's conduct is motivated by ill will or spite towards the plaintiff or if the defendant's conduct exhibits a reckless or callous disregard of the plaintiff's rights (see *Smith v. Wade*, 1983). Likewise, in the Civil Rights Restoration Act of 1991, Congress authorized an award of punitive damages only if the defendant engaged in a discriminatory practice "with malice or with reckless indifference to the federally protected rights" of the plaintiff.

In some types of civil rights actions, the amount of punitive damages that may be awarded is limited by statute. In the Civil Rights Restoration Act of 1991, for example, Congress enacted a sliding scale, which limits the total amount of compensatory plus punitive damages a plaintiff may recover to between $50,000 and $300,000 based on the number of employees employed by the defendant. Even if there is no statutorily imposed dollar limit on the amount of punitive damages a plaintiff may recover, the Supreme Court has held that a grossly excessive punitive damage award violates a defendant's rights under the Due Process Clause of the Fourteenth Amendment (see *BMW, Inc. v. Gore* 1996).

See also Disabilities, Right of Persons with; Civil Rights Act of 1866; Civil Rights Act of 1871; Civil Rights Act of 1964; Civil Rights Restoration Act of 1991; Due Process Clauses; Fourteenth Amendment (1868); Section 1983 Actions

Bibliography

Cook, Joseph G., and John L. Sobieski, Jr. 1997. *Civil Rights Actions.* New York: Matthew Bender and Company.

John L. Sobieski, Jr.

Q

QUAKERS

The historical influence of the Religious Society of Friends, or Quakers, on American civil liberties and civil rights can be attributed to their unique belief system. According to Harriet Hyman Alonso, "the Quaker faith was most influential and most widespread" among early American religious influences for three reasons (Alonso 1993, 22). These include the faith's "social responsibility component, its philosophy of nonviolence, and its recognition of each individual's equality before God" (Alonso 1993, 22). Quakers have always believed that Jesus Christ was neither male nor female and that God abides in each person (Alonso 1993, 22). Accordingly, the faith naturally perpetuated the notion of equality on the basis of both race and gender, as God was in everyone equally. This led to the Quaker belief in the Testimony of Equality, which stipulates that all human beings are seen as equal before God and therefore entitled to individual dignity and equal rights before secular authorities.

The Peace Testimony is a key concept of the religion. This pacifism is deeply rooted in the colonial history of the United States. Even prior to the Revolutionary War, the Quakers refused to fight, and this often stirred resentment in other colonists who felt as though they *did* have to fight to protect the Quakers (Alonso 2003, 23). By the time of the Revolutionary War, this resentment had grown considerably, and the Friends' offer of aid to casualties on both sides of battle sometimes resulted in their "being run out of their homes," or being "treated as traitors and penalized as such" (Alonso 2003, 23).

This legacy is all the more interesting because other religious groups were exempted from service in the Revolutionary War. The unique discrimination against the Quakers may have had to do with their religious beliefs. Typically, Quakers believe that the emphasis on Christ within everyone is more important than a focus on the Biblical discussion of the virgin birth, death, and resurrection of Christ. Moreover, many Quakers do not believe in a literal hell, or in the Bible as the sole source of spiritual guidance. This has always created tension with some more mainstream Christian denominations. Furthermore, opposition to war is usually unpopular—with Vietnam being a notable recent exception. During the Vietnam War, Quakers were prominent in the antiwar movement.

By the time of the Civil War, Quakers were allowed to obtain conscientious objector status along with other peace activists. Indeed, "in his original proposal for a Bill of Rights, James Madison included the following clause: 'no person religiously scrupulous of bearing arms shall be compelled to render military service in person.'" Certainly, though, the Friends have not always had an easy time even in this capacity as sometimes they have been forced to work in labor camps or have been given the option of serving as "guinea pigs" for lab tests if they chose not to fight; something that most individuals thought only the Nazis conducted during World War II.

Many famous Quakers have protested on behalf of the freedoms and equality of everyone despite race or gender. Early colonists such as William Penn and signatories to the Declaration of Independence and the Constitution included Quakers—the most notable of whom was probably Thomas Paine. It is also believed that Friends were the first group in this country to speak out against slavery in an organized manner, in Germantown, Pennsylvania in 1688. Elizabeth Chandler was an early Quaker abolitionist who wrote, "Will Christian sisters and wives and mothers stand coldly inert, while those of their own sex are daily exposed, not only to the threats and revilings, but to the very lash of a stern, unfeeling taskmaster?" (Quoted in Alonso 1993, 26). Other active Quaker abolitionists included Sarah and Angelina Grimke. Angelina Grimke suggested "that it was the 'duty of woman, and the province of woman, to plead the cause of the oppressed in our land'" (quoted in Alonso 1993, 32).

Lucretia Mott was also an abolitionist and an advocate of women's rights. She worked together with Elizabeth Cady Stanton and several other Quaker women to convene the Seneca Falls Convention, which produced the Declaration of Sentiments of 1848. Fashioned after the Declaration of Independence, the language is very similar to the Declaration of Independence, as is the text. A list of grievances follows a preamble, which asserts, in part, that "all men and women are created equal …" (quoted in Kolmar and Bartkowski 2005, 71). Quaker women were strong supporters of the Nineteenth Amendment (1920), which enfranchised women, and continued to support the movement for gender equality under the law.

Contemporary Quakers remain active in the antiwar movement, the abolition of capital punishment, prison reform, and the gay rights movement. These issues are not new to the Quakers, however, as they have always supported a progressive agenda in national policy and especially in the field of civil rights and liberties.

The Quakers have a rich historical tradition that is rooted in their faith. Two of the integral beliefs of the Quaker doctrine are the Testimony of Peace, which guides their pacifism, and the Testimony of Equality, which underlies their egalitarianism. Although they are a small religious minority that has suffered popular opprobrium and even religious persecution, the Quakers maintain steadfast dedication to the propositions that all persons are created equal and that all people are entitled to "life, liberty, and the pursuit of happiness."

See also Abolitionist Movement; Declaration of Independence; Equality; Gay Rights Movement; Madison, James; Nineteenth Amendment; Paine, Thomas; Religion, Freedom of; Seneca Falls Declaration; Stanton, Elizabeth Cady

Bibliography

Alonso, Harriet Hyman. 1993. *Peace as a Women's Issue.* Syracuse, NY: Syracuse University Press.

Kolmar, Wendy K., and Frances Bartkowski, eds. 2005. *Feminism Theory: A Reader.* 2nd ed. Boston: McGraw Hill.

Lori Maxwell

QUINLAN, KAREN. *See* Right to Die; Substituted Judgment, Doctrine of

QUIRIN, EX PARTE (1942)

In June 1942, some six months after the United States entered World War II against Nazi Germany, Japan, and Italy, the German High Command landed eight soldiers on American beaches to sabotage military bases. Upon the capture of these would-be saboteurs, President Franklin D. Roosevelt issued an executive proclamation that barred such persons from civilian courts and ordered their trial by a secret military tribunal. When the defendants petitioned for a writ of habeas corpus, the Supreme Court, in a brief per curiam decision, unanimously upheld the government's position. A few days after this ruling, six of the eight defendants were executed by electrocution in Washington, D.C. Two months later, in October 1942, the Supreme Court, in an opinion by chief Justice Harlan F. Stone, provided a more detailed rationale for its original holding that the president's proclamation and the action of the military tribunal were not in violation of the Constitution. While public opinion at the time supported the decision, constitutional and Supreme Court scholars saw the decision as weak and without constitutional support. Originally relegated to the shadows of history, the *Quirin* decision has become pertinent once again in light of America's War on Terrorism.

Quirin, Haupt, Dasch, and five other persons landed in the United States on or about June 13, 1942. Four landed at Amagansett Beach on Long Island, New York; four landed on Ponte Vedra Beach, Florida, near Jacksonville. All eight had been to the United States previously. Haupt claimed he was an American citizen by virtue of his parents becoming citizens while he was a minor. Dasch became an American citizen by serving in the U.S. Army. All eight admitted to receiving saboteur and espionage training in Germany. The eight landed wearing German military uniforms, which they immediately buried along with explosives. The Long Island group was spotted by a Coast Guard patrolman, whose later announcement began a nationwide hunt for the other four. Dasch, upon arrival in New York, telephoned the FBI to inform them of the plot. The FBI dismissed his story. Dasch then went to FBI headquarters in Washington to inform in person. As he was being shown the door, Dasch opened his suitcase to show the $84,000 in cash inside—payment by the German High Command for the operation. After being promised a pardon in return for information, Dasch spent the next eight days being questioned. The last of the eight was captured on June 27.

On July 2, President Roosevelt issued a proclamation stating that all those who act under the direction of any nation at war with the United States were subject to the jurisdiction of a military tribunal. All eight were tried before such a tribunal. While the tribunal was in session, the defense attorneys filed a petition for a writ of habeas corpus. An extraordinary session of the Supreme Court heard the petition on July 29 and July 30. Roosevelt made it clear that the eight would not have their cases heard before a civilian court regardless of the decision. The Supreme Court avoided the constitutional crisis by finding in a unanimous decision (8–0, as Justice Frank Murphy took no part in the case) that the military tribunals were properly constituted and that the July 2 executive order was constitutional.

Ultimately all eight defendants were found guilty. Burger was given life, Dasch was given 30 years. The other six were put to death by electrocution. Beyond the effects on those eight defendants, *Quirin* was almost universally seen as a relatively insignificant decision. Thus, it languished in the annals of the Supreme Court until the recent War on Terrorism began. In *Hamdi v. Rumsfeld* and *Rumsfeld v. Padilla,* two high-profile terrorism cases argued before the Supreme Court in 2004, the government relied on *Quirin* as a rationale for holding accused terrorists without giving them access to civilian courts. Hamdi and Padilla were both U.S. citizens, as was Dasch (and arguably Haupt) in the *Quirin* case. Hamdi and Padilla were both "enemy combatants" according to the government, as were the eight Nazi saboteurs. Thus, reasoned the U.S. government, a military tribunal could be used to try these two. In *Hamdi v. Rumsfeld* (2004), the Supreme Court avoided *Quirin* by holding that Hamdi had the right to challenge the "enemy combatant" label in court. In *Rumsfeld* v. *Padilla* (2004), the Court did not reach a decision on the merits of the case. Instead, the Court found that the petitioner had improperly filed against Rumsfeld when he should have filed against the person directly responsible for his confinement. Thus, the *Quirin* decision still stands and may be cited and used as precedential authority in future cases involving the use of military tribunals.

See also Habeas Corpus; Roosevelt, Franklin D.; Stone, Harlan F.; Terrorism, War on

Ole J. Forsberg

QUOTAS, RACIAL. *See* Affirmative Action

R

RACE, DISCRIMINATION BASED ON. *See* Abolitionist Movement; Affirmative Action; *Brown v. Board of Education* (1954; 1955); Black Codes; Busing Controversy; Civil Rights; Civil Rights Act of 1866; Civil Rights Act of 1870; Civil Rights Act of 1871; Civil Rights Act of 1875; Civil Rights Act of 1964; Civil Rights Act of 1988; *The Civil Rights Cases;* Civil Rights Division, U.S. Department of Justice; Civil Rights Movement; Civil Rights Restoration Act of 1991; Death Penalty and Racial Discrimination; Discrimination; Discrimination by Private Actors; Douglass, Frederick; Du Bois, W.E.B.; Emancipation Proclamation; Equal Employment Opportunity Commission; Equal Protection Clause; Fair Housing Act; Federalism and Civil Rights and Liberties; Fifteenth Amendment; Fourteenth Amendment (1868); Fourteenth Amendment, Section 5 of the; Grandfather Clause; Hate Crimes; Hate Speech; *Heart of Atlanta Motel v. United States* (1964); Housing, Discrimination in; Interracial Marriage; Jackson, Jesse; Jim Crow Laws; *Katzenbach v. McClung* (1964); King, Dr. Martin Luther, Jr.; Ku Klux Klan (KKK); Lincoln, Abraham; Literacy Tests; Little Rock Crisis; *Loving v. Virginia* (1967); Malcolm X; Marshall, Thurgood; Baker Motley, Constance; National Association for the Advancement of Colored People (NAACP); Parks, Rosa; Peremptory Challenges; *Plessy v. Ferguson* (1896); Poll Tax; *Powell v. Alabama* (1932); Public Accommodation, Places of; Public Support for Civil Rights and Liberties; Racial Gerrymandering; Racial Profiling; Radical Republicans; Reconstruction; Reparations for Slavery; Restrictive Covenants; *Reynolds v. Sims* (1964); Rodney King Incident; Segregation in Public Education; Sharpton, Alfred Charles; *Shelley v. Kraemer* (1948); Slavery; Southern Poverty Law Center; Thirteenth Amendment; Truth, Sojourner; Voting Rights Act of 1965; Washington, Booker T.

RACIAL GERRYMANDERING

Racial gerrymandering refers to the deliberate distortion of district boundaries for racial purposes. For a century after the American Civil War, decennial reapportionment of congressional districts sought to limit minority representation. The effect can clearly be seen in the number of African Americans serving in Congress. From 1870 to 1901, a total of 22 blacks were elected to the national legislature. However, intimidation of black voters and Jim Crow laws combined to reduce the number of black legislators to zero between 1900 and 1929 and just seven between 1929 and 1966.

The Civil Rights Movement in the United States began in the 1950s and produced a number of legal and legislative victories in the 1960s. In its ruling in *Gomillion v. Lightfoot* (1960), the U.S. Supreme Court applied the Fifteenth Amendment to overturn an Alabama law that changed the city boundaries of Tuskegee so as to exclude all but a handful of black voters.

Probably the most significant law passed on the issue of minority representation was the 1965 Voting Rights Act. Not only did the law remove a number of discriminatory procedures, which inhibited voting, but it prohibited gerrymandering of districts on account of race or color. Although more blacks were being elected to Congress following the latter law, the 1980 census revealed that the 17 U.S. House districts represented by blacks were shrinking. This led to a series of 1982 amendments to the Voting Rights Act of 1965, which were interpreted by many as requiring states to construct new districts with black majorities whenever possible.

After the number of congressional districts with a majority of African American residents rose to 32 following the 1990 census, it was clear that racial gerrymandering was being used to increase minority representation. Opponents to that practice filed suits in several states, contending that it violated the Equal Protection Clause of the Fourteenth Amendment. The initial constitutional challenge to reach the Supreme Court was *Shaw v. Reno* (1993), which set the tone for a series of decisions on racial gerrymandering.

Shaw v. Reno involved an effort by the state of North Carolina to satisfy U.S. Department of Justice demands to augment the number of congressional districts with a majority of African American residents. While the Court determined that the shape of the district in question had violated traditional district principles—including geographical and political considerations such as compactness, contiguity, and preservation of governmental boundaries—it nonetheless upheld the concept of minority-based districts provided that they met "strict scrutiny" standards. Such districts had to be based on a compelling state interest and the legislation that established them had to be narrowly tailored.

Shaw v. Reno was followed by a number of Supreme Court rulings on the same issue at different levels of government, including *Johnson v. DeGrandy* (1994), *Holder v. Hall* (1994), *Miller v.*

Johnson (1995), *Bush v. Vera* (1996), *Shaw v. Hunt* (1996), *Meadows v. Moon* (1997), *Lawyer v. Department of Justice* (1997), and *Hunt v. Cromartie* (2001). All but the *Lawyer* and *Meadows* cases were decided by five-to-four votes, and all but the *Lawyer* and *Hunt v. Cromartie* cases rejected the minority districts proposed.

Despite the ongoing controversy over racial gerrymandering, the number of black members in the national legislature reached an all-time high of 42 in the 109th Congress, including four freshmen. Barack Obama of Illinois, elected in 2004, became the nation's fifth African American U.S. senator.

See also Discrimination; Equal Protection Jurisprudence; Fifteenth Amendment; Free and Fair Elections; Jim Crow Laws; Reapportionment; Representative Democracy; Strict Scrutiny; Voting Rights Act

Bibliography

Burke, Christopher M. 1999. *The Appearance of Equality: Racial Gerrymandering, Redistricting, and the Supreme Court.* Westport, CT: Greenwood Press.

Clayton, Dewey M. 1999. *African Americans and the Politics of Congressional Redistricting.* New York: Garland Publishing Company.

O'Brien, David M. 2003. *Constitutional Law and Politics: Struggles for Power and Government Accountability.* New York: W.W. Norton.

Samuel B. Hoff

RACIAL PROFILING

Racial profiling happens when police departments and others in legal authority base their actions on the *race* rather than the *behavior* of an individual. Simply put, racial profiling occurs when the police target minorities for stops to determine whether they have participated in criminal activities. Scholars have examined racial profiling from several perspectives. Some have considered whether racial profiling is exacerbated by certain characteristics such as age (Meeks, 2000). Others have explored the possible connection between racism, profiling, and bias-based law enforcement (Rudovsky, 2001).

In addition, a number of scholars have sought to ascertain how often racial profiling occurs (Lundman and Kaufman, 2003).

Racial profiling is a controversial issue in American policing and law enforcement. In 2000, the American Civil Liberties Union Web site (http://www.aclu.org/profiling) stated that:

One of the ACLU's highest priority issues this year is the fight against the outrageous practice of racial profiling. Our recently released report, "Driving While Black: Racial Profiling On Our Nation's Highways," documents this practice of substituting skin color for evidence as a grounds for suspicion by enforcement officials.

Profiling has been used by many police departments. The practice of profiling in the descriptive sense is using an interpretation based on fact, which can serve a legitimate purpose for law enforcement agencies. However, when the profiling is not based on fact and is based largely on stereotypes or solely on race or ethnicity it becomes unconstitutional. Some police departments admit that they practice racial profiling to identify potential criminals. They have accepted this practice as a necessary evil of modern-day policing. Some police forces state that profiling is a necessary law enforcement tool, and that when used effectively, it helps control criminal activity and assists in the protection of police officers.

In June 1999, President Bill Clinton directed federal agencies to collect data to be turned over the United States Justice Department to determine if law enforcement was engaged in racial profiling and if so what steps could be taken to eliminate this practice. Specifically President Clinton stated, "Today I am directing my Cabinet agencies to begin gathering detailed information on their law enforcement activities. The Justice Department will then analyze this data to assess whether and where law enforcement engaged in racial profiling and what concrete steps we need to take at a national level to eliminate it anywhere it exists." Taking a lead from President Clinton, the governor of Kentucky ordered a study to determine whether racial profiling was a problem in state law enforcement in May 2000. Governor Patton said, "Stopping or searching individuals on the basis of race is not an effective law enforcement tool nor is it a defensible strategy for police protection" ("Governor Paul Patton Orders Study," 2000).

In the wake of the September 11, 2001 tragedy and subsequent controversies, Arab Americans have been targeted by the FBI and other law enforcement agencies using racial profiling. Arabs have been the target of racial profiling because the perpetrators of the terrorist actions were Arabs who were also radical Islamic fundamentalists. Some of the tactics used have infringed on the civil liberties of those thought to be affiliated with terrorist organizations.

In particular, civil libertarians were dismayed by the post-9/11 passage of the USA PATRIOT Act, which gives law enforcement agencies unprecedented powers in the name of fighting terrorism. A number of Arab groups, worried that their members are being unfairly profiled and monitored, banded together to challenge the constitutionality of Section 215 of the USA PATRIOT Act. As of this writing, however, and approximately two years after the case was filed, no decision has been reached as to whether the suit will be allowed to continue. The Patriot Act has awakened the ire of many people who are against various forms of profiling. This act allows authorities to listen to personal phone calls in attempts to obstruct the communications of terrorists and potential terrorists.

The phenomenon of racial profiling does not just surface in the law enforcement and the criminal justice system. Racial profiling can be seen in banking with regard to loan applications. It can be seen in the hospitality industry regarding service in restaurants, and also in educational opportunities and housing, where minorities are largely considered as more risky investments by certain housing and educational entities.

See also American Civil Liberties Union (ACLU); Civil Rights Movement; Equal Protection Clause; Federal Bureau of Investigation (FBI); Housing, Discrimination in; Terrorism, War on; USA PATRIOT Act

Bibliography

Bennett, Lerone. 2003. *Before the Mayflower: A History of Black America.* Chicago: Johnson.

"Governor Paul Patton Orders Study to Determine If Racial Profiling Exists." 2000. *The Advocate* 22, no 3 (May).

Lundman, Richard, and Robert Kaufman. 2003. "Driving While Black: Effects of Race, Ethnicity, and Gender On Citizen Self Reports of Traffic Stops and Police Actions." 41 *Criminology* 195.

Meeks, Kenneth. 2000. *Driving While Black: What to Do If You Are A Victim of Racial Profiling.* New York: Broadway Books.

Rudovsky, David. 2001. "Law Enforcement by Stereotypes and Serendipity: Racial Profiling and Stops and Searches Without Cause." 3 *University of Pennsylvania Journal of Constitutional Law* 296.

F. Erik Brooks

RACISM. *See* Abolitionist Movement; Affirmative Action; Baker Motley, Constance; *Brown v. Board of Education* (1954; 1955); Black Codes; Busing Controversy; Civil Rights Movement; Death Penalty and Racial Discrimination; Discrimination; Discrimination by Private Actors; Douglass, Frederick; DuBois, W.E.B.; Emancipation Proclamation; Grandfather Clause; Hate Crimes; Hate Speech; Housing, Discrimination in; Interracial Marriage; Jackson, Jesse; Jim Crow Laws; King, Martin Luther, Jr.; Ku Klux Klan (KKK); Lincoln, Abraham; Literacy Tests; Little Rock Crisis; *Loving v. Virginia* (1967); Malcolm X; Marshall, Thurgood; National Association for the Advancement of Colored People (NAACP); Parks, Rosa; Peremptory Challenges to Prospective Jurors; *Plessy v. Ferguson* (1896); Poll Tax; *Powell v. Alabama* (1932); Public Support for Civil Rights and Liberties; Racial Gerrymandering; Racial Profiling; Radical Republicans; Reconstruction; Reparations for Slavery; Restrictive Covenants; Rodney King Incident; Segregation in Public Education; Sharpton, Alfred Charles; Slavery; Southern Poverty Law Center; Thirteenth Amendment; Truth, Sojourner; Washington, Booker T.

RACKETEERING AND RICO LAWS

The Eighteenth Amendment, known as the Volstead Act, or prohibition, led to the rise of organized gangs that prospered from illegal bootlegging activities. In 1933, with the passage of the Twenty-First Amendment, the Volstead Act was repealed. With prohibition ended, these firmly entrenched gangs turned to loan sharking, gambling, narcotics, and prostitution and began infiltrating legitimate businesses. Congress recognized that because common-law crimes and legislative acts defining crimes focused on particular acts of wrongdoing, it was necessary to criminalize such ongoing activities by organized groups. Thus in 1970, Congress passed the Racketeer-Influenced and Corrupt Organizations Act, known as RICO, which is codified at Title 18, United States Code sec. 1961, et seq.

The law was aimed at the Mafia, particularly the Capos, who were insulated by layers of subordinates. Prior attempts at prosecution often failed because it was difficult to tie the upper echelons of organized crime to specific acts. The remedy fashioned by Congress was to punish association with a criminal enterprise, based on proof of a pattern of racketeering activity. Since then, the scope of such prosecutions has expanded to drug cartels, corrupt politicians, banks, investment firms, and even political protesters.

With the advent of RICO, the government has succeeded in prosecuting the heads of a criminal enterprises even though it cannot attribute any direct criminal conduct to those persons. It is the existence of the racketeering enterprise, proof of the defendant's association with that enterprise, and proof of a pattern of racketeering activities that can lead to a conviction.

RICO specifically seeks to prohibit: (1) participating in an enterprise through a pattern of racketeering activity; (2) using income derived from a pattern of racketeering activity to acquire an interest in an enterprise; (3) conducting the affairs of an enterprise through a pattern of racketeering activity; and, (4) conspiring to commit any of those offenses. (18 U.S.C. § 1962 (a-d)).

An *enterprise* need not be criminal in nature. An enterprise does not have to have a particular name, nor must it be registered or licensed. Although it may be, it does not have to be a commonly recognized legal entity, such as a corporation, a trade union, a partnership or the like.

A political office may also qualify as an enterprise. In political corruption cases the government has named such as entities as "the Office of the Mayor" or "the Office of the Governor" as RICO enterprise participants if the office holder is accused of heading a racketeering enterprise (18 U.S.C. § 1961[4]).

There does not have to be a formal structure to the enterprise. An enterprise can also be an individual or simply a relatively loose-knit group of people or legal entities. These are referred to as "association-in-fact" enterprises. The enterprise must constitute an ongoing organization whose members function as a continuing unit for a common purpose of achieving the objectives of the enterprise.

Association with the enterprise must be knowing but need not reach all activities of the enterprise or exist for its entire duration. In a prosecution, the government must prove that a defendant was associated with the enterprise at some time during the period indicated in the indictment. When Congress created the RICO Act, the phrase "association-in-fact" enterprise was intended to apply directly to the Mafia because a Mafia family is not a formal legal entity nor is it an individual, rather it is a "union or group of individuals associated in fact although not a legal entity." Corporations and their subsidiaries allegedly engaged in criminal activities have also been named as association-in-fact enterprises. Most courts will accept any informal group as an association-in-fact enterprise so long as the group possesses three characteristics: (1) some continuity of structure and personnel; (2) a common or shared purpose; and (3) an ascertainable structure distinct from that inherent in the pattern of racketeering.

Once linked to an enterprise, proof that the enterprise has engaged in these criminal actions on at least two occasions establishes the requisite pattern of racketeering activity. The government can successfully prosecute the Mafia Don under RICO even if the Don has never personally engaged in any criminal behavior. The Don can be convicted because he operated and managed a criminal enterprise that engaged in these crimes.

To prove that a defendant has violated the RICO statute, the government must establish beyond a reasonable doubt each of the following five elements of the offense: (1) that the enterprise existed as alleged in the indictment; (2) that the enterprise affected interstate or foreign commerce; (3) that the defendant was associated with the enterprise; (4) that the defendant engaged in a pattern of racketeering activity; and, (5) that the defendant conducted or participated in the conduct of the enterprise through that pattern of racketeering activity.

Two specific crimes committed by members of the enterprise within 10 years are all that is needed to show a pattern of racketeering activity. The racketeering activity is comprised of the criminal activities in which the enterprise engages—"any act or threat involving murder, kidnapping, gambling, arson, robbery, bribery, extortion, dealing in obscene matter, or dealing in a controlled substance ... which is chargeable under State law and punishable by imprisonment for more than one year."

Thus, these types of enumerated offenses can be violations of either federal or state law. In fact, many prosecutions are based solely on proven violations of state criminal statutes alone; particularly in those instances where the judicial interpretation of proof needed to convict under a state statute is less demanding on the prosecution than under the federal counterpart. Often these are state offenses that may not even have been formally charged as crimes. Thus, RICO effectively expands federal jurisdiction to include criminal acts previously within the exclusive province of the states.

The racketeering acts must be interrelated, and proof of disconnected acts is not sufficient to support a RICO conviction. Racketeering acts are related if the government demonstrates that the acts had the same or similar purposes, results, participants, victims, or methods of commission. Proof may also include that the acts are interrelated by distinguishing characteristics and are not isolated events. Proof does require that the defendant played some part in the operation or management of the affairs of the enterprise.

The use of RICO has evolved. Prosecutors, who previously were unable to convict corrupt public officials or corporate executives because of the absence of direct evidence of the official's participation in the crime, have now turned to the RICO Act to obtain convictions. It is often difficult to prove that a public official has received benefits to which he or she is not entitled in exchange for the awarding of public contracts. Utilizing RICO, prosecutors now strive to show the loose association of an enterprise with benefits flowing to the official in the nature of bribes or extortion. Convictions are more easily obtained.

As an example of RICO's use in a political corruption case, a mayor who conspires with representatives of a company seeking to privatize municipal services may be convicted under RICO with proof that bribes or kickbacks were tendered or accepted; or upon proof that the mails were employed to advance a fraudulent scheme that would deprive the citizens of the honest services of the Mayor ("honest services" mail fraud, 18 U.S.C. §1346); or, similarly, if extortionate threats were made to induce the private company to pay bribes. The receipt of expensive gifts or gratuities by a politician, offered or accepted with the intent to be corruptly influenced, can form the basis of a RICO indictment.

Fraudulent accounting or billing practices that employ the mails (mail fraud, 18 U.S.C. §1341) can link private corporations to violations of the RICO Act. In addition, the act has formed the basis for civil actions targeting illegal or corrupt practices. In civil RICO actions, the lesser standard of proof (preponderance of the evidence) applies, rather than the criminal standard (proof beyond a reasonable doubt.) The former requires only that more likely than not the evidence supports the plaintiff's allegations against the defendant.

Two of the legal scholars involved in the dispute over RICO's original intent are G. Robert Blakey of Notre Dame, a drafter of the act, and Craig Bradley of Indiana University. Bradley argues that Congress overreacted and mistakenly created a statute that is overly broad and constitutionally deficient. Blakey believes that RICO was created to apply beyond the target of organized crime, but he too recognizes the threat that the unbridled use of RICO can pose to civil liberties (see Blakey 1998).

Conspiracy to violate the RICO Act is charged as a separate crime, in addition to the substantive RICO violation (18 U.S.C. §1962[c]). Proof of participation in a RICO conspiracy requires the following: (1) that an enterprise existed as alleged in the indictment; (2) that the enterprise affected interstate or foreign commerce; (3) that the defendant was associated with or employed by the enterprise; (4) that the defendant knowingly and willfully became a member of the conspiracy. The defendant need not have agreed to commit two racketeering acts or actually have committed two such acts.

Whether convicted of the substantive RICO count or RICO conspiracy, the penalties are potentially severe. Each crime carries up to 20 years in prison. In addition, fines can be astronomical and criminal forfeiture can be imposed. The government can seek to forfeit the proceeds of a RICO enterprise. Houses, bank accounts, stocks, cash cars—any tangible property can be seized to satisfy the forfeiture order. The statute authorizes restraining orders and injunctions prior to conviction to prevent the transfer of potentially forfeitable property.

The broad interpretation of interstate commerce permits RICO to function effectively at the federal level. Yet, states have found a role for RICO and state laws operate on both a criminal and civil basis where activities are limited to intrastate activities. States have followed Congress's lead by enacting their own forms of racketeering laws. Connecticut, as an example, punishes similar types of criminal enterprises under its Corrupt Organizations and Racketeering Activity Act. In New Jersey, one may be charged under a similar scheme as a leader of organized crime.

Defending RICO charges is complex. The law is complicated and constantly developing. Federal investigators will link seemingly unrelated and sometimes ancient investigations with current investigations to support the claim of an enterprise and racketeering activity. Wiretaps, video surveillance, the use of cooperating witnesses (usually close friends and allies) and intense financial investigations are weapons in the government's arsenal. In the cyber age, federal law enforcement has armed itself with computer sleuths. Utilizing sophisticated computer programs, hard drives are analyzed. E-mails, financial records, and Web sites visited are retrieved and reconstructed despite the best efforts to have deleted them. Secret grand jury subpoenas are issued for financial records, and witnesses are called to provide testimony or produce documents. Those subpoenaed are warned not to reveal the existence of the subpoena or their testimony with a threat of prosecution for obstruction of justice. Drawing on the skills of specially trained agents of the IRS Criminal Investigation Division (CID), bank records, brokerage accounts, accounting files, and the like are microscopically examined.

There have been various constitutional attacks on RICO, principally involving claims that the act is impermissibly vague, in that it fails to give adequate notice that one may be subjected to prosecution. The courts have found that the act does not offend the Due Process Clauses of the Constitution.

See also Common Law Background of American Civil Rights and Liberties; Compulsory Process; Due Process Clauses; Due Process, Procedural; Grand Jury; Indictment; Internal Revenue Service (IRS); Prohibition; Reasonable Doubt Standard; Speech, Freedom of; Vagueness Doctrine

Bibliography

Blakey, G. Robert. 1998. "Enlarged RICO Threatens Right of Free Speech." *The Human Life Review* 24: 38.

Bradley, Craig M. 2003. "When is Political Protest a RICO violation?" *Trial* 39: 72.

Richard T. Meehan, Jr.

RADICAL REPUBLICANS

In the aftermath of the Civil War, the Republican Party dominated the national political scene under Abraham Lincoln. Not all members of his party believed that Lincoln's ideas, though, were appropriate for the Reconstruction of the South and the region's reassimilation into the United States. In fact, the Republicans split into two deeply divided factions over the issue of Reconstruction. The more punitive faction became known as the Radical Republicans.

The Radical Republicans were never a majority within the party but they developed a strong following behind passionate and principled leadership. Lincoln, and his successor Andrew Johnson, favored a lenient approach to the Reconstruction issue, believing that the top priority should be putting the war's brutality behind the United States and working to bring the South back into the Union as wholly and quickly as possible. The Radical Republicans, many of them the most strident abolitionists in the party prior to the Civil War, believed that the South should be punished severely for the twin crimes of slavery and secession. The Radicals also believed that the protection of civil rights for former slaves was paramount to the South's readmission into the Union.

The Lincoln and Johnson plan for Reconstruction was designed to let Southern property owners regain their land quickly, and allowed states where at least 10 percent of the population had taken an oath of loyalty to the Union to regain statehood. After Lincoln's assassination, Johnson's presidency saw an even more lenient approach to Reconstruction. Johnson supported emancipation and an end to the slave trade through the Thirteenth Amendment, but as a concession to the South he refused to come out in favor of the Fourteenth Amendment's citizenship or the Fifteenth Amendment's voting rights extension to freedmen.

The Radical Republicans, led most prominently by Thaddeus Stevens, Frederick Douglass, and Horace Greeley, supported a harsher penalty for the South. Stevens favored giving Congress the ability to redraw Southern state boundaries and decide on their representation in the legislature. Greeley, one of the Republican Party's founders, was a famed abolitionist pamphleteer who believed that equal rights must be extended to African Americans. Radical Republican proposals included the Civil Rights

Act of 1866, which undermined Black Codes designed to prevent freed slaves from fully exercising their individual rights. The Radical Republicans further created an enforcement mechanism, the Freedmen's Bureau, over President Johnson's veto. The Fourteenth and Fifteenth Amendments both came about as a result of the Radical Republican agenda.

The Radical Republicans' most significant contribution to the post-Civil War era was the impeachment of Andrew Johnson. Johnson actively resisted Radical efforts to impose ever harsher penalties on the South, including ousting Radical Edwin Stanton from his Lincoln Administration position of secretary of war. Radicals had passed the Tenure of Office Act, which required Senate approval of such removals. The Tenure of Office Act became the cornerstone of the charges against Johnson—charges which also included the pardoning of traitors (who were likely Confederate soldiers) and impeding the implementation of the Fourteenth Amendment.

The Senate came within a single vote of the two-thirds necessary to remove Johnson from office. With an unappealing replacement in Benjamin Wade of Ohio and only one year remaining in Johnson's term, the Radical Republicans failed in their move to extract the president.

Within 10 years of Johnson's impeachment, the Radical Republicans saw their influence wane. While they passed the Civil Rights Act of 1875, their numbers and support had diminished because the population saw the Radical Republicans as becoming too enamored of increasing government power.

See also Abolitionist Movement; Black Codes; Civil Rights Act of 1866; Civil Rights Act of 1875; Douglass, Frederick; Fifteenth Amendment; Fourteenth Amendment; Reconstruction; Slavery; Thirteenth Amendment

Bibliography

Benedict, Michael Les. 1973. *The Impeachment of Andrew Johnson.* New York: W. W. Norton.

Leonard, Elizabeth. 2004. *Lincoln's Avengers: Justice, Revenge, and Reunion After the Civil War.* New York: W. W. Norton.

Reichley, A. James. 2003. *The Life of the Parties.* 2nd ed. Lanham, MD: Rowman and Littlefield.

Chapman Rackaway

RATIONAL BASIS TEST

The United States Supreme Court has introduced a number of different levels of scrutiny in an attempt to provide some clarity and guidance in the resolution of legal claims. Typically, cases involving civil rights and liberties fall under one of three broad tests: rational basis, intermediate scrutiny, or strict scrutiny. The rational basis test, otherwise known as "ordinary" or "minimum" scrutiny, is the lowest standard of review. When employed by the Court, the burden falls primarily on the individual to demonstrate that the challenged governmental action does not even meet a minimum level of rationality. Put differently, the judiciary approaches cases warranting the rational basis test with the presumption that the government's initiative is constitutional.

Regarding civil rights and liberties, the Court assigns heightened levels of scrutiny (primarily strict scrutiny) to cases involving fundamental rights. Nonfundamental rights, on the other hand, trigger the rational basis test. For example, the Court has insisted since the mid-twentieth century that certain economic "rights" are neither fundamental nor worthy of the Court's heightened protection. As a consequence, the High Court evaluates legislation that potentially interferes with the economic interests of individual citizens by employing the rational basis test. Consider the Court's treatment of legislation regulating the process of filling prescriptions for eyeglasses in *Williamson v. Lee Optical* (1955). Respondents claimed that the law violated the liberty provision of the Fourteenth Amendment's Due Process Clause. In rejecting that challenge, the majority of the Court argued that the law "need not be in every respect logically consistent with its aims to be constitutional. It is enough that there is an evil at hand for correction, and that it might be thought that the particular legislative measure was a rational way to correct it." The majority concluded its analysis by reminding the parties to the case that minimum scrutiny—or the rational basis test—was the appropriate level of review.

In Equal Protection analysis, the Court reserves the rational basis test for instances in which the alleged discrimination is aimed at groups with a sufficient voice in the political process. The elderly, for example, constitute a class of citizens who, according to the Supreme Court, enjoy disproportionately high protection through the ordinary political channels. Thus the courts insist that they do not require special *judicial* protection. In *Massachusetts Board of Retirement v. Murgia* (1976) the Supreme Court upheld a Massachusetts law mandating that state police officers retire at the age of 50. Rejecting the respondent's call for heightened judicial scrutiny, the Court concluded that mandatory retirement at 50 was "rationally" related to the government's legitimate objective of maintaining a young and fit police force. In contrast, the judiciary employs a heightened level of scrutiny in those cases where a specified group, because of its minority or disadvantaged status, does not find adequate protection through the state or federal legislatures.

When applying the rational basis test, the judiciary will require the government to demonstrate two things: a "legitimate" governmental interest, and means that are "reasonably" or "rationally" related to the stated governmental objective. On most occasions the government will be able to satisfy the requirements of rationality; however, there have been occasions in which the government's interest was neither legitimate nor was the enactment reasonably related to the government's objectives (see *Romer v. Evans,* 1996). In those instances the judiciary is obliged to reject the legislation as unconstitutional.

See also Age Discrimination; Due Process Clauses; Due Process, Substantive; Economic Freedom; Equal Protection Clause; Equal Protection, Economic; Equal Protection Jurisprudence; Fourteenth Amendment (1868); Fundamental Rights; Liberty; Strict Scrutiny

Bibliography

Chemerinsky, Erwin. 1997. "Breakdown in the Levels of Scrutiny." *Trial* 33: 70.

Levinson, Sanford. 1992. "Tiers of Scrutiny—From Strict through Rational Bases—and the Future of Interests: Commentary on Fiss and Linde." *Albany Law Review* 55: 745.

Wexler, Jay D. 1998. "Defending the Middle Way: Intermediate Scrutiny as Judicial Minimalism." *George Washington Law Review* 66: 298.

Beau Breslin

RAWLS, JOHN (1921–2002)

Born in Baltimore, Maryland, in 1921, John Rawls received a B.A. degree from Princeton University in 1943. After serving in the armed forces 1943-1945, he returned to Princeton and received a Ph.D. in 1950. He taught at Princeton, Cornell, and the Massachusetts Institute of Technology before being appointed the James Bryant Conant University Professor at Harvard in 1979.

Rawls is generally considered the most influential political theorist of the twentieth century. His most important work is *A Theory of Justice* (1971) in which he proposed to "carry to a higher order of abstraction the traditional theory of the social compact as represented by Locke, Rousseau, and Kant." Rawls' theory, which he later referred to as "justice as fairness," was in large measure a response to utilitarianism, the predominant moral philosophy in the modern era.

In Rawls' version of the social compact, the state of nature, a notion common to the classical social contract theorists, was replaced with what he called "the original position"—a logical construct disassociated from images of preorganizational human existence. In this rarefied atmosphere, the parties in the original position—that is, the individuals committed to creating a just society—were to select first principles.

To prevent the principles chosen from being influenced by the particularized self-interest of the parties, Rawls added to the original position the notion of "the veil of ignorance," the purpose of which was to eliminate the influence of facts unique to the individual. When behind the veil, Rawls submitted, "no one knows his place in society, his class position or social status, nor does anyone know his fortune in the distribution of natural assets and abilities, his intelligence, strength, and the like." Lacking such knowledge, the individuals would be unable to skew the principles so as to serve their own advantage.

At the same time, Rawls assumed that the parties in the original position would be motivated by self-interest, even though they remained ignorant of what their self-interest would be once the veil of ignorance was lifted. He reasoned that, lacking self-knowledge, the rational individual would choose those principles believed most likely to serve her best interests irrespective of her specific proclivities or place in society.

While denied all particular information about themselves, the parties in the original position were afforded a wealth of general facts about human society. Rawls referred specifically to knowledge of political affairs, economic theory, the basis of social organization, and the laws of human psychology. "Indeed," he noted, "the parties are presumed to know whatever general facts affect the choice of the principles of justice."

For Rawls, unlike his classical forbears, the idea of the social contract was no more than a metaphor, because no contractual bargaining actually occurred. Indeed, once the parties in the original position are reduced to ratiocinating entities they become indistinguishable, and therefore they would be expected to reach the same conclusions, at least in matters of first principles. Thus the process proposed by Rawls could be undertaken by a single individual; bargaining became superfluous.

Two principles emerged from behind the veil of ignorance, and in their final version were articulated as follows:

a. Each person has an equal claim to a fully adequate scheme of equal basic rights and liberties, which scheme is compatible with the same scheme for all; and in this scheme the equal political liberties, and only those liberties, are to be guaranteed their fair value.

b. Social and economic inequalities are to satisfy two conditions: first, they are to be attached to positions and offices open to all under conditions of fair equality of opportunity; and second, they are to be to the greatest benefit of the least advantaged members of society.

So stated, the first principle—the liberty principle—was given lexical priority. That is, liberty was to be maximized before addressing questions of social and economic inequality, and no decisions regarding the latter would be acceptable if they resulted in a diminution of basic liberties. The two parts of the second principle were likewise lexically ordered, with the equality of opportunity principle taking priority over the distribution principle. Much of *A Theory of Justice* was devoted to the derivation and interpretation of these two principles.

Rawls' version of the social compact theory differed from the classical model in another sense. For Locke and Rousseau, the social compact was associated with the creation of political states. Once the agreement had been reached, the theory had in large measure fulfilled its purpose. Rawls' notion did not imply a similar limited focus. Because the theory was ultimately rich in detail, it might serve as a template for assessing the extent to which a society had achieved justice as fairness. Moreover, particular decisions of executives, legislatures, and courts might be appraised in terms of their congruence with the principles of justice emerging from the original position. In his later writings, Rawls discussed the implications of his theory for particular decisions of the Supreme Court, and the abortion controversy.

When introducing his second major book, Rawls observed that in *Theory*, "the social contract tradition is seen as part of moral philosophy and no distinction is drawn between moral and political philosophy." In *Political Liberalism*, essentially a series of loosely connected lectures, Rawls acknowledged that he had not adequately dealt with the problem of stability in the just society. The redirection in his thinking had been foreshadowed by an article, "Justice as Fairness: Political not Metaphysical," published in 1985. The problem as he saw it by the 1993 publication of *Political Liberalism* was this: "A modern democratic society is characterized not simply by a pluralism of comprehensive religious, philosophical, and moral doctrines but by a pluralism of incompatible yet reasonable comprehensive doctrines." The resulting tension was the continuing challenge presented to the pluralistic society. Rawls asked: "[H]ow is it possible for there to exist over time a just and stable society of free and equal citizens, who remain profoundly divided by reasonable religious, philosophical, and moral doctrines?"

In *Political Liberalism,* he introduced what he referred to as three main ideas. First, he proposed the idea of "an overlapping consensus," which entailed drawing a distinction between "comprehensive religious, philosophical, and moral doctrines" on one hand, and a political conception of justice on the other. Whereas the comprehensive doctrines might prove irreconcilable, a commonality of belief might be sufficient to generate an overlapping consensus. Thus, for example, while Christianity, Judaism, and Confucianism may differ widely in their core beliefs, they may nonetheless agree that individual freedom of conscience is essential. This common recognition might be incorporated into a political conception of justice. There might, of course, be religious doctrines which do not share this value, whose adherents believe, like Aquinas, that all heretics should be burned. Rawls responded that such doctrines were not reasonable, by which he meant not that they were necessarily incorrect but that they could not be accommodated in a pluralistic democratic society. In *Theory of Justice,* he had said that in extreme cases—those in which belief seriously threatened the lives and liberties of others—society was not obligated to tolerate the intolerant.

The second main idea developed in *Political Liberalism* was the priority of the right over the good. In this context, *right* referred to matters of political justice, and *good* referred to comprehensive doctrines. "[O]ne common theme of liberal thought," Rawls observed, "is that the state must

not favor any comprehensive doctrines and their associated conception of the good." As an obvious example, the state must not establish a religion as a governmental institution, nor favor one or more religions over others. Of course, whether something is a matter of right or good may be controverted, as when the state permits (or not) abortions, or prohibits (or not) same-sex marriages.

Moreover, a plausible argument may be made that the liberal society envisioned by Rawls with maximized rights and fair equality of opportunity will be less congenial to conservative comprehensive doctrines, and that these may not survive. Rawls responded to this concern by noting the distinction between political and comprehensive liberalism. "Justice as fairness honors, as far as it can, the claims of those who wish to withdraw from the modern world in accordance with the injunctions of their religion, provided only that they acknowledge the principles of the political conception of justice and appreciate its political ideals of person and society."

Rawls' third main concept in *Political Liberalism* was the idea of public reason. "Public reason," according to Rawls, "is characteristic of a democratic people: it is the reason of its citizens, of those sharing the status of equal citizenship." In contrast, "nonpublic reasons are those of associations of all kinds: churches and universities, scientific societies and professional groups." Stated otherwise, public reasons are reasons uninfluenced by special interest or theories of the good. They are reasons that might have been generated from behind a veil of ignorance. Now, however, Rawls found it unnecessary to resort to this heuristic device. Rather, he merely entreated the arbiter of justice to employ only arguments which would satisfy the definition of public reason, notwithstanding that she harbored nonpublic reasons which for her were more compelling.

Rawls allowed that the constraints of public reason did not apply to all political questions but only those involving "constitutional essentials." He acknowledged that this caveat meant that the limitation would not apply to most political questions. This compromise appeared less motivated by principle than to temporize, at least in the short run. Rawls said: "If we should not honor the limits of public reason here, it would seem we need not honor them anywhere. Should they hold here, we can then proceed to other cases." He suggested that the foremost exemplar of public reason should be the United States Supreme Court.

Finally, Rawls acknowledged that he was persuaded that an "inclusive" as opposed to an "exclusive" view of public reason was to be preferred. By this he meant that citizens might "present what they regard as the basis of political values rooted in their comprehensive doctrine, provided they do this in ways that strengthen the ideal of public reason." Examples of this were the abolitionist movement and the Civil Rights Movement, both of which incorporated religious reasons in their arguments. Neither group, Rawls explained, went against the idea of public reason. "[O]r rather, they did not provided they thought, or on reflection would have thought (as they certainly could have thought), that the comprehensive reasons they appealed to were required to give sufficient strength to the political conception to be subsequently realized."

Rawls' third doctrinal work was a small book entitled *The Law of Peoples* (1999), wherein his attention ventured beyond the creation of the reasonably just society. *The Law of Peoples,* however, was not a theory of international law. Rather, it fell clearly within the ambit of his earlier work. For analytical purposes, he recognized three categories of nation states: (1) reasonably just societies (that is, societies modeled after justice as fairness), (2) "decent hierarchical societies," and (3) indecent or "outlaw societies." Within the second category were societies that respected human rights by not engaging in torture, slavery, or religious persecution, for example. But they fell short of the reasonably just society for any number of reasons, such as an absence of democratic governance, or the establishment of a state religion. Outlaw societies were dictatorial and tyrannical and egregiously denied human rights.

In truth, no actual society may fall unambiguously into any of the three categories. They are in large measure hypothetical, but are nevertheless sufficient for Rawls' theoretical purposes. His concern was the proper relationship between reasonably just societies and those falling short of the ideal. The relationship between reasonably just societies could be expected to be amicable and cooperative. At the other extreme, outlaw societies should not be tolerated. Whether this entailed isolationist policies, such as economic embargos, or forcible intervention in the case of the abuse of human rights would depend on the magnitude of the injustice. Most problematic was the middle category. Rawls maintained that it was unreasonable for just societies to refuse to cooperate with any society that had not achieved the ideals of political liberalism. Nor was it their obligation or right to impose justice as fairness from without. So long as such societies had achieved a threshold level of decency, the configuration of political regime was a matter of self-determination for the affected people.

See also Civil Rights Movement; Conscience, Freedom of; Equality; International Law; Liberty; Locke, John

Bibliography

Rawls, John. 1971. *A Theory of Justice.* Cambridge, MA: Harvard University Press.

Rawls, John. 1985. "Justice as Fairness: Political not Metaphysical." *Philosophy and Public Affairs* 14: 223.

Rawls, John. 1993. *Political Liberalism.* New York: Columbia University Press.

Rawls, John. 1999. *The Law of Peoples.* Cambridge, MA: Harvard University Press.

Joseph G. Cook

RCFP. *See* Reporters Committee for Freedom of the Press

REAPPORTIONMENT

Reapportionment refers to the process every 10 years when state legislatures and local governments are required to redraw district lines for members of the United States House of Representatives, state legislators, and local elected officials to reflect changes or shifts in population. The reapportionment and redistricting process is constitutionally mandated, growing out of the right that individuals have to vote and to elect their representatives.

Article I, Section 2 of the Constitution mandates that the federal government undertake a federal census every 10 years for the purposes of apportioning representation in the House of Representatives. Because of population growth, or interstate or intrastate shifts in population, the decennial census is a way to determine how many House members each state should receive. Yet while the census would result in reapportioning the correct number of House members for each state, nothing in the plain text of the Constitution required states either to make House districts of equal population size, or to redraw state legislative lines to reflect changes in population.

Despite these constitutional mandates, public officials often wish to control the apportionment process to their benefit, drawing lines that will favor their reelection. Such a process is often called *gerrymandering*, named for a salamander-shaped state district created in 1812 by Massachusetts Governor Elbridge Gerry.

During the nineteenth century the majority of the population across the country lived in rural areas, thereby giving farm communities significant political representation both in Congress and in state legislatures. By the early to middle twentieth century the population centers had shifted to the cities, yet state legislatures, still controlled by rural interests, refused to reapportion and redistrict after the census. The result was that rural areas with smaller populations than the cities had far more representatives, and they refused to give up political power that reapportionment and redistricting would produce. In addition, many states, particularly in the South, did not want to reapportion and give more seats to urban areas because urban areas were more heavily populated by African Americans. Efforts to forestall reapportionment thus had a racial motive attached to them.

Efforts to challenge the malapportionment at the legislative level were futile and in 1946 the Supreme Court, in *Colegrove v. Green*, was asked to declare the numerical inequality in the apportionment of Illinois congressional districts unconstitutional. Writing for a plurality, Justice Felix Frankfurter stated that apportionment issues were nonjusticiable political questions best handled by the legislatures and not the courts. For Frankfurter, redistricting was a "political thicket" best avoided by the courts.

But in 1962 the Supreme Court reversed itself. In *Baker v. Carr* (1962), the Court rejected the reasoning in *Colegrove* that reapportionment issues are political questions. Instead, the Court held that issues alleging malapportionment raise important constitutional questions that needed to be addressed by the judiciary if legislatures failed to act. In addition to *Baker*, the Court had a few years earlier in *Gomillion v. Lightfoot* (1960) used the Fifteenth Amendment to strike down a districting scheme in Alabama meant to dilute African American representation. For the Court, race was not a permissible factor to consider in reapportionment.

After *Baker*, the Supreme Court ruled on numerous reapportionment issues. In *Reynolds v. Sims* (1964) it stated that the right to vote was diluted if some districts were more populous than others and that state legislative seats must be drawn according to a "one person, one vote" standard. In reaching this conclusion, the justices stated that: "Legislators represented people, not trees or acres." In *Wesberry v. Sanders* (1964), the Court mandated that congressional districts must be apportioned so as to be numerically equal, and in *Avery v. Midland County* (1968) the principle of one person, one vote was applied to local government units. Moreover, in *Lucas v. 44th General Assembly of Colorado* (1964), the Court rejected state analogies to the United States Congress where the Senate was apportioned by geography and the House by population. In *Lucas*, the Court mandated that all legislative seats must respect the one person, one vote standard. In subsequent cases such as *Karcher v. Daggett* (1983) and *Brown v. Thomson* (1983) the Court arrived at positions mandating strict numerical equality for congressional districts, but up to approximately a five percent deviation from equality at the state level was permitted in order to accommodate local governments and preclude the breaking up of political subunits.

By the end of the 1960s the courts had become significantly enmeshed in the middle of the political thicket. Not only did the thicket include general orders to redistrict according to specific standards, but because of the failure of most legislatures to act, state or federal courts actually took the responsibility of redrawing district lines in all of the states from the 1960s onward.

But starting with the passage of the 1965 Voting Rights Act, reapportionment had to confront another issue—race and representation. The Voting Rights Act (VRA) was passed in1965, with subsequent reauthorizations in 1970, 1975, and 1982. One goal of the act was to increase voter registration and turnout among black voters, especially in the South, where they had long faced persecution and legal barriers to franchise. The VRA had many provisions: Sections Two, Three, and Five placed a moratorium on the use of literacy tests, Section Two made illegal any action that diluted voting rights, and Section Five mandated preclearance of any new procedures with respect to voting without first obtaining clearance from the attorney general or a federal district court in Washington, D.C. Yet despite the importance the original VRA placed on voting rights, one matter had not been adequately addressed: the election of minority officeholders.

Starting with *United Jewish Organizations of Williamsburgh v. Carey* (1977), the Supreme Court began using the VRA to mandate that apportionment plans draw lines to accommodate the creation of seats to which people of color might be elected. The line of argument was also addressed in the 1982 VRA reauthorization, and subsequently in *Thornburg v. Gingles* (1986), which seemed to mandate, under certain conditions, that reapportionment and redistricting would be required to create what was called "majority-minority" seats in order to enhance the chances of minority candidates being elected. By the end of the 1980s, then, race appeared to be an important factor again in redistricting.

In *Shaw v. Reno* (1993) the Supreme Court confronted the emerging role of race in redistricting. Upset by what seemed to be an oddly drawn congressional district in North Carolina, Justice Sandra Day O'Connor stated that it appeared to her that racial considerations seemed to be the only possible explanation for its shape. While she acknowledged that factors such as population, compactness, contiguity, and respect for local subdivisions were traditional and acceptable factors to consider when redistricting, she stated that considering only race when reapportioning violated the Fourteenth Amendment's Equal Protection Clause. This case, and subsequently *Miller v. Johnson* (1995), came close to suggesting not only that race was never to be considered when drawing district lines, but that if the VRA mandated that legislative seats be apportioned for that purpose, then that law itself might be unconstitutional! In *Easley v. Cromartie* (2001), however, the Court retreated from this stance, finding ways to accommodate race so long it was not the sole factor used in apportionment and so long as it was used in conjunction with the other traditional districting criteria O'Connor had noted in *Shaw v. Reno*.

One last area where apportionment has been challenged addresses the traditional problem of gerrymandering for political purposes. In *Davis v. Brandemer* (1986) the Supreme Court ruled that in some circumstances, the use of party affiliation to apportion seats might be unconstitutional. Examples of the use of redistricting for political purposes were seen in states such as Colorado and Texas when, after decennial apportionment had already occurred after the 2000 census, new party majorities in both states led both legislatures to again redraw lines in the majorities' favor.

While *Davis v. Brandemer* held some promise at trying to prevent one party or incumbents from entrenching themselves by doing what occurred in these two states, the Court in *Vieth v. Jubelirer* (2004) retreated from that case. In *Vieth*, four Justices voted to overturn *Davis,* while five voted to overturn its test for political gerrymandering. This left it unclear whether the Court wanted to police these issues in the future. As a remedy to this type of partisan apportionment, some, such as California Governor Arnold Schwarzenegger, have called for the creation of nonpartisan districting commissions, such as may be found in Iowa, to draw new lines after the census.

See also *Baker v. Carr* (1962); Equal Protection Clause; Fourteenth Amendment (1868); Frankfurter, Felix; Literacy Tests; O'Connor, Sandra Day; Racial Gerrymandering; *Reynolds v. Sims* (1964); Voting Rights Act of 1965

Bibliography

Grofman, Bernard, and Chandler Davidson, eds. 1994. *The Quiet Revolution in the South: The Impact of the Voting Rights Act, 1965–1990.* Princeton: Princeton University Press.

Keyssar, Alexander. 2000. *The Right to Vote: The Contested History of Democracy in the United States.* New York: Basic Books.

Stephenson, Donald Grier, Jr. 2004. *The Right to Vote: Rights and Liberties under the Law.* Santa Barbara, CA: ABC-CLIO.

David Schultz

REASONABLE DOUBT STANDARD

It is axiomatic in the American system of criminal justice that a defendant is to be presumed innocent and that the prosecution has the burden of proving the defendant's guilt beyond a reasonable doubt. This standard of proof differs markedly from the "preponderance of evidence" standard that is the norm in civil trials. By definition, the preponderance standard means a degree of certainty greater than 50 percent. That is, there is more evidence in favor of a proposition than against it. The reasonable doubt standard is much stricter, although courts and commentators are understandably reluctant to quantify it in terms of the degree of certainty.

The reasonable doubt standard emerged in English and American courts in the eighteenth century and by the nineteenth century was well established in the common law. While the reasonable doubt standard is not explicitly addressed in the U.S. Constitution, the Supreme Court has held that it is an implicit guarantee. In *In re Winship* (1971), the Court anchored the reasonable doubt standard in the constitutional requirement of due process: "Lest there remain any doubt about the constitutional stature of the reasonable-doubt standard, we explicitly hold that the Due Process Clause protects the accused against conviction except upon proof beyond a reasonable doubt of every fact necessary to constitute the crime with which he is charged." Noting that it "plays a vital role in the American scheme of criminal procedure," the *Winship* Court insisted that "the reasonable-doubt standard is indispensable to command the respect and confidence of the community in applications of the criminal law." The Court stressed the need for the ordinary citizen to believe "that his government cannot adjudge him guilty of a criminal offense without convincing a proper fact-finder of his guilt with utmost certainty."

But what exactly is "reasonable doubt"? How should a trial judge instruct a jury as to the meaning of this standard of proof? Clearly, the elimination of reasonable doubt is not tantamount to achieving absolute intellectual certainty as to the defendant's guilt. Traditionally, courts have often used the term *moral certainty* in defining the reasonable doubt standard. A classic example is *Commonwealth v. Webster* (1850), where the Massachusetts Supreme Judicial Court said that before convicting a defendant, jurors should have "an abiding conviction, to a moral certainty, of the truth of the charge" based solely on the evidence introduced by the prosecution. The *Webster* charge, as it came to be known, served as a model for courts to follow, but in the modern era it has been criticized for placing more emphasis on the emotional reaction of the juror, as distinct from a strictly intellectual evaluation of the evidence.

In *Victor v. Nebraska* (1994), the Supreme Court held that trial judges have wide discretion in instructing juries on the meaning of the reasonable doubt standard. In evaluating jury instructions on this issue, the question is whether the court's instruction, taken as a whole, conveys a correct sense of the concept of reasonable doubt. In *Victor*, the Court avoided defining "reasonable doubt" directly but said that trial courts must avoid definitions of reasonable doubt that permit juries to convict a person on a standard that is less than what is required by due process of law.

In only one instance has the Supreme Court found an instruction on reasonable doubt to be unsatisfactory. In *Cage v. Louisiana* (1990), the Court invalidated a jury instruction given by the trial judge in a capital murder case. The judge had instructed the jury that reasonable doubt is

… founded upon a real tangible substantial basis and not upon mere caprice and conjecture. It must be such doubt as would give rise to a grave uncertainty, raised in your mind by reasons of the unsatisfactory character of the evidence or lack thereof. A reasonable doubt is not a mere possible doubt. It is an actual substantial doubt. It is a doubt that a reasonable man can seriously entertain. What is required is not an absolute or mathematical certainty, but a moral certainty.

The Supreme Court held that the equation of reasonable doubt with "grave uncertainty" suggested to jurors "a higher degree of doubt than is required for acquittal under the reasonable doubt standard." The Court also expressed concern about the classic term *moral certainty* and suggested that *evidentiary certainty* would be a preferable alternative. However, four years later in *Sandoval v. California* (1994), the Court upheld a reasonable doubt instruction in a capital case where the judge employed the "moral certainty" formulation. The challenged instruction was as follows:

Reasonable doubt is … not a mere possible doubt; because everything relating to human affairs, and depending on moral evidence, is open to some possible or imaginary doubt. It is that state of the case which, after the entire comparison and consideration of all the evidence, leaves the minds of the jurors in that condition that they cannot say they feel an abiding conviction, to a moral certainty, of the truth of the charge.

In upholding the challenged instruction, the Supreme Court assumed it was unlikely "that the jury understood the words moral certainty either as

suggesting a standard of proof lower than due process requires or as allowing conviction on factors other than the government's proof." However, the Court continued to express reservations about the use of the term *moral certainty* and noted that it has been eliminated from the instructions given in federal courts.

The Model Jury Instructions adopted by the U.S. Court of Appeals for the Ninth Circuit provide the following treatment of the reasonable doubt standard:

Proof beyond a reasonable doubt is proof that leaves you firmly convinced that the defendant is guilty. It is not required that the government prove guilt beyond all possible doubt.

A reasonable doubt is a doubt based upon reason and common sense and is not based purely on speculation. It may arise from a careful and impartial consideration of all the evidence, or from lack of evidence.

The Federal Judicial Center has proposed a model jury instruction that describes reasonable doubt as requiring that the jury be "firmly convinced" of the defendant's guilt. In her concurring opinion in *Victor v. Nebraska* (1994), Justice Ruth B. Ginsburg endorsed this formulation. It is unlikely, however, that American courts will universally adopt a model instruction on reasonable doubt. And even if they did, it would not be likely to make a significant difference in the behavior of juries. Determining guilt or innocence will always depend on the perceptions, reasoning, and conscience of the individuals in whose hands the fate of an accused person rests.

See also Accused, Rights of the; Due Process, Procedural; Fifth Amendment; Fourteenth Amendment (1868); Presumption of Innocence

Bibliography

Mulrine, Thomas V. 1997. "Reasonable Doubt: How In The World Is It Defined?" *American University Journal of International Law and Policy* 12: 195.

Shapiro, Barbara J. 1991. *Beyond Reasonable Doubt and Probable Cause: Historical Perspectives on the Anglo-American Law of Evidence.* Berkeley: University of California Press.

John M. Scheb II and Otis H. Stephens, Jr.

REASONABLE EXPECTATIONS OF PRIVACY.

See Privacy, Reasonable Expectations of

RECONSTRUCTION (1865–1877)

The Civil War's end saw a significant need to rebuild the war-ravaged South. In both infrastructure and social fabric, the South was ravaged and in need of repair. The southern state governments, embarrassed and hurting from the Civil War's damage, were not cooperative partners in Southern reassimilation into the United States. Much of the political controversy over Reconstruction centered on the extension to and protection of civil rights to newly freed slaves in their transition to being fully recognized citizens.

The defeated South would not abandon the vestiges of a slaveholding society willingly and moved to restrict the rights and liberties of the freed slaves. Former Confederate states passed Black Codes that restricted the civil rights of many former slaves. Under the Black Codes, freed slaves were forbidden from owning property outside of city limits (which would have invalidated government plans to grant 40 acres of land to former slaves), marrying between the races, or starting businesses. Into this context, President Abraham Lincoln proposed a plan to rebuild the South that became commonly known as Reconstruction.

Reconstruction under Lincoln would be a fairly benign affair. Lincoln (and his successor, Andrew Johnson) supported folding the former Confederate states back into the Union as quickly as possible. After dividing the old Confederacy into five militarily ruled districts, Lincoln intended to end military rule as soon as possible and to initiate the election of legitimate governments.

The Radical faction of the Republican Party favored a much more punitive approach than Lincoln, imposing harsh penalties on the South and basically giving African American citizens of the South equal rights to their white counterparts. The Radicals were never a majority of the Republican Party, but they had numerous legal successes and came within one vote of ousting President Andrew Johnson during his impeachment trial.

The legal portion of Reconstruction involved a series of acts that were designed primarily to protect the civil rights of African Americans from southern government actions similar to the Black Codes. The Civil Rights Act of 1866 was a specifically designed remedy for the Black Codes, and the so-called Civil War Amendments (comprised of the Thirteenth, Fourteenth, and Fifteenth Amendments to the U.S. Constitution that ended slavery) made former slaves U.S. citizens and extended the franchise to those new male citizens. The Radicals also added a Freedmen's Bureau as an ombudsman to help former slaves and followed the 1866 Civil Rights Act with additional civil rights legislation in 1870, 1871, and 1875.

Republicans won control of all state governments and passed a variety of state-level civil rights laws legalizing interracial marriage over the Black Codes' efforts, as well as creating schools for African American children and other civil rights protections. Literacy rates increased as a result of schooling, and African Americans began to advance socially. In many cases former slaves were appointed to or won prominent positions in state governments, primarily as state senators or state legislators.

Reconstruction formally ended as a result of a political deal. Rutherford B. Hayes and Samuel Tilden were locked in the aftermath of one of the closest and most contentious elections in American history in 1876. When a state sent two separate sets of electors to Congress, the election looked to be deadlocked. Southern states agreed to accept the Republican Hayes as president if military occupation by the North was withdrawn.

The end of Reconstruction began a period of regression for civil rights. Without the Radical Republicans in Congress and carpetbagging Northerners keeping a watchful eye on Southern states, their governments ignored or played a willing part in the subjugation of civil rights. Separate facilities quickly became the norm, the African American elected representatives were soon out of office, and restrictions on property ownership and political participation became commonplace.

See also Black Codes; Civil Rights Act of 1866; Civil Rights Act of 1870; Civil Rights Act of 1871; Civil Rights Act of 1875; Fifteenth Amendment; Fourteenth Amendment (1868); Lincoln, Abraham; *McCardle, Ex Parte* (1869); Radical Republicans; Slavery; Thirteenth Amendment

Bibliography

Foner, Eric.1988. *Reconstruction: America's Unfinished Revolution.* New York: Harper Collins.

McPherson, James.1991. *Abraham Lincoln and the Second American Revolution.* New York: Oxford University Press.

Chapman Rackaway

RED SCARE. *See* Clear and Present Danger Doctrine; Clear and Probable Danger Doctrine; Communist Party USA; Criminal Syndicalism; Espionage Act of 1917; House Un-American Activities Committee (HUAC); McCarthy, Joseph R.; *Schenck v. United States* (1919); Smith Act

REED, STANLEY F. (1884–1980)

Stanley Reed was Franklin Roosevelt's second appointment to the United States Supreme Court, replacing George Sutherland, one of the Court's ultraconservative justices. Reed served a little over 19 years on the Court—from 1938 to 1957. During that time he wrote 231 majority opinions, 20 concurring opinions, and 88 dissents (Burger 1981). Unlike many of the other Roosevelt appointees, he was neither colorful nor temperamental; rather he was hard-working, modest, and unassuming. He was courtly in his dealings with people although he had a strong stubborn streak (Canon, Greenfield, and Fleming1995).

Reed studied law at the University of Virginia, Columbia, and the Sorbonne, but never obtained a law degree. He was admitted to the bar by studying in a law office in his hometown of Maysville, Kentucky, where he also practiced law. Although a Democrat, he was brought to Washington by the Hoover Administration as counsel for the Federal Farm Board and later as general counsel to the Reconstruction Finance Administration. He remained in government as solicitor general during the Roosevelt administration (Fassett 1994).

As solicitor general, Reed argued many of the cases involving the constitutionality of Franklin Roosevelt's early New Deal legislation before the High Court. With a second vacancy on the Court, Reed was a logical choice for several reasons: (1) he was only 53; (2) he had shown his loyalty to the New Deal as solicitor general; (3) he had an impressive legal reputation; and (4) he was uncontroversial (Abraham 1992).

Reed was opposed to judicial policy making. He did not believe that judges should usurp the role of the political branches of government. The result was that he was somewhat conservative as a justice. C. Herman Pritchett, in his classic 1948 book *The Roosevelt Court,* considers Reed only slightly conservative on economic issues and substantially conservative on individual rights issues. Overall, Pritchett claims that Reed "… stands as the most moderate member of the right wing [of the Court]" (Pritchett 1948).

Reed supported some individual rights claims. He wrote the opinion in *Smith v. Allwright* (1944) which struck down the white primary system. He also wrote *Morgan v. Virginia* (1946), which invalidated segregated interstate buses. Apparently with great reluctance he decided to join the rest of the Court in *Brown v. Board of Education* (1954) (Fassett 1994). It may be that Reed personally held traditionally Southern segregationist racial values. On one occasion, for example, he refused to attend the Court's annual Christmas party when he learned black staff members at the Court had been invited (Lazarus 1998).

Reed was the lone dissenter in *McCollum v. Board of Education* (1948) where he rejected the majority's view that the state could not allow religious teaching in public schools. Reed argued that separation of religion from public life was not grounded in history. His views were somewhat vindicated when the Court backtracked on its strong separationist views in *Zorach v. Clauson* (1952) (Fassett 1994). After his retirement, Reed sat in over 250 cases on the U.S. Court of Appeals for the District of Columbia and for the U.S. Court of Claims (Burger 1981). Today he may be best remembered for his caution in *Brown v. Board of Education*, although overall he was a conservative Roosevelt New Dealer and an advocate of judicial restraint.

See also *Brown v. Board of Education* (1954;1955); Conservatism; Discrimination; Judicial Activism; Judicial Restraint; Liberalism; The New Deal; Roosevelt, Franklin D.; Segregation, *De Facto* and *De Jure; Smith v. Allwright* (1944); Warren Court; White Primary

Bibliography

Abraham, Henry. 1992. *Justices and Presidents*. New York: Oxford University Press.

Burger, Warren E. 1981. "Stanley F. Reed." *Yearbook of the Supreme Court Historical Society*. Available at: http://www.supremecourthistory.org/myweb/81journal.reed81.htm. Accessed 8 November 2003.

Canon, Bradley C., Kimberly Greenfield, and Jason S. Fleming. 1995. "Justice Frankfurter and Justice Reed: Friendship and Lobbying on the Court." *Judicature* 78: 224.

Fassett, John D. 1994. *New Deal Justice: The Life of Stanley Reed of Kentucky*. New York: Vantage Press.

Lazarus, Edward. 1998. *Closed Chambers*. New York: Random House.

Pritchett, C. Herman. 1948. *The Roosevelt Court*. New York: MacMillan.

Anthony Champagne

REHABILITATION ACT OF 1973. *See* Disabilities, Rights of Persons with; Disability Rights Organizations

REHNQUIST, WILLIAM H. (1924–2005)

William Hubbs Rehnquist was the 16th Chief Justice of the United States. He was elevated from associate justice by President Ronald Reagan in 1986 and served the fourth-longest tenure as Chief Justice in American history.

Born in Sherwood, Wisconsin, on October 1, 1924, Rehnquist was influenced by the strong Republican affiliation of both his parents. After graduating high school, he attended Kenyon College, but his education was interrupted by service in the U.S. Army Air Corps during World War II. In 1946, he enrolled at Stanford University, where he earned a bachelor's and master's degree in political science two years later. In 1950, he enrolled at Harvard University, where he received a master's degree in government that year. Returning to Stanford in 1950, he earned his law degree within two years, finishing first in his class.

Rehnquist began his legal career by clerking for Supreme Court Justice Robert Jackson during 1952 and 1953. He then practiced law in Phoenix, Arizona, for 16 years. He worked on the presidential campaigns of Republicans Richard Nixon and Barry Goldwater. After Nixon's election in 1968, Rehnquist was appointed as an assistant attorney general in the Office of Legal Counsel. In 1971, he was nominated to replace retiring Supreme Court Justice John Marshall Harlan (the younger). Rehnquist was confirmed by the Senate by a 68–26 vote on December 10, 1971. He took his seat as an associate justice on January 7, 1972, the same day that another successful nominee—Lewis Powell—joined the Supreme Court. After the retirement of Supreme Court Chief Justice Warren E. Burger in 1986, Rehnquist was nominated and confirmed for the Chief Justice post later that year.

During his service as an associate justice, William Rehnquist displayed a strident conservatism that often left him as the lone dissenter in case rulings. As the court itself moved to the right of the political spectrum, he more often joined the majority. While leading the Supreme Court as Chief Justice, Rehnquist appears to have moderated somewhat, at least in comparison to the views of his conservative colleagues Antonin Scalia and Clarence Thomas. Though many important cases were decided by the Rehnquist Court, by far the most memorable was *Bush v. Gore* (2000), which effectively ended the Florida recount following the close presidential election that year. Beyond that ruling, Rehnquist will probably be best remembered for presiding at the impeachment trial of President Bill Clinton in 1999, joining Salmon Chase as the only other chief justice to perform that role.

Scholars will also remember Rehnquist for the four books he authored on the history of the Supreme Court, including one on the impeachment of President Andrew Johnson in 1868 and another on the disputed presidential election of 1876.

After being diagnosed with thyroid cancer in 2004, Rehnquist's deteriorating health led to widespread speculation that he would be the first justice in 11 years to leave the Supreme Court. Ironically, Associate Justice Sandra Day O'Connor—the first women to serve on the Court and a classmate of Rehnquist's at Stanford Law School—garnered that distinction when she delivered the surprise announcement of her retirement in July 2005. Rehnquist died on September 3, 2005 and was replaced by his former clerk, Judge John Roberts.

See also Burger Court; Burger, Warren E.; Conservatism; Harlan, John Marshall, II; Jackson, Robert H.; Judicial Restraint; O'Connor, Sandra Day; Original Intent, Doctrine of; Powell, Lewis; Rehnquist Court; Scalia, Antonin; Strict Scrutiny; Thomas, Clarence

Bibliography

Schwartz, Herman, ed. 2002. *The Rehnquist Court: Judicial Activism on the Right.* New York: Hill and Wang.

Witt, Elmer. 1990. *Guide to the U.S. Supreme Court.* Washington, DC: Congressional Quarterly, Inc.

Yarbrough, Tinsley E. 2000. *The Rehnquist Court and the Constitution.* New York: Oxford University Press.

Samuel B. Hoff

REHNQUIST COURT (1986–2005)

The Rehnquist Court came into being on September 26, 1986 when Associate Justice William H. Rehnquist was sworn in as chief justice to fill the vacancy left by Chief Justice Warren E. Burger's retirement. The Rehnquist Court ended when the chief justice succumbed to thyroid cancer on September 3, 2005.

One commentator has observed that the Rehnquist Court was "the most conservative Supreme Court since before the New Deal" (Schwartz 2002, 13). The Rehnquist Court was in-

deed a conservative Court, due not only to the ideology of the chief justice, but also to the conservatism of Antonin Scalia (appointed by President Reagan in 1986) and Clarence Thomas (appointed by the elder President Bush in 1991). The Rehnquist Court's conservatism was clearly evident in decisions protecting private property rights (e.g., *Nollan v. California Coastal Commission,* 1987), delimiting the power of the federal government vis-à-vis the states (e.g., *United States v. Lopez,* 1995), upholding drug-testing programs (e.g., *Von Raab v. National Treasury Employees Union,* 1989), approving "drug courier profiling" (*United States v. Sokolow,* 1989), and restricting state prisoners' access to federal habeas corpus review (e.g., *McCleskey v. Zant,* 1991). One of the Rehnquist Court's more strident critics, Erwin Chemerinsky, after reviewing the Court's decisions across a range of civil rights and liberties issues, concluded that "[f]rom the perspective of public interest law, the Rehnquist Court, simply put, is a disaster" (Chemerinsky 1999, 37) and that "when we talk about the Rehnquist Court and justice, it really is an oxymoron" (Chemerinsky 1999, 53).

Exaggerated characterizations by some of its liberal critics notwithstanding, the Rehnquist Court was not nearly as conservative as it might have been, due in part to President Clinton's two appointments (Justices Ruth Bader Ginsburg and Stephen Breyer) and also to the fact that two of President Reagan's appointees (Sandra Day O'Connor and Anthony Kennedy) turned out to be more moderate than many observers had expected. Indeed, throughout the Rehnquist era, only Rehnquist, Scalia, and Thomas consistently voted in a conservative direction.

Throughout the tenure of the Rehnquist Court there existed a solid bloc of four reliably liberal votes. In the late 1980s, the liberal bloc consisted of Justices William Brennan and Thurgood Marshall, both icons of the Earl Warren era, and two Republican appointees, Harry Blackmun (appointed by President Nixon in 1971) and John Paul Stevens (appointed by President Ford in 1975). From the early 1990s through 2005, the liberal bloc included

Justice Stevens, the two Clinton appointees, Ginsburg and Breyer, along with Justice David Souter, appointed by the elder President Bush in 1990. Although in five-to-four decisions rendered by the Rehnquist Court, it was most often the four liberal justices in dissent, in many important cases the liberals were able to persuade one or two of the Court's more moderate justices to join them.

Clearly the most powerful members of the Rehnquist Court were its two moderates, Justices Anthony Kennedy and Sandra Day O'Connor. Swinging between the liberal and conservative blocs, these two centrists provided the key votes to forge majorities. Not only did Kennedy and O'Connor prevent the Rehnquist Court from overturning *Roe v. Wade* (see *Planned Parenthood v. Casey,* 1992), they provided crucial votes in cases expanding gay rights (see *Romer v. Evans,* 1996; *Lawrence v. Texas,* 2003), promoting the strict separation of church and state (see, e.g., *Santa Fe Independent School District v. Doe,* 2000), and recognizing the due process rights of military detainees in the war on terrorism (see *Rasul v. Bush,* 2004).

Although the Rehnquist Court was more likely to side with police, prosecutors, and prison officials than with persons accused or convicted of crimes, it maintained the Warren Court's major precedents in the criminal justice arena, chief among them *Mapp v. Ohio* (1961), *Gideon v. Wainwright* (1963), and *Miranda v. Arizona* (1966). Indeed, in *Dickerson v. United States* (2000), the Court explicitly reaffirmed *Miranda* in an opinion written by Chief Justice Rehnquist.

The Rehnquist Court also surprised many observers in rendering two important liberal decisions involving the death penalty. In *Atkins v. Virginia* (2002), the Court divided six-to-three in holding that the execution of mentally retarded inmates constitutes cruel and unusual punishment in violation of the Eighth Amendment. Three years later, in *Roper v. Simmons* (2005), the Court split five-to-four in striking down the death penalty for offenders who were juveniles at the time of their crimes.

Its putative conservatism notwithstanding, the Rehnquist Court also rendered a series of significant decisions protecting First Amendment rights. Indeed, the Rehnquist Court's five-to-four decision in *Texas v. Johnson* (1989), in which the Court struck down a state law making it a crime to burn the American flag, was surprisingly reminiscent of the Warren era. Similarly, *American Civil Liberties Union v. Reno* (1997), which invalidated congressional efforts to curtail indecency on the Internet, struck a blow for freedom of expression in this new medium.

Finally, it should be noted that the Rehnquist Court advanced the cause of women's rights, largely due to the influence of its two female members, Sandra Day O'Connor and Ruth Bader Ginsburg. In *United States v. Virginia* (1996), for example, the Court struck down Virginia Military Institute's longstanding policy of limiting admission to males. Justice Ginsburg, writing for the majority, expressed the view that the Fourteenth Amendment does not countenance "artificial constraints on an individual's opportunity."

After two decades of decisions, the Rehnquist Court left a rich jurisprudential legacy, especially in the First Amendment, Fourth Amendment, Eighth Amendment, privacy, and equal protection areas. It was, in the end, a Court largely controlled by two moderate justices, and thus it is not surprising that the Rehnquist Court's impact on civil rights and liberties was neither consistently liberal nor conservative.

See also Abortion, Right to; Accused, Rights of the; Affirmative Action; Brennan, William J., Jr.; Breyer, Stephen; Burger Court; Burger, Warren E.; Conservatism; Cruel and Unusual Punishments Clause; Death Penalty and Mental Incompetence; Death Penalty and the Supreme Court; Death Penalty for Juveniles; Drug Courier Profiles; Drug Testing; Due Process, Procedural; Eighth Amendment; Equal Protection Jurisprudence; First Amendment; Flag Burning; Fourteenth Amendment (1868); Gay Rights Movement; Gender-Based Discrimination; *Gideon v. Wainwright* (1963); Ginsburg, Ruth Bader; Habeas Corpus, Federal; Internet, Free Speech on the; Judicial Activism; Judicial Restraint;

Kennedy, Anthony; *Lawrence v. Texas* (2003); Liberalism; *Mapp v. Ohio* (1961); Marshall, Thurgood; *Miranda v. Arizona* (1967); The New Deal; O'Connor, Sandra Day; Privacy, Constitutional Right of; Property Rights; Rehnquist, William H.; Reproductive Freedom; *Roe v. Wade* (1973); *Romer v. Evans* (1996); School Prayer Decisions; Separation of Church and State; Speech, Freedom of; Terrorism, War on; *Texas v. Johnson* (1989); *United States v. Lopez* (1995); War on Drugs; Warren Court; Warren, Earl

Bibliography

Belsky, Martin H., ed. 2002. *The Rehnquist Court: A Retrospective.* New York: Oxford University Press.

Chemerinsky, Erwin. 1999. "The Rehnquist Court & Justice: An Oxymoron?" *Journal of Law and Policy* 1: 37.

O'Connor, Sandra Day. 2003. *The Majesty of the Law: Reflections of a Supreme Court Justice.* New York: Random House.

Schwartz, Herman, ed. 2002. *The Rehnquist Court: Judicial Activism on the Right.* New York: Hill and Wang.

Tushnet, Mark. 2005. *A Court Divided: The Rehnquist Court and the Future of Constitutional Law.* New York: W.W. Norton.

Yarbrough, Tinsley E. 2000. *The Rehnquist Court and the Constitution.* New York: Oxford University Press.

John M. Scheb II

RELIGION, FREEDOM OF

One of the distinguishing features of American society in the twenty-first century is the great diversity of religious beliefs and practices that coexist peacefully. The contemporary United States is characterized by a degree of religious diversity not found in any other nation on Earth. As people from all parts of the globe have immigrated to this country, they have brought with them their religious beliefs and practices. By and large they have found a country in which they can hold these beliefs, congregate with others for worship and ritual, and even proselytize without fear of sanction or reprisal. Of course, America's record is not perfect in this regard, and many instances of religious persecution appear in our history. At various times in America's

past, Baptists, Catholics, Jews, Mormons, Jehovah's Witnesses, and other sects have been subjected to harassment, calumny, and even official denigration. Today, however, there is far greater social tolerance of religious diversity. Because human beings can be given to zealotry, intolerance, persecution, and even warfare in the name of God, this tolerance must be regarded as one of the major accomplishments of American culture. This tolerance is by no means perfect or complete. In recent years, there has been a growing intolerance of those who practice Islam, especially after the terrorist attacks of September 11, 2001. However, any intolerance for Islam in the United States pales in comparison to the widespread and official hostility toward Judaism, Christianity, Hinduism, and Buddhism in the Islamic world.

The First Amendment to the United States Constitution provides that "Congress shall make no law respecting an establishment of religion, or prohibiting the free exercise thereof.... " That the protection of religious freedom was of fundamental importance to the founders is underscored by the fact that the Religion Clauses are listed first among the safeguards contained in the Bill of Rights. As David Fellman has observed, "[I]t is in the area of religious belief and worship that man in the emergent modern world first staked out a claim to the free exercise of an important right which the state may not lawfully invade" (Fellman 1965, 3). The Religion Clauses not only reflect the strong desire for religious freedom held by eighteenth-century Americans, they also protect and foster the religious diversity that exists in America today. Certainly the judicial enforcement of these constitutional provisions has bolstered America's cultural commitment to religious freedom and tolerance.

There is widespread agreement, at least in the abstract, as to the value of the Religion Clauses of the First Amendment. Nevertheless, there is equally broad disagreement about what these clauses specifically require, permit, and forbid. Some of the Supreme Court's least popular decisions are in the realm of government involvement with religion, specifically in the areas of school prayer and the public display of religious symbols. One must recognize, however, that these decisions are often as misunderstood as they are unpopular. Some see judicial decisions requiring governmental neutrality in matters of religion as manifestations of hostility toward religion. Others bemoan the increasing secularization of politics and government and view it as the source of moral decline of American society. On the other hand, there are some who refuse to acknowledge the important role that religion played in the formation and development of this country and see every official acknowledgment or accommodation of religion as a step toward the institution of a theocracy. As in other controversial areas of civil rights and liberties, the courts must steer a middle course, bearing in mind the rights and interests of the minority without departing too dramatically from common societal values.

See also *Abington School District v. Schempp* (1963); American Civil Liberties Union (ACLU); Americans United for Separation of Church and State; Anti-Defamation League (ADL); *Bob Jones University v. United States* (1983); *Cantwell v. Connecticut* (1940); Catholicism and Anti-Catholicism; Church of Jesus Christ of Latter-day Saints; Church of Jesus Christ, Scientist; Conscience, Freedom of; *Employment Division, Department of Human Resources v. Smith* (1990); *Epperson v. Arkansas* (1968); Establishment Clause; *Everson v. Board of Education* (1947); Evolution/Creationism Controversy; Freedom from Religion Foundation; Free Exercise Clause; Jehovah's Witnesses; *Lemon v. Kurtzman* (1971); Moment of Silence Laws; Nation of Islam (NOI); Native American Church; Quakers; Religion, Official Endorsements of; Religious Displays on Public Property; Religious Freedom Restoration Act; Religious Schools, Government Aid to; Religious Tests, Prohibition of; *Reynolds v. United States* (1879); Roger Williams, Plea for Religious Liberty; School Choice Programs; School Prayer Decisions; Separation of Church and State; Seventh-Day Adventists; Southern Baptist Convention (SBC); Speech, Freedom of; Sunday Closing Laws; Tax Exemptions for Religious Organizations; Ten Commandments, Public Display of; Unitarian Universalism; *West Virginia Board of Education v. Barnette*

Bibliography

Carter, Stephen L. 1993. *The Culture of Disbelief.* New York: Basic Books.

Fellman, David. 1965. *Religion in American Public Law.* Boston: Boston University Press.

Kramnick, Isaac, and R. Laurence Moore. 1996. *The Godless Constitution: The Case Against Religious Correctness.* New York: W.W. Norton.

Lambert, Frank. 2003. *The Founding Fathers and the Place of Religion in America.* Princeton, NJ: Princeton University Press.

John M. Scheb II and Otis H. Stephens, Jr.

RELIGION, OFFICIAL ENDORSEMENTS OF

The relationship between government and religion has a storied history in America. Among its first settlers were English religious dissidents looking for relief from the established Anglican Church. These immigrants sought religious freedom, but it often was freedom on *their* terms. The early Massachusetts Bay Puritans, for example, chafed under Anglican domination in England, but—established in the New World—asserted their Calvinist principles through the engine of the state. This led Roger Williams to flee and establish Rhode Island as a more religiously tolerant colony. Generally, American colonists were Christians, and their theistic notions frequently manifested themselves in governmental support for religion through taxes and symbolic affirmations of faith.

Cycles of "great awakenings" giving way to more secular periods marked colonial and early national American history. After the Revolution, states struggled with these tensions and embedded a variety of views on religious freedom in their public law. This battle was particularly hard fought in Virginia where Madison wrote the Memorial and Remonstrance Against Religious Assessments and Jefferson shepherded the Virginia Statute for Religious Freedom through the state legislature. After adoption of the Constitution, the Bill of Rights was added to limit the power of the federal government.

The first two clauses of the first of its amendments stated that "Congress shall make no law respecting the establishment of religion, or prohibiting the free exercise thereof." The Supreme Court held these clauses applicable to the states in the 1940s, and heightened the constitutional dimensions of the debate over the proper relationship between religion and government.

One dimension of this debate revolved around governmental endorsement of religion. Its first manifestation occurred in *McCollum v. Board of Education* (1948). Here, Illinois allowed students to leave secular classes before the end of the school day, provided they attended classes of religious instruction. Justice Black, for an eight-to-one Court, held that this practice violated the Establishment Clause as understood in *Everson v. Board* (1947). However, in *Zorach v. Clausen* (1952), a six-to-three Court—over Black's dissent—upheld a program that sent students *off campus* for instruction. Justice Douglas' majority opinion held that "We are a religious people whose institutions presuppose a Supreme Being…. When the state encourages religious instruction or cooperates with religious authorities by adjusting the schedule of public events to sectarian needs, it follows the best of our traditions."

The tension between the "wall of separation between church and state" and accommodating religious traditions has plagued the Court since. Because Americans are among the most religious people in the world (Wills 1990) and the First Amendment has been read to require a "wall of separation," it is not surprising that governmental endorsements of religion are both common and conflictual. Following *McCollum and Zorach,* the earliest phase of this struggle came in public schools. As Establishment Clause doctrine evolved, however, the battle lines moved to include governmental acknowledgements of the Deity itself.

The ambiguity of the "released time" cases did not carry over to the Court's treatment of governmental endorsement of religious practices *in* schools. Most prominent here are the battles over school-sponsored prayer. *Engel v. Vitale* (1962)

saw Justice Black (a Baptist) and a six-person majority (Frankfurter and White did not participate) strike down a state-composed, nonsectarian prayer, saying that "it is no part of the business of government to compose official prayers for any group of the American people to recite." After enormous public outrage on the heels of *Engel,* a full Court decided *Abington School District v. Schempp* (1963) the next year. *Schempp* involved Bible reading at the outset of the school day. Again, Justice Stewart (Episcopalian) was the only dissenter. Justice Tom Clark (Presbyterian) wrote for the majority and held that a governmental action had to have a "secular purpose" and "a primary effect that neither advances nor inhibits religion" to pass muster under the Establishment Clause. The concurring justices who wrote opinions—Douglas (Presbyterian), Brennan (Catholic), and Goldberg (Jewish)—combined to represent a broad canvass of Western religions. Symbolically, at least, this reinforced the core message of the decision: the Constitution is not *hostile* to religion, but its demand for neutrality required government to stand clear of it.

Although public reaction to the school prayer decisions remained decidedly critical, the Court cleaved to this position. In *Wallace v. Jaffree* (1985) ("moment of silence"), *Lee v. Weisman* (1992) (graduation prayer), and *Santa Fe School District v. Doe* (2000) (prayer before a high school football game), it has consistently struck governmentally prompted prayer in public schools. In *Edwards v. Aguillard* (1987), it also struck down a Louisiana law requiring coterminous teaching of creationism with evolution. However, in a line of cases beginning with *Widmar v. Vincent* (1981), the Court allowed—largely on free exercise grounds—private groups to use school facilities for prayer meetings outside the confines of the school day, provided that school authorities do not encourage religious activity.

Beyond the schoolhouse, the Court has been more tolerant of governmental accommodation of religion. *McGowan v. Maryland* (1961) and *Braunfeld v. Brown* (1961) saw the Warren Court uphold Sunday Blue laws against Establishment and Free

Exercise Clause challenges. The early Burger Court allowed tax breaks for religious property—a nod to the role churches play in America—in *Walz v. Tax Commission* (1970). That Court also let stand an *explicitly* religious practice in *Marsh v. Chambers* (1983): a state-paid legislative chaplain who prayed over the Nebraska legislature and ministered to members who wished it.

Religious holidays—days on which most government agencies close down—have come before the Court in the form of seasonal displays. In *Lynch v. Donnelly* (1984), the Court held five-to-four that a city-sponsored Christmas display, including a crèche and Christian figures, was constitutionally permissible. It argued that the context of the display was crucial, though precisely *what context* (the holiday season or the physical setting of the religious symbols) was unclear. *Allegheny County v. ACLU* (1989) addressed this point in finding a crèche inside a courthouse was unconstitutional, but a menorah—grouped with a Christmas tree, poinsettias, and a "Salute to Liberty" sign—outside it was not. The long-term viability of this decision is uncertain, however, as only Justices Blackmun and O'Connor agreed to the rationale of the controlling opinion and neither remains on the Court.

With the rise of the "religious right" in the mid-1970s—part of the ongoing cycle of public assertions of religiosity in American life—issues of governmental endorsement of religion gained political traction. As de Tocqueville noted, eventually in America political issues become legal ones. Recent manifestations of this include the removal of Chief Justice Roy Moore of the Alabama Supreme Court because of his refusal to remove a Ten Commandments monument he had installed in the Court building, and the Supreme Court's decision to sidestep the "under God" controversy in the Pledge of Allegiance case, *Elk Grove v. Newdow* (2004). Reminiscent of the Solomonic decision in *Allegheny County* is the Court's recent treatment of state-sponsored displays of the Decalogue. In *Van Orden v. Perry* (2005), by a five-to-four majority with Chief Justice Rehnquist writing, the Court upheld a six-foot monument engraved with the Ten Commandments. The same day, with Justice Breyer moving from the *Van Orden* majority to give the dissenters in that case a majority in *McCreary County v. ACLU* (2005), Justice Souter wrote for another five-to-four Court and struck down a display of gold-framed copies of the Decalogue in courthouses in two Kentucky counties. The seemingly schizophrenic faces of this area of law remain.

In a pluralistic society, when one set of interests arises to press its claims on government, those opposed to its claims mobilize as well. In a legalistic and rights-based culture with a rich tradition of religious practice, those claims often end up before the courts. In the American context, where justices are appointed by presidents with attachments to organized interests, the battles that rage in the political system will continue to find their way into the Supreme Court. History tells us that government's relationship with religion is no exception to this rule.

See also *Abington School District v. Schempp* (1963); Black, Hugo L.; Blackmun, Harry A.; Brennan, William J., Jr.; Breyer, Stephen G.; Burger Court; Burger, Warren E.; Clark, Tom; Evolution/Creationism Controversy; Douglas, William O.; Establishment Clause; *Everson v. Board of Education* (1947); First Amendment; Frankfurter, Felix; Free Exercise Clause; Goldberg, Arthur; Jefferson, Thomas; Madison, James; Memorial and Remonstrance (1785); Moment of Silence Laws; O'Connor, Sandra Day; Pluralism; Rehnquist Court; Rehnquist, William H.; Religion, Freedom of; Religious Right; Religious Schools, Government Aid to; School Prayer Decisions; Separation of Church and State; Souter, David H.; Stewart, Potter; Tax Exemptions for Religious Organizations; Ten Commandments, Public Display of; Virginia Statute for Religious Freedom; Warren Court; Warren, Earl; White, Byron R.

Bibliography

Wills, Garry. 1990. *Under God.* New York: Simon and Schuster.

Joseph F. Kobylka

RELIGIOUS DISPLAYS ON PUBLIC PROPERTY

Can government display religious symbols on public property without violating the First Amendment's Establishment Clause, which prohibits government from "respecting an establishment of religion"? The leading test to measure Establishment Clause violations derives from *Lemon v. Kurtzman* (1971). There the Supreme Court announced that governmental action must have a secular purpose whose primary effect must neither inhibit nor enhance religion. Such action also must not foster "excessive entanglement" between government and religion. Although the Court has selectively invoked *Lemon* in developing its complex and patchy Establishment Clause jurisprudence, a general rule emerges about governmentally sponsored religious displays on public property: these displays violate the Establishment Clause if they send a religious, rather than secular, message, which the government appears to endorse. Defining "religious" is difficult, and measuring governmental endorsement depends on elusive variables such as the nature of the display, its location, or how an "objective" person might interpret it. Judicial decisions have consequently been divided, uneven, and often unpredictable.

For example, in 1984 a closely divided (5-4) Court upheld municipal sponsorship on public property of the nativity scene during the Christmas holiday season. Speaking through Chief Justice Warren E. Burger, the Court in *Lynch v. Donnelly* (1984) treated Pawtucket, Rhode Island's manger scene as just one of many of the figures and decorations traditionally associated with Christmas—along with Santa Claus, reindeer, candy-striped poles, and colored lights—that the city sponsors to celebrate the holiday and its origins. In the Court's view, the origin and message of the crèche had melded into the city's overall secular holiday season and celebration and did not impermissibly advance religion in violation of the Establishment Clause.

Five years later in *Allegheny v. American Civil Liberties Union* (1989), the Court ruled on another city's display of a crèche, and also a Chanukah menorah, both located separately on public property in downtown Pittsburgh. The Court fractured on the official reasoning, but a (five-to-four) majority this time *prohibited* the crèche, and a different (six-to-three) majority upheld the menorah. Justice Harry A. Blackmun announced the judgment in an opinion joined in parts by individual justices who comprised a fragmented majority. The gist of Blackmun's position was that "the effect of a crèche display turns on its setting," and unlike Pawtucket's, Pittsburgh's "crèche ... is the single element of the display on the Grand Staircase" of the Allegheny County Courthouse, the county seat of government. Thus, "the county sends an unmistakable message that it supports and promotes the Christian praise to God that is the crèche's religious message." The menorah fared better, having been placed on the steps of the Pittsburgh City-County Building next to a Christmas tree and near the mayor's sign saluting liberty. This made the difference, as Blackmun explained: "[T]he display of the menorah is not an endorsement of religious faith but simply ... the city's secular recognition of different traditions for celebrating the winter holiday season."

These cases illustrate the difficulty in trying to accommodate a strong public interest in recognizing religious traditions. The Ten Commandments are a Judeo-Christian symbol, even though to many they have a secular significance: representing the foundation of law and legal codes. In *Stone v. Graham* (1980) the Court struck down a Kentucky law requiring posting the Ten Commandments in public school classrooms, even accompanied by the inscription: "The secular application of the Ten Commandments is clearly seen in its adoption as the fundamental legal code of Western Civilization and the Common Law of the United States." The Court countered that "The Ten Commandments are undeniably a sacred text in the Jewish and Christian faiths, and no legislative recitation of a supposed secular purpose can blind us to that fact." As with the placement of a crèche or a menorah, however, would location of the Ten Commandments somewhere other than in public school classrooms make any constitutional difference? State-sponsored prayer in the public schools is clearly unconstitutional, but the Court ever since *Marsh v. Chambers* (1983) has concluded that no violation takes place when a state-paid chaplain convenes legislative sessions with prayer and benediction.

In the summer of 2001, Chief Justice Roy Moore of Alabama's Supreme Court furtively installed a nearly 5,300-pound granite monument of the Ten Commandments in the rotunda of the state's judicial building. In a federal lawsuit that followed, U.S. District Judge Myron Thompson ordered the monument's removal. On August 20, 2003 the U.S. Supreme Court, as expected, rejected Moore's emergency plea to bypass ordinary appellate procedure and refused to intervene. The next day all eight of Moore's colleagues on the Alabama Supreme Court overruled their chief and directed officials to remove the monument. The Ten Commandments adorn judiciaries elsewhere in the country, for instance, on a plaque in the state courthouse in West Chester, Pennsylvania, and on the court seal in Richmond County, Georgia. Neither, however, is prominently displayed nor as obtrusive as that which commanded national and international media coverage. Moore and hundreds of supporters publicly resisted the court order, proclaiming in public their religious motives. Many were arrested, and he was eventually suspended from the bench. In late August 2003 the monument was removed from the rotunda of Montgomery, Alabama's Judicial Building, but the issue is very likely to return to the nation's highest tribunal.

On June 27, 2005, the final day of its 2004–2005 term, the Supreme Court addressed the display of the Ten Commandments on public property, though not via the politically charged Alabama case. In *Van Orden v. Perry* from Texas and *McCreary County v. American Civil Liberties Union* from Kentucky, a sharply divided Court (five-to-four) circumvented its earlier ruling regarding the Ten Commandments in public school classrooms and made it easier for government to display that symbol elsewhere on public property. In general, the Court focused on context and motive: If the placement of the Decalogue is arranged in such as way as to convey a secular message, there is no constitutional violation; if, on the other hand, the display expresses endorsement of religion, it violates the Establishment Clause. Obviously, each case will have to be decided on its particular facts, and the facts were sufficiently different in these two cases to produce different results.

Prohibiting expression on public property just because of its message could violate the free speech guarantee of the First Amendment, but if the message is religious, does the Establishment Clause compel government to exclude it from a public forum? The Court's response in this area has been very clear and consistent: the free speech guarantee forbids viewpoint discrimination, and the Establishment Clause does not demand that government exclude religious messages conveyed on public property. In *Widmar v. Vincent* (1981), for example, the Court (eight-to-one) insisted that a state university's facilities, opened for extracurricular activities of registered student organizations, must be equally available to registered religious student groups. The Court extended this principle in later cases to cover student access to public elementary, middle, and high school facilities and to funding allocated by public universities to their students. And when a state allowed the Ku Klux Klan to mount a cross on public property in front of the capitol, the Court in *Capitol Square Review Board v. Pinette* (1995) found no violation of the Establishment Clause. If public grounds are available as a public forum, the Court reasoned, the Free Speech Clause did not permit viewpoint discrimination, and the Establishment Clause did not require the state to ban the KKK's cross.

Creating "bright line" constitutional rules has been difficult in the field of religious displays on public property. The phrase "In God We Trust" stands undisturbed on U.S. currency, and the Supreme Court still opens its public sessions with a plea that "God save the United States and this Honorable Court." No doubt traditions involving these religious invocations will be challenged in court. Some religious displays are more contentious than others, and keeping government and religion separate in the United States will be even more challenging in post-9/11 America.

See also Blackmun, Harry A.; Burger, Warren E.; Establishment Clause; First Amendment; Ku Klux Klan (KKK); *Lemon v. Kurtzman* (1971); Religion, Freedom of; Religion, Official Endorsements of; School Prayer Decisions; Separation of Church and State; Ten Commandments, Public Display of

Bibliography

Carter, Stephen L. *The Culture of Disbelief.* 1993. New York: Basic Books.

Hensley, Thomas R., Chris E. Smith, and Joyce A. Baugh. 1997. *The Changing Supreme Court: Constitutional Rights and Liberties.* St. Paul, MN: Wadsworth/West Publishing.

Wills, Garry. 1990. *Under God.* New York: Simon and Schuster.

James Magee

RELIGIOUS FREEDOM IN MILITARY SERVICE

The constitutional protection of religious liberty provided by the First Amendment applies in principle to the armed forces and military personnel, but like First Amendment freedom of expression, the scope of this protection is more limited than in the civilian context. The courts usually defer to military determinations that regulations and actions, which may tend to support religion or limit religious practices, are necessary to sustain the morale, discipline, and readiness of the armed forces. However, the judicial deference normally afforded to such determinations is not absolute, and the courts may intervene when the connection to military requirements is deemed too tenuous to justify the infringement on constitutional protections.

The First Amendment's Establishment Clause does not prevent the armed forces from establishing and supporting chaplains and religious facilities, based on military necessity. In *Katcoff v. Marsh* (1985), the U.S. Court of Appeals for the Second

Circuit noted that chaplains have served continuously in the military since the Revolutionary War, and the chaplaincy corps was an institution familiar to the Constitution's Framers . The transient nature of military service, and the frequent deployment of military personnel to isolated and foreign places, continues to justify the existence of a chaplaincy corps, since its absence would adversely affect the morale and discipline of military personnel. Indeed, the existence of a chaplaincy corps is often necessary to allow military personnel to exercise their religious beliefs.

On the other hand, in *Anderson v. Laird* (1972), the D.C. Circuit Court struck down military regulations requiring mandatory chapel attendance by cadets and midshipmen at the three federal service academies. The academies asserted that such attendance was essential to instill into cadets important values of service and honor, and thus constituted an important part of the education and training of future officers. The circuit court, however, found that mandatory attendance at religious services frustrated the clear intent of the Framers in abolishing governmental compulsion of church attendance. Eliminating this requirement would also have the effect of enhancing the free exercise rights of cadets and midshipmen. Any asserted connection between mandatory chapel attendance and the needs of the military was therefore insufficient to support such a direct infringement on religious liberty.

In cases involving the First Amendment's Free Exercise Clause, the courts have expressed a similar approach of extensive but not unlimited judicial deference to the military. In *Goldman v. Weinberger* (1986), the United States Supreme Court upheld an Air Force regulation that prohibited the visible wear of religious apparel by military personnel while in uniform. The Court refused to second-guess the Air Force's determination that standardized uniforms were essential to maintain the discipline, unity, and readiness of military units. (In response to widespread criticism of this decision, Congress subsequently instructed the military to change its regulations to allow the wearing of "neat and conservative" religious apparel with the uniform so long as it does not interfere with the performance of military duties.)

However, in *Hartmann v. Stone* (1995), the Sixth Circuit Court of Appeals refused to apply judicial deference and struck down an Army regulation that prohibited family child care providers on military installations from engaging in religious practices in their homes during day care hours. The court first rejected the Army's assertion that the ban was mandated by the Establishment Clause of the First Amendment, since allowing such practices would promote religion. The court determined that the regulation was essentially secular in nature, and involved virtually no entanglement with religious activity. The court then rejected the Army's claim of judicial deference, and found the relationship between family child care and the need to foster military discipline and readiness to be sufficiently attenuated to make the regulation an impermissible restriction of the family members' First Amendment free exercise rights. Among the factors leading the court to abandon the standard of judicial deference in this case were the location of the activities (family housing), the individuals involved (spouses and children rather than military personnel), and the nonmilitary nature of the activity (instruction and care of children).

These cases illustrate the continuing latitude given by the courts to military policies and decisions affecting religious liberty. Such latitude will not be applied, however, where the relationship between the limits on religious liberty and the special requirements of the armed forces is simply too tenuous to support even the most deferential review. Military regulations and policies that accommodate religious practices within reasonably defined parameters relating to morale, discipline, and readiness will usually survive constitutional scrutiny.

Mark D. Welton

RELIGIOUS FREEDOM RESTORATION ACT (RFRA)

In *Employment Division v. Smith* (1990), the U.S. Supreme Court considered whether an Oregon law criminalizing the use of peyote, even for sacramental purposes, violated the Free Exercise of Religion Clause of the First Amendment. This case brought into question the precedent of *Sherbert v. Verner* (1963), in which the Court held that the state's denial of unemployment compensation to a Seventh-day Adventist who was discharged by her employer because she refused to work on Saturday violated her rights under the Free Exercise Clause. It is the practice of the U.S. Supreme Court to request and entertain amicus briefs when it is considering the possibility of overturning precedent. Although some amicus briefs were filed, including one by the Native American Church, the Court's decision in *Smith* surprised many national religious freedom organizations that did not file briefs. There had been little or no indication by the Court that it was poised to revisit *Sherbert*. The Court, however, declined to apply the balancing test adopted in *Sherbert* and held that criminal laws of "general applicability" are valid even if they incidentally restrict religious practices.

Almost immediately a number of concerned organizations began to work with members of Congress to develop legislation that would blunt the effects of the *Smith* ruling. These included Americans United for Separation of Church and State, the Baptist Joint Committee on Public Affairs, the National Council of Churches, and the National Association of Evangelicals. They and over 40 other religious and secular groups formed the Coalition For Free Exercise of Religion and established the goal of restoring the *Sherbert* rule. The result was the Religious Freedom Restoration Act (RFRA), a bipartisan measure that was encouraged and signed into law by President Clinton in November of 1993. RFRA applied to any "branch, department, agency, instrumentality, and official (or other person acting under color of law) of the United States…, any state, or … subdivision of a state."

RFRA's stated purposes were to reestablish the *Sherbert* test and "guarantee its application in all cases where free exercise of religion is substantially burdened." Congress intended that any person whose religious freedom was intruded upon by any level of government would have a "claim or defense" against this governmental action. The philosophical basis of the law was revealed both in the wording of the statute and in the debate surrounding its adoption, both of which employed the language of the founders emphasizing free exercise of religion as "an inalienable right."

The *Smith* case was specifically identified in the statute as the impetus for the Congressional act. The doctrine overturned by *Smith* was described by RFRA as a "workable test for striking sensible balances between religious liberty and competing prior governmental interests." Perhaps the most important point in the legislation was that "laws neutral toward religion may burden religious exercise as surely as laws intended to interfere with religious exercise." This provision was aimed directly at Justice Antonin Scalia's argument that laws of general applicability do not exempt people whose religious beliefs may be adversely affected.

Congress based the statute on its constitutional duty to enforce the principles of the Fourteenth Amendment "by appropriate legislation" as applied to state efforts that deny the freedoms afforded in the amendment. And the language is very precise:

Government shall not substantially burden a person's exercise of religion even if the burden results from a rule of general applicability [unless the government can show that the burden] (1) is in furtherance of a compelling governmental interest; and (2) is the best and least restrictive means of furthering that interest.

City of Boerne v. Flores (1997)

Meanwhile, in the early 1990s a case was developing that provided a convenient opportunity to test the constitutionality of RFRA. The St. Peter Apostolic Church was stopped by the city of Boerne, Texas, from leveling its facility and building a new church because the existing building was protected as an historical landmark. The Archbishop, P. F. Flores, sued on the ground that RFRA protected the church from this kind of governmental restriction. The city argued that RFRA was unconstitutional. The federal district court

agreed, but the Court of Appeals reversed and the city successfully petitioned the Supreme Court for review.

Justice Anthony Kennedy's majority opinion dismantled the Fourteenth Amendment basis for RFRA in a six-to-three decision. He stipulated that although Congress can enforce the Fourteenth Amendment with legislation, its authority to do so is not unlimited, as noted in *Oregon v. Mitchell* (1970). Although the Court had approved the Congressional enforcement authority of the Fifteenth Amendment, which duplicates the Fourteenth Amendment's "appropriate legislation" language, Kennedy insisted that the Voting Rights Act of 1965 challenged by South Carolina in 1966 was necessary to remediate decades of racial discrimination in voting (see *South Carolina v. Katzenbach* [1966]). He declared that RFRA was a Congressional attempt to "decree" and "alter" the meaning of the Free Exercise Clause via the enforcement clause of the Fourteenth Amendment. He asserted that "Congress does not enforce a constitutional right by changing what the right is." Unlike voting rights in the South, religious freedom did not have the same kinds of examples of despotic denial by the states. Instead RFRA changed the Constitution. Of course, what he never said was that RFRA overturned *Smith*, which had changed the Constitution.

Kennedy appeared to enjoy giving Congress a civics lesson by emphasizing that "our national experience teaches us that the Constitution is best preserved when each part of the government respects both the Constitution and the proper actions and determinations of the other branches." This not-so-subtle reprimand included reference to *Marbury v. Madison* (1803) as he sought to explain the separation of powers concept while invoking judicial review. In sum, Justice Kennedy concluded that "it is this Court's precedent (*Smith*), not RFRA, which must control."

In a concurring opinion Justice Scalia fashioned a debate about who should resolve these issues: the Court or the people via their representatives? The answer to this rhetorical question was obvious.

Justice Sandra Day O'Connor, joined by Justices David Souter and Stephen Breyer, wrote an impassioned dissent. She proclaimed that *Smith* was "wrongly decided" and should be revisited. Curiously, she conceded to the substance of much of Justice Kennedy's reasoning about the enforcement clause of the Fourteenth Amendment. After making that concession, she returned to her call for a review of *Smith* and its harm to religious liberty. Perhaps recalling Scalia's placement of the Free Exercise Clause as secondary to free speech in *Smith,* O'Conner insisted that historically the Court had always given both "special constitutional status."

Flores makes it clear that six justices (Rehnquist, Ginsberg, Kennedy, Stevens, Thomas, and the architect of *Smith,* Scalia) supported this reduced status for free exercise. And three justices (Breyer, Souter, and its staunch defender, O'Connor) wanted to restore free exercise to its pre-*Smith* status.

A major irony of this case is that two months after *Flores* the church and the city reached a compromise whereby 80 percent of the old building was preserved but the church was allowed to expand the facility.

Recent Legislative Developments

An additional irony was the pairing of Republican Orrin Hatch of Utah and Democrat Ted Kennedy of Massachusetts as the leaders in the Senate effort to pass a new RFRA. These strange bedfellows, along with others, pushed for the passage of the Religious Liberty Protection Act (RLPA). Even the Republican-dominated House of Representatives passed the bill by a vote of 306–118. Some Senators were concerned, however, that the protections proposed under the law were susceptible to abuse by prisoners and people who sought to deny rights to gays. For this reason, the vote on RLPA was delayed and a watered-down version, the Religious Land Use and Institutionalized Persons Act (RLUIPA), passed and was signed into law by President Clinton in 2000.

This statute has not been immune to controversy. Section 3 of RLUIPA, which concerns prisoners' religious rights, was brought before the United States Supreme Court in *Cutter v. Wilkinson*

(2005). Here, the Court concluded that Section 3 did not violate the Establishment Clause of the First Amendment. At this writing, challenges to other provisions of the Act are still pending.

Since *Smith* and *Flores,* more than 20 states have passed their own versions of RFRA. Additionally, the 1993 version of RFRA still applies to the federal government because that portion of the act was unaffected by the *Flores* interpretation of the Fourteenth Amendment.

See also Americans United for Separation of Church and State; Breyer, Stephen G.; *Employment Division, Department of Human Resources of Oregon v. Smith* (1990); Establishment Clause; First Amendment; Fourteenth Amendment (1868); Fourteenth Amendment, Section 5 of the; Free Exercise Clause; Ginsburg, Ruth Bader; Interest Groups; Kennedy, Anthony; Native American Church; O'Connor, Sandra Day; Prisoners' Rights; Rehnquist, William H.; Religion, Freedom of; Scalia, Antonin; Separation of Church and State; Souter, David H.; *South Carolina v. Katzenbach* (1966); Stevens, John Paul; Thomas, Clarence; Voting Rights Act of 1965

Bibliography

Chemerinsky, Erwin. 1998. "The Religious Freedom Restoration Act Is a Constitutional Expansion of Rights." *William and Mary Law Review* 39: 601.

Magarian, Gregory P. 2001. "How to Apply the Religious Freedom Restoration Act to Federal Law Without Violating the Constitution." *Michigan Law Review* 99: 1903.

Van Alstyne, William W. 1996. "The Failure of the Religious Freedom Restoration Act under Section 5 of the Fourteenth Amendment." *Duke Law Journal* 46: 291.

Joe Bill Sloan

RELIGIOUS RIGHT

A term often interchanged with "Christian Right," the Religious Right is a social movement consisting of people of faith whose primary political objective is to mobilize conservative religious people to political action. The primary goals of the

Religious Right are focused on moral reform efforts encompassing social issues such as abortion, gay rights, and public indecency. Though not exclusive, the Religious Right is today largely composed of Christian fundamentalists and other religious conservatives.

History and Composition

While the Religious Right experienced a resurgence in effort, followers, and political success in the mid-1980s and early 1990s, the social movement itself was far from new. The Religious Right was spawned in the early twentieth century in reaction to Charles Darwin, his theory of evolution, and the problems that modern science posed for biblical literalists. The assault on evolutionary theory and modern science culminated in the 1925 Scopes trial in the small town of Dayton, Tennessee. This famous case, commonly known as the "Monkey Trial," pitted anti-evolution crusader and former presidential candidate William Jennings Bryan against Clarence Darrow, then the most famous defense attorney in America. Bryan offered his assistance to Tennessee in its prosecution of local science teacher John Thomas Scopes, who had allegedly violated the state's recently enacted ban on the teaching of evolution in the public schools. Darrow defended Scopes against this charge and in the process enticed Bryan into testifying as an expert witness on the Bible. While Scopes was ultimately convicted of violating the anti-evolution law, the trial is best known for the heated exchanges resulting from Darrow's probing cross examination of Bryan on the literal interpretation of various passages from the Bible. Bryan's difficulty in answering many of Darrow's questions was embarrassing both to Bryan personally and to the fundamentalist movement in general. As a result of this highly publicized trial, the Religious Right temporarily abandoned politics and efforts to change society on a large scale.

The contemporary Religious Right movement traces its origins to the 1970s when evangelical Christians were encouraged by Jimmy Carter, a former Georgia governor and active Baptist, to become active in politics. The Religious Right tasted short-lived victories on local and state issues in opposing "secular humanism" in school textbooks and in supporting laws requiring the "balanced treatment" of evolution and creation science in the public schools. These victories, coupled with success at the national level in helping to defeat the Equal Rights Amendment, encouraged religious leaders to mount a grassroots campaign to fight back against the losses they had experienced at the hands of the Warren Court and liberal legislatures. Various religious leaders set their sights on reversing what they saw as a trend in the Supreme Court for protection of pornography and abortion and disdain for Christianity and God.

Seizing on the potential political power of conservative religious Americans were a handful of religious leaders, such as Jerry Falwell, Pat Robertson, and James Dobson. Founder of Liberty University and pastor of Thomas Road Baptist Church in Lynchburg, Virginia, Falwell formed the Moral Majority in 1979, urging conservative Christians to use their political power by voting their religious beliefs. Due to poor fundraising, a complacent constituency, and a backlash against certain televangelists, the Moral Majority folded in 1989.

With the demise of the Moral Majority, Pat Robertson, a televangelist, Baptist minister, businessman, and 1988 presidential candidate, moved quickly to form the Christian Coalition. Robertson was determined to establish a newer, more powerful grassroots religious right organization to counteract what he and his allies perceived as the growing menace of secular liberalism. The Christian Coalition was composed of conservative Christians seeking to change American politics through the electoral process, lobbying, and various protest activities. Though Pat Robertson was the architect of the Christian Coalition, he handed the responsibilities of director over to a lesser-known and younger individual, Ralph Reed, who was largely responsible for increasing the Christian Coalition's numbers and political influence throughout the 1990s.

The Religious Right would not have been the powerful political force it was in the 1990s if not for Dr. James Dobson and Christian radio. James Dobson is the director of Focus on the Family, a Christian organization devoted to spreading the word on "pro-family" issues. Dobson's success and popularity with the Religious Right stems from numerous parenting and family books, along with a program aired on thousands of radio stations across the United States. In addition to the more benign topics, such as how to raise children, Dobson's radio program and other ministries campaign against same-sex marriage and other gay rights initiatives, public indecency, pornography, and feminism. Members and followers of Focus on the Family are also usually affiliated with one or more other religious right organizations, such as the Family Research Council, Eagle Forum (Phyllis Schafly), Concerned Women for America (Beverly LaHaye), American Family Association (Don Wildmon), and the Traditional Values Coalition. These groups all share the common goal of bringing moral reform to the United States.

Policy Aims

Though the Religious Right has interests in tax policy and foreign affairs, its primary area of concern is domestic social policy, including abortion, education, and gay rights.

With abortion politics, the Religious Right calls for the overturning of *Roe v. Wade* (1973). Therefore, religious right organizations demand that nominees to the Supreme Court must be clear in opposing a right to abortion. In addition to its national focus, the Religious Right has been working at the state level on placing restrictions on the right to abortion. In recent years, banning late-term abortions has been of special concern.

The Religious Right has supported the return of school-sponsored prayers to the classroom ever since the Supreme Court ruled school-sponsored prayers unconstitutional in 1962. More recently, the Religious Right has vigorously supported school vouchers. Although the Supreme Court has upheld the constitutionality of vouchers, no federal voucher program has

thus far been enacted. A number of states, however, have adopted some form of school vouchers.

Finally, gay rights has always been an issue of major concern for the Religious Right. In 2003, the Supreme Court held in *Lawrence v. Texas* that a state law criminalizing homosexual sodomy violated the defendants' rights under the Due Process Clause of the Fourteenth Amendment. This widely publicized and highly controversial ruling mobilized the Religious Right in full force and no doubt contributed to its active participation in the 2004 elections.

Conclusion

The Religious Right has been an extremely successful grassroots organization, leaving its mark on a wide array of social issues. Through voter education efforts, candidate recruitment, protest activities, and media-savvy strategies, the Religious Right is a force to be reckoned with in American politics. Research from the 2004 presidential election suggests that the Religious Right's efforts to get its supporters out to the polls on Election Day helped President George W. Bush win a second term. These grassroots efforts have been so successful that the religious left has begun to adopt many of the strategies currently employed by the Religious Right. As they say, imitation is the highest form of flattery.

Bibliography

Green, John, Clyde Wilcox, and Mark J. Rozell, eds. 2003. *Christian Right in American Politics: Marching to the Millenium.* Washington, DC: Georgetown University Press.

Marsden, George. 1980. *Fundamentalism and American Culture.* New York: Oxford University Press.

Reed, Ralph. 1994. *Politically Incorrect: The Emerging Faith Factor in American Politics.* Dallas: Word Publishing.

Rozell, Mark J., and Clyde Wilcox, eds. 1995. *God at the Grassroots: The Christian Right in the 1994 Elections.* Lanham, MD: Roman and Littlefield.

Wilcox, Clyde. 1996. *Onward Christian Soldiers.* Boulder, CO: Westview Press.

Kyle Kreider

RELIGIOUS SCHOOLS, GOVERNMENT AID TO

The extent to which government aid to religious schools violates the Establishment Clause of the First Amendment has been examined by the U.S. Supreme Court in several cases over the last 50 years. Initially, the Court allowed state aid that served to benefit children, as long as parochial schools were not the primary beneficiaries. With the advent of the *Lemon* test in 1971, however, the Court imposed severe limitations on the types of state aid given to nonpublic schools. This approach is often referred to as a "separationist" approach as it seeks to maintain a sharp division between church and state. More recently, the Court has come full circle in upholding aid programs that are neutral in their application; an approach referred to as accommodation because aid programs are directed to benefiting children, not religious schools.

Between 1790 and 1945 the Supreme Court heard only three cases involving the relationship between church and state. It was not until the Establishment Clause of the First Amendment was incorporated into the concept of liberty embodied in the Fourteenth Amendment in *Everson v. Board of Education* (1947) that aid to parochial schools by state governments could be considered by the Court. Thus, when the Court decided *Everson,* it wrote on a veritable clean slate. This case presented the question of whether a New Jersey statute authorizing reimbursement to parents of money spent for bus transportation of their children to school, even if they were transported to parochial schools, was constitutional. In the majority opinion, Justice Hugo Black cited Thomas Jefferson's view that the Establishment Clause was "intended to erect 'a wall of separation between church and State.'" Despite invoking Jefferson's wall of separation which seemed to imply a total division between church and state, Black upheld the statute. He reasoned that since the state did not actually contribute money to the schools, it did not support them; therefore, there was no Establishment Clause violation. Black subscribed to the child benefit theory under which

government aid that assisted children attending parochial school did not violate the Establishment Clause because the children were the primary beneficiaries of the aid, not the school.

The *Everson* decision pleased many proponents of aid to parochial schools. They were equally pleased by the Court's decision in *Board of Education v. Allen* (1968). In this case, the Court ruled that a New York law requiring public authorities to lend secular textbooks to students in all elementary and secondary schools, including parochial schools, was constitutional. Justice Byron White applied guidelines set forth in prior Establishment Clause cases to distinguish between permissible and impermissible involvement of the state with religion. In order for a law to withstand a constitutional challenge under these guidelines, it was required to have a secular purpose and a primary effect that neither advanced nor inhibited religion. The New York law, according to White, met these requirements because its purpose was to augment educational opportunities for all students and because providing textbooks did not directly advance religion. White also cited Black's child benefit theory with approval because here, as in *Everson,* the children benefited from the aid, not the school.

At the time *Allen* was decided many parochial schools were facing funding crises due to increased educational costs, which in turn led them to request financial assistance from state governments. States were willing to oblige simply because it was cheaper for them to assist church-related schools than to absorb those students into the public school system should they be forced to shut down (Savage 2004, 112). This situation led many states, including New York, Pennsylvania, and Ohio, to offer direct aid in the form of subsidies for teacher salaries, reimbursement for tuition, and tuition tax credits. The *Allen* ruling along with positive reinforcement from both President Nixon and Congress gave hope to parochial schools and state officials that such programs would withstand constitutional challenges (Savage 2004, 113). The first challenges to these programs, which came to be known as "parochiaid," reached the High Court in the 1970s during the Burger Court era.

According to Ivers, parochiaid was *the* church-state issue that defined the Establishment Clause jurisprudence of the Burger Court (Ivers 1991, 69). The Burger Court inherited only two precedents concerning parochiaid, *Everson* and *Allen*, and it "fashioned an establishment clause jurisprudence governing the relationship between the public purse and parochial schools that departed from those cases" (Ivers 1991, 69) because it was less willing to allow state assistance to private schools. The initial parochiaid case decided by the Burger Court concerned both direct and indirect aid given to parochial schools by Rhode Island and Pennsylvania. In *Lemon v. Kurtzman* (1971), the Court formulated a three-pronged test that would guide the Court's inquiry into both this case and subsequent Establishment Clause cases. The *Lemon* test, as these guidelines would become known, was based on prior Establishment Clause jurisprudence. Under the guidelines, laws or policies implicating the Establishment Clause must: (1) have a secular purpose; (2) have a primary effect that neither advances nor inhibits religion; and (3) avoid excessive government entanglement with religion. Government action that failed any part of this test would be invalidated by the Court. The Pennsylvania and Rhode Island statutes offered several forms of aid including teacher salary supplements, textbooks, and instructional materials, none of which could be used to fund salaries or instructional supplements for religion classes. The Court ruled that these statutes violated the *Lemon* test; more specifically, they created excessive entanglement between church and state. With regard to the Rhode Island law, Chief Justice Warren Burger, who authored the majority opinion, pointed out the difficulty faced by teachers who normally teach religious subjects in a parochial school setting, when they had to teach secular subjects for which state aid was provided. To ensure that teachers remained neutral, continuing state surveillance was necessary to enforce compliance with the conditions; thus creating

impermissible entanglement. The Pennsylvania law had the further defect of providing financial aid directly to the private school. Because there were reporting requirements and state surveillance, Burger found that there was excessive entanglement.

Two years later, the Court continued its stringent approach to parochiaid in three cases, which centered on attempts by state legislatures to aid parochial schools in accordance with the *Lemon* test. The leading case was *Committee for Public Education and Religious Liberty v. Nyquist* (1973), which concerned three New York programs designed to aid parochial schools. These programs provided: (1) direct monetary grants to nonpublic schools for maintenance and repair work needed for school facilities; (2) tuition reimbursements for indigent parents whose children attended private schools; and (3) tax credits on tuition payments for parents who did not qualify for tuition reimbursement. The Court invalidated all three programs because they did not have a secular purpose as required by *Lemon*. Justice Lewis Powell wrote for the majority that the state did not attempt to limit repair and maintenance of facilities for secular purposes. Moreover, the other programs, even though they benefited parents more so than schools, still had the effect of promoting religion.

In a companion case, *Sloan v. Lemon* (1973), the Court invalidated a Pennsylvania statute providing tuition reimbursement to parents because it also impermissibly advanced religion. According to Powell, the bottom line was that the intended consequence of the tuition subsidy was "to preserve and support religion-oriented institutions."

In the third case decided in 1973, *Levitt v. Committee for Public Education and Religious Liberty* (1973), the Court considered a New York policy that allowed for the appropriation of 28 million dollars for reimbursing nonpublic schools for numerous activities, including maintaining pupil enrollment and health records. The most costly expense was related to reimbursement for testing and grading both state-mandated and teacher-prepared tests. The Court held that this reimbursement unconstitutionally advanced religion because the tests were not for secular subjects only but had religious content.

Parochiaid cases decided by the Court in the mid-1970s dealt with further attempts by state legislatures to provide aid in accordance with the Court's precedents. The policy at issue in *Meek v. Pittinger* (1975) was enacted by Pennsylvania in response to the adverse ruling in *Lemon*. This program allowed loaning textbooks, instructional materials, and providing counseling, testing, and hearing and speech therapy along with other secular services, to parochial schools. The Court upheld the textbook loan program because it was very similar to the program upheld in *Allen*. The other provisions, however, were found to violate the Establishment Clause. The Court noted that the almost 12 million dollars appropriated by the state for loans of instructional materials and equipment "necessarily results in aid to the sectarian enterprise as a whole" and thus impermissibly advances religion. The auxiliary services were problematic due to the supervision required to ensure that the personnel administering the services were doing so in a nonideological manner. This situation, according to the Court, created excessive entanglement and the program was struck down.

After *Meek*, Ohio enacted a law that authorized the state to provide nonpublic schools with books, instructional materials and equipment, standardized testing and scoring, diagnostic services, therapeutic services, and field trip transportation. In *Wolman v. Walter* (1977), the Court upheld the textbook provision and the testing and scoring services; the textbook provision was indistinguishable from similar provisions upheld in *Allen* and *Meek*, while the testing and scoring services were upheld because parochial school personnel were not involved in either drafting or scoring the exams. Additionally, no payment was given to private school personnel for administering the tests. These two factors were sufficient to distinguish this case from the provisions struck down in *Levitt*. The Court also upheld the speech and hearing diagnostic services as well as therapeutic services because they were not conducted on private school property. The Court struck down the provisions loaning instructional materials and equipment to parochial schools because it was similar to the provisions it struck down in *Meek*. The field trip provision was also invalidated because the private school determined the timing and destination of field trips; therefore, in the Court's view, there was an unacceptable risk of fostering religion.

The Court's attempts to prevent state involvement with parochial school education made it very difficult for states to provide assistance to those schools. The Court's parochiaid decisions in the 1970s evinced several principles. First, the Court upheld its rulings in *Everson* and *Allen*, thereby allowing bus transportation and books as well as other services to parochial school students if these services were provided to *all* children regardless of what school they attended. Second, the Court upheld aid that would not result in close supervision of the religious schools by the state. Third, any type of direct financial assistance was likely to be struck down. Fourth, indirect aid in the form of monetary incentives for parents impermissibly advanced religion. Fifth, any type of aid that required public employees to perform services on school property was invalidated because it advanced religion. Those basic principles provided a backdrop for the parochiaid rulings of the 1980s.

During the 1980s, the Court decided several important parochiaid cases. Two cases in the early 1980s signaled that the Court was ready to "retreat from the separationist principles on which most post-Lemon cases had been decided" (Ivers 1991, 75). In *Committee for Public Education and Religious Liberty v. Regan* (1980), the Court considered the constitutionality of a New York law that required the state commissioner of education to reimburse nonpublic schools for the costs of meeting state-mandated requirements, including state tests. This law, in order to avoid the constitutional flaws of *Levitt*, did not reimburse nonpublic schools for preparing, administering, or grading teacher-prepared tests. Moreover, state expenditures were audited to ensure that only the actual costs incurred in providing the secular services were reimbursed out of state coffers. By a six-to-three margin, the Court upheld this law. Justice White found *Wolman v. Walter* controlling and held that because the non-public school had no input over the content of the tests, nor did the grading of the tests by nonpublic school employees give the school any control over the outcome of the tests, there was no constitutional violation. This situation convinced the majority that the tests could not be used as part of religious teaching.

In *Mueller v. Allen* (1983), the Court upheld a Minnesota statute permitting taxpayers with children attending public or private school to deduct expenses for tuition, textbooks, and transportation. Justice William Rehnquist's majority opinion stressed that the law met the three requirements of the *Lemon* test. First, the tax deduction had the secular purpose of ensuring that the state's citizenry was well educated. Second, the deduction did not advance religion because it was available for educational expenses incurred by all parents regardless of where their children attended school. Also, aid was provided to the schools as a result of decisions made by individual parents, not the state. Third, there was no excessive entanglement because there was no "comprehensive, discriminating, [or] continuing state surveillance" in this program.

With its rulings in *Regan* and *Mueller*, the Court appeared to be approaching an accomodationist position on state aid to parochial schools. However, in 1985 it returned to its separationist tendencies in *Grand Rapids School District v. Ball* (1985) and *Aguilar v. Felton* (1985). These cases offered a new interpretation of Title I of the Elementary and Secondary Education Act of 1965, which provided federal funds to public schools for remedial reading and math instruction to children from indigent families regardless of what school they attended. In *Ball*, two specific programs were in question: (1) a shared time program that allowed secular courses to be offered to private school students during the school day in the private school classrooms that the state leased. These courses were taught by public school employees, although several had previously

taught at private schools; and (2) a community education program that provided courses at the end of the school day in subjects such as humanities and chess. Private school teachers were employed by the state to administer this program. Justice William Brennan found that both programs had the effect of promoting religion in three ways. First, the instructors paid by the state "may subtly or overtly indoctrinate the students in particular religious tenets at public expense." Second, the union of church and state inherent in the state provision of courses in private school buildings "threatens to convey a message of state support for religion to students and to the general public." Finally, the programs subsidized the religious function of the schools by taking over a substantial portion of their responsibility of teaching secular subjects.

In the companion case, *Aguilar v. Felton,* the Court struck down a New York program that sent public schoolteachers and other professionals to religious schools to provide remedial instruction and guidance service. This program also contained a system for monitoring religious content in the publicly funded classes. Brennan found that this program would require a "permanent and pervasive state presence in the sectarian schools receiving aid" and would thus violate the excessive entanglement prong of the *Lemon* test. These 1985 rulings were the zenith of the strict separation required by the Court in government aid to religious schools.

Personnel changes on the Court in the early 1990s led to rulings that were more permissive in allowing states to assist parochial schools. In *Zobrest v. Catalina Foothills School District* (1993), the Court upheld the use of a federally funded sign language interpreter in a Catholic high school. Chief Justice Rehnquist wrote that: "We have consistently held that government programs that neutrally provide benefits to a broad class of citizens defined without reference to religion are not readily subject to an Establishment Clause challenge just because sectarian institutions may also receive an attenuated financial benefit." Here the majority found that disabled children, not the religious schools, were the primary beneficiaries of the federal aid.

In *Agostini v. Felton* (1997), the Court continued down the accomodationist path by overturning its prior rulings in *Aguilar* and *Ball*. Those decisions created a problem since Title I required public school employees to provide services to disadvantaged children who were pupils at parochial schools, but the public school employees were not allowed to enter the private school buildings. As a result, New York City spent over $100 million to put computers in mobile vans which were parked outside the schools in order to comply with the Court's prior rulings in *Ball* and *Aguilar*. In *Agostini*, Justice Sandra Day O'Connor wrote that the Court's understanding of the criteria used to assess whether aid to religion had an impermissible effect had changed. As a result, *Aguilar* and *Ball*'s shared time program were no longer "good law." O'Connor's view was that public funds could be used on behalf of all students for secular purposes without violating the Establishment Clause. She also argued that public school teachers could offer instruction on private school premises and remain free from any religious connection. Moreover, she argued that it was possible for school boards to devise administrative rules to ensure neutrality. Finally, O'Connor asserted that there was no reason for parents to assume that the board of education was involved in or connected to religious education. In other words, there was no outward appearance of church-state commingling. For those reasons, the Court explicitly overturned the prior rulings and adopted an accomodationist stance with regard to government aid to religious schools.

Four years later the Court would determine that the *Meek* and *Wolman* rulings were also "no longer good law" in *Mitchell v. Helms* (2001). In this case the Court upheld the use of tax money to purchase computers for parochial schools. The case centered on Chapter 2 of the Education Consolidation and Improvement Act of 1981, which provided federal money to local school districts for the purchase of educational materials and equipment, including computers, with the expectation that school districts will provide an

equal amount of funding to local, nonprofit private schools. Justice Clarence Thomas wrote for a plurality of four that a general aid program should not be invalidated as a subsidy of religion because it is neutral in its application. He wrote that, "A government computer or overhead projector does not itself inculcate a religious message, even if it is conveying one." Thomas, a Catholic himself, noted that the exclusion of parochial schools from neutral aid programs was rooted in "bigotry" against Catholicism. O'Connor agreed with the outcome in this case but believed Thomas' opinion had gone too far and would seemingly allow government to fund parochial schools on an equal level with that of public schools.

After the Court's post-*Agostini* decisions, many commentators speculated as to whether the Court's modified stance on these issues would allow for state aid in the form of school vouchers. The Court had the opportunity to address the constitutionality of vouchers in *Zelman v. Simmons-Harris* (2002). In this case, Cleveland, Ohio had established a voucher plan in an effort to rescue its failing public school system. Under the guidelines of this program, indigent parents could obtain a state voucher for 90 percent of the cost of private school tuition. During the 1999–2000 school year, 96 percent of the students in the voucher program enrolled in church-related schools. The federal district court and the Sixth U.S. Circuit Court of Appeals invalidated the program because its primary effect advanced religion. The Supreme Court, however, upheld the program. Chief Justice Rehnquist's majority opinion emphasized that prior rulings had never prohibited programs involving private choice. Here, the government aid is neutral because *any* parents of school-age children have the opportunity to avail themselves of the vouchers to attend *any* school.

Thus the Court has become more open to government aid to religious schools than it was in the past. The Court has rejected the metaphor of a high wall of separation between church and state, especially for aid programs that benefit children rather than religion.

The Court's view on the Establishment Clause and state support of private church-related colleges has taken a different trajectory. The Court's rulings in this area are based on the recognition that there is a significant difference between church-related colleges and church-related elementary and secondary schools. College students are adults and are therefore less susceptible to religious indoctrination. Moreover, many religious colleges support and promote academic freedom and an open marketplace of ideas. These conditions reduce the possibility that government aid will, in fact, promote religion. In *Tilton v. Richardson* (1971), which was handed down on the same day as the *Lemon* ruling, the Court upheld Title I of the Higher Education Facilities Act of 1963, which provided aid for the construction of college and university buildings and facilities devoted solely to secular purposes. Chief Justice Burger wrote that the relationship between church and state in this situation had less potential for realizing the evils against which the Religion Clauses were created to protect.

The Court relied on the *Tilton* ruling to uphold a South Carolina law in *Hunt v. McNair* (1973). The law allowed the state to create an agency to issue revenue bonds to finance construction of secular facilities at both secular and sectarian colleges and universities. There were restrictions on the use of such funds for private schools in that the facilities could not be used for religious instruction or worship. The law did not violate the *Lemon* test because it had a secular purpose and did not advance religion. Additionally, there was no entanglement because only minimal state oversight was required to determine whether the money had been properly spent. The Court has also allowed the direct payment of state funds to private colleges that did not use funds for religious purposes and offered degrees in a wide range of programs. (*See Roemer v. Board of Public Works,* 1976.) Ten years later, the Court ruled in *Witters v. Washington Department of Services for the Blind* (1986) that a blind student could use a state tuition grant to fund his education at a private Christian college. State aid to religious schools has thus varied with the philosophies of the justices on the Court as well as the level of education benefiting from government funding.

See also Black, Hugo L.; Brennan, William J., Jr.; Burger Court; Burger, Warren; Establishment Clause; *Everson v. Board of Education* (1947); First Amendment; Jefferson, Thomas; *Lemon v. Kurtzman* (1971); Powell, Lewis F., Jr.; Rehnquist, William H.; Religion, Freedom of; Separation of Church and State; Thomas, Clarence; White, Byron R.

Bibliography

Ivers, Gregg. 1991. *Lowering the Wall: Religion and the Supreme Court in the 1980s.* New York: Anti-Defamation League.

Savage, David. 2004. *The Supreme Court and Individual Rights.* 4th ed. Washington, D.C.: CQ Press.

Kara E. Stooksbury

RELIGIOUS SOCIETY OF FRIENDS. *See* Quakers

RELIGIOUS TESTS, PROHIBITION OF

Article VI of the United States Constitution provides that "no religious Test shall ever be required as a Qualification to any Office or public Trust under the United States." In a letter published in the *Connecticut Courant* December 17, 1787, Oliver Ellsworth, one of the delegates to the Constitutional Convention, insisted that the Religious Test Clause was not intended as an affront to religious beliefs. Rather, explained Ellsworth, "the sole purpose and effect of it is to exclude persecution and to secure to you the important right of religious liberty."

Because the Religious Test Clause referred only to federal offices, states remained free to require religious tests as conditions of holding public office or securing public employment. At the time the U.S. Constitution was adopted, most states did have such requirements. Most of these religious tests required a statement of belief in God or an acceptance of Christianity. Delaware's test was more specific, requiring office holders to profess a belief in the Holy Trinity.

Even today, several state constitutions contain religious tests for public office, although they are no longer enforced. The Texas constitution contains a provision that many would regard as self-contradictory, stating, "…nor shall any one be excluded from holding office on account of his religious sentiments provided he acknowledge the existence of a Supreme Being."

The U.S. Supreme Court first examined the constitutionality of religious tests for state office in *Torcaso v. Watkins* (1961). At issue in *Torcaso* was a provision of the Maryland constitution stating that "no religious test ought ever to be required as a qualification for any office of profit or trust in this State, other than a declaration of belief in the existence of God…. " The appellant, Torcaso, was denied a commission as a notary public because he refused to acknowledge the existence of God. Writing for the majority, Justice Hugo L. Black concluded that the "Maryland religious test for public office unconstitutionally invades the appellant's freedom of belief and religion and therefore cannot be enforced against him."

Similarly, in *McDaniel v. Paty* (1978), the Court invalidated a Tennessee statute barring priests and ministers from serving as delegates to state constitutional conventions. In an opinion announcing the judgment of the Court, Chief Justice Warren E. Burger explained that the historical origin of state bans on clergy holding public office "was primarily to assure the success of a new political experiment, the separation of church and state." Nevertheless, Burger concluded that the ban violated the First Amendment right to the free exercise of religion.

Torcaso v. Watkins and *McDaniel v. Paty* have rendered unenforceable all similar state religious tests and restrictions on clergy holding public office.

In the summer of 2005 the issue of religious tests surfaced in a very different context. When some Democrats in the U.S. Senate suggested that Judge John Roberts' devout Catholicism might render him unacceptable as a member of the Supreme Court because he might feel a religious obligation to overturn *Roe v. Wade* (1973), Roberts' supporters were quick to charge that this amounted to an unconstitutional religious test. The issue was soon mooted by the Senate's overwhelming support for Roberts' appointment as chief justice.

See also Black, Hugo L.; Burger, Warren E.; Conscience, Freedom of; Free Exercise Clause; Religion, Freedom of; *Roe v. Wade* (1973); Separation of Church and State

Bibliography

Dreisbach, Daniel L. 1996. "The Constitution's Forgotten Religion Clause: Reflections on the Article VI Religious Test Ban." *Journal of Church and State* 3: 263.

John M. Scheb II

RENDITION CLAUSE. *See* Extradition, Interstate

RENO, JANET (1938–)

Janet Reno was born July 21, 1938, in Miami, Florida. Her father was a Danish immigrant who worked as a police reporter for the *Miami Herald*. Reno spent most of her childhood on an Everglades homestead, where she was raised by a mother described as hard-drinking, foul-mouthed, and eccentric. Reno's mother had worked as a reporter, occasionally wrestled alligators, kept snakes as pets, and was a kind of local celebrity. Reno attended Cornell University, where she majored in chemistry, and then Harvard Law School, where she was one of 16 women in a class of 500. After graduating from Harvard in 1963, Reno initially had difficulty in finding law positions because of her gender, but did practice with two Miami firms before entering government service in 1971 as staff director of the Judiciary Committee of the Florida House of Representatives.

During the middle and late 1970s, Reno ran unsuccessfully for the Florida legislature, worked at the state attorney general's office, and engaged in private practice. In 1978 she was elected to the office of state attorney for Dade County. The election was remarkable not only in that Reno was the first woman to hold such an office in the state, but that she, a liberal Democrat, was elected in a traditionally conservative Republican county. She faced a challenging situation after four white men she prosecuted for beating a black man were acquitted in 1980. This verdict resulted in deadly riots. However, she salvaged her image and became known for her interest in children's rights and her prosecution of "deadbeat dads," as well as for the establishment of the Miami Drug Court in a city famously ridden with drug-related crime. While some described her as a formidable adversary, others accused her of being soft on crime. She once remarked, "My highest priority is to protect the rights of the guilty, not to convict the guilty" (Rohter 1993).

In 1993 President Bill Clinton nominated her for the position of U.S. attorney general, and she was sworn into office in March of that year. She was the first woman to hold the office. After Clinton left office, Reno ran unsuccessfully for Florida governor in 2002. Reno was diagnosed with Parkinson's disease in 1995.

Reno supporters claim that her tenure in the office of attorney general was responsible for many positive developments. This tenure was, however, plagued by controversies in which Reno was sharply criticized by various groups; these included the standoff at Ruby Ridge, the siege of the Branch-Davidian compound, and the return of Elian Gonzalez to his father in Cuba.

In August of 1992, Bureau of Alcohol, Tobacco, and Firearms (BATF) agents; FBI agents; an alleged white separatist, Randall Weaver; and his friend Kevin Harris engaged in a firefight at Weaver's home in Ruby Ridge, Idaho. An FBI sniper, who believed that he was acting under orders to "shoot on sight," wounded Weaver and then shot Weaver's wife in the head while she stood unarmed and holding her infant daughter in the door of their cabin. Weaver was ultimately cleared of all major charges and filed a number of civil claims against the federal government. Reno approved a $3.1 million dollar settlement for the Weaver family in 1995. Also in that year, Reno signed an order that removed some of the uncertainty from federal law enforcement agencies' rules of engagement and reinforced the principle that federal agents were to avoid killing anyone who does not pose an immediate threat.

Perhaps the source of the greatest controversy surrounding Reno was the federal siege of the Branch Davidian compound in Waco, Texas, in 1993. The Branch Davidians, a religious cult under the leadership of David Koresh, a man claiming to be Jesus Christ, were suspected of illegal weapons stockpiling, polygamy, and child abuse. BATF agents raided the Davidian compound in February 1993, commencing a 51-day siege. The FBI applied to Reno for permission to use tear gas to clear the compound; Reno assented but specified that no pyrotechnic substances were to be used. Nonetheless, after tanks forcibly inserted CS gas (tear gas) capsules into the compound, the entire structure ignited and burned. Between 72 and 86 people died in the fire, including several children. Although the FBI initially asserted that the fire was started within the compound, in 1999 it admitted that the CS capsules used in the attack may have contained forbidden pyrotechnic material. Reno's credibility was seriously damaged by both the event and the 1999 admission. In 1993, Reno took full responsibility for the disaster and offered to resign, but President Clinton declined her offer.

In November 1999, a six-year-old Cuban boy whose mother's attempt to emigrate to the U.S. from Cuba ended with her death, was found clinging to inner tubes off the coast of Florida. The boy, Elian Gonzalez, was released to relatives in Miami. Elian's father, Juan Miguel Gonzalez, had no prior knowledge of his ex-wife's plans, and did not consent to Elian's participation. Juan Miguel asked that Elian be returned to him in Cuba, and Fidel Castro demanded the same. The situation was complicated by questions of lawful custody, of the mother's intentions for the boy, of the father's rights to his son, of Castro's influence over Juan Miguel, of Elian's possible status as a refugee, and of the right of his Miami relatives to petition for asylum on his behalf. In a brouhaha involving the Florida courts, the Immigration and Naturalization Service (INS), the president, the vocal Cuban-American community, fathers' rights advocates, Elian's Miami relatives, Castro, and the opinions of just about everyone in America, Janet Reno determined to enforce the ruling of a federal court to return Elian to his father. Reno has often stated that she worked for a peaceful solution to the conflict, but that the home of Elian's Miami relatives and the crowd which perpetually surrounded it created a hostile environment in which to enforce the law. Federal agents raided the Miami house shortly after 5:00 A.M. on April 22, 2000, and removed the boy. An agent was photographed reaching with one hand to take Elian from another man, while the agent pointed his gun at the terrified boy with the other hand. The raid did little for Reno's reputation generally or as a children's rights advocate.

A significant legacy of Reno's tenure as U.S. attorney general lies in the area of antiterrorism measures. The 1993 bombing attack on the World Trade Center in New York immediately preceded her oath of office, and she was succeeded in office by John Ashcroft, spokesperson for the USA PATRIOT Act and its controversial counterterrorism provisions. During her term in office, Timothy McVeigh and his co-conspirators bombed the Murrah Federal Building in Oklahoma City, and Al Qaeda bombed American embassies in Kenya and Tanzania. According to Reno's testimony before the 9/11 Commission in 2004, her department worked to implement some of the information-sharing measures and increased FISA powers which later became part of the USA PATRIOT Act. During that testimony, Reno also described the increasing intersection between intelligence work and law enforcement work that the threat of terrorism has produced. According to Reno, "In 1994, at our request, Congress passed the first statute prohibiting the provision of material support to terrorist activities. After the bombing of the Murrah Building, the Department [of Justice] developed a comprehensive anti-terrorism package, which Congress passed the next year as the Anti-Terrorism and Effective Death Penalty Act." This 1996 act contained a number of provisions, some relating to domestic fundraising for terrorism and increased law enforcement funding, but more famously included reforms to habeas corpus law, expediting the process for the execution of convicted terrorists.

See also Ashcroft, John D.; Death Penalty and the Supreme Court; Drug Courts; Federal Bureau of Investigation (FBI); Foreign Intelligence Surveillance Act (FISA); Habeas Corpus; Terrorism, War on; USA PATRIOT Act

Bibliography

Anderson, Paul. 1994. *Janet Reno: Doing the Right Thing.* New York: John Wiley.

Rohter, Larry. 1993. "Tough 'Front-Line Warrior.'" *New York Times* (12 February): A1.

Kara E. Stooksbury

RENO V. AMERICAN CIVIL LIBERTIES UNION (1997)

In 1996, Congress passed the Communications Decency Act (CDA), which made it a crime to knowingly transmit "obscene or indecent" content to any recipient under 18 years of age. Various interest groups, including the American Civil Liberties Union, immediately challenged the constitutionality of the CDA on First Amendment grounds, arguing that this measure would effectively prevent them from engaging in constitutionally protected expression on the Internet. A three-judge panel of the federal district court agreed and ruled that the disputed provisions of the CDA violated the First Amendment. On appeal, the Supreme Court upheld that decision, dividing seven-to-two. Writing for the Court, Justice John Paul Stevens concluded that, with respect to cyberspace, "the interest in encouraging freedom of expression in a democratic society outweighs any theoretical but unproven benefit of censorship." The Court's opinion in *Reno* left open the possibility that a more narrowly tailored statute, that is, one limited to prohibiting *obscenity* as distinct from *indecency,* might pass constitutional muster. Congress responded by enacting COPA, the Child Online Protection Act. Unlike the act invalidated in *Reno v. ACLU,* COPA applies only to Internet communications of a commercial nature. Moreover, it restricts only "material that is harmful to minors," which it defines in terms of the definition of obscenity articulated by the Supreme Court in *Miller v. California* (1973). Nevertheless that law too was challenged on First Amendment grounds.

See also American Civil Liberties Union (ACLU); First Amendment; Internet, Free Speech on the; *Miller v. California* (1973); Obscenity and Pornography; Reno, Janet; Speech, Freedom of; Stevens, John Paul

Maria Fontenot

REPARATIONS FOR SLAVERY

The issue of slavery was politically contentious throughout United States history until the Civil War ended the "peculiar institution." Before the Civil War was even over, the notion that former slaves were entitled to reparations for the atrocities they had endured existed. As he marched through Georgia, General William Sherman was joined by former slaves. While still in the field, Sherman with the support of the War Department issued Special Field Order No. 15, which set aside land previously owned by whites for former slaves. This land was divided into 40-acre tracts. Sherman also allowed former army service animals, including mules, to be borrowed for help in managing the land. Thus, the original proposal for slavery reparations became known as "forty acres and a mule." Later, President Andrew Johnson rescinded the offer of land and consistently opposed any congressional proposal that offered land as a form of reparation.

Since the end of the Civil War, the issue of reparations has been periodically raised by civil rights leaders. Notably, Dr. Martin Luther King, Jr., called General Sherman's promise "a check which has come back marked 'insufficient funds.'" Since the late 1980s there have been attempts to secure reparations for the evils of slavery. The impetus for the renewed interest can be traced to reparations the United States government made to individuals of Japanese descent placed in internment camps during World War II. The Civil Liberties Act of 1988 acknowledged the injustice of the internment policy, apologized for its implementation, provided funds for public education in order to prevent any future internment, and offered remuneration. The government granted

redress payments to 82,219 individuals; 28 refused to accept the payment, while fewer than 1,500 could not be located (Bryan 2003, 603). The total amount of compensation was over one billion dollars.

Shortly after the act's passage, Representative John Conyers (D-Michigan) introduced legislation that would establish a commission to study the issue of reparations for African Americans. According to Conyers' web site (www.house.gov/conyers), the legislation, known as H.R. 40 after the proposed 40 acres and a mule, has four goals: (1) to acknowledge the injustice of slavery; (2) to establish a commission to study slavery along with the racial and economic discrimination against freedmen; (3) to study the impact of that discrimination on African Americans who are currently living; and (4) to have the commission recommend to Congress appropriate remedies. The support for this legislation has increased over the last 15 years. Currently there are more than 40 co-sponsors; a dramatic increase according to Conyers. Conyers asserts that there were four million African slaves and their descendants who made a valuable contribution to the growth of the United States from 1619 to 1865, but were not compensated for it. Moreover, African Americans have since been victims of discrimination based on their ancestors' status as slaves. His commission would study the history of slavery and the responsibility, including compensation, of the U.S. government toward the descendants of slaves.

An additional argument by those in support of reparations is that an official apology from the U.S. government is a useful starting point primarily because slaves and their descendants suffered much more than the Japanese Americans interned during World War II. Proponents argue that this gesture, which has been proposed in Congress but has never had adequate support, would bring some degree of closure to the descendants of slaves.

While many argue that reparations should be given, there is some disagreement over what form they should take. Some have suggested that direct payments to any American of African descent is appropriate since they have all been subject to the vestiges of slavery through discrimination. Others have argued that government programs should be established for educational and job training purposes. Additionally, the government could fund grants to black community-based organizations. Some strategists have also proposed pursuing the issue at the international level from a human rights perspective to overcome legal hurdles that exist in the United States such as standing and problems with the statutes of limitation.

Those opposed to reparations suggest that any comparison to the situation faced by Japanese Americans is inappropriate because in that program, the individuals who were actually harmed received the compensation, not descendants several generations removed. Moreover, Japanese Americans were not compensated for racial discrimination per se. Others argue that reparations have been paid through civil rights legislation and affirmative action programs designed to remedy the effects of past discrimination. Some, such as conservative columnist Thomas Sowell, contend that reparations represent an attempt to victimize African Americans.

The issue becomes more complex when reparations are demanded from individuals instead of the government. From a legal perspective, no one currently living owned slaves and those whose ancestors did represent a small number of people. Some critics contend that whites should not be required to compensate African Americans because many whites fought for the North in the Civil War and were active in abolitionist societies in an attempt to free those in bondage. While many who argue against reparations base their opinions in law, much of the rhetoric has taken on racist overtones. In sum, the issue of reparations for the descendants of slaves has become part of the contemporary debate over civil rights in the United States.

See also Affirmative Action; Black Codes; Civil Rights Movement; Equality; Japanese Americans, Relocation of; King, Martin Luther, Jr.; *Korematsu v. United States* (1944); Slavery; Thirteenth Amendment

Bibliography

Balfour, Lawrie. 2003. "Unreconstructed Democracy: W.E.B. Du Bois and the Case for Reparations." *American Political Science Review* 97: 33.

Bitker, Boris I. 1973. *The Case for Black Reparations.* New York: Random House.

Bryan, Chad. 2003. "Precedent for Reparations? A Look at Historical Movements for Redress and Where Awarding Reparations for Slavery Might Fit." *Alabama Law Review* 54: 599.

Reed, Adolph L., Jr. 2000. "The Case Against Reparations." *Progressive* 64: 15.

Robinson, Randall. 2000. *The Debt: What America Owes to Blacks.* New York: Dutton.

Kara E. Stooksbury

REPORTERS COMMITTEE FOR FREEDOM OF THE PRESS (RCFP)

Civil rights and anti-Vietnam War demonstrations during the 1960s contributed to an unprecedented wave of government subpoenas to reporters who, in the course of covering such activities, had gained the confidence of protest leaders. *New York Times* reporter Earl Caldwell was subpoenaed by a federal grand jury seeking information about the militant Black Panthers, who allegedly had made assassination threats against President Richard Nixon. The subpoena demanded that Caldwell bring with him all his notes and tapes concerning the group.

When Caldwell challenged the broad scope of the subpoena, the district court struck a compromise whereby Caldwell would be not be compelled to reveal his confidential sources or information unless the federal government could show a compelling and overriding national interest in the information and that such information was not available by other means. Despite this grant of a conditional privilege, Caldwell still refused to appear before the grand jury, arguing that his sources would not know what he said behind the closed doors of a grand jury and might no longer trust him. Caldwell was found in contempt of court.

Caldwell's situation, as well as that of other subpoenaed journalists, mobilized leaders in the journalism community to provide legal assistance for reporters facing First Amendment battles. In 1970, a group of prominent journalists, including J. Anthony Lukas, Murray Fromson, Fred Graham, Jack Nelson, Ben Bradlee, Eileen Shanahan, Mike Wallace, Robert Maynard, and Tom Wicker, formed The Reporters Committee for Freedom of the Press to solicit contributions for legal fees and to recruit attorneys for pro bono work.

The committee first worked from a desk in the pressroom at the U.S. Supreme Court until support from foundations and news organizations enabled the RCFP to rent its own office space. From its inception, the committee began fighting a number of free speech battles, intervening in court cases and fighting to keep President Nixon from retaining sole custody of his presidential papers.

Since its 1970 founding, the RCFP has played a role in virtually every significant press freedom case that has come before the Supreme Court—from *Department of Justice v. RCFP* (1989), concerning interpretation of an exemption to the Freedom of Information Act, to the landmark gag order case of *Nebraska Press Association v. Stuart* (1976) to the question of whether a parody can cause emotional distress in *Hustler Magazine v. Falwell* (1988). In addition, the committee has gone to the aid of reporters and other media workers in hundreds of cases in federal and state courts. The RCFP also has become the leading advocate for reporters' interest on Internet issues. By its own count, the RCFP serves approximately two thousand working journalists every year. And since its founding, no reporter has ever paid for the committee's help in defending First Amendment rights, which the committee cites as its proudest achievement.

Education about First Amendment rights and federal and state statutes affecting journalism is another important aspect of the committee's mission. State and federal agencies, members of Congress, and educators regularly seek the committee's expertise. RCFP publishes *News Media and the Law*, a quarterly legal review, a biweekly newsletter, and various handbooks on media law issues. It also sponsors a 24-hour hotline. The committee makes many of these materials available at no cost to users on its Web site at www.rcfp.org.

See also First Amendment; Freedom of Information Act; Gag Orders; *Hustler Magazine v. Falwell* (1988); Internet, Free Speech on the; Press, Freedom of the; Speech, Freedom of

Dorothy Bowles

REPRESENTATION, LEGAL. *See* Counsel, Right to

REPRESENTATIVE DEMOCRACY

Representative democracy is a form of government in which citizens choose representatives through free and fair elections to make decisions on their behalf. This is distinguished from a direct democracy in which citizens participate directly in the making of public policy. The United States can be characterized as a representative democracy, in that voters select representatives to serve in Congress, the 50 state legislatures, and numerous local boards, councils, and commissions.

With the Mayflower Compact in 1620, the tradition of legally established government began in America. For the next 156 years, America would be a colony of England, required to abide by the rule of the monarch, a hereditary king or queen. However, many of the colonists who helped settle America were fleeing from England to escape the oppression of the monarchy and to create better lives for themselves. As America grew and organized and the colonists became increasingly frustrated with the demands of the king, the call for independence from England escalated. Immediately after independence was declared in 1776, a committee of Congress drew up the Articles of Confederation, the first constitution of the United States. Because this instrument of government could not formally go into effect until all 13 states had ratified it and because this unanimity was not achieved until 1781, the Articles served as the de facto basis of national government during the most critical years of the American Revolution. The Articles of Confederation were barely adequate as a wartime constitution. With final American victory and the signing of a peace treaty in 1783, the inherent weaknesses of the Articles posed a major threat to the perpetuation of a union of states. Under the Articles Congress lacked the power to tax and to regulate commerce among the states or with foreign countries. The national government consisted of a one-house congress in which each state had one vote. There was no separate executive branch and no independent system of courts. The national government exercised no powers over individual citizens. Responding to what they regarded as an emerging political crisis, the Framers of the American Constitution, meeting in Philadelphia in the summer of 1787, decided that they must create a system in which citizens had a voice in their national government. Accordingly, they created a combination of direct representative democracy (the U.S. House of Representatives) and indirect representative democracy (the U.S. Senate, selected by popularly elected state legislatures).

The term democracy, Greek for "rule of the people," was invented by the ancient Greeks in the early sixth century b.c. It defined the type of government that existed in Athens at the time, a system of majority rule by an assembly of male citizens who voted directly on decisions—direct democracy. From the beginnings of democracy in ancient Greece to the present, numerous forms of democracy have emerged, such as direct, participatory, representative, and deliberative. It is important to recognize that the form of government a country creates frequently reflects an overlapping of ideologies, political systems, and economic systems. Through a process of constitutional development, a country may adopt the form of democracy best suited to meet its needs. The United States, Germany, Canada, and the United Kingdom are representative democracies, but each has adopted the form of democracy that best reflects its own unique history and needs.

In representative democracies, citizens elect leaders who convey the interests and desires of the citizens within the representative governmental process. Since our founders were concerned with preventing any one segment within the government

from gaining too much power, they strove for a system of checks and balances. The system of checks and balances in the United States includes an independent judiciary to provide a balance against too much power being held by the representatives, staggered elections to guard against any extreme shifts in political climate, and an electoral college to select the president. With staggered elections, American voters elect a president (via the electoral college) every four years, senators every six years, and representatives every two years. The electoral college consists of delegates from each state based on the total number of senators and representatives that state has. Originally, the person receiving the most electoral college votes was elected president, and the person receiving the second largest number of electoral votes was elected vice-president. In the case of a tie in the electoral college, the House of Representatives would choose the president. The electoral college, however, has changed over time, and it has come under attack because representation is not equally shared. No matter what the population of a state, each state has two senators and at least one representative. As a result, in 1990, each electoral vote in Alaska was equivalent to approximately 112,000 people, while each electoral vote in New York was equivalent to approximately 404,000 people. Therefore, it would take almost four votes in New York to equal one vote in Alaska. This has resulted in some politicians calling for changes to or elimination of the electoral college.

From its beginnings in Greece and Rome, democracy has withstood many challenges and remains the most successful form of government. Since 1900, the United States, the United Kingdom, Sweden, and Switzerland have had unbroken reigns of democracy. Germany has been a democracy since 1949, and Canada is another successful democracy. The United States government has evolved over the years. This adaptability is a desirable aspect of representative democracy because it allows for changes in the governmental system as society changes. Revisions to the U.S. government include the end of slavery, establishment of a woman's right to vote, furtherance of civil rights, and, more recently, term limits and balanced budget amendments. Representative democracy can be messy and contentious, but it has proven to be an extremely effective means of governing pluralistic, conflictual societies like that of the United States (see Rosenthal, Loomis, Hibbing, and Kurtz 2002). One reason for this is that elected legislatures are more deliberative than impulsive; they do not respond only to transient popular majorities but to a wide spectrum of interests (Haskell 2000).

In 1997, more than 60 percent of the world's population lived in a democracy, around 25 percent in a Communist state, 10 percent under a military junta, and the remainder under autocracy in a one-party state or monarchy. The biggest threat to democracy in the twentieth century was fascism, which became the constitutional form of government in both Germany and Italy. These fascist governments invaded neighboring peaceful democratic countries in the 1930s and 1940s and attempted to take them over. Although many Americans at the time believed that communism was the primary threat to democratic governments, the communists never overthrew a democratic government that had been in place in a country for more than three years.

In the twenty-first century, the primary threats to democracy have come from vocal and extremely radical religious groups. These groups have incorporated terrorism, including the horrific attack of 9/11 on the World Trade Center and the 2004 subway bombing in Spain, to propel themselves and their goals into the media spotlight. Despite strident rhetoric and acts of terrorism by these groups, the majority of people in the world today live under some form of representative democracy.

See also Abolitionist Movement; Articles of Confederation; Civil Rights; Constitutional Democracy; Liberalism; Slavery; Terrorism, War on; Women's Suffrage

Bibliography

Haskell, John. 2000. *Direct Democracy or Representative Government?: Dispelling the Populist Myth.* Boulder, Colorado: Westview Press.

Rosenthal, Alan, Burdett A. Loomis, John R. Hibbing, and Karl T. Kurtz. 2002. *Republic on Trial: The Case for Representative Democracy.* Washington, DC: CQ Press.

Nissa Dahlin-Brown

REPRODUCTIVE FREEDOM

The judiciary, most notably the U.S. Supreme Court, plays a crucial role in interpreting the extent of civil rights. A single Supreme Court ruling can change the very nature of a right throughout the entire country. There is no explicit right to privacy listed in the United States Constitution; rather it is an implied right established via precedent. The Supreme Court initially acknowledged protection under the Fourteenth Amendment's Due Process Clause for personal privacy and freedom from governmental intrusions in the areas of marriage and reproduction in the 1920s. Until the last half of the 1800s, contraception and abortion were virtually unregulated by law in the United States. In 1873, the federal Comstock Law was enacted to prohibit interstate mailing of materials considered to be obscene, which included information relating to birth control as well as contraceptive devices.

In 1879, Connecticut enacted a law that made it illegal to use any type of birth control (drugs, medicinal article, or instrument) for the purpose of preventing conception. It was not until *Griswold v. Connecticut* (1965), that the Court overturned the Connecticut statute on the basis of a denial of the right of privacy of married couples. *Griswold* only applied the right of privacy to married individuals in relation to contraceptive use. *Eisenstadt v. Baird* (1972) extended the right of privacy in relation to contraceptive use to unmarried individuals. Justice William J. Brennan contended that, "if the right of privacy means anything, it is the right of the individual, married or single, to be free from unwarranted governmental intrusion into matters so fundamentally affecting a person as the decision whether to bear or beget a child."

With regard to abortion rights and reproductive freedom, jurisdiction over abortions historically resided with the states rather than with the federal government. By 1900, most states had some type of criminal offense linked to abortions. However, states generally exempted from prosecution therapeutic abortions preformed by physicians to save the life of the mother. In 1973, the U.S. Supreme Court granted review in *Roe v. Wade* and *Doe v. Bolton.* The majority in *Roe* held that the state's compelling interest in preventing abortion and protecting the life of the mother outweighs a mother's personal autonomy only after viability. Before viability, it was held, the mother's liberty of personal privacy limits state interference due to the lack of a compelling state interest. Thus, the trimester approach was applied to abortions: (1) during the first trimester of a pregnancy the decision regarding an abortion is left up to the women and her doctor, (2) in the second trimester states may regulate abortions but only in a manner that relates to the safeguarding of the health of a women, and (3) in the third trimester, the state's interest is of preserving the life of the unborn child.

Several states tried to lessen the impact of the *Roe* decision by implementing restrictions on the availability of abortions. These regulations and restrictions came before the Court in *Akron v. Akron Reproductive Health Center* (1983). The Court struck down several restrictions requiring (1) that abortions be performed in hospitals; (2) that minors must obtain "informed" consent from at least one parent; and (3) that women must wait a mandatory 24 hours before obtaining an abortion. The majority of the Court reasoned that these rejections did not further a compelling interest of the state. However, the Supreme Court overturned parts of this decision in *Planned Parenthood of Southeastern Pennsylvania v. Casey* (1992).

In *Casey*, the Court reaffirmed the essential holding of *Roe v. Wade,* although it abandoned the trimester framework the Court had developed to judge the constitutionality regulations in this area. In *Casey*, the Court adopted the "undue burden" test, holding that restrictions on abortion would be invalidated only if they impose an undue burden on a woman's right to obtain an abortion. Applying this test, the Court upheld requirements that: (1) a woman wait 24 hours between consenting to and receiving an abortion;

(2) a woman be given state-mandated information about abortion and offered state-authored materials on fetal development; and (3) minors' abortions be conditioned upon the consent, provided in person at the clinic, of one parent or guardian, or upon a judicial waiver. Although maintaining the right to choose under *Roe,* the Court veered away from the right to choose as a fundamental right.

Reproductive freedom is not only subject to judicial interpretation, but also subject to congressional statutes. In 1976, Congress first adopted the Hyde Amendment, which banned the use of federal Medicaid dollars for abortions. This legislation severely limited poor women's access to reproductive health care. In 1977, the Hyde Amendment was revised, allowing Medicaid funds to be used in the case of rape, incest, or severe endangerment of a woman's health. In what some considered a major setback to reproductive health for indigent women, the Supreme Court, in 1980, upheld the Hyde Amendment in *Harris v. McRae* (1980), ruling that "a woman's freedom of choice [does not carry] with it a constitutional entitlement to the financial resources to avail herself of the full range of protected choices."

Organizations and interest groups continue to be driving forces behind legislation dealing with reproductive freedom. Reproductive freedom is by no means a definite freedom or right, and to this day remains a salient political issue. For some, reproductive freedom is a personal choice and should be free from government involvement. For others, reproductive freedom is a moral issue, and the "right to life" should receive protection via government involvement. Political parties have also felt the division brought about by the pro-life/pro-choice pull. Many people on both sides of the argument want to know how specific candidates feel about abortions and in many cases cast votes based on the single issue of pro-choice or pro-life. Currently on the forefront of the reproductive freedom debate is that of possible pro-life Supreme Court appointments. Anti-choice forces are counting on new appointments to the Court in the next few years to overturn *Roe v. Wade* (1973). It should be noted that a decision by the Supreme Court to overturn Roe would not result in abortions being made illegal; that would require state legislatures to change existing abortion laws. However, the federal protection for a women's right to choose would no longer exist. Instead, states would have the power to determine whether they would allow abortions and what restrictions should be applied.

See also Abortion, Right to; Brennan, William J., Jr.; *Griswold v. Connecticut* (1965); Pro-Choice Position on Abortion; Pro-Life Movement; Pro-Life Position on Abortion; *Roe v. Wade* (1973)

Bibliography

Colker, Ruth. 1992. *Abortion & Dialogue: Pro-Choice, Pro-Life, and American Law.* Bloomington: Indiana University Press.

Hull, N. E. H., William James Hoffer, and Peter Charles Hoffer, eds. 2004. *The Abortion Rights Controversy in America: A Legal Reader.* Chapel Hill: University of North Carolina Press.

MariAnna, Cara J. 2002. *Abortion: A Collective Story.* Westport, CT: Praeger.

Kimberly Gill

RESTITUTION

Victims of crime often suffer economic loss, a problem not addressed by such traditional criminal sentences as imprisonment, fines, or probation. The remedy urged by the victim rights movement and adopted in some form by every state and by the national government is restitution, by which the criminal compensates the victim with cash payments and the return or replacement of property or services. Restitution laws commonly authorize compensation for such verifiable financial costs or losses as stolen or damaged property, medical care, missed work, counseling, and, in cases of homicide, funeral expenses. During recent years, state courts have imposed restitution on some 30 percent of defendants sentenced to probation.

The concept of restitution has deep historical roots. It is found, for instance, in the Code of Hammurabi (circa 1700 b.c.) and in the Bible: ("If a man shall steal an ox or a sheep or kill it or sell it, he shall restore five oxen for an ox and four sheep for a sheep" [Exodus 22:1]). For centuries restitution has played an important role in Native American law, and it was championed by British philosopher and criminal justice reformer Jeremy Bentham.

Advocates of restitution argue that it meets society's need for punishment and the victim's need to recoup economic losses. They argue that it promotes rehabilitation by having the criminal assume responsibility for the economic loss and that it is a rational intermediate sanction when probation is insufficiently severe and imprisonment too severe.

Critics of restitution argue that it works only when criminals are caught and convicted, but the majority of offenders are never caught and many of the apprehended are never convicted. Moreover, they contend, many criminals are so poor that it is pointless to order restitution. Critics allege that restitution has a strong class bias inasmuch as it tends to be an alternative to jail that only wealthier defendants can afford. They argue that restitution often goes unpaid, further embittering and revictimizing the people it purportedly helps. Victims, counting on restitution, may delay bringing a civil suit for damages only to find later that the statute of limitations has expired.

Critical decisions about restitution may come at different stages of the judicial process. The prosecutor may agree not to prosecute if the offender voluntarily pays restitution. Most often, restitution is a sentence imposed along with probation, but some parole boards are authorized to order it as a condition for release from prison.

Although restitution unquestionably helps some victims, there are numerous problems with it. Often, the defendant is so impoverished that the judge simply rules this remedy out. Some victims, unaware of their right to restitution, fail to request it even when the defendant has sufficient income. Obtaining restitution requires overcoming a series of hurdles that may deter even knowledgeable victims: proving dollar loss, completing detailed paperwork, holding often lengthy hearings, and the like. Moreover, the victims may be more interested in putting the crime behind them and may resist becoming dependent upon their victimizers. Overworked prosecutors may find seeking restitution to be so time-consuming that they are relieved to see the victim forego it.

Research indicates that it is common for victims to collect much less than half the restitution due them. One reason is that in about a third of the states, judges are required to order restitution for certain types of crime without regard to the offender's ability to pay. Offenders may find that once they have paid fines and court costs, they have nothing left for restitution, or they may lose their jobs. Restitution is often a condition of probation, but probation officers don't often seek revocation for failure to pay. Commonly, both probation officers and judges have huge caseloads, which would only be aggravated by time-consuming revocation hearings. Moreover, the jails are already overcrowded and imprisonment makes the payment of restitution even less likely.

Restitution can, of course, be collected without relying solely upon the ability of offenders to make regular payments. Restitution is sometimes taken from the prison earnings of inmates, and some states divert money from inmates' bank accounts and tax returns. A number of states have established "restitution centers," where offenders live while working in the community and paying their victims. Vermont, with one of the lowest restitution collection rates in the nation (about 13 percent), has decided to experiment with the state itself paying restitution, then collecting from offenders.

Restitution should not be confused with community service or victim compensation programs. With community service, offenders perform such services as picking up trash on public property or working at a homeless shelter. It tends to be used when there is no particular identifiable victim (e.g., drunken driving in which there is no accident, no injury, and no property damage). Also, community service is sometimes used for persons who fail to pay court-ordered restitution. Another alternative is a state-sponsored victim compensation program, which provides that the government, not the criminal, will pay victims of

violent crimes even if nobody has been convicted and there was no economic loss.

See also Bentham, Jeremy; Probation and Parole

Bibliography

Acker, William M., Jr. 1994. "Making Sense of Victim Restitution: A Critical Perspective." *Federal Sentencing Reporter* 6: 234.
"Development in Law: Alternatives to Incarceration." *Harvard Law Review* 111: 1944.

George Kiser

RESTORATIVE JUSTICE. *See* Crime Victims, Rights of

RESTRICTIVE COVENANTS

African Americans were the primary but not the sole targets of Jim Crow segregation in the area of residential discrimination. Mexican Americans, Asian Americans, and Jews were often subjected to a range of exclusionary practices designed to sustain all-white neighborhoods. By the turn of the twentieth century, residential segregation laws had become so widespread in the South that in many locations there were few places where blacks and whites could reside in the same area. The National Association for the Advancement of Colored People (NAACP) targeted residential segregation as the primary contributor to ghettoization in America and the group brought a test case to enable African Americans to live in the residential neighborhood of their choice. The city of Louisville, Kentucky, passed an ordinance that established exclusive residential zones for blacks and whites on the grounds that segregated neighborhoods will prevent the deterioration of whites' property values and promote the public peace. In *Buchanan v. Warley* (1917), Buchanan, a white property owner, brought a lawsuit to enforce the sale of a lot to a black person on the grounds that the ordinance violated the Due Process Clause of the Fourteenth Amendment. The Supreme Court, in a unanimous opinion authored by Justice Day, held that the Fourteenth Amendment and the Civil Rights Acts of 1866 and 1870 "operate to qualify and entitle a colored man to acquire property without state legislation discriminating against him solely because of color."

The *Buchanan* ruling was a short-lived victory in the sense that whites resorted to other discriminatory practices to prevent blacks from residing in their neighborhoods. One exclusionary practice that was common in areas outside of the South was the use of the restrictive covenant (Vose, 1959). Restrictive covenants, which were private agreements, contained contractual language that bound successive purchasers not to lease or sell their property to anyone but members of their own racial or ethnic groups. In 1921, 30 whites in an area of Washington, D.C., mutually covenanted and agreed that their properties should not be sold to blacks. Corrigan, who was white, agreed to sell her property to a black woman, and Buckley sued to enforce the covenant. Corrigan argued that the restrictive covenant violated the Fifth, Thirteenth, and Fourteenth Amendments. In *Corrigan v. Buckley* (1926), the Supreme Court found that "none of these Amendments prohibited private individuals from entering into contracts respecting the control and disposition of their own property." The *Corrigan* ruling legalized restrictive covenants for the next two decades.

The NAACP successfully challenged the constitutional validity of restrictive covenants in the landmark case of *Shelley v. Kraemer* (1948) and its companion case, *McGhee v. Sipes* (1948). In *Shelley* and *McGhee*, blacks from Missouri and Michigan respectively had purchased homes from whites whose properties were subject to restrictive covenants that prohibited whites from selling their properties to blacks or Asians (in the Missouri case) or to any person who was not white (in the Michigan case). The other white owners whose properties were also subject to the restrictive covenants brought lawsuits to prevent the black homeowners from taking possession of their properties. The legal question presented before the Supreme Court in *Shelley* was whether the Equal Protection Clause of the Fourteenth Amendment prevents the judicial enforcement of restrictive covenants based on race in state courts. In a unanimous opinion, Chief

Justice Vinson agreed with the black petitioners' arguments when he found that, "It cannot be doubted that among the civil rights intended to be protected from discriminatory state action by the Fourteenth Amendment are the rights to acquire, enjoy, own and dispose of property." Chief Justice Vinson ruled that although restrictive covenants standing alone do not violate the Equal Protection Clause of the Fourteenth Amendment, when white property owners attempt to enforce the agreements in state courts, "the action of state courts and judicial officers in their official capacities is to be regarded as action of the State within the meaning of the Fourteenth Amendment."

Hurd v. Hodge (1948) was decided in a separate opinion on the same day *Shelley* was announced. In *Hurd*, white property owners brought suit to enforce the terms of a restrictive covenant in Washington, D.C. Black petitioners attacked the judicial enforcement of the restrictive covenants as violative of the Due Process Clause of the Fifth Amendment. The Supreme Court declared the restrictive covenants involving the District of Columbia invalid under the Civil Rights Act of 1866 and on the grounds that the agreements were inconsistent with United States public policy.

The Supreme Court relied on the principle in *Shelley* when it declared that a white property owner could not be sued for damages by another white property owner for failing to observe a restrictive covenant. In *Barrows v. Jackson* (1953), Justice Minton, in a 6–1 opinion, asserted that, "To compel respondent to respond in damages would be for the State to punish her for her failure to perform her covenant to continue to discriminate against non-Caucasians in the use of her property." The majority found that the imposition of damages by a state court would constitute state action as in *Shelley*.

The landmark case of *Shelley v. Kraemer* was a significant one because it invalidated the use of racially restrictive covenants to exclude racial and ethnic minorities from residing in their neighborhoods of choice. The principle elaborated in *Shelley*, that state judicial enforcement of restrictive covenants constituted state action, was criticized by legal scholars as an example of judicial overreaching. Some scholars argue that the *Shelley* principle is inconsistent with the precedent of *The Civil Rights Cases* (1883), where the Supreme Court ruled that the Fourteenth Amendment does not reach private acts of discrimination, only state or governmental action. In *Shelley,* the Supreme Court transformed the state action doctrine into an instrument for prohibiting private racial discrimination, but in reality, the *Shelley* principle was limited in its application to the restrictive covenant cases.

See also Civil Rights Act of 1866; Civil Rights Act of 1870; *The Civil Rights Cases;* Due Process Clauses; Equal Protection Clause; Fifth Amendment; Fourteenth Amendment; Housing, Discrimination in; Jim Crow Laws; National Organization for the Advancement of Colored People (NAACP); Segregation, De Facto and De Jure; *Shelley v. Kramer* (1948); State Action Doctrine; Thirteenth Amendment; Vinson, Fred M.

Bibliography

Davis, Abraham L., and Barbara L. Graham. 1995. *The Supreme Court, Race, and Civil Rights.* Thousand Oaks, CA: Sage Publications.

Vose, Clement. 1959. *Caucasians Only: The Supreme Court, the NAACP, and the Restrictive Covenant Cases.* Berkeley: University of California Press.

Barbara L. Graham

RETRIBUTION

In its most literal sense, the term *retribution* means something demanded or given in repayment. Not to be confused with the similar term *restitution,* retribution refers to the ancient idea that the criminal must pay for wrongs perpetrated against society. The biblical phrase "an eye for an eye" (see Leviticus 24:17–20) is often invoked in this regard. Another oft-used phrase is that criminals must be given their "just deserts."

Concurring in *Furman v. Georgia* (1972), Justice Potter Stewart observed, "The instinct for retribution is part of the nature of man, and channeling that instinct in the administration of criminal

justice serves an important purpose in promoting the stability of a society governed by law." Justice Stewart was expressing the traditional view that the desire for revenge is part of human nature and that if the state does not adequately punish offenders then people will resort to vigilantism.

Defenders of retribution point out that it entails more than societal revenge against those who perpetrate antisocial acts. Properly understood, retribution entails proportionality in punishment. As Justice Antonin Scalia noted in his concurring opinion in *Ewing v. California,* (2003), "Proportionality—the notion that the punishment should fit the crime—is inherently a concept tied to the penological goal of retribution."

For the most part, judicial exposition of the concept of retribution has taken place in the context of capital punishment. Justice William J. Brennan, a stalwart opponent of the death penalty, generally accepted the notion of retribution as justification for criminal punishment, but believed that it was inadequate as a justification for the death penalty.

Of course, retribution is not the only justification for the imposition of the criminal sanction. Writing for the Supreme Court in *Williams v. New York* (1949), Justice Hugo L. Black observed, "Retribution is no longer the dominant objective of the criminal law. Reformation and rehabilitation of offenders have become important goals of criminal jurisprudence." In the 1950s and 1960s, the idea that offenders could be rehabilitated gave rise to a plethora of programs designed to reform criminals. Rising crime rates of the 1970s, combined with the meager results of such programs, swayed the mass public away from rehabilitation and back toward the ancient idea of retribution.

Public attitudes notwithstanding, liberal commentators continue to question whether retribution, which they see as little more than legalized vengeance, is a legitimate goal of a criminal justice system based on the rule of law and the dignity of all persons (see, e.g., Golash 2004). These critics often call for a restorative as distinct from a retributive model of justice as well as greater emphasis on addressing the social and economic underpinnings of crime.

See also Black, Hugo L.; Brennan, William J., Jr.; Conservatism; Cruel and Unusual Punishments Clause; Death Penalty and the Supreme Court; Death Penalty, Crimes Punishable by the; Eighth Amendment; *Furman v. Georgia* (1972); Liberalism; Scalia, Antonin; Sentencing, Proportionality in; Stewart, Potter

Bibliography

Golash, Deirdre. 2004. *The Case Against Punishment: Retribution, Crime Prevention, and the Law.* New York: New York University Press.

Judah, Eleanor Hannon, and Michael Bryant. 2004. *Criminal Justice: Retribution vs. Restoration.* Binghamton, NY: Haworth Press.

John M. Scheb II and Otis H. Stephens, Jr.

REYNOLDS V. SIMS (1964)

For many decades prior to the 1960s, the boundaries of state legislative and U.S. congressional districts around the country remained largely unchanged in spite of vast population shifts from rural to urban and suburban areas. In most instances, the effect of this malapportionment was to artificially inflate the influence of rural voters and depress the influence of voters in urban areas. Yet the Supreme Court was not solicitous to constitutional challenges in this area. In *Colegrove v. Green* (1946), the Supreme Court dismissed a challenge to the malapportionment of congressional districts in Illinois. Speaking for a plurality of justices in that case, Felix Frankfurter characterized such challenges as "political" rather than "justiciable" questions. Challenges to malapportionment nevertheless continued. Finally, in *Baker v. Carr* (1962), the Court changed course dramatically, holding that Tennessee voters could bring suit in federal court to challenge the malapportionment of their state legislature. That decision touched off a flurry of litigation as voters around the country filed suit to challenge the apportionment of state legislative districts as well as congressional districts.

In *Gray v. Sanders* (1963), the Supreme Court struck down Georgia's county unit system used in statewide primary elections. Under this system the voting power of the state's most populous counties was drastically reduced. After noting that the Fourteenth and Fifteenth Amendments prohibit dilution of votes based on gender or race, the Court asked rhetorically, "How then can one person be given ... ten times the voting power of another person in a statewide election merely because he lives in ... the smallest rural county? "

In another case originating in Georgia, *Wesberry v. Sanders* (1964), the Court upheld a challenge to the apportionment of that state's congressional districts. Reversing a federal district court's dismissal of the case, the Supreme Court remanded the case for trial, holding that congressional districts should be drawn so as to be equal in population. The Court based its holding on Article I, Section 2 of the U.S. Constitution, which provides that "[t]he House of Representatives shall be composed of Members chosen every second Year by the People of the several States ..." and that "Representatives ... shall be apportioned among the several States which may be included within this Union, according to their respective Numbers...."

In *Reynolds v. Sims,* the most famous of six companion cases decided on June 15, 1964, the Court took another giant step in bringing about the "reapportionment revolution" of the 1960s. Voters from two urban counties brought suit challenging the constitutionality of the existing apportionment of the Alabama legislature, which had not been significantly altered since 1903. When the lawsuit began, Alabama's 67 counties were represented by a 35-member senate and a 106-member house of representatives. The population of senate districts varied from 15,417 to 634,864; house districts ranged from 6,731 to 104,767.

The district court declared the existing scheme unconstitutional and ordered reapportionment. The court imposed its own plan by combining features of two different plans adopted by the legislature. State officials appealed, claiming that a federal court did not have the authority to affirmatively reapportion the legislature. Plaintiffs also appealed, because in their view the plan adopted by the district court did not go far enough toward achieving population equality across districts.

Given what the Supreme Court had said in *Baker v. Carr, Gray v. Sanders,* and *Wesberry v. Sanders,* there was little doubt that the Court would interpret the Equal Protection Clause of the Fourteenth Amendment to require states to apportion their legislative districts on the basis of equal population. It was not surprising that Chief Justice Earl Warren's opinion for the Court in *Reynolds v. Sims* held that "the Equal Protection Clause requires that a State make an honest and good faith effort to construct districts, in both houses of its legislature, as nearly of equal population as is practicable." Observing that "the right of suffrage is a fundamental matter in a free and democratic society," Warren insisted that "any alleged infringement of the right of citizens to vote must be scrutinized."

The only dissenter, John M. Harlan (the younger), objected to what he perceived as a departure from the intentions of the framers of the Fourteenth Amendment. Justice Harlan asserted that "neither those who proposed nor those who ratified the Amendment believed that the Equal Protection Clause limited the power of the States to apportion their legislatures as they saw fit." As a matter of historical record, Harlan was likely on solid ground. Indeed, Chief Justice Warren did not say that the Court's interpretation of the Fourteenth Amendment was based on the intentions of its framers. Like another of the Warren Court's great constitutional pronouncements, *Brown v. Board of Education* (1954), the interpretation of the Fourteenth Amendment adopted in *Reynolds v. Sims* appears to have been more an expression of the High Court's sense of substantive justice rather than the intentions of the framers of the Fourteenth Amendment.

See also *Baker v. Carr* (1962); *Brown v. Board of Education* (1954; 1955); Equal Protection Clause; Fifteenth Amendment; Fourteenth Amendment (1868); Frankfurter, Felix; Racial Gerrymandering;

Harlan, John Marshall, II; Reapportionment; Warren Court; Warren, Earl

Bibliography

Ball, Howard. 1971. *The Warren Court's Conceptions of Democracy: An Evaluation of the Supreme Court's Apportionment Opinions.* Madison, NJ: Fairleigh Dickinson University Press.

Cortner, Richard C. 1972. *The Apportionment Cases.* New York: W.W. Norton.

     John M. Scheb II and Otis H. Stephens, Jr.

REYNOLDS V. UNITED STATES (1879)

Polygamy, the practice of multiple marriages, dates back thousands of years. Polygamy came under fire in the United States as a result of hostility to the Mormon Church. Initially, polygamy was not a central aspect of the Mormon faith. However, Joseph Smith, a key prophet in the Mormon Church, engaged in polygamy, and, by 1852, it had become a central tenet of the Mormon faith. Mormon polygamy "provoked the ire of powerful organizations, including the eastern media establishment and the Republican Party, which linked the issue of polygamy with that of slavery" (Gillett 2000, 506). As a result, Congressman Justin Morrill introduced legislation in 1862 "to 'punish and prevent the Practice of Polygamy in the Territories of the United States … and [to disapprove] and [annul] certain Acts of the Legislative Assembly of the Territory of Utah'" (Gillett 2000, 509). This legislation, part of the Morrill Act, made polygamy punishable by fines of up to five hundred dollars and by imprisonment for up to five years.

Mormon historians contend that *Reynolds v. United States* was a test case stemming from an agreement between the Mormon Church and the federal government to determine the constitutionality of the antipolygamy statute. According to this view, George Reynolds, Brigham Young's personal secretary, "'agreed to test the statute and cooperate in his prosecution in return for the government's agreement not to seek a harsh punishment'" (Gillett 2000, 511). Initially, Reynolds was tried and convicted by the Utah territorial court in 1874. This conviction was overturned by the Utah Supreme Court, however, because the grand jury was impermissibly chosen by federal instead of state guidelines. Because Reynolds' polygamous actions were a matter of public record, he was arrested in October 1875. He was convicted, and ultimately the case was appealed to the United States Supreme Court.

Chief Justice Morrison Waite wrote the Court's opinion. The central question posed by this case was whether religious belief could be accepted as a justification for a criminal act. Waite noted that the government could not enact a law for the Utah territory that violated the Free Exercise Clause of the First Amendment. He pointed out that the Constitution itself did not define the term religion, so he looked to colonial and early American history for a definition. Waite relied extensively on the views of Thomas Jefferson as providing a foundation for the guarantees concerning religion contained in the First Amendment. He specifically cited Jefferson's letter to the Danbury Baptists in which Jefferson suggested that the First Amendment erected a "wall of separation" between church and state. From the views expressed in this letter, Waite suggested that "Congress was deprived of all legislative power over mere opinion, but was left free to reach actions which were in violation of social duties or subversive of good order." In other words, there is a distinction between religious belief, which is protected by the Free Exercise Clause, and religious action, which is not necessarily protected.

Waite also examined the history of polygamy, albeit selectively. He stated that polygamy had always been "odious" in the northern and western nations of Europe and that until the rise of the Mormon Church, had been confined to Asia and Africa. Moreover, under English common law a second marriage was always void, and was treated as an offense against society punishable by death. According to Waite, "[I]t is impossible to believe that the constitutional guaranty of religious freedom was intended to prohibit legislation in respect to this most important feature of social life." He stated that

marriage was such a significant social institution that it provided the basis for the principles of government. Waite concluded that the antipolygamy law was constitutional and that no exception could be made for Mormons because to allow exceptions "would be to make the professed doctrines of religious belief superior to the law of the land, and in effect to permit every citizen to become a law unto himself. Government could exist only in name under such circumstances."

This case is significant because the Court created a distinction between belief and action; a distinction that has occasionally been applied in subsequent cases. In *Employment Division v. Smith* (1990), for instance, Justice Antonin Scalia relied extensively on the holding in *Reynolds* in upholding a generally applicable criminal law despite the limitations it imposed upon free exercise of religion. Despite the Court's holding in *Reynolds,* polygamy continues to be practiced in Utah, largely due to nonenforcement of laws prohibiting the custom. Some observers have contended that the decision needs to be reexamined in light of more recent decisions concerning the right to privacy. The argument is that the anti-Mormon sentiment prevalent in the nineteenth century was central to the outcome of the case; therefore, it should be reevaluated under more modern precedents with greater emphasis on privacy and religious freedom.

See also Church of Jesus Christ of Latter-day Saints; *Employment Division, Department of Human Resources of Oregon v. Smith* (1990); First Amendment; Free Exercise Clause; Jefferson, Thomas; Religion, Freedom of; Scalia, Antonin; Separation of Church and State; Waite, Morrison Remick

Bibliography

Gillett, Todd M. 2000. "The Absolution of *Reynolds:* The Constitutionality of Religious Polygamy." *William and Mary Bill of Rights Journal* 8, no. 2: 497.

　　　　　　　　　　　　　　　　Kara E. Stooksbury

RFRA. *See* Religious Freedom Restoration Act

RICO LAWS. *See* Racketeering and RICO Laws

RIGHT/PRIVILEGE DISTINCTION

A constitutional right is a legitimate expectation grounded in a nation's fundamental law that a particular action or decision is shielded from governmental interference. To say it is a legitimate expectation means that one can reasonably expect that a court of law will support this expectation in the event of litigation. In the American context, most constitutional rights are set forth explicitly in the text of the federal and/or state constitutions. However, some rights (notably, the right of privacy) are recognized by the courts as implicit constitutional rights (see *Griswold v. Connecticut*, 1965).

A constitutional right cannot be revoked without altering the constitution or achieving a reinterpretation from the highest court of review. A privilege, however, is an opportunity that may be revoked by its grantor. An attempt to grant or revoke such benefits often results in highly contentious arguments over policy and procedure.

One question that arose from the right/privilege distinction was whether the state could require the surrender of constitutional rights in exchange for a privilege. Furthermore, courts have had to determine whether the grantor of a public or private benefit must respect rights such as due process or equal protection when rescinding such privileges as employment licenses, entitlements including public assistance, and public jobs (Smolla 1982).

Justice Oliver Wendell Holmes, Jr., speaking for the Massachusetts Supreme Court in *McAuliffe v. City of New Bedford* (1892), clearly differentiated between a right and a privilege. Justice Holmes noted that former police officer McAuliffe had a right to free speech as a private citizen. McAuliffe, however, did not have the right to be employed as a policeman or to enjoy due process of law before being fired for violating a city police regulation banning political speech. Holmes wrote, "The petitioner may have a constitutional right to talk politics, but he has no constitutional right to be a policeman." According to Holmes, the officer gave up his right to free speech in exchange for the privilege of being a police officer.

But more than 30 years later, Justice George Sutherland of the Supreme Court wrote that mandating waiver of a constitutional right in order to accept a privilege, such as employment, might "compel a surrender of all" rights and that the "guarantees embedded in the Constitution of the United States may thus be manipulated out of existence" (*Frost and Frost Trucking Co. v. Railroad Commission of the State of California*, 1926).

Not quite 30 years after that case, the United States Supreme Court upheld the suspension of a physician's license, asserting that a state legislature could require high standards of character and law observance from people seeking to obtain and keep medical licenses (*Barsky v. Board of Regents*, 1954). The Court indicated that in some cases public interest demanded "a high degree of reasonable governmental regulation" even if constitutional rights and private sector activity were in question (Van Alstyne 1968, 1444).

Since then the courts have gradually expanded the protection of public sector privileges. In *Goldberg v. Kelly* (1970), the Court held that a recipient of public assistance must be given notice of his right to a hearing and other due process rights prior to the termination of benefits. Justice William Brennan, writing for the Court, famously critiqued the right/privilege distinction, stating, "It may be realistic today to regard welfare entitlements as more like 'property' than a 'gratuity.' Much of the existing wealth in this country takes the form of rights that do not fall within traditional common-law concepts of property." And in *Perry v. Sindermann* (1972), Justice Potter Stewart stated that "even though a person has no 'right' to a valuable governmental benefit and even though the government may deny him the benefit for any number of reasons, there are some reasons upon which the government may not rely. It may not deny a benefit to a person on a basis that infringes his constitutionally protected interests ..." More recently in *Rosenberger v. Rector and Visitors of University of Virginia* (1995), the Supreme Court held that the University of Virginia could not deny student groups funding (a privilege) based on their views of those groups' religious viewpoints because that kind of viewpoint discrimination would be a denial of the right of free speech.

Right/privilege jurisprudence and history suggest that a government entity may require a person to waive some constitutional rights in exchange for state-granted privileges, such as public benefits, state employment licenses, or state jobs. While courts remain uneasy about applying the right/privilege distinction, scholars and jurists report that "the doctrine has shown an uncanny ability to reconstitute itself in spite of the best efforts of scholars and jurists to bury it" (Smolla 1982, 69) by "indirectly restrict[ing] liberties such as free speech through the device of granting governmental benefits 'with strings attached'" (Smolla 1990, 323).

See also Brennan, William J., Jr.; Due Process Clauses; Due Process, Procedural; Due Process, Substantive; Equal Protection Clause; First Amendment; Holmes, Oliver Wendell, Jr.; New Property; Privacy, Constitutional Right of; Property Rights; Public Employees, Constitutional Rights of; Speech, Freedom of; Stewart, Potter

Bibliography

Smolla, Rodney A. 1982. "The Reemergence of the Right-Privilege Distinction in Constitutional Law: The Price of Protesting too Much." *Stanford Law Review* 35: 69.

Smolla, Rodney A. 1990. "Sixth Annual Symposium of the Institute of Bill of Rights Law: Preserving the Bill of Rights in the Modern Administrative-Industrial State." *William and Mary Law Review* 31: 321.

Van Alstyne, William V. 1968. "The Demise of the Right-Privilege Distinction in Constitutional Law." *Harvard Law Review* 81: 1439.

Rosalie R. Young

RIGHTS. *See* Abortion, Right to; Accused, Rights of the; Animal Rights; Arms, Right to Keep and Bear; Assembly, Freedom of; Bill of Rights, American; Civil Rights; Counsel, Right to; Disabilities, Rights of Persons with; Due Process, Procedural; Due Process, Substantive; Economic Freedom; Gay Rights; Group Rights; Hearing, Elements of a; Immigrants and Aliens, Rights of; Individual Rights; Latino Americans, Civil Rights of; Liberty; Marriage, Rights Pertaining to; Native Americans, Civil Rights of; Natural Law and Natural Rights; Parental Rights; Petition, Right of; Press, Freedom of the; Prisoners' Rights; Privacy, Constitutional Right of; *Pierce v. Society of Sisters;* Pro-Life Movement; Pro-Life Position on Abortion; Property Rights; Public Employees, Rights of; Public Trial, Right to a; Religion, Freedom of; Reproductive Freedom; Sex Offenders, Rights of; Speech, Freedom of; Speedy Trial, Right to; States' Rights, Doctrine of

THE RIGHT TO DIE

Questions concerning the ability of an individual to determine the time and manner of his or her death have created much controversy in the United States. End of life decisions have become more complicated due in part to advances in medical technology. New technology was often viewed as prolonging the inevitable demise and suffering of the patient; thus, some patients and their families began to assert that courts and legislatures should recognize a right to die in order to protect individual liberty in personal decision making (Jost 2005, 12) and thus minimize individual suffering and governmental interference.

Discussions of the "right to die" can become confused when distinctions between killing, murder, manslaughter, suicide, assisted suicide, and euthanasia are conflated. Key distinctions include the physiological cause for death, the agent of death, the agent's intentions, the means of death, and the deceased's wishes. Murder and manslaughter are criminal acts. According to Chief Justice William Rehnquist's opinion in *Washington v. Glucksberg* (1997), Anglo-American law has punished or disapproved of both suicide and assisting a suicide for over 700 years. Early influential legal writers, including Henry de Bracton and William Blackstone, recognized suicide as a criminal act. This line of thought influenced colonial America where suicide was considered a crime. Since success meant the person escaped punishment, burial restrictions were imposed and family assets were seized. Punishment ended in the 1850s and by the mid 1900s, suicide was de-criminalized. Assisting a person to commit suicide, however, remains subject to prosecution.

The term "euthanasia" stems from two Greek words: *eudaimonia* which means well-being and *thanatos* which means death. Euthanasia, therefore, means a "good death" wherein death is preferable to continued living. Euthanasia differs from assisted suicide in that the person who dies is not actively involved in ending her life. Philosopher Dan Brock first described six kinds: voluntary passive, voluntary active, involuntary passive, involuntary active, non-voluntary passive, and non-voluntary active. Though definitions can vary (often causing disagreements), Brock labeled euthanasia as voluntary when a person freely and knowingly asks to die. It is involuntary when a person asks not to die. It is non-voluntary when no request is made. Passive euthanasia means death is caused by the person's underlying disease or injury; active euthanasia means death is caused by a direct human act (e.g., injecting KCl or smothering). Passive euthanasia is often known as "allowing or letting the person die" while active euthanasia is known as "causing the person to die" and is often referred to as a "mercy killing."

A legally protected right to die would mean someone wishing death can be helped to die by another person who won't be held criminally or civilly liable. The weak version of this right would permit a second party to help; the strong version would obligate such help. By the 1960s, a right to die movement was beginning to form in the U. S.. This movement was influenced by a spate of articles and books that broke the societal taboo of discussing death and by "the emphasis on individual self-realization and the equal-rights movements for blacks and women" (Jost 2005, 12). Several high profile cases and laws during the 1970's ushered in the movement in full.

Between 1973 and 2005, seventy-four state and federal cases reflected the right to die debate in the U.S.

According to the health ethics community, this debate began with "Dax's case" in 1973. Dax (Donald) Cowart was severely burned in a propane gas explosion. Over 65% of his body was covered with third degree burns and he repeatedly asked healthcare providers to stop life-saving therapy. Although judged competent, his requests were ignored because physicians believed that he was giving up too quickly and that they had a professional responsibility to keep him from dying. Tort damages were recovered, but Cowart could not find a lawyer to litigate for treatment discontinuation. Cowart went on to earn a law degree himself and even though he was able to enjoy a meaningful life, he has consistently maintained that he should have been allowed to decide for himself whether to live or die.

The first litigated case involved 21 year old Karen Ann Quinlan who became irreversibly comatose as the result of a suspected drug overdose and consequently required mechanical ventilation and artificial nutrition and hydration (hereafter "ANH"). Her life expectancy was one year. Her parents, devout Catholics, requested cessation of ventilation after consulting their priest and considering Karen's wishes (she had previously said she would not want mechanical life-support). When her physicians countered that it was standard practice to continue such measures, her father sued to have the ventilator removed. The New Jersey Superior Court held that stopping ventilation was a medical decision to be made only by physicians. The New Jersey Supreme Court, however, overturned this ruling and the United States Supreme Court denied review. In *In re Quinlan* (1976), the New Jersey Supreme Court unanimously ruled that withdrawal of the ventilator, under the circumstances, would not constitute a criminal homicide.

In its ruling, the New Jersey Supreme Court drew heavily on the U.S. Supreme Court's decisions in *Griswold v Connecticut* (1965), *Stanley v Georgia* (1969), *Eisenstadt v Baird* (1972), and *Roe v Wade*

(1973), which recognized a constitutional right of privacy and affirmed the right of personal choice in fundamental life matters. The court had little difficulty extending the logic of these decisions to encompass Karen Quinlan's decision to remove the life support system. Moreover, the court held that Karen's incompetence did not abrogate her right of privacy; a guardian could exercise that right on her behalf. State law recommended next-of-kin as alternate decision-makers and Mr. Quinlan's grief did not compromise his candidacy as guardian. Yet Karen's prior remarks were considered inadequate and too remote to be probative. The state's competing duty of *parens patriae* and the medical profession's right to follow practice standards were held to decrease relative to an increasing right of privacy, degree of bodily invasion, and likelihood of deterioration. Technically, her death would be due to respiratory failure; therefore, it would not qualify as a homicide. Since exercising a legal right was constitutionally protected, no risk of criminal or civil prosecution existed. This protection also extended to third parties. The court concluded that ventilation could be stopped without risk of prosecution as long as the guardian and family agreed about discontinuation, the medical team agreed recovery was impossible, and the hospital's ethics committee concurred. The court included the ethics committee as a check on possible inappropriate motives of family and physicians as well as a means to diffuse responsibility for such a grave decision.

In 1976, Karen's ventilation was discontinued. She breathed independently and remained comatose for eight years until her death from pneumonia in 1985. The significance of the New Jersey Supreme Court's ruling, however, is still relevant in the debate concerning a constitutional right to die. According to Clarke, the *Quinlan* decision was "forward looking" in four ways. First it acknowledged that life-sustaining treatment had regularly been withheld or withdrawn from patients by families and health-care providers in agreement with the patient's express or implied wishes without sanction of civil law. Second, it

held that the federal right to privacy was broad enough to allow an individual to decline medical treatment, even if it resulted in death. Third, it allowed a guardian to assert an incompetent individual's privacy rights; thus, removing the right to make that decision from the medical community. Fourth, it emphasized that in determining whether treatment should be withdrawn, the critical factor was whether the individual had a reasonable medical probability of returning to a meaningful life as opposed to a mere biological existence (Clarke 2006, 393-394). This ruling had a significant impact on the societal debate over the right to die.

The publicity surrounding the plight of Karen Quinlan led to a movement in state legislatures to protect the wishes of terminally ill individuals who did not desire to be on life support. In 1976, California became the first state to enact a living will statute. A living will, or advance directive, allows an individual to refuse medical treatment while still competent to make that decision. Although the first law was not enacted until 1976, there were several antecedents to legislative policies concerning the right to die. According to Smith, these included "a papal declaration; the formation of the Euthanasia Educational Council and similar groups intent on promoting refusal of treatment; the creation of the Hastings Center and the Kennedy Institute on Ethics (research centers designed to consider frontier issues in biomedical ethics); hearings by the U.S. Senate Committee on Aging; numerous proposals and declarations issued by prestigious organizations such as the Harvard Medical School, the American Medical Association, and the American Hospital Association" (Smith 2002, 75). The lobbying efforts that began in 1967 were realized with the California Natural Death Act in 1976 (California Health and Safety Code § §7185 to 7194.5). Although the act was limited in scope, its action in this policy field spread to other states. The law stipulated that a valid living will could only be executed fourteen days after two physicians agreed that the patient had a terminal illness. The law's definition of terminal illness excluded a diagnosis of persistent vegetative state or irreversible coma. The directive was valid only when witnessed by at least two people not related to the patient and not affiliated with any medical facility. Moreover, a state ombudsman was required to determine that a nursing home patient was of sound mind and operating without coercion.

Forty-six states adopted living will policies after California, and in the 1980s, states began to supplement their living will policies in order to overcome some of the limitations inherent in those policies (Smith 2002, 77). Health care proxies allow individuals to designate an "agent" to make medical decisions on their behalf should they become incompetent or unconscious. "By 1992, all 50 states and the District of Columbia permitted either living wills or health-care proxies, or both" (Jost 2005, 13). The utility of living will laws has been questioned, however, because doctors in 40 states are allowed to refuse a patient's advance directive that requests the use of life-sustaining measures. This part of the law is necessary, it is argued, to prevent disputes among the patient's family over whether to continue treatment. Living wills are also problematic from the standpoint that it is difficult, if not impossible, to anticipate all possible treatment options before one is actually in a position where a decision needs to be made. The limitations of living wills opened the door for health-care proxies.

The United States Supreme Court weighed in on the issue of state regulations concerning a patient's wishes in *Cruzan v Director, Missouri Department of Health* (1990). This case presented the first opportunity for the High Court to deal with the right to die. Previously, the Court had turned down the appeal in *Quinlan*, along with appeals in at least two other state cases that involved end of life issues (Colby 2006, 285). In *Cruzan* the Court affirmed the Missouri Supreme Court's ruling against discontinuation of ANH in a non-terminal, non-permanently vegetative patient. Nancy Beth Cruzan sustained severe injuries, including brain damage due to lack of oxygen, in an automobile accident. Four years after the accident, her parents requested that the hospital remove her feeding tube. The hospital refused without a court order. Cruzan's parents sued and won at the state trial court which held that someone in Cruzan's condition had a fundamental right under both the state and federal Constitutions to direct or refuse the withdrawal of death-prolonging procedures. The trial court also found that Cruzan's comment to a former housemate that she would not wish to continue her life if sick or injured unless she could live at least a halfway normal life suggested that she would not wish to continue ANH. The Missouri Supreme Court, however, reversed the trial court's decision holding that the neither the state constitution, nor the federal constitution embodied an unrestricted right to refuse treatment. This court also ruled that Cruzan's statements were not solid evidence under the Missouri Living Will statute, and that the state's interest in preserving life was sufficient to require "clear and convincing evidence" of an incapacitated person's wishes before terminating life support.

The Supreme Court affirmed the decision of the Missouri Supreme Court by the narrowest of margins (5-4). Chief Justice Rehnquist wrote for the majority that a competent person had the right to refuse unwanted life-saving treatment. However, the Court also found that Missouri could impose a standard of clear and convincing evidence of the patient's wishes before treatment was discontinued. Rehnquist stated that Missouri's interest in the preservation and protection of human life and the procedural safeguards instituted by the state were legitimate in order to prevent potential abuses.

After the Court's ruling in this case, a second trial was held. New witnesses came forward as a result of the publicity and testified that they believed that Nancy Cruzan would not want to live her life under those conditions. The state lost and decided not to pursue an appeal. Within hours of the December 14, 1990 ruling, Nancy Cruzan's feeding tube was removed and she died twelve days later.

Also in 1990, Congress passed the Patient Self-Determination Act. The Act required health-care institutions that accepted Medicare or Medicaid funds to inform patients of their right to plan for their death and thus encouraged adults to document choices about acceptable and unacceptable medical treatments in case they became incompetent. If a living will or advanced directive was presented to institutions or professionals it was to be honored. Prior to this federal legislation, many states had passed similar laws.

The issue of assisted suicide is part of the debate over the right to die and was galvanized in the 1990s, in part due to the actions of one doctor. Beginning in 1990, Dr. Jack Kevorkian, a retired pathologist, facilitated suicides for terminally ill people by connecting them to a machine from which they could then self-administer lethal medications. Dr. Kevorkian (who was nicknamed "Dr. Death") was tried six times prior to being convicted in 1999 of second-degree murder and sentenced to 10-25 years in prison (*People v Kevorkian* 2002). The state was successful in obtaining the 1999 conviction because Kevorkian videotaped himself lethally injecting a terminally ill man and sent the videotape to the CBS television show *60 Minutes*. He thus crossed the line from passive to active euthanasia. Kevorkian admitted that he had helped more than 130 people to die.

While the Supreme Court's ruling in *Cruzan* established that a person had the right to refuse life-sustaining treatment, the extent to which individuals could receive assistance in ending their lives was unclear. In *Vacco v Quill* (1997) and *Washington v Glucksberg* (1997), the U.S. Supreme Court unanimously upheld New York and Washington laws banning assisted suicide. In *Vacco*, the plaintiffs claimed that the state's criminal statute making it a felony for one person to assist another in committing suicide violated the Fourteenth Amendment's Equal Protection Clause because no substantive difference existed between refusing life-saving treatment and requesting assistance in dying. The Supreme Court, however, disagreed. Chief Justice Rehnquist wrote that the practices of assisting a suicide and refusing medical treatment were different types of actions. The Equal Protection Clause prohibits treating people in a similar situation differently; no one may assist a suicide and anyone may refuse medical treatment. There was, therefore, no violation of the Equal Protection Clause. The Court also held that preserving the physician's role as healer, and preventing abuse especially among vulnerable people were legitimate state interests that outweighed any right to assisted suicide.

In *Glucksberg*, the Court, using very similar reasoning to *Vacco*, held that the Due Process Clause did not protect a fundamental liberty interest for assisted suicide and the state's prohibition of assisted suicide accorded with important state interests. Rehnquist pointed out that while laws regarding punishing suicide had changed over time, it was and has always been a crime to assist in a suicide. This point was significant as the Court looks to deeply rooted traditions when determining whether an activity is protected by the Due Process Clause. Acknowledging the complexity of the issue, the Court recommended that state courts and legislatures work toward local consensus about the ethical and legal justification for and against a protected right to die.

While these rulings allowed states to ban physician-assisted suicide, it also allowed states to enact their own policies legalizing physician-assisted suicide if they wished. Oregon became the first state (and as of this writing the only state) to allow physicians to assist terminally ill patients to end their lives. In 1994, Oregon voters (by a 51% majority) passed the Death with Dignity Act through a referendum. The law imposed stringent requirements before a doctor supplied the patient with a prescription for a lethal dose of medication. The law stipulates that the patient must be at least 18 years of age, an Oregon resident, capable of making decisions, and suffering from a terminal illness that will lead to death in six months. If a patient meets those requirements, he or she must make a written request that is signed and witnessed by at least two people in order to prevent a patient from being coerced into making the request. The physician is required to give the patient information about the risks and consequences of taking the medication. Additionally, a second doctor is required to confirm the diagnosis, the decision making capacity of the patient, and the voluntariness of the request. Physicians whose actions conform to the mandates of the law are exempt from criminal and civil prosecution. From the time of the law's implementation in 1998 to the end of 2005, 246 Oregon patients chose to end their lives.

After the Supreme Court's rulings in *Vacco v. Quill* and *Washington v. Glucksberg*, Oregon voters reaffirmed the law in a referendum in 1997. 60% of voters approved the law; a nine point increase from the initial referendum. The law was amended in 1999 to alleviate concerns that depression would motivate patients to request to end their lives. The law now requires that physicians make a determination that patients do not suffer from depression before they are eligible for a prescription.

When the Bush administration came into office in 2001, there was an effort to undermine the Death with Dignity law. Attorney General John Ashcroft sought to void the Oregon law through the 1970 Controlled Substances Act (CSA) (21 U.S.C. § 801 et seq). This law allows the federal government to regulate the non-medical use of drugs. Ashcroft issued what became known as the "Ashcroft Directive" which prohibited health-care professionals from dispensing doses of lethal medication in order to facilitate suicide because suicide was not considered a "legitimate medical purpose" under the CSA for prescribing medication. The directive also provided that physicians who dispensed narcotics for the purpose of suicide could have their licenses suspended or revoked. When the legality of this action was challenged in federal court, Ashcroft lost twice; once in federal district court, and once before the Ninth Circuit Court of Appeals. By the time the case was appealed to the U. S. Supreme Court,

Ashcroft had resigned as attorney general and was replaced by Alberto Gonzales who continued the suit.

In *Gonzales v. Oregon* (2006), the Supreme Court ruled 6-3 that the CSA does not allow the Attorney General to prohibit doctors from prescribing regulated drugs for use in physician-assisted suicide under a state law which permits it. Justice Anthony Kennedy wrote for the six member majority that the attorney general's actions were not authorized by either Congress or the CSA. Kennedy stated that Ashcroft's actions were "beyond his expertise and incongruous with the statutory purposes and design." Kennedy pointed out that through the CSA, Congress regulated the practice of medicine only to the extent that it prohibited doctors from writing prescriptions as part of drug dealing and trafficking which obviously was not the case here. Moreover, the regulation of medical practices and medical licenses was the responsibility of state governments, not the federal government. As a result, accepting the attorney general's argument that he had the authority to interfere with the Oregon law would "effect a radical shift in authority" from the states to the federal government to define general medical practices; an outcome that Congress did not authorize or intend in the CSA.

The controversy over the right to die also garnered nationwide attention in a case involving Theresa (Terri) Schiavo who sustained severe brain damage in 1990 after a potassium imbalance (the cause of which was never determined) caused her heart to stop beating. Eight years later, her husband, Michael Schiavo, petitioned to have her feeding tube removed. Terri's parents, however, sought an injunction to prevent the removal of the feeding tube. Although a number of reasons have been given, the once cordial relationship between Schiavo and Terri's parents apparently turned sour after he won a lawsuit against the doctors who were treating Terri's infertility prior to her cardiac arrest. Michael received a $300,000 judgment for loss of consortium (which was overseen by an independent trustee and which he had no control over, unless she died; if they divorced, then her parents would inherit it.). Terri received $750,000 which was placed in a trust to cover her continuing medical expenses (Shepherd 2006, 303).

In 2000, Circuit Judge Robert Greer ruled that the feeding tube could be removed, because under Florida law, the spouse has the authority to make those types of decisions. Michael's statements about Terri's wish not to be kept alive through artificial means were sufficient evidence of Terri's beliefs and justified removal of ANH. This ruling was upheld by the Florida Court of Appeals in June 2003.

The case became highly politicized when public officials at both the state and federal level attempted to intervene to "save" Terri.

The Florida legislature passed "Terri's law", granting an injunction against removal of ANH in response to her parent's public appeal and allowing Florida Governor Jeb Bush to intervene; he did so and the feeding tube was reinserted (Chapter 2003-418 House Bill 35-E). The injunction was ruled unconstitutional by the state supreme court in September 2004 because it violated separation of powers since the legislature was intervening in a pending judicial case (*Schiavo* SC05-460). The feeding tube was again removed in March 2005 when in an extraordinary weekend session, the U.S. Congress became involved and passed "the Schiavo Measure" requesting a federal court to intervene (Jost 2005). President Bush took the rare step of returning from his vacation to sign the law. The federal courts, however, consistently followed the initial holding allowing the feeding tube to be removed. When the U.S. Supreme Court refused to hear the case, the legal process was exhausted.amidst extensive publicity, Schiavo died on March 31 thirteen days after ANH was stopped.

While the Schiavo case broke no new legal ground, it nevertheless affected the right to die debate in the United States. According to Shepard, the right to die issue had settled down before the controversy surrounding Schiavo because com-

mentators and activists in the field had "moved on to issues of physician-assisted suicide, palliative care, and suits for wrongful living" (Shepherd 2006, 300). Shepard asserted that the challenges leveled at the Florida law allowing the spouse to make end of life decisions could result in changes in state laws governing such decisions. She pointed out that during the controversy surrounding removing Terri's feeding tube, the Florida legislature considered, but did not pass, legislation that would make it more difficult to remove ANH than other forms of medical treatment; a move contemplated by several other states as well (Shepherd 2006, 300).

The right to die issue, much like the abortion issue, represents one of those areas where personal liberty and governmental authority are in conflict. Those who believe that individuals who are terminally ill or who, like Karen Ann Quinlan, Nancy Beth Cruzan, and Terri Schiavo, will never recover from injuries to live a meaningful life, also believe that it is the individuals' choice, not the government's, to decide how to end their suffering. In advocating a right for the terminally ill to die, it has been argued that physician-assisted suicide preserves death with dignity because trained medical professionals are in a better position to determine the exact dose of medication needed to end life without imposing further harm to the patient.

On the other side of the debate are those who believe that it is legitimate for government to protect life regardless of the quality. Otherwise, they argue we are on the proverbial "slippery slope" to involuntary euthanasia and a culture that values death over life. They argue that it has historically been the responsibility of government to protect life and by allowing actions such as removal of life support and physician-assisted suicide the government is sanctioning murder and thus demeaning life that was given by God.

The inability of the law to resolve this conflict of morals and values insures that the debate over the right to die will continue for some time in American society.

See also Abortion, Right to; Ashcroft, John; Blackstone, William; *Griswold v. Connecticut*; Kennedy, Anthony; Living Will; Privacy, Constitutional Right of; Reproductive Freedom; Rehnquist, William H.; *Roe v. Wade*; Suicide, Doctor-Assisted; Suicide, Right to

Bibliography

Clarke, Annette E. 2006. "The Right to Die: The Broken Road from Quinlan to Schiavo. " *Loyola University Chicago Law Journal* 37: 385.

Colby, William. 2006. "From Quinlan to Cruzan to Schiavo: What Have We Learned? " *Loyola University Chicago Law Journal* 37: 279.

Harrison, Maureen, and Steve Gilbert, eds. 1997. *Life, Death, and the Law: Landmark Right-To-Die Decisions.* Carlsbad, California: Excellent Books.

Jost, Kenneth. 2005. *CQ Researcher*. "Right to Die. " Vol. 15, Number 18. May 13, 2005.

Rosenfeld, Barry. 2004. *Assisted Suicide and the Right to Die: The Interface of Social Science,*

Public Policy, and Medical Ethics. New York: American Psychological Association.

Shepherd, Lois. 2006. "Terri Schiavo: Unsettling the Settled. " *Loyola University Chicago Law Journal* 37: 297.

Woodman, Sue. 2001. *Last Rights: The Struggle Over the Right to Die*. New York: Perseus Publishing.

Barbara J. Russell

RIGHT TO WORK LAWS

By enacting the National Labor Relations Act of 1935, Congress legalized unionization and collective bargaining in industries that affect interstate commerce. Without question, unionization and collective bargaining have resulted in important gains for American workers. However, not all employees wish to join labor unions. Some prefer to be "free riders" who benefit from collective bargaining agreements without paying union dues. Others are simply opposed philosophically to compulsory unionization.

Section 14(b) of the Taft-Hartley Act of 1947 affirmed the right of states to pass "right to work laws" under which employees cannot be forced to pay union dues as a condition of employment. Nevada's right to work law, enacted in 1952, provides:

No person shall be denied the opportunity to obtain or retain employment because of nonmembership in a labor organization, nor shall the state, or any subdivision thereof or any corporation, individual or association of any kind enter into any agreement, written or oral, which excludes any person from employment or continuation of employment because of nonmembership in a labor organization (Nev. Rev. Stat. § 613.250).

Similar laws exist in about half the states, mainly in the South, Midwest, and West. These statutes are stridently opposed by the labor movement on the grounds that that they decrease union membership, reduce the bargaining power of unions, and ultimately work to depress wages. However, many Americans, especially in the South and West, view compulsory unionization as antithetical to traditional notions of individual freedom.

In 2005, Senators Joe Wilson (R-North Carolina) and Trent Lott (R-Mississippi) introduced a bill to create a national right to work law. If enacted, this measure would repeal provisions of federal law that permit collective bargaining agreements to provide for the termination of workers in unionized workplaces who refuse to pay union dues. Due to intense opposition from organized labor and the Democratic Party, the legislation was pronounced "dead on arrival" by many political observers.

See also Economic Freedom; Individualism; Liberty

Bibliography

Farber, Henry S. 1984. "Right-to-Work Laws and the Extent of Unionization." *Journal of Labor Economics* 2: 319.

Moore, William J. 1998. "The Determinants and Effects of Right-To-Work Laws: A Review of the Recent Literature." *Journal of Labor Research* 19: 445.

John M. Scheb II

ROADBLOCKS AND SOBRIETY CHECKPOINTS

The discussion of the constitutionality of roadblocks begins with the prohibition-era case of *Carroll v. United States* (1925) and the later case of *Brinegar v. United States* (1949). Although these early decisions did not directly address the issue of roadblocks or checkpoints, they did imply that the wholesale stopping and searching of vehicles without probable cause contravenes the Fourth Amendment.

In *Carroll,* the Court upheld a warrantless vehicle search by federal agents on the basis of probable cause. The Court, however, stated that "It would be intolerable and unreasonable if a prohibition agent were authorized to stop every automobile on the chance of finding liquor," thereby subjecting law-abiding drivers to "the inconvenience and indignity of such a search."

In *Brinegar,* the Court cited *Carroll* and affirmed Brinegar's conviction for the violation of the Liquor Enforcement Act. But the Court warned, "This does not mean, as seems to be assumed, that every traveler along the public highways may be stopped and searched at the officer's whim, caprice or mere suspicion." In a strongly worded dissent, Justice Robert Jackson stressed that any exception to the Fourth Amendment should be based on the "gravity of the offense." Regarding the use of a roadblock to search every vehicle for a kidnapped child, Jackson stated that he would attempt to uphold such a roadblock search if "executed fairly and in good faith;" but conversely, he would not make such an attempt for a roadblock that involved a "universal search to salvage a few bottles of bourbon."

The first case to specifically examine the Fourth Amendment issue of checkpoints was *United States v. Ortiz* (1975). The question before the *Ortiz* Court involved its earlier holding in *Almeida-Sanchez v. United States* (1973). In *Almeida-Sanchez,* the Court ruled that the mere fact that a vehicle was near the border did not constitute probable cause for a warrantless search of the vehicle.

Therefore the Fourth Amendment did not support vehicle searches by roving Border Patrol units.

In upholding the reversal of the defendant's conviction, the unanimous Court applied the reasoning from *Almeida-Sanchez* to permanent Border Patrol checkpoints which were either at the border or its "functional equivalents." The Court found that the discretion given officers at the checkpoint for full searches of vehicles was without probable cause and so was "not consistent with the Fourth Amendment." Given that the search of an automobile was a "substantial invasion of privacy," the Court noted that guarding privacy from "official arbitrariness" demanded that probable cause be "the minimum for a lawful search." Writing for the Court, Justice William H. Rehnquist stressed that the Court's decision was confined to full searches and did not prohibit checkpoint stops for the purpose of investigating a person's citizenship.

A year later in *United States v. Martinez-Fuerte* (1976), the Supreme Court again dealt with permanent checkpoints utilized by the United States Border Patrol. At issue was whether, when officers had no reason to believe that a particular vehicle contained illegal aliens, stopping the vehicle was unconstitutional. Another issue was whether operation of such checkpoints required prior authorization by judicial warrant in order to insure Fourth Amendment protections.

Using a balancing test, the Court ruled that briefly questioning occupants of vehicles in order to determine status or citizenship did not violate the Fourth Amendment. Consequently such checkpoints did not require a warrant. While the Court acknowledged that checkpoint or roadblock stops are seizures within the meaning of the Fourth Amendment, it reasoned that requiring such stops be "based on reasonable suspicion would be impractical" because of the heavy flow of traffic through the checkpoint. Noting that the nature of the intrusion was limited and detention brief, the Court stated that the subjective intrusion-creating concern or fear in the lawful traveler of a checkpoint is less than that of roving patrols; hence the public interest and law enforcement need outweighed the limited intrusion. Justice William Brennan, joined by Justice Thurgood Marshall in a strongly worded dissent, stated that the Court's decision "virtually empties the [Fourth] Amendment of its reasonableness requirement" with a balancing test "that overwhelms the individual's protection against unwarranted official intrusion by a governmental interest said to justify the search and seizure."

The issue of sobriety checkpoints, familiar to most drivers today, finally reached the Court in the case of *Michigan Dep't of State Police v. Sitz* (1990). In 1986, the Michigan Department of State Police established a Sobriety Checkpoint Advisory Committee to examine the use of sobriety checkpoints. The committee developed guidelines for checkpoint operations, site selection, and publicity. These guidelines approved checkpoints along state roads that required all vehicles passing through to be stopped and drivers briefly examined for signs of intoxication. If an officer at the checkpoint detected signs of intoxication, the motorist would be directed to a location out of the traffic flow. At this location, an officer would check the motorist's driver's license and car registration and, if necessary, conduct a series of field sobriety tests. If the field sobriety tests and the officer's observations indicated that the driver was intoxicated, an arrest would be made. All other drivers would be permitted to continue through the checkpoint.

The Court, by a six-to-three vote, reversed the lower courts and held that the use of such sobriety checkpoints did not void the protection of the Fourth Amendment. The Court noted that in *Sitz*, the lower courts erred by misreading the Court's previous cases, such as *Martinez*, with regards to a roadblock's "degree of 'subjective intrusion' and the potential for generating fear and surprise." According to the Court, the "fear and surprise" to be taken into consideration was not that of the intoxicated driver who was to be stopped by such a checkpoint, rather it was the "fear and surprise" of the innocent motorist by the "nature of the stop." Further the Court found that when evaluating the effectiveness of such law enforcement techniques, the language of *Brown v. Texas* (1979) serves as the guide. However, *Brown* does not shift decision-making about use of law enforcement techniques dealing with "serious public dangers" from publicly accountable officials to the courts. The Court said that for Fourth Amendment purposes, the "choice among such reasonable alternatives remains with the government officials who have a unique understanding of, and a responsibility for, limited public resources, including a finite number of police officers."

In dissent, Justice Brennan, joined by Justice Marshall, wrote that, "Some level of individualized suspicion is a core component of the protection the Fourth Amendment provides against arbitrary government action." Further, Justice Brennan found that the need for law enforcement to prevent intoxicated drivers from operating vehicles on public roads was an insufficient reason for dismissing the component of individualized suspicion. Justice Brennan continued that "The needs of law enforcement stand in constant tension with the Constitution's protection of the individual against certain exercises of official power." Consequently it was the "predictability of these pressures that counsels a resolute loyalty to constitution safeguards." In his dissent Justice John Paul Stevens warned that "unannounced investigatory seizures are, particularly when they take place at night, the hallmark of regimes far different from ours."

In the years following *Sitz*, law enforcement attempted to expand use of roadblocks by including interdiction of illegal drugs as a legitimate public safety purpose. Often the purpose of these roadblocks was clearly indicated, such as sobriety/drug checkpoints, while at other times they appeared to be typical sobriety checkpoints, yet their true purpose was interception of illegal drugs. As use of these roadblocks became widespread, the question of their constitutionality divided the federal Courts of Appeals because the Supreme Court had not directly addressed the issue of such roadblocks. The majority of circuit courts believed that the Court's previous dicta indicated that such a roadblock was unreasonable, and therefore unconstitutional. But at least one circuit thought otherwise. Consequently, the final determination was left to the Supreme Court.

In *City of Indianapolis v. Edmond* (2000) the Supreme Court considered the constitutionality of a checkpoint program used by Indianapolis police for the primary purpose of interdicting illegal drugs. The checkpoint was operated in much the same manner as the sobriety checkpoint in *Sitz*, except that a drug-detection dog was walked around the outside of the vehicle that was briefly stopped. The City of Indianapolis contended that even if the primary purpose of the checkpoint to seize illegal drugs was questionable, the lawfulness of the checkpoint's secondary purpose (i.e., verifying driver's licenses and vehicle registrations, and intercepting impaired drivers) legally legitimized the checkpoint. However, the Court was not swayed. The Court noted that while the Fourth Amendment might allow an "appropriately tailored" roadblock in an emergency situation as an exception, a checkpoint used by law enforcement to "pursue primarily general crime control purposes" requires some level of individual suspicion. By a six-to-three vote, the Court deemed Indianapolis' checkpoint program to be unconstitutional.

Recently, the constitutionality of roadblocks reached the High Court again. In *Illinois v. Lidster* (2004) the Supreme Court addressed the Fourth Amendment issue of a roadblock set up by police for the purpose of gathering information one week after a deadly hit-run accident. A week to the day after the death of a bicyclist, law enforcement officers established a roadblock at about the same time of night and location of the accident in an effort to obtain information from the public regarding the accident. As vehicles approached the roadblock, drivers were asked if they had seen anything the week before and were given a flyer requesting information about the fatality. Each stop lasted approximately 10 to 15 seconds.

As Lidster approached the roadblock in his vehicle, he swerved, almost striking one of the officers. When the officer detected the possible odor of alcohol on the Lidster's breath, he directed him to pull over. Another officer administered a field

sobriety test and subsequently arrested Lidster for driving under the influence. During trial, Lidster argued that the evidence against him was obtained by means of a checkpoint that violated the Fourth Amendment. Because the lower courts were divided on the issue, the Supreme Court agreed to hear the case.

The Court rejected the lower courts' use of *Edmond* in determining the roadblock's constitutionality. The Court found that, contra *Edmond*, the roadblock's purpose was not to discover evidence of a crime by occupants of the vehicles, but rather it sought information about other individuals' criminal activity. Therefore, the Court stated that the proper test for this "information-seeking" type of roadblock was its reasonableness. In the previous case of *Brown v. Texas* (1979), the Court had stated that "[t]he reasonableness of seizures that are less intrusive than a traditional arrest ... depends 'on a balance between the public interest and the individual's right to personal security free from arbitrary interference by law officers.' " In *Lidster*, the Court examined the facts and noted that the nature of the crime being investigated was "grave," the roadblock was "appropriately tailored" for the type of investigation being conducted, and more importantly, "the stops interfered only minimally with liberty of the sort the Fourth Amendment seeks to protect." Consequently, applying its balancing test of reasonableness from *Brown* to the facts in *Lidster*, the Court determined the roadblock constitutional and overturned the ruling of the Illinois Supreme Court.

These cases demonstrate that, while exceptions exist to the Fourth Amendment with regard to the use of roadblocks or checkpoints, their use must always be balanced against the rights of the individual. Conversely, these cases show that oftentimes an individual will sacrifice his liberties for either his own protection or the protection of the community. At times when the public demands that the government act to make their lives safer, the Supreme Court helps ensure that individual liberties and rights are not disproportionately eroded.

See also Automobile Stops and Searches; Border Searches; Brennan, William J., Jr.; DUI Field Tests and Breath Tests; Fourth Amendment; Jackson, Robert H.; Marshall, Thurgood; Privacy, Reasonable Expectations of; Probable Cause; Rehnquist, William H.; Stevens, John Paul; Stop and Frisk; Warrantless Searches

Fermin De La Torre

ROBERTS, JOHN. *See* Precedent, Doctrine of; Rehnquist Court

ROBINSON V. CALIFORNIA (1962)

Much of the progress in the field of civil rights and liberties has been slow and steady, the result of inexorable force being gradually brought to bear against obstacles. Other progress has been fairly rapid, often the result of legal cases. One example of the latter phenomenon is *Robinson v. California*. An account of that case belongs in this book because the case increased the protections available for individuals against the state's power.

Robinson arose out of the arrest and conviction of a man for violating a California statute, the relevant part of which prohibited persons from "being addicted to the use of narcotics." Apparently pursuant to a police stop, the constitutionality of which was not addressed by the court because the case was decided on the basis of the Eighth rather than the Fourth Amendment, that man was observed by two officers. They noticed on his arm needle marks, skin discoloration, and a scab, which they interpreted as indications of narcotic use. The police seemed not to have sufficient evidence to charge him with use or possession of narcotics. As a result, as the court pointed out, Robinson was charged with having a status (drug addiction) rather than as having committed an act such as the use of narcotics or a continuing act such as possession of them. The statute also made conviction easier for another reason. Under it the injections that were proved by the marks on Robinson's skin and that the jury found were evidence of addiction need not have occurred in

the jurisdiction that tried Robinson. He merely had to be in the jurisdiction while he had an addiction. In fact, as an apparent addict he could have been charged as long as he was not cured of the addiction.

Robinson's attorneys attacked the statute and thus the arrest and conviction on the grounds of two constitutional provisions. One was the Eighth Amendment: "excessive bail shall not be required, nor excessive fines imposed, nor cruel and unusual punishments inflicted." The other was the Fourteenth Amendment, which specified, in part, that "nor shall any State deprive any person of life, liberty, or property, without due process of law." The Supreme Court had previously incorporated several provisions of the Bill of Rights into the "liberty" component of the Due Process Clause of the Fourteenth Amendment, making them applicable to the states. The *Robinson* case provided the justices with an opportunity to add the "cruel and unusual punishments" provision of the Eighth Amendment to the growing list of Bill of Rights provisions thus incorporated. The nub of the litigation was the question of whether the jail sentence inflicted on Robinson was cruel and unusual punishment.

To understand the significance of *Robinson* in that context it is necessary first to understand in rough terms the history of the case law on cruel and unusual punishments. On its face, that prohibition seems forceful. However, in the early cases the United States Supreme Court repeatedly held that its effect was solely to prohibit punishments that at the time of the writing of the Constitution had been held to be cruel and unusual. That is, for a long time that clause merely maintained the status quo of English common law. In 1910, however, the court held that to pass muster under that phrase punishment must be proportional to the criminal act. That holding, of course, extended the reach of the cruel and unusual punishment prohibition. The court in *Robinson* went a step further, holding that even a very minimal punishment is cruel and unusual if it is a response to an act that should not be punished at all. The Court wrote, "even one day in prison would be a cruel and unusual punishment for the 'crime' of having a common cold."

The Court's analogy to a cold is typical of its reasoning in this case. It was striking off in a new direction, so there were few precedents to follow. Rather, it relied on analogies and appeals to public policy concerns and common sense. It pointed out that the statute in question punished a status, not an act. It alluded to other statuses, the punishment of which would certainly be cruel and unusual: "it is unlikely that any State at this moment in history would attempt to make it a criminal offense for a person to be mentally ill, or a leper, or to be afflicted with a venereal disease." It follows, suggested the court, that punishment for the status of narcotic addiction, another kind of illness, would similarly run afoul of the pertinent prohibition. Moreover, the Court also noted that that addiction could be contracted "innocently or involuntarily." In a concurring opinion Justice William O. Douglas painted a horrifying picture of newborn infants who are addicted to heroin because their mothers were so addicted. It makes little sense to punish a status that has been involuntarily attained.

Later courts disagreed on the basic meaning of this case. Some interpreted it as prohibiting punishment for crimes that are predicated on a status. Others interpreted it as prohibiting punishment for involuntary acts. Under the latter interpretation the case has a broader applicability. Regardless of the way in which it is used as a precedent, the case is important. One can imagine a statute that criminalized a different kind of status, membership in a political organization, on the grounds that members of that organization have a propensity toward antisocial acts. *Robinson* would be an insurmountable argument against the constitutionality of such statutes.

See also Bill of Rights, Incorporation of; Common Law Background of American Civil Rights and Liberties; Cruel and Unusual Punishments Clause; Douglas, William O.; Due Process Clauses; Eighth Amendment; Fourth Amendment; Fourteenth Amendment (1868); Precedent, Doctrine of

Jack Stark

RODNEY KING INCIDENT (1991)

In the early morning of March 3, 1991, the beating of an unarmed African American man was captured on videotape. This widely reported attack on Rodney King at the hands of officers of the Los Angeles Police Department shocked the United States and the world. The videotape lasted approximately 81 seconds. The altercation led to two criminal trials and a civil trial against the officers. The Rodney King incident was the catalyst for serious dialogue on the issues of race, police brutality, and racial profiling.

King had led police on a high-speed chase in the San Fernando Valley. Once he pulled over, he was ordered out of the car. King was brutally beaten as Sergeant Stacey Koon, the supervising officer, oversaw the attack. King was kicked and beaten on his head and body by several Los Angeles police officers. Moreover, police officers hit King more than 56 times with batons and stunned him several times with a Taser stun gun (Tobar et al. 1991). These events and some other less publicized police brutality cases brought national print and broadcast media scrutiny. The amateur videographer who recorded the incident attempted to report it to the appropriate authorities but was allegedly turned away. After the incident, inaccurate police reports surfaced. Eventually, the officers involved in the beating of Rodney King were indicted. The officers who were indicted included Sergeant Stacey Koon, Officer Laurence Powell, Officer Theodore Briseno, and Officer Timothy Wind. Three of these officers had been named in prior excessive force complaints (Berger, Timnick and Soble 1991). It is probable that if this incident had not been captured on videotape, it would not have been prosecuted. Prior to the King incident, Los Angeles had settled one excessive force claim against Officer Powell for $70,000. He had also been accused of beating a handcuffed prisoner and cursing at an African

American motorist simply for driving in a white neighborhood (Cannon 1997). Officer Briseno had also been charged with using excessive force on a handcuffed child abuse suspect and in 1987 was suspended.

Officer Briseno is seen on the videotape stepping in between Laurence Powell and King. Briseno said that he was trying to intervene and stop the beating. He also maintained that he was instructed to move back so that he would not get zapped by the Taser stun gun (Newton 1992). On the videotape, Officer Wind is seen kicking King six times and beating him with his baton several times. It was later determined that he was acting under the orders of Sergeant Koon. During the trial, Officer Wind emerged as the prosecution's most consistent witness. Wind was tried twice, but was acquitted on both occasions.

Officers on the scene stated that Rodney King led police on a hundred-mile-per-hour car chase that endangered the lives of the passengers in King's car, the police officers, and innocent bystanders. Officers also stated that King seemed to be under the influence of some kind of narcotic and attacked the police officers. They further maintained that King was not effectively contained by electric jolts from the Taser stun gun. They also contended that they stopped swinging their sticks as soon as King surrendered.

On April 29, 1992, the state court located in Simi Valley, California, acquitted the officers of assault with a deadly weapon charges. As a result of what the African American community at large saw as an unjust acquittal, rioting and looting occurred in Los Angeles and surrounding counties. In the aftermath of the acquittals, 54 people were killed and 2,383 were injured, with 221 of those injuries being critical (Church 1992). Also in the wake of the Rodney King incident and subsequent acquittals, 13,212 people were arrested for crimes associated with the rioting and looting (Staten 1992). It was estimated that more than $700 million of damage was done in the county (Staten 1992). The rage exhibited by the African

American community expressed the sentiments that justice was not blind and even when crime is captured on tape, African Americans could not get justice. The reaction in Los Angeles also spurred violence, rioting, and looting in other cities across the country. King's most memorable moment occurred after the rioting when he said at a press conference, "Can't we all just get along?" (Chavez 1991). Subsequently, the officers were tried in federal court on federal civil rights charges. In April of 1993, Stacey Koon and Lawrence Powell were convicted of violating Rodney King's civil rights. Both officers were sentenced to 30 months in prison. In 1994, King was awarded $3.8 million in damages as a result of the civil lawsuit filed against the City of Los Angeles. Koon continued to believe throughout his trial that his actions were warranted and these actions may have saved Rodney King's life. Years after the initial incident, Koon maintained that he "would not change what happened one iota" (Mitchell 1994).

See also Racial Profiling; Force, Use of by Law Enforcement

Bibliography

Berger, Leslie, Lois Timnick, and Ronald L. Soble. 1991. "Officers Plead Not Guilty in King Beating." *Los Angeles Times* (27 March): B1.

Cannon, Lou. 1997. *Official Negligence*. New York: Random House.

Chavez, Stephanie. 1991. "The Year In Review. Los Angeles County: A Look Back." *Los Angeles Times* (28 December): 1.

Church, George J. 1992. "The Fire This Time." *Time Magazine* (May 11):18.

Mitchell, John L. 1994. "Koon Again Testifies That King Beating Was Justified." *Los Angeles Times* (27 April): B1.

Newton, Jim. "Briseno Breaks Silence About King Beating." *Los Angeles Times* (23 August): B1.

Staten, Clark. 1992. "Three Days Hell In Los Angeles." *Emergencynet News* (29 April).

Tobar, Hector, Richard Lee Colvin, Ashley Dunn, John Johnson, and Claire Spiegel. 1991. "Witnesses

Depict Relentless Beating." *Los Angeles Times* (7 March): B1.

F. Erik Brooks

ROE V. WADE (1973)

Prior to the 1800s, abortion was widely practiced in the United States and was even considered a relatively safe medical procedure. During the 1800s, states began to criminalize abortion and, by 1880, legal abortions were no longer attainable for most women. Anti-abortion laws were prompted by medical and economic considerations as well as religious concerns. Abortion policy remained essentially unchanged for almost a century, but pressure began to mount for abortion reform during the 1950s and 1960s.

A series of incidents in the early 1960s led to significant easing of the abortion restrictions in some states. Among other things, the abortion reform movement was spurred into action by women who had taken a drug called thalidomide that led to serious birth defects as well as an outbreak of German measles, a disease that often leads to blindness, deafness, or mental retardation in babies when contracted by their mothers during the early stages of pregnancy. These medical concerns focused the public's attention on the restrictiveness of abortion laws. During this time, the women's movement also played a significant role in demanding reform of abortion laws, arguing that abortion rights were a necessary concomitant of women's rights and women's equality. Additional pressure to reform abortion laws arose because hundreds of thousands of abortions were being performed illegally. These abortions often took place under dangerous conditions, and many women suffered long-lasting injuries and even death.

Between 1967 and 1970, a number of states enacted abortion reform legislation, including Colorado (the first), followed by New York, California, Hawaii, North Carolina, Alaska, and Georgia. Governor Ronald Reagan signed the California law in 1967. The laws differed, but most permitted abortion under limited circumstances for victims of rape or incest, cases of severe fetal deformity, or when the woman's life or health was threatened.

By 1973, Texas had not reformed its abortion law; it banned all abortions except one necessary to save the woman's life. The less-restrictive Georgia statute permitted an abortion under limited circumstances. When these laws were challenged in the Supreme Court in *Roe v. Wade* (1973) and *Doe v. Bolton* (1973), the Court had to decide whether they violated the guarantees of the United States Constitution by infringing upon a woman's right to privacy.

The Supreme Court's ruling in *Roe v. Wade* and *Doe v. Bolton* was grounded in two earlier decisions: *Griswold v. Connecticut* (1965) and *Eisenstadt v. Baird* (1972). In *Griswold v. Connecticut,* the Court, by a seven-to-two vote, invalidated a Connecticut law prohibiting the use of contraceptives by married couples. Announcing the opinion of the Court, Justice William Douglas stressed that the law directly infringed on the relationship between husband and wife. The Court found that the marital relationship was within a "zone of privacy" that was protected by the Constitution from the state's intrusion and the law forbidding the use of contraceptive devices infringed on the right to privacy.

A few years later, in *Eisenstadt v. Baird,* the Court invalidated a Massachusetts law that barred the distribution of contraceptive devices to individuals. The Court ruled that a married couple's privacy, established in *Griswold v. Connecticut,* belonged to single persons as well. Speaking for the majority, Justice William J. Brennan stressed that the right of privacy applies with special force to an individual's decision to bear and raise a child.

Roe v. Wade arose when Norma McCorvey, a pregnant carnival worker, sought an abortion in her home state of Texas in 1969. When she consulted a doctor, McCorvey was told that abortion was illegal in Texas "except for the purpose of saving the mother's life." With no money to travel out of state, she sought a lawyer to arrange a private adoption and was referred to two Dallas-Fort Worth attorneys, Linda Coffee and Sarah Weddington, who had been looking for a plaintiff to challenge the Texas abortion law in federal court. They took her case, arguing that restricting the right to abortion unconstitutionally infringed on a woman's fundamental right to privacy.

The Court was asked to decide whether the privacy right articulated in *Griswold v. Connecticut* extended to the right to decide whether to terminate a pregnancy. Speaking for a seven-to-two majority, consisting of Chief Justice Burger along with Justices Douglas, Stewart, Powell, Brennan, and Marshall, Justice Harry Blackmun agreed that the right to privacy encompassed a woman's decision to terminate a pregnancy. But, he added, although the right was fundamental, it was not absolute. The state had an interest in regulating abortions and the woman's right must be balanced against the state's interest in the health and safety of the woman and the fetus.

Texas advanced two reasons in support of its abortion law. First, it argued, the law protected the woman from the medical risks of abortion; second, it protected the fetus. Agreeing that these were important rationales, the Court emphasized that when a fundamental right, such as the right to privacy, was involved, the state can only restrict the right when it has a "compelling" reason to do so. Roe's attorneys maintained that the state did not have a compelling reason to control a woman's decision to have an abortion. The state contended that in the absence of a threat to a woman's life, it had a compelling interest in protecting prenatal life. The Supreme Court rejected both views.

To support its claim, Texas asserted that the fetus was a person protected by the Fourteenth Amendment, but the Court was not persuaded because there was no evidence that the Framers of the Constitution had contemplated protection of the unborn. The state also maintained that because life began at conception, its compelling interest in prenatal life arose at that point and continued throughout the pregnancy. Citing the dispute among religious, medical, and philosophical perspectives about the beginning of life, the Court proclaimed itself unable to define the onset of life. It refused to accept the state's theory of when life began as a justification for its abortion restrictions. However, while the Court rejected the state's claim that its interests in maternal health and fetal life were compelling throughout the pregnancy, it acknowledged that these interests became compelling at specific stages in the pregnancy. This led to the adoption of the trimester approach, the principle that abortion regulations must vary with the stage, or trimester, of pregnancy.

In the trimester framework, because abortion carried very little medical risk when performed during the first three months of pregnancy, the state had no compelling reason to regulate the procedure beyond requiring that the physician be licensed. Therefore, during the first trimester, Justice Blackmun said, the decision must be left to the woman and her physician without state interference. Because abortion is more dangerous during the second trimester, the state could enact regulations reasonably related to maternal health during this stage of pregnancy. Such regulations might specify the place where the abortion may be performed or the type of procedure. Finally, the Court held, the state had a legitimate interest in potential life, which becomes compelling when the fetus was viable, that is, when it was able to live outside the mother's womb. It determined that viability began at about seven months, or around twenty-eight weeks, but noted that a fetus may be viable even earlier, possibly at twenty-four weeks. To further its interest in protecting the fetus during this trimester, the Court held that the state may prohibit an abortion entirely unless it was "necessary to preserve the life or health of the mother."

After applying the standards of the trimester approach to the Texas abortion law, the Court declared it unconstitutional because it only permitted an abortion necessary to save the woman's life. In doing so, the law failed to distinguish among the stages of pregnancy and did not recognize that women's right to privacy conflicted with the state's interest. Therefore, the Court concluded, the law violated the Fourteenth Amendment's Due Process Clause by infringing on the woman's right to privacy.

Justice Stewart concurred with the majority opinion, but wrote separately to emphasize that reproductive freedom is a liberty guaranteed by the Due Process Clause of the Fourteenth Amendment. He reviewed the cases establishing a constitutional right of privacy, asserting that the right of "personal choice" in intimate matters involving marriage and the family, including the right to choose to terminate a pregnancy, was squarely within the Fourteenth Amendment. In his view, there was no question that the Texas abortion law directly infringed on a woman's individual liberty. But he also recognized that the state's legitimate interest in protecting the health and safety of the woman permitted it to regulate abortions to the same extent it regulated other medical procedures and even to prohibit abortion outright near the end of the pregnancy. Justice Stewart believed the Texas law was outside these boundaries and the state's interest did not justify its almost total ban on abortion throughout the pregnancy.

Justice William H. Rehnquist dissented from the majority opinion. He rejected the Court's declaration that a woman had a fundamental right of privacy that embraced her decision to terminate a pregnancy. He also disapproved of the Court's mandate that the state must have a compelling reason to restrict that right. Acknowledging that the right to choose an abortion may be encompassed within the meaning of the liberty guarantee of the Fourteenth Amendment, he emphasized that the state may absolutely deny access to abortion as long as it does so in a manner consistent with due process of law. In his view, the Due Process Clause allowed state legislatures to decide the type of abortion regulation to enact. A reviewing court must uphold such a regulation, if it were found to be rationally related to a legitimate state interest. Given these parameters, he believed the Court should have left the specific provisions of the Texas abortion policy to the judgments of its state legislators. Finally, he noted, the Court should

not have declared the entire statute unconstitutional because it would present no constitutional problems during the woman's last trimester of pregnancy.

In the companion case of *Doe v. Bolton,* the Court determined the constitutionality of Georgia's abortion statute. The Georgia law was not as stringent as the Texas law. Georgia allowed women to obtain certain "necessary" abortions such as when a pregnancy threatened a woman's life or would cause her serious and permanent injury, when a fetus would be born with serious and permanent mental or physical defects, or when the woman became pregnant as a result of rape. In addition to these substantive provisions, the law contained procedural guidelines. The law required that in addition to the woman's own physician, two other physicians must examine her and state in writing that the abortion was "necessary." All abortions had to be performed in hospitals accredited by the Joint Commission on Accreditation of Hospitals (JCAH) and required advance approval from at least three members of the hospital's abortion committee. The law limited abortions to Georgia residents, authorized hospitals to deny admission to women seeking abortions, and allowed physicians and staff members to refuse to participate in the abortion.

The case arose when the abortion committee at Atlanta's Grady Memorial Hospital denied Mary Doe's application for an abortion on the grounds that it was not medically necessary. Doe was a 22-year-old indigent woman with a history of mental illness. She already had three children—two in foster care and one who had been placed for adoption—because she was unable to care for them. Her constitutional challenge to the Georgia law in federal court was joined by physicians, social workers, nurses, and several members of the clergy.

Speaking for the same seven-to-two majority, and applying the standard developed in *Roe v. Wade,* Justice Blackmun reaffirmed the view that a woman does not have an absolute right to an abortion. However, he emphasized, the Georgia statute swept too broadly in restricting her right to terminate her pregnancy. He agreed with the lower court ruling that in exercising their "clinical judgments" to determine whether an abortion was "necessary," physicians must be able to base those judgments on a variety of factors, including the woman's "physical, emotional, psychological, [and] familial" status as well as her age.

The Court struck down the procedural requirement that all abortions must be performed in an accredited hospital because there was no evidence that to be safe, an abortion had to be performed in an accredited hospital, or even in a hospital at all. Moreover, the law failed to exempt first-trimester abortions from the hospital requirement. Similarly, it invalidated the rules mandating that two additional physicians certify the necessity of the abortion and that a hospital committee approve the abortion in advance because they served no legitimate state interest and "unduly" restricted the woman's right to privacy. Moreover, the Court held that the residency requirement infringed on the woman's constitutional right to travel and was irrational as well.

Justice Douglas concurred with the majority but wrote separately to stress that the restrictions on a woman's access to abortion were too broad and the woman's physician should be the only judge as to whether an abortion should be performed. He believed that although the state may view an abortion as a medical procedure, the woman's right to privacy demanded that it limit itself to setting standards for the physician's qualifications.

Chief Justice Burger also concurred with the majority, agreeing that the Georgia and Texas statutes violated the Fourteenth Amendment because they impermissibly restricted abortions necessary to protect the health of pregnant women. He indicated, however, that in his opinion, a state may be permitted to require two physicians to certify the need for an abortion because that would not "unduly burden" the woman.

Justice White, dissenting for himself and Justice Rehnquist, accused the majority of allowing women to terminate their pregnancies for almost any reason "or for no reason at all," even excusing them from having to demonstrate that their health was at risk in any way. He accused the majority of showing greater concern for the mother's "convenience" than it did for the life of the fetus before it was viable. Like Justice Rehnquist, he charged the Court with creating a new constitutional right for pregnant women and said there was no justification for usurping the power of elected state representatives to decide for the state citizens how to protect human life.

After 1973, almost two hundred bills were introduced in state legislatures, and, by 1975, 32 states enacted more than 50 abortion-related restrictions. These included: specification of where and by whom abortions could be performed; informed consent requirements; recordkeeping and reporting requirements; waiting periods; parental consent and notice laws; and funding restrictions. For the most part, with the exception of the latter two areas, the Supreme Court continued to uphold the basic principle of a woman's freedom to choose to have an abortion and ruled that such laws impermissibly restricted the woman's right to privacy.

See also Abortion, Public Funding of; Abortion, Right to; Blackmun, Harry A.; Brennan, William J., Jr.; Burger Court; Burger, Warren E.; Douglas, William O.; Due Process Clauses; Due Process, Substantive; Feminist Movement; Fourteenth Amendment (1868); Fundamental Rights; Gender-Based Discrimination; *Griswold v. Connecticut* (1965); Judicial Activism; Liberty; Marriage, Rights Pertaining to; Marshall, Thurgood; Powell, Lewis F., Jr.; Privacy, Constitutional Right of; Pro-Choice Position on Abortion; Pro-Life Movement; Pro-Life Position on Abortion; Rehnquist, William H.; Rehnquist Court; Reproductive Freedom; Stewart, Potter; White, Byron R.

Bibliography

Luker, Kristen.1984. *Abortion and the Politics of Motherhood.* Berkeley: University of California Press.

Mohr, James C. 1978. *Abortion in America*. Oxford: Oxford University Press.

Rubin, Eva. 1987. *Abortion, Politics, and the Courts*. Westport: Greenwood Press.

Susan Gluck Mezey

ROMAN CATHOLIC CHURCH. *See* Catholicism and Anti-Catholicism

ROMER V. EVANS (1996)

In what may well have been a transforming moment in the struggle for gay rights, the U.S. Supreme Court struck down Colorado's controversial Amendment 2, which banned state and local government from providing various legal protections for gays and lesbians. The amendment resulted from a statewide referendum and overturned ordinances enacted by Denver, Aspen, and Boulder that forbade discrimination on the basis of sexual orientation in such areas as housing, employment, education, social services, and the enjoyment of public accommodations. The Colorado Supreme Court ruled that Amendment 2 violated the Equal Protection Clause of the Fourteenth Amendment, and the U.S. Supreme Court affirmed that ruling.

Writing for a majority of six justices, Anthony Kennedy asserted that "Amendment 2, ... in making a general announcement that gays and lesbians shall not have any particular protections from the law, inflicts on them immediate, continuing, and real injuries that outrun and belie any legitimate justifications that may be claimed for it." Justice Kennedy concluded that Amendment 2 was unconstitutional because "it identifies persons by a single trait and then denies them equal protection across the board." This suggests that Kennedy, as well as the other moderate members of the Court, might have been more sympathetic to a measure that merely outlawed preferential treatment (i.e., affirmative action) for gays and lesbians.

In dissent, Justice Antonin Scalia argued that Amendment 2 "is not the manifestation of a 'bare ... desire to harm' homosexuals, but is rather a modest attempt by seemingly tolerant Coloradans to preserve traditional sexual mores against the efforts of a politically powerful minority to revise those mores through use of the laws." Scalia attacked the reasoning of the majority, saying that the Court's opinion "has no foundation in American constitutional law, and barely pretends to." Nevertheless the Court concluded that "it is not within our constitutional tradition to enact laws of this sort." Writing for the Court, Justice Kennedy opined that "a law declaring that in general it shall be more difficult for one group of citizens than for all others to seek aid from the government is itself a denial of equal protection of the laws in the most literal sense."

See also Affirmative Action; Equal Protection Clause; Fourteenth Amendment (1868); Gay Rights Movement; Kennedy, Anthony; Public Accommodation, Places of; Rehnquist Court; Scalia, Antonin; Sexual Orientation, Discrimination Based on

Bibliography

Hasian, Marouf A., Jr. 1997. "'A Stranger to Its Laws': Freedom, Civil Rights, and the Legal Ambiguity of *Romer v. Evans* (1996)." *Argumentation and Advocacy* 34: 27.

Rich, Stephen M. 1999. "Ruling by Numbers: Political Restructuring and the Reconsideration of Democratic Commitments After *Romer v. Evans*." *Yale Law Journal* 109: 587.

John M. Scheb II and Otis H. Stephens, Jr.

ROOSEVELT, ELEANOR (1884–1962)

Eleanor Roosevelt began her social activism very early and made it a lifetime pursuit to strive for advances in civil rights and fight violations of civil liberties. She exerted the greatest influence while she had the platform as First Lady during Franklin Delano Roosevelt's administration. During her 12 years in the White House, she served as an advocate for equal opportunities for all and was a critic of governmental policies that impeded this goal. As a "roving ambassador" (Biles 2001, 376) for her husband, Mrs. Roosevelt traveled the United States making speeches and analyzing the effectiveness of New Deal policies. It was during these activities that the First Lady's attention was drawn to the problem of institutional racism, especially in terms of how New Deal policies discriminated against African Americans. One specific policy that attracted her attention was the Subsistence Homestead Administration's refusal to allow African Americans into Arthurdale, the first New Deal settlement community for the poor located in Arthurdale, West Virginia (see Black 2001, 89). Mrs. Roosevelt believed that education, housing, and employment are basic human rights and should be available to all without regard to color (Black 2001, 93). Discriminatory elements of governmental programs such as this led her to a partnership with Walter White of the National Association for the Advancement of Colored People (NAACP). In Mrs. Roosevelt, the NAACP had a strong ally, and this created for them a powerful lobbying forum within the White House and provided access to the president through a series of public and private meetings arranged by the First Lady.

Early in her advocacy work for African Americans, Mrs. Roosevelt did not denounce segregation policies (she changed her position on this later with regard to desegregating the military), but she did work hard to provide equal opportunities for all races as well as the development of economic policies to help create a level playing field (Black 2001, 93). Throughout her work as First Lady, Eleanor Roosevelt fought for multiple programs and policies to help African Americans, including her role in advocating the inclusion of African Americans more fully into the Federal Emergency Relief Administration; supporting the NAACP-sponsored Costigan-Wagner antilynching bill (to the disdain of her husband's administration); promoting the National Sharecroppers Week; championing the creation of the Fair Employment Practices Commission; and helping organize the National Committee to Abolish the Poll Tax (Black 2001, 90–93).

During World War II one of the glaring problems in the military was the practice of discrimination and segregation policies against African Americans. Mrs. Roosevelt believed that it was impossible to "fight racism abroad while tolerating it at home" (Goodwin 1994, 626). Even though the military would not become completely desegregated until 1948 under an executive order signed by President Truman, the First Lady put enough pressure on her husband's administration so that the War Department began making all government-owned and government-operated buses available to all members of the military. In addition, the War Department ended the policy of having military recreational areas designated by race (Goodwin 1994, 627).

In her post–White House years, Eleanor Roosevelt continued her efforts in the civil rights arena using her newspaper column, radio show, and speaking engagements as platforms for her message. During this time, she became a member of the NAACP Board of Directors and of the Congress of Racial Equality. She also chaired the platform hearings on Civil Rights for the 1956 Democratic National Convention (Black 2001, 93).

As part of her White House role as "unofficial ombudsman or intermediary between troubled citizens and the government" (Biles 2001, 377), Mrs. Roosevelt also focused on women's rights. Even before her husband's election, she was a member of a cadre of women political activists within the Democratic Party. As a member of the League of Women Voters and the Women's Trade Union League (considered to be a militant women's group), Eleanor Roosevelt fought to make sure New Deal policies did not discriminate against women. She fought against the stereotype that the woman's place is in the home, and she was an advocate for the movement to hire women in factories. She played a key role in garnering government funds for day care facilities as well as getting localities to fund after-school programs and community laundries. "If there was no Eleanor Roosevelt, women would still have gone to work, but the conditions under which they worked would have been far less conducive to the preservation of home life, and their resulting productivity would have been substantially lower" (Goodwin 1994, 628). Mrs.

Roosevelt was also a key advocate for the federal government hiring more women, the end result of which was several high-level appointments of women to federal government administrative positions (including Frances Perkins as secretary of labor) and the hiring of over four thousand women as postal workers (Truman 1995, 62). Even though Mrs. Roosevelt did not support the Equal Rights Amendment, she was prominent in advancing the cause of women's rights especially as they pertained to the work place, and she continued her efforts after she left the White House, serving as the chair of the President's Commission on the Status of Women in 1961.

In her post-White House years, Eleanor Roosevelt continued her work as an advocate in the United States, but she also began to turn her attention to global issues. In 1948 President Truman appointed Eleanor as a delegate to the United Nations, where she helped draft the Universal Declaration on Human Rights. The basic understanding of the declaration was that "all men and women everywhere were born free and equal in dignity, entitled to basic human rights and freedoms without discrimination" (Black 2001, 164). Through her work around the world helping to advance the cause of civil rights and to fight for the basic civil liberties of all humans, Eleanor Roosevelt become known as "a humanitarian reformer and tireless fighter who blended conflicting forces into unassuming, simple humanness" (Hareven 1968, xii).

See also Civil Rights; Congress of Racial Equality (CORE); Discrimination; Equal Rights Amendment; Equality; Feminist Movement; Gender-Based Discrimination; International Law; National Association for the Advancement of Colored People (NAACP); The New Deal; Roosevelt, Franklin D.; Universal Declaration on Human Rights (UDHR)

Bibliography

Black, Allida M. 2001. "Civil Rights." In *The Eleanor Roosevelt Encyclopedia*, eds. Maurine H. Beasley, Holly C. Shulman, and Henry R. Beasley.89–96. Westport, CT: Greenwood Press.

Biles, Roger. 2001. "New Deal." In *The Eleanor Roosevelt Encyclopedia*, eds. Maurine H. Beasley, Holly C. Shulman, and Henry R. Beasley. 375–379. Westport, CT: Greenwood Press.

Goodwin, Doris Kearns. 1994. *No Ordinary Time.* New York: Simon and Schuster.

Hareven, Tamara K. 1968. *Eleanor Roosevelt: An American Conscience.* Chicago: Quandrangle Books.

Truman, Margaret. 1995. *First Ladies.* New York: Random House.

Alissa Warters

ROOSEVELT, FRANKLIN D. (1882–1945)

Franklin Delano Roosevelt (FDR) ranks among the greatest presidents in American history, but his record on civil rights and liberties is less than stellar, drawing one commentator to suggest that he "displayed a consistent lack of leadership" (Irons 1984, 693) pertaining to these issues. This is not to say that FDR held no regard for civil rights and liberties. Rather, his great concern for the constitutional rights of all Americans was tempered by the stark political realities of the time. For an administration mired with a broken economy, and in the latter years a World War, Roosevelt did not go above and beyond in order to further the cause of civil rights and liberties in the United States. In fact, he presided over one of the worst violations of civil rights and liberties with the internment of Japanese Americans during World War II.

Many calls for advances in civil rights legislation began with the implementation of the New Deal policies. These policies visibly neglected the needs of both women and African Americans. A push led by Roosevelt's wife, First Lady Eleanor Roosevelt, began to force the administration's hand on women's issues, especially in regard to the request for nondiscriminatory measures within federal government programs. Although Franklin Roosevelt played little role in the women's equality movement at the time, he did appoint more women to high-level administrative positions than any one of his predecessors (McElvaine 2002, 309). In fact, he appointed the first female cabinet member, Secretary of Labor Frances Perkins.

FDR's New Deal policies, however, did not fully take into account the needs of African Americans. In many cases, New Deal policies discriminated against African Americans. The First Lady was instrumental in bringing these realities to the attention of President Roosevelt. At the urging of his wife, President Roosevelt signed an executive order in 1935 that barred discrimination in the Works Progress Administration, one of the cornerstone policies of the New Deal (Goodwin 1994, 163).

FDR refused, however, to lend his backing to the Costigan-Wagner antilynching bill, a bill the First Lady had supported. FDR's opposition to the antilynching bill highlights one of his failures on civil rights. For years the National Association for the Advancement of Colored People (NAACP) fought for a federal antilynching law. And even though FDR personally disdained the practice of lynching, he did not throw his political weight behind the bill due to political considerations. The political realities were twofold. First, Roosevelt did not want to alienate his Southern white constituency. Second, Roosevelt held to the Jeffersonian idea that law enforcement should be left up to the state and local governments and outside the realm of federal government powers (Irons 1984, 695).

Even though he failed to support the antilynching legislation (which did not pass through Congress), FDR did sign Executive Order 8802 in 1941, an order that called upon all federal government employers and labor unions for the defense industry "to provide for the full and equitable participation of all workers in defense industries, without discrimination because of race, creed, color or national origin" (Goodwin 1994, 252). He also created the Fair Employment Practices Commission to investigate any complaints and violations under the executive order. This was the first presidential action on civil rights since the Civil War (Goodwin, 627). These measures, however, were taken by FDR only after the threat by African American groups around the country to conduct a massive march on Washington, D.C.

Although FDR was pressured to end segregation in the military (which did not take effect until the Truman administration) through the First Lady's advocacy, he did approve of the War Department's move to open up government buses to all races and to end the military practice of having separate recreational areas designated by race. Toward the end of World War II, FDR took the unprecedented step of signing into law the GI Bill of Rights, which was designed to provide all returning military personnel a chance to obtain the occupational training and education that they would have had access to if they had not served in the military (Goodwin, 512). Roosevelt was actually willing to end desegregation of the military, but pressure from within the administration, such as from Secretary of the Navy Frank Knox, who threatened to resign, forced FDR to relent and not to push the issue (Maney 1992, 157–58). The realities of war soon made it a necessity for the administration to become more stringent on antidiscriminatory measures because of the need for African Americans to fill the void in the labor shortages at home and in the military during the war. Roosevelt tried to convince his armed services leaders that they were wasting manpower by confining African Americans to menial positions, but he never pushed the issue (Maney 1992, 158).

One of the main reasons he did not press the matter of civil rights for African Americans was the political reality that he needed to appease white Americans, especially white Southerners. White Southerners propped up the New Deal coalition, and FDR needed to maintain their support. He also was aware that across the country racial upheavals were taking place, led mainly by white Americans. FDR felt that these types of demonstrations were adverse to maintaining a unified front during the war. He felt that any racial discord in the United States was an advantage for the enemies the United States was fighting abroad (Maney 1992, 157). Therefore, FDR rationalized his lack of movement on civil rights as support for the war effort. "In short, the war had presented Roosevelt with the unwelcome problem of racial tension; but the war also provided him with an excuse for postponing the day of reckoning" (Maney 1992, 159).

The Roosevelt administration also faced civil liberties challenges. When FDR entered the White House, he granted amnesty to all those who were held prisoner under the Espionage Act enacted during World War I. All those who had been imprisoned or deported for dissenting against the government were, in effect, granted full civil and political rights, and the Supreme Court held that they had been punished for speech that the First Amendment protects.

Even with this move forward for the protection of civil rights and liberties, in 1941 FDR presided over one of the most horrid violations of civil rights and liberties in United States history with the internment of over 110,000 Japanese Americans during World War II. After the Japanese attacked Pearl Harbor on December 7, 1941, a debate ensued within the administration concerning the growing call to imprison all Japanese Americans. Attorney General Francis Biddle could find no evidence of a threat to national security and argued against internment, stating that "the program was based on public hysteria and racial prejudice." But officials in the War Department labeled any American of Japanese descent an enemy to the United States because of his race. The concern of the officials in the War Department was more influential, and on February 19, 1942, FDR signed Executive Order 9066, which gave the Army the power to create "military areas" along the West Coast from which "any persons may be excluded." It was understood that the order only applied to Japanese Americans. Those that were excluded (the majority of whom were American citizens) from the designated areas were forced to leave their homes and jobs and move inland to "relocation centers." None of them were told of any charges, given any access to the courts, told where they were going or how long they would be detained, or that the government was permanently confiscating their property and belongings, leaving them to rebuild their lives after the war. One commentator has noted: "[T]hrough

it all, he (Roosevelt) displayed a striking indifference not only to the constitutional ramifications of internment but also to the human tragedy involved" (Maney 1992, 161). The Supreme Court upheld the executive order two years later in *Korematsu v. United States* (1944). In that ruling, the Court held that even though racial classifications are always suspect, the government had a compelling interest in protecting the American people during a time of war.

Civil rights were "the great unfinished business of American democracy at the end of the war" (Goodwin 1994, 627). As Peter Irons indicates, however, to adequately review Roosevelt's record on civil rights and liberties, both his accomplishments and failures need to be examined. In this examination, his accomplishments in the area of civil rights pale in comparison to the obvious violations during Roosevelt's tenure as president. As Irons points out, "[T]he 'moral tone' set by Franklin D. Roosevelt in the crucial area of civil rights and liberties was regrettably one more of disdain than determination" (Irons 1984, 722). On the other hand, it must be recognized that through his eight appointments to the Supreme Court, FDR set in motion a virtual constitutional revolution that would lead to the dramatic expansion of civil rights and liberties via judicial interpretation of the Constitution.

See also Civil Rights; Discrimination; Espionage Act of 1917; *Korematsu v. United States* (1944); The New Deal; Race, Roosevelt, Eleanor; Civil Rights and Liberties During Wartime

Bibliography

Goodwin, Doris Kearns. 1994. *No Ordinary Time.* New York: Simon and Schuster.

Irons, Peter. 1984. "Politics and Principle: An Assessment of the Roosevelt Record on Civil Rights and Liberties." *Washington Law Review* 59: 693.

Leuchtenberg, William E. 1963. *Franklin D Roosevelt and the New Deal.* New York: Harper and Row.

Maney, Patrick J. 1992. *The Roosevelt Presence: A Biography of Franklin Delano Roosevelt.* New York: Twayne Publishers.

McElvaine, Robert S. 2002. *Franklin Delano Roosevelt.* Washington, DC: CQ Press.

Pritchett, C. Herman. 1948. *The Roosevelt Court.* New York: Macmillan.

Alissa Warters

ROUSSEAU, JEAN-JACQUES (1712–1778)

"Man was born free and everywhere he is in chains." This famous line—the beginning of Rousseau's *The Social Contract*—could also be considered the thesis of his political philosophy. Because Rousseau focused on the social contract and civil liberties and rights, he greatly influenced both the American and French Revolutions. Yet, some have accused Rousseau of being contradictory.

To begin, Rousseau borrows one key component of Thomas Hobbes' philosophy in the exposition of his own social contract: that man is guided chiefly by a focus on self. Rousseau terms it "self-love" rather than Hobbes's term "self-preservation," but the primary focus is inward. However, Rousseau soon parts company with Hobbes because he disagrees that man is inherently evil; Rousseau instead champions the goodness of man.

This goodness coupled with man's self-love form a fertile ground for a civil society, according to Rousseau. He believed that the combination of these traits would engender in men sympathy for the plights of those who were less fortunate than themselves and encourage all to work together in harmony to promote a civil society in which everyone could prosper. Subsequent critics, of course, charged that a man who truly loved himself would want freedoms, but that a state would require the voluntary giving up of freedoms to a government of some type, and that these two principles were in conflict.

The brilliance of Rousseau, though, is that he anticipates this problem in his own work: "The problem is to find a form of association which will defend and protect with the whole common force the person and goods of each associate, and in which each, while uniting with all, may still obey himself alone, and remain as free as before"

(Ebenstein and Ebenstein 455). However, he never fully finds a solution to this problem, as will be discussed later. One component of his plan for a viable society is that the new social contract would hearken back to the ancient political system of Sparta, which emphasized a stern morality, patriotism, and militarism. However, the size of the society was never clearly defined; it could not be too small, but it especially could not be too large. Once a society became too large, then there was a threat that the legislature might not truly reflect the General Will of the citizens. One wonders then how applicable Rousseau's *Social Contract* would be among today's Western industrialized nations. In the United States for instance, Congress does not always reflect the will of the American people.

Rousseau further elaborated on his ideal society in another of his works, *Discourses on Inequality*. While his view of legislative control was clearly majoritarian-based, he had seen the potential for abuse this could cause. So he was a strong advocate for minority rights. He was firmly against slavery. As a protector of civil rights, he also knew that there were more subtle ways that a man could essentially be owned. He wrote of these in another work: *Discourse on Political Economy*. Here, he discussed property and the potential for abuse inherent in property ownership. Of course, we know that this later became a worrisome problem for the American Founding Fathers, who ultimately dropped the line "life, liberty, and property" from the Declaration of Independence—preferring the less controversial, if less empowering, "life, liberty, and the pursuit of happiness" instead. Rousseau felt as though all men should be able to work to secure a reasonable amount of property, but that excessive property ownership by a few would essentially mark a return to a feudal type of system where men would be economically owned or bound to work the land for others. In other words, he is anticipating a monopoly of sorts. If the American Founding Fathers interpreted Rousseau more conservatively than his writings would indicate, the French did just the opposite. They used him as their justification for the French Revolution, which he might have supported, as well as for the many atrocities of the war, which he certainly would not have.

Now the paradoxes with Rousseau really begin to show. In *The Social Contract,* Rousseau had written that "…the general will is always right and always tends toward the public utility" (Cohen and Fermon 1996, 284); this is clearly a majoritarian view. Conversely, it is obvious that his predilection to protect civil rights and civil liberties led him—in some instances—to champion minority rather than majority rights. This is a problem that had plagued philosophers for years. Indeed, the problem of the "tyranny of the majority" over the minority was the central focus of John Stuart Mill's revised utilitarianism.

Patrick Riley brilliantly explores the various paradoxes in Rousseau, while concluding that they are inherent in any democratic theory. Notable are three key paradoxes: (1) Rousseau's admission that there is inherent tension built into a social contract when one must give up freedom to live in a free society; (2) the utilitarian dilemma between majority/minority protections; (3) the difficulty of pinpointing Rousseau as a liberal or conservative. He believed all men are inherently good, and he sought to protect civil liberties and rights, by virtue of which he displayed liberal traits, however, he seemed more conservative when he suggested a re-creation of ancient Sparta with its militarism, patriotism, civic religion, and focus on morality. Riley describes these paradoxes thusly:

Here of course he got himself into the paradox of insisting on the willing of the essentially non-voluntaristic politics characteristic of antiquity. He got himself, that is, into a philosophical paradox of willed non-volunteerism; but if this paradoxical concept, the general will, a will which is the corporate "will" of a whole society, a will to stop being willful cannot be philosophically defended, it can at least be unraveled with interesting implications for all voluntaristic … not to mention democratic theories which are always hard pressed to fuse what is wanted with what is intrinsically good (Riley 2001, 168–69).

In other words, Riley is agreeing with all of Rousseau's critics that there are paradoxes

within Rousseau's work, just as Rousseau himself anticipated. However, Riley is arguing that these paradoxes are endemic to the very idea of a social contract (an agreement between the people who consent to give up some freedoms in order to live under the protection of the government that they elect) and a democratic society—not to Rousseau's work specifically.

Another key work of Rousseau's was *Emile,* in which he wrote extensively on his views of education—views that were very outside of the mainstream for his time. Indeed, he is considered the father of Romanticism for ushering in a new social period. Rousseau was vehemently opposed to the formal education and tutors of the day—advocating, instead, experiential learning. He felt that high society corrupted the morals; ironic, considering that he was the toast of Europe. Alternatively, he believed that experiential learning, in addition to serving as a great equalizer, taught humility and would teach young men how to become better citizens as well (Ebenstein and Ebenstein 2000, 455).

In conclusion, Jean Jacques Rousseau, the father of Romanticism, influenced both the American and French revolutions. He was a civil libertarian and civil rights advocate ahead of his time, and yet his sympathy for the conservative militarism of ancient Sparta seemed to indicate a stark conservatism as well. He has been accused of being paradoxical, and his ideology is indeed difficult to pinpoint. However, as Riley suggests, the other contradictions may reflect more on the endemic messiness of huge democratic societies trying to include everyone's voice rather than on Rousseau himself. Rousseau, probably more than anyone, would appreciate this "struggle"—after all, he predicted it.

See also Conservatism; Declaration of Independence; Hobbes, Thomas; Liberalism; Locke, John

Bibliography

Cohen, Mitchell, and Nicole Fermon, eds. 1996. *Princeton Readings in Political Thought.* Princeton, NJ: Princeton University Press.

Ebenstein, William, and Alan Ebenstein. 2000. *Great Political Thinkers: Plato To The Present.* 6th ed. Fort Worth, TX: Harcourt College Publishers.

Morris, Christopher, ed. 1999. *The Social Contract Theorists.* Lanham, MD: Rowan and Littlefield.

Riley, Patrick. 2001. *The Cambridge Companion to Rousseau.* Cambridge: Cambridge University Press.

Lori Maxwell

RUNYON V. MCCRARY (1976). *See* Civil Rights Act of 1866